ABRAHAM
KUYPER

Collected Works in Public Theology

GENERAL EDITORS
JORDAN J. BALLOR
MELVIN FLIKKEMA

AbrahamKuyper.com

PRO
REGE

LIVING UNDER CHRIST'S KINGSHIP

Volume 1: The Exalted Nature of Christ's Kingship

ABRAHAM
KUYPER

Edited by John Kok with Nelson D. Kloosterman

Translated by Albert Gootjes

LEXHAM PRESS

ACTON INSTITUTE
FOR THE STUDY OF RELIGION AND LIBERTY

Pro Rege: Living under Christ's Kingship
Volume 1: The Exalted Nature of Christ's Kingship

Abraham Kuyper Collected Works in Public Theology

Copyright 2016 Acton Institute for the Study of Religion & Liberty

Lexham Press, 1313 Commercial St., Bellingham, WA 98225
LexhamPress.com

Originally published as *Pro Rege of het Koningschap van Christus*, door Dr. A. Kuyper. Kampen: J. H. Kok, 1911–1912.

Print ISBN 978-1-57-799654-5
Digital ISBN 978-1-57-799723-8

Translator: Albert Gootjes
Acton Editorial: Nelson D. Kloosterman, John Kok
Lexham Editorial: Brannon Ellis, Abigail Stocker, Joel Wilcox
Cover Design: Christine Gerhart
Back Cover Design: Brittany Schrock
Typesetting: ProjectLuz.com

CONTENTS

GENERAL EDITORS' INTRODUCTION

In times of great upheaval and uncertainty, it is necessary to look to the past for resources to help us recognize and address our own contemporary challenges. While Scripture is foremost among these foundations, the thoughts and reflections of Christians throughout history also provide us with important guidance. Because of his unique gifts, experiences, and writings, Abraham Kuyper is an exemplary guide in these endeavors.

Kuyper (1837–1920) is a significant figure both in the history of the Netherlands and modern Protestant theology. A prolific intellectual, Kuyper founded a political party and a university, led the formation of a Reformed denomination and the movement to create Reformed elementary schools, and served as the prime minister of the Netherlands from 1901 to 1905. In connection with his work as a builder of institutions, Kuyper was also a prolific author. He wrote theological treatises, biblical and confessional studies, historical works, social and political commentary, and devotional materials.

Believing that Kuyper's work is a significant and underappreciated resource for Christian public witness, in 2011 a group of scholars interested in Kuyper's life and work formed the Abraham Kuyper Translation Society. The shared conviction of the society, along with the Acton Institute, Kuyper College, and other Abraham Kuyper scholars, is that Kuyper's works hold great potential to build intellectual capacity within the church in North America, Europe, and around the world. It is our hope that translation of his works into English will make his insights accessible to those seeking to grow and revitalize communities in the developed world as well as to those in the global south and east who are facing unique challenges and opportunities.

The church today—both locally and globally—needs the tools to construct a compelling and responsible public theology. The aim of this translation project is to provide those tools—we believe that Kuyper's unique insights can catalyze the development of a winsome and constructive Christian social witness and cultural engagement the world over.

In consultation and collaboration with these institutions and individual scholars, the Abraham Kuyper Translation Society developed this 12-volume translation project, the Abraham Kuyper Collected Works in Public Theology. This multivolume series collects in English translation Kuyper's writings and speeches from a variety of genres and contexts in his work as a theologian and statesman. In almost all cases, this set contains original works that have never before been translated into English. The series contains multivolume works as well as other volumes, including thematic anthologies.

The series includes a translation of Kuyper's *Our Program* (*Ons Program*), which sets forth Kuyper's attempt to frame a Christian political vision distinguished from the programs of the nineteenth-century Modernists who took their cues from the French Revolution. It was this document that launched Kuyper's career as a pastor, theologian, and educator. As James Bratt writes, "This comprehensive Program, which Kuyper crafted in the process of forming the Netherlands' first mass political party, brought the theology, the political theory, and the organization vision together brilliantly in a coherent set of policies that spoke directly to the needs of his day. For us it sets out the challenge of envisioning what might be an equivalent witness in our own day."

Also included is Kuyper's seminal three-volume work *De Gemeene Gratie*, or *Common Grace*, which presents a constructive public theology of cultural engagement rooted in the humanity Christians share with the rest of the world. Kuyper's presentation of common grace addresses a gap he recognized in the development of Reformed teaching on divine grace. After addressing particular grace and covenant grace in other writings, Kuyper here develops his articulation of a Reformed understanding of God's gifts that are common to all people after the fall into sin.

The series also contains Kuyper's three-volume work on the lordship of Christ, *Pro Rege*. These three volumes apply Kuyper's principles in *Common Grace*, providing guidance for how to live in a fallen world under Christ the King. Here the focus is on developing cultural institutions in a way that is consistent with the ordinances of creation that have been maintained and preserved, even if imperfectly so, through common grace.

The remaining volumes are thematic anthologies of Kuyper's writings and speeches gathered from the course of his long career.

The anthology *On Charity and Justice* includes a fresh and complete translation of Kuyper's "The Problem of Poverty," the landmark speech Kuyper gave at the opening of the First Christian Social Congress in Amsterdam in 1891. This important work was first translated into English in 1950 by Dirk Jellema; in 1991, a new edition by James Skillen was issued. This volume also contains other writings and speeches on subjects including charity, justice, wealth, and poverty.

The anthology *On Islam* contains English translations of significant pieces that Abraham Kuyper wrote about Islam, gathered from his reflections on a lengthy tour of the Mediterranean world. Kuyper's insights illustrate an instructive model for observing another faith and its cultural ramifications from an informed Christian perspective.

The anthology *On the Church* includes selections from Kuyper's doctrinal dissertation on the theologies of Reformation theologians John Calvin and John a Lasco. It also includes various treatises and sermons, such as "Rooted and Grounded," "Twofold Fatherland," and "Address on Missions."

The anthology *On Business and Economics* contains various meditations Kuyper wrote about the evils of the love of money as well as pieces that provide Kuyper's thoughts on stewardship, human trafficking, free trade, tariffs, child labor, work on the Sabbath, and business.

Finally, the anthology *On Education* includes Kuyper's important essay "Bound to the Word," which discusses what it means to be ruled by the Word of God in the entire world of human thought. Numerous other pieces are also included, resulting in a substantial English volume of Kuyper's thoughts on Christian education.

Collectively, this 12-volume series will, as Richard Mouw puts it, "give us a much-needed opportunity to absorb the insights of Abraham Kuyper about God's marvelous designs for human cultural life."

The Abraham Kuyper Translation Society along with the Acton Institute and Kuyper College gratefully acknowledge the Andreas Center for Reformed Scholarship and Service at Dordt College; Calvin College; Calvin Theological Seminary; Fuller Theological Seminary; Mid-America Reformed Seminary; Redeemer University College; Princeton Theological Seminary; and Southeastern Baptist Theological Seminary. Their financial support and partnership made these translations possible. The society is also grateful for the generous financial support of Dr. Rimmer and Ruth DeVries and the J. C. Huizenga family, which has enabled the translation and publication of these volumes.

This series is dedicated to Dr. Rimmer DeVries in recognition of his life's pursuits and enduring legacy as a cultural leader, economist, visionary, and faithful follower of Christ who reflects well the Kuyperian vision of Christ's lordship over all spheres of society.

Jordan J. Ballor
Melvin Flikkema

Grand Rapids, MI
August 2015

EDITORS' INTRODUCTION

Transposing a book from another time (early twentieth century) and another language (Dutch) into contemporary English is a delightful, but challenging process. That latter feature requires us to clarify for our readers a number of translation and editorial decisions designed to enhance this English edition of *Pro Rege*. These decisions, naturally, involve alterations, subtractions, and additions.

When citing Scripture, Kuyper employed either the Dutch *Statenvertaling* or his own paraphrase of the text. Consistent with our goal of producing a contemporary English edition of this work, we have used the English Standard Version (ESV) of the Bible, unless otherwise noted. To aid the reader, at some points we have replaced Kuyper's paraphrase with the actual text of the ESV, and we have supplied (in brackets) those specific textual references, of either Scripture citations or paraphrases, that were absent from the original. The renderings of various doctrinal standards, such as the Heidelberg Catechism, are taken from the versions appearing in *Reformed Confessions of the 16th and 17th Centuries in English Translation*, 4 vols., ed. James T. Dennison Jr. (Grand Rapids: Reformation Heritage Books, 2008–14). The editorial style conforms to the *Chicago Manual of Style*, 16th edition.

In the footnotes, the opening formula "Note by the author" identifies notes from Kuyper himself. All other notes are editorial additions to these editions. These brief editorial notes have been added throughout in order to identify persons, terms, schools of thought, or events mentioned in the original that might be unfamiliar to contemporary readers.

Other stylistic alterations have been made for ease of reading and for the sake of appearance. Italics are used less frequently in the English edition than appear in the original. More importantly, large paragraphs and long sentences have been divided, and subordinate clauses have occasionally been rearranged to render accurately the emphasis present in Kuyper's original. Sections within chapters were originally unnumbered; numbering has been added to aid readers in finding specific references.

Bringing significant intellectual works into the modern day by way of translation frequently confronts the translator and editor with matters involving sensitive sociocultural views and associated language. As times change, so do modes of expression. This pertains to Kuyper's work as well. For example, where possible we have opted for a responsible, though by no means rigorous, use of gender-neutral nouns and pronouns (for example, speaking of "people" rather than "men"). Where necessary and only infrequently, infelicitous formulations have either been altered for the modern ear or omitted altogether.

For some time now, translators and publishers have been laboring diligently to provide the English-speaking world with access to the formative writings of Dutch cultural theologian Abraham Kuyper. Combined with his seminal volumes on *Common Grace*, and with his 1898 *Lectures on Calvinism*, these three volumes of *Pro Rege* constitute an essential resource for faithfully transposing Kuyper's insights into a modern key. Being far more than a mere supplement to his works on common grace and worldview Calvinism, these volumes of *Pro Rege* are fundamentally correlative and complementary to those well-known works. In other words, these three major works of Kuyper are mutually interpretive.

In contrast to the somewhat philosophical and sweeping timbre of *Common Grace* and *Lectures on Calvinism*, *Pro Rege* offers teaching textured specifically for the church in the world, that is, for Christians living life *coram Deo*, in the presence of God. Because Christians share in Christ's own anointing as Chief Prophet, Only Priest, and Eternal King (Heidelberg Catechism, Lord's Day 12, Q&A 33–32), they are called and may expect, among other things, "with a free conscience [to] fight against sin and the devil in this life, and hereafter in eternity [to] reign with Him over all creatures." Until then, Christians live *pro Rege* within various spheres of human cultural activity, such as family, business, labor, art, science, education, and politics. As Kuyper's title confesses and these volumes explicate, such living before God entails submitting to his pervasive sovereignty, to his gracious claims, and to the present kingship of Jesus Christ over the entire world and its history.

John Kok
Nelson D. Kloosterman

VOLUME INTRODUCTION

These three volumes constitute a complete, unabridged English translation of Abraham Kuyper's *Pro Rege*. The publication of *Pro Rege* represents a major step forward for Kuyper scholarship. For years, English-speaking readers have depended on relatively few sources for understanding his theology. This inevitably led to distortions of his perspective and a certain one-sidedness of interpretation. Together with the other volumes in this series, students and scholars of Abraham Kuyper now have direct access to many more key works.

Like other triptychs, such as *Common Grace* and *E Voto Dordraceno* (a study of the Heidelberg Catechism), Kuyper takes a central theme and explores it over hundreds of pages. In *Pro Rege* his chosen theme is the kingship of Christ. Hearkening back to Calvin and confessions of the Reformed churches, we recall that Jesus Christ holds three offices: prophet, priest, and king. While liberal Christians favor the portrayal of Jesus as a prophet and pietist Christians embrace the image of Jesus as savior and healer of souls, little attention has been paid to Christ's royal office. With *Pro Rege*, Kuyper aims to fill that theological gap.

Though Kuyper divides his work into three volumes, he organizes *Pro Rege* according to two principal rubrics: the kingship of Christ in his exaltation, and the kingship of Christ in its operation. The first deals with the biblical notion of Christ's kingship as well as the consequences of the fall (and the advent of modernity) on the recognition of his kingship. The second rubric studies how Christ manifests his kingship across the various spheres of human existence.

Among Kuyper's most famous expressions is "there is not a square inch in the whole domain of our human existence over which Christ, who is Sovereign over all, does not cry: 'Mine!'"[1] In a way, *Pro Rege* may be read as a commentary on this peroration from his 1880 address on sphere sovereignty. Kuyper explores the significance of the royal office of Christ for numerous spheres of life, including the individual, family, and the church, but also the arts, the sciences, and the state. This wideness of vision distinguishes *Pro Rege*. Christ is king not only in the church, but in all spheres of life: "The dominion of Jesus' kingship extends also to family, society, state, scholarship, art, and every other sphere of human activity."[2] We continue to read and appreciate Kuyper today because of his broadness of perspective, which he upholds without falling into moralism or biblicism.

DEVOTIONAL THEOLOGY

Reading academic theology is frequently difficult and demanding. Theologians, like scholars in any field, tend to pile up qualifications whenever they make theological assertions. Such circumspection wards off misunderstandings but comes at the price of accessibility and comprehensibility. Most theological texts make few accommodations to readers, presenting their findings in unadorned academic prose. As a director of Christian education of my acquaintance once remarked about the Presbyterian Church (USA) *Book of Confessions*, "It's as dry as a bone!"

Nothing remotely similar can be said about *Pro Rege*. Kuyper shows that for theology, too, these bones may live. He composed these articles for readers of *De Herault* (The Herald), a weekly paper for members of the Reformed churches. He first published them from 1907 to 1911, eventually collecting them as an independent work in three parts printed in 1911 and 1912.[3] The history of its composition explains the format of the book, which is composed of hundreds of short chapters of several pages each.

---

1. Abraham Kuyper, "Sphere Sovereignty," in *Abraham Kuyper: A Centennial Reader*, ed. James D. Bratt (Grand Rapids, MI: Eerdmans, 1998), 488.
2. Abraham Kuyper, *Pro Rege: Living under Christ's Kingship*, 3 vols. (Bellingham, WA: Lexham Press, 2016–), 2.II.19.
3. Tjitze Kuipers, *Abraham Kuyper: An Annotated Bibliography 1857–2010*, ed. Barend Meijer, trans. Clifford Anderson with Dagmare Houniet (Leiden: Brill, 2011), 430.

Kuyper writes with narrative flair, resorting frequently to homespun analogies and metaphors. Would we think today, for example, of using the relationship between Napoleon and his army as an analogy between Christ and the church?

> Napoleon can serve as an example for the unity between Christ and his army, yet a wide gulf continues to separate them. Napoleon was able to animate his troops and work on them from the outside, but he could not enter them. He always stood before or beside his troops—he in his being, and they in theirs. But Christ actually enters his believers, the King really does live and rule in the heart of his people, and he really is in them and they in him, so that their lives are forged together into a more exalted unity.[4]

When paging through *Pro Rege*, it is important to keep its original audience in mind. Kuyper was not writing for academic theologians, but for the so-called *kleine luyden*, that is, the rank and file of the Calvinist community in the Netherlands. He was perfectly capable of writing academic prose—just take a look at *The Encyclopedia of Sacred Theology*.[5] By contrast, *Pro Rege* takes up a space somewhere between theology and inspirational literature. Kuyper always begins his short chapters with a brief citation from Scripture. His approach is not exegetical, but he makes frequent references to scriptural verses to ground his claims. More than anything, Kuyper intended his readers to ponder his book as they would a devotional. While readers may plow straight through *Pro Rege* to mine the books for the perspective they shed on Kuyper's (neo-)Calvinism, a better approach would be to read them slowly over time. The occasional repetition and reiteration assist deliberative readers with keeping the main arguments in mind while Kuyper leads them down many interesting byways.

ENCROACHING SECULARISM

Kuyper adopts a distinctively somber tone in *Pro Rege*. He opens the first volume with several chapters comparing Christianity and Islam, generally to the detriment of the former. Why is Muhammad—whom all Muslims acknowledge is only a prophet and not divine—held in far greater social

---

4. *PR* 2.I.9.
5. Abraham Kuyper, *Encyclopedia of Sacred Theology*, trans. J. Hendrick DeVries (New York: Scribner's, 1898).

esteem in (Middle) Eastern nations than is Christ—whom Christians confess to be the Son of God—in Western nations?

The pessimistic tone may surprise readers accustomed to reflecting back on the late nineteenth century as a silver age of Calvinism in the Netherlands, fully capable of standing alongside the golden age of the seventeenth century. Was this not the period during which Kuyper and his colleagues established their great, enduring institutions—the Anti-Revolutionary Party, the Reformed Churches of the Netherlands, and the Vrije Universiteit Amsterdam, among many others? Contemporary neo-Calvinists sometimes look back wistfully at the successes of this period as they seek to revive a cultural Calvinism adapted to our era.

Kuyper, however, sees signs of weakness and decay everywhere. He would have been dismayed but not surprised to see how the "Christian pillar" in the Netherlands shrank, then toppled during the past hundred years. Though Kuyper takes pains to argue that genuine Christians—those in the sanctuary of the temple—cannot fall away, the "crowds in the forecourt" may easily abandon Christianity under the pressures of the modern world. The accelerating cultural changes he describes—ranging from the successes of the physical and medical sciences to globalization and the growth of capitalism—remain with us today. Indeed, the post-Christian world Kuyper foresees has largely become the world in which we now live.

While Kuyper is popularly known as a cultural Christian, he could be as sharply critical of the shallowness of Christianity as better-known critics like Dietrich Bonhoeffer or Karl Barth. A society that accepts everyone and every institution as exemplifying Christian virtues inevitably fails to witness to the kingship of Christ. In such a society, there is no need for witness or for any kind of missional church.

> Almost all people have been baptized, and according to the census records they all profess the Christian religion. This pushes the witness of Christ away into a corner. There is no need to witness among Christians, but everyone is a Christian—so why would you ever have to bear witness? But this perspective hides a lie. True believers know all too well that not everything that is called Christian actually is Christian.[6]

---

6. *PR* 2.I.4.

Kuyper's animosity toward a superficial cultural Christianity emerges most clearly in his arguments against a national church in volume 2 of *Pro Rege*. A national church assumes that the entire population is baptized and belongs, to a greater or lesser extent, to the Christian faith. Kuyper makes the straightforward point that a national church excludes members of other religions from membership, though it frequently requires them to pay church taxes. Making a less obvious point, he asserts that a national church misunderstands the witness to Christ's kingship in the church. The church is Christ's vehicle for overcoming the nationalisms introduced after Babel; it should not become captive and subservient to them.

No doubt Kuyper's downbeat estimation of the Christianity of early twentieth-century Dutch culture reflected his situation after leaving political office in 1905. As leader of the Anti-Revolutionary Party, he had lost a hard-fought reelection campaign. He then toured the Mediterranean, visiting many states with Muslim majorities. He published his impressions in a two-volume work titled *Around the Mediterranean Sea* in 1907 and 1908.[7] His hopes for a return to active political life were dashed when Theo Heemskerk (1852–1932), the next prime minister from the Anti-Revolutionary Party, excluded him from his cabinet in 1908. Moreover, he endured a fundraising scandal in 1909 (the so-called *Lintjesaffaire*) that effectively ended his political career, despite being formally cleared of the charges. In the autumn of his life, Kuyper knew all too well the shortcomings and failures of the Christian society that he had put so much energy into fostering.

A superficial historiography of the "long nineteenth century" recounts how its optimism and progressivism foundered unexpectedly and tragically on the fields of Flanders during the Great War. While Kuyper does not foresee that great conflagration, his skeptical evaluation of the possibilities and limits of the Christian culture bears little trace of false optimism. In volume 3 of *Pro Rege*, he explores the increasing divergence between secular society and Christian society. Kuyper rejects the idea that Dutch culture, despite its roots in the Reformation, is straightforwardly Christian. The divisions between Christians and non-Christians is growing even sharper—to the detriment of Dutch society as a whole.

---

7. Abraham Kuyper, *Om de Oude Wereldzee*, 2 vols. (Amsterdam: Van Holkema en Warendorf, 1907–1908).

However, Kuyper is no Oswald Spengler, one of Kuyper's contemporaries and author of the classic *Decline of the West*—for Kuyper the decline of Christendom in the West may also serve as a backhanded compliment to the kingship of Christ, whose reign shines all the more brilliantly against society's fall away from Christ.

SOME THEOLOGICAL QUESTIONS FOR KUYPER

Kuyper's *Pro Rege* is daring and provocative. He takes theological risks, advancing speculative ideas and pushing concepts to their limits. In this sense, Kuyper is not a Kantian theologian—he does not carry out a *Critique of Theological Reason* before advancing theological claims. To modern readers, especially those taught by Karl Barth to refrain from theological speculation, Kuyper's proclivity to speak empirically about the creation before and after the fall may lead to consternation.

A good example of this speculative tendency emerges in his discussion of Jesus' miracles. According to Kuyper, Jesus worked wonders not through his divine nature, but through his uncorrupted human nature. Like Adam before the fall, Jesus could see the essence of things and could exercise mental dominion over the natural world. However, his powers exceed the first Adam's. In the person of Jesus Christ, human nature has grown from its incipient seed into a mature organism. The miracles of Christ demonstrate what God intended for all humanity before the fall and exemplify its overcoming. In what may strike us today as faintly humorous, Kuyper speculates that paranormal abilities like hypnosis and psychokinesis linger as witnesses to the original powers of human beings before the fall. Though their practitioners have perverted these primordial powers into magical forms, Kuyper perceives their uncorrupted seeds amidst the noxious weeds. Striking a more serious note, Kuyper returns to these analogies in volume 3 of *Pro Rege* to explain how Jesus's form of knowledge exceeded our corrupted human understanding without relying on divine omniscience. In doing so, Kuyper lays the basis for the difference between science in its unredeemed and redeemed manifestations, and redemption has restored the minds of Christian scientists to something approaching the immediate knowledge that human beings possessed at the creation.

Kuyper's understanding of the relationship between the rule of Jesus Christ and the rule of the Triune God will also likely provoke comment, especially among professional theologians. According to Kuyper, we must draw a distinction between the kingship of Christ in the church and the rule of the Triune God in the world. In the church, Christ rules directly. He is the king, and his people—members of the church—are his subjects. By contrast, Christ's rule is indirect in the world. The spheres of creation—among them the family, the institutions of civil society, and the state—belong to the Creator. By grace, the light of Christ spills over from the church to illumine and restore the primordial intentions of the Creator in the creation: "He who originally ruled there is thus not Jesus our King, but rather our Triune God, who has created everything, instituted everything, and bound everything to his ordinance."[8] For readers not familiar with the heady theological debates about the doctrines of Christology and the Trinity, these passages may prove the hardest-going in *Pro Rege*, but the distinction Kuyper introduces between church and world is fundamental to his theology of the kingship of Christ.

The organic metaphors also provide Kuyper with a dynamic concept of law. This dynamism allows him to reject what has become known in North America as dominion theology. The confession of Christ as king does not mean reinstituting Deuteronomic law and subjugating non-believers to Holy Writ. While opposed to Darwin, Kuyper held an evolutionary view of history and revelation. Creation is growing toward its *telos*; law develops just as all knowledge develops. So returning to biblical law is not an option for modern Christians, though we may learn from the deep principles at play in the Mosaic law. If nothing else, the English translation of *Pro Rege* will correct misperceptions about the relationship between Kuyper and the dead-end known as theonomy (à la Rousas J. Rushdoony, not Paul Tillich).

The difference between organic and mechanical government plays an important role in his understanding of the sovereignty of Christ. Like his colleague Herman Bavinck (and like the apostle Paul), Kuyper resorted frequently to organic metaphors of seedlings, growth, development, and flowering. In the creation, God implanted the seeds of a differentiated culture. God patiently allows history to take its course so that these teleological forces may come to fruition. In his royal office, Christ both ingrafts believers onto his flowering vine in the church and tends to the cultural garden of creation by removing the weeds that have choked its native plants. This distinguishes the government of Christ from all human government, which cannot restore the organic unity of people and creation,

---

8. *PR* 2.III.1.

but only can force them to obey the law by mechanical means such as police, the courts, and the military.

Finally, Kuyper's approach to Judaism also raises questions. He regards nations and nationalism as emerging from the consequence of the fall. Jesus, though born a Jew, is not simply King of the Jews. He is King of all humanity:

> The Christian religion never was Jewish, even though it arose out of Israel. It was the religion of humanity, it had a general human character, and it was intended to win for Christ our entire human race—all people. And so it was to be, in the fullest sense of the term, the religion of the world, without any restrictions based on nationality. This is the universalism fundamentally opposed to Jewish particularism.[9]

Where does this leave modern Jews in Kuyper's theology? For Kuyper, a continued existence of the Jewish nation is a theological anomaly. While his universalism has many positive aspects, especially as it inherently undermines any hierarchies of races and cultures, does it come at the cost of an implicit anti-Judaism?

A HIERARCHICAL UNIVERSE

Nothing separates Kuyper from modern readers as much as his hierarchical vision of society. The metaphor of the kingship of Christ, of course, is intrinsically hierarchical. Indeed, among Kuyper's main points is that Christians are *subjects* of Christ. If Christ is the Good Shepherd, then we are his flock:

> This also explains why, in our circles, there is such an emphasis on our title as subjects. That title derives from the honor that Christ's kingship deserves. Whether we speak of Christ's possession, of Christ's flock, of the sheep of his pasture, or of his subjects, it all comes down to the same thing, and serves always to point out that you must be fully conscious of your total dependence on your King.[10]

It is problematic that he sees hierarchies as pervasive throughout the created order. God has not created all people equal, he contends.

---

9. *PR* 1.II.14.
10. *PR* 2.II.18.

The Creator has ordered the nations and peoples of the world by differentiating their talents and abilities:

> There is no equality among people. What is a quiet housekeeper compared to a philosopher like Augustine when it comes to knowledge? What is a farmer behind his plow compared to men such as Plato or Kant when it comes to knowledge?[11]

As an empirical point, it is hard to argue against this assertion (though we may ask whether philosophers always demonstrate greater practical wisdom). But what makes these differences? Are the differences due to the ordering of creation, or to structural inequalities in society that sinfully repress and discourage the housewife and the yeoman from developing all their God-given talents and abilities?

Judging Kuyper's views on class, gender, and race requires a decent understanding of his historical world. Kuyper holds views that we find completely unacceptable today. Mustering such passages is easy. For instance, Kuyper occasionally engages in reification of racial prejudices, ascribing strong nerves to the Japanese and "Mongols" while claiming that blacks suffer from weak nerves—with Europeans clustering somewhere in the middle.[12]

The stumbling blocks just keep piling up. Contemporary missiologists will cringe, for instance, when reading Kuyper on the connection between Christian missions and the success of European colonialism:

> Just as the Netherlands has colonies outside of the kingdom,
> so Christ's kingdom has the entire world as its colony, while
> he works on that world in a way that brings blessing, soothes,
> and energizes.[13]

But Kuyper's views on missions should not be extrapolated from such comments alone. Later in *Pro Rege* he also chastises churches for not becoming directly involved in missions and argues for a greater sense of enculturation when planting churches abroad. "Anyone who forces upon the inhabitants of Asia and Africa a church whose form is equivalent to what the European church has developed in its historical circumstances,"

---

11. *PR* 1.III.24.
12. *PR* 1.I.6.4.
13. *PR* 1.III.16.

he wrote, "denies the difference in the nature and character that exists between nations and peoples according to the very ordinance of God."[14]

And, of course, we have to consider his bourgeois perspective on the family, which clearly delineates roles for husbands, wives, children, and servants. Kuyper does not idealize the family; he acknowledges that many families, including "Christian" families, fail to live according to the divine mandate. Still, his idealization of the nineteenth-century family—along with barbed comments about feminized husbands and masculinized wives—dates his treatment of Christian society more than any other topic in *Pro Rege*. Writing during the first wave of feminism, Kuyper has nothing positive to say about the movement:

> We must consider feminism as nothing less than an attempt to turn what is actually a matter of deterioration, falsification, and degeneration into a basic principle and to exaggerate it consciously.[15]

By contrast, we find it hard not to turn the tools of ideological critique back on Kuyper's depiction of family life. Could Christ really command such wastage of human gifts and talents as the strict division between the male as breadwinner and the female as housekeeper effectuates? Here, as elsewhere, we must question the links Kuyper makes between nineteenth-century bourgeois values and supposed mandates of creation.

But we should not overlook the progressive social dimensions of his vision of Christ's kingship. In his study of numerous spheres of society, Kuyper has a sharp eye for the effects of elitism on ordinary citizens. Using a paradoxical (but biblical) argument, he contends that subservience to Christ ennobles the poor, downtrodden, and weak. Despite a patriarchal perspective on the family, Kuyper aims for a socially engaged Christianity:

> Poverty alone has already impoverished family life so bitterly and rendered it unable to meet its calling. Think of the many families where fathers are absent from early in the morning until late at night, such that they rarely see their children and are hardly involved in their upbringing at all. There is nothing in human life that has escaped sin and misery, and yet the family more than anything else has suffered bitterly under

---

14. *PR* 2.II.20.
15. *PR* 2.III.7.

them. It is the calling of the Christian religion to intervene here as well, and to effect a restoration of what has been damaged and wrenched from its proper context.[16]

Kuyper asserts that the church should not let any members go hungry. If poor members of the church lack anything necessary for their material welfare, wealthier members of the church should supply it. While Kuyper also acknowledges the social mission of the church outside its walls, he believes that social justice should start within the church. On a political level, he contends that the government should require industry to provide workers' compensation insurance, given the high rates of debilitating injury in modern factories.

If we press further, we may also find that Kuyper's blithe assumptions of a hierarchical universe run counter to a deeper and more significant emphasis in his thought—namely, the role that social forces play in binding the human race together. As opposed to families and nations, which divide human beings from one another, society tends toward universalism. Kuyper is struck by how "the life of society, after it has been shut up within limited spheres, gradually expanded to form a single, all-encompassing sphere that is beginning to approach the general sphere of the entire human race."[17] In keeping with this perspective, despite concerns about "world cities" found in *Pro* Rege, he unabashedly favors the cosmopolitan life of the city over traditional village life, where the circles were smaller and the possibilities for social engagement much fewer. His own career path, which led him out of the small town of Beesd into the wider spheres of Amsterdam and The Hague, underscored this preference for city life. How does society's drive toward universalism affect the series of hierarchies he describes? Kuyper argues that a universal society need not erase all particularism. Families and nations will continue to exist even as the financial system, journalism, sports, and public opinion become increasingly global. However, we may expect that the process of globalization will undermine many forms of particularism, effacing differences between "more" and "less" civilized peoples. As scholars have frequently remarked, a parallel tension exists in Kuyper's *Lectures on Calvinism* between his arguments for the "comingling of blood" and his remarks about

---

16. *PR* 2.III.2.
17. *PR* 3.IV.4.

the differences between races.[18] Which tendency runs deeper in Kuyper remains an open question, though I personally believe that *Pro Rege* demonstrates that unity and universalism have the final word.

In sum, repristinating Kuyper is not an option for us. Kuyper himself argued against conservatism and false orthodoxy earlier in his career. As Kuyper contended in his 1870 farewell as he left brewing conflicts in Utrecht to pursue a more expansive vocation in Amsterdam, "it is our calling to hold fast what we have in Christ *in our own time*, not in theirs, and so it is from our own time that we must take the material with which to prepare that form today."[19] If anything, his remarks on colonialism and the role of women illustrate the danger of elevating transitory social structures to creational mandates. Kuyper was always a dynamic thinker. Christ had come to restore God's intentions in creation, yes, but those intentions unfold through a historical process. The dynamism of his theology must take precedence over his commitment to static social structures.

POLITICAL THEOLOGY

The publication of the English translation of *Pro Rege* is especially timely given the growing interest in political theology. While the term *political theology* has a disputed provenance, the German legal thinker Carl Schmitt (1888–1985) indelibly stamped the term when he published *Political Theology* in 1922. By *political theology*, Schmitt meant the transposition of theological ideas (such as "miracle" or "sovereignty") into the secular political realm.

Kuyper is sometimes typified as a *public* theologian in contrast to political theologians such as Schmitt and his successors. The distinction boils down to Kuyper's focus on the family, and especially the associations of civil society. Whereas political theologians typically consider the relation between individuals and the state (with perhaps the church as among the few mediating institutions), a public theologian explores the rich fabric of society that flourishes within (and often beyond) the state. But to call Kuyper a public theologian is not to deny that he also develops a political theology with a significant role for the state. Kuyper explicitly rejects libertarianism, with its philosophy of the sovereign individual. Indeed, a

---

18. See, for instance, Abraham Kuyper, *Lectures on Calvinism* (Grand Rapids: Eerdmans, 1931), 34–37.

19. Abraham Kuyper, "Conservatism and Orthodoxy: False and True Preservation," in *Abraham Kuyper: A Centennial Reader*, 82.

major goal of *Pro Rege* is to unfold a political theology that respects the integrity of the public sphere.

A key difference between Kuyper and Schmitt, however, is the former's relentless insistence on Christ's active rule. Christ is no *roi fainéant* or passive monarch. He rules dynamically across the spheres. This realism about the kingship of Christ sets Kuyper apart from Schmitt, who was interested in how theological ideas transform into political concepts. The reign of Christ is not just a concept or ideal. Kuyper criticizes Frank Thomas, a Swiss theologian who lectured that Christ's kingship is expressed in his moral influence over individual Christians, arguing, "You may never speak about Jesus' kingship in a metaphorical sense. Jesus' kingship is to be understood in an altogether proper sense."[20] Christ's kingship is not an imaginary ideal, but a real political truth. His kingship is our reality, whether we live in ignorance or acknowledgment of his reign. At the same time, and perhaps unpalatably to contemporary readers, Kuyper also insists on the reality of the demonic. The battle between good and evil, God and the Devil, forms the cosmic backdrop to *Pro Rege*. "Nothing has done more damage to the church's confession of Jesus' kingship," he contends, "than the marked increase in the indifference toward the spirit world, whether toward angels or of demons."[21] This cosmological drama will be brought to a definitive conclusion at the end of time, when Christ reveals himself as king in all his glory.

HOW IS CHRIST OUR KING TODAY?

A contemporary Christian cannot return to early twentieth-century Holland, just as Kuyper could not go back to sixteenth-century Geneva. The scientific progress, social revolutions, world wars, and economic developments of the twentieth century have shattered his world irrevocably. His call to confess the kingship of Christ in the church, society, and the state echoes from the past, inviting us to reflect anew with him, and sometimes against him, about Christ as our Lord and sovereign. But first we should take pains to understand him.

Kuyper opposed the French Revolution. He regarded the revolutionary slogan "neither God nor master" as the epitome of the modern rejection of God's sovereignty. In this stance, he formed a line with conservative

---

20. *PR* 3.IV.22.
21. *PR* 1.III.22.

thinkers from the previous generation such as Guillaume Groen van Prinsterer (1801–1876), who propounded a political philosophy he termed "antirevolutionary." Kuyper adopted this political philosophy and made it a centerpiece of his own theological politics.

We might think that we could infer from his sharp rejection of the philosophy of the French Revolution that his politics would be conservative or reactionary. But we would be wrong. In Kuyper's hands, antirevolutionary political thinking is fluid and, may we say, progressive. He had no desire to return to the *Ancien Régime* nor was he, for all his praise of the noble House of Orange, particularly enamored with the contemporary Dutch royalty. The past was as corrupted by sin as the present. Christians "could not simply fight for the existing order, since it was poisoned throughout," Kuyper contends, "and as long as they sought merely to ride the wave of reactionary conservatism in the battle against modernism, they imagined they were living in Zion's rest and so their cause was spoiled."[22] A Christian political party must be progressive as well as conservative. In *Pro Rege*, Kuyper accordingly underscores his support for liberal ideals such as constitutionalism, elections, and democratic representation, while maintaining a commitment to the tradition of Groen by distancing himself from the notion of popular sovereignty.

Most surprisingly, perhaps, for those who assume that Christian politics implies theocracy in some form or other, Kuyper rejects the concept of a Christian nation. While he can speak loosely of "Christian nations," by which he means nations where the majority of the population adheres in some degree to Christianity, he rejects the idea of a genuinely *Christian* nation. In his subsection on the state in volume 3 of *Pro Rege*, he argues that, despite the work of common grace, nation-states can never become Christian. A just legal system is necessary but not sufficient; "this is no reason to claim that the state became a Christian institution."[23] The fundamental problem is that nation-states divide peoples against one another. States forms barriers to the unity of the people of God. Thus he writes, "The Christian principle keeps calling out for the unity of the human race, and for that reason there is no room for the division into states in the kingdom of heaven."[24] Hence the need for Christian political parties—Christian

---

22. *PR* 3.V.7.
23. *PR* 3.V.6.
24. *PR* 3.V.6.

parties strive to make states conform as closely to the ideal of a Christian polity as possible, while also witnessing, by their very existence, to the fractures among citizens. For Kuyper, establishing a Christian nation is an eschatological event. Only the return of Christ the king will bring about Christendom—and, in so doing, abolish the sinful divisions among the nations.

Reading *Pro Rege* provides a window into a vanished world of Dutch order, puritanism, and, frankly, repression. Its author was a man of his times—but also a man who resisted the historical movement of his times. His vision of Christ the King was occluded by commitments to various bourgeois, Victorian ideals. But despite his failures in vision, he provided a witness to the kingship of Christ across all spheres of life. To learn from *Pro Rege* today, we must train our eyes on the radiant throne of Christ, assessing where Kuyper went astray and also what he got right.

Clifford Anderson

ABBREVIATIONS

GENERAL AND BIBLIOGRAPHIC

AKB	Kuipers, Tjitze. *Abraham Kuyper: An Annotated Bibliography 1857–2010.* Translated by Clifford Anderson and Dagmare Houniet. Brill's Series in Church History 55. Leiden: Brill, 2011.
CG	Kuyper, Abraham. *Common Grace.* Translated by Nelson D. Kloosterman and Ed M. van der Maas. Edited by Jordan J. Ballor and Stephen J. Grabill. 3 vols. Bellingham, WA: Lexham Press, 2015–.
KJV	King James Version
NKJV	New King James Version
PR	Kuyper, Abraham. *Pro Rege: Living under Christ's Kingship.* 3 vols. Bellingham, WA: Lexham Press, 2016–.
RC	*Reformed Confessions of the 16th and 17th Centuries in English Translation.* Compiled by James T. Dennison Jr. 4 vols. Grand Rapids: Reformation Heritage Books, 2008–2014.
SV	*Statenvertaling* ("States Translation" of the Dutch Bible, 1637)

OLD TESTAMENT

Gen	Genesis
Exod	Exodus
Lev	Leviticus
Num	Numbers

Deut	Deuteronomy
Josh	Joshua
Judg	Judges
Ruth	Ruth
1–2 Sam	1–2 Samuel
1–2 Kgs	1–2 Kings
1–2 Chr	1–2 Chronicles
Ezra	Ezra
Neh	Nehemiah
Esth	Esther
Job	Job
Psa (Pss)	Psalm(s)
Prov	Proverbs
Eccl	Ecclesiastes
Song	Song of Songs
Isa	Isaiah
Jer	Jeremiah
Lam	Lamentations
Ezek	Ezekiel
Dan	Daniel
Hos	Hosea
Joel	Joel
Amos	Amos
Obad	Obadiah
Jonah	Jonah
Mic	Micah
Nah	Nahum
Hab	Habakkuk
Zeph	Zephaniah
Hag	Haggai
Zech	Zechariah
Mal	Malachi

NEW TESTAMENT

Matt	Matthew
Mark	Mark
Luke	Luke
John	John

Acts	Acts
Rom	Romans
1–2 Cor	1–2 Corinthians
Gal	Galatians
Eph	Ephesians
Phil	Philippians
Col	Colossians
1–2 Thess	1–2 Thessalonians
1–2 Tim	1–2 Timothy
Titus	Titus
Phlm	Philemon
Heb	Hebrews
Jas	James
1–2 Pet	1–2 Peter
1–3 John	1–3 John
Jude	Jude
Rev	Revelation

FOREWORD

Pro Rege is being written with the aim of removing the separation between our life *inside* the church and our life *outside* the church that has arisen within our consciousness more sharply than is helpful. Within the arena of the church this could not be helped, since the confession of Christ as our Savior stands in the foreground. Naturally the Savior fixes the contrast between our being lost in guilt and sin, and the grace standing in opposition to that. And church life must be lived precisely in the fluctuation between these two poles. A church life that is conducted simply in terms of observing churchly duties becomes debilitated. If it aims principally at a lifestyle characterized by virtue, it exchanges its deeply religious character for a superficially moral character. The result has always been, and will always continue to be, that those who are spiritually engaged do not feel at home in their church; once they join up with like-minded folk in a more intimate circle, they will cause the flowering of sectarianism.

Christ's being Savior does not exclude his being Lord. Instead it has always been confessed within the arena of the church that the church is lost apart from the most holy preservation of its King, and that Christ rules in the midst of his own—not least of all in the church. From their very beginning, then, our Reformed churches have strongly sensed that need for the protection and government of their King.[1] At that point they

---

1. Although Kuyper also has in mind the Protestant Reformation of the sixteenth century, in his contemporary Dutch context he is referring to the *Gereformeerde Kerken* (Reformed Churches in the Netherlands), a denomination that came into being in 1892 as a result of union between churches that had seceded from the

were facing times of bitter persecution and uncommon confusion in every sphere. So it could not have been otherwise than that they confessed with zeal that our King guarded his church, and that they in their hour of need looked to the one who is seated at the right hand of the Father and is clothed with all power in heaven and earth for their salvation and protection. After the break with Rome, wherever the church had to be regulated once again and the need was sensed on every side for a higher authority, people continued to honor, in the person of the Savior, their King as well, to whose leading they surrendered without reservation. But things changed when persecution ceased, when public religion received the Reformed imprint, and when the Reformed churches eventually acquired a more established order.

This explains why, despite continuing to be confessed, the kingship of Christ at that point nonetheless lost its exalted significance for life. People heard less and less about the King and more and more about the Savior and Redeemer.

Coupled with this came changes in other areas of life. Once the ecclesiastical conflict was settled, Reformed people threw themselves into public social life. Life for them was of two sorts: life within the church and life outside the church. Justice was no longer being done to the unity of both. That rupture could have been prevented only if the confession of the kingship of Christ, proceeding from the church, had been recognized within popular consciousness as the governing power for the entirety of life. But this is precisely what did not happen. Instead, the kingship of Christ was pushed further into the background, and at that point this naturally caused the opposition between ecclesiastical life and public life to penetrate the consciousness of Reformed people in a very perilous way. Ultimately, it was as if Christ only had to do with the church, and that they did not have to take the importance of Christ into account outside the church.

That opposition prevailed until late in the previous [nineteenth] century. However, room for a better harmony in life has surfaced of late. This is how we conceived our Christian press, our Christian scholarship, our Christian art, our Christian literature, our Christian philanthropy,

---

Dutch Reformed Church in 1834 (the *Afscheiding*) and the churches that left the same denomination in 1886 (the *Doleantie*) under his leadership.

our Christian politics, our Christian labor organization, and so on.[2] In short, the understanding that Christ also lays claim to life outside the church gradually became commonplace.

At present we have reached the point where nobody among us wants it any differently anymore. The problem, however, is that people still seek [to locate] the Christian character of these various expressions of life too exclusively in Christian principles. This sense has to flourish more: that Christ himself is the one who, as our King, must impress this Christian hallmark on our expressions of life. Hence the need to awaken and fortify this understanding once again. This is the need that *Pro Rege* is attempting to satisfy.

This revived understanding gives rise to an altered relationship toward those who, while confessing with us the kingship of Christ, differ with us ecclesiastically.

In the ecclesiastical arena, in terms of the most refined formulations of the faith, people must share one meaning and one sentiment; therefore it could only be that groups of people had to separate into various churches. This is how the Roman [Catholic], the Greek [Orthodox], the Lutheran, the Reformed, the Baptist, and the Independent churches all came into existence, and no matter how hard people try, removing these differences will not succeed, at least not in the first place, in the ecclesiastical arena. But these ecclesiastical differences have for many years threatened to divide Christians in the public arena as well. Our only hope against this danger can be found in the universal confession of the kingship of Christ. This is the case because in the public arena, people are not dealing with those more refined formulations of the faith. In the public arena, communal Christian activity is possible with others, possibly even with everyone, who confesses the kingship of Christ—even though in the spiritual arena, and consequently in the ecclesiastical arena, we may have separated. Considering the deeper need (now appearing with increasing urgency) to unite together all sectors of Christianity in the conflict against unbelief and revolution, it is desperately necessary to place more emphasis on the kingship of Christ as governing all our living. In this sense as well, a

---

2. Among the massive literature, both primary and secondary, that explains Kuyper's vision for extending the principles of biblical religion to all of life, perhaps the best place to begin is with Kuyper's own *Lectures on Calvinism: The Stone Lectures of 1898* (1931; repr., Peabody, MA: Hendrickson, 2008).

study like that offered in *Pro Rege* seems required, if not indispensable, for our generation.

Since the articles appeared in *De Heraut*,[3] one can observe repeatedly how, more than formerly, Christ is being given his honor as King in various arenas. My silent prayer is that this may continue.

Like the earlier work, entitled *E Voto*,[4] the Latin title *Pro Rege* is also an abbreviation. Long titles are too burdensome for citation. The short titles of *Pro Rege* or *E Voto* are easily remembered and tell you immediately what document is being intended. *Pro Rege* means: *For Our King!*

After this initial volume, the subsequent two volumes will appear as soon as possible. Like *Common Grace*, this work will also consist of three volumes.

Kuyper

The Hague, 20 December, 1910

---

3. "The chapters of the three volumes [of *Pro Rege*] were initially published as articles in *De Heraut* [*The Herald*], no. 1514, January 6, 1907–no. 1723, January 8, 1911. The three series of articles from *De Heraut* were rearranged into seven series. The original number of articles was maintained, but each chapter was now given a relevant heading. The series was published weekly in *De Heraut* and was only interrupted, as usual, by biblical-theological meditations on major church holidays and by devotions during the summer holidays.

   "The first volume reprints the articles from *De Heraut*, no. 1514, January 6, 1907–no. 1572, February 16, 1908; and no. 1580, April 12, 1908. Eight articles (pp. 488–570) were mistakenly not reprinted (cf. 1905.21) and were delivered a few weeks later (see 1911.08). However, they were not included by the publisher in the first portion of the print run (the premium copies) of the first volume. Some owners of a p[r]emium copy ordered a private binding before 1911.08 was published, and when the publisher's bindings were available (cf. 1912.01) some probably forgot to provide their binder with the supplement. This is why there are bound premium copies from 1911.03 without 1911.08.

   "The first portion of the print run was intended for readers of *De Heraut*, who could sign up for one or two sets at half price (cf. 1892.17). The trade edition was then published without the words *premie-exemplaar* on the title page. Kuyper paid all the printing costs and thus owned the entire print run (KA 315)" (*AKB*, 1911.03, 430–31).

4. The full title is *E Voto Dordraceno. Toelichting op den Heidelbergschen Catechismus* (that is, in agreement with the wish expressed at the Synod of Dort, an explanation of the Heidelberg Catechism). This four-volume work was published first in *De Heraut* (*The Herald*) as a multi-year (1886–1894) series of articles. For more information, see *AKB*, 1892.17, 230–31.

THE DARKENING OF CHRIST'S KINGSHIP

CHRIST AND MUHAMMAD

As for me, I have anointed my King on Zion, my holy hill.

PSALM 2:6

In the distant land of Islam, nothing strikes you more strongly than the §1
faithfulness and ardor with which all the people hold high the name of
"the Prophet," the honor of Muhammad. In order to get a feel for this, you
should not go by the pale light that the crescent sheds on our archipelago of the East Indies. To admire that faithfulness, that devotion, in all its
warmth and inner beauty, you have to listen attentively in the Caliph's[1]
own country, in Istanbul and Brussa, in Khonia and Damascus, in Cairo or

---

1. Also spelled as *khalifah*, this was among the titles given to successors of Muhammad,
    and it referred to rulers in the Islamic world. For more information, see *OEIW*,
    1:387–94, s.v. *Caliph*. For this and subsequent notes, see also Thomas Patrick Hughes,
    Dictionary of Islam (London: W. H. Allen & Co., 1885).

Alexandria.[2] The foundation for life is and remains the old "Let's go, let's march, let's sing to the honor of God and his Prophet."[3]

Every time at the hour of prayer, day in and day out, the *muezzins*[4] without fail climb up to the gallery of the minaret or, if there is no minaret, take up a position near the mosque, and in the sight of all they recite their *azan,* or call to prayer, in song. Then, from thousands of mouths in every city, town, and village there resound all at one time the following words:

> God is great, God is great, God is great,
>> God is great, God is great!
>> I bear witness that there is no other God.
>> I bear witness that there is no other God.

This is for Allah. But without fail, this recitation is followed by these words to the honor of the prophet:

> I bear witness that *Muhammad* is the messenger of God.
>> I bear witness that Muhammad is the messenger of God.
>> Come to pray, come to pray.
>> Come to felicity, come to felicity.

In the morning at least, they also add:

> Prayer is better than sleep.

Once everyone has gathered in the mosque, these same words are repeated to introduce the prayer. Also in the *Iqama,*[5] the introduction to the actual prayer, they once again call out:

---

2. Brussa (modern Bursa), a city in Turkey located near Istanbul, was the ancient capital of the Ottoman sultans in the fourteenth century; Khonia (modern Konya, and the biblical Iconium) was an early capital of Turkic influence during the Seljuk period. It remains one of the most conservative Islamic cities in the Turkic world. For more information, see Abraham Kuyper, *Om de Oude Wereldzee*, 2nd ed. (Amsterdam: Van Holkema & Warendorf, 1907), 378–401.
3. Kuyper cites the French: "Allons, marchons, chantons en l'honneur de Dieu et son Prophète."
4. Also spelled *mu'azzin*, this refers to the Muslim official of a mosque who summons the faithful to prayer five times a day from a minaret. For more information, see *OEIW*, 4:91-92, s.v. *Muezzin*. See also Thomas Patrick Hughes, *Dictionary of Islam*, s.v. *Prayer*.
5. The *Iqama* or *Ikamet* refers to the second call to Islamic prayer, sounded immediately before the prayer begins.

I bear witness that *Muhammad* is the messenger of God.

I bear witness that *Muhammad* is the messenger of God.

The prayers will now begin.

Evidence of great religious seriousness accompanies the honor, the great honor shown toward Muhammad, for prayers in the mosque are always recited in an elevated tone that never drops. First the words, "In the name of God, the Most Beneficent, the Most Merciful!" are called out, followed by the so-called *Fatiha*:[6]

> All glory is to God alone, lord of the worlds,
> The Most Beneficent, the Most Merciful,
> The King of the day of judgment.
> You alone we worship, and to You alone do we call out
>   for help.
> Direct us on the straight path.
> The path of those on whom you have bestowed your
>   grace.
> Those against whom your wrath has not broken out.
> Those who have not lost their way. *Amen*.

And so it goes, on and on, in a sacred and constantly elevated tone, until the *rak'ahs*,[7] or separate prayers, which are sometimes completed with nine supplications, such as in the *Nafl*.[8] Every second *rak'ah* is always followed by the commemoration of Muhammad, and that in no fewer than two instances:

First, they recite:

> To God be the worship of every tongue.
> To God be the worshipful position of our body.
> And to God be the worship of our almsgiving.

Then to the glory of the prophet:

---

6. Kuyper is here referring to the opening Sura of the Qur'an, which is very important to Islamic worship and an obligatory part of daily prayer, repeated several times throughout the day. For more information, see *The Qur'an: A New Translation*, by M. A. S. Abdel Haleem, Oxford World's Classics (Oxford: Oxford University Press, 2004).

7. A *rak'ah* consists of prescribed movements and words used by Muslims in their prayers.

8. A *Nafl* prayer is a supererogatory or optional Islamic prayer.

> Peace be upon you, O *Muhammad*, with the peace of God
> and his blessing!

This is still not the end. Again and again they add to the praise of
the prophet:

> I bear witness that there is no god but God.
> And I bear witness that *Muhammad* is the ambassador
> of Allah.

Among the many other examples that could be mentioned, there is the
Darud,[9] in which the exaltation of Muhammad returns once more, and
then even more abundantly than before:

> O God, bless *Muhammad* and his descendants, just as you
> blessed Abraham and his descendants.
> You, O God, are to be praised, for You are great!
> O, bless *Muhammad* and his descendants, just as your
> blessing was upon Abraham and his offspring.
> You are to be magnified, for You are great!

These prayers have to be recited five times a day, and Muslims who are
especially pious will add another two or three voluntary prayers, the so-
called *Ishraq*,[10] *Zuha*,[11] and *Tahajjud*.[12]

§ 2   Altogether, this adds up to approximately 1,800 prayers per year, and
for some Muslims over 2,500 prayers. In each of them, the commemoration of Muhammad occurs between four and ten times. This means that
every single worshiper commemorates the name of Muhammad more
than ten thousand times per year!

There is, of course, something mechanical at work here—how could
there not be? But the prayers are arranged in such a way that the body is
actively involved, with prescribed poses and motions to keep worshipers

---

9. This refers to the *Darud (Darood) Shareef* prayer, a common prayer known to the
   majority of Muslims, that is recited in two sections in the latter portion of the daily prayers.
10. The time for the *Ishraq* prayer begins ten to twenty minutes after sunrise, and con-
    sists of two *rak'ahs*.
11. The term *Zuha* refers to a period of voluntary prayer.
12. The *Tahajjud* prayer is said to be the most rewarding Islamic supererogatory prayer,
    rendered during the night; this prayer consists of twelve *rak'ahs*, though the num-
    ber is optional.

from drifting off into drowsiness and breaking the mechanical routine. If you carefully observe the elaborate prayers in the mosque and take note of the restful calm, earnestness, and warmth with which they are made, you will soon sense how the Eastern soul has a tendency for ecstasy capable of animating what would otherwise be mechanical.

On the upper gallery of the Hagia Sophia in Constantinople, the present writer observed a bell-ringer (who could not have surmised that someone was watching him) for more than twenty minutes. He said his prayers with a face and posture that testified to a zeal and earnestness that would be the envy of many a Christian.

Yet there is more.

Not only is Muhammad commemorated endlessly in prayer, but the respect shown to all who are thought to be in any way descendants of Muhammad also testifies poignantly to the way Muhammad's name and memory live on in every Islamic nation.

More remarkable yet is the fact, to which the preceding was only an introduction, that half-westernized Muslims still take up the cause of Muhammad. They will not tolerate those who diminish his high calling in any way and agree with devoted worshipers in their conviction that those who refuse to take up Allah's cause default on their own honor.

The indifference toward Jesus encountered in Christian countries, or cowardly silence when the Divine Founder of *our* religion is defamed, is virtually unheard of in Islamic nations when it comes to Muhammad.

The Chodchas[13] in Persia and India, we admit, place Ali[14] above Muhammad, but they are a sect that has adopted numerous Buddhist elements, including the transmigration of the soul. For that reason this exception does not alter the rule that, where Islam has been preserved in a pure form, it is Muhammad who receives all veneration.

---

13. Kuyper seems to refer here to Khojas, a diverse group of Muslims originating in South Asia.
14. The *Shi'ah* Muslims are followers of Ali, first cousin and son-in-law of Muhammad and husband of his daughter Fatimah. The Shi'ahs view Ali as the first legitimate Imam or successor to the prophet, which places them in religious opposition to Sunni Muslims. This division occurred after the death of Muhammad in 632. The 7th century leader Abdullah ibn Saba' is often viewed as the first *ghulat* for his purported ascription of divine status to Ali.

A decline in the splendor of Islam's religious life can indeed be observed. This is not in the country, nor in the more remote areas, but in such centers of social life as Constantinople, Cairo, Alexandria, or Algiers.

Many people in these cities have frequently visited the West or have even completed their studies in Paris and London. They returned with admiration for the Western lifestyle and attempted to introduce Western morals into their own homes. Of course, this meant a weakening of their religious consciousness. They no longer paid attention to the prohibition against drinking wine. Like numerous Reform Jews, they even ate pork. They are at times semi-modern people.

All the same (and that is why it is so illustrative!), you will never hear even these modernized Muslims utter a word from their lips that detracts from the honor of Muhammad.

Despite all their indifference and religious wavering, they sense very deeply the difference and contrast between the Christian and Islamic worlds. Virtually without any exception, they all defend the superior excellence of Islam. Even among the higher circles you will not find any group that would let you escape unpunished if you defame Muhammad.

In these higher circles there is complete freedom of expression and no impediment to presenting your aberrant views. The only condition is that you should not suppose that you may fall short in respect toward what is and remains sacred to them. If you do so for even a moment, you soon meet resistance and everyone takes up Muhammad's cause. In those homes and circles that are still truly Eastern, the respect for Muhammad is naturally an even more sensitive issue, just as it is in our own orthodox circles. However, what is so striking about Islam is that, also in those circles that have strayed the furthest, their allegiance to the founder of their religion remains unshaken.

Moreover, they are far from timid when they defend Muhammad and Islam. They know precisely at which weak points they can attack you and are very aware of the light that shines on their lives as Muslims. Down to the lowest classes they know the entirely distinctive significance of their religion. Thus armed, they can defend themselves very well. Especially the fact that Muhammad came after Jesus is for them the definitive proof that Muhammad also occupies a position above him.

Every statement that could diminish the honor of Muhammad is immediately thwarted by a response—not sharp or harsh, because Easterners remain polite, but no less decisive in their politeness. You shall not lay your fingers on Muhammad's honor and good name. As soon as Muhammad is violated, everyone stands up for Muhammad in his own way. For everyone, his is and remains *the* name among all great names of history that arouses quiet reverence.

That disposition encountered in Islamic countries soon grips believers who confess the name of Christ because their experience in their own country when it comes to Christ is so different. One feels ashamed of one's homeland. One bemoans the depth to which Christianity's power has sunk in one's own land. And one is grieved and distressed when recalling the tepidness, indifference, or even hidden hostility with which the memory of one's Savior and King is so often treated in that Christian land.

§ 3

Of course, this situation also does not escape the notice of those Muslims who often visit the West. Since they are used to the great reverence shown to Muhammad in their own country, they initially do not know what to make of the unsparing and unbounded boldness with which Christ's great honor is attacked in Christian countries. Muslims hear and know that Christians in their confessions place Christ much higher than Muhammad. Muslims honor Muhammad as messenger, prophet, apostle, but they do not deify him. For that very reason Muslims expect to find a much deeper, worshipful reverence for the God-man in Christian countries.

But how this conflicts with reality! They find an entire body of literature intended to pull down the great honor of Christ. They notice the deeply hostile comments that testify of hatred for Christ rather than love for him. They see that in certain circles Christ's name is either systematically silenced or at best derided. In the circles of academics and artists they may not find that hostility or mockery, but instead a refined (and thus abominable) dethroning of Christ that reduces him to some religious genius who may have been good back in his time but is now outdated and subject to sharp criticism even on an ethical level.

On Java[15] it is similarly known that nothing hinders or obstructs the work of mission as much as the unchristianity of so many among the European population who call themselves Christian. Doing so may benefit their public and social status, but their walk and their talk fails to show

---

15. Java is an island of Indonesia. The Dutch colonized Indonesia and in the 1670s began to control a number of Java's Islamic kingdoms. Throughout the nineteenth century, Java was intensively developed. In Kuyper's day, the Reformed Church was committed to doing mission work in Indonesia, especially on the island of Java.

even the slightest bit of reverence for Christ. You hardly need to guess what kind of an impression you make on a Muslim when you try to entice him to bid Muhammad farewell and come over to your religion, when these are the examples he has in mind of what your religion allows.

This is so repulsive to the knowledgeable Muslim because he in his own way honors not only Muhammad, but also Moses and Jesus. He gives more honor to Jesus Christ as the prophet sent by God than do many Christians; acknowledges in him much that is divine and miraculous; and does not think for a moment about seeing Jesus as just another teacher. The Qur'an indeed speaks about Jesus—and not all that briefly. That Christ's status among the intelligentsia of Christian countries is even lower than it is for these Muslims amazes and confounds them. It leaves a lasting impression on them as to the inferiority of our holy religion, and makes our mission work among them all but impossible.

§ 4 This series of articles is entitled *Pro Rege* and expresses our desire to sound forth a summons for the honor of our King.

Muslims witness for their prophet, but we profess about our Messiah that he is not only the greatest Teacher and our only High Priest, but also *our eternal King*.[16]

"Lord of lords and King of kings" is his highest title, and our constant desire is one day to rule with him as anointed kings.

You call him your Savior, Redeemer, Surety, and you delight in the redemption and salvation he obtained for you. But all of this has to do with *how he has benefited you,* to save you from perdition. But Christ is more— he is also your King. Saying so expresses the honor due him, but also expressed *what you must be for Christ*. The kingship of Jesus comes to you with a demand. It demands faithfulness, allegiance, and submission. It demands of you—especially in this Christian nation—that you confess him, that you stand up for him, and that you plead for the honor of his Name.

However, precisely regarding this demand there is a frightening and appalling contrast between what almost everyone in Islamic nations feels, claims, and does for the prophet, and what the leading inhabitants of Christian countries feel, claim, and do for the King whom God has given to us.

The confession of Christ's kingship has been so enormously weakened and diluted—not only among those who have fallen away from the faith of

---

16. This formulation derives from Heidelberg Catechism, Lord's Day 12, Q&A 31.

their fathers, but also among believers—that it sometimes seems to have been forgotten even in the preaching of the word. Although great homage is paid to the Lord as Prophet and High Priest, complete devotion and loyalty to him as the *anointed King* no longer grips the hearts of the people. His kingship has disappeared from view, even among believers.

For that reason, we want to bear witness for our King and issue an appeal on his behalf. Not as though a single series of articles can undo the disruption that has built up over a number of years. But at least the will and the attempt may be expressed. Since God's Word testifies to us that Jesus Christ "rules as King until all enemies will be subjected under his feet" [see 1 Cor 15:25-27], so too *through* that Word and *for the sake of* that Word the homage, faithfulness, and devotion may be awakened for our King once again. All of these are increasingly withheld from him due to the hostility displayed by many and the lukewarm attitude of all.

Our queen reigns over fewer Christians and more Muslims than the §5 Sultan of Turkey in Europe and Asia combined. England leads with sixty-three million Muslims in Hindustan[17] and Pakistan; however, after England, the Dutch crown extends over by far the greatest number of Muslims. In European Turkey, the sultan governs four million Muslims, and another sixteen million in Asia—but that total of twenty million Muslims is easily surpassed in number on Java alone. This comparison between the devotion that people in Islamic countries feel for the prophet and the devotion expressed in a Christian nation for our divinely anointed King is particularly relevant for us Dutch people. If we must regrettably confess that in Islamic countries, despite sectarian influences and all kinds of religious decline there, the crescent continues to shine brightly while on the whole the splendor of the cross has dimmed, is there then not cause once again—and more consciously than before—to issue an appeal in our *Heraut* on behalf of the honor of our King?

The Muslims' religious allegiance, ardor, and devotion to the prophet are so strong that even earnest statesmen perceive and recognize the possibility that one day, sooner or later, the Caliph may issue a call for a holy

---

17. This name refers to the region of the upper and middle Ganges valley, between Punjab and Bengal. In Kuyper's day, British colonialism, exercised through the East India Company, was enjoying significant economic and political control in this and other regions of modern day India.

war that will almost certainly be heeded far and wide.[18] This is connected to the belief derived from the Qur'an that Muslims may gird the sword for their religion when necessary. Yet even apart from this unreasonable element, we see a spiritedness and enthusiasm whose embers continue to glow in the hearts of all those men and women who belong to Islam.

The waters of flagging zeal may well flow over the glow of these embers temporarily to dampen them, but they cannot extinguish them. When a broad stream of water is aimed at a lake of fire, new flames shoot out again from the smoldering ground; so it is with Islam.

And even if we hope that God will keep such evil fanaticism from ever breaking out among us, we would still stand higher in our Christian countries if faithfulness to and ardor for our divinely anointed King were to dwell so deeply in the hearts of everyone that, where *his* honor and *his* glory were concerned, a similar spiritedness would glow in hearts and a similar enthusiasm would unite all believers together into one holy, impenetrable battle line.

Even in tranquil times, when Christianity was not exposed to direct attack, our honor as people who confess Christ would require of us such testifying for our King. How much more, then, in the twentieth century, which already in its first decade been sharply characterized by nothing more than the all but hatched plan in every country—also in ours—to drive back the Christian religion from the place of honor that it has achieved now for almost fifteen centuries!

18. The fear that the Ottoman Caliph might invoke a "holy war" against European colonial powers (at German instigation) was widespread during the lead up to the Great War (World War I; 1914–1918). For a critique of this fear, see Christiaan Snouck Hurgronje, *The Holy War "Made in Germany"* (New York: G. P. Putnam & Sons, 1915).

DARKENING AMONG CHRISTIAN NATIONS

Then Pilate said to him, "So you are a king?" Jesus answered, "You say that I am a king. For this purpose I was born and for this purpose I have come into the world—to bear witness to the truth. Everyone who is of the truth listens to my voice."

JOHN 18:37

The States of Europe still count as Christian nations. In the East [of Europe] there are also several million people who follow Islam; a Jewish diaspora is spread throughout all countries; among the Laplanders and Finns in northern Scandinavia we even find pagans. But taken together, they do not constitute as much as four percent of the European population, of which ninety-six percent register themselves as baptized. This applies to the Netherlands as well. According to the latest census figures, there are 104,000 Jews in our country, and another 80,000 claim no religion at all, but altogether they constitute not even 3 percent of the 5.5 million inhabitants of our land.[1]

§ 1

---

1. Kuyper is presumably relying on the 1909 census (Centraal Bureau voor de Statistiek. Uitkomsten der negende tienjaarlijksche volkstelling in het Koninkrijk der Nederlanden gehouden op den een en dertigsten December 1909. The Hague, 1910–1911).

The name of Christ is no doubt applied to our country all over the world as well. Statistics indicate that the overwhelming majority of the Netherlands still belongs to him. These reports are not coming from the outside, but the heads of families themselves provide the figures in a census. People themselves officially reported that they have been baptized and belong to Christ. Admittedly, the family heads did not report anything personal about their faith or the faith of those they represent, but they did report belonging to the Dutch Reformed Church, the Roman Catholic Church, the Reformed Churches in the Netherlands, the Lutheran Churches, and so on. And by reporting this, they were showing that they wanted to be considered as officially belonging to them. Virtually without any exceptions, all of these churches statutorily acknowledge that they confess and honor Christ as King. Everyone knows that this is the case for the Reformed Churches. It is just as certain with respect to the Roman Catholic Church. And no matter how one wiggles and squirms, the large Dutch Reformed Church still recognizes no official confession other than the Confession of Guido de Brès, the Heidelberg Catechism, and the Canons of Dort, in which Christ's kingship is clearly recognized.[2] Therefore, if we do not go by personal relationship but by official numbers and use the official documents as our basis, the entire population of the Netherlands—with the exception of a tiny three percent—officially counted itself as belonging and wanting to belong to those Christian churches that fly the banner of Christ's kingship in their official confession.

But if you now contrast those numbers with the painful reality, where can you find officially in our country or in its leading circles even a small remnant of homage for Christ as our King?

§ 2 We do admittedly find a remnant in the recognition of Sunday as a special day and in the celebration of the commonly acknowledged Christian holidays. Not Friday, as with Islam, or Saturday, as among the Jews, but the first day of the week is considered the day of rest. Even those who have in fact broken entirely with Christianity insist—for the sake of the lower working class—on a weekly day of rest and are in favor of Sunday being that day. Sunday is the day of Christianity, hallowed by Christ's

---

2. Guido de Brès was the principal author of the Belgic Confession (1561), one of the Three Forms of Unity along with the Heidelberg Catechism (1563) and Canons of Dort (1618–19), honored by churches in the continental Reformed tradition. It was so named because it originated in the Southern Netherlands, now known as Belgium.

resurrection from the dead. The same is true of the Christian holidays. The Puritans in Scotland wanted to do away with these holidays, not out of faithlessness to Christ but out of their excessive spiritual fervor. Quakers and other sectarians likewise drift away on that current of overly excited spiritualism. But in national life, the Christian holidays managed to hold their place, in spite of a certain amount of protest against maintaining the first and especially the second day following Pentecost as holidays. However, in the lives of most people as well as in an official sense, the feast of Jesus' birth, the feast of his resurrection from the dead, the feast of his ascension, and the feast of the outpouring of the Holy Spirit are the days that, together with Good Friday as a day of commemoration, break up the normal course of daily life. They are recognized by the government in matters of law, policy, and administration. On the face of it, this fact is of little importance; nevertheless, the official character of these holidays lends it some weight. One could hardly say that Christ is, through this, really receiving the homage that is due to him. But this circumstance does prove that the Christian tradition is so deeply rooted in the country's life that, just as with the census figures, the Christian character of our nation comes to expression in at least a nominal way.

In the second place, something of that Christian tradition is officially embedded in our Education Law,[3] which calls for children to be raised in not only social but also Christian virtues—although already at this point the definition changes. It is a historical fact that the Law was intended to reduce Christianity to a purely ethical factor, consciously severed from the trunk of our faith in Christ as our King. Virtues were placed in the foreground, and it was at most acknowledged that the Christian standard for ethical life recommended itself highly. However, what *Christian* virtues might be in distinction from *social* virtues was not even indicated. Soon the "Christian" was absorbed entirely into the social, and in many schools a system of social virtues was established on a foundation that *contrasted* with Christianity far more than it was built on faith in Christ.

---

3. In 1857, the Dutch Parliament passed a law requiring state schools to educate students in both general Christian and social virtues. Some were convinced that this aided and abetted growing religious liberalism in the Netherlands, fueling an initiative, under the leadership of Guillaume Groen van Prinsterer (1801–76), that led to the eventual founding of Christian schools free of state influence. See Jan Bank et al., *Dutch Culture in a European Perspective*, vol. 3: *1900: The Age of Bourgeois Culture* (Assen: Royal Van Gorcum, 2004), 328.

As a result, those schools were avoided precisely by those who continued to embrace the kingship of Christ. Instead they became the Lost City of Gold (El Dorado) for the part of the population that had wandered away from Christ in order finally to seek shelter in the tents of skepticism and Social Democracy.

This all but exhausts what still reminds us, at least on an official level, of the Christian character of the state. Although there are a number of countries where even Parliament is still opened with prayer in the name of Jesus, in our States General no prayer is held at the opening of a session. The [annual] throne speech still refers to "God's blessing," but in a vague formulation that even ministers who have declared themselves atheists do not find objectionable.[4] No thought is given to laying one's hand on the Gospel when swearing oaths. If someone dares to refer to the Christian foundations of our nation's life as much as a single time in an official address, it always arouses protest. Even a purely historical reference to groundwork of our national character has at times been found offensive. And where in an official context a certain weak recognition of the Christian element can still be found, it is never more than formal and traditional without any trace at all of the recognition of Christ as God's anointed King.

§ 3   Are things any different or better when we leave the official terrain and continue our examination in the public square?

There are three groups in our society. The first is composed of those who find refuge in quiet and oblivion; the second consists of those who do participate in the broader national life, yet without setting the tone; finally, there is a small, yet highly influential group that is always in the foreground, speaks the supreme word in all matters, takes leadership in every field, and is said, both here and abroad, to represent the Dutch spirit.

Though few in number, this highly intellectual circle sets the tone for public opinion; the second, broader stratum has its say in the exchanges and markets, but involves itself less in public life; while the by far most

---

4. Similar to the annual State of the Union address delivered by presidents to the United States Congress, the throne speech is delivered annually by the reigning monarch to a joint session of the Dutch Senate and House of Representatives gathered in The Hague. The speech is a statement of policy for the coming parliamentary session, and often contains references to God and the need for his blessing upon the nation.

populous lowest stratum devotes itself almost entirely to home life, the office, and small business.

The leading circle, though small, includes professors at state and local universities and at the technological college;[5] those who teach at the *gymnasium* and advanced high school level; writers in the public press; public servants; artists and art critics; members of the States General, as well as statesmen more broadly defined; CEOs of large corporations; keynote speakers at meetings—in short, it is made up of all those who on account of their position or talent stand in the foreground of public life.

Is this tone-setting group inspired in word and deed by the kingship of Christ in a way that compares even closely with the Muslim faith, where even the most aberrant continue to call out for Muhammad with one voice? Does public life show you that maintaining Christ's name is what pushes and drives each and every representative of our national life in this influential circle? Do you notice even a general indignation when the name of Christ as our King is disparaged? Do you feel that in the public square of our Christian nation the honor of Christ weighs upon each and every heart? Do you get the sense that, whatever comes our way, the life of our nation, which arose from Christian action and still finds its firmest root in Christ, may never be torn away from Christ, but must always find its power-renewing concentration in him? Is the loyalty there that still faithfully and courageously clings to Christ, despite deviation and differences, and will not ever allow the deep significance of his holy name for us as a nation and as a people to be diminished?

Regrettably, this is not the case at all!   § 4

Even though Christian parties are undertaking powerful actions to defend Christ's honor, the circle that continues to this very day to set the tone for public life no longer calls out for the kingship of God's anointed King in any arena whatsoever. Not only has that ardor disappeared, but even the recognition that there is cause for such ardor has worn away. Every Islamic nation still takes pride in its prophet, but in our Christian country it is instead the silence about and resistance to the divinely anointed King that determines public opinion.

---

5. Dutch, *Technische Hoogeschool*. Historically, a technical college in the Netherlands provided industrial vocational technical training for those entering the fields of engineering, electronics, mechanics, and technology.

One will still hear people acknowledge, at least when they for whatever reason cannot not mention Jesus, that he evidenced a higher and more refined religious consciousness than did such founders of world religions as Confucius, Buddha, and Muhammad. They are not disinclined to allow Jesus the highest place of honor among the religious geniuses. As a human being, the Rabbi of Nazareth is thus indeed spoken of with a certain amount of respect. We are not yet at Voltaire's *écrasez l'infâme*.[6] There is likewise a general recognition that Christian ethics are to be preferred. But in public life there is no regard whatsoever for Jesus' kingship, and people in fact no longer know anything about it. And however high the esteem may be for Jesus' religious and ethical consciousness, no one hesitates to declare that there exists a greater religious and ethical consciousness than was found in him. People are already recommending it to us.

This partial veneration of Christ as an ethical teacher is found especially in the limited circle of those under the care of modernist preachers—men, that is, who must more or less still speak *ex officio* about Christ. But as a rule you will no longer find even this in that leading circle. There you are more likely to come upon a harsh reality that is so independent of all Christian tradition that people are simply silent regarding Christ. Nothing in their heart inclines them to him. In their self-satisfaction, people no longer see any reason to broach the subject. Their entire being and most of their thinking goes on without him. Jesus no longer has a place in their lifeview. They are almost completely dead to Christ. In their scholarship, art, literature, and press, you find next to nothing left of a holy desire to feel rich in Christ, to look up to him in wonder, and to find strength in honoring Christ. What then would those in this public circle feel for Christ as the King anointed by God? They can, for the most part, no longer even conceive or understand what it means to honor Christ as our King.

---

6. Voltaire was the assumed name of François-Marie Arouet (1694–1778). The phrase *écrasez l'infâme* means "crush the infamous." For Voltaire, this phrase referred to the abuses of the people by the royalty and the clergy, but especially to the superstitions taught by the clergy. This was expressed in one of his most famous quotes: "Superstition sets the whole world in flames; philosophy quenches them." See Geoffrey Parrinder, *The Routledge Dictionary of Religious and Spiritual Quotations* (New York: Routledge, 2001), 24. Voltaire's commitment to atheism and deism prompted his lifelong attacks against every institution and belief associated with religion. For a more detailed account, see Jim Herrick, *Against the Faith: Essays on Deists, Skeptics, and Atheists* (Buffalo, NY: Prometheus, 1985).

And indeed, there is still more. Christ was "appointed for the fall and rising of many" [Luke 2:34]. People can evade and avoid him and to attempt to silence him completely, but in history, in the life of the nation, and in reality, they nevertheless come into contact with Christ repeatedly.

There are still people who confess Christ. In history, one is time and again confronted with great events that revolved around the honor of Golgotha's cross. Even in today's literature, press, and politics one confronts thorny issues that are in some way tied up with Christ, with those who confess him, or with his importance in the past. There is the church-state relationship; the penetrating question of education; the issue of universities; the matter of elections and of government appointments. There are also great religious and ethical problems that no one can begin to address without confronting the one Name that has so decisively influenced these matters for eighteen centuries. Both in the Netherlands and elsewhere, one is confronted with these issues. They appear to be more and more thorny and difficult to resolve. For that reason, many in this circle are unwillingly forced in spite of themselves to disclose how they feel about Jesus.

What does this bring to light? What comes out? What is it that moves these leading minds? What else but a deep-seated aversion to God's entire special revelation—revulsion for every part of the confession that has come to us as doctrine from that special revelation! There is no mention of the Trinity, of God revealed in the flesh, and of salvation through the blood of the cross. If God himself testifies in Psalm 2:[6], "As for me, I have set my King on Zion, my holy hill," a smile of unbelief forms on their lips. And if some still dare to defend the cause of Christ's honor as our King, then no weapon of scorn, contempt, mockery, and derision is spared to try to break their influence, stifle their speech, and dampen the courage of their faith. An enmity is expressed that does not refrain or back down from anything. It never rests until the footstool of Christ as God's anointed King has been overturned and crushed.

In this circle there may well be noble people who disapprove of such unholy action and who judge that the freedom they desire for themselves should be given also to those who confess Christ. However, what these more philosophical and calmer opponents have in common with their wild and harsh counterparts is that they look down with a certain pity on the backwardness of believers. They see Christianity as an outdated point of view that they themselves have outgrown. They see those who continue to hold to such an outdated Christianity as lagging in their development and expect that, as long as the process continues consistently, all that is now called orthodox or swears by orthodoxy will ascend to a higher view and forever abandon that illusion of the Christ in which they once dwelled. In America and England, the situation is still different. In Germany, the population has not come this far, either. In Roman Catholic countries such as Belgium, Italy, and Spain, one still finds a somewhat different state of affairs. In our country, however, by far the greatest majority of leaders in the public square have no respect even for historic Christianity anymore. Just as in France, an unsparing spirit more and more thrashes about as it tries to convert Christianity into modernism, simply hushes it up, or else sets itself tooth and nail against all that is still called Christian by virtue of the history of the past centuries.

It is thus no exaggeration, but an incontrovertible naked truth, that no voice raises itself in the circle of our leaders on behalf of Christ as our divinely anointed King. Just look at the mainstream press and literature. See what scholarship produces. Come to lectures, attend meetings, and listen to conversation—you will hear almost nothing about Jesus, and where his name is mentioned, no call is sounded on behalf of Christ as the King given to us by God.

This may have struck and bothered you in your own country, and yet you will never be as painfully impressed by it as when you spend some time in Islamic countries.

There you will find calls for Muhammad as prophet in all social ranks and classes. Indeed, even here a weakening in the orthodoxy of Islam may be detected. Also there you will notice a drop-off in religious life. Especially in Europeanized circles you will observe an indifference to Islamic rituals and ceremonial regulations, at least when people are on their own. But in the public sphere and in private conversation with Christians, there is an unflagging zeal to stand up for Muhammad's honor and to exalt him as the prophet given by God.

By contrast, you encounter in our Christian nations a lukewarm indifference, a relaxing of the spirits, and indeed an aversion to what has been revealed in Christ, so that in our public life no spark of enthusiasm can so much as flicker on behalf of Christ as our God-given King. Are you not confronted then with a raw reality that cuts and wounds you in your very soul?

I.3

DARKENING IN
THE CHURCH

Let Israel be glad in his Maker; let the children of Zion rejoice in their King!

PSALM 149:2

Even if almost none in those leading groups whose spirit is governed by the spirit of the age call out for Christ as our King anymore, you would think that at least among those who confess Christ a call would resound day and night for the majesty of our Lord. §1

Yet disappointment awaits us here, too, and you find a deafening silence where you first expected to find joyful exultation from the lips of all.

There is, let it be understood, no lack of reverence for Jesus as our Messiah among those who confess his holy name. Such praise more than anything else will overwhelm you; all the same, it is not this subject with which we now intend to deal. At this point, we want to speak about Christ's *kingship*, the throne from which he rules, and the crown of purest gold that has been placed upon his head. We thus raise an insuperable complaint because not only outside of the forecourt, but even in the very holy place, the recollection of Christ's kingship has waned and the inspiration for it has nearly died out.

In their unceasing worship, in their never-ending praise, and in their readiness to stand in service for him who is clothed with glory and majesty at God's right hand, the angels of God understand that he who, as our High

Priest, gave himself as a sacrifice to reconcile us to God is "most highly exalted" exactly for this self-sacrifice; nor do they ever forget that he has been given "a name that is above every name" so that every knee should bow before him and every tongue sing to honor him [see Phil 2:9–11]. But here on earth there is only a vague awareness of the majesty of the Lord's kingship—not that anyone even thinks of denying it, of course. Far from it! That majesty continually comes to us from God's Holy Word. We confess it in our confession of faith. We teach it to our children from the Catechism. A number of songs popular in our midst also render it due homage. In their sermons, our preachers likewise do not fail (at times) to speak of it. Who of us would not earnestly and even heatedly defend the kingship of Christ when it is intentionally attacked?

§ 2 While we gratefully recognize this, it is not at all what we really mean. Even the people on Madura know that our queen rules the Dutch Indies.[1] On Java they acknowledge it, too, and tell it to their children. When the queen's authority is assailed and our troops are mustered in order to restore it, the Madurese and Javanese courageously fight alongside us and not infrequently give up their lives.

But if you now compare the respect for royal authority on Java with the spiritedness and enthusiasm with which the entire nation welcomes the queen in springtime at her entry into the capital of the Netherlands, you will feel, taste, and perceive that this is like day and night, like joyful cheering and detachment, like a driven national spirit and resigned compliance.

Should not holy enthusiasm for our King on high, anointed by God, far surpass any national ardor for even the best of all earthly kings in spirit and in exalted tone and in fire set ablaze by the Holy Spirit? And if by this natural demand you measure the zeal for the majesty of our heavenly King even among believers, do you not come to the painful realization that we have fallen short in our love?

Indeed, there is zeal for the cause of Christ. Zeal burns everywhere, albeit with different levels of intensity, to recruit for Christ, to extend blessing in the name of Jesus, and through his power to be surpassed by none in dedication and acts of mercy.

All the same, this is to seek the Messiah, to proclaim the Savior, to praise and commend the Redeemer, the Surety, the Atoner of sinners. Is this the

---

1. Madura is an Indonesian island off the northeastern coast of Java. In 1743, sovereignty over this island was given by treaty to the Dutch.

same thing as honoring his *kingship*? Do you not feel the deep difference that runs between the two? Do they not widely diverge?

To seek salvation as soon as that painful sense of being lost is awakened in you. To take refuge in the Messiah as soon as you abandon the false appearance of imagined holiness and see your need for salvation. To seek atonement in the Lamb of God who carries the sins of the world as soon as sin begins to oppress your soul with its deadly weight. Yes, to rejoice and exult in the salvation you have received as soon as you feel deep in your soul that you are a child of your God, sprinkled with the blood of atonement—where else can you locate the cause, desire, and motivation for all of this than in a holy egotism? In all these things it is a love for yourself that drives you.

This is not a mistaken self-love. On the contrary, your self-love was mistaken as long as you kept your distance from your Messiah, stood on your own, and sought to satisfy your ideals in the world. All the same, that self-love is and remains a desire and drive to be snatched from the waters of perdition now that you recognize that it is as though you are drowning. You were sick, and you came to the only Physician. You felt yourself sinking away under the wrath of the Holy One, and you clung to the hem of your Messiah's garment in order to be saved from the depths of destruction. You saw everlasting death before your eyes, and in faith you bound yourself onto the one who overcame death through life. O, how wonderful that is, and the angels of God rejoiced over you! Yet, however earnestly and piously this may be understood, it is still all a matter of your own salvation, atonement, and bliss. Everything revolved around you, your salvation, your entrance into eternal life. Your Messiah in all of this was *about you and for you*. But that you need to be, exist, and live *about and for Jesus* was not yet part of the picture.

Even if things progressed and Christ's love aroused in you a burning §3 love for him who loved you so deeply; even if thanksgiving welled up in your heart and you broke out in a song of praise and worship; indeed, even if for Jesus' sake you continued to fight against sin and sacrificed your money, possessions, strength, time, energy, and devotion in the work of Christian love—even then, all of these things stand on the same line with the feeling of thanks and obligation you have toward a doctor who raised you up from a deadly illness, with the thanks and obligation you feel toward someone who saved you from drowning. It is and remains a feeling that flows from your soul because *you* have been saved, *you* have been freed, and good has been done to *you*. In a strict sense, it remains the sacrifice of praise, thanksgiving, and honor to Jesus as your only *High Priest*. But is your *King* not entirely different, and is he not much more than the Priest who atones for you?

The same applies when you draw and call others to the Messiah. A mother who draws her child to Jesus from an early age and tries to instill in him or her a boundless devotion for Jesus is concerned first of all to lead that child to enjoy salvation and to partake of the heavenly inheritance. Those who call the unrepentant in their neighborhood and from among their circle of relatives and friends to Jesus, and plead with them to turn to Christ, are concerned first and foremost with their salvation. Similarly, those who go out to seek the lost, to bring light into their darkness, and to save them from perdition, aim at adding them and at being themselves a means in God's hand to bring them from the kingdom of this world into the kingdom of the Son of God.

Everything directed at finding, drawing, and adding those who are lost points to Jesus as the instrument of salvation—to Jesus as the means to redemption, salvation, the healing of diseases, the anointing of wounds, the sanctification of souls, and the obtaining of eternal life. What drives and animates is consistently a love for those who are lost. It is a matter of knowing that the Physician is there and that the medicine that can save from death stands ready. And now, because you see that there are so many who do not know the Physician and who have never put the holy medicine to their lips, you set that Physician with his eternal love and the unfailing power of his saving grace before their eyes and bring that medicine to their lips so that they may drink deeply from it and be saved by it. Yet what does bringing people under Jesus' high priestly grace have to do with honoring his kingship?

We must point out that we do not make this observation as if there lies hidden in all these things something that is less good and noble, too egotistical, or too altruistic. If that holy selfishness and noble egoism are not at work in you, you debase yourself and bring dishonor to your God as your Creator. If you feel no thirst in yourself to raise up those who are lost, you likewise neglect how you are connected to your fellow creatures. Of course, Christ was also anointed as our eternal High Priest, and those who have no desire to be impressed by the exaltedness of his priesthood will never be able to honor and worship him as King. But even if the honor of Christ as our High Priest cannot be neglected for even an instant,

God's Holy Word does make a distinction here and tells you deliberately and emphatically that God anointed him not only as High Priest, but also as our eternal King. How then can you continue to harbor the illusion that, as long as you honor Jesus as High Priest, the honor of the King may leave you indifferent?

What has been said above applies all the more to those who go no further than Jesus as Prophet. Their number is unfortunately constantly increasing. Such (in essence) half-believers could be excluded from the circle of true believers, but we will not do this. Since thousands upon thousands refuse to honor the greatest Prophet and Teacher in Jesus and place their own learning above the Word of him who was given to us by God as the revelation of the greatest wisdom, it is much more fitting that we joyfully take into account those who, in their exasperation with the false wisdom the world offers, at least still defend Jesus as our greatest Prophet. To go no further is indeed to weaken our confession most sinfully, to dislodge the cross, to be blind to what must always be the center and core of our holy confession. However, the people in this group still take up Jesus' cause—even if for no more than one third of the whole truth— and of them, too, the following words hold true: "Do not despise them. Whoever is not against him is for him" [see Luke 9:50]. Especially in times when faith is numb and emotions are paralyzed, we should be thankful to recognize this witness for Jesus, even if we feel that witness to be too faint and even if those who make it refuse to follow us all the way.

§ 4

For that reason, we must also make room in our present discussion for those who, in their coldness to the deep mystery of divine justification, refuse to warm their hearts by the High Priest's heart, expecting all the strength they need from the Word that went out with power from Jesus' lips. [We must make room] for those who delight in his high ethical ideal and raise themselves up by this ideal in order to enter into communion with their God through Jesus' unique religious consciousness. This group of people is to be included as long as they—and this condition cannot be discarded!—in honoring Christ as our High Priest do not trace the elevated character of his ethical-religious revelation back to a spark of genius in him, explaining it on the basis of his elevated status among other human beings. They must consciously and resolutely confess that he is God revealed in the flesh, and [they must confess] that for that reason the full, greatest, absolute, and unsurpassable revelation of God has been given to us in him. If Thomas' confession ("My Lord and my God!" [John 20:28]) falls silent, every confession will drop lifeless to the ground, all communion with believers will be undone, and every call for the Greatest Prophet will turn into a ready lie.

§ 5   Given this proviso and the ensuing spiritual struggle, it is undoubtedly very important that there still is a broad circle in which at least the divinity of Christ is honored, the comprehensive reach of his revelation is still resolutely confessed with sincerity, and, countering the errors of our times, the ethical and religious relevancy of the gospel is defended with conviction. Those who swear by the Word of the Messiah may still be at quite a distance, but they are no longer that far from the Kingdom of God. If the greatest Prophet is only known better and understood more intimately in his Word, he automatically leads to the only High Priest.

But as thankful as we may be that, also in these circles, a warm plea is often made for the excellency of the gospel, as highly as we value these voices and do not hesitate to admit that many of those who have found the High Priest come up short in showing honor to Jesus as the Highest Prophet, still none of these things has anything to do with the honor due to Christ as the King anointed by God. The fact remains that, in this more reflective group of people, the real and warm-hearted jubilation for Jesus as our King unfortunately hardly ever arises.

§ 6   It is also something else to recognize and honor Jesus as the Head of the body, even though this can come close to the recognition of him as King. The Head of the body is a mystical-organic concept, and it points to the organic communion of those who are one in faith, hope, and love. Every communion can be compared with a body, and the image of the body right away makes us think of the image of the head.

For this reason, many of those who have an eye for the mystical life, who seek communion with God's saints, and who experience in that communion the unifying and inspiring work of Christ are especially glad to honor Christ as the Head of the church. They feel and notice through this communion that Christ exercises a guiding influence. Regrettably, this conviction is all too often desecrated by comparing it with philosophical theories. It thereby loses the gold dust from its wings. Yet, even where this has not happened and Christ's honor as Head of the church continues to be understood in a purely mystical fashion, it is something entirely different from his kingship. An earthly prince like William the Silent[2] can be the head of his nation temporarily in that he thinks on its behalf, injects the nation with ardor and courage, and leads it to victory, but these things still do not as such make him a king.

The recognition of Jesus as Head of the church is expressed in an even weaker way when that headship is limited to his church, as was often done in the ancient opposition against the papacy. Not wanting to recognize anyone as Christ's governor on earth, many are inclined to retreat straightaway to Christ himself, to point to him alone, and to cover everything the church does with Jesus' name. But however much this does indeed come close to his kingship, limiting Christ to the churchly domain[3]—which in our circles has such a simple form—keeps one from seeing the majesty of him who as our King is seated at God's right hand. That limitation fails in every way to raise the soul up to the greatness of the majesty of Jesus' kingship. Indeed, the domain of the church is also included in his kingship, but the former reveals itself in such a deficient human form, in so small a field, with such elusive power, that it does not give rise to even the faintest hint of the majesty that shines in Christ's full kingship.

By now it should be clear why we complained that Jesus' kingship is not only being ignored, denied, and attacked in the outside world, but that the glory of his kingship is also waning inside all believing circles.

§ 7

People honor Christ as God revealed in the flesh; they kneel before him in worship; they swear by him as the Greatest Prophet; they approach him as the only High Priest; they let themselves be animated by him as the Head of the body; in church affairs [the legitimacy of] every act is deduced from him, and him alone; and the kingship of Christ in his eternal majesty and glory, too, is indeed confessed, recognized in the confessions, and even emphatically and earnestly defended over against anyone who tries to deny it. But confessing, not-denying, and even recognizing and

---

2. William the Silent was one of the names given to William I, Prince of Orange (24 April 1533–10 July 1584; he is also known as William of Orange). William was the main leader of the Dutch revolt against the Spanish Habsburgs, marking the start of the Eighty Years' War, which resulted in the political independence of the United Provinces in 1648. William became Prince of Orange in 1544, founding the House of Orange-Nassau and becoming the ancestor of the monarchy in the Netherlands.

3. The Dutch word used for "domain" in this and the following sentence is "regiment," referring to an ordered and governed arena.

pleading for something, is altogether different from taking it up into the very existence of your soul and living out of it.

Precisely this last element is missing. We do not mean to say that this is the case for everyone. We make no judgment about anyone's personal position before his Messiah. To do this, you would have to know someone's innermost life—and who knows this for more than a number of one's closest friends? How many of you know this even of your own children or of yourselves? Our judgment can be based only on the expression, manifestation, and external activity of the Christian life. In making this judgment, we cannot keep silent about the fact that, in the Islamic world, a more powerful and persistent appeal is made on behalf of Muhammad the prophet than there is among us on behalf of Christ as our King whom God has anointed.

This weakens us and undermines our power, and above all it represents a failure to give to Jesus the all-surpassing honor that we owe our King as his subjects.

THE GENERAL APOSTASY

Unless the apostasy comes first.

2 Thessalonians 2:3

It was thus from two sides at once that the honor shown to the kingship of §1 Christ sank and fell. In the broad circles of the intelligentsia the splendor of that kingship was almost entirely extinguished, while among believers it also waned. That latter aspect also must be pointed out emphatically. People are easily tempted to shove the whole responsibility for this situation onto the world and to think that they get off scot free, but precisely that would break the force of this observation. We do not mean this generally in the sense of the absolute need for humility when one prepares for spiritual action. The call for humility has unfortunately shown itself to be most in vogue among those who resist all concerted action tooth and nail. They preach humility constantly and add that action could commence only after there was humility. And because that humility was never thought to run deep enough, they could never get around to doing anything.

This is nothing less than apprehension putting you to sleep! It is true that a deadly serious tone will give rise to humility about *personal* sin and *personal* unfaithfulness in everyone. But humility with regard to national ills, social wrongs, or being lax and lukewarm, is a state of mind that at most only a few prophetic, priestly people can muster—something

29

unthinkable for people at large. You may be able to impress on a large group for a few minutes in a meeting or assembly that there is a broad communal level of guilt about which we should be ashamed, but that impression is soon dispelled by the diverse issues of daily life. Those who are concerned not about the world of their imagination but about the real world in which most people live their daily lives, must realize that psychologically such *general* humility about some *general* states of affairs— unless action against that evil follows immediately—never is or can be anything more than a morning mist that hangs for some time over one's conscience but is soon driven away by the wind of the day.

By contrast, such general humility is not only imaginable, but is in fact a duty, and represents a force to reckon with when those who are ready to launch a major defensive or offensive assault urge everyone at that very moment to bow down and confess their guilt before God and to perform the intended action not under any illusion concerning their supposed holiness, but in the power of the Lord of lords. On the other hand, those who discourage all action while appealing constantly for humility—not, we repeat, over *personal* but *communal* guilt embedded in the universal human condition—are either unfamiliar with the world of psychology or else deceive themselves and others. Such an appeal for humility goes up in a smoke of words and in the end reaches neither conscience nor mind. Their pleas are more likely to weaken and quench all holy zeal, leading to nauseating complaints and passive resignation.

At the great moments of history an impressive humility reigned in and of itself. At such times, humility was indeed present and worked miracles, but at the very same time the decision was made to spring into action. On the battlefield, even the most hardened soldier feels no smaller than when the first canon blast rumbles through the air. We thus have not pointed to the absence of honor for the kingship of Christ among believers in order to stifle courage, but rather so that we can gain better insight into the current situation and learn from this knowledge how we should proceed.

§ 2   By this time, it should be evident that we are in a period of *general apostasy*. We do not intend for our readers to understand that we are now faced with that great apostasy which will bring us closer to the end of all things. The Father has placed the times and events under his own power, and it remains a risky venture to announce the imminent end of time as long as the special signs are absent. History shows us that even the most pious often failed in this. It always became apparent after the fact that God's ways are higher than ours and that he once more parted the clouds to let the light through again, even though many Christians were convinced that history had come to the ultimate extinction of the light.

But even if Christianity has undoubtedly erred countless times when it imagined the end of the world to be at hand, we also have to acknowledge that we have a tendency to shut ourselves up in our own circles and be blind, because things go well within that small circle, to the general decline in the spiritual world. Many Christians do indeed rage against public opinion, are unsparing in their condemnation of the rise and increase of all kinds of social sins, and are bothered by the impudent expression of unbelief. However, they refuse to open their eyes to the *general* character of this decline and take no account of the threat this general situation poses in the end for the next generation in our own Christian circle as well. In Zion they are not worried, and while they do condemn the decline among others, they imagine themselves to be safe within their own circle. This is precisely why they do not understand the world that lies outside of their own small circle, and for that reason they are likewise powerless to exercise a positive influence.

This false illusion under which believers live is nowhere more evident than in their internal quarrels and bickering, and the tone in which such quarrels are often conducted. It almost never happens—or can happen— that everyone agrees on everything. Our individualism is too strong to allow this. The unique circumstances and sensitivities arising out of the past are too lasting in their impact. That is why the derivation of our conclusions based on what all believe together is too fluctuating and uncertain. But if you look at the questions and issues over which believers have battled each other during the last fifty years and note the bitterness with which that battle over these issues—which to a degree continues even today—has been fought, then you can hardly escape the impression that you are watching a mighty enemy coming out to lay siege to and occupy a small fortress. Meanwhile the leaders and soldiers in that fortress are not at all busy preparing a solid defense but are instead nearly at each other's throat over the decision of whether the barrack's façade should be constructed in Renaissance or Gothic style.

We do not, of course, claim that such issues are in themselves unimportant, nor do we deny that in times of peace such matters can be weighty and significant. However, one cannot remain silent about the fact that,

§ 3

when the enemy is at the gate, the importance of these questions fades away. People who in such times do not first of all do everything to prepare themselves to defend the fortress against the enemy have not understood either their duty or their calling. There are many today who do not do this, but continue exhausting their strength in settling issues of second, third, or even fourth importance, and it is all too clear that their eyes have been blinded to the threatening danger; they do not see it. For that reason, they imagine that they can afford a luxury that can be ours only in days of total peace.

As a result, love cools, people no longer win over but push away, and to those on the outside they give the disastrous impression that, if you want to admire and enjoy the powerful rule of Christ's love, you should certainly not seek shelter in the tents of believers. The *odium theologicum*, or the sharp bitterness with which theologians are accustomed to waging war against each other, has regrettably become proverbial. Even today we can continue to bemoan the lamentable division in the East between Nestorians,[1] Catholics, Greek Orthodox, Armenians, Copts,[2] Marionites,[3]

---

1. Nestorianism involves the doctrine that Jesus Christ existed as two persons: the man Jesus and the divine Son of God. This doctrine is identified with Nestorius (c.386-451), Patriarch of Constantinople. In this view the humanity of Christ suffered separate from his divine nature. The Nestorians also rejected the title of Theotokos (Mother of God) for Mary, choosing instead the title Christotokos (Mother of Christ). Nestorianism was condemned at the Council of Ephesus in 431, leading to the Nestorian schism, which separated the Assyrian Church of the East from the Byzantine Church.

2. "Coptic" means "Egyptian," and the Coptic Christians are the native Christians of Egypt, constituting the largest Christian community in the Middle East. The Orthodox Church of Egypt is Coptic and has been described as monophysite (believing that Christ possessed one nature, virtually denying his humanity), though some prefer to be described as miaphysite (believing in one composite, conjoined nature from two). The Coptic Orthodox Church became separated from other Christians after the Council of Chalcedon (451), whose decisions regarding the natures of Christ became the standard view of subsequent Roman Catholic, Eastern Orthodox, and Protestant churches.

3. Though spelled by Kuyper as "Marionites," this likely refers to the Syriac Maronite Church of Antioch. It is an Eastern Catholic Church in full communion with the Roman Catholic Church. Maron was a fourth-century monk and a contemporary and friend of John Chrysostom. He left Antioch for the Orontes River in modern day Syria to lead an ascetic life, accompanied by many of his followers. After the death of Maron in AD 410, his disciples dedicated a monastery to his memory and formed the Maronite Church. The Maronites affirmed the Chalcedonian formula regarding the natures of Christ, for which they were severely persecuted by some

and whatever other groups there may be, which because of theological infighting leaves Christians powerless under Islam. There, too, when the enemy was at the gate, Christians did not see the danger threatening their community, and as a result their descendants have for twelve or thirteen centuries reaped the bitter fruit of the way in which Christians of all stripes sinned, spoiled, and erred when Islam arose. The issues dividing the Christians in the East were in themselves very important as well, but they failed to see that, where the existence and flowering of Christ's church itself is at stake, all other issues surrender their weight and importance. How you should dress is in the same way not unimportant, but if you find yourself bedridden with a fatal illness and stare death itself in the eyes, you would reprove your family and relatives if they were to fight at your bedside over whether Christians should dress as Europeans in the East or wear Eastern clothing, rather than devoting their combined attention and love to saving your life.

For that reason, it must earnestly be pointed out to believers that their small circle cannot be hermetically sealed off from the greater spiritual world and that, in this spiritual world, action has been undertaken which is starting to look more and more like a continually advancing apostasy from Christianity. More than that, it must be made clear that a situation is being created in which not only the Christian religion, but religion as a whole increasingly surrenders its influence. In all parts of society religious life is falling apart, and this manifests itself more clearly in each successive generation. This can be seen not only in the broad circle of the baptized, but also among Jews and, in part, even among Muslims. In all of the three great monotheistic religions united against paganism's worship of many gods or of a god-in-everything (that is, polytheism and pantheism), an unmistakable deadening and collapse of religious consciousness is now evident.

For all three, the cause is equally clear. Neither among Christians nor Jews nor Muslims does the apostasy extend to the entire population. As a general observation, one can note that a considerable group in the middle and lower classes continues to maintain the age-old historical traditions. For the Christians, we see this most clearly in our own country. For the

---

of the monophysite party in Antioch. Controversy continues to this day regarding whether the Maronite Church held to monothelitism (that Christ and God have only one will) or to miathelitism (Christ's will was fully united to God's will).

Jews, this is confirmed by the large groups of orthodox Jews in Amsterdam, and especially by what one sees among the Jews in Poland, Russia, and Romania. For the Muslims, the decline in religious life at present touches only a thin upper stratum of those who live in a modernized society. However, in the higher social strata an entirely different spirit has gradually gained influence. It leads away from faith everywhere, closes the eyes to the world of the invisible, and has attempted under the name of *the modern spirit of the age* to establish an entirely different life- and world-view. This modern spirit of the age continually trickles down, first to the middle strata, and then all the way down to the lowest strata of society. It is like a drop of ink on a blotter that spreads out in concentric circles.

We must distinguish within this modern spirit of the age between a cynical-materialistic stream and an idealistic-mystical stream; though the second is so weak and insignificant compared to the first that it neither agitates nor assists. It is the cynical-materialistic stream that advances with leaps and bounds to bind spiritually more and more of our sons and daughters of the next generation. There is an intellectual circle as well that may not be idealistic, but comes close to both cynicism and materialism. Yet it too is so small that it hardly leaves any trace of itself within the broader stream. And even if you combine all who are more idealistically oriented, more intellectually developed, and more mystically inclined, these three groups together still form no more than a negligible minority that has almost no influence on the masses.

The quiet hope that modern theologians once harbored and of which they were fully convinced—namely, that they would gradually succeed in making our entire nation religiously sensitive again through a higher religion—ended up being a fatal fiasco. What was recently declared at the anniversary celebration of the *Dageraad*[4]—that is, "The Christians sang, 'High, on high, lift up your heart above! Here below is there nothing: ...,'[5] but we declare the opposite, 'What you seek is indeed down here';

---

4. The *Dageraad* (*Daybreak*) was a periodical, subtitled "A magazine devoted to the spread of truth and enlightenment in the spirit of natural religion and morals." This organ of the society of freethinkers was founded on October 1, 1855, with the objective of liberating people from the oppression of religion and morality by means of reason and science. Its nineteenth and final volume appeared in 1897–1898.
5. These are the words of a famous and familiar Dutch hymn, "'t Oog omhoog, het hart naar boven, hier beneden is het niet!" composed by Jodocus van Lodenstein (1620–77), a Dutch churchman renowned for his piety and accomplishments

we work only for this earth."—betrays the tone-setting spirit of society's upper strata. The purposes of everyone are united and focused on this earthly life, and in this earthly life one person may work for money and possessions alone, another for art and beauty, a third person for academia, a fourth for sports, a fifth for pleasure. But despite their differences, all of them are united in three respects: namely, that the thing they seek is to be found here on earth, in this world; that we are to limit ourselves to this earthly sphere of life; and that it is best not to muse, consider, think, or speak of whatever may be beyond, within, or above it. After all—so it is thought—no one knows anything about it anyway, and whoever claims to have some knowledge is either clever but deceptive, or else honest but ignorant.

There are countless causes at work in this, but the main one is the decline and fall in the activity of the religious consciousness. Those who clearly recognize this will also realize that the evil is not limited to the modernist circle but has also touched our own circle albeit, thank God, to a smaller degree. §4

No matter how the faith life of Christians concentrates itself personally in the conversion of their souls to the Triune God, in our Christian circles we also are subjected to influence from various currents. There are times when the spiritual sets the tone for public life as a whole; at other times people live spiritually more in the past; these are followed by yet other times that see regression and weakening; and in the end comes the period of spiritual decline.

Everyone who reads about the time of the Reformation and compares it with what we currently see around us will sense this. In the sixteenth and seventeenth centuries, religion was the primary issue in life not only among believers, but also among those who were opposed to them. The religious standard was determinative, and the importance of religion surpassed everything else. People felt at home in it, talked about it, read about it, and with courage and perseverance made the greatest sacrifices for it. It is for that very reason that religious life among believers had a depth of which later generations can only be jealous.

---

in hymnody. For more information on Van Lodenstein as poet and hymnist, see Carl J. Schroeder, *In Quest of Pentecost: Jodocus van Lodenstein and the Dutch Second Reformation* (Lanham, MD: University Press of America, 2001), 89-98.

But as early as the second half of the seventeenth century, a change occurred. In the first half of the eighteenth century, one saw barrenness where earlier roses and lilies had flourished. And by the end of the eighteenth century, that barrenness had virtually sunk into total demise and death. Since then there has been that wonderful *Réveil*,[6] which brought a new awakening. And after the time when the *Réveil* turned more to national action, things have flourished to a degree for which we cannot give enough thanks. But whatever we make of it, the contrast with the sixteenth century remains. Things are not as they used to be. The current situation is lower in degree, level, and tone, and you continually perceive how in more than one circle that tone is dropping lower and lower.

This is now what the Lord has apportioned to us in his almighty sovereignty. The century in which we live, as well as the second half of the last century, is dominated more by matter than religion. The religious movement in the general mindset lacks that holy energy that it used to have in bygone times. This is the case in all countries and can be noticed throughout the entire world. The very atmosphere of religion is heavy, and we who breathe in it no longer drink in full and overabundant measure from the spiritual oxygen that brought our forefathers their great vitality. There may be some signs pointing to favorable change in the religious atmosphere, but until now such signs have been more like an evening breeze than a storm that shakes the trees of the forest and sweeps the dust from their leaves.

God's grace is not prevented from being and remaining capable of strengthening the personal life of faith also in that languid atmosphere, from keeping it healthy, and inspiring it with holy zeal. But you should never imagine that the atmosphere you breathe has no influence on you. The dullness of that atmosphere dampens even the strongest faith life to a certain degree, and it has especially disastrous effects in the broad group of believers where personal faith life is not yet sufficiently strong. And if we are seeing this unmistakably among groups of believers, then among groups where there is no decisive faith, the oppressive atmosphere can only have been more deadly in its effect. When the waters in the stream of the religious are high, people in worldly circles are also lifted up by

---

6. The Dutch *Réveil* (awakening, renewal) was a part of the cultural and religious revivals occurring in England, Switzerland, and France during the nineteenth century. Willem Bilderdijk (1756–1831) is considered the father of the *Réveil*, and Groen van Prinsterer became one of its most accomplished advocates.

that stream, and by virtue of that they automatically live higher. But if, as is now the case, the level of that stream plummets, then everything will drop and in the end reach a mark so low that *all* religious influence will fall away entirely from these broader groups. The more we become aware that we are dealing with a general evil under which we ourselves suffer as well, the more thankful we will be for what the Lord has left to us, and the more ready we will be both to have pity on the spiritually poor from those other groups and to be a blessing to them in the power of God.

HUMANITY IS GREAT

They set their mouths against the heavens, and their tongue struts through the earth.

PSALM 73:9

§ 1   While the call that "The Prophet is great!" continues to resound loudly in the countries of Islam, the *Pro Rege—Great is our King!*—is dying out more and more in our Christian nation. It not only died off among the groups that set the tone for public life, but also among believers it has undergone a painful weakening, though for different reasons. As we discussed in the last chapter, in the atmosphere of religion the thermometer of religious life shows a decline in its intensity and glow. Compared to the spirit of the past centuries, the modern spirit of the age has deprived religion of its prominent significance. The modern spirit of the age still salutes religion, but then from a distance. Just as there is among the masses a group of artistically inclined people, so also the existence of a group of piously and mystically inclined people is respected.

For the main life stream, however, these small groups are of only secondary importance. Religion does still exercise a certain moral-purifying influence in the public arena and receives the prize for alleviating various kinds of need, and even that group of artists exercises in its own way a certain noble influence on the masses. However, both art and religion exercise marginal influence on the spirit of the age. The powerful wind that drives the current of life and determines its course originates from material interests, the intellect, and technology's control over nature. The heroes of religion can be found in the days of the martyrs; for the different fields of art we find the greatest glory represented by Dante and Shakespeare, by Michelangelo and Rubens; the heroes of the modern spirit of the age are the great philosophers, leading scientists, and those who can work magic with electricity and technology.

This turnaround in the state of affairs must be clearly understood. Those who wish to live powerfully and to exercise power over life must begin by understanding the stamp imprinted on the forehead of the life of their times in its basic principles. At present, those basic principles are not the religious ones; the situation is rather that an anti-religious feature is becoming mixed into the life of our times. This anti-religious feature results partly from hostility toward God and partly from hostility against the "elite," but even more from the present century, whose face has been lined by the attempt to cut everyone off for good from a return to religion's rule.

Is it not possible to explain the cause of this, as serious and lamentable as it is? §2

Is one not struck immediately by the way man as man has grown from a dwarf into a giant compared to the past centuries with regard to his power and ability, to his knowledge and know-how, to his dominion and subjection of the power of nature? Is one not likewise struck by the sudden spurts and shocks in which this growth took place? There is undoubtedly a contrast between man and the world in which he moves. Can it be disputed that, until the middle of the eighteenth century, man was almost like a martyr before nature when you compare his control over nature then to what man was able to accomplish in the second half of the nineteenth century and up to this point in the twentieth century?

Our power, our dominion over nature and its powers, is more than fourteen times what it was less than half a century ago. Whereas people earlier lived under a certain feeling of inferiority and weakness over against the power and forces of nature, at present humanity stands over nature with a magic wand in its hand and knows how to cast spells over it. The former fear gave way, and in its place has come an unwavering feeling of power that totters on the edge of overconfidence. Humanity has won one triumph over nature after another. Earlier people saw themselves as toys in the hands of nature, but now they are its masters. Although by far not every force of nature has been subjected under our feet, the victory already attained is so pervasive, comprehensive, constant, and progressive that the mastery that has been won prophesies future triumphs.

Already humanity senses that its triumph will soon be complete. It continues in every area of life. No year fails to surprise us in terms of the victories won and discoveries made. And the fruits and blessings reach through into every corner of society. Man and woman, young and old, rich and poor all profit from it. Everyone enjoys it. A consciousness entirely different from before has penetrated through to all ranks and positions. And even those believers who look with dismay at the consequences of this unceasing progress benefit as much as others do from the advantages offered by this new situation. Whether they want to be or not, they are likewise subject in their inner consciousness to its overwhelming influence.

This change in the state of affairs can only have a negative effect on the state of religion. Although we do not concede Schleiermacher's principle that religious consciousness consists in a feeling of absolute dependence, it cannot be doubted that the feeling of dependence on a higher power has always been one of the most powerful factors.[1] The dependence on God Almighty was most deeply felt in the mastery that nature exercised over our human existence. Epidemics, sickness and death, shipwreck and flooding, lightning strikes and earthquakes, devastated crops, destruction by vermin, spoiling by cold, scorching through heat, vast distances—altogether, they created a feeling of impotence and inability. Whenever the level of need arose, there manifested itself in every circle a tendency, a need, and a drive to seek refuge in a higher grace. A sick man's prayer was never more fervent than when the doctor seemed to be powerless. Epidemics immediately caused the pews to fill again in houses of prayer. Shipwreck saw even the most calloused sailor sink to his knees. Earthquakes led people to go to church right away. Distress taught people to pray time and again. Religion did not find greater support anywhere than in the feeling of a constant inferiority before nature and in the potential for new dangers.

Add to this the abuses that were due to nature's power over human life—the constant wars, the ever recurring famines, the unbridled lust for theft and murder, the threat of fire, the insurrection and mutiny and the

---

1. See Friedrich Schleiermacher, *The Christian Faith*, ed. H. R. Mackintosh and J. S. Stewart (New York: T&T Clark, 1999 [1830]), §4.

resulting fears—then you will understand how this tiny humanity used to dwell in constant worry, living from one day to the next, constantly overwhelmed by the somber premonition of what the next day could bring. Because of this, in the general mindset there always remained an understanding of one's smallness, together with an urge to seek help and rescue from the One who, stronger than both man and nature, can offer help in need and rescue when there is danger. This accounts for the general religious character that life used to have, the stamp which religion, with its days of thanksgiving and prayer, placed upon all public and private life.

It is important that we are properly understood on this point. Pure religion grows out of a root that is holier than distress and worry; it comes from the work of the Holy Spirit. And both now and in the days of our fathers, the hidden communion that those who know God enjoy with him finds its origin in a special operation that proceeds from God to the souls of his elect. It should never be forgotten, however, that religion has two spheres. In truly pious men and women it personally bears a most particular character. It can be compared to art in the sense that neither religion nor art ever come to a higher and purer expression than by inspiration, and such inspiration in religion and art has always worked in a limited circle alone. §3

However, this is only one of two spheres—the one in which religion shines in its full and pure radiance. Beside, or rather around it, there extends a second and much wider sphere that may not penetrate to the core of the soul, but which is nevertheless unmistakable and highly important. In this wide circle of religion, its stimulus does not reach as deep, is considerably less constant, and depends much more on the external. This sphere forms, as it were, the forecourt of the holy temple. And precisely because in this forecourt the spiritual affections and sensations do not touch the core of holiness and the feeling of guilt and awareness as deeply, in this second sphere religion depends much more on the feeling of dependence, on the need for rescue and release from life's basic perils, and on the moral effect that religion has on individuals, family, and society as a whole. As a result, the following difference exists between these two religious spheres: the first, which reigns in the holy place itself, maintains its own power and character at all times, for all people, and under all circumstances; in the sphere of the forecourt, the stream of religion rises and falls, going up when need runs high and down when that need has been satisfied. Those who live in the first sphere of the holy place pray constantly and unceasingly; in the second sphere of the forecourt, prayer falls silent or turns into idle chattering when things go well, only to become more intense, upright, and bold when the need returns.

We see the result before our very eyes. In the narrow circles of the pious, religion has barely suffered any damage. In the holy place it still is what it always was. And however high humanity's power over nature and the ordinances of life may eventually reach, the intimate—the spiritually intimate mystery of religion—remains in this small circle what it has always been: to walk with God, to enter into his holy community, and to live in secret communion with him. But in the sphere of the forecourt things have taken a very different course. At present, the need is much lower, and so there is less prayer. An increased awareness of power led to a diminished sense of powerlessness, so that the need to seek help from God declined. Consciousness of one's own strength keeps people from drawing near to the Strong God. When there is sudden and unexpected need, that old consciousness does return, but it no longer has its former significance and disappears as quickly as it arose. People feel themselves to be less dependent, and for that reason they no longer experience that old drive to call upon and honor the Almighty.

§ 4   Do not say that this decline in the feeling of dependence, this decrease in sensing the need for supernatural deliverance, may well touch the world but does not harm the church of Christ. You are mistaken if you imagine that this feeling of smallness, powerlessness, helplessness, and dependence is not an integral element in all of religion. Read the Psalms, the Prophets, and the Gospels, and time and again you will find this prevailing theme: "You are my strength, my rock and tower, my refuge in the darkest hour. Your praise I sing and shout abroad, O mighty Fortress, loving God!"[2] Ask the most pious of the pious, and every single one of them will confess that nothing drew them more to God than that feeling of deep dependence. Children who learn for the first time to bow their knees know no other religion and cannot know any other religion than that which arises from that feeling of deep dependence.

Here, too, nature precedes grace. In the hidden corners of a child's soul there may well have been a spiritual operation from God that potentially

---

2. This quotation combines elements from two psalms according to their 1773 rhyming. The first two lines are part of Psalm 59, stanza 10; the last two lines are part of Psalm 73, stanza 14.

implanted the seed of true faith, and yet in the foreground of that child's consciousness there remains, even in the circle of believers, the need for help and deliverance and blessing. This is also how it continues in the later years, sometimes even when that child has reached the age of maturity, until a higher urge is awakened in the soul and God himself unveils his holy presence, entering into the communion of the Holy Spirit with that child.

Even when that higher perspective has been reached and faith has begun to spread its wings to ascend to the Exalted, the needs of this life, difficulties in earthly affairs, worries about the future, or new dangers continue to inspire faith's wing-strokes with renewed strength. Need uncovers sin. Sin, as it is being uncovered, seeks grace. And in this way even in the holy place, life's needs and the deep feeling of dependence continually drive the soul toward its God. The forecourt's sphere retains its animating power even for those who have penetrated through to the sphere of the holy place. Indeed, necessity, smallness, and dependence first exercise their full influence on those who are allowed to dwell in the holy place. The church of Christ is not a gathering of living believers alone. The sacrament of infant baptism recognizes also the seed of the church. And so the church of Christ will remain a mixed body until the very end, and also in the church the forecourt will remain distinct from the holy of holies.

The mastery won over nature, and the regular pattern established in our human life, could for that reason not avoid being of great influence on the church of Christ. Even those added to the church are affected by it, but the entirely new relationship in which we find ourselves over against the powers of nature must have an especially deep effect on the youth, on the next generation, and on those who, even when they have reached the age of maturity, continue to keep their distance. Had this generation lived in the sixteenth century, its religious situation would be entirely different than it is now.

But also conversely, had the sixteenth century possessed our control over the powers of nature, the tone of its religious life would have been much weaker than it now appears to us in history. Human beings remain human. People as such remain virtually unchanged throughout all centuries. What differences there may be from one century to another come precisely from the distinctive influences exerted upon them. It would, for that reason, be unfair to your surroundings if you attribute the things that now bother you only to wickedness and malevolence, while explaining the tone that used to reign as the result of devotion and piety alone. A life factor as strong as powerlessness before nature, or the power that has now been won over it, cannot remain without influence on the way in which religious life manifests and presents itself. We who still closely hold to the faith of our fathers would be unfair toward our less fortunate contemporaries if we were to see nothing but wickedness in the absence of religion in them. We will make it impossible to work effectively on them if we do not make a more serious attempt to comprehend and understand their lack of religion. All rebellion against religion is a wicked act of the soul, but this wickedness is by nature hidden in each person's heart and was also found in the souls of the past generations. The question is rather whether the influences tempering or fostering this wickedness now work in an entirely different manner compared to before.

§ 5   Once the question has been put this way, there can be no difference of opinion as to whether the triumphs over the forces of nature and the forces of communal life—won by intellect, skill, knowledge, and know-how—effected a radical change in the way we think, in our view of the world and of life, and with that also in the place of religion. Our dependence declined; our power increased. The great forces of nature that used to overpower and overwhelm are now subject to us and at our service. Humankind can work magic with them. Various kinds of distress that used to strike down are now all but turned aside and hardly appear anymore. All kinds of resources have been discovered against the distresses that still remain, and they are generally applied to believers and unbelievers alike. A bright stroke of sunlight has broken through the clouds that used to darken life. What the preceding generation did not know has been revealed to us. Through the microscope our eyes see what theirs did not see, and our arm reaches ten times as far as theirs. Distances have shrunk; separation between one country and another has been undone by various means of powerful communication. Almost every barrier that used to offer resistance has been broken through. We stretch out our wings in all directions as never before. How, then, can those who are fully aware of humanity's growing power today and know no higher grace still feel what the previous generations felt? Still believe that they are small in the face of hardships that no longer exist? Or have a sense of being unimportant and dependent now that their impotence has fallen away? Given the way things have turned out, that feeling of profound dependence—which in most people never had a deeper root than fear and concern—had to weaken in a generation that has overcome these hardships and feels in many respects as if it can even govern the future.

Do not deceive yourselves. Insofar as this feeling of dependence had no other basis than the awareness of being powerless and small, it also suffered serious damage in the circle of believers. Almost all who look inside themselves will be forced to witness that their inner awareness as well has undergone a change that is in many ways remarkable. To convince yourself of this, just look at an intimate record from the days of our fathers in which someone writes his soul's experiences in this regard. When you then compare his experiences to what goes on in your own soul, you will all too often recognize that within his heart something was oppressing him that you no longer experience, and when you attempt to trace this change back to its cause, you will always return to the conclusion that it results from the new relationship in which we stand today over against nature and life's distresses.

This alone explains how the decline in the energy of religious life is a general phenomenon found—albeit in unequal measure—in all countries, among all peoples, and with Christians as well as Jews and Muslims.

THE RELIGIOUS SENSE DIMINISHED

And they have no rest, day or night.

REVELATION 14:11

§ 1   The universal dominion that we have achieved over the powers of nature has stimulated humanity's feeling of power and thus has significantly weakened humanity's feeling of dependence. Therefore, it *had* to lead to a dampening of religious life, to a reduction in the sphere of piety, to a cooling of the devotion of many. It is here that the root cause of religion's decline and unbelief's swift increase lies, and for that reason we placed it up front. Yet humanity's dominance and supremacy over nature is not the only cause of the ebb in the tide of religious life. That victory over nature's power has produced much more to erode religion. Let us first focus our attention on the loss of the calm and quiet in which the pious life used to flourish so abundantly.

The book of Revelation says about those who are lost in their corruption that "they have *no rest*, day or night" [Rev 14:11]—and this in contrast to the wonderful promise that "there remains a Sabbath rest for the people of God" [Heb 4:9]. Time and again, the Word of God points to the precious rest for our hunted and tortured heart. The Sabbath, as day of rest, comes every seven days to bring quiet into our lives, and as our Catechism expresses so beautifully, it gives us a foretaste of the eternal

Sabbath with God.[1] "A dry morsel *with quiet*" [Prov 17:1] seemed to the poet of the Proverbs a desirable lot, while the Preacher observed: "Better is a handful *of quietness* than two hands full of toil and a striving after wind" [Eccl 4:6]. In the song of the Good Shepherd, the psalmist sings: "He leads me beside still waters" [Psa 23:2]. In the Lamentation over Jerusalem, it says, "My eyes will flow without ceasing, *without respite*" [Lam 3:49], while Baruch complains to Jeremiah: "I am weary with my groaning, and I *find no rest*" [Jer 45:3]. The apostle from Tarsus suffers so bitterly under the *lack of rest* for his spirit and body [2 Cor 2:12; compare 2 Cor 7:5]. While in the prophecies to Israel it was already said: "*This is rest*; give rest to the weary; and this is repose" (Isa 28:12), our peace appeared in Christ so that he could declare to us: "Learn from me, for I am gentle and lowly in heart, *and you will find rest* for your souls" [Matt 11:29].

Not all rest to which we have alluded here is equal. Deepest is the rest that tames the unrest of the tumultuous passions in the hiddenness of the soul and that brings us peace with our God. Then follows the rest that saves us from the lack of peace inflicted on us by others. There is also rest from destiny's pursuit, whether it takes shape in the bitterness of the enemy, the cruelty of disappointment, painful loss, or sickness. Furthermore, there is the rest that overcomes the doubts in our heart and calms the world of our thoughts, senses, and imagination. The rest that is already enjoyed here on earth then ascends to the higher rest of the eternal Sabbath that will be enjoyed in the house of our God.

In whatever degree or form, under whatever blast or anxiety, whether from the inside or the outside, our spirit may be overcome by unrest, tumult, lack of peace. From the very depths of our souls there constantly arises the desire for rest, for peace, for quietness. This manifests itself most frightfully in the insane, the over-agitated, the strained, and the distressed, who in the end forget themselves and God and seek refuge in suicide. Jesus said of the demon-possessed that they wander among the graves *seeking rest* [see Luke 11:24]; it is no different for the spirit of the man who must always go further, is never left alone, and is consumed inwardly by a thirst, hunger, and bitter craving for rest. That hunger and

---

1. As the Heidelberg Catechism describes the fourth commandment (Lord's Day 38, Q&A 103), Sabbath observance requires, in part, "that all the days of my life I rest from my evil works, allow the Lord to work in me by His Spirit, and thus begin in this life the everlasting sabbath (Isa 66:23)." See *RC* 2:794.

desire for quiet and calm for the stirred-up spirit is especially characteristic for the people of the East, from which the Scriptures came to us.

§ 2   When God extinguishes our light so that night follows day, long shadows spread over our cities and towns. With the hours of the night and
the darkness in which life becomes enveloped, we gain the rest of sleep.
It is a steady cycle in our lives by which God's mercy gives new grace to
his people—when the eyes are closed and our tired limbs stretched out
and the hunted spirit sinks into stupor. The rest of sleep spans a third
of our existence. One who dies at the age of ninety will have spent nearly thirty years in sleep's rest as it gives reanimation, quickening, and renewal of the strength that was spent. Indeed, the quiet grave is a sweet
attraction in the rest that it brings. Marnix's motto "The rest in the hereafter," "*repos ailleurs*," gets rendered on gravestones as "*Here rests....*"[2] These
things always, in all manners and in various tones, express that insatiable
desire, poignant craving, and unquenchable thirst for rest. Rest for our
conscience, rest from our sins, rest from our labor, rest from our fellow
human beings, rest from our enemy, rest from destiny's pursuit.

In order to attain the quiet flourishing and soft thriving of a pious
life, we have a great need for the enjoyment of that rest. However they
may have fallen short, hermits, ascetics, monks, and the Desert Fathers
never intended to do anything except withdraw from the world's tumult
and upheaval in order to seek communion with their God in silence and
prayer. They attempted by their separation to still live in the world, but as
if the world did not exist for them; they were ready to abandon the whole
world rather than be robbed by that world of eternal rest, of rest for the
soul. "Alone, but together with God" was likewise the way in which those
Protestants who avoided the monastery pointed to the path leading to the
quiet of the Zion of God.[3]

In the countryside where the world's tumult is at a much lower level,
the pious life could always find a place of refuge when the din and clam-
or of the big cities stifled it. Because of the rest it brought to the street,

---

2. Kuyper is referring to Philips of Marnix, Lord of Saint-Aldegonde (1540–1598), who
    studied theology under John Calvin and Theodore Beza in Geneva. He took up the
    cause of the Reformation in the Netherlands, was a prominent Dutch literary au-
    thor, and wrote one of the earliest Dutch Bible translations.
3. Here Kuyper refers to a formula associated with lines from "Eensaemheyd met
    God" by Jodocus van Lodenstein.

business, and family, the Lord's Day was always the day on which the life of piety came to greatest expression.

In their childhood before entering the world, or else in old age after having withdrawn from it again, people always found it much easier to listen to the heavenly voice than when they threw themselves into the full stream of life during their years of vigor. The custom, found especially in Russia, of withdrawing at times to a house of seclusion for a few weeks and living for God alone, still protected to a degree the richness of the mystical life in that powerful empire. To pour out their souls before their God, the pious still seek solitude continually; and once they have withdrawn themselves to the inner room and closed the door and thereby found a place and room of rest, the soul opens itself up for prayer in the presence of the Lord. The disproportionate piety found especially in the inland shipping business is also worthy of note. Isolated from the world, these people drift about on the waters and find in their seclusion a rest that cannot be found on shore.

This does not mean that godliness and piety cannot flourish also in the busiest lives. The lives of such men as De Ruyter[4] or Marnix of St. Aldegonde witness this. But then piety is awakened precisely because of the tension caused by the tremendous responsibility they wake up to after falling asleep. God can be found also in storms and thunder, but the greatest majority of people meet God first in the quiet whisper of a cool breeze. A quiet life fosters piety; rest that surrounds us causes the godly life to awaken. But in the tumultuous and foaming waters of life, the dove that wants to fly finds no place to rest its wings [see Gen 8:9].

§ 3

With this in mind, look now upon what the world and human life have become through our dominion over the powers of nature; then you will understand how this dominion has contributed to the decline of religious life during the past century. At this point, we are not speaking of those who are consciously born again. In their lives there is a greater power of the Spirit at work that can resist all assaults, even though these do cause people to suffer. Those who have been regenerated, however, stand in the holy place, while we are now referring only to the great mass of those

---

4. Michiel de Ruyter (1607–1676) is one of the most famous and skilled admirals in Dutch history. De Ruyter is most famous for his role in the Anglo-Dutch Wars of the seventeenth century. He fought the English and French in these wars and scored several major victories. The pious De Ruyter was very much loved by his sailors and soldiers.

who have never made it further than the forecourt. In bygone centuries they too were religiously oriented, while at present they are by and large entirely alienated from all religious participation. We are appealing for compassion toward these people, whose impiety you may be inclined to judge harshly after you look at yourself.

What a difference, distinction, and contrast there is between that multitude of baptized people then and now! And what else is it but a massive overstimulation of the nerves that has come in the place of an earlier calm and rest? Just consider how the mental institutions are filling up and the suicide rates increase. Unrest in thought, unrest in the soul, unrest at home and business, always hunted, never time to finish one's work in calm, always that pulsing in our blood and electrical current in our nerves that overstrain our entire lives. Nearly everyone is chased out of the house early every morning, many no longer even take their meals at their own table, and so we no longer enjoy the atmosphere of the home or gather together around the Word of God when we ought to give thanks to him for what we just enjoyed. Formerly, the first perimeter of rest included the home. Next, a second perimeter of rest was the neighborhood around the home, which people left only a few times a year; and when people did leave home, the national border was the last perimeter of rest for virtually everyone.

But now every perimeter of rest has been dismantled. Electrical wires connect cities and towns to each other, and one country to another. Rail tracks span an entire continent. Mail ships cross all seas. Local markets are no longer anything but subsidiaries, there are no markets at all anymore in this country except as auxiliary links, and everything has been drawn together into an all-encompassing global market with which every businessman or tradesman has to deal. Activity is no longer even limited to a single continent. Europe and America form one sphere of activity, and Africa, Australia, and Asia are seeking to join the tumult that drives and absorbs everything. People in villages do not notice this, but visit a world city and you will see how thousands upon thousands gallop through it during the daytime, as well as throughout the evening with the help of lights. They even add a part of the night to that already tumultuous day. There was a time when mail was delivered at most once per day, but now as many as eight to ten daily deliveries constantly inundate you with new messages and new questions. The telegraph overwhelms you with urgent messages. The telephone distracts your attention from your work.

It is no longer possible to walk calmly through the big cities, but electric trams are waiting to transport you from one side of the city to the other in one large sweep. Everything is done in haste without leaving you time to think; you have to grasp quickly what someone is presenting to you and decide immediately.

Then there are those endless meetings, assemblies, and reunions. All kinds of interests counting on your support and cooperation—participation in business, market, science, literature, art, politics. Your entire existence is quartered every single day of your life. You can no longer keep your work separate. Everything is thrown together, as three or four matters claim your attention at one time. Then you have to leave home again for a meeting elsewhere, and once you are spent and can no longer continue, you make a trip to try and recharge your strength. Like a leaf that falls from the branches and is driven about restlessly by the autumn winds, so the lives of businessmen in those great world cities are tossed about in complete and ceaseless restlessness, not just for several days, but every year time and again.

For a while people sought rest in the stupor of alcohol, but they found no contentment and now strive instead to avoid wine and liquor. However, they still pursue muscular strength in order to maintain the life that strains their nerves. They see sports as supplying those greater powers. Yet sports, too, increase the unrest. Bicycle, motorbike, automobile, soon hot air balloon and airplane will increase the tension of life. Even when it comes to war fought on sea or land, the past can hardly compare to the current incredible deployment of power. What a crew on a battleship undergoes in the heat of battle cannot even be imagined by those with ordinary nerves. It is reported to be like the gates of hell.

Not all nerves, we admit, are everywhere the same. In Japan, for example, nerves are hardly ever shaken or shocked. Africans, by contrast, are more easily shaken than we are. The tough nerves of Japanese soldiers and mariners are a large reason for their power in the current war.[5] As Europeans, we are somewhere between these two extremes: less easily stimulated than the Africans, our nerves we are three times more sensitive than the Mongols. As central and western Europeans, we also suffer

§ 4

---

5. This possibly refers to the Russo-Japanese War (1904–1905).

much more from our nerves than those in the East.[6] It should furthermore be noted that this sensitivity and irritability of the nerves increases from one generation to the other. Born to parents already victim to this high level of nervous tension, children are born with a greater sensitivity. If this is allowed to continue, within two or three generations' time the irritation of life will be disquietingly high. One French writer was already led to prophesy that the world will, in the end, be populated only by insane people.

Our description above is not meant to excuse the lack of piety found among the great masses. Whoever they may be, all who do not live in piety before God stand guilty. However, from a human perspective, one may still ask whether you yourself feel how this overstraining of mind and nerves clearly impedes the fostering of a sense of religion and a common godliness. People live in small houses; they no longer have their own room in which they can quietly pray. The exercise of piety as a family has fallen away, and no one has time to participate anymore. On Sundays people want to catch up on what they could not get to during the week, or else they seek respite and relaxation out in nature. Their nerves have been so shaken that they can no longer sit quietly under the preaching of the Word. Rest continues to elude them. There is no place, no time for seclusion. No one even thinks of turning in upon himself anymore.

Everything hurries and chases through head and heart. Not even a single moment remains for the soul to be lifted up to God because such a demand is constantly made on the capacities of our thoughts and feelings. Billowing clouds block out the world of the eternal. The earth's light shines so brightly and sharply that people no longer look up to God's starry heavens in the firmament. Nothing impresses them any longer. Humanity itself has become so mighty, while the world around us has been so subjected, that people no longer ask for anything from the almighty Source of all things. The conscience does speak, but the clamors of the world drown out its whispers. In reaction to this overstrained life, there comes the wild and bewildered laugh; that laugh brings mockery; and when they die—so people say—that restless chasing will finally end. This is why death without the prospect of eternity is seen as something almost desirable.

---

6. These kinds of culturally-bound stereotypes are fairly common in Kuyper's writing. On his treatment of three main people groups (European, African, and Asian), see *CG* 1.41.1, and the volume" editors' introduction to *CG*.

Then there will be no eternity to follow. Such a prospect is what people now hope for with a near-Buddhist craving.

If you now look at the three successive generations around you, you §5 will see how the destruction of religion has advanced. All three generations have, just as before and throughout all ages, a large number of entirely indifferent and corrupt characters who are only out for money and pleasure. They do not count. They never did set the tone, and do not now, either. But consider in those three generations the better families of higher standing, the people of greater nobility, and what do you see?

Among the older generation on the way to the grave you will see some surviving remnant of an earlier piety. The elderly are not as orthodox as before, but they are not entirely detached from the Word either. They pray at home. They impress upon their children respect for what is holy. God's blessing is something they do not want to do without. They still believe in his providential ordering of all things. They still have religious ideals. In such families there still is a certain religious life, even if it is weakened, bleak, and waning.

With the second generation in the vigor of adult life, however, things are already different. The Bible is gone, church attendance and the sacraments are not part of the picture, and prayer at the table is a thing of the past. This generation has rid itself of all these things. A certain amount of respect for the holy can still be detected, but this is almost entirely dissolved into a moral ideal with at most a touch of the mystical. At times there is also spiritualism or theosophy,[7] but for the greatest majority by far, there is a cold, chilly, and frigid numbness. They do not even think about practicing religion, about seeking God's hidden communion. In undisguised indifference they keep their eyes set on the road before them without ever raising their eyes anymore.

With the third generation—young people who will soon reach adult age—the situation is even more frightening. For them all religion is a singular peculiarity of a small group of backward people. They are indeed interesting, those strange self-contained people who go to church and pray. The new generation does not mock them. They are simply an interesting, never-disappearing phenomenon in life. But the third generation itself

---

7. The term *theosophy* refers to any philosophical mysticism where knowledge of God is available only through some kind of mystical acquaintance or experience. See *The Oxford Companion to Philosophy*, ed. Ted Honderich, 2nd ed. (New York: Oxford University Press, 2005), s.v. *Theosophy*.

has done away with religion. For them, science is everything. Science decides. They walk by its light. It has provided the ideal. The times of old, with their legends and mysteries and imaginary dreams, have passed. The modern life is for us, they say. Modern man does indeed have more noble inclinations, he does indeed want to raise the human to a higher level, to live for an ideal goal, but he no longer knows religion. Religion is an extinguished phenomenon, a remnant of the past to which modern man looks back with a melancholic curiosity.

The life that surrounds you thus unfolds ever more clearly. As lord and master of the forces of nature rather than slave and victim, humanity no longer feels itself dependent but sovereign. Precisely that power over nature has turned our human existence entirely on its head, roused it out of its earlier rest into nerve-wracking action, and so removed from life those very tranquil, restful, isolating, calming features that used to lead to seclusion, to reflection on one's situation, and to retreat into the conscience. The evil result is that religion, which cannot do without rest and quiet, has lost more and more of the terrain where it used to be able to flourish even among the unregenerate. The powerful current of the world's modern life has unearthed the root of religion, pried it loose and lifted it out, and now sweeps it along like a tree that has been uprooted from the river bank.

DISTRACTED THINKING

Of making many books there is no end, and much study is a weariness of the flesh.

ECCLESIASTES 12:12

Religion no longer occupies the place it used to in social and public life. §1
In the sixteenth century, nearly all of life revolved around religion, but
now a dark shadow oppresses it. The atmosphere that at that time was
favorable to religion now in fact suppresses it. In the forecourt, religion
has been hushed up. The waters in the sacred stream are at a lower level.
Modern life, as a whole, no longer works along with the holy, but against
it. Whatever heights the present century may have achieved, these have
nothing to do with religion. As a result, more and more of those who only
went along for the ride are beginning to abandon the purely historical
faith that was handed down to them, and those whose faith is personally
rooted in regeneration feel that life no longer carries them on its waves;
instead, they become increasingly weary as they have to swim against
the current.

To explain this change in the state of affairs, we pointed, first of all, to
the rapid and uncontested dominion over the forces of nature that the last
century gave us. Through it, the feeling of dependence on a higher power
declined perceptibly among the majority of people, who are not inclined
to further reflection anyway. After this, we focused our attention on the

restless unrest of modern times, which over-stimulates the senses and so disrupts the tranquility in which religious reflection ought to germinate. At this point, we now add a third cause for the general dampening of the life of religion, which could be referred to as *the human mind's preoccupation with all things*.

The human mind is amazingly multifaceted, and throughout history there have always been people who have the ability to extend their minds in almost every direction, to occupy themselves with all kinds of things virtually simultaneously, to focus their mind so well that one thing almost never drew them away from another. Most people, however—especially the common masses—are not like that. Instead, the great majority of people are quite limited as to the outlets for their mind. They have no perspective on a continent or country, or even a province or world city. They live, so to speak, with their mind in a town or something even smaller. Their horizon extends no further. Their mind does have within it the seeds for wider developments, but these seeds do not sprout. They can occupy themselves with no more than a very limited number of things at once, and when they do spread their mind too thin, in the end they master nothing. At times their mind manifests itself in a remarkably powerful way and not infrequently shows a surprising resilience.

But in order to reach that level, such people have to focus all of this resilience on a single point. They are or at least can be strong, but only by concentrating, by mustering all of their forces in one area. And they cannot take it when there is too much to distract them. When this does happen, they are distracted in their mind so that the secret of their strength disappears. The concentration of their mental power is for them what the Nazirite crown was for Samson, and when Delilah removes the source of their power, that power is broken, and often irretrievably at that [Judg 16:19-21]. We have noted that there are some who do not suffer from this at all, but they constitute a great exception. And even if there are quite a few others who manage to a certain extent to avoid the threatening weakening of their mind, for the majority in all circles of society—by far the greatest majority in fact—it holds true that a lack of concentration severs the tendon of its power.

On reading of your homeland's history, you stand astonished at how, in earlier times, not only the heroes who stood front and center, but also the wider class of common people displayed in all areas such a powerful character, such wondrous energy, such virile strength—all of this, of course, without much if any help, with inferior schools, and with tools no longer worth looking at. Whenever someone was sought for a difficult task, volunteers were never lacking. It is as if they simply grew out of the ground. The book of history shows them doing well in everything they undertook, acquitting themselves of their tasks admirably, and reaching the mark for which they aimed. They are a picture of living valor and are a somber contrast to the persistent absence of people worthy of this name in the present times. Our people know more, comprehend more, attempt more, but the fountain of their personal strength now drips, whereas it used to leap, splash, and flow. Of all nations, England has maintained its method of concentrated upbringing for the longest, and for that reason it has at its disposal comparatively the most vigorous personal power. There is thus no lack of power, but the strap that holds the arrows together has come off; and due to this lack of cooperation, the overwhelming power that the past used to display is no longer there. What was once still able to exercise an extraordinary power when joined together now lies diffused and has, for that reason, become weak. The mind's concentration within itself, which used to create wonders, is no longer there. The lack of concentration avenges itself in the dispirited stumbling that we now witness.

For the time being, however, there is nothing that can be done about this. The spirit of the age, the standpoint on which our current society is based, the factors governing our lives, all permit no other outcome. Knowledge used to be very limited; the field to which human knowledge extended was narrowly enclosed. And even in the time of the polymaths—that is, men of science who sought to know all that could be known—one did not need a telescope to survey their field of knowledge. That is no longer the situation today, however. Human knowledge has broadened, widened, and expanded so incredibly that the principle requiring division of labor is self-evident. Nowadays, general knowledge, general development, is a great exception. The entire body of intellectuals has divided into various groups of specializations, and each group sets out to investigate one particular corner of the immeasurable field. Consequently, the study of that specific selected corner is now nearly infinite in its depth. People choose one particular subject for research or study, and they devote themselves entirely to it and consider it from all possible angles so that in the end it reveals all its secrets to us. In our time, a polymath—someone who encompasses all learning—is entirely unthinkable. Even in their own corners, people have a thorough knowledge of only a single part, and most

§ 2

have to be content to soak up the more general details for the other parts. But the sum of acquired knowledge is immeasurably great, extending so inscrutably far over the entire field and so inscrutably deep down to the foundations that the sum of acquired knowledge passes far over our heads; this is precisely because that body of intellectuals who work in this way is now at least ten times bigger than before.

The result was that the upbringing and education of the following generation took on an entirely different form than before. It was no longer possible to limit education to passing on a certain number of capacities. The field in which our young men and women today are expected to be at home continues to grow. As a result, the subject areas continually increase in number and scope. Ever more is demanded from their budding brains. And the inauspicious exams by which people intend to test their education have for many become a test of torture that is more likely to dull the mind than to enlighten it. There are no borders and limits to the questions that can be asked in examinations, and the old exams that aimed at general development are known only from the memory of others. As a result, nearly all examiners hardly get anything more from the young examinees than the shortcuts they exchange with each other, which in themselves constitute a deadly blow to real study. In this way, the human mind is distracted at an early age and divided in all directions. A deep immersion in any study whatsoever has become unfeasible. The mind itself is no longer formed. It no longer teaches itself to assemble and to collect. Concentration of the mind's resilience becomes ever rarer. In Latin we call such a phenomenon *multa non multum*—acquaintance with many facts without real knowledge. However, we have to go along with that stream. You would remain an outsider in life if you were unable to talk about at least the most general facts in every field of knowledge. Even in England they are beginning to yield, even though they held out the longest there. The world that used to be so small has now become immeasurably large, and of that large world we are expected to have at least a general grasp or else we will be lost.

§ 3　　If many schools already overburden the minds that have become imbalanced and lack any sort of training for a powerful concentration, the printing press then persecutes us throughout our entire lives by preventing us from making even the smallest beginning in concentration.

The printing press is, as such, one of the greatest blessings we have ever received. The press unlocked for the broader circles of society the field of knowledge that was once accessible to only a few. It is the means *par excellence* to carry the light of knowledge out into the most hidden circles of society. However, we may not forget that this same printing press also captivates our minds in a way that dulls them.

Consider, first of all, the daily press. Every morning, and often every evening as well, the newspaper is delivered to your house to keep you abreast of all that is happening in the world. In bygone times, it was often the case that with even the most serious wars, the vague details of a great but distant battle took some ten or twelve days to arrive. Now the newspapers inundate you that same day with increasingly extensive reports and force your mind to follow the entire course of the war down to the smallest details. The war now distracts you. You become involved in it, and whether you want to or not, your mind is occupied with it hour after hour. This is true not only with wars, but with literally everything. You follow step by step all that happens in the parliaments of other countries. Everything is laid out for you in detail, together with the chances of success or failure. The development in other countries grips and interests you, and a part of your mind is once again unwillingly and imperceptibly occupied by something that lies beyond the sphere of your life. You are similarly informed of all the crime and folly in your own country and outside of it. The main events of the justice systems in all countries are summarized for you. You are introduced to every new phenomenon in art and literature. A summary of everything noteworthy in science is communicated to you. The ins and outs of the social dilemma across the world stage demand your attention. Sports and matches take you captive. And the worldwide special events in agriculture, industry, commerce, and shipping are brought to your attention.

Not everyone, it is true, grazes as greedily as others do in all of these pastures. Most people cannot handle it, cannot keep up; they skip, no longer read, and ignore the regular grass in favor of their favorite leaf of clover. But even this choice that they are forced to make from all that is available shows how overwhelming the wave of reading material is. And even if many limit themselves to a single leaf of clover, there is also a wide circle of people who want to nose around a little in everything; not a few people simply *must* stay up to date on nearly everything and so plow their way every morning and every evening through that mountain of information.

There are also magazines, whether weekly, biweekly, monthly, or quarterly. You are hardly even halfway through the first issue before the next one appears. The magazines are becoming thicker and thicker, and more varied in content. It is so interesting that you have to read it, because everyone is talking about it. It is like a giant restaurant in which you lose the right to choose your meal and have to be content with the courses set before you from a fixed menu. Other people decide what you are to read; you do not. It is precisely this kind of reading material prescribed by others which delights the mind deprived of its will so much that new magazines and weeklies are constantly added, again laying claim on a few hours of your already short week.

Up to this point, I have spoken only of the periodic press. In spite of its extensiveness, it forms only a small part of the great mass of literature that rushes over you. Not only what is produced in our own country, but also products from all other countries offer themselves to you in original language editions, or else in translation. With every visit to your local bookstore you are overwhelmed by piles and piles of books. In reading groups, books are circulated by the stack. There are the necessary reference books for your field, but also and especially general books of which everyone must be aware—particularly those that garner widespread attention and that everyone is talking about. Every year again, each country produces an independent catalog of all the books published in it during that one year, and for our small country alone that catalog already forms a rather fat volume. This continues from one year to the next. By the time you reach the age of fifty, the books published during your lifetime alone will fill a massive library. Of course, you could block that stream by not buying or reading. However, no one wants to fall behind, and everyone seeks to be a child of her time. Not to be ignored are those books that draw you irresistibly like a magnet. Fiction especially is too powerful for many. They cannot leave it alone. Once they have been swept up by a novel, they do not lay it down before they have turned the last page. These novels, too, lay a claim on their minds, distract and draw them away from the concentration of their own mind. And to think that we have not said anything yet about the immoral literature that seduces especially the younger generation and distracts their minds and passions!

§ 4   When comparing this with the circumstances in which our fathers lived, you will hardly be able even to imagine the comparative rest and calm in which they passed their days. Daily newspapers were only beginning to appear, and those that did circulate were still rare and small in size. You could finish them in no time. At first there was no mail delivery, then only once in two days. There were no magazines for sale. Only a few families had foreign literature. And the literary industry in an entire year produced only a small quantity of mostly Latin books, some pamphlets, and a small amount of poetry. There never was that stream of literature that rushed in over them like a tidal wave, lifted them up, and engulfed them. People read the same book two or three times, and libraries had no more than a very limited number of writings.

The human mind was thus left to itself for the largest part of the day, or it lost itself in discussion. People decided what they wanted to read, obtained that work with difficulty, and because it was generally written in such a bland style, they would really have to want to read it in order to find it engaging. They never stuffed themselves—they ate more sparingly, frugally, and simply, but remained lord and master of their table when it came to the choice of the food for their mind. As a result, time remained for inner reflection, for thought, for mental recalibration. The mind's concentration thus occurred automatically, and at times diversion, distraction, and relaxation had to be pursued intentionally in order to avoid the powerful urge to occupy oneself with one's own mind. The mind remained its own master. There was no restless knocking at its door. It was more the exception than the rule when another mind reached through into the quiet chamber of the soul in order to seize the quiet thinker. A person's mind was indeed engaged, busy, and active, but it was not constantly occupied by whatever the printing press delivered to each and every person. While today we have to deal with something that resembles a parcel service where anyone who writes something drops a parcel off, in former times, one received only what had been ordered, so that the mind had a life of its own to shape character and resilience.

Wishing to return to those days makes no sense. It is not going to happen. Doing so would reek like the soot of a candle snuffer. What we have today developed logically from what was back then. It was God's design that life would be extended, widened, and expanded. And in the end, we will see that the human mind, in spite of what so overwhelmingly occupies us today, has what it takes to reclaim its freedom. We live in a period of transition, and things moved so quickly that our minds were not prepared for it. We lost our balance. Each of us must, on the one hand, exert ourselves to participate in the life of our time, while on the other hand we must continue to protect the freedom of our mind and force it to concentrate on what matters.

§ 5   This is beyond the reach of most, and that is something you need to keep in mind when you judge the decline of religion in society. Those who have entered the holy place continue to be safe, but the masses who still linger in the forecourt suffer the harmful effect of the squalls that howl by day. The traditional faith that the majority received in the past (and which can be distinguished from the personal faith of God's own children) is not in a position to weather such storms. Those who stand in the forecourt know much and are busy with and interested in many things, but their mind is no longer free. Their minds are inundated, occupied by the sheer amount of knowledge and information about all sorts of things that bombard them day after day. They feel the pressure this puts them under, and for that reason they need entertainment and relaxation more than others do. However, they do not have the calm, rest, or isolation to withdraw into themselves and to concentrate. Their minds are constantly occupied with all kinds of things, not because this is what they seek or want, but because all of this attacks them, rolls over them, overpowers them, and occupies every corner of their heart and thoughts unasked. They no longer live, but are overcome by life. They no longer have a choice, but must take what is put before them. It disturbs them; it divides them in their inner being. They have to think what others think. They are taken captive. They are no longer themselves.

If what inundated them had served to confirm religion or at least to focus their attention on it, the departure from the faith of the fathers would not have been so deadly also among these broader ranks. However, the opposite was in fact the case. For the greatest majority, the wave that engulfs them has nothing to do with religion. Everything comes from the world and has to do with the world. There may well be a place for the soul—and in fact there often is—but then as it struggles down here on earth, the soul gawks at outward appearances and debases itself. And where there is a higher aim, where the noble flares up and the ideal is allowed to shine, things still remain limited to this life alone, without any attention for a higher and eternal destination. To the extent that religion is spoken about, most of those discussions break religion down—whether they undermine the very foundation of religion, or else deliver those who profess religion up to shame and mockery.

There is thus almost nothing from that entire inundating stream that works either to confirm the faith received or arouse deep religious reflection, and even less to entice humanity to seek and thirst after its God.

People were already estranged from the church. Holy Scripture has been set on the bookshelf for good. Religious works are thought to be too heavy and boring. They are not exciting or relaxing. That is why increasingly even women, who continued to hold to the old tradition for some time, turned away from the Christian religion. At times they still find a new stimulus in spiritualism or theosophy, but more often they simply turn their back on religion altogether. And how could it be otherwise? Religion, first of all, demands a concentration of the mind. Without concentration of the mind, prayer is not possible. A formulaic prayer may still be spoken before a meal, or the Lord's Prayer be rattled off, but what is no longer possible is a prayer from the heart, from the very depths of the soul, a search of the finite mind for the Infinite. Since their minds are occupied, people no longer turn in toward themselves. They no longer want to. They are afraid to. Moreover, their attention is too distracted. The mind is always too full, too occupied, too overburdened. Schoolwork already makes them unaccustomed to concentrating. People renounce the concentration of the mind in all of life. They have not been formed for it. They are no longer capable of it. Where almost everything in the forecourt draws people away from God and next to nothing stimulates the heart to lift itself up to God, can any religion worthy of its name still survive?

It should not be forgotten that all religion is a penetration with the innermost part of the soul into the unity of all things, in order to comprehend the unity of the One from whom everything comes. For that reason, to take delight in godliness you must ascend from the many, the varied, the endlessly distinct, to the coherence of all these things, penetrating through to the One from whom everything comes. However, achieving precisely that composition and entry into this oneness, crossing the boundary separating the finite from the infinite, is something that those who stand in the forecourt hardly ever manage anymore. The mass of the things overwhelming them is too great. When you speak with them, you feel that they are not only too distracted, too taken up with particulars, but also that the internal spring for directing one's religious life upward has become unhinged.

This circumstance may not harm the assembling of believers in the holy place, but it does indicate that the crowds in the forecourt will dwindle away in a matter of years. People will even abandon the fore-court in favor of what lies behind and beyond it in the life of the world. The number of believers will not decrease. Our King will always defend and preserve his people. The holy place will not empty out. However, even if not entirely empty, the forecourt will be unpopulated for the most part. The historical, purely traditional faith will continue to decrease in power and reach. In older families, you still find the historical faith, but sons and daughters have more or less turned away from it. With the grandchildren, the situation will be even worse. They will be entirely estranged from it, and even Jesus' name will be a strange sound to them. Some have already reached that stage—not many perhaps, but their number is increasing. And their number will continue to grow. There is no power to hold them back. Things will return to the way they were in the days of the apostles, with a circle of personal believers in the holy place, but then placed in the middle of a society that inwardly and even outwardly is being estranged from historic Christianity. Such a process moves slowly, but once it is in motion it will continue without rest. God's exalted design will execute all these things in order to expose all *apparent* Christianity in its idleness and weakness, and instead to bring to greater illumination the divine power at work in the small flock. This power alone is sufficient, even amidst the endless distractions of the present day, to cause those who fear God to delight in the spiritual communion of their souls.[1]

---

1. *Note from the author*: In the *Zuider Kerkbode* Dr. Wagenaar [L. H. (Lutzen Harmens) Wagenaar (1855-1910) was a *Gereformeerd* pastor and historian; he served as the editor of the *Zuider Kerkbode* from 1899 to 1908] questions whether our distinction between Christians in the forecourt and Christians in the holy place is justified. We suggest that the learned Doctor keep in mind that this is not a doctrinal distinction, but a practical one. It is a fact that in our country an innumerable number of people confess Christ, and it is also a fact that in this multitude there are some for whom that confession possesses a spiritual reality, while there are others for whom that reality is absent. The distinction we made was intended to point only to this phenomenon.

THE GREAT WORLD CITIES

Alas, alas, for the great city!

REVELATION 18:16

We have seen the contrast in the human situation between then and now in three aspects. Humanity used to be powerless in the face of nature's forces; now humanity has dominion over them. Humanity used to be locked up in a small, tranquil world; now we participate in the restlessness of the entire globe's life. Similarly, we used to be limited in knowledge; today we are overburdened with knowledge. Applied to the religious life, humankind's powerlessness made them dependent; life's rest caused them to turn in upon themselves; and the small amount of knowledge acquired led them to reach greedily for the knowledge revealed. Conversely, the current awareness of power has weakened the feeling of dependence on the Almighty; the restless, outward-directed activity leaves no time for the life of one's own heart's inner room; and the sheer weight of finite knowledge drives back the craving for knowledge of the Infinite.

§ 1

As will become clear later on, this was not how things had to be, and our being created in the image of God should instead have led to the opposite outcome. However, the guilt of the past and the sin of the current generation would not allow for anything else. Our strength in every field, our feeling of being at home everywhere, and our knowledge of everything has given glory to our "I" and left almost no room for the general sense of the glory of God and of Christ. That ban was, of course, broken wherever regeneration intervened, but faith's general instinct for the things unseen, which used to have the most leverage in human life, lost its power so that religious life declined everywhere in significance and power. This does not mean that faith's instinct has disappeared altogether. The spark remains. However, the layer of ashes covering that spark prevents it from glowing.

Since the former concentration of life and consciousness in united adoration was lost, there automatically arose a desire and need to find that concentration of life in something else. However much an undue individualism may have fragmented our life, the drive for unity and coherence will not permit itself to be erased. That need for unity arises from our very existence. However divergently and sometimes contradictorily the inclinations and faculties of our souls may express themselves, our one and only essence still comes to expression in everything. And even today, if people would rather avoid speaking of the *soul* and accustom themselves to referring time and again to their *I*, this *I* is and remains the unity in our own existence.

§ 2   Humanity cannot, however, find rest in the unity of the personal *I*. Instead, one person's *I* works against another person's *I* in a way that loosens and unbinds, and this explains the continuous search for an imposing power to unite us in spite of our differences and divergent life expressions. Religion used to be that power. This is something that did not begin with Christians, but clearly manifested itself already in ancient Israel, and even in the pagan world. Local gods bind local and national life together, but the Greeks, for example, also had the higher notion of Jupiter, who hovered over and above the local gods and gave a certain unity to them. That unity reached a still higher level, however, when worship of the only true God entered this world. That worship was summed up in the worship of Christ, and a time followed when all human life indeed concentrated itself in the worship of Christ. Not only personal and family (both immediate and extended family) life, but also the life of the schools, trade guilds, city life, the life of art and skilled labor—all these things were sanctified and found their unity in Christ. There was thus unity, there was coherence, there was concentration, and precisely this gave human life greater harmony, like a holy nimbus shining from the invisible world upon this world of the visible.

Nowadays, by contrast, that coherence has been broken, that unity is gone, that concentration has been lost, and that holy harmony has faded away. The waters are so troubled that the mire rises up from the bottom, and the waters no longer reflect what shines in the firmament. Clarity has been lost. Everything around us has become murky. Everything is one great turbulent sea whose waves are whipped up by the wind and cannot find rest.

At a time when these things are erupting and breaking down, the un- §3
dying need for unity and coherence nevertheless does show itself again, even if it works in a very different way. While formerly people strove for spiritual unity, now that unity has to bear a visible, material character. It used to come to us from the invisible world, but now it roots itself in the world before our eyes. It does not seek its concentration in the Jerusalem that is above but in the mighty *world city* that encompasses all of human life. That striving was already present in the ancient world, in Jerusalem and Athens, in Babylon and Rome. But though there are similarities, there are also differences between then and now. Jerusalem and Athens were not world cities because of their enormous, gigantic dimensions, nor because they encompassed all of human life in their bosom, but because they excelled spiritually. As cities, they were rather small. However, Jerusalem shone through Zion's monotheism, Athens through its artistic genius. Babylon and Rome were indeed powerful cities and to a degree the prototype for world cities, but still in an entirely different way than we might think. Even if it was for a false god, the temple always remained the center. There was power, there was decay that had crept in, there was the bulk of wealth, there was decline in morality; yet notwithstanding all of our doubt and skepticism, there was still something holy that bonded everything together. But even already in their tempered state, the prophet saw the danger that lay in such powerful cities. When applied to Rome, "Babylon" remained the name for the wicked city that gave the nations to drink from her poisonous cup; the contrast between Babylon as the world city and the Jerusalem that is above inspired the seer on Patmos.

However, antiquity never knew the world city as we know it now—as a concentration of all of human life that has rid itself of all that might appear to be higher or sacred. In our world cities, it is the world city it-self, without something higher or more ideal, that has become the cen-ter point, the dominating power of human life. That is not the case for the smaller cities, like the ones we also have in the Netherlands. Urban self-deception may want to suggest that Amsterdam is a world city, but every well-informed person knows that the world cities are Paris, London, and Berlin for Europe, and New York for the American world. They are concentrations of millions of inhabitants that draw in all the activity from the entire nation unto themselves, and consider the rest of the nation with all its cities and towns as a dependent territory over which they wave their scepter. These cities in fact respect no national boundaries and attempt, each in their territory, to subject the life of all nations to themselves. Paris is the world city of opulence, London the world city of trade and commerce, Berlin the world city of human knowledge, and New York the world city of money. From all sides, people flock to those world cities. From every corner of the earth, people go on pilgrimages in order to feel themselves fully human for the first time in those world cities. The magnetic power of these world cities draws everything to them. They supply the watchword that must sound throughout the entire world and set the tone of life in even the remotest regions. Those who miss out on the pilgrimage to the world cities do not count as full human beings. There, in those world cities, people can live their own lives; everything that happens outside merely mimics the life of those world cities. The world cities rule and govern every area of human existence. There, in those world cities, the wine is poured out—and as the Seer says, all have become drunk on her wine. Those who set the tone are "clothed in fine linen, in purple and scarlet, adorned with gold, with jewels and with pearls" [Rev 18:16]. All of this is according to the old model that the prophets and the Seer on Patmos portrayed with such powerful language.

§ 4   When the former concentration of human life under the shield of Christ was lost, the concentration that the world city gave us in its place could not be anything but unholy. Regarding such a city's description, the prophet already indicated that it could be nothing other than "a meeting-place of unclean spirits ... a storehouse of what is unclean and detestable" [see Rev 18:2]. It could not be otherwise. The seed of sin is found in the heart of every man. The more people you gather together in one place, the more the unholy fuel for the fire of sin is piled up into an unholy heap. Those who imagine that this is so only in Paris demonstrate at once a naïveté concerning human nature and an ignorance of the facts. In the capital of England, evil is piled up just as high. Berlin does not lag behind in any respect. And in New York, sin's shameful forms even celebrate satanic orgies. In each one of those cities a deep pit of iniquity is found in every moral and material field. Of course, this is not to say that these cities are such in their entirety. Each has a civilized and very tasteful façade, but behind it nearly unbridled and limitless evil is brewing, and in wildly billowing clouds noxious gases spread out in every direction.

The reason for this is that shame can be hidden. In the country and in small cities, people know you by name and face. Self-respect thus forces you to self-control. A holy feeling of shame is thus like a guardian angel that keeps the wild passions in check. With their millions upon millions of inhabitants, however, people can lose themselves completely in world cities. No one knows them. They are left to themselves and thus lose sight of shame's guardian angel. They see that nothing bothers anyone anymore, and so they rejoice with them in their drunken orgies. Night is turned to day, and day to night. People no longer have their own name and reputation. They lose themselves in the wanton masses. Among both men and women, sin thus takes on increasingly flagrant forms. For whom would you deny yourself? From whom would you hide? The result is one great sport of sensual self-abasement in which the one tries to outdo the other. People drink, gamble, and debase themselves until every higher form of human nobility has been trampled underfoot. Nothing causes them to shrink back any longer. Nothing awakens the conscience any longer. People know this about each other, and the guilt of others causes them to feel safe in their own guilt. No unholy "brother" will later despise you for it. Children know this about their fathers and mothers. Brothers and sisters know this about their older siblings. It is an unstoppable train of sensual pleasure and opulence that lures and draws everything along with it. The natural result is that the most godless and criminal elements come creeping and crawling to these cities from across the entire country, and even from countries far away. There, these people find a world after their own heart, and once they have nestled in the city, they celebrate every wicked passion to their heart's content.

All the glory of human life comes to be contracted in these inwardly corrupted world cities. In them, artistic endeavor opens its temple and gives honor and gold to its priests and priestesses. Art's pleasure celebrates its greatest triumphs there. Soloists with beautiful voices, instrumentalists who play so skillfully, and the impressive décor and acting of many theatre productions enchant their audiences. What is the life of an artist in a provincial city compared to the triumphal careers of many artists in one of our world cities! In architecture, sculpture, and painting,

§ 5

the monumental palaces and richly furnished museums of the world cities surpass whatever else there may be in the entire country. The forms of life have been raised there to the highest degree of refinement. Banquet halls shimmer and shine with their choice dishes and fine furnishings. Fabrics and garments have the kind of cut and color, harmonious texture, and opulent adornment, for which you will search elsewhere in vain. Scholarship flourishes there as well. Each world city parades its university and shows off its well-furnished primary and secondary schools. You will find associations, societies, and clubs for every field of learning. Every evening, meetings, lectures, and conferences about all forms of human scholarship draw a choice audience.

The government unfurls its power in the world cities. An army of police officers and soldiers maintains order and tranquility. The government lights up the canals and streets and alleys brightly until deep into the night. For speedy communication, it offers you subways, numerous tramlines, and vehicles under its supervision. It offers drinking water that rivals mountain brooks in purity, and it offers protection against the sicknesses that result from filth and poisonous bugs. Without any intervention from the government, you also feel at home everywhere in those world cities. One barroom after another is waiting to accommodate you. Everything has been thought of. Every need in life has been provided for.

The composition of life in such a world city then also far surpasses the concentration of life in your towns and small cities. In those world cities, there is not only a concentration of the life of the entire nation and of the entire world, but also a concentration of life within the city itself. In the countryside and in our small cities, people live their own lives in their own house, and in that quiet home life develop a family mindset, devotion, and mutual attachment. But in a world city the home is an incidental matter. All too many leave home in the morning and do not make their way back until long after midnight. The home is a shelter for when they want to sleep or when they fall ill. People do not live at home but in the city. They eat lunch at the office or in a restaurant, and at night husband, wife, and children are found in the theater, concert hall, or bar, to return home only to sleep. In this way, life becomes more and more externalized, transferred to the public sphere; and in that public sphere, personality is lost, the sense of family is lost, the bonds of blood are loosened more and more, and religion no longer has a place to set its feet. How then can life still be gathered under Christ as our Head in every area of life? Art bans him. Science reduces him to a rabbi from the past. And in its endless tumult, society, ever wicked, creates an ethical standard for itself that has no eye for the soul and denies the body nothing.

§ 6

The strong concentration of life in a world city—which continually circumvents the unity in Christ and in fact consciously turns against the unity of life in Christ—therefore seeks unity in *a spirit of its own*. It does not seek it in a spirit of its own from above, or even a spirit embodied in a powerful personality, but in a nameless spirit, a spirit that cannot be visualized, and yet a spirit whose overpowering and compelling power can be felt in every area of life. No one resists the power of that spirit. All who want to be involved accommodate themselves to it, not only in major things, but down to the smallest details, to fashion, to appearance, to language, and to expressions. People are addicted to this spirit. No one dares to resist. People follow each other like a flock of sheep, even though this spirit constantly undergoes change. What was fashionable and customary ten years ago is now long out of style. Almost every five years, this one, all-dominating spirit takes on new forms, whether it be the things people wear or eat, the institutions they visit, or the places they go to at night. The minute the form has changed, thousands and even ten thousands willingly follow, and no one even thinks of following a set rule from ten years ago anymore. The spirit differs between Paris and London, between Berlin and New York, and those who move from Berlin to Paris quickly change their Berlin-ways and slavishly adopt the spirit of Paris. It is still possible to identify who sets the tone for fashion. The man or woman who every spring and fall prescribes the cut and color of your clothes can be identified by name. But for all other things, the tone is set by unknown people. No one can say for sure why customs and lifestyle change once again at that particular time and in that particular way. However, the result remains the same. The spirit haunts and dominates, and everyone submits to it, and all who are up with the times try to follow.

Beneath it all, a unity of spiritual direction thrashes and works. All those forms and habits and customs, as varying and changing as they may be, are still the expression of one and the same purpose, one and the same will, one and the same direction, which is unconsciously guided. Nothing is isolated. There is a link between all things. There is not only outward and formal concentration, but also a concentration in unity of spirit in all who guide, direct, and lead. There are thus philosophers who imagined that they could express the unity of the dominating spirit in their system, and while they did indeed exercise influence on deep thinkers, they were mistaken in imagining that it was their thinking that created the spirit. Instead, their system gave expression only to what had already been aroused in the spirit of the nation and gradually came to clearer consciousness in the spirit of an entire world city.

Those who peek behind the curtain know that, in all of this, on the one hand, the strength that God placed in our human essence and, on the other, all kinds of satanic influences are wrestling with each other, and that this wrestling produces the tone-setting spirit for each successive period. Over the course of the last century, that spirit departed more and more from the sacred path, and now it occupies itself more and more clearly with the organization of a spiritual human existence that forsakes God in everything and turns away from his holy will. Whether that ungodly development will once again be hindered, pruned, weakened, and subjected to a higher spirit, we do not know. It could very well be that we are on the road to the revelation of the "man of lawlessness" [2 Thess 2:3]. It could also be that the current governing spirit will once again sink away for some time. But whatever the future may bring, it is at any rate certain that our entire human development for the time being stands under the sign of the world city, and that the tone-setting and dominating spirit that goes forth from those great world cities more and more sets its stamp on our entire human existence. It is the spirit of the world city that, carried out into our cities and towns, will more and more govern the entire expression of our human life.

It is this spirit, this unity, coherence, and concentration, that presses upon those who are up with the times; it seeks to reproduce itself in all parts of the world. Christian Europe has dethroned the One who was once its King, and the world city has become the queen under whose scepter people willingly bow down. It is no longer the spirit from above that raises us with a *sursum corda*, arms us against sin, and opens the gates of eternity to us.[1] That spirit from above still governs in the small circle, among those who have remained faithful to their King. But the spirit governing the masses is a spirit from the world, which encloses life within the limits of this world, and which more and more takes possession of the human heart, even among those who confess Christ. The world city is

---

1. *Sursum corda* is Latin for "lift up your hearts," and is the opening phrase for the traditional Eucharistic prayer in Christian worship.

the splendid temple of that spirit from the world. And from that temple of the world's spirit people don't even fight against the kingship of Christ anymore. A battle would have roused those who are zealous for Christ's kingship out of their slumber. No, a better approach would be first to spiritualize that kingship of Christ entirely, then to pass over it in silence, and finally let it be forgotten. This is how the terrain was set free. Europe forgot that it had once enjoyed harmonious unity for the expression of all of life in Christ, and as a result the doors of the heart were opened wide to the majesty of the new queen, Babylon, who would give us her unity of spirit and her modern composition of human life in its glory.

THE QUEEN OF THE WORLD

Without natural affection.

2 TIMOTHY 3:3 KJV

§ 1 We have intentionally drawn a sharp line of distinction between the small flock and the great masses that some churches still have on record. It is a simple fact that the circle of those personally raised to life was always smaller compared to the wide circle of those who only went along nominally without consciously living along. But because a link does remain between that small and wide circle, we spoke of the small group in the holy place and of the broader group in the forecourt. Among those who dwell in the holy place, religion of course continued to live in unbroken power; but among those who wander in the forecourt, religion continues to sink to an ever lower level by the decade. For many, in fact, the moment of apostasy has already come. They themselves notice that the faith handed down to them no longer grips them anymore; that properly speaking, they no longer even belong in the forecourt—and so the one, and then the other, slips out of the forecourt. Some seek a new stimulus for higher consciousness in a Buddhist temple or in spiritualism, but the great majority go without religion until their dying day.

We have pointed to this gradual drop in religion's current in the wide bed of life's river, not so much to come down hard on those who have fallen away, but rather to illustrate the way in which time and circumstances among the masses at one time stimulate religious feeling and at another time dampen it, without the centuries introducing any change worth mentioning in the state of the unregenerate heart. Among all nations and in all centuries it is and remains the same human being with precious seeds for a higher disposition, but also with the powerful seeds for the most frightening sin and error in the poisoned heart. Time and circumstances used to be favorable for maintaining a certain general religiosity, but the same time and circumstances have now become more and more unfavorable for the flourishing of the same general religiosity. The result was a decline in the significance that religion held in public life, as well as an ever-expanding doubt and indifference; finally, there was the growing apostasy, not among believers, but among those who were merely following along. This decline can sometimes be seen in one and the same family when the very elderly members still go to church, when the second generation still harbors a certain respect for the religion handed down to them, while the grandchildren grow up entirely outside of all religion.

Man's higher disposition, however, still prevents every higher aspiration, every search for a communal ideal, from being lost. Christian society used to find that higher aspiration, that communal ideal, in Christ; but people now seek and find it in a more pressured life in this world known as modern life. There surges and rules in modern life a communal spirit that gives to life unity of tone and unity of purpose, and that communal spirit reveals itself in the great world cities. From those world cities, it occupies land and nation so as to conquer entire countries gradually. From the world cities proceeds a mode for life, a lifestyle, a lifeview, which once again binds the wandering spirits together into a certain unity. Those world cities are the reincarnation of what Scripture refers to as "Babylon," and today this modern Babylon, like a queen, increasingly subjects and governs our modern society in all of life's expressions. Her ways are so tyrannical that no one who wants to be up with the times and to feel included even dares to resist her life ordinances. The worldly man slavishly follows her fashion, her lifestyle, customs, and lifeview. In its powerful organization, the kingdom of the world thus elevates itself against the kingdom of Christ. People feel that whatever influence the church still exercises on life only stands in the way of the pursuits of the kingdom of the world. Such influences only constitute bonds from the past that prevent the modern spirit from spreading its wings out in freedom and gladness.

This explains the gradual anticlericalism that seeks to push the church's influence back in every terrain and cannot rest until every influence from the bygone general Christian life has been broken and done away with. Science, art, sensual pleasure, and greed must all work together as instruments in the service of that general world spirit, which ever more powerfully modernizes all of life and existence and which emanates from modern Babylon to celebrate its unimpeded triumphs.

It is this spirit that unites all participating nations internationally into a single whole and gathers the entire civilized world under one scepter. It thus usurps the place once occupied by the dominion of Christ, and from which the kingdom of Christ is now increasingly being squeezed out. The kingdom of Christ had at one time managed to win a place for itself in the heart of the nations. Lower passions did indeed thrash about at that time, but the gospel was able to remain their master and to bind all baptized nations together in higher aspiration. But this is no longer the case. An entirely different spirit has taken over the heart of the people. An entirely different unity of spirit has arisen to unify and govern them. The spirit proceeding from Christ no longer stands at the center of life, but the modern world spirit has now become authoritative. And that modern spirit of the age, which is either indifferent or hostile to all religion, finds the focus of its power in the modern-day Babylon of our world cities; and while each is different, they nevertheless harmoniously cooperate.

§ 2   It used to be that when the mind of Christ set the tone on the great world stage, it connected to the natural life given in the nature of our human existence. Each person lives in natural bonds: in the bond of immediate and extended family, the bond of the life of one's neighborhood, the bond of one's vocation, the bond of national life. People were able to develop their individuality powerfully, but always within these natural bonds. These bonds came to expression in what is called *natural love*. Outside of those natural bonds, there were indeed other bonds of friendship and like-mindedness, but natural love was and remained the backbone of social life as a whole. It was in the love of parents for their children, of children for their parents, of sisters and brothers for each other, and of members of one family and generation for each other; in the love for one's town and city; in the love for one's business or work; in the love for one's province and homeland—in all these things there came to expression the natural love that bound all things together, could fill an entire nation with zeal, and supplied guidance and direction in life.

In the entire broad terrain where this natural love functioned and united and animated, it was impossible to suppress one's inner awareness that all of these bonds by which people felt united with others were placed on us from above. You did not choose your parents, but were born to them. Care for the life and nurture of one's children was a task imposed on us by a higher hand. Love for and obedience to one's father and mother was experienced in the conscience as a duty placed upon one by God. Sisters and brothers were seen as having been placed together with us in one and the same family by God's design, and the bonds of blood had their draw. The cry that "You, O All-Governing King, have determined the place of each one's dwelling, the sphere wherein he must work,"[1] lived in everyone's heart—especially since people relocated and moved very little. Father and son often worked in the same trade, and the bonds of the trade guilds were all but interwoven with the bonds of the family. And when peace was disturbed and the homeland came under threat, one's love of country was like an electrical spark that set the entire nation ablaze. All human existence was thus composed of bonds of natural love, and the interconnection of these bonds presented itself as a consequence of higher ordination. Natural love was experienced as something innate, as worked in us by God, and as a matter of uplifting worship.

The Christian religion never meddled with these bonds. In fact, it caused the unity of our human race to triumph repeatedly over a narrow-minded patriotism. It extended mercy and compassion to the foreigner as well. And Christianity never forgot that there can be cases in which those who love their father and mother more than Christ would be unworthy of him. But all of this was nothing more than a necessary corrective to the abuse that a selfish or sinful interpretation of natural love could bring about. That being said, the Christian religion constantly connected to the life of the immediate and extended family, to local, provincial, and national society, and imbued every vocation with its sanctifying power. It did not wrest natural life from its place, did not push it aside, did not consider it as indifferent; but infused it with its spirit, drew it back to its original purity, and offered itself as a complement to it.

---

1. These lines or close variants appear in numerous hymnals from the period. See, for example, *Het Boek der Psalmen, nevens de gezangen, bij de Hervormde Kerk van Nederland in gebruik* (Amsterdam: J. Brandt en Zoon, en P. Proost, 1851), 25.

§ 3   Human life slid over the edge of the grave. It could not and should not be seen as being finished within this short existence. For some, a period of sixty or seventy years could be called an existence. But what of those ten thousands, and even millions, who died young or hardly reached maturity? The human heart screamed out for an eternal existence. Life with its brevity, with its full measure of human misery, with its overabundance of injustice, could not be what *life* is all about. For that reason, human existence came to be considered by all as beginning here, but never ending here. Rather, the perception was that life only began and came into existence here, and only afterward to reach its full, endless development in an eternal existence. People took dying and the enormous power of death into account. And the question of what the hereafter will be weighed heavily on everyone's heart and placed their inner life before the Judge of the living and the dead. Our entire earthly existence lost itself in its smallness, in its being almost insignificant, compared to the endless eternity whose gates were opened to us at death. And this decisive moment of the *memento mori* ["remember that you have to die"] was automatically connected to our appearance before the Almighty, and thus it caused our stained and sinful existence to step back for his holiness.

As a result, there were questions and problems for which this earthly life did not offer even the semblance of a solution. But precisely at this point, the Christian religion offered itself in order to fill this void in our existence with the treasure of divine light and divine compassion. Expectations that otherwise had a vague form now obtained a definite shape. The Christian religion paved a way for us through the dark shadow of death. The temporal was now firmly connected to the eternal. Our existence acquired more depth and breadth. Even as it stood before the gate of eternity, man's heart retained its feeling of rest. Life here and life hereafter were joined together in holy unity. A single spirit could penetrate both. And the spirit that would animate our human life, both here and later with its entrance into eternity, was the spirit of Christ who, seated at God's right hand, was clothed with all power over the living and the dead. In this way there was unity—the coherence of our entire existence in one holy harmony that shone upon us from Christ as the King of all. It automatically found its point of connection in that natural love placed by God as the Creator of all in our heart and in our human relationships. In this way religion sanctified life, and life led to religion.

For the modern spirit of the age, of course, natural love would not do. That spirit of the world too wants to join life together in tight bonds. After all, without tight bonds neither unity nor power nor dominion are imaginable. Natural love, however, could not hold on to its place. The modern spirit of the age proceeds rather from the assumption of the free individual, the equality of individuals, and the contractual bonding together of individuals based their own choice and will.

This spirit of the world cannot take its starting point in anything that lies beyond the world. It seeks and finds the secret of its strength in the world itself. In that world, it is of course humanity that rules, and human will and choice must organize this modern world. Going with people's free will and choice is simply required as soon as you take the individual as your point of departure. Every bond arising from birth, family, lineage, locale, or from whatever else, would in the end still be owing to a higher power; these thus make the individual unfree and define them not from within, but by something external to them. To acknowledge a power that defines us, be it outside of, behind, or above us, would not leave decisions regarding who we are and our destiny in our hands, but would place these in a higher hand and, in the end, lead once again to the celebration of religion. And this is precisely what people do not want. It would constitute a regression into the error of the previous generations. It would once again make us dependent on all kinds of influences worked upon us from a higher world. But of this we are convinced: our life must be explained from this world and must be tied to this world. Life must and will remain a life from and for the kingdom of the world. There may be things that influence us, and perhaps even entirely control us, but they are and will remain influences that proceed either from nature or from one person upon another.

Whatever the case may be, these influences must always arise from either the world or humankind; and in the latter case of human domination [they must] be rooted in the choice and will of human beings. Admittedly, one person exercises influence over another, and not all of us can remain our own lord and master. But that influence of one person upon another must and may not arise from the dictates of a higher order. It must find its root in a human discovery, a human story, a human choice, a human act. You may retreat as far back into history as you like, but as deep as you go to examine the mutual influence people exercise on each other, the push, the impulse that once went out—and continues to work itself out in you—must always have come from an individual and must likewise reach and touch you as an individual. There is a special, most complex psychology of the masses, and even now the secrets hidden from us by this psychology of the masses have scarcely been revealed. One thing is certain, however: One can deal only with individuals and the fortuitous bonds that one individual creates with another.

§ 4   In this way, the organic life connection of generations is pushed aside by a contractual, almost mechanical life connection of individuals, and natural love is neglected from the very outset.[2] The bond of marriage and the bond binding parents to their children have become weaker and weaker. People are no longer even willing to admit that by virtue of their birth, children have the duty to honor their parents. A common conception is that parents pay for the sensual pleasure that led to their children's birth by feeding and raising their children, while no obligation is thought to result for children. This implies a fundamental corrosion of the natural love between parents and children.

As a consequence, family life loses its nature and character. It can even be set aside if necessary. Where family life continues to exist, it is the fruit of the will of those who are married or live together, but no higher ordinance or deeper basis exists for life any longer. Sisters and brothers may love each other, but they may just as well not. The bond that unites them is entirely a matter of happenstance; it came into existence without and outside of their will, and it is the fruit of the acts of others for which they are not responsible.

In this way the constancy of family life, and thus the very foundation for all of social life, is put out of joint, and the solidarity of inhabitants of the same place or of fellow citizens becomes even looser. The division of nations and peoples creates false distinctions that have come down to us from an error-filled past, and everyone's ideal should be to call for a single world republic that has a universal social character and encompasses the entire human race. Anarchists and socialists who really claim to be

---

2. This distinction between *mechanical* (*mechanisch*)—which will at times be translated as *artificial* or *contractual*—and *organic* (*organisch*) functions significantly throughout Kuyper's entire paradigm. The contrast expressed by these two terms involves, on the one hand, the use of tools and operations external to the object to which they are applied, with a view to altering or improving that object, as distinguished from such change being effected by way of energies and laws inherent to what is being changed.

without a homeland go the furthest of all, but in their plans they in fact express no other ideas than those that the modern spirit of the age impresses upon all circles as a basic principle. The world city is the ideal. All commerce and trade spans the entire earth. All life ideals are international. And the one spirit of the world breaks through all national dividing walls so as to break them down in the end. Is a single language for the entire world not being developed already?[3]

In this way the old bonds become ever looser and diminish in significance, while conversely, an entirely different bond is being advanced among people that is neither God-ordained nor created in our nature, but proceeds from human choice and volition. In place of the organic bond that God created in life itself comes an external and artificial bond that arises from the subjection of everything and everyone to the modern world spirit. This is a bond not of blood, nor of the treasure handed down to us by history, nor of communal local life. Rather, it is a bond resulting from forcing people to think alike, from maintaining the same habits and manners, from harboring the same ideals, from enslaving themselves to one mode of fashion, from entering into the same style of life, from exerting themselves for the same innovations, from being animated by the same life spirit—and above all, from breaking one and all with what in the Christian religion was at one time holy to all.

And these efforts do indeed conflict with the natural order of things. The organic bond put in place by God cannot be discounted. It continues to exist, and so it must be said that modern global living lacks its natural basis. You can see it already in the senseless attempt to do away with the fundamental difference between man and woman, which certainly avenges the former undervaluing of women, but whose denial of woman's own essence makes it the laughingstock of nature's unconditional demand. But even if the spirit of the modern age is repeatedly challenged by the nature of things, it refuses to surrender. In the end it assails that nature as such, and for that reason it yields the sad outcome that in the modern citizen of this world the spiritual will and purpose increasingly are at odds with the natural basis of our existence.

---

3. The linguist L. L. Zamenhof published a book describing Esperanto, an artificial, politically neutral language intended for global use, in 1887. It appeared in English translation the following year as *Dr. Esperanto's International Tongue*, trans. Julian Steinhaus (Warsaw: Ch. Kelter, 1888).

The tenacity with which the Christian tradition continues to survive in the face of this modern spirit of the age (not among believers, but among the masses) can be explained, in particular, from the fact that the Christian religion coincides with the natural order of life, while the modern spirit of the age conflicts with it. The Christian religion follows the natural order, while the modern spirit of the age breaks with it. The modern spirit nevertheless continues to conquer a remarkable amount of terrain. This would be unthinkable in a sinless society that lives according to its created order. All sin, however, is always an attempt to seek freedom from the bonds created by God. That cry of emancipation cited in Psalm 2 sounds time and again: "Let us burst their bonds apart" [Psa 2:3]. Modern life aligns itself with this sinful side of our fallen nature. This does not occur without a certain intrusion of a higher purpose that will at some point bear the fruits God has willed for it. The masses, however, are lured not only by what is attractive, but also by what is sinful in the modern spirit of the age. Hidden within fallen man, there is from the very outset enmity toward God, and it is in this trait of the human heart that the world spirit finds its unexpected and powerful ally in thousands of hearts from every corner of the earth.

It thus remains a matter of Babylon against Jerusalem. Both are, of course, taken as types: The queen of the world against the King anointed by God over his Zion!

THE POWER
OF MONEY

You cannot serve God and mammon.

MATTHEW 6:24 NKJV

When Holy Scripture speaks of money as an unholy power, it does not brand it as *the golden calf*, but as *mammon*. The image of a calf cast from pure gold that Israel erected beside the altar in the desert was intended as a sensual representation of the Creator of heaven and earth. People did not expect gold from it, but gave their gold for it. The battle for or against the power of money thus has nothing to do with the golden calf. A particular group unfamiliar with Scripture first began to introduce the term *golden calf* as a reference to fascination with money, purely for its sound. Our Lord Jesus, by contrast, in a clear and conscious way, summarized the dark, shadowy side of monetary existence as a whole in the word *mammon*. And by the juxtaposition that "You cannot serve God and mammon," he forcefully rejected and condemned it, showing the extent of its anti-religious propensity.

§ 1

Money can entice one to all kinds of sin; in fact, there is almost no sin imaginable to which it does not entice. However, this is merely the consequence of the core corruption money brings as soon as it becomes for someone what his God alone can and may be for him. That struggle also goes on for a long time in the heart. Our human heart needs a point of support on which to depend, rest, lean, and rely; and from which it derives the peace, rest, and calm of life. At first, things fluctuate. At one time the heart finds this support in God, at another time in money or capital. Then follows a period of constant swinging back and forth, depending on the afflictions and dangers threatening us. As long as they can be countered with money, God takes second place. But if the threatening affliction or danger takes on a character against which gold can no longer fight, then in most people our God's name once again rises to the surface as the heart again seeks comfort in the God it had forgotten.

For many, their adherence to money gradually becomes so dominant that it begins to rule their entire soul and all their senses. The more money people have at their disposal, the more assured and certain they feel in their capacity for managing such a monetary treasure. They begin to look down almost in pity on those poor souls who have hardly any money and who seek consolation in prayer and thanksgiving and in their dependence on a purely imaginary God. They do not begrudge them this, since these poor souls after all need something in order to keep going in their poverty-stricken state. The rich, however, feel themselves to be beyond that. Those poor souls chase after a dream, while these folk hold on to reality. Gold is the real god, so why would we also add the unreal God of the imagination?

The contrast thus becomes sharper and sharper. Religion is for the poor and destitute who gaze at mere semblances, but money and gold constitute the real power for those with possessions. It is their rock, their support, and their strength. In this way, money first comes to stand beside religion; then there follows a period when money drives religion out of the heart; and in the end, a mystical veneration for money itself arises in the heart. At first one serves both God and mammon. Then the soul becomes entirely monetized until all religion appears to be erased. In the end, not only the worship of God falls away forever, but under a different form something of that old worship reappears and develops into a sort of religious veneration of money *and* mammon. This is exactly how Christ said things would go. First, you try to serve both God and mammon. This cannot be done, however, and is impossible in the long run. You cannot serve God and mammon. For that reason, if you do not want to break with mammon, the religion of your God can only die off in your monetized heart, so that in the end nothing remains but the money-god, mammon.

The sad process that affects individuals addicted to money becomes reality for entire social circles and even countries. Especially those countries that are devoted to the business of wholesale trade and banking experience over time the incredible power that money has. In that way, they ultimately become so impressed by that enormous world power that only in periods of high spiritual elevation in the circles of this powerful commercial world does one still see a religious tone reign. §2

In the sixteenth and early seventeenth centuries, there was an elevated religious tone among the merchants who moved in droves from Flanders and Wallonia to Amsterdam. However, as soon as the great pressure that the Spanish tyranny exercised on the conscience had passed and the acquired capital had grown, our merchant circles also largely lost the love for religion. While *hac nitimur, hanc tuemur*—that is, "On this book we lean, this book we defend"—originally meant the Bible, people soon began to mock that meaning and with a smile argue that the book they leaned on and defended was the book of the Exchange. Mercurius, the ancient god of trade, was elevated; the God of our fathers who had freed us was forgotten. Money displaced worship of the Only True One. Godliness went into hiding; in the end, no one turned more fiercely against religion than that powerful circle of merchants and stockbrokers of what at the time was our leading commercial city.

From the exchange, the reversal in thought and in the aspirations of the conscience gradually spread to all of national life. They would say, "Our nation's welfare came from the sea." Our national existence depended on commerce. Commerce wielded enormous power through its influence on the High Councils of State. The corruption of wealth soon trickled down from the higher to the lower classes. Soon the upper and lower bourgeois classes became infected, and in the end religious zeal could survive only in the class of the "little people" and in the countryside. Not that people openly exalted mammon—not at all! Appearances were maintained. Both God and mammon would be served. But that is impossible, and so the time came when unbelief—atheism—gained a stronger foothold; the time when the religious character that had once been so dominant wore away in this part of the nation.

Over the course of the last century, this ugly phenomenon has spread out in ever widening circles and has gradually assumed a worldwide character. World life in its entirety now stands under the sign of money-power. In the international community there is hardly any sensitivity for higher §3 interests anymore. Almost all governments openly show that their only goal is to increase their population's riches and welfare. This orientation in government policy has pushed material and financial interests to the foreground. All conflicts between states, whether they involve war or not, aim at obtaining the greatest possible financial advantages for their own country. This spirit has penetrated downwards and placed its grasp on all levels of society. The battle, the fierce struggle of the so-called proletariat against capital, had no other cause. From those wide circles the same thirst for money worked its way into families and people. The lust of the current generation is to accumulate wealth, to better one's position, and to have at our disposal the greatest amount of money possible.

It is no longer the man from a family of high standing, the man of character and high intelligence, the man of noble spirit, who presides at the nation's table. The place of honor is now reserved for the merchant, for the one who has much money, for the millionaire. This passion has proved itself to be so infectious that even families of standing have cast their higher calling aside and now strive to match the financial power of the *nouveau riche*; yes, even kings and princes exert themselves to earn honor and respect among the money magnates by acquiring as much capital as the magnates do—or even more. Without wealth you are nothing. All doors are open to those with immeasurable capital, and so they automatically climb higher and higher on the social ladder. Wealth covers everything; without wealth you are helpless. It is especially in our great world cities that the greatest amount of ready capital gives influence and ensures dominion, even in the international struggles between nations.

§ 4   In all of this, it should be kept in mind that capital grew to a hitherto unknown superpower through the gradual development of the credit system. Amounts of capital that previously entire countries scarcely had at their disposal are now in the hands of a single person or family. Billionaires, who can now be found in America by the dozens, or else in the great banking houses of London, Paris, and Berlin, were once entirely unknown. Some have managed to scrape together and collect sums that would once have surpassed the full budget of entire countries. Half a century ago our national budget was just over fifty million. Some magnates now have more than that, not just in total capital but in annual income. Money used to be said to reproduce through interest, but the credit system has by now grown so incredibly that, if a house or family simply acquires two-hundred million or so, it already knows that its enormous assets will be doubled within a quarter century assuming that the credit system is allowed to run its course. If the credit system is already stretched so tightly that there is the occasional drop, bad speculation, or crash, such a crash usually affects the small borrowers much more than the great magnates. The latter are, after all, up-to-date on everything, see the crash coming, and cover themselves for it; and even if they too suffer loss, the damage is recovered more quickly than they themselves had ever thought possible.

For this reason, the magnetic power emanating from money has become so bewitchingly great that talented and energetic young men increasingly feel themselves drawn to banks or to the other institutions that the financial markets have created. It is more the exception than the rule when a top man of power devotes himself to other interests. What are the wages you can expect for service to church or state compared to the high salaries dealt out in the commercial sector? In this way, the great strength of the human spirit increasingly comes to be concentrated in the circles of banking and commerce. Real financial geniuses throw themselves into the gold trade, while the rest of the country has to suffice with various second rate talents that can hardly match the influence emanating from *haute finance*.[1]

Indeed, hidden within money is a magical power that thereby enchants people. Hardly anything cannot be turned into money anymore, and you can scarcely conceive of anything that is not available for money. Money is the universal means of exchange. Everything that allures, fascinates, and awakens desire can be exchanged for, valued as, and calculated in terms of money. What is more, while the power of money used to be bound to gold as metal, money has now thrown that bond off as well. Value is no longer measured in metal but paper. The available gold is amassed in bank vaults. A mint of paper currency is then printed whose value is backed up by—though not always literally tied to—this storehouse of gold, such that a rich person in America or England can produce the amount needed at will with no more than a signature on a slip of paper from their checkbook. This brings human power to its greatest heights. People no longer pay in actual coin, but write a word, and through that word they create and call into being whatever legal tender they may need at any given time.

§ 5

---

1. This phrase literally means "high finance," and today refers to the twenty-four-hour trading within the global financial system. For more on this, see Jason P. Abbott, *Routledge Encyclopedia of International Political Economy*, ed. R. J. Barry Jones, vol. 2, *Entries G–O* (New York: Routledge, 2001), s.v. "haute finance."

All recently emerging forces have placed themselves in the service of that monetary power. While our power over nature has grown incredibly, that great power constantly demands more capital in order to mine recently discovered resources, to set up railroads and mail service, to promote means of transport and communication, and to provide industry with the ways and means to flood the worldwide market with its products. This forces national governments to acquire, with new and massive loans, the funds necessary to better organize social life at home or in their colonies. The increase of knowledge at our disposal demands ever more expensive arrangements in order to continue research in all areas; and every new scientific discovery requires new capital in order to apply that finding practically. The ease of production raises the standard of living and constantly creates new needs even for civil life, which, if they are to be met, in turn cry out for capital. Money's power has thus become a world power that ignores the borders of land and nation, spreads its wings out over all of human life, lays claim to everything, and increasingly penetrates into some of the most unknown corners of the world. It makes everything dependent on it, imposes its law on all lives, and consolidates in the great world cities in order to give life a bewitching glow, to have a temple there in its honor, and to rule the entire world from that base.

§ 6   How could such a miraculous power not have influenced people's inner life? Could such a power have raised itself to a splendor and glory as never before without poisoning the human heart itself? The entire public sees before its eyes how the power of money is flourishing, developing enormously, causing everything to bow down before it, and triumphing over anything and everything that offers resistance. Especially in America, you see how a throne stands ready for everyone—even the common citizen—in money's palace, if only they work resolutely, cleverly, and resourcefully. A considerable proportion of those who now have gold by the handful were ignored citizens ten years ago. There is no hierarchy there. Even those who begin with nothing can soon place on their heads the crown of the money king. This is why everyone everywhere hunts feverishly to get ahead, to climb the social ladder, and to be counted soon among the world's powers. The desire for pleasure exercises pressure, and every sensual pleasure can be had for money as well.

This explains the increasing hunger for gambling. Is stock market speculation, after all, not a form of gambling? Do governments themselves not constantly encourage gambling with option loans and lotteries?

Many already love sports to begin with, but gambling is also a kind of sport. So why should this sport alone be condemned? Gambling, playing for money, wins for itself an ever-increasing circle of worshipers in both the upper and lower circles. While it is just one of the many ways to become a man of fortune, it is a means that demands the least amount of effort. But where one person wins, another always has to lose. People are willing take that risk, however. Financial suicide cannot be separated from service to mammon.

A bewitching power thus works upon the unguarded heart, lulling more noble inclinations into an ever deeper sleep. It recognizes in greed alone a world power that far surpasses all normal dimensions and increasingly takes on a nearly almighty, nearly divine character. People admit that it is for this world alone; with the grave, this power slips away irrevocably from its owner. But what harm is there in that? After all, people want to live for this world alone and be taken up in it. The one passion they have is to be able to shine here on earth, to have had enjoyment here, to have achieved greatness here. Greatness does not come from the soul's nobility, from dedication to higher things, or from self-sacrifice for an ideal; it comes through power, and it is in money that this power is hidden. Those who have money have the entire world at their feet. Money may be a cruel power for those who have it, but it also makes you lord and master in the circles of this world.

How could the worship of him who created heaven and earth ever survive when faced with the enormous growth of money's power in the unregenerate human heart? Worship of the only true God reaches very deep. It does not tolerate you placing your confidence in some creature, in something other than him alone. However, we are faced with a mystery at this point. It pleased God in his unsearchable design to allow the power of money to establish its throne on earth and to wave its scepter over the kingdom of this world. And—let us not hide the truth—in money, there rules a power that closely approaches God's omnipotence, at least insofar as the satisfaction of the needs and wants of one's outer life is concerned. God himself mysteriously raised that power to life in order to confront us more than ever before with the choice for or against him. After all, you can expect all you desire from the power of money; you can ask and receive it from mammon. This places you before the question that your God asks you in your conscience: Is it your determined choice to reject all these things, to recognize that they are nothing, and to place your only, unwavering, and full trust in me as your God?

Former generations faced the same choice, of course. But the level of temptation was lower because mammon's power was so small and insignificant compared to God's omnipotence. Money did exist, but it could do so little. Now, in contrast, it can sometimes do everything. And as long as you feel no deeper need in your soul, money—mammon—provides for you in all your needs, in all your necessities, and in all your wants. And when these are met, it makes you feel as if you have a power that is unspent, is virtually inexhaustible, and has almost no limits; and this strokes your human ego. For precisely that reason, given the current state of the struggle, you need to be much stronger in spirit now in order to cast mammon down to earth and to bow down before God alone, to love him only, and merely to trust in his omnipotence.

Was it not inevitable that the dollar-king would come to occupy in many hearts the place that King Jesus had at one time won for himself? The kingship of Jesus was and is the embodiment of human life in its more noble, spiritual, and higher aspirations. His is the kingdom of heaven, which stands opposed to the kingdom of the world. Anything that is external, material, sensual, can occupy a place only of second order in his kingdom. In Jesus' kingship, the spiritual is always the starting point, the end, and the means in order to reach that end. The kingdom of monetary power stands diametrically opposed to that kingdom. It is its opposite, reverse, its counter-image, and denial.

King Jesus certainly is and remains sovereign in everything. No power of mammon will ever prevent him from winning the souls of those who have been given to him by the Father. For that reason, we exclude from our discussion here and elsewhere those who are regenerated by the Spirit. But if we disregard them and look only at the masses, who must begin the battle with nothing but their sinful heart, do you not feel, see, sense with irrepressible pity how this destitute human race no longer has any power within itself to wrestle against mammon's enormous power? And do you not hear the sad laments, the anguished cries for help that go out to the Exalted One, but also to you, for release and rescue from the clutches of a society oppressed by mammon?

I.11

THE DOMINION OF ART

The sound of harpists and musicians, of flute players and trumpeters, will be heard in you no more, and a craftsman of any craft will be found in you no more.

REVELATION 18:22

The book of Revelation portrays the life-determining influence emanating from today's world city against what lies outside her gates with the following brief phrase: "All nations were deceived by your sorcery" [Rev 18:23]. This influence is indeed a powerful sorcery whose work no one can fully explain. This power has much greater effect on life than the power that ancient Babylon, Tyre, or the Roman Empire were ever able to exert. It is a power that not only subjects and rules, but at the same time molds life into its spirit, forms humanity after its model, and thus attempts to imprint on our human development its own stamp rather than the stamp of nature and history. The apostles of this power proclaim that they have chosen humanity's ideal ahead of the Christian ideal. Humanity has been placed in the foreground—that is, humanity with its power over nature, its near omnipresence, and its pervasive knowledge. Once it had gained such power and climbed so high, humanity made the world city the seat of its glory, threw off the bonds of nature so as to replace them with the new unity of style, fashion, high life, or whatever it is called.

§ 1

That new type of humanity has its own magic formulas, its own fascinations, its own language and art, partly even its own ideals, the highest of which is to become not like Jesus but like Croesus.[1] The goddess Fortuna is quietly worshiped. Even if the members of the proletariat have lately begun to organize themselves against the idol named Capital, the child of Fortuna, they too are in their innermost being driven by nothing other than the thirst for gold. And it always is humanity that ascends, humanity that announces itself in its royalty. And humanity, in treading upon nature, encompasses the entire world and possesses a near omniscience and sits enthroned on the throne of the world city. Here, too, there is an enthroned-humanity,[2] just as Christianity worships Christ. But the Jerusalem above is replaced by a Babylon on earth, and the king is not crowned by the almighty God, but self-proclaimed. Instead of the Holy Spirit's power, the power of gold and money subjects everything to itself. The lord here is not the Man-king at God's right hand, through whom and in whom God is great, but the self-satisfied enthroned-humanity who plays with Fortune and has cut through every bond that existed between itself and the Creator of heaven and earth. The contrast to the kingship of Christ is thus complete.

Kingship as such has not been abandoned, but Christ has been dethroned and people have perched themselves like real Jacobins on the throne and placed the crown on their own head.[3] This process was not arbitrary, but driven by an internal necessity. The human race cannot exist without a king. Once it had closed its eyes to the glory of Jesus' kingship, the presence of sin—together with the disposition of our human nature—could mean only one thing: that with the help of purely worldly factors, humanity would proclaim itself king of nature, king of the world, and king of all of human life.

It is a mistake, however, to think that everything loftier and more ideal has altogether disappeared from human life. The fact that we have been

---

1. Croesus (595–547 BC) was a Greek king renowned for his wealth. In Greek and Persian culture, "Croesus" became a synonym for a wealthy man.
2. In this and subsequent chapters, Kuyper uses the unique phrase *de mensch-koning* in reference to the exalted position of the human race at creation and in paradise. Rather than render this phrase as *the man-king*, the rendering of *enthroned-humanity* highlights the royal identity, status, and calling of the entire human race.
3. The Jacobins were a political club during the French Revolution who defended values of republicanism, universal suffrage, popular education, and the separation of church and state.

created in the image of God means that this can never happen. While this may have happened for the base individuals from the group that is captivated by its fascination for lower motives, this is not so for the nobler element. God has so determined our human race that, in addition to the stalk and chaff, there is always a bud that sprouts from the top. There has always been and there will always be a spiritual aristocracy, a circle of people who have a more elevated orientation, who have finer needs, and who cannot rest before those finer needs are also satisfied.

When I say this, I am not thinking of that mystical current we find in modern life. That mystical current arises from dissatisfaction with what lies before our eyes. It represents a break with the modern principle of life, a renewed attempt to connect with the eternal and infinite. And whether that mystical current manifests itself in spiritualist, theosophical, or Buddhist tendencies, it is always the expression of dissatisfaction with the treasure of this earthly life; a striving for what is higher, a longing to go a-Maying in what lies above and beyond our worldly life. That is why it remains an exception; a small mystical oasis in the midst of a rationalistic and materialistic desert. It never sets the tone. It is in hiding. It does not rule life.

By contrast, what does set the tone and does function as an instrument for the new enthroned-humanity's dominion is *art*, and it is through art that modern life attempts to satisfy its thirst for the ideal. That is not so strange. In fact, it almost speaks for itself that wherever religion goes into hiding, art presents itself to take its high place. Religion and art are closely related, and both flourish best where they can exist in mutual harmony. But if religion is taken away, art soon makes itself the lord of the entire domain. It grows through hypertrophy like a miracle tree and absorbs into itself all of power and sap that belong to religion. What art and religion have in common is that they depend on inspiration. Everything we can do with the power of our hands in the practical, or with the power of the mind in the rational, lies trapped within the finite; only art and religion can extend their wings so as to rise above it. Religion finds its fountainhead in our hearts through a higher sensitivity that lays hold of our inner life. Faith laughs at the bonds of the sensuous and finite, and immediately reaches through the clouds to lay hold on the infinite. All nobler art does exactly the same. It does not flourish in its high spheres unless two actions occur at once: a grasping from above, and a laying hold immediately of what is elevated above normal life. Just like religion, through faith,

§ 2

gives and possesses certainty in its domain, so also art finds its power in this sense of certainty. Art does not hesitate. It does not doubt. It is stirred up by the higher, it grasps the higher, it displays or sings or acts it out, and it hovers over life as a kingly power. This is why art arose from the spheres of religion and first entered the world from that sacred sphere. First came temples, then monuments and palaces. First came psalms and hymns, then national anthems and epics. It is for that reason not strange, but entirely natural and necessary, that where society leaves and abandons religion, art comes to take its place.

Art can either serve or rule. People can take hold of art as a means for pleasure rather than a means to higher exaltation. When discussing modern Babylon as type, we already pointed to humanity's submission to the sensuous impulse to revel in what a lower art offers it to stimulate its sensual desires. This was initially nothing more than an attempt to experience the prickle that is present in art. People sought distraction, relaxation, and diversion. They took music as it was, the theatre as it offered itself, songs as they were sung, fiction as it portrayed scenes from life with honor and virtue.

It goes without saying that such ordinary food could not satisfy the taste, which soon found itself over-stimulated. It contained too much that was noble, too little that was sensual. That is when the arts began to diminish; which turned them into a servant of the passions. They must not just flatter and embolden, but stimulate and excite. Art needed to do the same as alcohol: to over-stimulate. And once it had over-stimulated, it simply had to become even more extreme in order to satisfy the passions that were also increasing. The result was the baseness in theaters, the domination of the nude and sensual in painting, the shameless debasement of sculpture, the hyper-erotic tone in music, the dirty realism in fiction, the hyper-sensuality in dance, the excesses in music that throw all of the senses into confusion—in short, the result was a beastliness in art far surpassing anything that had ever been produced in pagan countries. The real priest in art's temple covered his face in shame as art traded its divine essence in for a demonic imitation.

What is more, money then began to wave its scepter over art. Debased, demonic art won for itself the highest whore's wages in order to expand its circle of influence continually. A decent theater production does not pay. A respectable novel does not sell. The shamelessness of the cynic's art, however, produces a fortune.

It was necessary to emphasize these observations so that art's univer-   §3
sal expansion might not be interpreted as evidence for a trend that leads
toward the ideal. This claim has been made all too often. You hear people
say it, but there is nothing to it and the opposite is in fact true. Debased art
debases humanity; it does not lift humanity up. We need to be on guard.

People are suggesting that the present age stands taller than earlier
generations because we have learned to appreciate the arts more, and because art has become a powerful factor in the development of our nation.
They even want, in the name of democracy, to bring art to the lowest classes of society. And while this may seem like a wonderful idea, the outcome
belies the lofty claims. In all such sensual art, it is not the lofty but the
base animal in man that is out for entertainment, sensual pleasure, freedom of the passions, and shameless enjoyment. Art's higher purpose is no
longer sought. A realistic novel is not devoured for its character portraits,
for its stylistic beauty, but for the vulgarities it contains. The clean pages
are skimmed, and those with vulgarity are read over and over again. It is
a matter of lust, not art. People do not gaze upon the exaltation of the holy,
but upon Satan's depths. While the spectators who seek to satisfy their
lust are no doubt guilty in this development, the same applies to the artists themselves, who dare to display the products arising from their own
lusts so as to stimulate the lusts of others, and who even deliver them into
their living rooms. Viewed as such, art is thus no proof at all of a nobler
orientation and of more ideal purposes, but a sign of our moral decay and
the decline of human worth.

And yet—and this is what we intended to note all along—the arts are
not entirely defined by this. On the contrary. A small circle of artists also
exists in which nobler purposes really do preside. It is a circle in which
people are fascinated by the magnificent, by real art that has come down
to us from the past centuries—fascinated by the things art created when
artists were still driven by the sacred and when scenes from the Bible,
the era of Christ and the virgin mother, of the apostles and martyrs, the
courage of epic heroes and knightly honor, inspired singers and sculptors. And even though that circle is rather small, its adopting of such a
noble viewpoint means that it still exercises an uncommon influence for
the good. In that chosen circle they no longer want anything to do with a
base art that debases itself and its audience. When they discover that our
age is poor in the nobler art that they seek, they reach back into history
to be built up and inspired by art works from the past. What is more, new

creations and projects are not lacking. Their beautiful, lofty creations in architecture, sculpture, painting, and music, also in our day, amaze the world. They may differ from the creations of past generations, and yet they remain largely in the same style, connect to it, and continue the line of those who went before them.

From our Christian perspective, we may not close our eyes to those who are working in these fields today. In fact, we must warn people not to be blind to them, since the pious have long had a tendency to protest against art's arrogance—and not without reason. One must, of course, remain critical. Nevertheless, wherever a nobler impulse, a nobler striving manifests itself in human life, it continues to demand our admiration. And as justified as we are to hate debased art, we must learn to value the high development that comes to expression in the love for nobler and higher art. Our love for our fellow human beings also lays a demand on us when they begin to wander astray. Even if we know and confess with all our heart that nothing but the lost son's return to his heavenly Father can bring salvation, sufficient salvation, we do have a higher calling that still commands us to rejoice and delight over every manifestation of an ideal tendency that we may observe. These phenomena, too, are revealed under a higher ordination, and they are a balsam that a higher hand pours over the current generation's spiritual wounds.

Our eyes must of course remain open to the limitation that dominates this artistic circle, the blindness to the sacred with which this circle's heroes have often been struck, and the nearly idolatrous veneration of art that has become the warp and woof for many of them. But even if we discount everything in this movement that has a destructive impact and is to be condemned without qualification, the fact remains that people in these circles do not bow their knees before mammon or sell their soul to lust. They are active and animated. Their untiring efforts represent a greater inheritance, a lofty ideal, an inspiration from above.

§ 4   Although we recognize this without any qualification, we are still bound to consider this phenomenon, too, in the context of its time. When we do this, we can unfortunately come only with a less favorable judgment. Art is related to religion, since both depend on higher inspiration. But even if the inspiration for art, just like religion, always comes from above and cannot flow to the artist from any other source, this does not mean that art itself acknowledges and recognizes this circumstance. In life, the opposite in fact holds true. It is a great exception to find even a single artist who prays for inspiration and afterward gives thanks for it; even rarer is the artist who, after he has expressed his soul and successfully given shape to the image he saw within himself, openly gives glory to God as the one who inspired him and urges his audience to glorify God rather than him. Even among the best artists, one instead commonly finds self-admiration and a desire for incense to be burned to their talent. One altar after another is erected; one incense bowl after another is lit. But almost without exception, these are for the priest in art's temple and not for the God whose humble priest the artist ought to be.

Of course, we have to be careful not to come down too hard on the artists. After all, what you observe among them you see also among scholars and businessmen. Conceit and the desire for glory reside in each and every person's heart, while jealousy stimulates self-admiration. For those who are rich in talent, have great genius, overflow with gifts, it is twice as difficult to stay humble. Nevertheless, even if we admit that we are to a certain degree dealing with a universal phenomenon, it can hardly be denied that artists in particular seem to suffer from the glorification of self and each other; it is particularly in their circle that one will be hard pressed to find homage for the One who gave artists their inspiration.

If we already find a serious deficiency among architects, sculptors, painters, and musicians, the situation is twice as serious among poets and writers. The latter must transform their inspiration into images, those images into words, and those words into a deliberately artistic form. Theirs is the world of thought, and in that world of thought, consideration is to be given to what people experience, perceive, assimilate, and produce. For this reason, it is precisely in their circle that the question "From where does my inspiration come?" cannot remain unanswered. Those artists who work in poetry and prose and who have discarded all faith in the living God need a surrogate to replace the God they have discarded. They look for it mystically in pantheism and in its slogan that everything is actually divine and is God—all of nature, all of humankind, and every expression of human life.

However, they cannot stop at this general mystical feeling. While architects and musicians can stop here, artists whose tool is the word cannot. An inspiration leading to conscious art in the word must itself come from something that is conscious. The God-who-is-in-everything must therefore be more narrowly determined. And because the inspiration animating the artist drives and pushes him to the beautiful, he can reach no other conclusion than that the divine-in-everything is the beautiful, and that beauty is fundamentally divine. People thus come to look at beauty as god, at the beautiful as the divine, and veneration of the beautiful automatically passes over into the worship of beauty. However, this worship, too, remains vague and uncertain as long as no conscious life is discovered in that beautiful thing. The beautiful, as such, has no *I*, while a higher, animating inspiration can only come from a conscious *I*. As a result, the artist has to go and seek this conscious *I*-revelation of the beautiful in a person, and in this case in the person of the artist.

In short, those who refuse to know of a master who formed them will end up worshiping themselves and seeing in themselves the self-revelation of the beautiful, of the god of the beautiful, while artists of a lower stature will in the end find their God in the great Artist who formed and inspired them.

All of this means that the King of kings, the Greatest Architect and Artist, has been dethroned in art as well, and the artist-man erects a throne for himself from which he intends to rule as a higher spirit.

Will artists who have become a god to themselves still acknowledge a higher law? This may indeed be true for those whose works still follow the law of the beautiful that is imposed on them by the art schools of the past. However, even they do not fully submit to it, either. This would be recognizing a power over and above them to which they must submit, and this is the very thing that goes entirely against the basic foundation of the self-inspired artist-god who wants at once to be both god and priest. They never can nor will admit that a law of the sacred also exists to rule over their art, or at least to set limits on their art or to guide their choices regarding its purpose and the use of its resources. And this is where even the more ideal art reaches out for the self-debasing art. Everything, even the law of the sacred, must step back before art. Art must rule—it must rule over every realm of our human existence.

It should be noted that the veneration of art has taken heart, soul, and senses captive, even in our best circles of society. In fact, in the highest circles people have the greatest esteem for those who are fascinated by art, plead the cause of art, and make sacrifices for art. The only result can be that the one-sided exaltation of art, understood and practiced in this way, continues to unravel the threads of the faith that has been handed down, causes respect for the sacred to weaken. It thus also undermines the Christian foundations on which, until now, state and society have rested for over a thousand years.

Art's arrogant kingly dominion, even in its most ideal interpretation, diminishes Christ's kingship more and more.

THE UNDERMINING OF CHRIST'S KINGSHIP

BY THE GRACE OF GOD

Authority over me.

JOHN 19:11

Does Scripture include the government among those authorities that can §1 suppress the kingship of Christ in order to set themselves up in its place? Many—without thinking—claim that this is indeed the case, but they are entirely mistaken. The authority of the government is not included in the kingship of Christ. Of course, government authority can turn itself against his kingship and attempt indirectly to undermine it, though it too is in fact called to serve the glory of Christ. All the same, this is not at all to deny the need for the careful consideration that must be given at the very outset to the distinction on earth between Christ's kingship and government authority. We will expand on this later, but in order to avoid possible misunderstandings it is necessary already at this point to sketch the main argument.

Jesus' words that "All authority in heaven and on earth has been given to me" [Matt 28:18] are often understood as if the kings and princes of this earth likewise derive their governmental authority from Christ. Roman Catholics even developed this notion in such a way that all sovereign majesty would be derived from Christ, and for that reason the Vicar of Christ on earth also possessed the crown and scepter to forgive and take away sins. The intent was not to deny that the government ruled by the grace of God; rather, the commissioning and transfer of authority was understood *mediately*. Government authority was indeed held to be an authority from God, but one that came to the magistrate in the name of the Father through Christ (that is, mediately).

The Reformed view instead emphasized that the assignment of authority to the government had an *immediate* character, and that Christ was not to be seen as an intermediary in this regard. Reformed theologians never developed this point, but treated it simply from two perspectives. First, in the battle with Roman Catholic theologians regarding the authority of the pope over sovereigns; and, in the second place, in their resistance to the Remonstrants who conversely sought to permit the government to exercise authority in the church, a *ius in sacra* [right in sacred things], and attempted to derive that authority from the power that came to the government from Christ. So Reformed theologians have hammered out this issue only to the extent that it was a subject of controversy in the spiritual battle of those days. They never explored its depths.

This was left for our own time, when the contrast between the *mediate* and *immediate* character of government authority has arisen on its own through the struggle against the modern spirit of the age. The Reformed did develop the contrast to the extent that they pleaded and insisted plainly and clearly on the immediate character of government authority as deriving directly from God. Their point of departure and foundation was the apostolic explanation in Romans 13. No apostle has made the authority of Christ shine more impressively in all its glory than did the apostle from Tarsus. Yet in Romans 13, when he was determining the proper relationship to the government of those who confess Christ, he did so using expressions that omitted all reference to Christ and devoted not even a single letter to any origin for government authority other than the Triune God. Christ is not mentioned even once in this entire context. In contrast, the name of God is placed in the foreground five times in these few verses: "For there is no authority except from *God*, and those that exist have been instituted by *God*. Therefore whoever resists the authorities resists what *God* has appointed.... [The government] is *God's* servant for your good." And finally, government is "the servant of *God*, an avenger who carries out God's wrath on the wrongdoer." The name of the Lord Jesus Christ is not even mentioned in Romans 13 until the last verse, yet in these words—that is, "But put on the Lord Jesus Christ, and make no provision for the flesh, to gratify its desires"—Paul is speaking no longer of government authority but of its spiritual influence.

Confirmation of this can be found in Jesus' words to Pilate. John 18:36 shows that Jesus presented himself to Pilate neither as the Redeemer from sin nor as the fulfillment of prophecy, but rather as King. Jesus' work as Prophet and High Priest retreated into the background so that Jesus could present himself as King over against the emperor's representative. It is not relevant to dismiss this by insisting that Pilate gave opportunity for this with his question, "So you are a king?" Jesus did in fact choose to answer that question. His response was decisive: "I am not only a king, but for this purpose I was born and for this purpose I have come into the world" [see John 18:37]. Jesus not only emphasized his kingship, but he spoke with equal emphasis about his kingdom—in such a way that he gave a further description of the unique and special character of the nature of both that kingship and that kingdom. The power of his kingship lay in this, that he had come "to bear witness to the truth" [John 18:37]. His kingdom was to be distinguished from the kingdom of earthly sovereigns in that their kingdom was the world, and in that they had armed powers at their disposal in order to defend it. Jesus' kingdom, by way of contrast, was not from the world and his servants were not allowed to fight for him with the sword. Jesus confirmed this characteristic of his kingship and kingdom with his final words: "My kingdom is not from the world" [John 18:36]. The kingdom of kings and emperors came from *here*, but Jesus' kingdom did not.

But there is more. Jesus did not say to Pilate that he was going to become King, that he would inherit his kingdom only through his resurrection and ascension, and that he would be crowned in that way. No, he positioned himself *as* King over against the emperor's representative—as the King anointed by God over against the kingdom of the world. But while he stood before Pilate in the full majesty of his kingship, he acknowledged that the Roman emperor had authority over him, authority from above, authority from God. In fact, Pilate's authority was such that he could detain him or release him in the emperor's name, and even deliver him over to death according to the law of the Roman emperor. It is clear that Pilate sinned when he condemned Jesus to death, but he sinned only insofar as, in his office as judge, he pronounced a death sentence upon Jesus that was not in accord with justice, but contrary to justice.

This explains why Jesus added: "He who delivered me over to you has the greater sin" [John 19:11]. In Jerusalem, legal jurisdiction was mixed. There was the Sanhedrin's jurisdiction, on the one hand, and that of Roman law, on the other. With regard to the factual evidence, the Roman judge could not ignore the verdict of the Sanhedrin. Therefore, a double responsibility rested on the Jewish court that brought Jesus before Pilate's court as someone upon whom the Sanhedrin had pronounced the death sentence. Pilate did sin, but the sin of the Sanhedrin was even greater. But even if there was mixed jurisdiction with a resulting twofold measure of sin, nothing prevented Jesus from acknowledging without qualification that, as governor to the emperor of Rome, Pilate had authority over him, and that it was God who had given the Roman emperor this authority over him. Pilate of course remained responsible for the verdict and was supposed to determine whether it was just or unjust. But if he really did see Jesus as a pretender who sought to raise himself up in order to undermine the emperor's authority in Palestine, Pilate had the authority to destroy this resistance against his authority. With his words, Jesus thus makes a twofold pronouncement. He claims, on the one hand, that he is King, and on the other hand, that even as King over the kingdom of God, he is subject to the authority of the government, which the government has received not from itself but from God.

§ 2   In light of the above, we can only conclude that there is a twofold kingship, that both proceed directly from the Triune God, and that they run parallel to each other. On the one hand, there is the kingship of the world that proceeds directly from God and calls governmental authority here on earth into being. On the other hand, there is the kingship of Christ that is not from here—not from the world and reigning elsewhere—but that reigns here and proceeds just as directly from God. Government authority has been ordained by God. Alongside it, "all authority in heaven and on earth" has been given to Jesus as King of God's kingdom. Both kingships will come to an end one day. The earthly kingship will end when this world ends, because it is from the world and belongs to the sphere of the world; but the spiritual kingship will likewise end when "the Son himself delivers the kingdom to God the Father, so that God may be all in all" [see 1 Cor 15:24, 28].

So here we see a twofold derived sovereignty. The original sovereignty, the primordial majesty, rests in the Triune God and in him alone, because he is Creator of heaven and earth. But from this original sovereignty that resides in God alone, a twofold sovereignty is derived. First, there is the sovereignty of the government that is God's servant, reigns by his grace, and, as his servant, even has the right of life and death over its subjects. Secondly, there is the sovereignty of Christ in his kingdom, so that in his kingdom everyone is subjected to him for God's sake—not only those who acknowledge him as King, but also those who deny him or have never even heard of his kingship. As a resident of Palestine and a citizen in Israel, Jesus was subject to Pilate and to the Roman emperor, and they were able and permitted to judge him according to worldly justice. However, both Pilate and the Roman emperor were likewise subject to Jesus as King over the kingdom of God, and when his day comes, Jesus will judge them both. Government authority in and of itself, however, is not part of the kingdom of Christ. It runs alongside it, it runs parallel to it, but it is not taken up into it. It stands independently alongside it. This explains the independence of the government from the church, but also the independence of the church from the state. State and church are two spheres that are both ordained by God, but in such a way that the sphere of the world is and remains subject to the government for the organization of the state; by contrast, the other sphere, the spiritual one, is and remains subject to Christ for every human society.

An objection to this could be drawn from Jesus' kingship over Zion. In the days when Psalm 2 was sung, Zion represented a national authority, a national sphere, the chosen people of Israel. This psalm describes a battle between Israel and the heathen nations. The neighboring nations want to destroy Israel, and as God's people, Israel must survive nationally against them. In this context the psalm tells us that God has anointed his Messiah "on Zion, his holy hill" [see Psa 2:6], and that the nations will not be able to do anything against Zion. Rather, they are instructed to "Kiss the Son, lest he be angry, and you perish in the way, for his wrath is quickly kindled" [Psa 2:12]. If Zion is understood, as indeed is often the case, as the type for every nation and every people that will honor God, one must conclude that Jesus is anointed as King over each and every nation, and that the old covenant's stipulations for Israel must in fact be applied to every kingdom or every republic. From there, one would be forced to deduce that Christ is the real ruling authority over the Netherlands, over England, and over all other countries.

It is, by now, hardly necessary to point out that this entire understanding of the meaning of Israel, of Zion, of the Messiah, and of the order God established in the land of the patriarchs is entirely incorrect. Israel is a symbolic phenomenon. Symbolically, Israel was and remained God's people even when sacrifices were offered to idols in all of Jerusalem's streets. But this symbolic nation would be replaced by the real nation only when the Messiah came, and the true Israel—not of the circumcision of the flesh, but the circumcision of the heart—was gathered from all nations. In this vein the apostles also clearly insisted that the real, actual Zion is the Zion that is above, the heavenly Jerusalem; that the Messiah's people have been bought by his blood; and that not the children of Abraham, but those born of the Spirit are *the Israel of God*.

Consequently, it is clear that a twofold dispensation exists. There is a figurative, symbolic dispensation in which one could see no more than shadows and figures, a dispensation that continued until the Messiah had come. Alongside it, there was the essential dispensation when the shadows and figures fell away and the spiritual kingdom made its entry. This explains the most exceptional situation of the earthly government's authority in Israel, to which the government authority of no other nation can be compared. In Israel there was a theocracy. It was immediate rule by God. "The LORD is our judge; the LORD is our lawgiver; the LORD is our king" [Isa 33:22]. This likewise explains why in Israel miracles were constantly necessary as a direct manifestation of the theocratic authority that governed Israel. By contrast, in the other nations there was no theocracy, but a derived and commissioned sovereignty whereby law proceeded from the sovereigns themselves and justice was instituted and sealed by the government. Israel alone, not those other nations, could be the type and symbol of the kingdom of Christ; Israel alone could be the type and symbol of the people of the Lord. And only Israel's nation-state could foreshadow the state comprising the spiritual kingdom. For that reason, one may never make a direct inference from the situation that existed in Israel to the life of nations and peoples. This is not meant to deny that the theocratic legislation given to Israel does not contain much that applies to all nations. But the difference has to be clearly maintained so that the theocratic and symbolic character of Israel will not be neglected, and also so that something unsuitable for us might not be transferred to the life of our nation; it is neither a theocratic nor a symbolic nation.

§ 3   These things can be considered from yet another perspective. Article 36 of our Belgic Confession was entirely correct to say that government authority extends to the restraining of sin. "We believe that our gracious

God, because of the depravity of mankind, has appointed kings, princes, and magistrates; willing that the world should be governed by certain laws and policies; to the end that the dissoluteness of men might be restrained, and all things carried on among them with good order and decency."[1] You need only to imagine for a moment what the world would look like if sin had not brought about its great destruction in order to be convinced that there then would have been no place for government action. Where sin is absent, law is entirely unnecessary; all people would have the law written on their hearts and would never will anything or do anything but the will of God. There would be no need to administer justice where no transgression existed and where no conflict could arise. Without sin, there would be no curse, and thus no illness or destruction through the elements of nature; and so there would be no need for all the measures currently undertaken by the government in order to protect our health and security.

War between nations would be unthinkable where everyone lived in peace. The division and separation between nations would never have arisen. No fleet or army would ever be outfitted. What we call private initiatives, which are today so often impeded by ignoble rivalry, would exert a full and sufficient power to arrange everything necessary for life. The society of the household, as it would have developed in the family, would have functioned patriarchally to supply everything needed to regulate society. And if you consider one by one all of our departments of general administration, you would come to no other conclusion than that one after the other would be entirely unnecessary in a situation without sin. The earthly dispensation of government authority thus functions in an unspiritual situation where the consequences of sin for public life must be overcome and where evil must be curtailed with violence if necessary. This earthly dispensation is, after all, characterized particularly by the use of coercion. It opposes sin with a mighty arm and, if needed, with the sword.

But what does any of this have in common with the kingship of Christ, with the spiritual kingdom, with the kingdom of heaven? We will see below that this may not be taken to suggest that the kingdom of Christ evaporates into vague ideas and spiritual sentiments because of that. However, the fundamental difference between a worldly authority that applies force

---

1. *RC* 2:447.

by the sword and the spiritual nature of the kingdom of Christ, which has no servants who bear the sword, is not of the world, and has no outward front but is within you, may not be lost from sight for even a single moment. Indeed, the kingdom of Christ opposes sin as well, yet it does not attack sin from the outside, in transgression's wildly growing underbrush, but at its core and root. It does not prune the tree, but heals the cancer in its root. Finally, the kingdom of Christ does not vanish as sin is overcome, but only then for the first time shines with greater splendor.

Both kingdoms diverge widely in origin, nature, means, and purpose. Each has its own its own domain and sphere of power and their ends are entirely distinct. They are not analogous, but each represents its own kind. How could government authority then ever be derived from the kingship of Jesus?

§ 4   The spirit that opposes the sacred does indeed attempt to undermine also the earthly institution of government, to wrest it from God's grasp, and to turn it against him. People call out loudly that continuing to speak about a "king by the grace of God" is a worn and dated notion. More and more people are convinced that it is humanity itself, based on what it considers wise, that organizes a state and appoints governments to rule over it. The increasingly popular notion is that the people themselves determine law, that their will is the highest expression of will on earth. Law, so it is said, is what people approve as law. No one is allowed to speak any longer about a legal principle possessing eternal validity. To avenge the transgression of justice as prescribed by Romans 13 is itself considered injustice—criminals are not seen as being guilty but as themselves being victims of another person's guilt. In short, all nations set out on the road to emancipation while they sing a song beginning with the words, "Let us burst their bonds apart" [Psa 2:3]. This overturning of every certitude likewise turns against the Holy One and culminates in an audacious attack on the kingship of Christ.

This does not mean, however, that this act of popular sovereignty is, as such, an act of turning against Christ. It does not turn directly against Christ, but against the majesty and sovereignty of God; it is only in its effect and consequences that it also turns against the kingship of Christ. For that reason, in the broader context of our argument, the frenzy of popular sovereignty may not be enlisted as one of the fundamental forms in which the spirit of the age manifests itself so as to set up its own kingship in the place of Christ's kingship. This form of evil does not lead to the denial of Christ's kingship, but to the direct denial of God—that is, to atheism. Popular sovereignty does not say in its heart: "I take the place of Christ"; rather, it says something far different: "I identify my own heart as the heart of God. I will be my own god." A nation that acknowledges: "Our king rules over us by the grace of God," is therefore at least a Christian nation; a nation that cries out: "Away with that prince who rules by the grace of God!" does not thereby cast off its Christian garment, but becomes entirely godless.

HUMANITY'S DOMINION OVER NATURE

You have crowned him with glory and honor.

PSALM 8:5

§ 1   The question that arises now is whether the enormous development that humanity has gradually achieved is a bold and arrogant attempt on its part to grasp the unattainable, and should be condemned; or whether the possession of this majesty already lay in the calling received from God, and its accomplishment deserves to be applauded.

It is clear that Jesus' kingship has been suppressed in the life of the nations. The nations' "shepherds," as their leaders can be called, are no longer inspired by the call for Jesus. Even within the church's walls the songs of praise that once went up for Christ as the King of glory have diminished in tenor and tone. We explained this disappointing phenomenon by pointing out that the stream of godly life—the current of religion—has undeniably receded in its banks everywhere. And lest believers exalt themselves in pride above the skeptics and unbelievers, we went on to admit that a minimizing of grace can be detected among us as well, and that especially the zeal for Jesus' kingly glory has been stifled all too much. The distinction between believers in the holy place, nominal believers in the forecourt, and unbelievers who have even withdrawn themselves from the forecourt, was intended to point to the differences evident between what we observe in our smaller circle and in the broader surroundings of the nation. Moreover, in order to warn against pride and to caution people not to judge the drifters or skeptics too harshly, we attempted to provide an explanation of the general error in the current of religious consciousness that was based on the reality we observe.

If we are going to be able to work also for the good in our national surroundings, and if the greater masses are once more going to understand something of the honor for Jesus' kingship, then denouncing all the evils of the human heart is hardly fitting. Exercising influence demands sympathy, and sympathy for those who have strayed grows only when you clearly and plainly see that the current of general human consciousness is governed everywhere by the times and circumstances. The times and circumstances in the days of our fathers were as remarkably advantageous for an interest in religion as they now are utterly disadvantageous to it. Such sympathy also arises when you, acknowledging that you too share in that disadvantage of the times, feel that you share the same fate as those who have fallen away, and therefore also the wrath; but even more so when you give voice to the searching love in your heart for those in the forecourt and for those whom you have seen already stray outside the forecourt.

In order to explain the lot common to us all, we then emphasized three undeniable facts. The first was the supremacy over nature that humanity managed to win for itself in such a short span of time. That power saw more growth in the last century alone than in the eighteen preceding centuries of the Christian era combined. As a result, the feeling of dependence, which constitutes the broad context for godliness in general, experienced a remarkable decline. We pointed, in the second place, to the horizon that used to be largely enclosed within national borders, but which has now broadened to include, surround, and draw the entire world together into a single field of vision. And in the third place, we pointed to the astounding increase of our human knowledge, not so much in depth and height as in length and breadth. Afterward, we illustrated how these three factors set in motion a restlessness that shattered the quietness for which the pious heart longs, and that disrupted the quiet, hidden communion with the world above. We further pointed out how, where humanity's great sense of self-importance grew as described above, and where the circumstances became increasingly disadvantageous to religious life, a human kingship imperceptibly came to power, leaving no place for the kingship of Christ. That kingship of humanity established a throne of glory for itself in the world cities, and from that seat it now rules over entire nations and peoples by what people refer to as the *modern spirit of the age*. This modern spirit of the age pushed the work of the Holy Spirit into retreat, just as the kingship of humanity had done with the kingship of Christ. Misled by this great delusion, however, the enthroned-humanity itself became a slave of the mammon-king. While modern people did turn to art in order to satisfy their more ideal needs, their love for art soon turned into the worship of art. The enthroned-humanity bowed down before the god of the beautiful and became lost once more, this time in idolatrous worship of the idol of beauty.

§ 2   This places before us an entirely different question, namely, whether humanity sinned when it strove for that higher mastery over nature, or whether it thereby fulfilled the calling given by God. We can only affirm that God himself called humanity to subject nature to itself; that in the time of its boundless dominion, Christianity all too often neglected that calling; and that, in this way, it is culpable for the fact that a power hostile to God and his anointed King has arisen in the supremacy that has been won over nature.

If you turn to the creation story, you will see immediately that humanity was called to have dominion. God said: "Let us make man in our image, after our likeness. And let them have dominion" [Gen 1:26]. This dominion was not only to be over the animal world that is mentioned first; after all, the text specifically says, "dominion over *all the earth*." All the same, it is only natural that the animals are mentioned first. Before man and woman appeared, the animal world was the highest and most powerful expression of created life. The plant world already stood above the elements and the dust of the earth. But did the lion not stand much higher than the lily of the field in terms of its power and the freedom of its movement? For this reason, it first had to be made clear that humanity was to be the king of creation over the animal world as well. The lion may well be the king of the forest, but humanity's dominion extends to include even the most powerful and splendid creatures in the animal world. This is all the more striking given that, measured in terms of physical power and size, the lion far surpasses humankind; the animal world gathers like an army around that single pair of human beings who were so weak in comparison. God's lofty idea to create humanity after his own image and likeness, after the creation of plants and animals, thus extended to the future course of this world's history when the exalted command went out for this apparently small and insignificant human race to be clothed with dominion over all the earth.

At the bottom of this lay the all-determining contrast between spirit and matter. In the higher animal world too, indeed even in insects like ants and bees, a mental[1] element has been created, yet it is weak, does not develop, remains what it is, is bound to its instinct, and lives by its own free choice to only a limited degree. In animals as such, the material still governs them. Things are entirely different for humankind. In human beings the spiritual element dominates. Humans are able to exercise physical power as well, but this is incidental, and the higher humans climb, the more they renounce the use of that physical power in order to concentrate all power in their spirit. God's resolution to give humanity dominion over all the earth thus rested on the irrefutable basic principle, included in the whole plan of creation, that spirit would rule over matter. Spirit would rule over flesh within human beings, and through that dominion of spirit over flesh, humans would exercise the spiritual superiority that gave them—as spiritual beings—dominion over the entire earth, over all of God's creation here below, over this whole world.

That basic principle is grounded even more deeply since the words spoken by God connected the spirit's dominion within a human being directly to the person's creation according to God's image and after God's likeness. As we already noted, spirit as such is also present in animals. Scripture repeatedly states that not only people, but also animals have souls. This is already clear in the creation account. In fact, it begins with the fish. "God," so we read in Genesis 1:21, "created every living *soul* that moves, with which the waters swarm."[2] In verse 24, we similarly read con-

---

1. Although the Dutch word *geest* is usually rendered in this work as *spirit*, Kuyper's use of these terms can often refer more generally to that which is distinguishable from the material, that is, to the *mind*, the *mental*, and the *rational*, as well as the *spiritual* sense.
2. In this context, Kuyper is citing from the *Statenvertaling*, which reads: "En God schiep de grote walvissen, en alle levende wremelende *ziel*, welke de wateren overvloediglijk voortbrachten, naar haar aard; en alle gevleugeld gevogelte naar zijn aard. En God zag, dat het goed was" (Gen 1:21 SV).

cerning the creation of the land animals: "'Let the earth bring forth living *souls* according to their kinds—livestock and creeping things and beasts of the earth according to their kinds.' And it was so."[3] This comes out still more clearly in verse 30: "And to every beast of the earth and to every bird of the heavens and to everything that creeps on the earth, everything that has a living *soul*."[4] So the difference between people and animals is not that we have a soul and they do not. A soul is something we have in common with animals, and our excellence lies not in our possession of a soul, but rather in that God himself breathed into us the breath of life and created us as the bearers of his divine image. *Spirit* is a general term and *soul* is an expression with a wide application. But what is impressed upon us as our unique stamp and our greatest distinguishing feature as human beings is not that we have a spirit or a soul, but that the very image of God is mirrored in the spiritual life of our soul. There is a progression within creation, from matter to plants, from plants to animals, and from animals to humankind. All of this proceeds from God and comes to life through his powerful Word, but the circle is not closed without humanity because God has impressed his own image on them.

§ 3   Humanity's higher calling came to expression not only in the decision of God's inner counsel when he said: "Let us make man," but it was likewise announced as a holy ordinance to human beings and given to them as a high command for their walk here below on earth. At their creation, humans no doubt felt small and almost powerless before nature's power and before the animal world surrounding them. Even if the destructive powers of nature had not yet been unleashed in paradise, the majesty of creation would have overwhelmed them so that they felt desolate and small over against the innumerable army of the animal world. Even if we assume that humans were not yet struck by the disruptive element when they saw these mighty animals, people still saw animals before and around them that were much greater in size and number. They immediately began to wonder what rank and place they would have in and over that world. To this question the Lord God immediately gave that newly-created

---

3. The Dutch version reads: "En God zeide: De aarde brenge levende *zielen* voort, naar haar aard, vee, en kruipend, en wild gedierte der aarde, naar zijn aard! En het was alzo" (Gen 1:24 SV).

4. The Dutch version reads: "Maar aan al het gedierte der aarde, en aan al het gevogelte des hemels, en aan al het kruipende gedierte op de aarde, waarin een levende *ziel* is, heb Ik al het groene kruid tot spijze gegeven. En het was alzo" (Gen 1:30 SV).

humanity an answer: "Be fruitful and multiply and fill the earth and subdue it and have dominion over [it]" [Gen 1:28]. God himself thus crowned humanity as king over his creation, over this entire world, and over all the earth. At that point, humanity did not understand what all that would involve. This ordinance of God was for humanity a completely unresolved enigma. As physically weaker human beings, slender, slim, and small in build, humans could move by taking only one step at a time. They had nothing at their disposal except their two hands; and yet they were not only to walk all over and possess the entire earth—that entire world—but also had to subdue it. This pointed to resistance, to opposition. It pointed to an exertion of force to break that opposition. Even if humans felt dependent on nature, they had to make nature dependent on them. Not only was it not allowed to dominate them, they were to have dominion over all of nature. They were to have such dominion that nature would eventually be fully subject to them. In doing so, their dominion, their kingly power, and their spiritual dominance would be fully realized.

In Psalm 8, David sang of humanity's dominion over nature as something that applies also to our fallen, sinful state. His song does not rejoice over humanity in paradise in its unfallen state, but rather humanity as it was in David's own days and as David knew himself as a man. This explains the deep amazement expressed in this psalm. David knows that he is sinful and sees the same in others around him—humanity in its brokenness and misery. He thus feels the depths of the contrast between small, sinful humanity and the majesty of the Lord of lords. And now he breaks out in song over the way God has established his praise even from the mouths of babies and infants, and how he throws back the enemy and the avenger through his power over the hearts of those who are his. The reference to "the enemy and the avenger" makes it clear that he is thinking of humanity in *his* day, and not in paradise. For this reason, he also exclaims: "What is man that you are mindful of him, and the son of man that you care for him?" [Psa 8:4]. It is exactly because of the sinful and fallen state of humanity that the contrast between what human beings are in themselves and what God calls them to be is so clear before his eyes. It is nevertheless of humanity in this state that David sings forth: "Yet you have made him a little lower than the heavenly beings and crowned him with glory and honor" [Psa 8:5]. Once again there is a reference to humanity's crowning, its being clothed with kingly dominion. This is clearer still in verse 6: "You have given him dominion over the works of your hands; you have put all things under his feet." To "put all things under his feet" is a set expression in the East for the power and dominion of the king, just as it is written of Christ that he will "put all his enemies under his feet" [1 Cor 15:25]. A number of commentators, including Calvin, would rather understand the phrase, "You have made him a little lower than the angels," as, "You have made him a little lower than God." The basis for this understanding is the usual use of the Hebrew word *Elohim* for God. It cannot be denied that from a poetical perspective this interpretation is much nicer, and that a comparison with angels seems a little unusual in this context. However, since both translations can be defended, we will not go further into the issue. Whatever the case may be, it is certain—and this is the main point we wish to make—that Psalm 8 also sings about a dominion bestowed by God upon humanity so as to set a king's crown on its head.

It should be obvious that the above cannot mean that each person on one's own is called to exercise this dominion to its fullest extent. A child cannot take on a lion. A weak woman cannot wrestle with the behemoth. No one person can on one's own, have dominion over all creation. What is given to man is in fact given to *humanity*, entrusted to our human race. Humanity must be fruitful and multiply. Hosts of human armies must grow out of this first human couple. It is not a matter of the individual man, but rather of his numerous children. Not in one generation, but throughout the successive generations dominion shall be established over nature. Only when it is understood in that sense will it appear to be true that humanity is stronger than all the powers and forces of nature that surround it. Not each person on his or her own shall be king, but humanity shall be clothed with dominion. Time and again, people will fall victim to the raging of nature's elements, be slain by lion or tiger, or be overwhelmed by waves; but humanity will have the upper hand in the struggle against wild animals and triumph over all powers and elements.

This is the reason David's song of praise is applied to Christ in the New Testament, because the real enthroned-humanity was first revealed in him. This very point makes it clear, however, that Christ's kingship is to be venerated in him not as Son of God but as Son of Man, and that it arises from the kingly dominion with which God clothed humanity in paradise. This dominion does not depend on physical strength, since a single bull can toss even the strongest man into the air or trample him. Nor does it depend on the human soul, since a lion's courage comes from its heart rather than from its maw or claws. No, it depends on our being created in the image of God. It is a dominion laid upon humanity by God, in which God himself is glorified through humanity.

According to the ordinance of creation, there is in this way no conflict at all between our God's supreme dominion and humanity's derived and commissioned dominion. Rather, the one flows forth from the other. In fact, dominion is such a vital characteristic in the image of our God, and so much the great sign of his sovereignty, that a creature created according to his image who does not have such derived dominion is simply unthinkable. This dominion over nature is not something added to humanity; instead, it is rooted in humanity's essence. Without that dominion, humanity could not bear the image of God. If humanity did not rule over nature, nature would rule over humanity. Not the human being, the creature with a spirit, would be master, but pure matter; the savage and wild creature without a spirit would master humans. The highest creature would be subject to the lower, and the image of God in humanity would be defrauded and turn into its opposite.

This very thing has too often been lost from sight. People far too one-sidedly look for the image of God in things spiritual and religious. They limit themselves to the sacred alone in trying to discover the expression of God's likeness in regenerated people. However, this neither can nor may be done. We confess about our God, first of all, that he is "God Almighty, Creator of heaven and earth."[5] His almightiness, his sovereignty, stands in the foreground. Those who lose sight of this end up in mysticism or, before they know it, lose themselves in the immeasurable depths of pantheism. His name is the Almighty, his title of honor is the Most Exalted One, and that almightiness is his dominion, his majesty over all creation, his royal-sovereign majesty with which he subdues under his feet everything that has been created. How can you imagine that there is a creature that bears his image and likeness if you remove from that creaturely image the main feature—the basic characteristic of the divine essence—and you retreat to the ethical and religious field? This is precisely why we have to emphasize that in the creation ordinance and in the creation account, when the image of God, according to which we have been created, is described, not a single word is spoken pertaining to either the ethical or the religious life. Instead, the full emphasis in depicting God's image in us falls solely on our kingly dominion over all the earth.

---

5. The first article of the Apostles' Creed.

II.3

PARADISE NO LONGER

And God said to them, "Be fruitful and multiply and fill the earth and subdue it, and have dominion over it."

GENESIS 1:28

§ 1   In order to understand fully the dominion of Jesus our King, we have to go back to consider the kingship that God conferred on man[1] at his very creation. Humanity's creation in the image of God included its anointing as lord and king of the whole earth and everything in it. This complete and comprehensive dominion is not something added to humanity's creation in God's image, but flows directly out of it. In fact, in God's creation ordinance this is the one and only consequence that is specifically mentioned of humanity's likeness in the image of God.

The creation ordinance does not end there, however. It does not simply say that of all creatures on earth, human beings are the most powerful in spirit, and for that reason they outshine all other creatures. No—immediately after being created, man is also given a command, and the purpose of this command is to lay upon human beings the duty to exercise, maintain,

---

1. In this chapter, the Dutch collective noun *mens* is often rendered as *man*. Since Kuyper usually has in mind the first man Adam specifically, this rendering is justified, instead of *humanity*, *human race*, and the like.

and expand the dominion given to them. We do not see even the smallest beginning of Sinai's law in the opening chapters of Genesis. At that time there was still no sin, not even the inclination to sin; it was only after the probationary command[2] [had been given] that the direction in which humanity would develop became clear. From the very beginning, humanity is instead given the command to fill the earth, to subdue the earth, and to exercise dominion over everything on this earth. The words are so majestic: "So God created man in his own image, in the image of God he created him; male and female he created them. And God blessed them. And God said to them, 'Be fruitful and multiply and fill the earth and subdue it, and have dominion over [it]'" [Gen 1:27-28].

These words reveal that the human race was destined to multiply to more than a billion in number. At the present time, there are already some one-and-a-half billion inhabitants on earth, while half of it is still empty or sparsely populated. The enormous growth of the human race was not to come only when sin broke out and death entered the world, but it lay within human destiny entirely apart from the question of sin. It was for this very purpose that the Lord God called man into existence on earth and placed him at the top of creation's ladder. This certainly could be understood merely as a blessing bestowed on man, since the intention to avoid marriage and to prevent the birth of children is imaginable only after sin's entrance into the world. But even if one conceives of this exclusively as a blessing, it remains the command, the Lord's ordinance clearly articulated in the duty imposed on man to subdue the world. "Fill the earth and subdue it" is a command that lays a demand on man, that shows him his workplace, and that calls him to exercise the powers given to him. Consequently, dominion over the earth may have come to man by nature, according to God's ordination, yet it did not drop into his lap. Man instead had to take hold of it, maintain it, and realize it. No worship was prescribed for man. His life in communion with his God would be a given as long as he lived in that sinless state. What is required of him, however, is that he must work out, in all its length, breadth, depth, and height, the dominion over nature given him in seed form in his being created in the image of God.

One should be careful to note that this task was laid on humanity's shoulders even before the curse came upon this earth. Human beings

§ 2

---

2. See *CG* 1.25.

would have dominion over creation in its original purity. For that reason, we should not think in this context of a struggle with wild animals or a battle against the elements. All of that came later. Rather, we should think of dominion through spiritual dominance and superiority, and through the exertion of the normal powers given to humanity. We still find some of this in animal tamers and snake charmers. Tamers rule over their tigers and lions by impressing and mesmerizing them. In order to tame them, they do indeed discipline, confine, and withhold food from them, but anyone without the tamer's mesmerizing power cannot subdue wild animals simply with those means. The ability to tame wild animals is now no longer a general human trait, but a special capacity that very few people have. It is an ability on the same level as the ability that some have to mesmerize and hypnotize people. Such an ability is a mystery that defies explanation, but it nevertheless displays a weak vestige, a sporadic remainder of the spiritual superiority over the animal kingdom that was originally given to humanity as a race. The animals were at first admittedly not wild, fierce, or ferocious. All the same, a single person with a small frame stood before an innumerable army of animals with their gigantic bodies. In fact, Scripture notes that in paradise the entire animal army came to Adam, that Adam stood among them as their lord and king without being hurt by them, and that he gave them names which were not random but corresponded to their nature. This points to humanity's great superiority over all creation and to a now lost ability to see through to the essence of all things. This knowledge of animals is entirely different from that of zoologists today, but much higher in value.

It goes without saying that the existence of many different animals was no coincidence. Each has its own reason for being, to which their physical build and environs are connected. Earth, air, and water are the three spheres of the earth's creation, and each of these spheres has its basic animal type. But each of these basic types—that is, whether they walk, fly, or swim—is further divided into numerous subspecies, each of which has its own appearance and corresponding purpose. God's creation was not an arbitrary game or guesswork in the hope that the beings created would turn out. No—each kind of animal is the peculiar expression of a unique thought of God. Each kind has its own calling to glorify its God. There is a sacred order in the animal world as well. At present we know almost nothing of it anymore. We can distinguish animals by their size, form, means of defense, or fur. But we can no longer comprehend why one distinct kind was created this way rather than that way in its distinguishing characteristics.

The creation account reveals, however, that their purpose lay in that very distinction of species. Why else would there be such an extensive description of the animals in the waters, of the animals that fly in the air, and of the animals that move on the ground? Our zoologists no longer have any of that higher knowledge. The connection between God's thoughts and the distinct forms of the numerous species escapes them all. This knowledge, however, was created in the first man. He saw the different species in their essence and gave them names to match. The dominion that Adam had over animals thus did not have its origin in the strength of his hand or even in the cunning by which he could master them. His power consisted entirely in his spiritual superiority.

§ 3

It is hardly surprising that only the animals are mentioned as the object of that dominion. Adam did, of course, also have a spiritual superiority over the plant world and over organic nature. In them, however, there is no activity. A plant is passive. A plant does not move. We cannot really speak of resistance and struggle in the case of plants. The simple fact that man had the power to pick flowers for decoration, or to pick fruits for food, does not lead to dominion. These things instead constitute use. These things constitute a taking of something that already belonged to man. The absence of any kind of resistance and struggle does not produce dominion. The same holds true for the mineral kingdom. Later, when the elemental power of nature arose after and as a result of sin—wreaking havoc through hurricane and storm, lightning, fire and flood, earthquakes and shifting plateaus, heat and frost—then powers threatening man with destruction also rose up against him from these spheres.

But in paradise, all of this was still unthinkable. In this sphere of creation there was as well no battle, struggle, resistance, or threatening danger at all. It was, for that reason, entirely natural and self-evident that the animal world alone could impress upon Adam the feeling that he stood before an entire army.

It therefore follows from the situation of the time that the creation ordinance explicitly mentions man's struggle with the animal kingdom, while it passes in silence over the plant world, the minerals, and the elemental powers of nature. Or more accurately, the latter are not skipped in silence but are telescoped into the general concept of the earth. In addition to the animals, the first man was also given dominion "over *all the earth,*" and it is written emphatically: "Fill the earth and *subdue it*." Aside from the animals that had already been mentioned explicitly, this could refer only to the remaining kingdoms and powers of nature; so humanity is indeed given dominion over the plant world, the world of inorganic nature, and the world of the elemental powers as well. The words "subdue the earth" do not refer to the hard toil of working the ground. The first reference to such toil comes after the fall: "By the sweat of your face you shall eat bread" [Gen 3:19]. Here as well [that is, in respect to the earth], Scripture points to dominion by virtue of superiority of spirit. Being created in the image of God, man is appointed as vicegerent under God over the entire visible creation here below. It is a dominion that he exercised through an innate knowledge of all of nature, which has now been almost entirely lost.

Almost entirely, we said—but not completely. We already pointed to the lion tamer and the snake charmer. But there is more. Reports from antiquity—about the wisdom of the Egyptians, for instance—in spite of their vague uncertainty still point to the presence of some kind of mysterious knowledge in certain circles that has since been lost, but which at that time still represented a real power. Such mysterious knowledge that lived on in tradition may well have been mixed with much superstition and magic, and as such may gradually have degenerated completely. But the outcome does not contradict that this knowledge points to something instinctive that continued to be effective long after paradise was lost.

Something similar, albeit of an entirely different nature, can be seen in nature poetry. Nature poets live with nature as no other people do. It is as if the distance between human nature and the nature that surrounds these poets has been reduced to much smaller proportions for them. They feel along with and for nature. They listen to and understand it when it speaks. They live with that nature in a mysterious and often very close communion, and they know how to draw beautiful things out of it that we would never find. This nature poetry is the reason why there remains also for us, to varying degrees and with certain limits, a life together with nature. Furthermore, the beneficial influence that nature's life and voice exercise on us likewise continues in significant measure. We hardly need to be reminded that in the book of Proverbs, too, as well as in some of the Prophets, and especially in our Lord Jesus Christ, living with nature and comprehending its voice come to expression, at times most poignantly. These are transmitted to Christianity thanks to the influence of Holy Scripture.

With the fall, however, the relationship between humans and nature, in which the kingdom of their dominion was established, underwent a fundamental change. Humanity's letter of nobility was not taken away from it. God did not declare that humans had fallen from their dominion. They remained king over nature. However, the fall did face humans with an entirely different situation, in which the power of their spirit was weakened and where nature raised itself up in total rebellion against them. Humanity was so weakened as humanity, and nature's rebellion was so great, that humanity's kingship over nature survived only nominally. It was true only in principle. The spiritual weakening was the result of their break with God. Humans had possessed power only because they held so tightly to their God. As long as the bond between their inner essence and their God remained undisturbed and intact, the power, capacity, strength, and instinctive knowledge flowed to them from God without interruption. As long as this situation remained, humans had a spiritual superiority over nature. But when humanity wandered away from God and distanced itself from him, it also distanced itself from the source of its strength. What used to flow through people's inner being as an unending stream of sacred power no longer came to them. Whereas people were initially strong in unbroken power, they now became weak and fragile, and they began to collapse. They no longer reigned by virtue of their nature. They now lacked the spiritual superiority that used to function automatically, and this decrease in power brought fear, anxiety, and concern. In paradise, human beings were like a firmly rooted oak tree; after the fall, they became a trembling reed. They were not only weak in the face of sin's temptation, but also weak in their dignity, their inner consciousness, their power and instinctive knowledge, and weak in the observations that came to them from nature around them.

This decrease in the feeling of power and capacity is accompanied by the awareness that nature, now that it has escaped from and turned against humanity's dominion, is ready to throw itself against humanity and to destroy it. Although we are used to the sound of thunder, try to imagine what it was like for Adam when the heavens first gathered in dark billowing clouds, when the clouds broke out in peals of thunder, and when flames of lightning shot down upon the earth.

§ 4

We often have too limited an understanding of the curse that came upon the earth. We should realize, however, that it represented nothing less than a full reversal in the order of nature. The solemn peace of paradise turned into restlessness, disruption, and unending turbulence. In the plant world, thorns and thistles sprouted. Poison entered certain plants and animals. Many of the most powerful animals began to display a ferocious wildness in their appearance. The daytime breeze in paradise turned into storms and howling hurricanes. The temperature that at one time was constant began to fluctuate drastically between cold and hot. The streams overflowed their banks and flooded pastures. Weeds and vermin began to wreak destruction. Poisonous bacteria started to threaten the life of people and animals. The earth was stirred up in its hidden depths, shuddered and shook, and spewed forth streams of glowing lava and fire. It was as if hell suddenly rose up from the depths and sought to throw its giant arms around nature and humankind in order to destroy and crush them.

Over against the destructive power that had been unleashed, there stood a single pair of human beings, sick with guilt, abandoned by God, small, broken, and disheartened. In paradise, their nimble fingers had by their spirit of mastery played the organ of nature, but now the organ's bellows had been torn to pieces, and their fingers seemed to be paralyzed, moving tremblingly over the rattling keys from which they could no longer draw forth that melodious, heavenly tone.

We who have never experienced the dominion of paradise can hardly even imagine the fear, the shock, the perplexity that must have seized Adam in that hour. All we know is that he fled, fled from his God who in his mercy came calling him in order to trace out with silver dots, before his eyes filled with the fear of death, the way leading to grace. At the end of the dotted line leading to grace, which God traced out for humanity, there radiated from a distance the kingship of the Son of Man. One born of Eve would one day bring down Satan's power, and so restore humanity's kingship over the nature that had now risen up in rebellion and establish that kingship forever.

But even if a star of hope was shimmering on the dark horizon, this was language that Adam could hardly understand. There he was, threatened by illness and death. God's entire creation now stood against him in rebellion. The king whom God had appointed for his creation here below, while not deposed, had in fact been dethroned. His lot was now to suffer for the sake of dominion. The struggle that had just begun would take on ever increasing dimensions. Suddenly, mighty, overpowering nature with its enormous strength was on the one side, while humanity, bowed down, disarmed and insignificant mortals, was on the other.

All the same, the creation ordinance still applied just as much as it had before. As much as it seemed that humanity had been destroyed, the high command continued unabated: "Yours must be the dominion over all the kingdom of the earth. Get up, multiply, fill all the earth, and subdue it." This is the terrifying meaning that nature now has for the human race. That wild, powerful nature throws itself upon humanity in order to destroy it. People attempt to cover themselves, to secure themselves, to protect themselves against its rage. But that is not enough. No, human beings must not only resist its attacks, but must also attack nature, throw themselves upon it, and may not rest before they have recovered their superiority.

The human race still possesses a spirit. Spirit must triumph over matter and may not submit before it. That spirit is from God, and God's honor depends on the spirit's triumph. There is not a single person who can accomplish this. It is the entire human race that has been given this giant struggle as its life task. And one day the Son of Man will appear at the head of the human race; he will lead the triumph and cause the power to recover dominion to flow out from him.

But that struggle will be a centuries-long struggle. And throughout those centuries, sickness, death, damage, destruction, and decay will continue to appear among the sons of men. Nature, now cruel and wild, will spare no power or effort to keep humanity from recovering its former dominion. The crying on earth will increase; there will be no end to pain and suffering. Nature will choose its victims from our human race by entire hecatombs.[3] It will stand firm for a long time, so that one would think that nature, not humanity, is triumphing. Anguish and despair will make themselves the masters of the whole human heart.

Nevertheless, throughout all of this, God will keep watch so that the spark of hope will not be extinguished in the human heart, so that the core of its power will not be completely broken. Spirit will continue to fight the power of nature. Not the tiger and the leopard, but the human

---

3. A hecatomb is a large number of people, animals, or things, especially as sacrificed or destroyed.

race will gain ground. Even if the streams appear to overwhelm it, humanity will in the end rule over the waters as well. And one day, humanity will in glory once again feel itself to be, not king perhaps, but still the master over nature and its awesome powers.

MIRACLES

Blessed be the Lord, the God of Israel, who alone does wondrous things.

Psalm 72:18

Miracles can be understood only when you give careful consideration to § 1
the painful struggles in which humanity, weakened by sin, became em-
broiled against nature, whose power was conversely strengthened by
the curse. Without miracles, the impression is given all too quickly that
nature is more powerful and greater and higher than spirit; this automatically leads to a fearful, idolatrous worship of nature. In the eyes of
a trembling humanity, nature slipped, without them noticing, into the
place that belonged only to the living God. It mattered little if the fear in
their hearts was owing to the suffering caused by nature itself or to the
presumed presence of evil spirits at work behind nature. That fear came
not from nature at rest but from nature in action, and in the end it makes
no difference whether that action came from nature itself or was wrought
by evil spirits. Whatever it may have been, the frightening question remained the same: "How can we escape nature's dominion when it rises up
in action?"

The sea was for many the image of choice. The sea is beautiful to behold from the beach or to sail upon in a small boat when its waters are at
rest. But it threatens helpless people with death and destruction when its
waves are piled up as high as mountains and come crashing down on the
beach. When at rest, nature provided refreshment, encouragement, and

benefit, but when its elements were thrown into disarray, nature in action aroused fear and upheaval. Weakened as it was, humanity could not help itself address that fearful terror; it even seemed as if its God was no match for nature. Worship of God became worship of nature in its power and upheaval, or in its animistic form it became a fear of the spirits that were able to produce evil magic with nature. That fear of God, not of nature or evil spirits, could stand or return only when a miracle intervened, when in factual occurrences God showed to the human race that he still had dominion over the power of nature.

Only if we understand this do we see the indispensability and significance of miracles. Miracles cannot be understood outside of the relationship in which they stand with sin and the curse. And it is safe to say that the refusal to believe in miracles has always been based on the inability or refusal to understand this most holy significance of miracles.

Desecrated by sin, humanity thus stood in a weakened state before nature in both body and soul. Its physical powers may not have taken a sudden drop, but they nevertheless dropped in a slow and gradual measure. Just consider for a moment the span of life. The span of human life was first measured in terms of centuries, sometimes as many as ten centuries; but it shortened and declined until, in the days of the patriarchs, it was virtually the same as the short span of our life, while in the song of Moses it even shortened to as few as seventy or eighty years [see Psa 90:10]. All kinds of illnesses arose. Hereditary sicknesses undermined the resistance offered by life in successive generations, as did poisons of all kinds. Many nations have recollections of a much stronger, much more powerful bygone generation—that of the Nimrods and Hercules, of giants and the descendants of Anak—and their descendants are no more than a deteriorated and weakened generation.

Their souls were weakened more seriously still. Rather than standing up together to attack nature, one person attacks another. Cain kills Abel. Murderous thoughts are fanned into flames. The conscience is stained, and the stained conscience kills courage. The noble sentiment, the proud awareness of being human and elevated high above nature, begins to suffer decline. Fear replaces courage. Anxiety diminishes the soul's inner resilience. Those who are tortured by anxiety lose spirit. It was, for that reason, entirely natural that humankind gradually felt itself increasingly weak and powerless before a nature that ruled and threatened all of life.

Human beings in their weakened state now stood over against a nature that had increased in power. To seek to understand the curse that came upon the earth is a difficult task. Perhaps it is best understood if you think of nature as having become insane through the curse. The insanity of some people is known to have increased their physical power in an amazing way. Three strong men have at times been insufficient to subdue a single madman. The same is at times true for drunkards. Before an insurrection or fight, the wild masses will often get drunk to increase their recklessness and courage, and exceptional efforts are sometimes needed to overpower a single wild drunkard. The insane, however, can on occasion experience an even greater increase in power. This is thankfully not the rule, but the rage of insanity not infrequently lends to its victim a physical power that far surpasses the normal bounds. The entire nature of such a wildly insane person is changed. Such a person seems to be entirely poisoned. The same person who earlier was calm and relaxed, who tenderly encouraged his family, suddenly attacks his wife and children or his father and mother, and wants to harm them and kill them. His entire mood, expression of life, and being has changed. He is like a destructive power to his entire surroundings, and those who try to seize or calm him suffer the wrath of that miraculously increased power.

Now that the curse has entered nature, it presents itself in the same way. Just as with the insane, it does experience times of calm and rest, but these are followed by times of wildness and rage in which the elements flare up and destruction threatens on all sides. Then the earth shakes, hurricanes roar, storm winds pile the waters high, rivers flow over their banks, and everything seems to be headed toward destruction. And as with the insane, nature's entire being has been completely changed by the curse. That which used to work for good has now become poisonous. Plants grow thorns and thistles. Animals rage with wildness and a desire to tear things apart. Illnesses and plagues spread. The entire essence of nature forms one organic whole, but corruption has crept into all its kingdoms and spheres. Destruction penetrates to the marrow, and from the marrow the poison of destruction spreads throughout all of its members.

It is therefore indeed like an insane person that nature now rises up against humankind. And whereas that same nature, in paradise, embraced the first man with love, under the grip of the curse it seems rather to throw itself on the man it used to love in order to harass, afflict, violate, and destroy him—and that while nature has become much stronger and more powerful. The plant world opposes him with poison and thorns, the animal world with claw and maw, the air with thunder and storms, and the depths with spewing fire and earthquakes. It is one raging colossus that seeks with all of its powers to cast humanity down. In that rage, its strength has been multiplied fourteen-fold. It howls and roars to try and terrify people. And, overcome by terror and shock, weakened humanity curls up into itself, crawls away, and like a turtle withdraws into its shell, shaking and shivering with fear.

§ 3   Fear has become the religion. The word *fear* can be misleading if by it we mean that tender and intimate feeling of love for our God. Ours is the religion that pours out a Spirit in us not so we should fall back into fear [see Rom 8:15], but in order to rouse an affection within us that causes us to whisper in holy reverence: "Abba, dear Father!" But look in the books of the old covenant, look at the patriarchs and Moses, the psalmist and the prophet, and you will see that the fear of God always stands in the foreground; fear is and remains the first and foremost form in which religion expresses itself. Even in the last prophetic book, in Malachi, the Lord asks: "If I am a master, where is my fear?" [Mal 1:6]. It could, in truth, be no other way. In the current circumstances, we can no longer imagine the anxiety and fear in which humanity lived after the fall, surrounded by a nature that had been poisoned by the curse.

Dependence is much too weak a word to describe the anxiety that the human race was prey to at the time. Given nature's unfettered, unrestrained power, it was angst, dread, mortal suspense, shock, fear—fear in the fullest sense of the word—that held humanity's spirit in its clutches. Those who in the midst of that angst went wild and fell away from their God soon began to see that overpowering nature as what is highest and all-controlling. This fear gave rise to the worship of nature or of the evil spirits who were thought to use nature to threaten humanity with destruction. However, where faith remained and people did not abandon their conviction that our God is even more powerful than nature—that it served him merely as an instrument—people directed their fear to God, such that the *fear of God* became the very essence of religion. The fear of the Lord is a word, an expression, that we can still maintain and use today, although its meaning has changed entirely. The Dutch words for "God-fearing" and "piety," [*godvruchtig* and *godsvrucht*], still point to fear [*vrees*] of God; the same is true of the German word *Furcht*. Religion is therefore literally fear of God. But in our minds that notion of terror and anxiety, of fright, has disappeared entirely. For us, fearing God stands over against fearing man, and it simply refers to quiet reverence for our God and his holy ordinances so as to submit ourselves to him as his creatures.

However, it is precisely at this point that miracles were needed.

Miracles arose out of the contrast between a weakened human race being confronted with a nature that was now wild and had grown in strength and destructive powers. People did not see God. He was the Invisible One. However, people did always have frightening nature around, in front of, behind, and above them. The impression left by nature was thus so overwhelming that it crushed humanity's courage. Who could take on nature? Who could rise up against it? Who could overpower and control it? People did, admittedly, continue to have faith. The Creator of heaven and earth had to be more powerful, and at times deliverance could be had from him through normal means. Time and time again, however, one question came up and could not be pushed aside: Is God, our God, really stronger than nature? Is he also lord and master over it? But when people pleaded and prayed, tormented themselves and brought sacrifices, and nature still overpowered them, their faith eventually began to cave in. Not God, but nature was sovereign, so they thought.

That scary, faith-draining conclusion can be broken only by miracles. Only when God produced wonders and signs that caused his sovereignty over nature to shine before the eyes of all did the fear of nature drop away and God become a refuge and rock, a high encampment for those who are his. Revelation in voice and speech preceded these signs and wonders. The fear of nature that caused people to doubt God's sovereignty finally gave rise to doubts about whether God even exists. The Invisible One could not be seen. Was he there? Where could he be discovered? How was he to be found? This was the point at which revelation came to our aid.

This was already so in paradise. God does not show himself, but he reveals himself. He speaks in the soul and to humanity. He then gives promises, and those promises are fulfilled. He announced judgment in the flood, and that flood came. He communed with the patriarchs as one does with a friend. For that reason, faith in the existence of God continued in the circle of those to whom he revealed himself. But this circle was small. There were very few who received this grace; and among the nations, faith in God declined. Nearly everyone fell away into the worship of nature or spirits. And now the nation must be called, the nation must be formed where faith in God will become the foundation for its existence. This is why the descendants of the patriarchs go into Egypt's crucible. And at the very time when they, fused together as one nation, are called to leave Egypt and enter Canaan and so to become the people of the Lord, miracles appear in great measure and in an overwhelming manner. In the memory of all the Israelites, miracles would remain the foundation of their faith and hope.

§ 4   First came the miracles performed in Pharaoh's palace; then the miracles of judgment over him and his people; and, ultimately, the powerful miracle when Israel walked through the Red Sea on dry land. Their clear purpose is the display of power—the display of power in order to inspire awe in Egypt and Pharaoh, the display of power in order to deliver Israel and to bind it in faith to the God of their fathers. Revelation precedes these miracles, once again, in God's self-revelation to Moses. God's holy existence must be deeply and powerfully impressed on him. Then follows the competition with the wise men of Egypt.

Pay careful attention here. There is no doubt that antiquity had received a knowledge, an instinctive knowledge of nature, and that, at the time, secrets still existed that gave people a certain amount of power over nature. It is easy to laugh this off as the figment of one's imagination, but Scripture teaches us otherwise. It says that the wise men in Egypt indeed performed things that we would not be able to imitate. This can be explained only as a mysterious and instinctive knowledge of nature's power that has since been lost. Yet, as ready as we are to acknowledge this, we cannot forget that it was mixed with all kinds of trickery and deception, and that the things the wise men of Egypt performed under the guise of magic in fact represented nothing more than the product of the traditional knowledge of nature. But even if this arcane knowledge served them well for some time, and even if Egypt's priests and wise men were able by that knowledge to raise Pharaoh's people to a higher cultural level, it was removed so that Moses and Aaron came to confront them with an entirely different power: namely, God's power of miracles. While the form of this power may seem strange to us, it had to be revealed as it was in order to expose the futility of the Egyptian mysteries. This first set of miracles countered the mystery that had continued to blossom in Egypt.

The situation, however, becomes more serious, and the miracles of judgment are then performed. These miracles are *mediate*, so to speak, because most of them are powers of nature that God used in order to complete his judgment on Pharaoh's pride. The Nile was the Egyptians' very renown and god. The same Nile now becomes the instrument that the Lord used to strike down Egypt's pride. This miracle is followed by the plagues from the desert, which can all be explained as a higher operation of nature. Yet that operation is so high and is exercised in such a way that even the Egyptians recognize a higher power in it—although once their initial fear has passed they sink back time and again into unbelief. This continues until the power touches even the firstborn and Israel passes through the Red Sea, so that, once the nation sees the Lord's capacity over the power of nature, Miriam breaks out in a song of praise together with the women. And Moses calls out: "Who is like you, O LORD, among the gods? Who is like you, majestic in holiness, awesome in glorious deeds, working miracles?" [Exod 15:11].

In order to understand the full significance of that powerful miracle, we do well to read the excellent work of Dr. [George Frederick] Wright, a highly qualified geologist. He has authored *The Ice Age in North America and its Bearings Upon the Antiquity of Man*, and *Greenland Icefields and Life in the North Atlantic*, and *Asiatic Russia*, among others—all works acclaimed for their scholarly character. Recently he has published *Scientific Confirmations of Old Testament History*.[1] On pages 83–115 of the latter work, he discusses the exodus from Egypt as a geologist and paleontologist, and he made us understand for the very first time what the significance of the miracles really was. Upon reading this work, you are struck by the fact that this majestic miracle at the beginning of Israel's history established Yahweh's sovereignty over nature and its power once for all as the foundation for Israel's entire religion. Religion in Israel returns time and again to this point. It always draws its power from it. Under the slogan that Yahweh is a God who works miracles, the Israelites set out to enter Canaan. Fear of the power of Israel's God overcame all of Canaan's inhabitants. It was

---

1. George Frederick Wright (1838–1921) was a Congregational clergyman and a professor at Oberlin Theological Seminary, first in New Testament language and literature (1881–92), and then in the harmony of science and revelation (until retirement in 1907). He authored works in geology, history, and theology. Early in his career he defended Darwinism, and later in life he became committed to a form of theistic evolution. The books mentioned by Kuyper are: *The Ice Age in North America and its Bearings Upon the Antiquity of Man* (New York: D. Appleton and Company, 1889; 5th ed., 1911); *Greenland Icefields and Life in the North Atlantic* (New York: D. Appleton and Company, 1896); *Asiatic Russia* (New York: McClure, Phillips & Co., 1902); and *Scientific Confirmations of Old Testament History* (Oberlin, OH: Bibliotheca Sacra, 1906). For more information, see "Wright, George Frederick," in *NSHE* 12:445.

the Lord's miraculous power that unnerved these nations, and this miraculous power that affects the soul gave Israel the upper hand in Canaan.

§ 5   Therefore, miracles were what preserved faith in the living God. Miracles are not incidental to the history of religion. They are not a decoration for history, something that we can easily do without. Rather, miracles take center stage: Faith is renewed and confirmed by miracles, and the fact that we may and can believe in the living God so many centuries later comes from the miracles that took place at Israel's beginnings and then throughout its history as well. All the same, you cannot measure or understand the particular significance of miracles if you do not go back to God's ordinance to man to subdue nature and the earth. Through sin and the fall, that crown of honor fell from humanity's head. Standing powerless and helpless before nature's unfettered rage, the human race had only one question: Would the God they worshiped give way before nature's unbridled power like humanity had, or would God remain nature's lord and master where humanity had surrendered? Could he cover and protect humanity against nature's unbridled power?

The response to this question could be given only by way of miracles. It had to be clear and publicly manifested that a power greater than nature could reveal itself in nature, operate in it, manipulate it, and make it serve a higher purpose. Revelation, word, and engagement with the soul were insufficient. It came down to power—to display of power, sovereignty, and supremacy over the awe-inspiring power of nature confronting the weakened human race. This is precisely what miracles, and especially those miracles that occurred at Israel's birth as a nation, brought us. This is also why our Reformed ancestors did not close the old covenant in order to seek spiritual strength only in the new covenant. No, they went back to Israel and its rise as a nation in order to honor in Israel's birth the powerful revelation of miracles. They understood that the phenomenon of miracles, for which there was no room in paradise, could not remain absent but had to come; and also that it *did* come when the paradise tradition had become extinct and the new faith life had to be raised up within Israel; so that one day all nations on earth would be blessed through Israel.

THE MIRACLES OF CHRIST

When the crowds saw it, they were afraid, and they glorified God, who had given such authority to men.

MATTHEW 9:8

The foregoing does not, however, exhaust the significance of miracles in Holy Scripture. Until now we have spoken mostly of the miracles accomplished directly or immediately by God himself. The purpose of these miracles was to display that God's sovereignty extended far beyond nature's power, which in itself is already astounding. Those who thought that nature's power was strongest fell away into idolatrous worship of it. Only those who saw and confessed that Yahweh's power far surpassed the power of nature bowed down in worship before the Invisible One. Everyone's heart was filled with fear. For those who worshiped nature, this fear remained anxiety and shuddering; while for those who believed in Yahweh's miraculous power, it became the fear of God. This still does not end our discussion, however. As such, we do not yet see the relationship between humanity's call to kingly dominion and the power of miracles as reported to us by Scripture. In order to gain clear and full insight into miracles, we must turn our attention to two other kinds of miracles: (1) the miracles performed by men of God, and (2) the miracles and signs of Christ.

§ 1

Concerning the miracles performed by the men of God, we will limit ourselves to the miracles and signs they themselves performed by virtue of a power given to them. This means that we will pass over the competing signs performed against Egypt's wise men, as well as other signs in which the men of God played no more than an external role. When Moses stretched his staff over the Nile or the Red Sea, he did not perform the miracle by the swing of his staff. Moses rejects this understanding emphatically. He gives God, and God alone, all the glory, and in his song of praise he sings: "At the blast of your nostrils the waters piled up; the floods stood up in a heap" [Exod 15:8]. Likewise, when he struck the rock instead of speaking to it, his very arrogance illustrated that, though he had to give the cue to announce that the miracle would follow, the power that brought the miracle about did not, as such, go forth from him.

Even if it is occasionally difficult to distinguish between those miracles that God himself performed immediately and other miracles that were also from God but with man as the vehicle or channel through which God worked his power, there is no doubt that such a distinction does exist. In the flood we have a miracle in which no person at all is involved and which occurred entirely outside of any human involvement. By way of contrast, the raising of the Shunamite widow's son happened mediately through Elisha. The conception of Christ in Mary's womb is an immediate divine miracle; the signs that the disciples performed when they were sent out into Israel are miracles for whose performance Jesus had given them the power. This second category of miracles that are performed mediately through the men of God has a more direct relationship with humanity's kingly dominion. In them, humanity is given power to triumph over nature and the results of the curse.

§ 2   This is a mystery that comes down to the power that spirit has over matter. Nowhere does this power come to clearer expression than in our power over our bodies. In all that we do through and with our bodies, it is not the body but the spirit in us that is working. Our spirit sets our body in motion, moves it, and makes it perform all kinds of acts. If one person takes hold of another's arm, both hand and arm serve only a mediate role while the real worker is the spirit in us. As soon as the spirit in us wants to let go of the person we hold, our hand and arm lose their power to grip. In all the work we do, our limbs and our senses have no more than a serving role. They serve our spirit, and the spirit in us performs the work by means of the limbs and senses. However, at the present time our spirit no longer has the capacity to operate without mediation on things outside of our body. Remnants of this power remain in the words we speak, or in the power of hypnosis that some people can exercise on others through a look, touch, or at times by the operation of one spirit on another.

Humanity, however, can no longer operate directly on the material nature that surrounds us. The guidewire along which that operation could at one time travel has been broken, and we now stand powerless before nature. Scripture constantly testifies that operations from the supernatural, spiritual world go out upon the earth—power for doing good by God's angels and for doing evil by demons. Nevertheless, fallen humanity stood powerless before these demonic influences. People saw before their eyes a person who was demon possessed, the victim of a demon, but were unable to deliver him from that demon. It is evident from the weak aftereffects of that instinctive power—which can still be seen in the pagan world even after paradise—that humanity originally did possess such an instinctive power. If you refuse to accept this possibility, you will be entirely unable to explain the reports that come to us from the pagan world. But that instinctive effect of humanity's original capacities gradually wore away, was increasingly lost, and eventually the human race was entirely powerless. One's spirit could operate only on one's own body, and on other spirits it could only exercise itself in speech or personal influence. The king of creation sank into inability, and even if he remained king in the eyes of God, he had lost his scepter and crown.

Now in this context, the miracles that God gave a few men of God to perform are uniquely significant. While most of these miracles also had saving power in them to counter misery, that was not their actual purpose. Misery was, after all, found throughout the entire nation of Israel, and more frighteningly yet among the other nations. If deliverance from misery had been the proximate purpose of these miracles, they would also have had to occur everywhere. But they did not. They were limited in number. They all took place in a small area, among one nation. They did not occur constantly, but only occasionally. They were performed by only a limited number of people, all of whom stood in a higher service and were interpreters of God's revelation. These miracles served to support the faith in this revelation, to impress a seal on that revelation, and to awaken the conviction that a higher power had descended on the nation.

This could just as easily have come to pass if all of these miracles had been performed by God himself. But that is not how things went.

In addition to the many miracles that God himself performed without an intermediary, others were performed through these men of God, partly to legitimate them as God's witnesses, but also partly to prophetically restore humanity—or the human spirit, if you will—in its kingly power over nature and over the world of evil spirits. They were a prelude to the triumph that would allow humanity to recover what it had lost. They caused something to shine again of the power and majesty with which humanity was clothed at creation. They showed humanity's susceptibility for a higher revelation of power on the part of the human spirit, as soon as the spirit within was raised in power by a higher Spirit.

These were not miracles that magic tries to feign. Scripture is keen on condemning all such miracles. All magic was to be banished from Israel. The demonic element mixed in with it was to be resisted in every way. Contrary to these semi-demonic miracles, Israel saw miracles performed by the human spirit, thanks to the elevation in power that God's Spirit brought to the spirit of man, that was not magical at all, but entirely in line with humanity's original supremacy over nature. Momentary glimpses of humanity's original nobility appeared in a few holy persons, prophetically representing the glory that would one day come. They represented breaking through the banishment that has oppressed the entire human race since the curse. That curse continues to oppress humanity in part, but one day it will be taken away.

Even Daniel in the lion's den makes you think of Adam in paradise. It was God's power that kept those wild animals in check, and this is and remains true for all the things we do. Heroes who defeat the enemy in battle return home in triumph and give glory to God, even though God used them to reveal this power. The very same thing that we see as a weak aftereffect in animal tamers, but which Adam had in full when he was in paradise—that is, the control over the spirit of animals—radiated suddenly and brightly in the miracle that God performed in Daniel. He stood in the lion's den as the man-king among the kings of the forest.

§ 3   The complete, unbroken majesty, however, came to expression only in the Son of Man. The old covenant miracles were connected to the coming of the Messiah. They showed from a distance what would come in Christ; but they were no more than a prelude. They recalled humanity's exalted position in paradise, illustrated that the restoration of this original power was possible, and prophesied that this power would one day return; but they could not manifest that power in its fullness. This could, had to, and would first happen when Christ himself appeared and when, in the Son of Man, sinless humanity—that is, humanity in its original unbroken power—once again appeared.

We must be careful at this point not to turn the miracles of the Son of Man into miracles of the Son of God. There is indeed a tendency to do this. Omnipotence belongs to God, and where the one for whom we, with Thomas, bow down as "our Lord and our God" [see John 20:28] appears, we tend to see nothing in the miracles and signs but the revelation of his divine omnipotence and to find in them nothing but proofs of his divinity. However, this understanding takes us away from the right path entirely. Jesus himself never pointed to his miracles as proof that he was God. He rather had to make it clear that it was the Father who sent him and that he thus performed a duty on earth and fulfilled the task laid upon him. He never drew a fundamental distinction between his own miracles and those for which he would equip his apostles. At one point he spoke the remarkable words that those who believed in him would perform greater deeds than these. Even of the forgiveness of sin, connected to a miracle of healing, the Lord said: "'But that you may know that the Son of Man has authority on earth to forgive sins'—he then said to the paralytic—'Rise, pick up your bed and go home'" [Matt 9:6]. And Matthew, evangelist and apostle, added that the crowds were amazed because God "had given such authority to men." For that reason, you immediately lose the proper perspective on all of Jesus' work if you do not continually remind yourself that he acted as *man*, in *our* nature, as *Son of Man*, and that in our midst he humbled himself, and even made himself nothing, and lived among us in "a likeness with a human appearance" [Ezek 1:26], even in the form of a servant [see Phil 2:7]. Christ did not have dominion on earth as Son of God and did not display his majesty as God, but acted as man, as one of us. He displayed no other power than what could come from man. He had to learn obedience. He came to fulfill the work to which the Father had called him. All of his power lay hidden in his spirit. Admittedly, the Holy Spirit was given to him in abundant measure. But to the very end, it was and remained a spiritual power that worked in, from, and through him within the limits of our human nature, bound to the ordinances that God himself had given to our human nature at creation. And even when Jesus said, "Do you think that I cannot appeal to my Father, and he will at once send me more than twelve legions of angels?" [Matt 26:53], he was not speaking as Son of God. Anyone revealing himself as God needed no help from angels. Instead, he was speaking as the Son of Man who would be saved from peril and death by the invincible angel armies.

In Jesus, restored humanity appears before us; and in that humanity, the power that the human spirit has over nature, matter, and demons, reaches its highest fulfillment. We cannot say that Jesus was like Adam, because in Adam human development found only its *beginning*, while in Jesus that development appeared in its *completion*. He was not only man, but the Son of Man. The central man. Humanity in its fullness; humanity in its richest and greatest power and ability. And even where Adam's power over creation sank and gave way at the very moment when the curse made this entire creation (so to speak) insane, the Son of Man possessed the human spirit's power raised and elevated to the highest degree so that he could control nature as it had been derailed by the curse.

Nevertheless, his power to do miracles remained a human power to the very end. That is, it was a power that falls within the framework of our human nature—provided, of course, that you do not understand that framework in its present terms, but as it was in Adam; and you must further picture the framework in Adam elevated to its highest fulfillment. In Jesus' miracles and signs we see a power come to expression and at work that far surpasses our power. But it is and remains a power that he received, a power that was *given* to him. You err if you identify that power as one that he had of himself as God. In his miracles and signs Jesus did not reveal himself in his divinity, but as the Son of Man. Even in his exaltation he is and remains the glorified Head of his church—that is, the glorified Son of Man, since he of course could not be glorified as God. Even of the glorification that came to him, the apostles testify that those redeemed by him will one day reign with him as kings and that our bodies, which are now in a state of humiliation, will be made like his glorified body.

At this point we cannot consider in greater detail the relationship and unity of Jesus' divine and human natures. But all the same, it was necessary for us to emphasize that it is entirely false to see the miracles and signs of our Redeemer as immediate divine miracles and to fail to recognize that they together form one miraculous display of power on the part of the man Jesus Christ, or more precisely, the Son of Man. As Adam was clothed with majesty, so Jesus stood before the demon world and all the kingdoms of nature—although, in him, that majesty was raised to its perfection, and even applied to creation in its bewildered state resulting from the curse. In him, the dominion, the kingly dominion, that had been lost in paradise was restored. In Jesus' miraculous power, the glory of the enthroned-humanity shone once again.

When Jesus was tempted and the wild animals surrounded him (see Mark 1:13), the glorious scene in paradise when Adam named the animals was relived. The temptation itself recalls the temptation of Adam and Eve in paradise, but where Adam failed, the Son of Man triumphed. Afterward, his battle is first of all directed against the demons. The casting out of demons is meant to break their power, and when Jesus sends out his disciples, he gives them specifically the power to cast out demons [see Matt 10:8]. That power of demons, just like the work of angels, is the power hiding behind nature. This demonic power was most clearly displayed in those poor souls who were possessed by a demon. This is the power that Jesus breaks, using a power that falls within the bounds of the human; his apostles, and before them, even his disciples, do the same.

From there, the power of the Son of Man continues to spread even wider. While in the desert the animals were subject to him, now also the fish in the water obeyed him [see Luke 5:4–10]. He likewise revealed his power over the plant world through the miracle at Cana, through the miracle of the multiplying of the loaves of bread, and also when he caused the fig tree to wither. He revealed his supremacy over inorganic nature by walking on the water and quieting a storm. The revelation of his power over the kingdoms of nature is not the end, however. Jesus also addresses the results of the curse. He liberates the blind, the deaf, and the mute from their bonds. Those who suffer from diseases find compassion and healing from their illnesses. And, finally, as often as three times he temporarily undoes the separation of soul and body caused by death. In the high priest's servant, Jesus does not heal someone who is sick, but a wounded man.

All of Jesus' miracles, therefore, constitute a unified whole. You would almost say that there was a plan to display in the Messiah the restored and complete power of the human spirit in its triumph—in full measure, in every way, and in all the kingdoms of the demons, of nature, and of misery. You understand that sacred cycle fully only when you see in these things the Son of Man victorious as *King* over all the opposition that exalts itself against man.

This is not meant to deny that every miracle can be considered in itself, that we can also admire in them Jesus' compassion for the unfortunate, his love for those who suffer. Jesus' miracles form a holy necklace in which each and every pearl has its own high value. Only when that pearl-string is taken as a whole, however, do you understand the miracles Jesus performed in their fundamental meaning and comprehend their deeper purpose. In order to reach this deeper understanding, you may not take your point of departure in godless humanity—in sinners—but in humanity as created by God in his image, crowned with glory and wonder, clothed with power and majesty, and anointed as king over his creation.

That humanity perished. That humanity could no longer be found. But even if it was hidden in the human nature overcome by curse and sin, the seed for all of these things was still embedded in our human nature. This was the nature that Jesus took on. He is the Seed promised to Eve. He is from the loins of Adam as concerns the flesh. His spirit received an allotment of power that causes all the glory of paradise to return in him, causes that glory to shine in its full splendor, and in that light makes the turbulence of curse and sin to fade—even to the point of triumphing over death. In this first revelation, the kingship of Christ is thus not a cloth in which he is wrapped, not an authority laid upon him from the outside. This kingship, rather, arises in him from his human nature, but then under the highest and richest spiritual conception. It is the enthroned-humanity from paradise that comes back to life in Jesus and surpasses its original state.

THE POWER GIVEN TO US

And he called to him his twelve disciples and gave them power.

MATTHEW 10:1

As we have seen, direct divine miracles restored faith in the position of God's omnipotence over and above the power of nature, which had fallen into insanity. Likewise, in the miracles performed by Christ, humanity's kingship over nature was restored. These two types of miracles must be sharply distinguished in terms of their significance. It is the majesty of the Lord of lords that is revealed at Horeb; but when Jesus quiets the hurricane on the Lake of Gennesaret, it is the Son of Man who subjects it to his will as king over nature. The miracles that Jesus performed have a significance of their own, which comes to particular expression in that he gave his disciples power to do the same, and even promised that they would do "greater works than these" [John 14:12].

§ 1

The first occasion we hear of this is when Jesus dismisses his disciples and sends them throughout the holy land to announce to the people of Israel that his kingdom has come. We read in Matthew that at that moment Jesus "gave them authority over unclean spirits, to cast them out, and to heal every disease and every affliction" [Matt 10:1]. Jesus himself referred to it as their journey to "the towns of Israel" [see Matt 10:23]. The disciples traveled throughout Israel and then returned to Jesus in holy ecstasy, rejoicing that the spirits were subject to them and that they too had been able to perform miracles. It would appear that they were a little too impressed by this, for Jesus warned them not to see this as the highest thing but rather to "rejoice that your names are written in heaven" [Luke 10:20]. What Jesus says clearly supposes that the miracles they had performed are indicative of a power belonging to the sphere of this life on earth, and that they ought to continually seek their highest ideal not in *this* state of life on earth, but in the future state of glorification.

Further explanation of this miraculous power is given to the disciples after Jesus came down from Mount Tabor after his transfiguration. Only three of his disciples were with him at his transfiguration, and Jesus had left the others at the foot of the mountain. During this time, a father came to the remaining disciples with his epileptic son who was possessed by a powerful demon and pleaded with them to free this poor child from it. The disciples attempted to do so, but did not succeed. When Jesus himself came down from Mount Tabor, the disappointed father walked up to him and called out: "Lord, have mercy on my son, for he is an epileptic and he suffers terribly. For often he falls into the fire, and often into the water. And I brought him to your disciples, and they could not heal him" [Matt 17:15-16]. Jesus then rebuked the demon who left the boy, and the child was healed from that hour on. Jesus did not stop there, however. He also rebuked his disciples and spoke these puzzling words to them: "Because of your little faith. For truly, I say to you, if you have faith like a grain of mustard seed, you will say to this mountain, 'Move from here to there,' and it will move" [Matt 17:20]. Jesus then also added: "This kind," that is, this kind of demon, "cannot be driven out by anything but prayer and fasting" [see Mark 9:29].

Thereby Jesus is expressing three things: (1) that the power of miracles given to the disciples was not a magical power, but came from faith; (2) that this ability from faith was an application of the power of the spirit upon the power of matter in its demonic underpinnings; and (3) that this ability could be increased through fasting and prayer. Therefore, the ability to perform miracles was no influx of divine power for which the disciples merely served as channels. Rather, the ability arose out of human nature, if only it were sanctified through faith and that faith were reinforced through fasting and prayer.

§ 2   We have to be careful not to skip too quickly over Jesus' powerful claim that the disciples would be able to uproot mountains if only their faith were like a mustard seed. Most often Jesus' words have been given a moral explanation in terms of what people refer to as "the faith that can move mountains." With this they mean no more than that faith, in the end, triumphs over all of life's difficulties, even if those difficulties are as high as mountains. Such an explanation, however, does not fit the context. It would indeed work if the context concerned the struggle that the disciples would face when Jesus had been taken away from them and they had to take his gospel out into the world. This is not the present context, however. It was a concrete event; there was an epileptic child who was also possessed by a demon, and the disciples had attempted in vain to free this child from that demonic power. Here Jesus saw a shortcoming in the faith of the disciples: "Because of your little faith you could not heal him." Jesus then identified the kind of faith and the kind of power of faith needed for them to heal people who suffered from such illnesses and to perform such miracles. This power of faith—that is, not to overcome moral difficulties but to heal the sick miraculously—Jesus described further by saying: "If you have faith like a grain of mustard seed, you will say to this mountain, 'Move from here to there,' and it will move" [Matt 17:20]. The common interpretation of that reason cannot be correct. Jesus' words concern a miraculous power, an unlimited power over illness, that is, a power to perform miracles.

Just as unlikely is the interpretation in which that faith like a grain of mustard seed indicates a very small, newly-born faith. While the grain of a mustard seed may well be one of the smallest seeds, in the context of this passage we find no such thing as a very small, newly born faith. Jesus in no way meant to deny that the disciples had faith. That they did have faith would already have been evident in the numerous miracles they were able to perform. Rather, Jesus rebukes them because their faith was not big enough; not big enough for this special type of demon. The demon here was a very powerful one that would not be cast out unless the power of faith was increased to a special measure through fasting and prayer. We must in this context, therefore, not think of the mustard seed in terms of its small size compared to other seeds, but in terms of an entirely different quality—namely, that such a great power can develop from a seemingly insignificant seed, that from that small seed an entire tree sprang up.

That this is what struck Jesus about the mustard seed is clear from Matthew 13:32. There, too, Jesus pointed to the mustard seed and said that while it may be the smallest of all seeds, once it has grown up it "becomes a tree, so that the birds of the air come and make nests in its branches."

Jesus was thereby teaching his disciples to consider mustard seeds from this perspective; that same understanding fits the present context. The disciples did have faith, but not enough power had sprouted from it. Just like the mustard seed, their faith, which in germ was very small, had to develop into an unbelievable power and become like a tree in whose branches the birds could nestle. The emphasis is thus on the surprising power, exceeding all expectations, that develops out of the mustard seed, and that must likewise develop out of the germ of faith. The disciples did not come up short in power because they did not have even a grain of faith. They certainly had that. Rather, it was because the growth of the stalk from the germ of their faith had not been strong enough.

When Jesus applies this to a mountain that can be thrown into the sea, he does not want people to play with magic, but rather he points out that the force that could develop from the germ of their faith would prove to be a power that defies any and every resistance of matter and of the demonic forces sheltering behind it.

The ability to perform miracles that Jesus conferred on his disciples was thus the power of the spirit implanted in our nature that had sunk through sin but was restored through faith and could be raised to a higher level through that faith. It is further evident that Jesus directs this ability of theirs, first of all, to the removal of the curse's consequences. The disciples will cast out demons and heal the sick—all illnesses, all sicknesses. The spiritual character of the power of their faith is then so much in the foreground that Jesus, who when healing illnesses penetrates through to the demonic influence of the curse, also causes the sacred in the power of their spirit to triumph over the demonic.

§ 3   In this context we should also pay attention to Jesus' words in John 14:11. Here Jesus points to the works that he had done. The one who does not believe in him because of his words may well believe in him because of his works. These works, of course, cannot refer to anything except his miracles. Jesus then adds: "Truly, truly, I say to you, whoever believes in me will also do the works that I do; and greater works than these will he do" [John 14:12]. These words make it clear that Jesus does not locate his miracles outside of his human nature so as to derive them from his divine nature. If that were the case, it would be impossible for the miraculous power in him to be manifested in his disciples as well, who of course had no more than a human nature. Jesus does not distinguish himself from his disciples and does not push them aside, but he chooses a field in which he and his disciples are one: he as Son of Man, they as children of men. However, this also makes it clear that the works that his believers would perform will likewise evidence a spiritual power over nature—meant to set it free from the curse—as well as over the demonic operation arising from the curse; and that they would exercise this power by virtue of their faith.

There is something more, however. Jesus says that this power will come upon his disciples because he is going to the Father [see John 14:12]. In doing these greater works, the believers thus do not stand on their own, free of Jesus. Rather, they are considered as one with Jesus, belonging to his mystical body and working with him as their Head.[1] The situation to which he refers would come when Jesus had died, risen, and ascended into heaven, and then sat down at God's right hand. However, Jesus continues: "Whatever you ask in my name, this I will do" [John 14:13], and in verse 14 he repeats it once more: "If you ask me anything in my name, I will do it." Thus, Jesus presents himself as the one from whom a power will go forth to work in his disciples and inspire them and those who will believe in him. He does not say: "God will do it," but rather, "I, the Son of Man, your Head and Lord, will work in the members of my spiritual body." Thus there is no question of a power or faculty that they themselves freely had at their disposal. It was to be a royal-human power that, seated in the Son of Man, would go forth from him to manifest itself in believers as members of the spiritual body. Although sinful humanity lost its kingship over nature, as nature lies under the curse, it was revived again in Jesus as the Son of Man, and now shines forth from him, our king, in his believers and comes to be manifested in them.

This convincingly shows how extremely superficial the generally common understanding is that Jesus' words had no other meaning or intention than to reveal his *divine* power. If that were the case, it would make no sense for his disciples likewise to receive the power to do miracles, since they were normal humans; and it is even more difficult to explain how

§ 4

---

1. "In Kuyper's thought, the mystical body of Christ is synonymous with the invisible church, the essence of which lies directly in God. The invisible church did not, however, exist only as a divine thought or idea. It existed outside of God as a separate entity." See Henry Zwaanstra, "Abraham Kuyper's Conception of the Church," *Calvin Theological Journal* 9 (1974): 160.

they could do even greater works than Jesus. This only makes sense if one understands Jesus' miracles as miracles performed by the Messiah—that is, by the one promised to the fathers, who had come from God and who, as the Son of Man, being one of us, partaking in our human nature, has revealed the restored and heightened power that was first laid by the Triune God in humanity by virtue of the creation ordinance. Only when Jesus' miracles are understood in this way do they have a direct relationship with creation, the fall, the curse, and the effect of demonic powers upon this world. This forms an indispensable link in the great work of salvation. Only in this way do Jesus' miracles have a place in the context of sacred history. And only when they are understood in this way do they govern the further development of human dominion over matter, over nature, over the curse, and over the demonic power that works in and through the curse.

Right after the apostles appear as the Lord's witnesses, they reveal that a power to do miracles, similar to Jesus' power, is also at work in them; and already in the first miracle—that is, the healing of the man born crippled—it becomes evident that they did not perform such miracles by virtue of some magical ability, but by their communion with Christ their King. "Why," asked Peter, "do you wonder at this, or why do you stare at us, as though by our own power or piety we have made him walk?" [Acts 3:12]. The God of the fathers had glorified Jesus and crowned him with majesty. It was in this Jesus that they believed, and it was the name of this Jesus—that is, his exalted majesty—that had saved and healed cripples. That miracle, too, occurred through faith. Faith is the restoration of our human nature's spiritual capacities not in itself but in communion with the Son of Man. That faith was at work both in Peter and in the crippled man. This faith, which after all broke the power of demons and connected us once more to God in Christ, was given from and through Christ to the apostles and to the lame man. This is why Peter added: "The faith that is through Jesus has given the man this perfect health in the presence of you all" [Acts 3:16]. The manifestation of this miraculous power in the apostles also made such an impression on the people that they carried the sick on their beds out to where the apostles passed by; and even though Paul had not been one of Jesus' disciples, it soon became evident that this power to do miracles was at work in him also. That power did not come from interaction with Jesus but was given through him, and only after his ascension to the right hand of God could it go forth in its fullness from him as the Head of the body, as the King of a new humanity. James' report that the elders likewise anointed the sick and prayed with them in order to try to heal their illnesses follows in that same line [see Jas 5:14], and even today people attempt to heal through prayer.

It is impossible to push aside all that is reported [about healings] as if it is simply nonsense and intentional deceit. If no healings had actually occurred, then especially those which were said to have happened at a particular time and to a particular person would not have maintained their credibility for so long. No one, therefore, has the right to deny, without searching further for evidence, the possibility that the power to do miracles, which was so frequently at work in the days of revelation, may also be at work today. All the same, we do have to resist the claim that today things must continue just as they did in the time of revelation, and then to twist this argument around so as to conclude that what no longer occurs in the same measure today also never happened in the past. With such an understanding, you will utterly fail to appreciate the truly particular and unique character of revelation. Israel as nation could be formed as God's people only through the mighty miracles at the Red Sea and at Horeb, but it does not in the least follow from that fact that every nation today ought to have a similar origin. Faith first had to be established in Israel; the other nations then took it over from Israel.

§ 5

In nature, too, there are so-called climacteric periods. A seed that sprouts and grows into a tree first has forms that later disappear without coming back. Children have characteristics entirely different from when they are adults, and in adults we see things that were entirely unthinkable in them when they were children. Old age in turn brings things that were not apparent in adulthood. The same is true for all of history. Throughout history we find a succession of distinct periods, each of which bears its own character, requires other facts, and has another goal. The same is true of the history of revelation. Here, too, a tree first sprouts and grows, and bears fruit only afterward. Miracles had their own significance in that first period in the history of revelation, but from it one may never conclude that the same phenomena had to be repeated in the same way in the second period of revelation—that is, when [revelation] was spread throughout the nations. We must also be particularly attentive to the fact that Scripture somewhere records that deceivers and even the Antichrist will perform signs as well [for example, 2 Thess 2:9]. Therefore, when we hear of miracles occurring among us, we have to pay careful attention to the source of the force that is said to be displayed in them.

However, as long as we pay careful attention to both the special character of the first period of the history of revelation and to the threat of demonic miracles, there is no reason to deny outright that a spiritual, healing power may also manifest itself in our days. We may not deny the possibility in and of itself that God may want to continue performing miracles, or that even now a power to heal the sick can exert itself through faith in Christ. This does not mean that we have to accept as true everything we are told. We have to decide by the facts, and those facts must be carefully examined. There is no room for gullibility. Rather, everything depends on two questions: (1) What power can our soul exercise on our body? and (2) What power can be awakened in us through faith?

The relationship between our soul and body has not been studied sufficiently. As mentioned above, the spirit of insane people sometimes doubles the muscular strength of their bodies. Though hidden to us, there must naturally be a point where the soul is connected to our nervous system. The soul then works on the muscle tissues through the contact it has with the nerves. The body does not see, hear, move, and pick up or drop something; the soul does all of these things through the body as its instrument. When a person sleepwalks, it is the soul that unconsciously guides the entire body. Courage is a characteristic of the soul, and history shows how often courage produces greater miracles than do the muscles of giants. Joshua and his people are told as many as seven times: "Be strong and courageous," which presupposes that an increased power can go forth from the soul onto the body. Who will then claim that the soul in certain circumstances does not have the ability to exercise a higher power on the body? Even doctors attach more value than one might assume to what they call the patient's morale. In and of itself, it is thus not at all impossible for the soul to undergo an intense process through which it has a healing effect on the body. The soul can undergo that intense process through faith—specifically, faith in one's own healing—and be inspired to healing by what it hears from and sees in others and through the soul's prayer for being allowed to share in that healing as well. Here, too, we see the spiritual influence that one person can exercise on another's soul. It is not true that we can approach the soul of others only by touching their body. Though miles from him, Napoleon's name was enough to inspire his armies, and biology and hypnosis convincingly testify to the direct influence that one spirit can have upon another. Faith in the one can directly awaken and strengthen faith in another.

A purely psychological explanation is not intended here. Faith in healing must be rooted in faith in Christ, and this soul-changing faith comes only from above. It is always in communion with Christ and through his name—as Peter says [see Acts 3:16]—that the healing we are speaking of in this context takes place. However, even if this prevents us from discarding all healing through faith's spiritual power in our days as being inconceivable and deceptive, we do not mean to deny that such healings often involve deception and fiction. Neither do we deny that there have always been certain people with the power of hypnosis who mixed it with a little bit of spirituality and thereby began to consider themselves as some kind of miracle workers, and in the process abused the gullibility of the superstitious crowds to their own glory and advantage. In any case, as will be further apparent, these spiritual healings do not hold the secret of the further development of Jesus' kingship over the powers of nature. That development lies elsewhere.

THE INCREASE IN OUR POWER

Until it was all leavened.

MATTHEW 13:33

§ 1   Given the above, we have acknowledged: (1) the miracles that occurred in the days of Jesus and the apostles had a significance that no longer applied after the completion of revelation; and (2) as a result, no one may say that miracles can no longer occur today. Christ our King lives at the right hand of God as the Head of the church and as the Head of humanity; powers go forth from him; and there is no reason why that power could not triumph over nature's resistance also at the present time.

But even if we maintain the possibility of miracles for now, we straightforwardly admit that neither the miracles performed by the apostles nor those recorded at a later time can be said to surpass or excel the miracles that Jesus himself performed. You need to think only of the miracle at Cana or the feeding of the multitude, the miracle on the Sea of Galilee, and the three people raised from the dead, to realize that the apostles' miracles in no way surpass them in glory. We do not thereby intend to detract in any way from the apostolic miracles; we do not downplay them; we do not deny their importance. But what we deny is that the apostles' miracles ranked above the miracles that Jesus himself performed. Since Christ emphatically declared that something greater and higher than was displayed in *his* works would go forth from his church [see John 14:12], the complicated question arises as to where we are to look for those "greater works" and where the "greater works" are to be found.

What the annotators [to the *Statenvertaling*] offer does not satisfy. They point to four things: to the fact that the apostles imparted the Holy Spirit through the laying on of hands; to speech in foreign languages; to the spread of the gospel throughout the Roman empire; and, finally, to what we read in Mark 16:17–18: "And these signs will accompany those who believe: in my name they will cast out demons; they will speak in new tongues; they will pick up serpents with their hands; and if they drink any deadly poison, it will not hurt them; they will lay their hands on the sick, and they will recover."[1] It is obvious that these things apply to every believer. It can only mean that such things would occur over the course of the centuries.

Nevertheless, we remain unconvinced that the above contains something greater than what was revealed in the miracles that Jesus himself performed. In any case, this cannot refer to spiritual things. The fact that Jesus' preaching was limited to Palestine, while Paul brought the gospel to Spain and Peter as far as Babylon, does not mean that the apostles did greater works. It is nothing other than the expansion and continuation of what Jesus began. In this respect, the apostles are no more than epigones. It may not be said of the Christian teachers who today bring the gospel to China and Japan that they are doing more than Jesus did. Nor can the laying on of hands be greater than when Jesus breathed on his disciples and said, "Receive the Holy Spirit" [John 20:22]. One may also not say that the disciples' speaking foreign languages or words was a miracle that they performed; rather, it was an expression of the soul that came spontaneously from their lips without any deliberation on their part in a moment of higher ecstasy. Moreover, who would ever claim that speaking other languages is greater than the calming of a storm on the Sea of Galilee or the feeding of the five thousand?

Regarding the *material* miracles to which our attention was shifted by the [annotators'] reference to Mark 16:17–18 (that is, picking up snakes, escaping harm from deadly poison, healing the sick), they are all of a lower order than the miracles that Jesus performed. At any rate, they do not surpass them. Snake charming is still being practiced in India. Unless you

---

1. Kuyper refers here to the Dutch SV annotations at John 14:12.

are content with generalities or superficialities, we can only conclude that the annotators do not do justice to Jesus' words and cannot satisfy those who read Scripture seriously.

For this reason, we would like to propose an entirely different interpretation. Our point of departure is an undeniable distinction in history: the distinction, the contrast between the instinctive, unwitting handling of nature's objects and the deliberate handling gained through practice.

In order to make this distinction clear, we will purposely take an example from daily life whose ordinariness will nevertheless make it accessible to all.

In bygone centuries, the Dutch kitchen was revered throughout Europe, and yet there were no cooking schools. Housewives, together with their servants, cooked delicious meals, but they taught themselves; they instinctively discovered how the food had to be handled in order to make the best meal. What defined the Dutch kitchen was its ability to make the taste of the natural produce from the field and of the meat come out more naturally than was done in other kitchens. In France, they still use "à la Hollandaise" to refer to the preparation of a dish that is not forced or overwhelmed by all kinds of sauces. Fish "à la Hollandaise" is pure fish, baked with butter, that has not been made unrecognizable under all kinds of sauces. Dutch housewives discovered this method of preparing food on their own and instinctively. They gave no deep consideration as to how it had to be done or why they did things in this way rather than another. What they did, they did instinctively and well. This instinctive talent has now been largely lost, and daughters preparing themselves for marriage or kitchen maids in training are sent to culinary school. There they must observe and learn. Everything is shown and explained to them. Cooking well is now no longer the result of a talent's natural inclination to discover by instinct what is good, but the result of a kind of schooling. What used to be done unwittingly and automatically is now deliberately acquired.

This same distinction carries through into all areas of life. Consider agriculture, for example. Isaiah says: "Give ear, and hear my voice; give attention, and hear my speech. Does he who plows for sowing plow continually? Does he continually open and harrow his ground? When he has leveled its surface, does he not scatter dill, sow cumin, and put in wheat in rows and barley in its proper place, and emmer as the border? For he is rightly instructed; his God teaches him" (Isa 28:23-26). This passage thus speaks of an agriculture that is experimental and entirely instinctive. It is a talent, a gift, a practical way of doing that God himself teaches to the farmer. No mention is made of an agricultural school or of intensive agriculture. But how things have changed in the current situation! In agriculture, too, a radical change occurred from an unwitting operation to a deliberate, acquired operation in which careful attention is given to one's actions. We have gained a thorough knowledge of the soil's chemistry, of seeds, and of all the factors at work in the growth of plants. The earlier, instinctive cultivation of the land and the instinctive handling of dairy and livestock have now been replaced by a totally different method where there is a reason for everything.

What we observe in agriculture is true for all areas of human life. In the past, children were raised—and not all too badly, at that!—without any pedagogical study; now we see recently married women at the point of birth reach for a pedagogical handbook in order to learn from it how to raise their children. In the Netherlands, industry used to flourish in remarkable measure, so that those who worked in it solidified our reputation throughout Europe as the teachers of the entire developed world in more than one field. However, at that time there were no trade schools, business schools, industrial schools, or factory schools. In the current situation of our impoverished industry, by contrast, everything is taught at schools, and no one can get anywhere anymore without a long list of schools. It used to be that all higher expressions in all areas arose from life itself, automatically and from instinctive aptitude, but now instinct has been flattened and *deliberate* learning has come in its place.

The same can even be observed in the field of art. The great artists used to appear unexpectedly. They built, chiseled, painted, made music, and sang at the urge of their own spirit; and their creations are still admired as the greatest of what the world of art has to offer. Rarely, however, had they read books on art, seldom had they visited art schools, and they had almost no knowledge of the history of art at their disposal. Everything in them came from holy inspiration. Today, by way of contrast, we have established art schools and academies, with books about real and false art that try to explain everything to you. Art criticism is enjoying its heyday, and you could fill entire libraries with books on aesthetics. All the same, this turnaround in the field of art has been unable to overturn the order of nature. Art is never something that can be learned. Art is nothing else but what arises instinctively from inspiration. Art is something automatic, or else it is not art. However, for that very reason, it is so indicative that even in this field the conscious life tries time and again to drive the unconscious and instinctive away.

All this taken together points to a most important evolution in our lives that grew up richly out of the instinctive during the years and centuries of our unconsciousness, and now, as the instinctive factor wanes, attempts to raise us, by deliberately probing into the composition of the laws of nature, to a higher, more united, and more powerfully dominating expression of life. The deliberateness in life today lacks the alluring power that the former instinctive life possessed in such a powerful measure; but it places us in a higher position, multiplies our power, and makes us into reasonable creatures capable of greater things. If in the past each and every triumph over nature stood on its own, at present our triumph over the power of nature is common property; it has become a manifestation of strength over against nature as such. We have penetrated through to its mysteries. We have discovered the order of its structure, the movement of its elements, and the laws that govern this movement. In the transition from an instinctive to a deliberate treatment of nature lies a general advance that gives humanity much greater power over nature.

§ 2 Similarly, it was entirely natural that our human life did not begin with deliberate expression, but with the instinctive. The expression is instinctive when God himself, directly and without mediation, shows humanity the way and causes its inner force to come out. This is precisely what Isaiah expresses when he says that God himself, in that first period, teaches and instructs the farmer. The deliberate life could not be the beginning, since deliberate knowledge of nature was still lacking. Had it been necessary to wait for it, human development would never have come, because no one had an analytical knowledge of nature and so there was no one who could teach it to others. This is why it was such an amazing act of grace that, during this first period of time, the Lord God enabled humanity to do such great things instinctively.

The dominion over nature that humanity had from its very creation was broken through sin and curse. It did not disappear all at once, however. For some time it still operated among all people in a weakened form, but its nature was eventually changed so that it developed into pagan magic and therefore died out. What did remain and what did carry our human development for many centuries was the inspiration of instinctive life that quickly raised our human life to a high level of flourishing. We stand in amazement at what the past century of scholarship has revealed about the high level of development that existed in ancient Egypt or in Canaan in Abraham's days.

By this we do not mean to deny that, also at that time, a certain amount of study was necessary. From the very beginning there was imitation, and all imitation is, of course, a form of study. However, the unique character of human development at the time came from genius, innate talent, and instinctive drive, while study only touched the surface and was incidental. Things could not stay this way for long, however. A much greater power over nature became ours when, by research and reflection, humanity penetrated through to the very essence of nature and learned to put the powers hidden within her into service. For that reason, there is no use in lamenting the loss of the poetry that at one time brought splendor to life but has now been replaced by cold and barren prose. The evolution into prose had to come in the end; it could not fail to appear. The siege laid at nature's outer gates could not go on forever. Humanity had to pass through those gates to enter the fortress, to look for its hidden powers, and thus to establish dominion over it from the inside.

This is the way in which things indeed progressed. After an initial period when the forces of paradise continued to linger for some time, instinctive life flourished in the second period, but by now we have entered a third period that expands our dominion over nature enormously and roots that dominion in investigation and in the knowledge gained from it. The difference is like the difference between Asians in Tibet, who try to heal the sick with amulets and spells, and the diagnosis made and medication prescribed by a trained physician today, after he examines the body's structure from the inside, identifying where the illness comes from by virtue of that greater and more complete knowledge. That is not to deny that also the sick in Tibet can be healed. We also do not mean to deny that certain means of diagnosis and medications that once were known are overlooked today. The study of medicine continues to pay too little attention to the history of medicine. All the same, everyone will feel that our knowledge of sicknesses and cures is now, thanks to the anatomy and physiology of the human body, on a much higher level and that, for this reason, we have a much stronger position over against illnesses in this time of deliberate investigation than when people relied on tradition and instinct.

For that reason, we should not return to that period of instinctive life, even though it remains fitting for us to honor its relative excellence.

Our rational power resides not in the unconscious but in the deliberate. Only those who approach nature with deliberate knowledge have a dominion over that nature that reminds us of our royal call to subdue it. Moreover, in the deliberate we do indeed find something greater compared to the past.

§ 3   Let us, in this context, consider Jesus' parables of the mustard seed and of the leaven.

These parables are commonly understood to refer to spiritual processes. But is this correct? Does not Jesus' teaching as a whole show that he always kept together body and soul, matter and spirit, the visible and invisible world, as being unified in their essential coherence? And what right, then, do we have simply to exclude from Jesus' prophecy in these parables everything that is tangible and that pertains to the body, to matter, and to the visible, and to limit ourselves to the spiritual alone? When Jesus speaks of the greater things that will come one day, he does so specifically in reference to his works; and among those works especially his miracles stand in the foreground—miracles that, in particular, revealed his power over *visible* nature.

Therefore, let us not separate what Jesus always joined together. He took humanity in its entirety, with both our internal needs and external miseries, and presented himself to us as the Savior and Redeemer— Redeemer from sin, but also Redeemer from the miseries that pursue us.

It is in this context that Jesus points to the mustard seed. It is such a small seed, but it germinates, grows, goes through a process; and the end of that process is a tree with wide-spreading branches that offer shade and protection to the birds of the air. This, says Jesus, is how it will be with the seed of the kingdom. First it is small, and after germinating it still seems tiny and vulnerable. But then it will spread itself. It will pass through a regulated organic process, and at the outcome it will stand at the center of the world like a tree with wide branches that offer consolation and protection to humankind in its sin and misery. Jesus therefore does not point to a stable situation where everything always remains the same, but to a progression through periods, to an expansion of influence, to a saturation of our entire life with that influence, and to a future in which it will become clear to all that the seed of the kingdom brings spiritual and material blessing. It is always a matter of the greater.

In the parable of the leaven, Jesus goes on to depict that same process for us in its hidden operation. The miracle is that the leaven is added to the flour, and after coming into contact with the flour, the leaven sets a powerful process in motion. Jesus does not direct us to the external act or instinctive handling of the baker, but to what happens to the flour through the powers residing in nature entirely independently of that baker. Jesus penetrates through to enter nature's secret and shows how there are forces in nature that set a process in motion on their own and complete it according to the laws of that process.

What right does anyone have to restrict this weighty prophecy about this process to the spiritual realm alone? Rather, are we not obliged to apply this process of the kingdom's forces to human society as a whole? Has the kingdom's force not made itself felt in every area of our life—in the spiritual, the social, and the material? And is not the process that manifests itself in all areas precisely the process of the leaven? Is not Christianity being carried forth into the world, coming into contact with the elements and laws of human life and through that contact modifying and changing life entirely? If you compare our life in Christian Europe and America with life in Asia and Africa, it will be most clear that the leaven of the Christian religion has penetrated through to the three measures of flour in all of life and has thereby raised our entire life in the spiritual, social, and material spheres to a high level, just like dough rises through the efficacy hidden in leaven.

If we take this as our starting point, we no longer have to ask for evidence. History and the present time show that it is only in Christian nations that the liberation and elevation of the [human] spirit has taken place, which, after also turning to the study and knowledge of nature, has also increased our power over nature in such an entirely wonderful way. While the Greeks and Romans were similarly occupied with the study of nature, and the Arabs also made significant progress, it is only in those countries where the Christian foundation freed humanity's spirit that science and the study of nature have taken off. Even if it is true that the study of nature now turns so reprehensibly against the Christian religion, it is and remains a plant that could sprout and shoot up in Christian soil alone. If we were to imagine Europe without Jesus and without Christianity, our place with respect to nature would be no different from that of the Chinese in the East or the Indians in southern Asia. We would be doing an injustice to Jesus' greatness if we were to claim that he neither foresaw, nor conjectured, nor knew of this course of events, this coming process. He was to be our King; to him was to be given all power in heaven and on earth. And so, when Jesus tells his disciples that the leaven that he will add to the three measures of flour will elevate our entire human life, is it not clear that this prophecy to his disciples has now come to full realization? Namely, as great as his miracles were, the fruit of his entering the world would produce greater and more miraculous works when we achieved the current level of dominion over nature through the unveiling of its secrets and the knowledge of its hidden forces.

MORE SHREWD IN DEALING WITH THEIR OWN GENERATION

For the sons of this world are more shrewd in dealing with their own generation than the sons of light.

LUKE 16:8

Humanity's dominion over nature was thus ordained already in paradise. Through the fall into sin and through the resulting curse, weakened humanity gave up this dominion over nature. In Christ as the Son of Man, however, it returns, and Christ restores it in three ways. First, he does this immediately by means of direct miracles, a power that continued to work for some time in his apostles. Second, he does this mediately by the higher development of the spiritual factors in our generation, in all countries where the Christian religion triumphs. And third, he does this in the end, at his return; this is related to this [present] topic, and the New Testament points to it time and again as an indispensable part of the great work of salvation. In short: (1) Jesus restores humanity's power over nature by miracles; (2) Jesus restores humanity's power over nature on a

§ 1

much wider scale and for longer by the light that shines upon the nations as the gospel transforms their lives; and (3) Jesus will one day raise nature, along with his holy ones, to its ideal by glorification.

The third element—regarding the end reached at Jesus' return—can be touched on here only in passing. To treat it more extensively would draw us too far from our topic. However, it should suffice to point to what Isaiah already prophesied, with a clear allusion to the situation in paradise, when he said that one day "the wolf shall dwell with the lamb, and the lion shall eat straw like the ox" [Isa 11:6, 7], and even that "a nursing child shall play over the hole of the cobra, and the weaned child shall put his hand on the adder's den" [Isa 11:8]. This is an Eastern poetic manner—but nonetheless powerful!—of portraying the full restoration of humanity's power over nature. This is a restoration that will be completed only when, at his return, Jesus will undo Satan's power forever, and all the resistance of evil spirits will have been broken down. But this will not happen until the end of time, when the struggle has been completed and the kingdom of glorification has won its triumph.

However, what is already at work in the present time is the restoration of humanity's mediate power over nature. This power over nature in the second period of its restoration is the power that we now have and is now at our disposal, and that experienced such a particularly remarkable breakthrough over the course of the last century. It is not the immediate power to do miracles that Jesus exercised while he was on earth. It is a power of an entirely different order, of an entirely different kind, of an entirely different operation. In his power of miracles, as well as the mediate power that Jesus now exercises over nature, spirit rules over matter; but in miracles spirit ruled over matter directly, while the same spirit now rules over matter mediately through the development of the human spirit. Although one may for the sake of brevity refer to it as the spirit's power over matter through science and technological aptitude, this description is not entirely accurate. It is less accurate because, alongside science, there is discovery, genius, energy and talent, determination and will. However, their results are all analyzed, probed, explained, and exposited in science and technological aptitude. This technological aptitude of which we speak is humanity's ability, the ability pertaining to the subjection of nature; it is something to which medicine and other aptitudes belong as well.

That mediate power that we have over nature—which is a miraculous power all the same, even if it is not a power to do miracles—has come down to us through and from Christ. The gospel of Christ has called into existence an entirely different, much higher development in the life of humanity's spirit. This great light has come to burn brightly in Christian countries alone; and from that newer, richer, higher development in the life of our spirit, a greater power over nature naturally arises for us through our knowledge and ability. This, too, we owe to Christ. This greater power went out from him. He brought it about in and through us.

Just as certain is the fact that this second, mediate restoration of power over nature that we owe to Christ is greater in comparison to the things Jesus brought about directly through his power in miracles. This power is not greater in the sense of manifesting a *higher* power. Nothing surpasses the calming of wind and storm on the sea of Gennesaret, the multiplication of loaves, and the raising of the dead. Nevertheless, the power that has now been given to us is indeed something greater when we consider its extent, scope, and longevity. Everything Jesus worked through his power of miracles was directed to one specific circumstance, for one specific sick person, to one specific demon-possessed person, and was limited to one specific place. By contrast, this second, mediate power over nature, which we now have, exercises its work and influence among all countries and nations equally from one century into the next. It is a blessing to thousands simultaneously in all their distress and diseases. It sounds strange to our ears that our power over nature surpasses Jesus' power in miracles. But this nevertheless allows us to explain fully how Jesus—knowing what he would bring about and establish in and through us through later development—could tell his disciples that they would perform things that were greater than those visible in his miracles.

The mistake that many made, which kept them from seeing this, was to attribute a power to Christ that remained alien to those who believed in him. They thought that whatever transpired outside of faith also lay beyond the sphere of Jesus' activity. What unbelievers accomplished in the arts and sciences was considered odious and the work of the Evil One. Jesus was left out entirely. His kingship was said to be limited to what pertained to the blessings of the soul for eternal life. The *world*, understood not only as a term for an unholy spiritual state but also as a reference to normal human life, was thought to lie beyond the domain over which Christ exercises his kingly power and dignity. That God so loved the world

§ 2

that he gave it his only-begotten Son not in order to condemn it but to save it [see John 3:16–17] was understood as pertaining to the elect exclusively. The world was left aside, and Jesus' coming was understood as salvific only in terms of bringing eternal salvation for the elect. Nobody saw that this understanding conflicted directly with what Scripture reveals to us about the restoration of paradise, about the new earth and the new heaven, and about the glorification of our bodies.

As a result, many were led to the false position where, on the one hand, they did not deny that we in Christian countries have arrived at a much higher expression of human earthly life; but on the other hand, they understood this apart from Jesus' kingship, without any causal relationship to Christ, and as being in enmity with Christ. The full, rich, all-encompassing meaning of "All authority in heaven and on earth has been given to me" [Matt 28:18] was neither seen nor understood. But if we broaden and expand our view, acknowledging that Jesus, as our King, has dominion over our entire human life, it can only be true that we owe to him both our spiritual development unto eternal life *and* our general human development, which has increased our power over nature and expanded our knowledge and ability so incredibly. We have convincing proof of this when we compare human development in pagan and Islamic life to what has been attained in Christian countries. Our spiritual awakening to salvation and our general human development in this life are not completely separate from each other. They represent two operations in a single organism that continually influence each other. And you fail to do justice to the honor due the kingship of Jesus if you refuse to honor his majesty as displayed in them both.

§ 3   All the same, it is not difficult to see how people came to deny Jesus' kingship in general human development. After all, it is irrefutable that unbelievers, more than believers, are responsible for general human development. It is no coincidence that it is more an exception than the rule today to find those who practice the natural sciences and technical aptitudes worshipping Christ as their Savior and Redeemer. The same phenomenon can be observed throughout almost the entire course of history, to use these words found in the Gospel of Luke, that "the sons of this world are more shrewd in dealing with their own generation than the sons of light" (Luke 16:8).

Because the older authorized Dutch Bible writes that they are "*more careful* than the sons of light," this expression is commonly not understood with sufficient depth. The misunderstanding results from the two meanings the word *careful* [*voorzichtig*] can have in the older Dutch language. First, as it does today, it means *cautiousness*, in the sense of paying attention to the consequences, thinking about the dangers to which one might be exposed. Thus, a person climbs carefully down a dangerous, steep mountain path. However, *careful* also meant something entirely different and was used in the sense of skillful, shrewd, intelligent, and clever. In a letter, a high-ranking person could therefore be addressed as: "To the careful _____." According to the French proverb "prévoir c'est gouverner," to govern well means to have foresight. It is this sense that the Greek word *phronimos* conveys in Luke 16:8, and the very same word is used in reference to the "wise virgins" [see Matt 25:2]. Instead of *careful*, it would be better to translate the Greek as "more wise, more shrewd."

Understood in this way, the verse expresses that the children of this world are more shrewd in the use of their spirit than the children of the light are in their field. That is, in worldly concerns—in all that pertains to the life of nature and to the visible world—the people of the world generally succeed in exercising greater power than the believers whom the text identifies as the children of the light. In no way does the text intend to express that this is worthy of reproach; it says that Jesus *praised* the judge who acted so shrewdly. The only thing the text establishes here is that this is the way things are: when it comes to the field of general human life, unbelievers on the whole display greater resilience than believers do. Nothing else is said. There is no indication that the situation could and should be otherwise. Similarly, there is no indication as to the cause. Rather, on the basis of life itself, of practice, of experience, the rule is established that this is the way things are. When it comes to general human life in this world, unbelievers as a rule far surpass believers.

The disciples would already have found confirmation for this in the old covenant. Abel prefers to walk in front of his lambs while deep in thought, but Cain exerts himself and drives his shovel into the ground. Of Cain it is said that he built a city [Gen 4:17], which would have been no more than a ramshackle dwelling with some kind of palisade to keep the wild animals out, although its construction still points to the first manifestation of technical aptitude. When Seth is later contrasted to Cain and his offspring, once more it is not in Seth's line of believers but in Cain's unbelieving offspring that Jabal, Jubal, and Tubal-cain appear as the great inventors of metallurgy, of musical instruments, and of woven tent cloths

[Gen 4:20-22]. Things continue in the same way. Egypt is a pagan land, yet it is their wisdom that Moses must learn, and it is in Egypt that Israel is formed into a nation. Bezalel and Oholiab were given special talent for building the tabernacle, but that talent was related to what was already known in Egypt about construction. When the temple was later built on Zion, no master builder was found in Israel, but Tyre's great architect Hiram had to come to build the house of the Lord. About the days of Saul, we even read that no smith could be found in Israel, which most likely means that the Israelites themselves did not practice metallurgy, but that their smiths, like the gypsies today, were traveling craftsman whom the Philistines drove outside the borders of Israel in order to weaken the nation.

In its time of glory, Israel therefore did not distinguish itself in a single field of science or art. Commerce was mostly in the hands of the Canaanites, and Israel's ships were insignificant compared to the fleets of Tyre and Sidon. Not only Egypt, but also Assyria, Babylon, and Persia—to say nothing of the Greeks and Romans—surpassed Israel in every field of science and technological aptitude. The richest collections in museums of ancient history have scarcely any artifacts from ancient Israel. Jerusalem's palaces would no doubt have been filled with uncommon wealth during the reign of Solomon, but all signs once again point to the use of foreign skill.

Similarly, in Jesus' time the newly founded cities of Caesarea and Tiberias were of foreign origin. And that was while Jesus surrounded himself with simple fisherman from the Sea of Galilee, without mention of anybody who excelled in intellect or art. Such higher intellects entered the sacred assembly only with Paul, Apollos, and Luke. Furthermore, with the exception of Paul's writings, the beauty of the Gospels and apostolic writings is not found in the fruit of scholarly learning, but in the spark of divine inspiration.

§ 4   This is not a haphazard circumstance but is easily explained by the psychological fact that, as a rule, the power of our spirit is too weak to embrace at once both the kingdom of heaven and the kingdom of general human life. If the spirit is too concentrated on general human development, the science and art that result from it stimulate the ego's sense of self-worth so much that it has no use whatsoever for becoming a child of

God. Newton[1] and Agassiz[2] still demonstrate how this pitfall can be avoided, but they remain exceptions; learning and art seem, as a rule, to elevate people's sense of power to such a degree that they can no longer even think about humbling themselves before God. The skepticism created in the heart through learning and art is accompanied by confusion in the spirit and a level of temptation that normal believers can hardly imagine. Humanity ends up being elevated too highly, and damage is thereby done to the reverence that should be shown to the exaltedness of the Lord of lords. We see how young men enter advanced education with a sound confession of Christ, only to return home as unbelievers at the end of their studies. Here life consumes almost the entire person so that no room is left for them to look upward anymore.

Among the children of the light (as the Gospel calls them), one instead all too often finds the tendency to avoid life out of a fear and concern that full participation in human life would in the end lead one to surrender and to lose faith. This tendency is witnessed most obviously in hermits, stylites, and cloister-dwellers. They seek God and want to enjoy communion with him; and since the world draws one away from that communion, they flee the world, flee all temptation, and withdraw from full participation in human life in order to be "alone, but together with God."[3]

This tendency to avoid the world and to set oneself apart from it may not take this extreme form in the broad circle of believers, but it remains as dominant as it was in all previous centuries. People may exaggerate when they say of the Anabaptists that they like to sit "with my book in a quiet nook," but there is still some truth to it.[4] Calvinists always had

---

1. Isaac Newton (1643–1727) was a deeply religious English physicist and mathematician. With discoveries in optics, motion, and mathematics, Newton developed the principles of modern physics. In 1687, he published his most acclaimed work, *Philosophiae Naturalis Principia Mathematica* (*Mathematical Principles of Natural Philosophy*), which has been called the single most influential book on physics.
2. Jean Louis Rodolphe Agassiz (1807–73), commonly known as Louis Agassiz, was a Swiss-born American naturalist, geologist, and teacher who contributed significantly to the study of natural science with his work on glacier activity and extinct fishes. He was a lifelong opponent of Darwinian evolutionary theory and was recognized as an innovative and prodigious scholar of natural history.
3. On these lines, see also *PR* 1.1.6.2n3.
4. This saying comes from Thomas à Kempis and is often used somewhat dismissively to criticize those who prefer a more contemplative life above a life of cultural engagement. The English rendering is meant to capture the rhyme of the Dutch, "*met een boekje in een hoekje.*"

another viewpoint, and praise may not be withheld from them for how they excelled in general human development by their confession of common grace. Even so, it can hardly be denied that, after their decline in the late-seventeenth and eighteenth centuries, they too showed a remarkably increasing tendency to separate themselves in groups, withdrawing from general human life.

At present there may be renewed improvement, but the tendency as such continues to manifest itself. And even if from our better vantage point we look on that tendency with disparagement, it does contain a holy principle in the desire for avoidance and separation. "For what will it profit a man if he gains the whole world and forfeits his soul?" [Matt 16:26]. When you enter the world, you constantly come into contact with the world understood as evil, with its unholy spirit, with its sensuous temptation, with the demonic background to the world's life. Although faith indeed conquers also this world, those who feel that they are too weak are better off to withdraw into the light than to stray from the path of life in the darkness of the world.

§ 5 This is something we must take into account throughout the course of history. All forces in the arena of the spirit must be mustered constantly to prepare for the spiritual war. Those who want to succeed in the world must constantly concentrate the force of their spirit on the material and visible. Each stream follows its own course. This is how it was, is, and will be. On the one side stands the powerful development of human knowledge and ability, promoted in particular by those who have concentrated their spirit's entire power on it. But this very concentration kept them estranged from the mysteries of the higher life. On the other side stands the powerful development of the life of the spirit as it is promoted especially by those who, as children of the light, concentrate all the exertion of their spiritual power on that eternal light.

There is in fact much that pleads for us to see nothing in this but the design of God. He is the most powerful dispenser of gifts and talents. And does not history show how it pleased him to dispense gifts and talents for our human knowledge and ability not to his people Israel, but to the pagan nations? Did Egypt, Babylon, Greece, and heathen Rome not have gifts of science and art that were withheld from Israel? Cannot that contrast we find between the sons of Seth and the sons of Cain be traced throughout the entire course of history?

When we reflect on our own times, do we not see before our eyes that this rule for the dispensing of gifts in science and art continues to apply? You may constantly plead for those who excel in science and art to fall down before the feet of Jesus, and you may time and again ask yourself gloomily why we [Christians] do not have such people. However, things remain as they are. The gifts and talents for general human development are dispensed in much stronger and greater measure to the children of the world than the children of the light.

Calvinism alone—when it flourished—broke that rule, and our recollection of Rembrandt's biblical paintings[5] and De Ruyter's heroic godliness[6] and Bilderdijk's poetic glory[7] makes us aware that there are exceptions not only in individuals but in entire groups who follow another direction of the human spirit, but these exceptions do not overturn the fundamental rule.

All the same, we should never lose sight of the fact that, even where this fundamental rule applies, neither the higher and richer light that shines in human matters, nor the resulting higher power over nature that comes to us, ever function outside of the design of Christ—even if in certain people this higher light and this higher power do turn against the kingdom of Christ. For that reason, we must honor also that general human development—now considered without its sinful turn—as a gift that has come to us from the cross.

---

5. Rembrandt Harmenszoon van Rijn (1606–69) was a Dutch artist of international renown, who produced numerous etchings and paintings that were popular throughout his lifetime, and remain so to this day. Rembrandt's greatest creative triumphs are exemplified especially in his portraits of his contemporaries, his self-portraits, and his illustrations of scenes from the Bible.

6. Michiel Adriaenszoon de Ruyter (1607–1676) was one of the most famous admirals in Dutch history. He was a pious man, known most for his role in the Anglo-Dutch wars of the seventeenth century.

7. Willem Bilderdijk (1756–1831) was a Dutch poet who had considerable influence not only on the poetry of the Netherlands, but also on the country's intellectual and social life. His contributions to Dutch poetry included his revival of Romantic poetic style, his insistence on the importance of feeling in writing poetry, and his deeply religious poems that inspired others to write theological poetry.

THE WORLD OF
THE SPIRITS

All these I will give you.

MATTHEW 4:9

§ 1   We saw previously that the Son of Man recaptured the kingship over nature in two ways: in the first place, *immediately*, by his power to do miracles; and in the second place, *mediately*, by the miraculous power that,
throughout the centuries, Christ raised up in humanity's knowledge and
ability in Christian countries. We saw that Jesus calls the latter "greater works" [John 14:12], which by his influence would be accomplished
through believers. We say that these things occurred by virtue of Jesus'
influence because he not only testified that they would do greater things
than he had done, but then he also added by way of explanation: "Because
I am going to the Father."

This important point requires further careful explanation. Although
there is no doubt that our greater knowledge and ability with respect to
nature arose only in the countries that came under the influence of the
Christian religion, this fact in itself still does not explain the relationship between our richer knowledge of nature and Jesus' influence upon
our hearts. It would have been possible to explain it if those who con-
veyed this knowledge had almost exclusively been believers. Instead, we
find ourselves confronted with the apparently internally contradictory

circumstance where, as we saw above, the study of nature and the inventive spirit needed to subdue it seemed to be absent among believers, and as a rule was found among unbelievers. As an inner contradiction, it is all the more poignant since Jesus testified: "Whoever believes in me will also do the works that I do; and greater works than these will he do" [John 14:12]. It will not do to seek to explain this superior power that we have over nature as proceeding from Jesus' kingly dominion and to separate it from faith. For that reason, we are confronted with the question of how to harmonize these two circumstances—namely, that Jesus draws a connection between our greater power and faith, and that on the whole the study of nature is absent where this faith is found, and often even turns against faith. There must be a link to harmonize these two apparently contradictory facts, but we still have to ask ourselves where this link lies.

In order to consider this question, we have to go back to Jesus' temptation in the wilderness. The Messiah appeared in order to reassume on our behalf, as Son of Man, humanity's kingship over this earth. But before Jesus began his public ministry in Israel for this purpose, a demonic spirit—the head of the demons, in fact—appears to him in the wilderness, claiming to possess the kingdom and saying that he has the power and inclination to give them to Jesus if only he bows down to worship him. We cannot shrug off these words of Satan as mere pretense, for Jesus himself called him the "ruler of this world" [John 14:30]. This title is on the same level as the title of king, but with this difference: the latter is too beautiful and noble to be applied to Satan. *Ruler* is a title for a violent man, and this is why Jesus does not say "the king," but rather "the *ruler* of this world is coming. He has no claim on me."

Jesus not only wrestled the ruler of the world in the wilderness over the matter of kingship and confessed on the way to Gethsemane that the struggle with Satan would not end until the cross, but throughout his three-year sojourn on earth we also see Jesus constantly at work breaking down the Devil's work. Casting demons out was in the forefront of Jesus' daily work, and while the power he gave to his disciples may have included the healing of the sick, its primary purpose was to cast out demons. In a moment of holy rapture, Jesus testified that he saw Satan fall like lightning from heaven [see Luke 10:18]. In fact, Jesus' battle with Satan is so much in the foreground that, in the short prayer he taught us, he emphatically included the petition: "Deliver us from the Evil One" [see Matt 6:13]. To remove Jesus' struggle with the Devil from the history of his life and to account for his powerful work "psychologically," based on something he did not say, while leaving out what he himself always saw as the background to his holy struggle, is to adulterate the reality of his having worked among us.

His apostles likewise constantly emphasize the struggle between the Spirit poured out by Jesus and the spirit of the satanic world. They oppose every attempt to turn the believer's struggle into an ordinary moral struggle. As those whom the Lord has freed, our struggle is not against flesh and blood but against "the spiritual forces of evil in the heavenly places" [Eph 6:12]. Even now Satan "prowls around like a roaring lion, seeking someone to devour" [1 Pet 5:8]. When the church's final triumph is revealed on Patmos, the spiritual drama culminates in one final release of Satan, only thereafter to complete the full defeat of all that is anti-Christian and anti-godly when he is thrown into the lake of fire [see Rev 20:10]. The "man of lawlessness" of whom Paul speaks in 2 Thessalonians 2:3 will function "by the activity of Satan" [2 Thess 2:9]. This [man of lawlessness] is a last-ditch attempt on the part of Satan to undergo human incarnation—just as, in Jesus, the Son of God became man, and the eternal Word became flesh—only to meet eternal destruction in this most extreme form of sacrilege. Luther said in this regard that Satan was like God's ape since, in his struggle with God over the possession of this earth and our human race, he imitates unto our destruction what the Triune God had in his compassion ordained for our salvation.[1]

§ 2   Meanwhile, later studies have completely uncoupled Jesus' appearance from this extremely important demon-filled backdrop that is functioning throughout Jesus' ministry. Everything pertaining to it in the Gospels and the apostolic writings is now being cast aside as an erroneous observation,

---

1. Luther refers to Satan as "God's ape" in numerous places, but Kuyper may have in mind here Luther's commentary on Genesis 37:9, in which Luther writes concerning visions, prophecies, and dreams: "For they do not always arise only from God but also from the devil, who is God's ape, and just as he is accustomed to awaken prophets, so he also stirs up visions and dreams, God permitting this in His wonderful counsel. But even when he speaks the truth through dreams, he is looking to something different from God's intent in this connection. God shows forth His Word and signs for the salvation and redemption of men, but Satan seeks the destruction and ruin of souls and the darkening of God's truth, and therefore he lies even in telling the truth." See Martin Luther, *Lectures on Genesis: Chapters 31-37*, ed. Jaroslav Jan Pelikan, Hilton C. Oswald, and Helmut T. Lehmann. *Luther's Works* (Saint Louis: Concordia, 1999), 6:331.

a figment of the imagination. People claim that these were superstitions common to the time when Jesus was raised and grew up, and that in the end he likewise imagined that there actually was a demonic spirit world. These same people insist, however, that we now know better, and so they transpose the Gospel in such a way that everything recounted in it about Satan and demons is given a psychological explanation. It should not amaze us that this often happens among the highly educated, since they see in Jesus no more than a great rabbi and a religious genius. They do not accept the Savior as the Gospels offer and represent him to us, but fashion a Jesus for themselves after their own liking and need.

What we do not understand and what goes against all rhyme and reason is the presence of scholars who call themselves "believers," who say that they honor Christ in his divinity, and who nevertheless hold the untenable position that Jesus succumbed to the errors of his time. The one, after all, entirely excludes the other. It is not possible to maintain that Jesus shared in the divine nature while admitting that he made mistakes. What some then claim in order to save themselves from this inconvenience—namely, that Jesus did know that these were errors of his time, but followed and conformed himself to these errors out of love and in order to gain access to their hearts—is a pure figment of the imagination that conflicts with the facts. The temptation in the wilderness was a struggle that he fought himself without involving a single one of his disciples, and it was the Holy Spirit who led him out into the wilderness for this struggle. When Jesus casts out devils, he does not conform himself to any erroneous notions; they in fact speak to him in this struggle. It was also without any prompting from the side of his disciples that, on his way to Gethsemane, Jesus said that the ruler of the world was about to make his final attack [see John 14:30]. And why would Jesus have included the petition, "Deliver us from the Evil One," in his prayer if he was not convinced that Satan exists and that he works upon human hearts?

All of these kinds of explanations are, for that reason, to be rejected unconditionally. Jesus' struggle with Satan to save the sheep of his pasture out of the clutches of the world is not a secondary but the primary purpose for Jesus' coming to earth. Sacred history, from paradise to the end of the ages, cannot be explained if Satan's struggle against God for humanity is not placed in the foreground as its all-determining motive.

It is for this very reason that, during Jesus' time on earth, demonic activity was more evident than it was in other times. The influence of the world of the spirit on this earth can rise and fall, and this principle applies to both the good and the fallen angels. Thus, when Jesus comes to earth and the spiritual struggle is at its decisive point, angels and demons both show themselves more clearly. For that reason, we would be removing Jesus' coming entirely out of its natural framework if we do not take full account of the influence of demons.

Upon considering these things carefully, we see that this question extends even further and pertains not only to the angels and demons, but to all spiritual life. Those who began by explaining demons away as a false product of the imagination, then discarded their belief in the existence of angels, did not stop there but proceeded by logical necessity to deny the existence of the soul as well, abandoned their faith in the immortal, and finally denied God's existence so as to be left in the end with nothing but nature, body, and matter.

The one is therefore tied to the other. Those who lock themselves in this finite world, enclose it in their finite thought, derive their standard from it, and now apply that standard in order to decide what is and is not possible, close the shutters of the window that gave us some insight into the spiritual world, and hence no longer see it. The measure for the visible is not suited to the spiritual. The spiritual is of an entirely different nature and, for that reason, works through entirely different powers and follows entirely different laws.

Scholars who insist on measuring spiritual matters according to the nature, forces, and laws that govern the material and visible can only conclude—if they are consistent—that there are no miracles or spirits, or even souls or a God. Just like fish perceive nothing of the beauty of cedar because their world is limited to the world of water, so scholars who bind themselves to the visible also perceive nothing of the beauty and magnificence of the spiritual world, because they are entirely taken up in the world that they can measure, weigh, and calculate. Moreover, even if they assume that there is a world of the beautiful and the good, and find their ideal in it, their starting point forces them finally to attempt to explain the ideal from the visible, as proceeding from matter or—more accurately— from cells or from what can be found in cells and gives them their being. They do not know or acknowledge a distinct and separate world with a structure of its own that, as a spiritual world, cannot be measured according to anything in our visible world. It would have meant the end of science's dominance. Science that sets itself up as a master above and against faith leads to a complete negation of the very existence of a spiritual world. The two exclude each other, and a half-faith that molds and conforms itself to such one-sided science forfeits the right to call itself faith.

A certain change in this tense relationship first came—at least to some degree—when people began impartially to describe phenomena connected to spiritism, telepathy, clairvoyance, and so on. To mention only two, Dr. Myers in his *Human Personality*,[2] and Flammarion in his *Forces naturelles inconnues*,[3] have carefully catalogued all the phenomena for which they thought there was abundant testimony through sufficiently reliable evidence. In the Netherlands, works of a similar nature have likewise appeared. There is thus a significant group that recognizes that enigmatic things indeed exist and mysterious forces are at work, and that it is fitting to study them even if the results of such a study are from the outset expected to disappoint, since our knowing intellect cannot penetrate that hidden world anyway. What we do gain by this, however, is that there are now also scholars outside the circle of believers who begin to admit that there must exist, entirely distinct from this earthly world, something like another spiritual world, and that certain forces from that world are at work on ours in a way that affects the souls and lives of many.

§ 3

It may not be much, but we have nevertheless made some gain. People are starting to get used to the idea that another order, distinct from this order, exists. People acknowledge that we stand in an entirely different relationship to this other world than to the normal world around us. People see how some detect nothing whatsoever of this other order and laugh about it, while others are in communion with and firmly believe in it. And people can no longer conceal that there is some agreement with what the prophets and apostles revealed about the existence of a higher, spiritual world order.

---

2. Frederic William Henry Myers (1843–1901) was a poet, classicist, philologist, and a founder of the Society for Psychical Research. In his own day, Myers' work on psychical research and his ideas about a "subliminal self" were influential, even though they were not accepted by the scientific community. Here Kuyper mentions his work, *Human Personality and Its Survival of Bodily Death*, ed. and abr. Leopold Hamilton Myers (London: Longmans, Green & Co., 1906).

3. Camille Flammarion (1842–1925) was a French author in the areas of astronomy, popular science, and psychical research. He sought to apply the scientific method to the study of spiritism and reincarnation, and spent more than sixty years investigating paranormal phenomena. Here Kuyper refers to his work, *Les Forces naturelles inconnues* (Paris: Ernest Flammarion, 1907).

This is not to say that the prophetic and apostolic revelation is the same as what comes to us from this spiritism, this clairvoyance, this psychic world. After all, one is most struck by the deep differences that run between them. However, what the two do have in common is that both revelation and spiritualistic phenomena presuppose the existence of another world order alongside this earthly life, and that there is indeed a way in which the forces and operations from this other world manifest themselves to us in our earthly existence. Even some half-believers, who were on the road to losing their faith, later admitted ecstatically that these phenomena testified to them of an immortal existence after death. The poltergeists in telekinesis seemed to them to be as reliable witnesses to immortality as Jesus' resurrection on the third day. Of course, true believers will never fall into such a palpable error. They experience an entirely different communion with the spiritual world than a medium does with the spirit world, and their faith rests not on the evidence of spiritists but on their spiritual bond of faith with God.

Although believers were entirely justified in refusing to attribute to these phenomena the special value that others attributed to them, in the context of the great struggle between faith and science, the study of these phenomena nevertheless has the advantage of having struck a damaging blow to the short-sighted pretense of the exact sciences that denies the possibility that another order than the one at work in our normal life can even exist. It is now admitted that another order may indeed exist and that certain forces from this other order that defy normal explanation may be at work. The spirit world, of which people now speak, automatically opens the way to believing in the existence of a spiritual world. This naturally raises the question as to how we are to think of this spiritual world and in what way that spiritual world operates on the visible world and, in particular, on human beings.

§ 4   A similar movement can be observed in psychology. Contemporary psychology has no use anymore for the vague data that used to be applied. It proceeds from the standpoint that what we refer to as psychological phenomena must come to expression through or in the body in one way or another. Insofar as these phenomena—healthy or sick, normal or abnormal—are manifested externally in a way that they can be seen and heard, then they can be perceived, touched, compared, interrelated, and used to draw certain conclusions. But even if many people prefer to explain all of these phenomena from physical causes, and even if a significant number admit that a distinct soul exists, they nevertheless constantly witness how material data are entirely incapable of explaining everything we perceive.

For that reason, people are forced to accept something else in humanity alongside matter and to acknowledge that the spiritual in humanity constitutes a life sphere of its own where its own influences are at work and where the normal laws of nature do not apply. Even in human thought life, in imagination, in the world of dreams, in artistic creations, in the sense of beauty, in moral motives, even in the administration of justice and power, there are phenomena shrouded in mystery. And when one considers the power of religion, the mystery of love, heroism, and many others, one is confronted with deeply impacting phenomena that, briefly stated, defy all explanation if one discards the notion of a spiritual world operating in humanity.

This, too, is why materialism is increasingly losing ground, even among more refined and deeper thinkers. A more ideal life interpretation is making headway. People feel and acknowledge that there is a mystical world with which they have a certain relationship. The *ignorabimus* (we will be at peace with our ignorance) of former times is making way for the tendency to seek a certain mystical communion with that world. There must be, so people now say, another sphere of spiritual life, the knowledge of which our heart thirsts for; they even open the doors of their heart widely so as to undergo the influences of the mystical world. This is the dominant mood among the more nobly educated, and it is only among the half-educated, among businesspeople, and in the revolutionary corners of our lower social classes, that we still find the obtuse materialism that half a century ago enjoyed nearly complete dominion, even in educated circles.

All the same—and this is characteristic of our time!—nobody wants to hear anything about the revelation that has come to us from this mystical-spiritual world in the Word of God. People seize upon what has come down to us from Buddhism, they deepen themselves in the study of theosophy, and they attempt to raise up the spirit of Hegel once more. They have an ear for everything. The only thing they remain firmly opposed to is the special revelation of God in prophecy, in Christ, and in his apostles. They admit that there may well be a spiritual world, that we may be related to it, and that it is most important to determine this relationship; however, that knowledge must come from us, from humanity—from one's own conjecture and invention, one's own thought, reflection, and meditation. We must owe all knowledge of it to ourselves. What is not allowed and what they do not want is that this knowledge would be revealed to us in a mysterious way by God.

Believers certainly share the blame for this. This is not to say that they, too, deny that revelation. Not at all. But the mysterious background of revelation has retreated into the shadows among them as well. Just ask yourself what the armies of angels still mean for people, and especially what significance the influence of demons and Satan still has for them. Many believers no longer take any of these things into account. They do not deny their existence, but for most such notions have been reduced to meaninglessness. If you take these elements away, the faith of these believers that has already shrunk remains as it was. Influence from the Holy Spirit on their soul—there is that, of course. But what has the casting out of demons by Jesus and his apostles become other than a psychological cure for epilepsy or other illnesses? In preaching as well, so much of the rich content regarding the spiritual world that was given to us in revelation has disappeared without a trace. And if, in order to explain the kingship of Jesus, you refer to Satan as the ruler of the world who robbed the Son of Man of what belonged to him only to return that dominion to its rightful owner at Golgotha and at the empty tomb, you are drawing your hearers toward a domain that has become entirely foreign to them. They never did understand Satan's power over this world and the spirits as a real power. As a result, neither could they understand what made Jesus' victory over Satan so great. This is the very reason why they failed altogether to see how, by sending his church out into the world, Christ broke Satan's spiritual power in that world, freed the spirit of man, and thereafter made it possible once again for the human spirit to bring nature into subjection.

The preparation for what we have observed so painfully among idealistic scholars—namely, their attempt to reach for the mystical in rejecting the revelation of God—was the fault of the church itself.

THE INFLUENCE OF
THE SPIRIT WORLD

Are they not all ministering spirits?

HEBREWS 1:14

Because we acknowledge the influence of the spirit world on our earth, §1
as Christ also bore witness to it, and therefore also accept the influence
exercised by Satan and his demons on our world as actually taking place,
curiosity then compels us to ask how and in what way we should think of
that influence. Apart from Scripture, however, we know absolutely nothing on this subject. It is a mystery to us. We see every day that one spirit
acts upon another, and it is very clear to us that our mind influences our
body. All the same, neither experience nor science can answer for us how
it is that one spirit influences another spirit or how our spirit influences
our body. The working of our mind on those of others, as well as on our
own body, takes place at a level where our powers of observation abandon
us. We are dealing here with feelings, impressions, emotions, sensations,
and we do not doubt for a minute that our spirit exercises an influence on
the minds of others and on our body.

Nevertheless, we cannot investigate how that happens. We are able
to observe the effect but the operation itself escapes us so that every attempt at analysis ends in failure. We clearly see that sometimes the one
person's spirit exercises a much greater and more rapid influence upon

the spirit of others than is usual. We likewise see that one person may be much more susceptible and receptive to such an operation than another. We even observe that one spirit can more easily influence a gathered crowd than those who make up that crowd could be influenced one on one. And yet we remain in the dark as to how this hypnosis or suggestive influence begins, what power is at work in it, and how it accomplishes its goal.

Even the game of love confronts us with an unresolved mystery—or so it seems, at any rate, when a single look turns out to be unforgettable and irresistible, and one encounter leaves such a deep impression on the souls of two young people that they feel irresistibly attracted to each other and their souls are drawn together by a magnetic force.

We have a spirit within us, and daily we come into contact with the spirits of others, and yet no one can say what that human spirit really is. A spirit is *something*, it exists *somewhere*, but it is immortal and therefore invisible. Every attempt to describe and define it fails. We can say what the spirit is not, but cannot say what it is. Similarly, we know that spirits exercise power, but how that power is found in them, how they spring into action, and to which laws they are subject, remain a mystery to us. We see that our soul must at some point come into contact with the most sensitive extremities of our nervous system, since it is through our nerves that the soul gathers the awareness of our existence and the perceptions of our senses. Where in our bodies that point of contact may be located, however, we do not know. Some claim that the soul is dispersed throughout the body, others state that it is seated in our heart, and yet others locate it in our brain. Surgery can remove entire parts of our body without our spirit suffering any harm, while when other body parts are hardly even touched we instantly lose consciousness. We can make guesses, we can have suspicions, we can develop theories, but what we do not have is certainty.

Yet even though almost every *how* remains unanswered here, and even though we cannot in any way account clearly for the way in which our spirit is able to influence our body, we do not doubt for even a second that this influence does occur. Every day and every hour of our life confirms this.

If we now apply this to the spirit world beyond the human circle, taking our point of departure in the fact revealed to us that such a spirit world indeed exists, then it is no more than natural to assume that the spirits from the world beyond this earth are somehow related to the human spirit. At the very least there is this relationship: namely, that they too are spirits;

and the basic mark of our spiritual existence, through which the spirit inside of us is distinguished from all that is visible, must also be found in those other spirits. Further than this, however, we cannot go. Our spirits may have certain characteristics that other spirits lack, and conversely, they may have attributes that are entirely foreign to us. Yet however great the divide may be, we must conceive of them as spirits and thus as beings whose basic existence matches our own spiritual existence.

This implies that it would not be out of the question or unnatural in any way if these spirits, too, could remain holy or could fall—if there were both good and fallen angels, holy spirits and demonized spirits. Of these spirits, too, we may assume that one spirit can exercise influence upon another, and that, as one such demonic spirit, Satan exercises an influence of dominion over the other demonic spirits. Similarly, we may assume that both good and evil spirits exercise influence upon the human spirit and that the good and evil angels exercise an influence upon us for good or for evil, respectively. Finally, it is entirely possible that, just as our spirit exercises an influence upon our body or upon matter, so also the good and evil spirits are capable of exercising an influence upon the perceptible and visible world. §2

The details found in Scripture raise this possibility to the level of certainty. It tells us that all spirits are ministering spirits. This means that they have a ministry to perform, that they are called to a ministry, that they received the attributes and powers necessary to fulfill this ministry, and that the angels' ministry is not limited to the sphere of heaven but also extends to this earth and to the world of humanity. Scripture tells us that an influence comes to us from the good spirits, that they exercise a power upon us, and that they fight alongside us in the great battle for the Lord's kingdom. They stand and cheer in the fields of Bethlehem Ephrathah, they yearn for insight into the plan of salvation, they are sent out "for the sake of those who are to inherit salvation" [Heb 1:14], and on the last day they will triumph with Christ and with those who have been saved by him. It is not as if they have their own separate life above while we live here below on earth, but they share in our experiences, rejoice with us or cry over us, and fulfill God's ministry toward us. The manner in which angels live alongside us is portrayed in the parable Jesus told, in which Lazarus was carried by them to Abraham's side [see Luke 16:22].

Just as the angels who remained standing exercise their influence upon our lives, Scripture likewise teaches concerning the fallen angels that they influence us, but then in the opposite sense; as demonic spirits they now work for our perdition. It is not as though it was their plan and intention to destroy us, but Satan envies God because of us and tries to draw us into his kingdom. Some refer to Satan as the brother of Christ in order to indicate that he is far superior to the other spirits. This superiority was the very thing that led him to rebel against God, and from that time forward his entire purpose has been to impede the progress of the kingdom of God and to establish his own kingdom. In order to attain this end, he also tries to claim the world of humanity for himself.

It goes without saying that Satan, because of his superiority, has great gifts and remarkable powers at his disposal. He had been called and destined to apply these gifts and powers in service to the Lord, but he retained them after his fall and now applies them against God and his Anointed One. After this power had become an unholy power, Satan displayed it in paradise when he seduced our entire human race to fall. Scripture reveals that he has been occupied incessantly ever since in sowing spiritual corruption among the human race, in frustrating God's work of saving grace, and in maintaining his own dominion on earth. He has become the ruler of this world [see John 12:31; 14:30; 16:11; 1 John 5:19]. The kingship over this earth that God had authorized for humanity has now gone over to him. Satan holds souls, peoples, and nations in his clutches through all kinds of unholy, mysterious powers, including magic and witchcraft. That unbounded demonic dominion held its own until Christ appeared. Then Satan doubled his efforts and prepared himself for a personal battle in order to maintain his dominion as the ruler of this world, over against that of the King anointed by God, and to frustrate the coming of the kingdom of heaven.

In order to develop this power, Satan influences other demonic spirits by subjecting them to his will and molding them to serve his purpose. In the same way, Satan works on people's spirits so as to seduce them, get them into his clutches, and corrupt the seed of piety within them. He also exercises influence on the physical and material, which is abundantly clear from those who were demon-possessed when Jesus walked on earth. Satan extended his power into Jesus' own circle when he brought down Judas and placed Peter in great danger; and these efforts to tempt and to seduce will continue without end, so that Jesus bids all Christians to pray: "Deliver us from the Evil One" [see Matt 6:13]. Satan's attacks come and go in waves. When Jesus lived on earth, they were particularly pronounced. The demonic influences were so over-abundantly evident in those who suffered from mental illness or epilepsy in those days that the demons themselves addressed Jesus and said: "Have you come to destroy us? I know who you are—the Holy One of God" [Luke 4:34]. But Jesus cast them out. On one occasion he even drove them into a herd of swine, and in their madness the swine plunged down the steep bank into the sea. This is a spiritual influence, a being turned and overwhelmed by way of spiritual dominance. Yet this spiritual influence extends to the body as well and is not limited to the spirit alone, but touches the entire human person. In the power that was exercised by Jesus, it extended even to the animal kingdom.

Those who think that it is no more than a great exception when spirits influence our lives will not understand, and for them this does not explain anything. Scripture, however, gives us no reason to maintain such a position. It describes Satan to us as a "roaring lion, seeking someone to devour" [1 Pet 5:8]. The spiritual forces of evil in heaven form a power with which we constantly do battle [see Eph 6:12]. Every morning and every evening again we must ask God to "deliver us from the Evil One" [see Matt 6:13]. Moreover, it is not only the life of our spirit that has been exposed to these unholy influences, but all of nature "was subjected to futility, not willingly, but because of him who subjected it" [Rom 8:20]. It has been subjected to "a bondage to corruption, so that the whole creation has been groaning together in the pains of childbirth until now" in that hope that it will one day "obtain the freedom of the glory of the children of God" [see Rom 8:21–22].

§ 3

This means that we are not dealing with an exceptional circumstance, but a situation of sustained corrupting influence exercised by demonic pressure on the sphere of this earthly life and felt by all throughout the earth. This pressure was a result of the curse; this pressure grew among the nations that had wandered away from God; this pressure was, at one point in time, broken at its core through the appearance of the Messiah; and thanks to the outpouring of the Holy Spirit, this pressure is tempered through the activity of God's church. But this pressure will be taken away completely only when Satan has been bound eternally and when the glory of God's children and of the earth, as the new earth under the new heavens, will dawn at Christ's return.

Spirit does not rest in matter, but spirit bears matter. It is God's omnipotence that maintains the composition of the universe through the majesty of his will. That omnipotence of God is omnipresent. No created spirit, no material atom, is preserved by anything other than God's omnipotence. At every point and at every moment in time, everything in creation is borne, maintained, and enabled to function through God's in-dwelling, omnipotent, and omnipresent power. But God is spirit [see John 4:24]. He is not visible or material. This means that it is the Almighty Spirit who created and upholds not only creaturely spirits, but along with the visible world also the visible coverings in which they are wrapped. And as far as science may penetrate into the essence and powers and laws of nature, it can never reach the spiritual substratum that carries and supports everything. Even in regard to the material, where everything seems to be a matter of movement and power, science can go only as far as the degree to which motion can be observed. Determining how God—who is a spirit—exercises his omnipotence in that material, or makes it to vibrate in that movement, lies beyond the reach of science. No one knows anything of it unless God reveals it to us, and anybody who has the need to formulate even a vague understanding of it must always and ever return to revelation.

§ 4   People did attempt these things apart from revelation, but this only led them from one error into the next. Those who were more superficially inclined sought refuge in what has become known as deism. They imagined that God at one point created the universe like a watch, and that this watch now always runs by itself entirely without and outside of God. Others refused to be satisfied with this superficial view and sought a way out in pantheism. They maintained that just as we are a body with a soul inside of us that fills everything with life, so too the universe is one immeasurable body and that the all-soul of that body is called god. The god of the Pantheists was thus taken up in everything, first coming to consciousness in humankind—a god without independence, without holiness, without self-consciousness. God became a dreaming spirit bound up within the universe. This was the wisdom offered by the world, and anyone who rejects God's holy revelation returns time and again to such wisdom.

Over against that pseudo-wisdom, however, Jesus and his apostles placed the divine wisdom, which has been kept hidden from the wise of the current age and which God has revealed to little children [see Matt 11:25]. In that wisdom revealed to us, the world of the spirits becomes apparent. It is not as if there is a small earth down here while God is high above us, without anything in between the two except the emptiness of death. Rather, all of God's creation is filled with rich and fascinating life. There are myriads of myriads of angels, thousands of thousands, as the seer on Patmos expresses it [see Rev 5:11], and God's omnipotence is even represented in the four cherubim. The innumerable spirits do not only rejoice and sing praises, nor are they marginal actors on the great stage of the universe. No, the spirits are "mighty ones" who carry out the Word of God. "All his hosts are his ministers, who do his will!" They have a ministry, a calling, a task, which always consists in "obeying the voice of his word" [Psa 103:20]. They neither slumber nor rest, but they are always active and always performing their ministry. They are carried by God's omnipotence, but God acts in them like a personal power. "He makes his messengers winds, his ministers a flaming fire" [Psa 104:4], that is, a center of power that is always active and at work. Christ has been appointed as the Head over these hosts, and under him these hosts of God's good angels battle all demonic influences, seek to overcome them, and one day will bring them down.

This activity is not something we may apply only to the spiritual sphere. §5 Nowhere in the visible world can we draw a line to separate the spiritual from the visible. In fact, Scripture repeatedly makes it clear to us that angels—especially the evil, demonic spirits—exercise an influence upon what is visible. It is through the visible that they attempt to seduce us and cause us to fall. Even the sin of pride, which is purely spiritual-satanic in its essence and at first blush not at all a matter of the visible, always clings to money and possessions, honor and power in the visible world. Over against the good angels, who unfailingly perform the ministry of their God, stand the fallen angels, who forsook serving their God and now have no other goal except to break his dominion, even though they still retain the powers and gifts God endowed them with at creation for the sake of their ministry to him. This means that they have retained the ability to contact souls, to entice them, to seduce them, to sway and influence our spirit, and further, to exercise influence upon the sensible and material. This may have been more apparent in those who were demon-possessed than it is to us today, but the "bondage to decay" to which the apostle refers [Rom 8:21] does continue, and every abuse in life that cannot be reconciled with God's love and holiness must likewise be explained from these demonic influences. A veil hangs over our life, and behind that impenetrable veil a struggle of spirits is taking place that escapes us entirely, and of which we can only observe its effect in our lives.

All superstition grew out of that mysterious background to life. People felt that a mysterious power was at work in our lives, and they felt the need to oppose that mysterious power. But instead of seeking help from God and from his good spirits against this pressing power, they tried to solve things for themselves and to exorcize evil through magic and witchcraft. This practice was, in fact, tantamount to serving and worshiping the demonic spirits themselves. People feared the power of these spirits, and so they sought to make them amenable. In certain groups this really did become public worship of the Evil One, of Ahriman,[1] or of something else. But regardless of their particular manifestation, this superstition and these devilish arts attempted to exorcize these demonic influences with the aid of the demonic. As a result, the spirit of the nations fell increasingly into the clutches of demonism. This yielded fear, not the liberation of the spirit. People sensed that a net had been cast over us, but they did not know how to cast it off. They felt as if a demonized nature now surrounded them.

This was why Moses spoke the following words: "These nations, which you are about to dispossess, listen to fortune-tellers and to diviners. But as for you, the LORD your God has not allowed you to do this. ... The LORD your God will raise up for you a prophet like me from among you, from your brothers—it is to him you shall listen" [Deut 18:14-15]. An initial break in the power of demons was thus already effected in Israel alone among all other nations. When the promised Prophet finally appeared and the voice declared at his baptism in the Jordan River that "this is my beloved Son, listen to him," the battle between Christ and Satan began immediately thereafter in the wilderness. It was on the cross that Satan's head was crushed; and when the Holy Spirit was poured out, this new power went out into the world through the church of the living God, in order to create an atmosphere in which the human spirit would be liberated and in which the freedom of the children of God would begin to unfold. For the first time, the human spirit's free development began to manifest itself, all superstition began to be driven back, and people managed—not through magic, but through investigation, through study by the sweat of their brow [see Gen 3:19]—to prepare the bread of knowledge and, in this way, to recapture his power over the power of nature.

---

1. Ahriman, also called Avestan Angra Mainyu ("Destructive Spirit"), is the evil spirit in the dualistic doctrine of Zoroastrianism. His essential nature is expressed in his principal title—Druj, "the Lie," which comes to expression as greed, wrath, and envy.

II.11

CHRIST AND SATAN

And he said to them, "I saw Satan fall like lightning from heaven."

LUKE 10:18

As a rule, it can be said, particularly of those who refuse to believe in the existence of Satan and his demons, that they are the ones who have fallen into his clutches. We see a paradox here in that Christ leaves no note unplayed in order to reveal his name and through this revelation to save, while Satan constantly exerts himself to stay hidden and to corrupt you through the mysterious influences that he can exercise upon you. Here light and darkness stand opposed to each other. Christ is that light whose rays shine further and further; Satan is the darkness that retreats ever more into the dark and shadowy places and that loses itself and this earth in the murky night. §1

To refuse to believe that Satan and his works exist is such a great danger because this very conviction presents him with the best opportunity to conquer your heart. It is undoubtedly a step in the wrong direction and a sign that faith is weakening when even the church of Christ and its preaching increasingly ignore the demonic powers. That this is happening, however, can easily be demonstrated. With the Lord's Prayer, everyone still prays: "Deliver us from the Evil One"; yet in their free prayers, people hardly ever appeal to God to protect us with his shield from Satan's poisonous darts.

Therefore, if the kingship of Christ is to regain its glory also in our eyes, it is imperative to state very clearly that Jesus himself saw the struggles of his life as one great battle against Satan, and that Jesus' view of himself should be determinative for us. To us, things must appear as they did to him, since that is the way they really are. Of ourselves, we know nothing that offers us certainty concerning the spirit world. But he who came down to us from heaven, from the spirit world, has the right to speak to us. What came to us from his lips was revelation, and everyone who confesses that Christ is the way, the truth, and the life must hold on to that revelation. Of course, people's beliefs about the existence of this spirit world have been and continue to be mixed with superstition, and this is something we constantly have to fight against. All the same, it is only short-sightedness and superficiality if you claim that belief in the existence of a demonic world is per se the product of one's imagination or a superstition. Throughout the ages, it was always those who were most spiritually inclined who also felt most poignantly that they were caught up in a great struggle for life with that demonic world.

The clear details given to us in revelation allow us to state the following: (1) A world of spirits exists beyond our human race. (2) These spirits form armies of angels and demons. (3) The demon armies are spiritually-organically under the dominion of Satan. (4) Angels and demons both received powers, gifts, and talents from their creator. (5) They were called to put these powers, gifts, and talents to use in the service of their God— not only to praise him, but also to be instruments of his kingdom administration. (6) Because of these spirits, numerous influences go forth upon the earth—and this not only upon spiritual life but upon the physical, visible, and material as well. (7) After the fall, the demons abused the powers and functions they had been given in order to bring the earth, and especially our human race, down to perdition. (8) Until Jesus appeared on earth, these demonic influences established Satan's dominion over all peoples and nations, with the one exception of Israel, so that he became the ruler of this world. (9) At that point in time, Christ came to destroy the Devil's works so as to become not the ruler of this world, but rather its Head and King. (10) The temptation in the wilderness, as well as the many demons cast out [by Jesus], are to be explained against this background. (11) The power of the ruler of this world was therefore essentially broken nineteen centuries ago, leading Jesus to proclaim: "I saw Satan fall like lightning from heaven" [Luke 10:18]. (12) The outpouring of the

Holy Spirit after Jesus' ascension meant that a holy spiritual atmosphere descended upon this world so as to drive back unceasingly the demonic atmosphere that weighed so heavily on the lives of the nations.

Scripture further testifies to us that Satan has been bound since that time. At the end of time, he will be unbound once more and released in the fullness of his demonic power [see Rev 20:7]. This important prophecy, however, establishes for us that at the present time Satan does not have his full power at his disposal. Not only does this mean that Satan never could or can do anything except with God's permission, but it also means more particularly that Christ's kingship will break down Satan's kingdom more and more, and that the work of his power is restrained by the spiritual atmosphere that rules in the church of the living God through the Holy Spirit and radiates from it into the world. By this, we do not mean to say that the power of Satan has already been destroyed and that it has already been doomed to complete impotence. The Lord's Prayer teaches us that the struggle undertaken by the Evil One to bring us down to perdition continues, and the apostle emphatically teaches us that, behind the works of flesh and blood, we must see the frightening battle in the heavenly spheres with the "spiritual forces of evil" [Eph 6:12]. After Jesus came down to earth, however, and after the Holy Spirit was poured out, a great change was effected; and thus we can identify two realms that are very clearly distinguishable: one is that of the unbelieving nations, where Satan's power continues to work as it did before. Alongside and over against it, there is the other realm covered by holy baptism, where all power is held not by the spirit of Satan but by the Holy Spirit.

This is portrayed in baptism itself. Baptism finds its origin in the ancient notion according to which, just as water washes impurity away from the body, clothing, and household goods, so purification came about on a religious level through sprinkling or immersion. Nearly all nations therefore have such purifications in their religious rites. Israel was well aware that its land and inheritance were set apart, sanctified, and purified compared to the land and inheritance of the Gentiles. When Gentiles were included into the state of Israel, they had to undergo proselyte baptism. This signified that before they became a part of Israel's nation state, they were figuratively cleansed from the contamination that clung to them because of their pagan origins. The symbolic meaning of proselyte baptism was all the more significant because, on the one hand, those being baptized were required to break off every bond and relationship with their home

§ 2

191

and family, but also in part because Israel bore the stain of sin both internally in the soul and externally in the body. The law of Moses draws a radical distinction between clean and unclean. Animals, the sick, corpses, and carrion could all render people unholy and unclean. Thus the Mosaic law prescribed an endless list of washings, purifications, and sprinklings, in order to portray that demonic influence corrodes not only the soul and the invisible, but also the body and the visible.

The preceding helps us to understand why the baptism of John, as well as the baptism of Jesus and his apostles, rattled Israel's national pride. This new baptism placed Israel among that which was unclean and unholy. It also prophesied of a new coming kingdom—that is, the kingdom of heaven—from which both Jews and Gentiles alike were excluded by nature, so that it was only through this new baptism that they could attain this high degree of purification needed to enter the holy terrain of the spiritual kingdom. For this reason, in the time of the early Christian church, holy baptism was also accompanied by so-called exorcisms. Baptizands first had to renounce Satan and to free themselves from his service and influence. If the baptizand was a child, this promise was made on his or her behalf by the godparents. There was nothing wrong with this practice as such, and in fact it had a rich meaning because it vividly displayed the meaning of baptism. This practice was out of place, however, in the second-generation church when children born to Christian parents were presented for baptism. Such children were not on the same level as the children of Jews and Gentiles. Born to parents who were already Christians, they were pure and holy. They were born not in demonic territory, but in the territory where the Holy Spirit rules. As a result, the custom of exorcism made no sense for them. This explains why our Reformed churches did not adopt this practice of exorcism.

Not enough consideration has been given to the question whether this ancient practice still ought to be maintained today when pagan, Jewish, and Muslim converts are baptized. These converts do not come from the holy courtyard but from beyond, and they enter the holy courtyard only through baptism. They are still literally "delivered from the domain of darkness and transferred to the kingdom of his beloved Son" [see Col 1:13]. A solemn understanding of the fundamental difference between that which is holy and which is unholy, therefore, suggests to us that in the case of the baptism of converts, whose circumstances are exactly the same as those of the earliest baptizands in the days of the apostles, we should retain some element of the renunciation of the Devil. In early baptism, the difference between the baptism of John and Christian baptism consisted in that the latter was done with the Holy Spirit.

Two things follow from the above. In the first place, children born of Christian parents are not transferred for the first time onto holy terrain but already come from it, so that there is no need for exorcism. Second, those who have been born on unholy terrain, and who through baptism first pass over to holy terrain, must break with the ruler of this world and honor Christ as King in his place. The entire doctrine of the covenant of grace rests on this distinction—where it is always necessary to understand the work of the Holy Spirit in the widest possible sense. Those who think only of the Holy Spirit's personal work in regenerating the soul overlook how his light radiates from the center point in our spirit over our entire life and how he creates in that life an entirely different atmosphere of human existence. If it is already true in part that Satan created such a demonic atmosphere in the life of pagan nations through his influencing souls, how much the more is this true for the Holy Spirit, who penetrates all of human life with divine omnipotence once he has chosen within the church a center point from which his work can radiate.

This does not mean in any way, however, that the line of demarcation §3 between the consecrated terrain of the Holy Spirit and the unholy terrain of the ruler of this world was unambiguously and sharply drawn from the very beginning and strictly maintained from that point in time onward. Where the church of Christ appeared in a flourishing pagan city like Corinth, initially of course, it represented nothing more than a tiny oasis in the moral wilderness. Those few Christians did not govern the life of the city. The life of the city first remained pagan, and at that time there was the real danger that the demonic influences would instead work their way from their pagan center into Jesus' church. This explains Paul's sharp and serious exhortations in his two letters to this church. At first only a few, then more and more people asked to be baptized; and in the end the entire population (with some exceptions) joined the Christian church, so that that church was even able to encompass public life.

In Central and Northern Europe, this process went even more slowly when the Christianization of entire tribes and whole nations took the place of the conversion of individuals. With such mass conversions, the Christian life could at first not help but be much more than an outward appearance, while the former pagan way of life, with its pernicious demonic influences, continued to survive, albeit now under a Christian guise. The continuation of the pagan life of former days was evident not only in persisting pagan customs and in lower moral standards, but also in the tendency to perpetuate the rule of demons through superstition. At times this took a coarse and flagrant form, and a kind of satanic worship was initiated. Asian influences in particular had a revolting effect, but the traditions of European nations similarly fostered attempts to search for demonic powers, to conciliate them, to enter their service, and at times even to worship them in shameful orgies.[1] This tradition manifested itself in all kinds of superstition, and it is most frighteningly remembered in the so-called witch trials.

The church, however—and through its urging, the government as well—was poignantly aware of the serious danger threatening Christianity from the side of these demonic influences. Nowadays people often assume that superstition was the result of nothing more than ignorance and false delusions; indeed, people can reach no other conclusion when they themselves refuse to believe that unholy spiritual powers do exist and operate. This standpoint was never taken by the Christian church, however. From the gospel, and from its Lord and Master, it knew that these demonic influences really do exist. The church does not doubt that such widespread, unholy phenomena hide an attempt on the part of Satan to disrupt the kingdom of Christ, to maintain his own influence, and to frustrate the advancement and expansion of the Holy Spirit's holy terrain. The mistake made at that time by church and government was not that they knew and felt that they faced an unholy, demonic power, but that they attacked it with sword and stake instead of on the spiritual level alone. The Christian church's fight against this demonic power for that reason forms a somber and dark page in its history. Demons were not cast out, as in the days of the apostles, through intense spiritual supremacy; instead, something that could be undermined and defeated only spiritually was persecuted by means of sword and fire. The liturgical formulary of our Lord's Supper showed the better way. In this formulary, demonic evil is attacked in its main artery, and it is acknowledged that traces of this evil can be found even in the church of Christ. Nevertheless, it resists this evil by church discipline and by suspension from the sacrament of the Lord's Supper.

---

1. For more on Kuyper's problematic judgments based on racial and ethnic stereotypes, see the volume editors' introduction to *CG*, as well as *CG* 1.12.10n4 and 1.41.1n3.

This spiritual combat worked so well that there is no other circle where superstition has been rooted out so effectively as in the circles of Calvinism. We do not mean to suggest that the government immediately stopped all violent repression, but the main movement of resistance did come from the churches and was purely spiritual in nature.

The remnant of demonic power was so dangerous because people §4 thought they could break it with the power of magic. This meant that, in the end, they sought in Satan the means to counter his own deadly work. This is superstition: it is the conviction that mysterious means are available in order to break the evil effects of demonic influence, be that in the temptation to sin, or where life is disturbed by illness or other malady in a person or animal, or by frightening apparitions. People sought a way out by using an amulet, talisman, spell, or incantation. Satan produced evil with magic; superstition attempts to outdo him with an even greater show of magic. People fought the demonic with demonic means, and so they actually reinforced the dominion of the demonic over human hearts. This may have passed under a different guise when the magical, saving power was attributed to a relic or some other sign derived from the Christian religion. However, because people did not try to remove demonic evil spiritually through the Holy Spirit but magically through some external, mysterious power, in essence the resistance they offered was no different from the original purpose of that magic.

It took centuries for superstition to pass out of public life in Christian countries. In pagan and Muslim nations, there are still numerous mysterious influences of demonic origin at work that are no longer found among us; and in these unbaptized nations, the superstition of renouncing demonic influences through magic continues unhindered. All the same, it would be a mistake to suppose that all superstition has been fully eradicated from Christian countries. Gambling, which is on the rise, promotes belief in the mysterious effect of fortune on our lives. In every big city we find card readers and fortunetellers, and they are consulted even by those in the highest classes of society. Throughout Europe, superstitious traditions continue regarding the number of people with whom one may sit at table or regarding the departure date for a ship; and in elite circles where the outpouring of the Holy Spirit is no longer experienced anymore, people abandon themselves to spiritism and clairvoyance, as if the light of these phenomena is greater than that of the gospel. We do not deny that these phenomena have an element of truth or that they deserve attention.

Evil enters when people push the gospel of Christ aside, and when they seek in these phenomena a higher revelation than what has been given to us in Christ. It should not be forgotten that Scripture teaches that Satan, too, will perform signs and wonders, and that the Christian conscience is therefore bound to test the spirits also in this respect [see 1 John 4:1].

Nothing can save us effectively and permanently from the dominion of these demonic and superstitious powers except the more powerful influence that goes forth from the Holy Spirit over private and public life. Seated at the right hand of God as our King, Christ poured out the Holy Spirit into our lives. In the church, whose Head he is, a spiritual power has thus been established, and this power's work and influence always serve as the instruments of his rule. Those influences of the Holy Spirit have extended beyond the limited circle of the living church. They have influenced national life, public opinion, law, morals, and traditions. These influences emanating from the Holy Spirit have thrown up a dam to stem the demonic tides. Due to Christ's continuing work, we are through his Holy Spirit gradually being freed from the demonic powers in public life. We no longer cling to the superstitious notion that we can fight the results of the curse with magic. Our spirit has been freed, and this liberated spirit has sensed within itself the enlarged capacity to penetrate the mysteries of nature through research, analysis, and ingenuity, such that we will be in a position to subject the mysterious powers of nature to us in the way that God had ordained.

Those who worship Christ as nothing more than the Savior of the souls of the elect fail to understand this. However, what we described above becomes like an epic story of Christ, the Lion from the tribe of Judah, for those who understand that all power—both spiritual and material—in heaven and on earth has been given to Christ. They understand that his divine battle was and is and will remain to the end the fundamental battle to cause Satan to fall like lightning from heaven, to wrest this world that belongs to God from Satan's power, and to cause the holy rule God exercises over this world, to Satan's dismay, to reach its completion. The dethronement of the ruler of this world, and the glorious unfolding of Jesus' kingship over the world, are what encompass and drive sacred history.

THE WISDOM OF THE WORLD

Has not God made foolish the wisdom of the world?

1 CORINTHIANS 1:20

By now we have gained a coherent overview. Spirit governs matter. Of all creatures on earth, the human being was the strongest spirit. At creation, therefore, God determined for humanity to be the king of the earth and to have dominion over all of nature. This was disrupted by Satan. Since he was an even more powerful spirit, he was able to exercise influence over humanity's spirit; he caused humanity to fall; and he intruded into humanity's entire life, as well as the life of all that lives on earth. Humanity thereby lost its kingship, and Satan set himself in its place. He pushed humanity from the throne of honor and sat on it himself. This is why Jesus even called him the ruler of this world. First it was prophesied against this ruler of this world that the seed of the woman would crush his head; then the nation of Israel was established, which was like a safe haven from this demonic power; and, finally, Christ himself appeared. He was the Son of God and the Son of Man; as man, he mobilized himself in the battle against Satan in order to remove him as ruler of this world and to dethrone him, and to regain as humanity's Head the kingship over this world that had been lost in paradise. This battle between the King whom God had anointed and the ruler of this world began with the temptation

§ 1

in the wilderness, passed through Gethsemane and Golgotha, and was settled in the resurrection of the Prince of life.

While Jesus was on earth, the demonic world was in great uproar. Many
people in the land were possessed by demons. The most hellish ideas took
hold of Judas, of Israel's high priest, and of the Roman governor. But with
his royal, spiritual superiority, Jesus took on the power of Satan and his
demons. He cast the demons out and gave to his disciples the power to cast
them out—not to cast demons out mediately, but immediately through
the direct power of his spirit.

This was not all, however. Both in the curse and in the misery that the
curse brought upon nature and humanity, there lay hidden the demonic power of the ruler of this world, such that Jesus directed his miracle
power also to the material sphere. He not only cast out demons but also
healed the sick, and he even demonstrated his spirit's superiority over nature. This, too, he did directly and immediately. On the Sea of Gennesaret,
he calmed the elements in a storm with nothing but his powerful word.
Finally, Jesus attacked death itself, and he did so most powerfully when
he called forth Lazarus from the grave. He called the daughter of Jairus
back to life from her deathbed, and the young man from Nain as he lay on
the funeral bier. Lazarus, however, was already in the grave. Jesus gave
his disciples this power of the immediate operation of the spirit, and in
the first Christian century miracles continued throughout the time of the
apostles. These things were only the beginning, and the beginning was
a prophecy of what awaits us at the end of the age. One day Christ will
return, and on that day the power of Satan will be completely destroyed;
paradise—and more!—will be restored, and the great wonder of the world
will come when this earth has become a new earth, to flourish forever under a new heaven before the face of God.

An interval of many centuries, however, separates the beginning and
the end. During the interval, Satan may in principle already be defeated,
but especially among the pagan nations his power continues to stir. This
was why Jesus ascended to heaven and received royal dominion at God's
right hand, while on earth he is forming a new humanity as his body that
lives from him at its Head. This congregation of the living God receives
the outpouring of the Holy Spirit, such that it lives from the Spirit and,
at the same time, spreads around itself an atmosphere of elevated and
holier human life. It is the city set on a hill that not only enjoys the light
itself, but also shines that light to the outside. The atmosphere of the Holy

Spirit pushes back the atmosphere of Satan's spirit. A Christian life in politics, society, science, and art developed particularly in Europe. Magic and witchcraft disappeared from the Christian circle, and the human spirit was freed from them. Humanity's spirit, now liberated, began by the sweat of its brow also to eat from the bread of knowledge, and through science to win back the dominion over nature that we now enjoy.

But instead of honoring Christ for that power regained over nature, the natural sciences began increasingly to set themselves up against our King as if we owed this supremacy to our own strength. We have to admit, unfortunately, that the Christian world also bears guilt in this. It became narrow-mindedly attached to the direct spiritual power at work in miracles; and it closed its eyes to the development of another spiritual power over nature that, through a process lasting more than two thousand years, came to humanity through ingenuity, the application of talent, and serious study. It refused to believe that the spirits could be freed; it was suspicious of experimental research, and continued to want to grasp with a special dispensation of miracle power what can be acquired only by the sweat of one's brow [see Gen 3:19]. It understood the reference to "sweat of the brow" as pertaining to agriculture alone, without realizing that it actually held for the application and efforts of all human power exerted through body and spirit. The result was that especially unbelievers applied themselves to the arena neglected by Christianity, which now began to turn in hostility against the natural sciences. This was the cause for the deep rift currently separating science and faith. Christ's church then withdrew itself in its powerlessness. The church no longer possessed the power of miracles and now surrendered to unbelievers the power of knowledge, while conversely scholars broke with the faith and set up their science as a strength of the people over against the kingship of Christ.

Gradually, however, this will change. Spiritual Israel emerges from its tents. It is beginning to see that it erred. It is beginning to break with its earlier narrow-mindedness. No longer reluctantly, but with thanksgiving it now accepts the growth in the power regained over nature. People sense at least something of the fact that Christ our King is active in reestablishing humanity's kingship over the earth. People begin to see the guilt of the past, and a new light begins to dawn. Christians begin to reach for the power of science. They are starting to feel that Christ's power is also at work in science and are ready to honor Christ as our King in it as well.

§ 2

This leads to a new danger. Once they have reconciled themselves with science, Christians in many circles swing over to the other extreme and imagine that they also have to adopt the theories of the natural sciences. Some have in fact already slipped from the mystery of the creation into the hypothesis of evolution. Of course, this forms a part of a period of transition whose only victims are among those who are spiritually superficial. True believers will not allow themselves to fall into this snare, and they draw a clear line of demarcation between the results science derives from study and the theories that are no more than the chimera of the spirit of scientists who have lost their way.

This brings us to the second point we noted earlier. In addition to the power gained over nature, it was especially the gradual increase of our knowledge that stimulated humanity's feeling of superiority, so that it exalted itself in pride above the gospel's humble meaning. Think back to the argument we offered for explaining the receding of the stream of religious life not only by our power over nature, but also by the increase of our knowledge and by the way in which science extended itself over nearly all fields of knowledge. Consequently, we must ask ourselves whether Christianity is in principle opposed to this lofty flight of the expansion of science and regards it with hostility, or whether this increase is a blessing from Christ even if scientists so often attempt to wrest it from Christ and even play it off against his kingship.

The first impression one gets is that Christianity does indeed attack science and does seek to banish it. Especially the apostle Paul has much to say about the foolishness of the wisdom of the world. "Has not God made foolish the wisdom of the world?" [1 Cor 1:20]. With these words he tears "philosophy" down from its pedestal. Those who are noble and wise in the eyes of the world do not strengthen the congregation; it is formed by simple, humble folks who are nothing in the eyes of the world. The apostle exposes the "debaters of this age" [see 1 Cor 1:20]. "For since, in the wisdom of God, the world did not know God through wisdom, it pleased God through the folly of what we preach to save those who believe" [1 Cor 1:21]. Greeks seek wisdom, and Christ is "a stumbling block to Jews and folly to Gentiles" [1 Cor 1:23]. It was to shame the wise that God chose what is foolish in the world [see 1 Cor 1:27]. God calls us not to be drawn away by philosophy, the deliberations of men, and the elementary principles of the world [see Col 2:8; Gal 4:9]. Furthermore, did not Christ himself praise and thank God that it pleased him to have "hidden these things from the wise and understanding and revealed them to little children" [Matt 11:25]? Jesus was so emphatic that he even added: "Yes, Father, for such was your gracious will" [Matt 11:26].

Scripture's attack on the wisdom of the world is so fierce and constant that it easily explains why those who adopted these words without further reflection and took such expressions entirely outside of their context came to hate all human science and to oppose all higher human knowledge. Sound preaching alone could avert this evil, but sound preaching was the very thing that could scarcely be found. Theology withdrew to its own arena, lost the connection with the other disciplines, and presented itself as a grand-mistress whose task it was to impede the unwelcome progress that the other sciences were making. All too often it forgot that our beautiful Confession says that we know God from two books: the book of Scripture, as well as the book of nature in which the majesty of the Lord of lords is revealed to us in golden letters.[1] Theology increasingly sought to rule by way of a coercion exercised by the church, supported by coercion from the state. This was why it became impoverished and emaciated, turned to stone, and increasingly found itself in an uneasy position with respect to the natural sciences, which were beginning to flourish mightily.

This view of things was entirely incorrect, however. Not only is it not in line with Scripture, but it is altogether in conflict with Scripture. Nowhere does Scripture suggest that all of our knowledge about nature and the world should be derived from Scripture. It posits that there are things that we can only come to know from nature, from the world, and from the course of the world; and that there are other things, about which nature tells us nothing, that can be known only from revelation. Rather than pulling down the knowledge of nature, Scripture instead expresses that God's great power and divinity can from the very outset be understood and comprehended from creation. It is the height of folly if you imagine that, with Scripture in front of you, you should be able to know

§ 3

---

1. See Belgic Confession, Article 2 (RC 2:425–26): "We know Him by two means: First, by the creation, preservation, and government of the universe; which is before our eyes as a most elegant book, wherein all creatures, great and small, are as so many characters leading us to 'see clearly the invisible things of God, even his everlasting power and divinity,' as the apostle Paul says (Rom 1:20). All which things are sufficient to convince men and leave them without excuse. Second, He makes Himself more clearly and fully known to us by His holy and divine Word, that is to say, as far as is necessary for us to know in this life, to His glory and our salvation."

from Scripture about nature, the life of the world, and its history without ever actually investigating nature or the life and composition of the world. You can only know the body by studying the body. You only gain knowledge of the earth's crust by digging in it. The plant world must be known from the plant world, the animal world from the animals; and similarly the history of the human world must be known from the past. Scripture does lead the way, of course; but aside from it we have, as sources for our knowledge, the entire kingdom of nature, the entire course of history, and the entire course of the development of capacities in human life. God is honored not by those who close the second book of nature to ponder Scripture alone, but by those who in quiet obedience zealously study the two books of Scripture and nature. Nature and human life in this world supply us with a storehouse of givens that God himself lays bare for us, and it would be a sin of omission to delight in Scripture while closing the other book of nature and human life and pushing it aside. All too many have done this, however, and the natural result is that society has seen the formation of two separate streams: the one insists, "I have enough in Scripture," and pays no attention to the book of nature; the other is just as one-sided, because it pushes Scripture aside and imagines that it can derive all knowledge from the book of nature and life alone.

That same contrast existed in the days of the apostles. In the Greco-Roman world, people knew nothing of Scripture and only looked to the science of their day for a way out; while conversely the Old Testament was the only source for the people of Israel whose involvement in science, in the strict sense of the term, was quite limited. The Jews did have many schools for scholars, but these schools were for the scribes who devoted themselves to the interpretation of the books of the Old Testament and to a somewhat scholastic series of stipulations that were based on those interpretations. As a result, as it is today, Scripture (that is, the Old Testament) stood alone on the one side, while philosophy, science, and the wisdom of the Greeks stood on the other. Since the gospel was incompatible with both the rabbis' interpretation of the Old Testament as well as the wisdom of the Greeks, the apostle turned against them both and wrote that the gospel can be nothing other than a stumbling block for Jews and folly to the Greeks.

It was a stumbling block to the Jews because it cut down their national pride. After all, they understood the Old Testament to mean that Israel's dispensation was permanent and lasting rather than prophetic-symbolic, and consequently they failed to see that it would pass away and terminate in Christ. They did think that a Messiah would come, but conceived of him as an earthly king who would sit on David's throne in Jerusalem. It was a hindrance and a stumbling-block to them when Jesus' coming and the apostles' preaching overturned the entire edifice constructed by their national pride, recognizing in Israel no more than a nation that was to prepare the way of salvation and calling it to enter the kingdom of heaven together with all the other nations.

Similarly, the gospel of Christ could only be folly to the well-educated Greeks. They thought that through their rational powers they could construct a scheme to explain the origin and existence of all things, and they were hurt and insulted when the apostle of Christ similarly toppled the edifice they had constructed and brought divine revelation to shine its light in the darkness of paganism. The wise and educated Greeks looked down with contempt on the idolatrous worship that the peasants and lower social classes practiced in the cities and villages of Greece. As civilized, educated, and developed people, they felt themselves to be above such idolatrous nonsense and referred to it as folly. When Christianity came as a new religion, they saw in it nothing more than the despicable religions that their countrymen practiced. That was why they labeled the gospel, too, as folly. When Paul hears of this, he does not shrink back from the label, but he embraces it and then turns it back on the wise men of those days. Not the gospel, but your wisdom is folly. You have shut yourselves off from the gospel because of what you think is wisdom. But the only true and real wisdom is found in that gospel, since it does not come from humanity's wisdom but from God's wisdom; this was why it pleased God to close the hearts of the Jewish scribes and the Greek sages to the gospel, and to call them to the folly of the world—to what the world sees as weak, ignoble, and insignificant.

But is the wisdom of the world, which Christ and the apostles rejected and even labeled as "folly," the same thing as the science of nature, of history, and of the wonderful system of human life? This is, of course, the decisive question for the issue under consideration. That question, however, must be answered with a resounding "no."

In order to understand this, you need only to consider the distinction between what all these sciences offer as the results of strict research and the system that they construct on their own and make to rest upon conjecture and presuppositions. Those results of experimental research are established and must be accepted by all, since it can be demonstrated to us that things are and work this way and not in another way. No one is able to deny that a lightning rod can draw and divert lightning to save a house; and those who still refuse to install a lightning rod on the peak of their roof do so not because they refuse to accept this fact, but because they suppose wrongly that people are not permitted to protect themselves from lightning strikes. Religious timidity neither adds anything to nor detracts anything from the recognition of the truth of observed facts. We are so disinclined to explain away such well-founded facts that we do not hesitate to use trains and electric trams, telegraph and telephone, and we are grateful for the help of doctors when they soothe the pains of an illness or accident and heal our wounds.

In the days of Paul, the wise men of Greece may not have advanced all that far in the study of nature and history, but they still made significant discoveries in nature and made remarkable progress in their knowledge of the human body and in the treatment of illnesses. In fact, the apostle was so indisposed to rejecting the acquired results that, during the second half of his journey through the pagan world, he was accompanied by the physician Luke. You would be hard pressed to find even a single word in his letters from which you could even remotely deduce that the apostle was opposed to science or, more specifically, the science of nature.

If you do somehow draw this conclusion from his writings, you simply do not understand him. When he commands us on the spiritual level to "test everything; hold fast what is good" [1 Thess 5:21], this fully applies in the present case as well. Not only should the study of nature and history, of the entire system of this world and of human life, not be disapproved, but it should be praised and encouraged. There is only one condition that must be observed without fail, namely, that we maintain only what is good and reject what is evil.

That was and today still is the duty of all Christians when they evaluate whatever presents itself as science. Even in that time, Greek science or wisdom mixed the fruit of two entirely different kinds of labor. First, there were the results derived from strictly regulated research; second, there were the thought systems concerning world and life erroneously constructed upon conjecture. The Greeks offered the latter to the world, however, as their wisdom and their philosophy. Thus, when the apostle turned against the Greeks' overinflated wisdom, he was not saying anything against strict science but rejected only whatever scholars and scientists presented about things concerning which they knew nothing.

II.13

SCIENCE IN CHRISTIAN COUNTRIES

In whom are hidden all the treasures of wisdom and knowledge.

COLOSSIANS 2:3

The difference between the real science of nature and the wisdom of the   § 1
Greeks that the apostle attacks in his letters comes out even in the French
and English languages. In France, the sciences occupied with the study
of nature in the strict sense of the word are referred to as *les sciences ex-
actes*, while in England these disciplines alone are commonly given the
name *sciences*.[1] Of course, in France and England they do not deny that the
historical and spiritual sciences are very valuable, but with the choice of
terms they do indicate that the latter are not to be placed on the same level
with the strictly natural sciences. The particular value of the results of
scientific study is that here people repeatedly arrive at results that, once
discovered, are established for all time and for all people and can no longer be doubted by anyone.

---

1. Kuyper refers here to what are often identified today as natural or "hard" sciences,
   in distinction from social, or what Kuyper otherwise calls "spiritual" sciences.

This should not be exaggerated, since explanations were often given in the natural sciences that people thought to be based immediately on the facts; thus they were widely accepted as true, although afterward it became clear that they depended on hasty observation or faulty generalizations. Many are convinced, for example, that the new electron theory is in the process of dislodging the very foundations of statics; and in the field of medicine in particular, time and again we see a procedure in high demand for a quarter century only to be widely abandoned as incorrect thereafter. We must for that reason establish a certain boundary here as well. All the same, if that one condition is observed, we should gratefully recognize that careful and ingenious observation in the natural sciences, understood most broadly, has uncovered certain facts, then discovered an operation of powers behind these facts, and finally found in this operation of powers a constancy that placed us on firm ground and that enormously increased the power over nature at our disposal.

These exact sciences, of course, possess a great degree of certainty. The field of investigation for these sciences is limited to the sphere of the finite; it does not occupy itself with the spiritual or with anything that surpasses the bounds of the finite. The exact sciences have hardly any place for the subjective, which plays a considerable role in the historical sciences. For that reason, those who are spiritually dead are left with the impression that the exact sciences are much more valuable than the sciences that occupy themselves with the sphere of faith. Many difficulties that prevent a unity of conviction in the spiritual field are absent from the exact sciences. If an observation is precise and the resulting conclusion is formulated accurately, everyone immediately agrees with the conclusion. There is no room for doubt, and everyone applies the result after it has been found and benefits from it. In the field of the natural sciences, careful observation and logically deduced consequences, whose accuracy can be verified by way of test cases, together provide us with a firmness and certainty in this area that falls entirely within the context of our finite thought. It is decisive for all people in the matter under investigation.

In saying this, we do not mean that faith is less certain. Nevertheless, in the spiritual field, and particularly when it comes to faith, the certainty and firmness are of an entirely different kind. In the spiritual, certainty depends on an inner disposition in the investigator, which no one else may have. Those who have such spiritual certainty can stand unmoved in that certainty themselves, but they cannot prove it to anyone with the exception of those who have the same disposition in their inner life. Therefore, on the one side we have the complete and universally demonstrable exact sciences that fall within the bounds of our finite thinking; on the other side are the spiritual disciplines whose results can only be grasped by those who have the necessary spiritual organ. Just like a blind woman cannot be the judge of color, or a deaf man the judge of acoustics, so someone who lacks that spiritual organ cannot evaluate or adopt the results of spiritual study. This circumstance has led the exact sciences to present themselves increasingly as science in the strictest sense of the word, and setting themselves off over against faith as the only reliable means for arriving at the truth.

No complaint would be raised against this circumstance if science had limited itself strictly to the visible and focused on the truth of visible things alone. However, it failed to meet these conditions. Researchers in the exact sciences constantly allowed themselves to wander into an arena that was not theirs, and they tried to construct all kinds of systems for which they simply lacked the support. Conversely, those engaged in the historical and spiritual-psychological sciences wrongly claimed for their science the same level of certainty as the natural sciences have. In doing so, this group mixed two very distinct fields and included them under the one name of science, proudly claiming that, even in regard to spiritual matters, its science could legitimately set itself over against faith, able to identify and determine what is true or false just as the exact sciences could.

Admittedly, this danger was less pronounced among top-notch scholars. They maintained a certain amount of modesty throughout; but among second- and third-rate scholars, and especially among those who did no research themselves but depended on the results of others, the boasting about science soon emerged from every side. This idolizing of so-called science became an annoying habit especially among unbelieving teachers and second-rate members of the press, and it is from these corners in particular that we see the glorification of science at the cost of faith. Conversely, it went without saying that everyone whose inner disposition and subjective existence was granted a higher capacity through the organ of faith thankfully and unhesitatingly accepted the irrefutable results of the exact sciences as new discoveries, but were critical of anything that presented itself in the spiritual field as a leading theory comprehending all spirits under the lofty but purloined title of "science."

§ 2   This was the way things were when the Christian religion arose in the pagan world of Greece and Rome. The apostles never discounted, not even with a single word, the results that the exact sciences had produced by that time. In fact, they did not even think of it for a second. No such trace can be found in any of the apostolic writings. What Scripture does address and attack as false science, as erroneous wisdom, as fake philosophy, is the illusion of certainty that unbelieving thinkers of that time imagined they could claim for a system resting on nothing but conjectures, suspicions, and assumptions. The object of the exact sciences is the visible, audible, and tangible world. This is their field of strength, and as long as they limit themselves to that and are based on accurate investigation, they deserve confidence, praise, and gratitude.

The exact sciences know nothing, however, about the origin of things, nothing about the spirit, nothing about the spiritual world beyond our earth, and nothing about the way in which the spirit can exercise its influence upon the body. The whole field of the spiritual—which is much higher, more complicated, and more subtle than the material—escapes the exact sciences and lies outside their field of investigation. The exact sciences can say nothing about a unifying plan in the course and history of this world. Humanity's destination after death and eternity itself lies hidden from them behind an impenetrable veil. Even the moral battle between the holy and unholy, the origin of that battle, the power determining that battle, and its final outcome, escape the exact sciences entirely. They have nothing to say about a divine providence governing all things. And once they arrive at the highest level (that is, religion) and at religion's sacred object of worship, they speak like a blind man would about colors; and if they want to be straightforward and honest, they should just admit their ignorance.

The people who practiced the exact sciences, however, could not bring themselves to this point. They sensed that these spiritual questions were much more important than the problems related to the visible sphere for which they managed to obtain certitude, and for that reason they were unable to confess their ignorance in this higher field. As a result, they appropriated for themselves the right to make lofty claims even in the spiritual domain. With their imagination, by conjecture and supposition, or through improbable mental gymnastics, they then formed a cleverly constructed conception about the spiritual and all kinds of spiritual issues, called it their system, and presented this foundationless, superficial construct as if it were *the* truth, *the* wisdom, *the* science, *the* philosophy. However, the simple fact that one philosopher after the other arose to dismantle the system of his predecessor and to set another system over against it demonstrated the fragility and unreliability of their construction. One school came to stand over against the other. Each school presented its own life- and worldview.

With these false systems they suppressed the true thirst for God in the human heart and drew the human spirit to pride, sensual pleasure, or eternal doubt. The result was that, with all of their puffed up wisdom, the most delicate seeds of the human heart withered, and the soul could not find peace in its endless struggle. When Christianity arose to breathe new life into the seed of the human heart and to supply, out of pure grace, the soul's endlessly wavering existence with the peace that comes from above and surpasses all understanding, the Christian religion could only set itself in sharp and fundamental opposition to all imagined wisdom that leads away from God. It had to uproot it, demonstrate its futility, drive it out of the human spirit, and thereby make way for what Scripture calls the establishment of the Christian consciousness.

From this it should never be concluded that Christianity adopted a hostile attitude toward bona fide science. It only means that Christianity, not wanting to see the way to the human heart obstructed, broke away from and undid what in fact was no science at all, and yet was presenting itself as such under false pretenses. The situation then was just as it is again today. We heartily applaud all that is truly science, but we say, "Shoemaker, keep to your trade!"[2] Any time we come upon systems built on suppositions and assumptions that attempt to explain or discard spiritual questions about which there can be no knowledge without faith, we deny it the label of "science" that it has usurped for itself, and from our side we try to posit over against it the Christian life- and worldview based on what God has revealed to us.

---

2. This rebuke was spoken by Apelles (fl. fourth century BC), an Alexandrian artist, to a shoemaker who, when asked for his opinion on the painting of a shoe, began to criticize other parts of the work: "A cobbler found fault with the shoe-latchet of one of Apelles' paintings, and the artist rectified the fault. The cobbler, thinking himself very wise, next ventured to criticize the legs; but Apelles said, *Ne sutor ultra crepidam* ("Let not the cobbler go beyond his last"). See "Apelles and the Cobbler," in E. Cobham Brewer, *Character Sketches of Romance, Fiction and the Drama*, ed. Marion Harland (New York: Selmar Hess, 1902), 1:56.

§3   You cannot know anything about Australia unless you have been there yourself, or if someone else who has been there tells you about it. The same holds true for the invisible world. We will see what it is like when we get there; and until that point in time we know nothing unless we receive a revelation from that invisible world, or unless someone who has been there comes down to us. Even regarding what goes on in the inner life of the spirit world, we know almost nothing. The apostle was right when he said that only the spirit of man knows what is in man [see 1 Cor 2:11]. Even famous people are such an intriguing mystery to us that people correctly observe that our life is too short to understand even a single person. For that reason, a human being, inasmuch as he is a creature, could know as little about what and who God is as a thrush in a cage hung on the façade of Gladstone's house could grasp, feel, or understand what went on in the head and heart of that great statesman.[3]

The real situation is different, however. Human beings, created in God's image, have been endowed with religious sensitivity and with the capacity to serve their God. In line with this, God does not allow them to wander about in darkness, but shines the light of revelation on them and allows himself to be known by them. In Christ, who was in heaven but came down to us from heaven, this revelation was raised to the highest degree possible in this world of sin; and only by virtue of it do we have the givens that enable us to build our knowledge in the spiritual field about God's greatness, the origin of things, the government of this world, the inner existence of our soul, our calling, our destination, and the future that awaits each one of us.

This was also why the revelation of Christ had barely entered the world before paganism fell wherever the Christian religion penetrated, and why the imagined wisdom that occupied the learned of those days was brought down. The first to embrace this lofty revelation were those who in the eyes of the world were small, simple, weak, and insignificant; but then the higher classes followed as well, and soon the triumph in the frightful and fierce battle with the loftily developed wisdom of the Greeks went to the power of revelation, and in this way to Christianity.

Then, lest this be passed over in silence, at an early stage a tendency crept in that led people to withdraw one-sidedly to the arena of revelation

---

3. William E. Gladstone (1809–98) was a distinguished British statesman and four-time prime minister.

and to undermine the importance of the exact sciences. It is not entirely unnatural that this happened. At that point in time, the exact sciences had not yet conquered their own territory; and everywhere they were mingled with and melded into what presented itself as wisdom, as a system, as the meaning of life. As a result, everything that at the time had the name of science fiercely opposed the Christian religion. By the nature of the case, the study that Christians undertook was first and foremost directed to driving back the attacks from the intellectualism of that age. Furthermore, violent turmoil caused that society suddenly to fall, and the Greco-Roman world that had once been so highly elevated was brought down. The stream of Christian religion flowed especially to the as-yet-uncivilized people of Central and Western Europe, and in this new world everything had to be rebuilt from the ground up. During that first period when the newly converted people groups were regenerated, there was no room at all for thinking about the development of science. Yet that first period had hardly passed before schools began to flourish and scientific study was resumed. Before long, universities were established and scholarship stretched its wings. Then the time came when the exact sciences began to grow new roots.

Similarly, you can see how, in the days of the Reformation, one of the first acts of government under the Christian rule of our Republic was to establish the academy in Leiden.[4] Take the lasting results of scholarship from the pagan academies of Athens and Alexandria, from the Islamic schools of Isfahan and Baghdad,[5] from the Jewish schools of Pumbedita and Tiberias,[6] and even from the great Islamic university in Cairo with its 10,000 students—if you compare them with the university's glorious existence in Christian Europe stretching back to the sixteenth, seventeenth, and eighteenth centuries, you cannot deny that science flourished and developed in the Christian countries more than anywhere else. An institution like the Calvinist university in Amsterdam abundantly demonstrates the importance attached to scientific development particularly in

---

4. Leiden University (*Universiteit Leiden*) was founded in 1575 by William I, Prince of Orange (1533–84).
5. Isfahan is the capital of the Isfahan Province in modern Iran. Baghdad is the capital of modern Iraq. Both are home to educational institutions of international repute.
6. Pumbedita was the name of an ancient city in Babylonia, famous for its Talmudic academy. Tiberias is located in Israel, north of the Sea of Galilee, and is known as one of Judaism's four holy cities.

Calvinist circles.[7] Similarly, anyone up to date with scientific literature from the Roman Catholic side cannot with honesty deny that scholarship flourishes there as well.

§ 4   Proof from history does not suffice, however. Here, too, we must go back to Christ and to Scripture. Someone may ask, for example: What does the plant world have to do with Christ? We can answer by pointing out that Christ is the eternal Word and that all things, including the plant and animal kingdoms, were created through this Word. God's eternal thoughts, which were embodied in all creation (and thus also in the plant and animal kingdoms), came to that embodiment only through the eternal Word. There is no flower or songbird that does not represent something specific in God's thoughts, and what every creature represents has been implanted and created in it through the eternal Word. Scripture does not lock Christ up within the sphere of grace or within the world of humanity; it places all creation—the visible and the invisible, both on the earth and beneath the earth—in direct dependence on Christ.

In the Old Testament, wisdom is already extolled—not as a human invention, but as eternally existing with God. "Ages ago I was set up, at the first, before the beginning of the earth. When there were no depths I was brought forth, when there were no springs abounding with water. Before the mountains had been shaped, before the hills, I was brought forth, before he had made the earth with its fields, or the first of the dust of the world. When he established the heavens, I was there" [Prov 8:23–27].

Nothing is therefore excluded from the Son. Whatever natural kingdom, star, or comet you can think of, even the first principles and very dust of the earth, everything stands in a direct—not indirect—relationship with Christ. There is no power in nature, nor any law governing that power, that does not proceed from the eternal Word. It is for that reason entirely unfitting to say that Christ dwells within the spiritual things, but that the natural sciences fall outside of and have no point of contact with him. In a sense, you should instead say that the more deeply knowledge penetrates into the essence of nature, the more it glorifies the majesty of the eternal Word.

---

7. This reference is to the *Vrije Universiteit Amsterdam* ("Free University"), founded by Kuyper himself in 1880. The ideal undergirding the institution was that its education would be free from the control of both church and state.

This combination is not forced. The apostle himself expresses it as clearly as possible when he says: "In Christ are hidden all the treasures of wisdom and knowledge" [Col 2:3]. It is important to note that he mentions not only wisdom, but also knowledge, and that he does not say that a part of knowledge, but all the treasures of knowledge and wisdom are hidden in Christ. Could it be any other way? He through whom all things were created, who placed within all creatures high and low the thoughts of God that they would express, and who implanted within every creature the powers, laws, and functions that made them what they are—how could he be estranged from anything in nature that is either material or spiritual? How could anything in creation exist or function that he did not bring to mind and effect? He not only knows and fathoms all nature, but he himself has also purposefully implanted in nature that which is in it. And what is the knowledge of someone like Linnaeus compared to the knowledge that Christ has by virtue of creation?[8] All study of nature, as well as psychology, anthropology, ethnology, or anything else, is the radiance of a new glory that is hidden in Christ. For that reason, even though the powerful increase in knowledge gained over the course of the last century has alienated from the faith those who are spiritually insensible owing to pride in their own wisdom, as confessors of Christ we accept all new knowledge—and in particular knowledge concerning nature—with thanksgiving. This is because we see in it the sacred mark of its origin and because we know that it is only a small part of "all the treasures of wisdom and knowledge" that are hidden in Christ [see Col 2:3].

---

8. Carl Linnaeus (1707–78), also known as Carl von Linné, was called "Prince of Botanists" and "Father of Taxonomy." He devised a binomial system of nomenclature, still used today, for identifying more than 12,000 species of animals and plants.

UNIVERSALISM

And this gospel of the kingdom will be proclaimed throughout the whole world as a testimony to all nations, and then the end will come.

MATTHEW 24:14

§ 1   Our time is marked, first of all, by the remarkable power that humanity has gained over nature; second, by the remarkable increase of our knowledge; but, in the third place, also by the all but magical appearance of new means of communication and transportation, through which the entire world, including all countries and all nations, has been taken up into the one great complex of human dominion. This, too, could only contribute to breaking down religious life and the Christian religion, and therefore the recognition of Jesus' kingship, where they had once flourished. We already pointed to this emphatically in [chapter II.6 above]. At this point, we would add that our increasingly rapid transportation has introduced greater mobility to our lives, has disturbed the peace of Sabbath rest, and has caused church attendance to decline. And anyone who visits Islamic or pagan nations is quickly led to compare our Christian religion with these false religions—a comparison that leads to reducing the complete opposition between them to a relative difference, to understanding Christianity and all other religions as one manifestation of a single religious idea differing in degree alone, and in the end (this merely in a restricted circle so far) even to raising those other religions above Christianity.

In the world religion congresses, this came to expression in a humiliating way for Christians.[1] The Buddhist priests did not exaggerate when they remarked that they had found more love for Buddhism in the Christian world than for Christ in Buddhist nations. The Persians were so bold as to insist that their Sufism appealed to modern Europe, while conversely one will be hard pressed to find even a single Persian Christian in Persia. And it can be observed how even baptized Christians often raise Islam above the gospel among our colonial magnates, or among the English authorities in Hindustan, Pakistan, and Egypt. This reversal has of course been a source of grief to those who faithfully confess the kingship of Christ, and once again we seriously need to consider whether the inclusion of the entire world into our human development should be viewed as something lamentable from a Christian perspective. Or should it rather be applauded as a demand arising from the Christian religion itself, such that we should condemn not the thing itself but only its abuse?

This question, too, requires careful examination. Believers are powerless before the religious destruction created by this new state of affairs—unless they have a clear understanding of the relationship in which Scripture places the Christian religion relative to the entire world's inclusion within the sphere of human activity. We observe how the nations' material interests are increasingly occupying the most important place. World power, as it is called, is starting to put pressure on all that belongs to a specifically national life. A cosmopolitan disposition arises, and it leaves no room for true patriotism anymore. A movement is even underway to mitigate the power of historical ethnic languages by means of a single artificial world language. Everything unique to and characteristic of one nation is being dissolved into what is general and common to all nations. The core and kernel that lies hidden in a specific life form is being weakened and lost. Furthermore, throughout the entire world a circle of modern life is being formed, presenting itself in the interest of "civilization" and "humanity" in order to renounce all obedience to any and every religion, but especially to Christianity. In most European countries this movement has already developed rather forcefully under the name of anticlericalism. This anticlericalism is making preparations to drive

---

1. Kuyper may be referring here to the World's Parliament of Religions held in 1893 in Chicago, Illinois, often identified as the beginning of formal global interreligious dialogue.

back Christianity in Italy and Spain, in France and Austria, in Germany, Belgium, and the Netherlands. In the end, this means nothing other than an increasingly decisive and hostile attempt to destroy the kingship of Christ.

§ 2   In its essence, what we observe at the present time is nothing other than the opposition between Israel's God and the idols. Nowhere in Scripture do we find even a hint to suggest that, although Yahweh may indeed have had a higher place than the other gods, the idols too, in spite of their lower rank, were worthy of worship as real gods. Scripture never relativizes the difference between the gods of the Gentiles and the one true God of Israel. Instead, it states the conviction over and over again that there is only one God and that everything that attempts to exalt itself as a god alongside or against Yahweh is to be counted among the idols and to be rejected. We neither dispute nor deny that all religions have something fundamentally in common with each other; but this cannot be explained from idolatry's comparative right [of existence]. It must be explained first of all from the fact that God implanted the *semen religionis* (that is, seed of religion) in our human nature; and in the second place, our entire human race brought a certain religious tradition with it out of paradise. Everything always goes back to the work of God, to what God placed in man by virtue of his creation in the image of God, and to what God revealed to man before and immediately after the fall. Idolatry, by way of contrast, is never characterized any other way than as a lie. It is pseudo-religion, a false religion, and it robs the living God of the honor that is due to him alone. All idolatry is therefore destined to be brought down and eradicated, and all idols must ultimately fall so that the dominion over the spirits comes finally to the King anointed by God and to none other.

The fundamental opposition between God and the idols must therefore necessarily be transferred to the opposition between the Christian religion and the false religions—and in a deeper sense yet, [to the opposition] between Christ as the King anointed by God and the unholy spirits that are succeeding in winning for themselves dominion over the nations. This exposes the demonic character of idolatry. The unholy spirit has nestled itself in these religions; and among all of them the Jewish and Muslim religions alone continue, albeit amid grave errors, to hold to the God of Abraham, Isaac, and Jacob.

At this point, it is irrelevant to ask whether a germ of truth still lies hidden in these pagan religions. Even in the most deplorable felon you may at times still find certain character traits that allure you. This is a result of what God implanted in human nature, and it does not excuse the crime of the felon any more than does the unholy spirit manifested in these idolatries.

Moreover, a distinction must be made between the philosophical ideas that were developed in pagan countries and became largely mixed with idolatrous religion and the idolatrous worship itself as it is controlled by a spirit of its own. Idolatry is in essence people being given up to—understood in a negative sense—as the apostle testifies [see Rom 1:26]. This is why idolatry always ended in doing things that are not fitting, and giving to those things the appearance of holiness. At bottom, therefore, all idolatry is motivated by a satanic impulse. Just as Satan freed himself from the living God and made himself a false ruler of this world, so he also wants false gods to emerge everywhere in order to challenge the power, majesty, and honor of God. And precisely because there is not just one idol, but numerous idols were set up all over, he maintained the power of unity and proceeded with a divide and conquer strategy.

The feature of the Christian religion that people call its universalism results particularly from the above. However, this universalism has been misunderstood by theologians who saw it as no more than the opposite of the Jews' particularism being promoted in the days of the apostles. We can think here especially of Paul's argument against those Jewish Christians who judged that one had to be circumcised and obey the law of Moses in order to become a Christian. With this, they incorporated the Christian religion into Judaism, supposing that Christianity had to enter the world as a Jewish religion. They believed that Judaism had to enter the world in order to incorporate many Gentiles into the Jewish nation, and that, since this religion was Israelite in origin, it was destined to remain Israelite and national-Jewish throughout its entire historical existence. This is a particularism that interprets Christianity as a special Jewish religion. §3

Over against this, Paul argued that Christianity had to break the bonds of a specifically national-Jewish life; that the true Israel is composed not of those born from Abraham, but of those who believe in Christ; and that spiritual Israel was not to join the one Jewish nation, but rather to embrace all the nations of the earth. The Christian religion never was Jewish, even though it arose out of Israel. It was the religion of humanity, it had a general human character, and it was intended to win for Christ our entire human race—all people. And so it was to be, in the fullest sense of the term, the religion of the world, without any restrictions based on nationality. This is the universalism fundamentally opposed to Jewish particularism.

This view was not that of Paul alone, but it came from the very heart of the Old Testament, such that Paul appeals to it constantly. Time and again the old covenant preached that Yahweh is not the national God particularly of Israel, but that he rules all countries and all nations from Zion. His dominion is not limited to Israel's small inheritance, but the entire world is under his dominion. He rules not only specifically over the nation of the Jews, but also generally over all the nations of the earth. He is the King of kings, the Lord of lords, and all nations are his property and subjected to his divine power and dominion.

The basic thrust of the old covenant is and remains: "Shout for joy to God, all the earth; sing the glory of his name. ... All the earth worships you and sings praises to you; they sing praises to your name. ... Who rules by his might forever, whose eyes keep watch on the nations. ... Bless our God, O peoples; let the sound of his praise be heard" (see Psa 66:1–8). And again: "Let your way be known on earth, your saving power among all nations. Let the peoples praise you, O God; let all the peoples praise you! Let the nations be glad and sing for joy, for you judge the peoples with equity and guide the nations upon earth" (see Psa 67:2–4). And elsewhere: "The Lord reigns; let the peoples tremble! The Lord is great in Zion; he is exalted over all the peoples. Make a joyful noise to the Lord, all the earth!" (Psa 99:1–2; 100:1). And as "the kings of the earth set themselves, and the rulers take counsel together, against the Lord and against his Anointed, saying, 'Let us burst their bonds apart and cast away their cords from us.' He who sits in the heavens laughs; the Lord holds them in derision. Then he will speak to them in his wrath, and terrify them in his fury, saying, 'As for me, I have set my King on Zion, my holy hill.'" Likewise the call goes out to the kings of the peoples and nations: "Now therefore, O kings, be wise; be warned, O rulers of the earth. Kiss the Son, lest he be angry, and you perish in the way" (Psa 2). And in order to make it clear that this does not refer to any kind of earthly dominion over all lands by Israel, but to Christ's dominion over all nations and peoples as our King, the Holy Spirit testifies in that same old covenant that *Lo-ammi* ["Not my people"] will become *Ammi* ["my people"; see Hos 1–3]—in other words, God will call peoples that are not his people to be unto him a spiritual people, a spiritual Israel, and this under the temporary rejection of the Israel according to the flesh.

When Christ had come, the first confession made by Simeon in the temple directly after Jesus' birth was that he is a "light for revelation to the Gentiles" [Luke 2:32]. Jesus' own preaching was entirely in line with this. He was not only the Good Shepherd to the sheepfolds of Israel, but he had other sheep who were not of this sheepfold and he had to go seek them as well. Even clearer is what Jesus told his disciples when he was about to be taken up from them: they would be his witnesses "in Jerusalem and in all Judea and Samaria, and to the end of the earth" [Acts 1:8], partly through the words they spoke and partly through their writing and through the effect of their preaching. In the Great Commission, Jesus emphatically declared: "Go therefore and make disciples of all nations, baptizing them in the name of the Father and of the Son and of the Holy Spirit" [Matt 28:19]. Earlier he had already foretold that the "gospel of the kingdom will be proclaimed throughout the whole world as a testimony to all nations, and then the end will come" (Matt 24:14). When he ascended into heaven and was seated at God's right hand, God glorified him "so that at the name of Jesus every knee should bow, in heaven and on earth and under the earth, and every tongue confess that Jesus Christ is Lord, to the glory of God the Father" [Phil 2:10–11]. In the Revelation that came on Patmos, a song of praise is raised by all who have been bought by the blood of the Lamb "from every tribe and language and people and nation" [see Rev 5:9], and the King anointed by God is glorified as the King of all kings and the Lord of all lords.

§ 4

This universalism is much grander than a universalism that merely protests the narrow interpretation according to which Christ would be the Messiah for the Jews alone. This grander universalism includes the great, powerful, and all-determining idea that the entire world, to the very ends of the earth, including all peoples and nations, constitutes one human race; that the entire world must be drawn together into a single life bond; and that God calls the entire human race in his anointed King to fulfill our lofty destiny. In order to understand the far-reaching implications of this universalism, you have to think of the world as the people in Jesus' day did. When we read in Luke 2 that Emperor Augustus issued a decree for the whole world to be registered, the decree pertained to a very small part of Africa, a somewhat larger part of Asia, and not even half of present-day Europe. This was the extent of the Roman emperor's rule, and his empire was understood to be the entire world. There was a vague awareness that certain barbarians lived and migrated outside of the empire's borders, but they did not count. They formed a wilderness surrounding the world empire's borders. There was no awareness of the unity of all human beings, nor did anyone understand the human race as something that encompasses all nations. The world as we know and understand it was still shrouded in mystery at that time. "The world" referred to only that small part of our earth that was subject to the scepter of the Roman emperor.

Against this background it is especially significant to note that Scripture constantly speaks of the unity of our entire human race. Jesus tells us that his gospel was to be carried out not only to the nations in the Roman empire, but to all nations [see Matt 28:19], and that his kingdom was to extend "to the end of the earth" [Acts 1:8]. With this, Jesus rejects the restrictive view by which the territory under the Roman emperor was understood to be the whole world, and over against it he places his kingdom that will extend well beyond the borders of the Roman Empire to *all* nations and even to the end of the earth. This is the first appearance of a cosmopolitan view, a broad understanding of the world that is being realized at the present time. We must understand the Gospel of John in the same light when it testifies that God so loved the world that he sent his only Son to save it [see John 3:16], or when the First Letter of John witnesses that Christ is the satisfaction "not for ours only but also for the sins of the whole world" [1 John 2:2]. The apostle Paul clearly perceived and understood this, as is evident from what he wrote in Colossians 3:11, namely, that in Christ there is no "Greek and Jew, circumcised and uncircumcised, barbarian, Scythian, slave, free; but Christ is all, and in all." The words "barbarian" and "Scythian" referred precisely to the clusters of remote, migratory nations, and they were intended to complete the notion of a single human race. In this context, it is also highly significant that the Old Testament Scriptures teach us about the entire human race, that it came from a single couple, that this race was dispersed into three clans after the flood, and that the nations were divided at Babel. They even record entire genealogies to exhibit for us the unity of all nations in the one progenitor of the entire human race.

§ 5   The absorption of every region of the earth and of every people and nation into a single, all-encompassing nexus of human activity by way of rapid communication and improved transportation is, therefore, not at all opposed to the fundamental genius of Christianity, nor is it something to be lamented by us as Christians. We cannot deny that this all-governing development of human life is and will be abused, and that at present it even turns increasingly against Christianity. But that should never lead us astray. On the contrary, the entire world's becoming taken up into one context and worldwide interchange realizes a thought, alien to paganism, that sprang from a Christian root, and is closely connected to the confession of true monotheism and of Christ as the King over the kingdom of the world. While this powerful image had not yet arisen outside of Israel and was obstructed through the idolatrous division and separation of the nations, within Israel a notion of the unity of our human race as it extends to the end of the earth had already budded. Although Israel continued to repress it because of its own narrow-mindedness, especially during the time of the Maccabees, none other than Christ himself emphasized it most decidedly as the wonderful idea of unity that was to guide the nations.

Seeing the entire world, the whole human race, and so all nations, peoples and tongues as one indissoluble organic whole called into being by God—and with it the calling to bring the unity of our human race to expression through communication and interchange—is a fundamental Christian thought, and could never be realized without Christianity. Rather than lamenting the dark side of the momentous events involved in its realization, we ought to greet this change in the history of the world with joy and to recognize in it a turn of events that could not fail to occur if the kingship of Christ is to come to the full splendor of its development.

That we as Christians are not ready to derive the full benefit from this circumstance, that this reversal has so overwhelmed and divided us as to leave us powerless, is something that we must lament before God as the result of our own fault. It is of no use to bemoan it. Only penitence within ourselves and awakening our Christian energy can be the medicine that promises a better future. Even the work of missions, which has already made such a contribution in this respect, but which continues to be too restricted and narrow in view of its high calling, must rethink that calling. However, it especially calls for self-examination on the part of Christian churches in the countries of Europe and America, so that they may return to Christ as their King anointed by God in order that, as the church sends its missionaries out into the foreign nations, the church itself may not be overcome with pagan ideas, lose its influence on its own people, and be ashamed when Buddhists or Muslims come from afar to observe Christ's church in Christian countries.

SPIRITUAL UNITY

So there will be one flock, one shepherd.

JOHN 10:16

§ 1 From the very beginning, missions embraced the noble thought that the Christian dispensation concerns the world, humanity, all peoples and nations—and it has never lost sight of this since. It set out for the remotest regions, and it went to countries from which nothing could be gained and to which the gospel alone could be brought. This did not commence in the nineteenth or twentieth century, but from the very beginning; and the deeper you work your way into Asia, the more historical indications you will find that testify of mission work that was already undertaken in the past. This great work also did not grind to a halt during the Middle Ages. After the Americas were discovered, missionaries immediately turned to the new world. At the end of the eighteenth century, in England we see a love for the original inhabitants develop apart from mission work; and while in the aboriginal societies this love may for a time have drawn abreast of missions, it never was able to match it and soon retreated entirely into its shadow. The mission activity of all churches reached its peak in particular in the nineteenth century, however, and it is at least as responsible as improved communication and greater commercial exchange for expanding our conception of the world and for making us aware that the entire human race forms a unity.

The activity undertaken by missions flows directly from Jesus' command to make disciples of all nations [see Matt 28:19], and from his ordinance that the gospel was to be preached "to the end of the earth" [Acts 1:8]. Consequently, not only the words of this ordinance, but still more the powerful activity resulting from that ordinance has revealed how the inclusion of the whole world and our entire human race within the sphere of our human activity is not at all in fundamental opposition to Christianity; it instead arose out of it and is being bolstered by it. What the ever-expanding merchant business is now doing out of material interests in order to unlock the entire world through trade is, in the end, nothing other than the continuation of what Christianity began centuries ago with a spiritual motive, so that we might hear psalms rising up from the ends of the earth to praise and worship the One who called this earth into existence out of nothing and created humankind to dwell in it as a unity.

Nevertheless, more than once mission endeavors and commercial activity led to intentional or also unintentional cooperation. One time missions would take the lead while the merchants followed; another time commerce would reach out first and end up promoting the interests of gospel preaching. English missionaries in particular entered virtually unknown areas, especially in Africa, in order to pave the way for English political influence. In the Netherlands the merchants initially looked down on missions, but this too has changed, so that both here and almost everywhere else the work of missions is valued highly by the merchant class and even by the state—not, however, for the results it gained in the spiritual domain, but because it supplied a point of entry to tribes unknown to us, facilitated interaction with these tribes in the interests of commerce and government, and set apart a group of converts among the native inhabitants on whom the ruling powers could count in times of tension.

The Dutch East India Company has historically been of great help for promoting not only the preaching of the gospel, but also the Christianizing of natives in the Dutch Archipelago. Even today almost the entire population of Ambon Island is Christian through the preaching of the past, and our government even enlists some of the Christian natives into the army because they can be counted on. Had the preaching been pursued with greater persistence, and had it been maintained in the nineteenth century also in the foreign colonies, Islam presumably never would have penetrated there and our rule would at present be much more firmly established. On New Guinea, Sumba, and other islands, mission activity is still the pioneer that establishes the influence of the Netherlands; and even in Dutch politics all parties are becoming increasingly convinced of the great usefulness of mission activity. The translation of holy Scripture into the native languages has greatly facilitated access to these nations, and the unity of our human race has likewise come to better expression in the family-tree of languages [that is, historical linguistics].

The Christian religion welcomes our increased power over nature as the fulfillment of a divine ordinance, and the increase of our knowledge in every field of life has been willed and favorably embraced by Christianity. In the same way (and even more emphatically), it may be said regarding the absorption of the entire world into the nexus of our human activity, that it is nothing but the realization of a noble idea that first came to expression in the Christian religion. It continues together with commerce and colonization to improve the awareness of the unity of our human race and of the rule of the Lord our God over the entire earth.

§ 2   Things proceeded differently when it came to Christ's church. In it a unity was announced that would soar high above the division and splitting of humanity into races, nations, and peoples that had arisen according to God's will with the confusion of speech at Babel. The unity of rule over the entire earth belonged to God, and no human ruler was to possess it. The confusion of speech at Babel was an intervention on the part of God in order to prevent the political unity of a world empire.

The ruler of this world, however, has attempted time and again to bring the unity of world rule under a single human ruler once more. One powerful ruler after another arose to drive the surrounding nations out before him with sword and fire so as to establish a single world empire. This pursuit already manifested itself among the kings of Persia, while under Alexander the Great the Greeks took it over from the Asians, and the Roman emperors finally managed to realize it temporarily over the largest part of the known world. The Roman Empire lived out of the conviction that the entire world was subject to Rome. Charlemagne then took this conviction over from imperial Rome, and after him the old German emperors attempted one more time to bring this all-encompassing idea to realization. Napoleon, too, was animated by this idea. He stood alone as general and fought with his troops on three different continents. Even today the notion of world dominion is not entirely strange to English imperial politicians.

We can also add that this same idea has come to life again in an entirely new form, since many harbor the cosmopolitan dream of uniting all peoples and nations into a single, great world republic. These are all attempts to resist the divine ordinance requiring the human race to continue living with its division into nations and peoples, by means of the haughty idea that we, as human beings, are more than capable of raising the entire human race to the full extent of its power under one rule and under one law.

The unity that God sought for humanity is, by contrast, a spiritual one, consisting in the one holy, catholic Christian church in all nations and among all peoples, with the purpose of bringing to expression a limited, a different, a spiritual—and therefore higher—unity. If you imagine for a moment what it would be like if this ideal had been realized and if all those throughout the entire earth and among all peoples who confess Christ could function in unity under one council, you can hardly even imagine the influence and power on the spiritual domain that could proceed from this one church of Christ.

To mention only one example, it is clear as day that nothing is more destructive to the influence of mission than the work carried out in pagan countries by three or four churches that begrudge the light in the eyes of the other and thereby leave an entirely unedifying impression on the local inhabitants. The realization of this high and beautiful ideal was most unfortunately broken when the first Christian emperor declared the Christian religion to be the religion of the state, turned the church into a state church, and thereby bound the freedom of Christ's church with the bonds of the nation state. The result of Byzantinism was that it broke the church's unity permanently and almost irreparably. The church had been intended to stand as a spiritual unity far above the division of our human race into nations and peoples, but to this end it had to remain free of the tight bonds that maintained the existence of various nation states among these peoples. The church was to remain universal, precisely thereby to bind the national differences together into a higher unity. However, by incorporating the church within the state and turning it into a national possession, Byzantinism robbed Christ's church of the high ideal that it had derived from its independence from national divisions. This was what broke the church's strength.

Although Rome sought as a spiritual power to make the national life and rule of different nation states dependent upon it, the Roman bishops should be applauded for attempting throughout to keep the church from becoming nationalized and for striving toward a church that, as a world church, would secure a spiritual unity for all nations. They failed to succeed in these efforts, because only a small part of Christianity remained within the unity of Rome. The Greek church was the first to fall away, and in the sixteenth century the churches of the Reformation were the next to leave Rome's unity—not to mention the small groups that lead an independent existence in Abyssinia, Egypt, Syria, and Asia Minor.

Whether this [splintering] could have been avoided cannot be investigated in the present context. Perhaps true unity would have remained had the bishops of Rome understood this unity in a more purely spiritual sense. Whatever the case may be, there is no question that the Byzantine notion of caesaropapism in particular, which arose one more time among the Eastern and Slavic nations, breathed new life into Emperor Constantine's basic position, even though it conflicted with the very foundation of the gospel and subsequently gave this position new power and dominance. This was clearly the case in Russia, in Turkey, and in Greece, but even the churches of the Reformation did not remain unaffected.

§ 3   In the sixteenth century, the princes of Germany significantly advanced the cause of the Reformation in their nation states and pushed it through; and with his gratitude for this support, Luther failed to see the latent danger that this circumstance posed to the purified churches. Through the influence of legal scholars in Germany, especially among the courts of the nobility, the Byzantine view of Emperor Constantine once more became powerful. Having been raised with this perspective, the German princes thought that they were hindered by the influence that the Roman bishop exercised upon their subjects. The princes tried to rid themselves of this obstructive influence and knew no better way than to set themselves up, as Emperor Constantine had done, in the place of the chief bishop. They even adopted the title of Chief Bishop, and to this very day the German sovereign is the *summus episcopus* of the state church.

As a result, in each country the church automatically became a separate church, and the church was once again nationalized and tightly tethered by the close bonds of national life. Every attempt to bring the churches of the various nation states under the unified rule of one communal council was soon abandoned. The church thus became a branch of the state, its own spiritual character was denied, and its independence was lost. The principle of *cuius regio eius religio* [whose realm, his religion] was adopted: he who governed the land could decide on the religious affiliation of the people. Every subject had to confess the religion of his prince. The identity of the church was absorbed into the identity of the nation. And in the end, not even a trace could be found anymore of Scripture's great intent to embody the unity of the human race in one catholic, Christian church of Christ in the very midst of the [world's] division into different peoples. There was an awareness that this concealed an error, and afterward frequent attempts were made to restore the unity of the church through the power of irenicism; but every attempt without exception ended in shipwreck. The churches were incorporated into the state, nationalized in a Byzantine sense, and the princes refused to let go of the spoils that they had captured. Caesaropapism maintained the upper hand.

In the Netherlands, the Remonstrant faction attempted to do the same thing, but the Calvinist spirit resisted. This resistance was inadequate, to be sure. The close coincidence between our war of liberation from Spain and the Reformation movement also brought our church into a national bond that was too tight, one that perpetuated the notion of a state Church and denied the freedom of the church's spiritual character. Even though we [as Reformed believers] also suffered damage, the international character of the Synod of Dort illustrated how the spiritual world-unity of the church of Christ was not abandoned in the Netherlands. People were convinced that the truth belonged to everyone, and that the churches in the Netherlands were for that reason not allowed to make a decision about the truth on their own or by virtue of their own power. This is why all foreign churches of Reformed confession appeared together with the Dutch churches at the Synod of Dort; and although not all that glittered was gold, the notion was still maintained that the church represents a unity among the many different nations. Had attention been given to this noble idea in the time that followed as well, our history would have taken an entirely different course.

As it turned out, however, the nation states soon regained the upper hand; general synods were prevented from assembling, and as a result our churches also fell away from the world church and were increasingly nationalized. Not in the good sense that the life of our nation came to be pervaded more and more by the spirit of the church of Christ, but in the pernicious sense that relationships with foreign Reformed churches were increasingly abandoned, we became a church group unto ourselves, and we no longer felt that we constituted a link in the great chain of churches by which Christ bound all of Europe together. This also explains how, with the best of intentions, King William I could presume that as sovereign king he had the right to impose a law on the Reformed churches, and how the state thought it could call into being the synodical system under which so many churches continue to groan today.

§ 4   All of these things are connected. According to God's will and ordinance, the division of people into nations and peoples must continue and is intended to give peoples their own national existence, which in turn allows each nation to develop, for the benefit of the entire human race, those characteristics and gifts that God has entrusted to each nation and to all the peoples that have arisen in the course of history. But precisely because of that division, the need to express humanity's unity remained. This was awkwardly tested in the various empires that were founded by world conquerors, but both fell away just as quickly. Then Christ appeared, visibly expressing, through the establishment of his one church, the spiritual unity that is so sorely needed for our human race in the midst of national divisions. This spiritual unity was maintained over three continents during the time of the apostles and during the persecutions, but Emperor Constantine most unfortunately perverted Jesus' high and holy idea by enclosing religion once again within the state and by binding it to the authority of the sovereign of the land.

The nationalization of different churches pushed Christ's exalted idea into the background, and even today we hear the appeal sounded among us as though the honorific title of *national church* could ever be an honorable title for the body of Christ. This has led the world to attempt once again to reach for the lost unity of the human race outside of Christ's church, and nowadays people are gushing about internationalism and attempting to realize this unity materially through faster means of communication and the network of commercial trade. This is injurious to the church of Christ because people now attempt on the material level to establish what the church was called to do in the spiritual domain. However, even this disdain can bring about healing—on the condition, however, that the church humbles itself, that it not rise up in hostility against that which establishes itself outside of its walls, and that it once again pursues the unity of Christ's church throughout the entire world as a holy ideal. This is something it must not pursue by pulling Christ down to the lower level of a religious pundit or a moral example, but by standing up once again with united power on behalf of the spiritual kingship of Christ.

THE COURSE OF THE CENTURIES

For you yourselves are fully aware that the day of the Lord will come like a thief in the night.

1 THESSALONIANS 5:2

We ask you, brothers, not to be quickly shaken in mind or alarmed ... to the effect that the day of the Lord has come.

2 THESSALONIANS 2:1–2

At the end of the first part of our appeal on behalf of Christ's kingship, we still need to consider whether Scripture allows us to understand the work of the kingship of Christ as a long historical process that by now stretches over two thousand years and could last even hundreds more.

§ 1

We already showed how, among the educated of our country in particular, the honor paid to Christ's kingship has suffered damage and declined, so that one would be hard pressed to find even a single person in our leading circles who is still concerned for that kingship—even in Christian circles his kingship has lost its exalted significance. After this, we outlined the causes that explain the decline in Christ's kingship; we pointed first to the diminished feeling of dependence due to the increase in humanity's power over nature, and next to the enormous increase and expansion of our knowledge. We pointed out how the current in the stream of our religious life had weakened in power and had even been bogged down through life's tense unrest, caused by increasingly rapid means of communication and by the absorption of the entire world within the sphere of our human activity. Finally, we emphasized how this decline in the stream of the life of piety was accompanied by a certain spirit that had awakened from the depths in order to overpower the leading of the spirits to establish for itself a throne in the great world cities, had then set up in them the worship of mammon, and had covered the resulting inner emptiness of the consciousness with the glory of art.

As would be expected, when Christians took note of this unholy development in life, they opposed it with good degree of hostility. Bemoaning the decline in our dependence on the power of nature, they attempted to proscribe science and withdrew from the breadth of life's activities in order to continue their life of piety in isolation and quiet rest. This made it seem as if the power of nature, the power of science, richer economic development, and the treasures of art were to be abandoned to the world as it dwelt in wickedness, and as if Christianity had nothing to do except to bemoan the ruins of Zion's walls and to await the return of Christ and the end of all things. People therefore imagined that they could be excused and that they could assign all the blame for this turn of affairs on the wicked world.

However, our argument attempted to show how untenable that response is. We demonstrated how we ought instead to be moved by pity for the many who wandered away and were swept along by the current such that they could no longer maintain their hold on the faith. We underscored how Christianity itself had become guilty of a weakening of faith within its own circle, and how the high and all-encompassing significance of the kingship of Christ in particular had sunk to much too low a level.

In order to make this case, we went back and considered humanity's kingship that, after being ordained by God at creation, was lost with the fall, but was destined to rise up again in the kingship of the Son of Man. Furthermore, we pointed out how in the meantime Satan had set himself up as the ruler of this world in order to frustrate the kingship of Christ by establishing humanity's false kingship. We likewise demonstrated how Christ had dethroned the ruler of this world in his death and resurrection and how he, seated at the right hand of God, had accepted the rule not only over his church and his elect but also over the peoples and nations, over the entire development of human life in both spiritual and material terms. And then how, as a result, we are also to welcome—in our increased power over nature and in the remarkable way science has flourished—an outcome that was not only willed by Christ but also effected through him and established under his dominion. We explained this globally by pointing to the influence of the spirits that, as much as it may hide behind the visible, continues to govern the course of events [in history].

This implies, however, that a lengthy historical process was not entirely foreign to Christianity but rather demanded by it—and this is the question we are addressing in the present chapter. The awareness of this process grew only very gradually among believing Christians. It all too often has been and continues to be assumed that the history of the world stood on its own. It is assumed that the church of Christ, in the midst of a history of the world that remains foreign to us, pursues its pilgrim journey and is constantly persecuted, threatened, and hindered by the world; that it is once again seduced to faithlessness through the world's wealth; and for that reason longs with a deep spiritual craving for the final salvation to be ushered in when Christ returns. This craving is seen over and over again in apocalyptic sects[1]—that is, groups that make the teaching of Jesus' return the center of their confession. All the while the rest of the church, though not denying his return, nonetheless does lose sight of and forgets it entirely in its contentment with the current situation.

We have to acknowledge that two apparently divergent lines in respect to this question seem to run through Scripture. On the one hand, Scripture gives the impression that the generation alive at that time was already to expect Christ's return; while on the other hand, it appears to suggest a lengthy historical process that must precede the return of Christ. Even in the writings of the apostles we see these two views running alongside each other. The apostle Paul in particular had the premonition that he would live to see the return of the Lord. From 1 Corinthians 15:51-52 it is evident that for some time he counted himself among those who would not see death, but would enter glory when Jesus returned without dying. More significant still, in the revelations that came to the apostle John on the island of Patmos, Christ himself says: "Hold fast what you have, so that no one may seize your crown" [Rev 3:11]. And when Paul writes in AD 52

§ 2

---

1. For the phrase rendered here and elsewhere as "apocalyptic sects," Kuyper uses the phrase *eschatologische secten*.

from Corinth to Thessalonica that "you yourselves are fully aware that the day of the Lord will come like a thief in the night" [1 Thess 5:2], these words may as such not contain an indication of time, yet it is difficult to escape the impression that Christ's return is very near. One cannot try to eliminate this impression from the apostolic writings. In different ways it is evident that in the early church people expected Christ to return from heaven soon to settle the final battle, and more than one apostle harbored this same expectation.

As decisive as we are in pointing to this, we must also remember that an entirely different perspective appears alongside that one. This perspective may not specify that the wait would last for many centuries, but it clearly does require a lengthy historical process to precede the return of Christ. It is remarkable that when Jesus' disciples tried to press him for more details about the establishment of his kingdom, he resisted them time and again. The Father has by his own authority fixed the times and seasons [see Acts 1:7], and neither the angels nor the Son know anything about them [see Matt 24:36]. The Lord even warns emphatically that false Christians will arise after his departure announcing that the day of Christ has come, and he therefore warns his church not to listen to these false rumors and points out that the end of days must be preceded by great events in world history. His parable of the yeast similarly points to a lengthy process. The yeast is put in the three measures of flour; only then does the process of fermentation begin; and this fermentation must run its historic course until the three measures of flour have been completely fermented by the yeast [see Matt 13:33].

While the apostle Paul initially thought that he would live to see that great day, his letter to the Philippians is indicative of a premonition that he would soon pass away. He even longs for it and writes that this is far better for him [see Phil 1:23]. It is for the sake of the church alone that he hopes for a slight lengthening of his life. In 2 Corinthians 5:1, he already states: "We know that if the tent that is our earthly home is destroyed, we have a building from God ... eternal in the heavens," and then he adds: "We groan, longing to put on our heavenly dwelling" [2 Cor 5:2]. No more than three years separate these letters [to the Philippians and to the Colossians]. The first letter to the church at Corinth was composed no earlier than AD 54, while the second was written no later than AD 57. For that reason, we should not imagine the apostle to have changed his mind in the intervening time, which in fact represented the years of his greatest activity. For him, the two could stand equally side by side.

Particularly remarkable is the fact that in the first letter to the church of Thessalonica, which he had founded shortly after his release from prison in Philippi, he writes that the return of Christ will be like a thief in the night [see 1 Thess 5:2], while in the other letter he writes that the return of Christ must be preceded by an entire historical process. The struggle between Christ and Satan must have run its entire course until Satan in the end, in a final desperate attempt, will embody the "man of lawlessness" [2 Thess 2:3]. And this cannot take place earlier because a power is hindering [the manifestation of the "man of lawlessness"]. On this basis, he emphatically warns [the Thessalonians] not to expect the return of the Lord in the immediate future. Those who claim that this is indeed the case only mislead the church. The rebellion must come first, and the man of lawlessness is yet to be revealed. Already when he was in Thessalonica, Paul had warned the believers there against this erroneous expectation. There is a mystery of iniquity [see 2 Thess 2:7]. There is a hidden demonic power that works to bring the church of Christ to perdition. But the full manifestation of that demonic power still awaits, and it will not come until later. For the moment, an irresistible power prevents its full eruption.

It is thus clear that these two understandings stood alongside each other from the very beginning of Christ's church. On the one hand, living with a sense of immediacy regarding Jesus' return; on the other hand, a clear understanding that much still had to happen before the final day would come, that the struggle between Christ and Satan had entered upon a historical course, and that the final day could come only after this process had been completed.

For those who live in time and measure everything according to time, §3 this seems to involve a contradiction. However, this contradiction forms part and parcel of the contrast between time and eternity. The psalmist verbalized this contrast with these well-known words: "With the LORD one day is as a thousand years, and a thousand years as one day" [2 Pet 3:8; see Psa 90:4]; and in the Revelation that came to John on Patmos, time and eternity are likewise placed alongside and over against each other when we read on the one hand: "Behold, I am coming soon" [Rev 22:7], while on the other hand, the historical process awaiting fulfillment is depicted as a book with seven seals containing the future events that would first be unfolded in the course of the ages. In eternity, and in everything that reflects the eternal, there is no time or measure of time. In the eternal, everything is immediately present. Eternity is something—as the name Yahweh indicates—that is, was, and shall be. Every distinction in time falls away. The past, the present, and the future collapse into the one eternity.

This is why in the book of Revelation, the scenes that were yet to be played out in the course of history are grouped as symbolical depictions by their kinds. These would occur not a single time, but time and again throughout the course of the centuries, in different forms in spite of their basic correspondence, until the end has come and the final events have been accomplished. Even though people were entirely correct to see the fulfillment of one of these seven seals in every great period of history, it was an error when those seven seals were restricted to one particular period, as if everything had occurred. The Revelation of John is what people call "dioramic." In these seven seals there is an undulation of history, but an undulation that progresses throughout the centuries, reappearing repeatedly with an identical fundamental shape, though with various tints and colors.

We stand before a mystery because everything that recedes into the eternal, that presents itself as eternal, and that raises us up into the eternal can make no other impression on those who live in time and measure everything according to time than that of being a mystery. It is impossible for us to free ourselves from the notion of time. This follows naturally from our finite existence. However, we all too often picture our immortal existence in the hereafter as an existence extending over an endless number of centuries. We even impose that concept of time on the Lord our God whenever we think of his sovereign counsel as something that is fixed for an entire sequence of centuries and is now being realized little by little. Yet we know this cannot be correct, because it means that we impute to the eternal One something that belongs to human existence alone. Every attempt to free ourselves from the concept of time and this sense of finitude fails. Only in moments of sacred tension and in the glow that comes when we lift our souls up in prayer can we have experiences that wrest us from the grasp of time's power and draw us up to a higher awareness.

Since Christ as our King sits enthroned in eternity and we still live in time, it can (and may) not be otherwise than that his return—if our longing to see the mystery unraveled is to remain vibrant—must at times, when seen in the light of the eternal, appear to us as if it is going to happen any moment now. Yet at other times, it appears to us as coming in the course of time, as part of the great historical process that the struggle between Christ and Satan—including the development of the church and the liberation of all of human life through the influence of the gospel—will traverse. The return of Christ raises an expectation that the radiance of eternity flashes like lightning in the present, while at the same time sending out a shower of sparks over the history of centuries, in the distant future.

From a practical perspective, all of this means that a Christian church that imagines the day of the Lord to be far off and lives in the conviction that this day will not come until many centuries have passed, will die entirely to the inspiration of the promise of the Lord's return, will be weakened internally, and will begin to behave as though its future lies here below on earth. Conversely, a church that every morning and evening anew expects Christ to return for judgment will give up its peaceful activity and suspend its efforts, will abandon its duty and calling, and will in the end lie buried beneath its strained predictions. The former can be observed in all of the powerful state churches where the preaching of the Lord's return no longer constitutes a stable ingredient, and whose members are no longer inspired in any way by the hope of Jesus' return. The latter can be observed in numerous apocalyptic sects and enthusiasts who band together in small groups and have lost their strength in the battle for the Christian position against the demonic world power. At first they live in nervous tension. They wait; they yearn. If the end is not this year, then surely the next! And when every expectation ends in disappointment, and when nothing happens even after years of waiting, their nervous tension turns into despondency while the ecstasy of their faith expires.

For that reason, just as in the days of the apostles, so also at the present time, the holy challenge for preaching and the holy challenge for the soul's inner life is to keep doing justice to *both of these* [perspectives] in the mystery of the Word and in the mystery of the conscience—both the "Behold, I am coming soon" [Rev 22:7], as well as "The rebellion comes first, and [then] the man of lawlessness is revealed" [2 Thess 2:3].

To this end, it is necessary to do away with the false separation that claims that Christ's kingship applies only to his church and not to the life and course of this world as well. Later on, in subsequent chapters, we will draw the line between the order of providence and the kingship of Christ. At this point, we are only registering our protest against the conception that has been so damaging to the honor due to Christ as our divinely

§ 4

anointed King—since it presents Christ, seated at the right hand of God, as the most powerful patron of his church; while conversely, it depicts the historical process of the world's life as something that occurs entirely apart from him. His statement "All authority in heaven and on earth has been given to me" [Matt 28:18] contradicts that dubious conception altogether; and from a historical and practical perspective this view has shortcomings as well.

The church and the world do not form two hermetically sealed spheres of life. The church is in the world. The church influences the world, and the world in turn influences the church. Every age brings changes to the face of human life; and whenever human life takes on a new form, the church is called to take account of the new situation, to address it, and to adjust its activity accordingly. The one gospel always remains the same, and the one body of Christ remains unchanged, but across the ages it speaks the language that each new age needs to hear. This is why the rule of King Jesus over his church is unthinkable unless his royal dominion extends over the life of the world as well, inasmuch as a spiritual power is at work in the life of the world that in part allows the light from God's church to shine upon it, and in part sets itself up as a demonic power against Christ. In this connection we have established that the new shape in which the world's life now presents itself is indebted to the reign of King Jesus in regard to the good and priceless things it brings, while it is restrained and countered by King Jesus insofar as there are demonic powers at work in it. For this reason, the church of Christ need not be despondent, regardless of the resistance offered against faith by modern developments. If the church understands the signs of the times, confesses its sins, and exalts Jesus' kingship to a position of honor once again, then even the developments seen in our times will not damage God's cause but serve the honor of our King.

THE KINGSHIP OF CHRIST ACCORDING TO SCRIPTURE

THE NOTION
OF KING

On his robe and on his thigh he has a name written, King of kings and Lord of lords.

REVELATION 19:16

All Christian countries, especially those found in the parts of Europe and America marked by baptism, should be continually filled with reverence for Christ as King. The respect for his majesty should govern all spiritual relationships of life. No name other than that of Christ as our King anointed by God should, at its very mention, arouse a greater ardor among people of every rank and walk of life, among every people and nation. There were times in bygone centuries when this was indeed the case. At present, however, this is no longer so. In the wide arena of our nation's life, the glory of Jesus' royal crown has been smothered. Although in the much smaller circle of faithful believers there is still no name that surpasses the name of Jesus, here too Jesus the Savior and Redeemer receives more honor and thanksgiving than does Jesus the King, whom God has given to us and to whom we owe all homage and allegiance.

§ 1

The general cause of this shortcoming in homage and sacred zeal appeared to be located in the general decline in the stream of religious life. Sacred worship, and the holy realities to which it refers, used to have a leading place in the estimation and esteem of all, including princes and nations. We do not mean to suggest that at that time the unholy never crept in and poisoned life, but the unholy was still experienced as sin; conversely, the holy, and therefore the majesty of Christ, did preserve its honor.

This is no longer the case today. At best one could say that there are only a few solemn events where religion's place and significance is acknowledged, but even there this recognition is more nominal than anything else. Today public esteem elevates material interests and public welfare, as well as science and art, modesty and philanthropy—but even there, philanthropy only in the sense that it comes from man and gives glory to him alone.

The explanation for this turn in the public's estimation seemed to us to reside in the fact that humanity's power over nature saw an especially miraculous increase in the nineteenth century, and that given the superiority over nature this garnered people felt liberated from the fear of the elemental powers that in large part had been the source of their fear of God. The fact that this ongoing increase in our power over nature made people hopeful, and in an ever widening circle canceled out the fear of God, initially produced the hostile relationship between faith, as it clung to the fear of God, and science, which continued to celebrate one triumph after another over the power of nature. This was why some in the circle of believers ascribed the increase in power over nature to a demonic power. A hostile attitude toward natural science began to manifest itself more and more among believers. They looked with troubled eyes at its steady stream of victories. They refused to see this triumph over nature as the fulfillment of a holy prophecy, and they denied that it was to be explained by the dominion of the mind of Christ over the life of the nations.

Gradually, two separate and distinct groups began to form. The one increasingly wandered away from the faith and took delight in their scientific success, so as to shape their entire life more and more according to the nature of that success. Over against this group stood another group that held onto the faith and lamented the increasing power over nature, tried to get rid of it, and could not understand it as anything other than a hostile power.

However great the divide between these two circles may initially have been, unbelievers slowly began to exercise more and more influence upon the circle of believers. Believers were unable to isolate themselves from the benefits to life that accompanied the dominion over nature. They too began to profit from and enjoy them. And as they imperceptibly experienced the influence of the developments of science, the firmness of their faith began to weaken; they felt the stream of religious life ebbing within their own circles as well. It was not without a certain amount of fear that they began to ask themselves what the outcome of this change in public opinion would be, especially for the next generation.

This gave rise to a disturbing situation also among believers. All kinds of discord arose as some sought resolution by yielding halfway to the success of science, imagining that the best way to preserve the faith was to find scientific support for it as well; others, overcome by an exaggerated hostility toward all science, withdrew into mystical isolation. This situation continued for more than half a century, weakened the group of believers and led it to retreat from public life until a reaction finally arose that led to a new, inspired revival of faith. At this stage, for the first time the happy moment dawned when, even among believers, people girded themselves for substantial development. They began to give a lucid account of the place that faith ought to occupy in the face of the overwhelming power of natural science. This was also the principal reason the kingship of Christ began to be discussed among us once again. We became aware that those who honored Christ as no more than Reconciler and Surety were actually suppressing the majesty of our King. Christ's kingship ought to receive its due not only specifically in terms of spiritual salvation, but also in human life more broadly. It had to be recognized that we really do have a King in Christ, to whom has been given "all authority in heaven and on earth" [Matt 28:18].

This was as far as we came in the first and second sections of *Pro Rege*. §2 In this third section we now intend to build the kingship of Christ up from the foundation of life itself by the light of revelation. We take our point of departure in the observation that Christ was always announced as *King*, and never as *Emperor*. While this may seem trivial, in fact it captures the essence of his majesty.

The earth's sovereigns have always tried to find an impressive way to express their sovereign majesty in a lofty title. In Turkey the sovereign calls himself a Sultan, in Persia the Shah, in Japan the Mikado, Tenno, or Tenshi; and when they came into contact with Europe, they did not present themselves as kings, but emperors. The word Sultan means *dictator*, Shah means *ruler*, Mikado, *honorable gate*, and Tenshi, *the messenger of heaven*. Because these sovereigns enjoyed such lofty titles in their own countries, for their international relations they did not want to be placed on the same level with the kings of small countries, and instead they reached for the loftiest available title in Europe, namely, the honorific title of emperor. They did understand a king as a sovereign, but then as one of a much lower rank. It is not a king who rules in Austria, Germany, and Russia; "czar" is nothing but a Slavic form of our word for emperor.

At times this desire to win influence with the lofty title of emperor became laughable. The sad fate of the royal family in Korea is well known, but even this sovereign of such a small and insignificant country proudly and loftily called himself the emperor of Korea. Before Brazil became a republic, it had an imperial throne as well; and when European influence attempted to establish itself in Mexico, the imperial crown was likewise applied to this republic. One could therefore say that, once the title of emperor arose, it was only natural that those who sought a lofty title for their sovereign immediately thought of the title of emperor.

This title was also known and used in Palestine in the time of Jesus. Christ's birth narrative begins by reporting a decree proclaimed by the Emperor Augustus. Jesus himself later said to "render to the emperor the things that are the emperor's" [see Matt 22:21]. At the judgment seat of Gabbatha, the Jews said, "If you release this man, you are not the emperor's friend" [see John 19:12]. Of Paul it is similarly reported that he appealed to the emperor when he faced the wrath of Jewish fanatics [see Acts 25:11–12]. Nevertheless, although in Jesus' day the title of emperor was commonly applied as the highest title of dominion and power, neither Jesus himself nor his apostles or evangelists ever applied the title of *Emperor* to Jesus' messianic majesty. Instead, they always used the honorific title of *King*. Even today it seems odd to speak of *Emperor* Jesus. Everyone instinctively feels that the title of King alone honors Jesus in his majesty.

This circumstance is all the more remarkable because the title of emperor, much more than king, would express the nature and extent of Jesus' dominion. *King* is a title used exclusively for the sovereign of a single nation, while *emperor* refers to a sovereign whose territory and dominion extends over many countries and nations, as well as their many kings. In England this was recently felt when Victoria received the title Empress of India.[1] In England, Scotland, and Ireland, she remained queen; but in

---

1. Victoria (Alexandrina Victoria; 1819–1901) was Queen of the United Kingdom of Great Britain and Ireland from 1837 until her death. After the Indian Rebellion of 1857, Britain's possessions and protectorates on the Indian subcontinent were

Asia she ruled over all kinds of people, nations, and sovereigns, so that for India she accepted the title of empress. Since Jesus' dominion is not at all restricted to a single nation or people but extends over all peoples and nations, as such it would only have been natural to assign to it the title of emperor. Nevertheless, this was not done. It is true that he is called not only King, but also the King of kings and Lord of lords [see Rev 17:14 and 19:16], and even the Ruler of the kings of the earth [see Rev 1:5]. All the same, Jesus is never referred to as Emperor.

The word *emperor* is closely related to the word *Caesar*, which in Greek was pronounced *kaisar*, leading to the German form *kaiser* and the Dutch *keizer*. Gaius Julius Caesar was the first to have the honorific title of Emperor, and the Greek, German, and Dutch words were all derived from his name. The Romans referred to Caesar as *Imperator* or *Augustus*, from which are derived the French word *empereur* and the English *emperor*. Irrespective of the particular form of the word, it always expresses that the one who bears this title is the head of a world kingdom rather than the ruler over a specific people. The Romans had a republic, and the chief of this republic, as the ruler of the nations in Europe, Asia, and Africa—that is, the entire known world of that time—declared himself through the imperial title to be the ruler or lord of the entire world. Some savage peoples did migrate beyond the borders of the Roman Empire, but they did not count. The chief of the Roman republic was lord and commander over all parts of the world that did count, and he expressed this by adopting the imperial title. This is one reason why the emperor was soon honored as a deity, and why he received the title *Dominus et Deus*, that is, Lord and God. The emperor's title thus expressed an entirely different meaning than the ruler of one country. The one holding this title was claiming world dominion for himself, so that the conviction prevailed for many centuries, extending even into the Middle Ages, that there could only be one emperor. There is one world, one world dominion, and therefore only one emperor.

When the great Roman Empire was divided between the East of Constantinople and the West of Rome, this was nothing less than an anomaly. And when the Byzantine Empire declined more and more under pressure from Islam, Charlemagne restored the Roman Empire by adding the title of emperor to that of the king of France. As such, he called

§ 3

---

formally incorporated into the British Empire. From 1876, Victoria used the additional title of Empress of India.

himself the *Römische Kaiser*, a title that the ancient German emperors likewise maintained. It was only at a later point in time that the original meaning of "ruler of the entire known world" began to weaken. Napoleon attempted to restore it. Even today the title of emperor, which was adopted in Russia, in Austria, and—recently again—in Germany, continues to be the honorific title for a sovereign who stands at the head of a very powerful territory whose strength and power far surpass ordinary kingdoms. The title of king soon seemed to be inadequate for such a powerful kingdom, and instead a claim was laid upon the title of emperor. This is also why the sovereigns from the East were not content with the title of king, and why in the European context they honored themselves with the title of emperor. As result, for everyone the name *emperor* has the sound of a much higher title and is expressive of a much greater power.

If you know this about the history of the imperial title, you will sense that, all things being equal, everything suggests the need to express Jesus' majesty with the title of Emperor. His dominion, too, does not simply extend over a single land, but it extends to all the lands of the earth. If the emperor of Rome was honored as *Dominus et Deus* (that is, as Lord and God), Jesus *is* Lord and God. While the emperor of Rome was the ruler over many kings, Jesus is the King of kings and the Lord of lords. While the emperor of Rome presumed to have this power, Jesus really does have it. His authority entails not national dominion, but worldwide dominion. And if ever someone could be called *Emperor* in a complete and literal sense, it is Jesus and no one else. What Jesus' apostles claimed about him was what the ruler of Rome thought he alone could claim. As such, nothing would have been more natural than for the apostles to have insisted that, when honoring Jesus, he could not be compared to one of the kings subjected under the emperor but to the emperor himself alone. If you asked yourself which sovereign power on earth is the fitting image and proper representation of Christ's power and majesty, it would as such not have been found in the kings of the Galileans or Germanic peoples, the Persians or Dacians, but in Rome's imperial palace alone.

§ 4   The fact that, in spite of the above, Jesus is never given any other title except King must be explained from the distinct meaning embedded in the concepts of king and emperor, respectively. The emperor embodies a dominion that is exercised by violence and domination. Legions set out from Rome in order with violence to subject one people after the other to the powers in Rome. There was no relationship between the vanquished peoples and the Roman emperor except a relationship of subjugation resulting from the superiority of the imperial forces. These nations all spoke languages unknown to him, had religions unknown to him, and lived according to customs and habits that were entirely in conflict with Roman customs.

The goal of his rule was not directed to the fortune of those peoples but consisted in the splendor of the emperor's power alone. There is no doubt that Rome introduced better order to those lands, more equitable justice, and at times even greater prosperity and higher culture; but the main goal was and remained for their treasures to flow toward Rome and for these peoples, checked by the threat of violence, to increase the splendor of the imperial crown. It was dominion over the world, but as Jesus expressed it in his words to Pilate, it was likewise a dominion *from* this world—that is, the dominion arose from this world, so that the struggle is continued with the violence of weapons.

Jesus placed his dominion over against it as a dominion that does extend over the world, but is not from the world. For that reason, the servants of his dominion could not, like the servants of the Roman emperor, fight for their Lord with the sword. This was part of the very nature of Jesus' dominion, which stood diametrically opposed to the nature of the emperor's dominion. Imperial dominion was not the image, but the caricature, of the world dominion that was given to Jesus. The nature of the Roman emperor's world dominion and the nature of Jesus' world dominion were mutually exclusive. In Rome we see no more than a shadow of the true essence of world dominion as it would be realized in Jesus. In the former, there was the violence of weapons, in the latter, the power of the Spirit. In the former, everything was sacrificed for the sake of one's own honor and greatness; in Christ, it was a matter of self-giving, devotion, self-sacrifice, self-abasement, and self-destruction—in order to bring eternal life to a people and to enrich them with the treasures of grace.

This is why Scripture applied the idea of king to Jesus and not the notion of emperor; although it goes without saying that no earthly title, not even that of a king, can adequately express the actual and particular nature of his majesty and power. Everything on earth, including the notion of king, has become adulterated and unnatural. That is why in Samuel's day a contrast was made between the true King of Israel (that is, Yahweh himself) and "the kings like all the other nations" [see 1 Sam 8:19–20]. For the same reason, the messianic understanding of kingship is from the very outset distinguished from the kingship of other nations, and not Saul but David becomes the first type of the Messiah-King.

Consequently, it is of little use to explain Jesus' kingship by drawing on the etymology of the words for *king* used in the original text of the Old and New Testament. By a false etymology, our dogmaticians have attempted to explain the Greek *basileus* as if it derives from "basis"—the foundation, the support of the people. Yet a better derivation has already indicated that this explanation does not work and that *basileus* simply means "one who goes ahead of the people"; it is roughly equivalent to "duke" [*hertog*]. You get no further with the Hebrew word *melek*—a word familiar to Bible readers through Melchizedek, the king of righteousness. Even if we were to suppose that the origin of this word suggests the meaning "counselor," we would get no further. After all, the word *melek* was already in use among the ancient Canaanites, and nothing suggests that it had a sacred origin. Holy Scripture uses words already found in the languages of the peoples; but it does not appropriate their meaning so much as infuse these words with the meaning that it wants to express. The correct interpretation of these words, then, is to be sought not on a linguistic basis, but from their actual usage.

And even if the Dutch word *koning* [king] is related to *kunne* [which relates to the Latin word *genus*], and thus appears to refer to a unity in origin and an affiliation with the people, bringing it much closer to the deeper sense of kingship than the Greek or Hebrew words do, the word *king* per se does not bring us any further. The word *king* came into existence entirely outside the circle of revelation and lacks any kind of sacred stamp. It is entirely coincidental that it comes closer [in its etymology] to the essence of kingship than the [corresponding] Greek or Hebrew words do.

DOMINION

You are my King, O God; ordain salvation for Jacob!

PSALM 44:4

A king embodies the notion of dominion. His dominion, unlike that of an emperor, is not gained through the power of weapons, but it is and remains a governing power. The concept of power is in fact what most characterizes a kingship, and it distinguishes a king from a prophet and priest. The notion of dominion is commonly expressed with the words sovereignty or exaltedness; but regardless of the expression used, a king's dominion is always first of all one of power, superior power, supreme power. Someone is a king by virtue of the possession of that power. We do not mean to deny that the notion of kingship includes many other things, but these may not push the main point to the side—thus reverence for that power should always stand in the foreground whenever we speak of Jesus as our King.

§ 1

Christ is not there for us, but we exist for the sake of Christ. Regarding earthly government, it can indeed be said that it exists for the sake of the people, rather than the other way around. This is always the case, as long as we understand government on earth in and of itself rather than as a body that bears the authority of the Lord. However, this cannot be applied to Christ as our King, and the reason for this is his divine dignity. We have been given to Christ by the Father. We are his possession. We do not belong to ourselves, but to Christ. We are his servants. It is precisely in this relationship that Christ's royal honor first comes to full expression.

It cannot be denied that the opposite is all too often apparent among believers, due to a one-sided emphasis on Christ's love extended to us in his work of salvation. In this redemptive work that Christ effected, his power retreats into the shadows behind his voluntary self-humiliation and his self-surrender in death. Here Christ gives himself for us, which might give the momentary impression that the only goal of his redemptive work was that we might be saved. This is not the case, of course. The main issue was the restoration of God's justice and honor; and it was only insofar as we are creatures of this God that the power and dominion over this world, also with respect to us, had to be contested with Satan and restored to God. Even when we read that God so loved the world that he gave us his only Son for its salvation [see John 3:16], we may not understand this to mean that it was our eminence that won us God's compassion. It means nothing else than that God could endure the disruption of his work, the desecration of his world, only on a temporary rather than a permanent basis; and that for this reason he reached for the highest possible means to restore his power and justice on earth, in this way to save the world from eternal destruction. This is why the apostle prays so solemnly: "We implore you on behalf of Christ, be reconciled to God" [2 Cor 5:20]. He does not say: "Accept the salvation that is offered to you. Do not pass up the opportunity offered to you to be assured of a blissful future." While this is something he could have said, those words would not reach to the bottom and foundation of the work of redemption. He does express that latter reality, however, when he says: "Be reconciled to God!"

All the same, initially the preaching of the gospel remains on the surface of things, and it emphasizes the salvation of man. This is only natural. The gospel is brought to those who have been estranged from God and continue to live in their sins without even thinking about it. Among them you would accomplish nothing with an appeal on behalf of God's honor. They do not understand what the honor of God demands, and their heart is not ready for that yet. They are often not at all unhappy with their worldly life, and they are instead afraid that if they enter the service of Jesus, they will have to give up the joy that the world offers them.

For that reason, evangelism, especially in its elementary forms, directs itself almost unfailingly to those with a less fortunate lot in this world, who suffer under the decay resulting from the sin in their hearts.

Few forms of evangelism are as pervasive as that of the Salvation Army, but it too directs itself first and foremost to the lost in the lower classes of society. In America, and to a certain degree in England as well, evangelism does dare to call men and women from the middle and upper classes to repentance; but after the partial disappointment of the *Réveil*[1] on mainland Europe—and, therefore, in the Netherlands—evangelism among those who are more highly refined, more cultured, and better educated has nearly come to a complete halt. Thank God, even in these circles there are still young and older people who convert to Christ, but they form a great exception, and this almost never happens as the result of regular evangelism. Nearly all evangelism efforts are directed almost exclusively to the social class of the poor and less fortunate, and especially to those who lead a publicly sinful life and to those who can be addressed about the life of their soul without bumping up against an imagined superiority.

The apostolic writings make it clear that the situation was the same for the early Christian church. "Not many were of noble birth, not many were powerful, not many were wise, but this is nothing" [see 1 Cor 1:26]. It naturally follows that evangelism tends to emphasize the frightening lot awaiting sinners after death. There is little to offer for the present life, at least not to those who do not yet understand what it is to enjoy a higher spiritual life and whose interest is almost entirely limited to what can improve and enrich their earthly existence. The question "What must I do to be saved?" [Acts 16:30] therefore comes to their lips automatically, and we should neither disapprove of it nor find it unnatural when someone who goes out to save the souls of those who are lost is driven by the answer to this question in particular. "Life in this world already gives you so little—be sure not to waste your eternal life as well. Come to Jesus, and through faith in him find your entrance to eternal happiness."

The result of this method of evangelism is an emphasis on the salvation of the soul, so that we are inclined to treat Jesus as we do a physician who saves us from a deadly disease. We are thankful to the physician, and from the very beginning we submit ourselves to what he prescribes. We willingly swallow the bitter medicine he gives us. However, once the deadly danger has passed, we regain strength and begin to feel more free; so we acknowledge the physician, pay him, and let him go in peace. That is why

§ 2

---

1. *Réveil* refers to the Reformed–evangelical revival of the early 1800s.

more than one evangelism effort has proved fruitless—once people have been brought to repentance, the converts are lost and left to themselves.

Such evangelism has too high an opinion of itself because it looks down on the church somewhat disparagingly, and fails to understand that converts need to be brought into the church, so that once embraced by the church they can get past the superficial sense of being saved and become devoted to the deeper life that comes to those who have been saved in their righteous state before Christ. If these things do not happen, Jesus may well be honored as Savior and Redeemer, but there is no place for his dominion over us or for us to be incorporated into his people.

The result is that more and more people imagine that Christ exists for our sake, while the much richer notion of our existing for the sake of Christ does not arise. Those who have sunk down in their sins are lost and want to enter eternal life, and it is Jesus who opens the way for them. That goal has now been accomplished. The Physician has fulfilled his task for the sick and he receives lofty praise in return. But once they are assured that after death they will indeed enter the paradise of God, Christ's work for them is finished, his task has been completed, and he stops being the governing element in their lives.

This is the very thing the church must resist. The church may not be content simply to bring the gospel to the lost. Instead, its primary calling is to lead those the Lord calls into a deeper understanding of God's intentions, from which the entire plan of salvation arose; and to lay the firm connection between Jesus and those who are saved, which is not complete at conversion, but only begins there.

Doing so depends almost exclusively on a kind of preaching that, after bearing witness to our heart of Christ as Prophet and High Priest, also shines the radiance of the King into the eye of our soul. It will weave the entirely new relationship—which must exist between those who have been saved, as those incorporated into the people of God, and the One who has been appointed by God as King over that people—into the mysticism of the human heart. The church has all too often fallen short in this regard. It made the mistake of not going any further than evangelism in its lower forms, and this is the main reason why a sense of the important significance of Christ's kingship is essentially lost to a considerable part of the congregation. Everyone knows, confesses, and understands that Jesus is our chief Prophet, who has fully revealed to us the truth about eternal things, and that he is our eternal High Priest, who has brought the sacrifice of redemption for us. However, the vast majority hardly understand that the greatest is yet to come in our confession of the kingship of Christ. They do honor Jesus as a patron who prays for them and gives them the certainty that the salvation that has been won for them will not slip from them. They see in Jesus' sitting at God's right hand the reward after the battle—the honor of the exaltation given to him by the Father. They also confess that Christ will return as Judge at the end of time. Those who have a somewhat deeper experience even sense that Jesus restrains the demonic powers. But left with little more than the sound of the name "king," they no longer sense, enjoy, or experience anything of the royal power with which Jesus is clothed, of the royal majesty in which he sits enthroned, of the royal dominion that he exercises over earth and in heaven.

Of course, this is not something that we can say of each person individually, but this statement does hold generally for the great majority on the basis of the way they express the life of their soul in word and song. This does not mean that Jesus does not have a high place—a very high place, even!—in the estimation of all, or that they do not constantly think and speak about Jesus with the highest reverence. It similarly does not deny that the hearts of many have a warm, tender, and fervent love for Jesus that expresses itself through sacrifice and thanksgiving, and thereby through consecration. What we do mean, however, is that among us the unique zeal that seizes a loyal people when they applaud their king—a zeal that, when it applauds the King of kings, ought to surpass by far all enthusiasm for earthly kings—is no longer what it used to be in former centuries, and that without a doubt increasingly falls short of Scripture's standard. People are no longer drenched with the sense, the notion, that we exist for the sake of Christ and for Christ, rather than that he exists for our sake. They no longer join ranks behind the only Commander or feel that they belong to the people who in living and in dying are committed to him.

A very shallow, unspiritual understanding of Christ's kingship naturally led to a slackening in zeal. A king embodies the highest power, but we also expect that highest power to manifest itself and make its presence known. If there is a king among the earth's sovereigns who remains hidden and in whose kingdom order and peace are constantly disrupted by invading enemies, whose people can no longer defend themselves, whose army shrinks back, and whose land is required to pay tribute—then all authority of and reverence for such a sovereign is gradually lost. And just as

§ 3

in France they used to speak of a *roi fainéant* (a king who does not budge), so the majesty of the kingship gradually dwindles away in every age and land when and where the king was no longer able to maintain himself through a triumphal display of power internally and externally.

For earthly kings, this is the only way things could be. The power on which earthly authority leans and through which earthly kingship manifests itself cannot do without a strong arm and is simply unthinkable without coercion. A sovereign who has no police force to repel evil within his borders, or an army to repel the enemy outside his borders, is unimaginable among earthly kings.

But if you apply this notion or something similar to Jesus' kingship, if you demand of it as well that, if it exists, it must manifest itself in the display and demonstration of a power residing in a strong arm, you need no further proof that by this standard the exalted kingship of Christ is slowly losing its honor. The church of Christ has been divided and split, and one sect or heresy arises after the other. Sin and transgression continue in the church. Even the priests in the holy place fall short in their faithfulness and sacred dedication. While the order is constantly disturbed on a spiritual level without Christ manifesting his power to restore it, one similarly finds hardly any trace of an attempt to repel the enemy threatening the holy domain from the outside. The Lord's flock seems instead to surrender itself to the overwhelming power of unbelievers and scoffers. It is as if Christ does not triumph over the world, but that the world instead triumphs over the Lord's cause. Entirely in line with the supposition that kingship can maintain its splendor only if it suppresses all resistance immediately and inspires universal respect for its law and rule, people began more and more to suppose that Christ's kingship was a nominal honorific title decorating the Savior, rather than a power that really exists and that we have to take into account throughout our entire life.

This standard, however, is not fitting and may not be applied. Every earthly kingship is mechanical in its orientation, while Jesus' kingship is organic. The resulting difference must govern our entire view of Jesus' kingship. Properly understood, there is only one who has power—the Triune God, the Creator of heaven and earth. The psalmist expressed this with joyful adoration in Psalm 44: "You are my King, O God!" [Psa 44:4]. This power belongs to God because every creature is his. His power is one that is founded on the very existence of things.

Whoever gives existence to something or someone is the lord and master over that thing or person in the fullest sense. This never applies fully when we as human beings give existence to a thing. Not even when singers spontaneously sing a song from their heart are they its creator in the full sense of the word. After all, they use thoughts and images derived from what exists outside of them, they sing in tones related to the poetry of all ages, and they express themselves in a language that they did not create but only found among their people. When we say of people that they bring creative thoughts or things to life, this is always meant in a derivative and restrictive sense alone, and we do not ever speak of people having an absolute power of creation.

In God, however, and in him alone, this creative power is absolute. Everything that exists was called into being by him without in doing so ever being bound to something other than himself, or ever making use of any factor that similarly and just as strictly did not owe its origin to him and to him alone. In us human beings God not only created our very being, but he also gave us our nature, as well as all the powers, gifts, talents, and abilities that distinguish one person from another. From that perspective there is nothing in all creation, whether stars or sun, matter or spirit, plant or animal, person or angel, that did not owe its being—and its being thus or so—entirely and exclusively to God the Lord when it came from his hand.

Divine sovereignty depends on this very thing. God could not create his creatures according to a law existing outside of himself, because such a law did not exist. God could no less create creatures with a view to something other than himself, since there was nothing aside from the Triune God. All creatures are, by virtue of their creation, in a state of full and complete dependence, and they cannot exist for any other goal than to glorify God and to serve him as a means or factor for the execution of his counsel. It similarly follows from this that, aside from God, there can be no power to which creation can be subjected in any way. There is only one dominion, and that dominion belongs to the Triune God. Similarly, there is only one power and majesty, the power and majesty of God. This power cannot be mechanical; by virtue of its nature it must be organic, since it finds its foundation in the origin and existence of all that has been created.

This is also why Scripture continually glorifies the Triune God as LORD. In Israel they avoided the name Yahweh because it was considered too holy; they chose the name "LORD" instead, which the translators of the authorized Dutch Bible used throughout in place of "Yahweh." The word Lord is not meant as a form of address, but as a majestic title intended to express God's absolute and complete sovereignty over all creatures. The titles "King" or "King of kings" were also substituted for it, but "Lord" remained the more comprehensive expression to declare in halting human speech the full extent of God's governing power, sovereignty, and claim over all people and things. A derived, transferred, and imposed authority can exist on earth, and this derived authority can maintain itself through coercion and violence. However, this is nothing more than a shadow of that unique and most exalted kingship that automatically came to and rests in God alone because of his omnipotence and by virtue of creation.

The kingship of the Son of God ought to be compared to this kingship of God rather than to earthly kingship. It is not the earthly standard of the world's sovereigns or rulers that must be applied, but the standard of the kingship of the Triune God. The simple fact alone that the earthly standard was applied Jesus can explain why people were disappointed by Jesus' kingship, missed the overwhelming manifestation of power that they were looking for, and therefore began to understand his kingship more in a nominal sense than as something real. The apostles, however, have given us sufficient warning of this. They immediately transferred the name and honorific title of "Lord" to the exalted Savior, and in their portrayal of Christ as the Head of the body they most clearly emphasized the organic character of his kingship.

DERIVED AUTHORITY

Know that the Lord, he is God! It is he who made us, and we are his; we are his people, and the sheep of his pasture.

PSALM 100:3

The distinction between organic and mechanical authority is most clearly illustrated in the contrast between parental authority over a child and that of a guardian over the same child. Parental authority came at birth and was grounded in that birth. It was in and with the child's life that authority was given to the parents. The authority of a guardian is entirely different. There need be no blood relationship or kinship at all between the guardian and the child. A guardian can be someone who is entirely unknown to the child and has nothing to do with him or her. The authority over that child does not originate with birth nor does it come with life itself, but it is conferred on the guardian by family agreement, law, or the appointment of a judge. The bond of authority between parents and a child exists automatically; the bond between a guardian and a ward is assigned by the authority of a third party. Something arising from the very process of life is called *organic*, while something composed through our invention, activity, or order is called *mechanical*; thus parental authority has an organic character while that of a guardian is mechanical.

§ 1

This same difference comes to even greater expression—or, the most complete expression—when you contrast the authority of an earthly king to the authority of the King of kings. There is no king on earth who rules except by virtue of the authority that either he himself or his ancestors acquired, or that was bestowed on him by others. His royal authority does not flow forth automatically and necessarily from the existence of his people or from their nature. However, the sovereignty of the Lord our God, which extends over everything, comes along with the very existence of his creatures. We simply cannot think of a creature without God's complete sovereignty extending over that creature. The notion of the Creator's sovereign authority is included in the very concept of a creature.

The nature of creatures means that a marked distinction arises between the two. Stars and angels are both God's creatures, and for that reason he has absolute authority over them. Both belong to God, exist for the sake of God and his honor alone, and their mode of existence, work, and lot are all determined by God. God determines the course of the stars and the path of the angels; and the rich language of Scripture applies this to the world of the stars in a vivid way when it is said of God that he "gives to all of them their names" [Psa 147:4], while the firmament is called to declare the glory of God [see Psa 19:1]. The same thing happens in Psalm 103. "Praise him, all you shining stars!" [Psa 148:3]. Dead nature does not exist. All of nature is carried from one moment to the next by God's spiritual power, and it is God who governs all the kingdoms of nature, enforces his law, and causes everything to answer to his holy will.

But as rich a significance as this may have, you still sense at once that God's authority over a star is of an entirely different character than God's authority over an angel. In the case of stars and all creatures without a soul, God powerfully imposes his will and law on them without encountering anything in the way of opposition or resistance. The situation is entirely different when we pass from soulless creatures to angels and people, that is, to creatures that are endowed with a soul. God's operation on the spirit of creatures with a soul does not exercise itself as a blind power, but rouses and awakens the spiritual element in humans and angels to cooperate with God's work and adjust themselves as an instrument of divine ability. By itself this already posits the possibility of resistance, opposition, and departure from the divine will; and this possibility is what lends a *moral* character to God's rule over all creatures that have been endowed with a soul.

Even if we may say poetically and figuratively that the stars and oceans are subject to divine authority, everyone will sense that, in the case of creatures without a soul, it is more fitting to speak of a power and capacity—properly speaking, there is authority only in reference to creatures with a soul. Only creatures endowed with a soul can confess: "The LORD is our judge; the LORD is our lawgiver; the LORD is our king!" [Isa 33:22]. While authority in the proper sense of the term arises first with creatures that have a soul, and while this means that we can speak of kingship in respect to that part of creation alone, the ground of this authority is and remains the same as the ground of [God's] sovereign power of disposition over those creatures without a soul. This is why Israel sings out in praise: "It is he who made us, and we are his; we are his people, and the sheep of his pasture" [Psa 100:3].

Another, no less important consequence similarly flows from this distinction between the differing character of divine sovereignty over creatures with and without a soul. Here we are thinking of the possibility for divine authority to work through a derived authority that one creature receives over another. For the moment, we will leave the angels out of the discussion because so little has been revealed to us about the way in which authority has been structured among them—except to remark that Satan's relationship to the rest of the demons conclusively proves that we can also detect in the angel world an authority on the part of a more powerful spirit over the less powerful spirits. §2

Aside from the angels, however, it is as clear as day that a derived, instrumental power is found almost everywhere among people. That man has power and disposition over things, plants, and animals already, by virtue of his existence, lies in the fact that he is made to feed on what the earth produces. In our earlier chapters, it became clear to us that God gave humanity dominion over nature—and this in a nearly absolute sense—and that this dominion is increasingly coming to realization in the findings produced by the science of nature.

This is not where things end, however. Not only did humanity receive dominion over the creatures on earth that do not have a soul, but among people there is also the dominion of one person over another person. In itself, it would have been quite conceivable that the situation were different. If every person were created like Adam, that is, if every person were to come into existence in an adult state and find at their disposal everything necessary for their life, there would be no reason why one person should have any say over another. If this were the case, there would be no immediate or extended family, no nation, no human race. There would be only individual people with equal rights, without any bond binding one person to another. There would be no room for one person to have authority over another, and all authority would be exercised immediately by God himself over each individual person.

This was not the way things were ordained, however, with the creation of humanity. The first man alone came into existence—in the full sense of the word—without any intervention on the part of another person, and it is remarkable how Scripture emphasizes that already with Eve this was not the case. For the rest, every person is born from other people, and by that very fact in one's origin and birth one already has a relationship to other people. One person does not stand independently of another, but one blood binds the lives of everybody together into a single unity. Family bonds bind people together in groups. No one stands independently and on one's own, but all people together form one human race; and within that human race an inequality comes to expression that calls into existence the authority of one person over another. The fact that a human being is born into this world as a helpless child automatically creates a superiority on the part of the child's father and mother. Parents therefore begin by caring for that helpless baby just like a lioness cares for her cubs.

Nevertheless, because people have a soul, something entirely different enters the equation. That difference does not consist in a stronger natural love and care, since the care of a hen for her chicks or of a tigress for her cubs not infrequently far surpasses the care that degenerate mothers or selfish fathers give to their children. Instead, the difference is that human authority involves a moral element. This moral element does not enter right away, since a child at first is not capable of it; however, it does come as soon as the child's ego is gradually awakened to self-consciousness as the child grows up. Once a cub is grown, the old lioness no longer cares for her cubs and every bond with them is broken. This is not the way things are with human beings. As children grow up, the care and duty of raising them grows and increases; and a child must respond by obeying, that is, by subjecting himself to the authority that has been placed over him.

People are thus found in a situation where, through the way in which he ordained the propagation of the human race, the Lord God installed fathers and mothers as the instruments by which he could exercise his high and divine authority over children. Parental authority cannot be original because, even if parents did procreate the child, the child did not receive his life and existence from his father but from God. God alone has supreme and complete authority over that child. God can take a child away from his father and mother through death, without his supreme authority over the child declining or diminishing in any way. But even if the supreme right of disposition over each and every child who is born belongs to God alone, in the normal course of life God has so ordained the birth and upbringing of that child such that she first honors her father and mother as the ones who bear the authority with which God has clothed them. This does not await a specific ordinance in the fifth commandment, but follows from the way in which children are born to their parents as helpless beings. God's authority is therefore exercised in two ways: the first, directly and immediately over creatures without a soul; the second, mediately through a human being as an instrument, and therefore as an authority that is derived and conferred, being manifested first in paternal and maternal authority.

A father's authority is what one could call a derived and instrumental authority, although it belongs to a regulated order. There are numerous other kinds of instrumental authority that likewise arise from the inequality among people, although a regulated order is entirely absent for these kinds. Such authority is most evident in genius, in talent, and in higher gifts of the spirit. A process of flowering and development occurs in this higher field of human life as well, and here too we see laws or norms, powers, and motives at work. Once they are brought to light, nothing remains for those who have not been endowed as richly except to follow the example and initiative of those who do have richer spirits. Especially in France, it is customary to honor such governing spirits with the title *master*—people do not do so unwillingly but willingly, and nothing is more normal for the followers of such a more powerful spirit than to laud them in their writings and to address them as *"mon maître."* We express the same thing when we say of certain prominent leaders that they have "gathered a following,"[1] which comes down to the same thing. Furthermore, at schools there are masters whom others join voluntarily as their students. §3

All this drivel about equality among people is therefore pure nonsense. Instead, we should say that no two people on earth are equal. For even if, particularly in the less developed nations, the differences between people

---

1. Dutch, *school maken*, literally "make school"

may be reduced to a minimum, every mother can tell her children apart and the external differences between them are always connected to differences of nature, disposition, and character.

In addition to the differences among people in kind, there is also an infinite difference of degree. This constitutes the reason why people of a higher degree automatically and imperceptibly not only exercise their influence, but also have authority over people who are endowed with a lower degree of the same qualities. You can see this already among boys who play in the street, where one is always the leader and obeyed, since most obtain authority primarily through obedience. This applies even to bands of thieves or robbers. There is never equality but always inequality, and that inequality always produces the exercise of and submission to that authority.

This is most evident in schools, and for that reason the man in charge used to bear the honorific title of master in order to express that he not only taught, but also possessed authority. Out of a misplaced feeling of wisdom this title was first considered outdated and then abolished, so that people spoke only of *teachers*, or at most of the *principal*. In the end this was recognized to be a mistake, and some opted to use the term *head* [*hoofd*] instead. However, there is no one who finds this new name appealing, and it has met resistance only among the regular teachers. The old name of *master* was by far most suitable because it expressed the notion of authority. Along this line, it is remarkable that while the name of *master* was discarded in the regular public schools, in France's more refined circles of the highly gifted it is still maintained for those with genius and talent.

Similarly, men who studied law write *master* before their names, and at one time the name of *master* was also used for doctors. After all, lawyers exercise a certain authority over their clients, and the same is true for doctors and their patients. The clients and patients themselves seek this authority out, and for that reason it consists in a choice they make on their own. But once it has been made, they willingly submit, and that very submission is the mark of authority. Thus in English as well as in French, we speak of doctors writing a *prescription*, while in Germany they refer to the same thing in similar fashion as a *Verordnung* [order, decree].

This instrumental authority without a regulated order is also derived and, just like the authority of parents, flows from God as the source of all authority. It is he who willed this inequality among people. It is he who calls into existence one person whose spirit is weak in drive and power, while he clothes another with the majesty of genius. Genius is not something we give to ourselves, and although we can sharpen and develop our talent, we cannot give it to ourselves. Through this most unequal distribution of gifts, the Lord God by the very nature of the case calls into existence an authority in life's spiritual terrain whose influence extends much further than the parental authority that is of a regulated order. Men like Luther and Calvin in the religious sphere, and Vondel, Cats, and Bilderdijk[2] in the field of poetry, did not turn themselves into authoritative spirits, nor were they appointed as such by others. They had this position by the grace of God, *gratia Dei*. There have always been unruly critics in this respect, just as every family seems to have at least one child who never ceases being contrary. Nevertheless, the authority of genius and talent is specifically marked by this, that the best have always willingly recognized it, and in the end it has overcome all resistance.

Of course, this twofold instrumental authority is not all that exists. Parental authority and the authority of genius did not suffice. Gradually broader groups also began to form. From the immediate family came extended family, from that came a clan, from a clan a tribe, from a tribe a nation. This produced, in addition to the bonds of immediate family, the bonds of the extended family, of clans, of tribes, and of nations; and these bonds could not exist without law, rule, and discipline. As result, there was ever greater need for an authority in each of those bonds that would be recognized by the entire group. Initially the development was patriarchal and followed the rights of the firstborn and of age, so that the necessary authority could be constituted as long as common descent and blood relations dominated the bond's formation. §4

This was no longer possible, however, when the distance separating the generations increased, and when need or violence required groups estranged from each other to live together in a national bond. It was at first on a small scale that different groups joined together, as when we read in the context of Israel's entry into Canaan about a large number of kings who each ruled over a single city. One such king was Melchizedek, who reigned over Salem alone. But the nature of the case meant that these

---

2. One nineteenth-century writer, with whom Kuyper may have been familiar, ranked Willem Bilderdijk (1756–1831), Jacob Cats (1577–1660), and Joost van den Vondel (1587–1679) highest among the Dutch national poets. See A. Schwartz, "The Literature of Holland during the Nineteenth Century. Part I and Part II," *Macmillan's Magazine* 33, November 1875–April 1876, 155–64, 267–74.

small formations could not survive, and gradually they joined into larger groups uniting millions and millions of people. Here in particular a bond of a well-regulated order was necessary, but this was unthinkable without a powerful man who would stand at the head.

This is why kings of nations arose. Also, these kings exercised nothing other than the divine authority of government, but—and this constitutes the foundational difference with respect to the authority of parents—the character of their authority was not organic but mechanical. The resulting situation may have been entirely suited to the fallen human race, but it still did not correspond to the creation ordinances. The nation did not come from the king. He was not the natural, organic head of his people, but had been set up as a head to those who formed the body. This contrast between the actual situation and God's original ordinance came to expression in Samuel's protests that the people had sinned and rejected God because they wanted a king "like all the nations" [1 Sam 8:20]. God was the Lord of Israel because he had made it into a nation. This was an organic concept. The kings of Gentiles had not made their nations; this was a mechanical aberration.

Something else played a role as well. The division and separation of our human race into separate and distinct nations resulted from sin, and it was indeed in this way that the unity of the human race was broken. In the beginning, the first Adam was not only clothed with fatherly authority over his family, but he also held universal authority over the entire human race. The same can to a certain degree be said about Noah after the flood as well. After him, however, the unity of our race was lost. There was no common bond to unite the entire human race anymore, and for that reason there was no king of humanity who could instrumentally and organically represent God's authority over the entire human race.

Attempts may have been made later on to fill this void with an empire that was intended to be universal, but as we described it above [in chapter III.1], this was an act of arbitrariness and violence that meant no more than the subjection of the weaker nations to the military power of a more powerful nation. It was the incorporation of as many nations as possible into one nation, and the purpose of this incorporation was not to bring the rich treasure of the entire human race into one harmonious development but to have that one nation whose king held the most power to rule over all other nations.

Although it did and still does please God—in spite of the division of the nations and their development in the brokenness of sin—to use the mechanical instrument of an ordained kingship as the instrument by which he exercises his rule over the nations, it goes without saying that such a kingship never could and never can realize the lofty ideal embedded in the creation of the entire human race from one blood. This defective situation will exist only as long as sin continues. One day this situation will end. The ideal must and will be realized. It is this realization of the human ideal that calls and appeals for a King who is bound organically to his nation and who gathers to himself—from all nations and tongues—the one nation that can represent the entire human race. And that King is Christ.

III.4

NO SPIRITUALIZATION

For to us a child is born, to us a son is given; and dominion shall be upon his shoulder, and his name shall be called Wonderful Counselor, Mighty God, Everlasting Father, Prince of Peace.

ISAIAH 9:6

§ 1   The original power of rule, supremacy, and sovereignty thus resides in the Triune God alone. Only he who created and preserves all things can claim this for his honor, and he alone has the say and the right of disposition over everything that exists. He does with his creatures whatever he wants; and there is no right whatsoever that any creature, however highly positioned it may be, can exercise to limit or decrease God's supremacy and right of disposition in any way. This is why God is entirely free to exercise his high authority and to have it function as it pleases him. It could have pleased him to exercise this divine authority immediately everywhere and always, but it could just as well have pleased him to assert his high authority mediately through one spirit upon another, so that the angel or person whom he has clothed with authority serves as his instrument. God opted for the latter. He rules children through their fathers and mothers, students through their teachers, weaker spirits through geniuses, tribes through their chiefs, and nations through their sovereigns.

Sin's entrance, however, was the reason that his government through human instruments suffered numerous shortcomings. On the one side, there is abuse of authority, as in despotism; while on the other side, resistance and disobedience are aroused to rebellion. This disrupts the natural operation of the instrumental authority that God has instituted, so that what should operate organically and of its own degenerates into a relationship of coercion and violence. Instrumental authority becomes more and more detached from the bond of life, becomes mechanical, and operates more through a show of force than through spiritual factors.

Something of this can already be seen in families, but it is particularly evident in the dominion exercised across larger and wider circles—especially the dominion held by the earth's sovereigns over the nations. These sovereigns and their houses often do not even belong to the nation itself, but have come from outside. Without police force and army, no dynasty could survive throughout the centuries. More frightening yet was the struggle that came when one people rose up against another people, one nation against another nation, and so one king against another king. This led to a division and splintering that automatically caused the frightful pain of war, so that the violence displayed as show of force received even greater emphasis. And although attempts were made to end this division and splintering by reuniting many nations into one empire under a single emperor, the result was never anything more than dominion on the part of one nation over the others, or an artificial unity in part of the world—one that was forged by the sword.

Over against it, however, the ideal of creation remained in the human heart through revelation. [This ideal was] to acknowledge and honor without reserve the supremacy of God over our entire human race as a unity, and over all the circles of immediate and extended families, of clans, and of tribes within that unity. The Lord is our King, the Lord is our Lawgiver, the Lord is our Judge. This authority is exercised directly through the Triune God insofar as it includes the right of determination and the government of providence, but it is instrumental and exercised through human beings clothed by God with authority insofar as it must regulate and govern our human life externally. He did not clothe them with that authority by a direct appointment, but through the place each occupied in their circle by virtue of life itself. A father has this authority as the founder of his family and the progenitor of his offspring; where he is not present, this authority is held by the mother; and where she too is absent, the older brothers hold this authority over their younger siblings. God's instrumental government over our entire human race had to be established according to this example. A King had to come who would stand at the head of the entire human race, but who also by virtue of who he was could be the organic head of the human race. He was to be a second Adam who would be what the first Adam was, but then in a higher sense.

It was likewise from the pursuit of this ideal that Israel's messianic ideal arose. It did not arise out of the thoughts and contemplations of Israel, a nation that never managed to rise above its own exclusiveness; even Jesus' disciples still spoke about the reestablishment of the kingship in Israel. It was an ideal revealed by God to the more powerful spirits in Israel and fulfilled in Christ as the King of God's kingdom. But in the kingdom of Christ, all national differences between Greeks, Jews, and barbarians fall away, and only the unity of regenerated humanity remains. In this dispensation, there is in his kingdom no external show of force; its lofty authority rests on a spiritual foundation. In the kingdom of Christ, there is no artificial construction, but a *body* is formed—that is, a nation naturally composed in an organic way, whose all-governing Head is Christ, by virtue of his very being.

§ 2   Christ is also the Savior, the Reconciler of our sins, our Savior and Redeemer; but he is all of these things only as a means to attain the great goal that is and remains the establishment of the kingdom of heaven, a kingdom in which he is King. For that reason his royal honor and dignity are not added to his work as Savior but constitute the final goal to which everything is being steered, directed, and driven. The one kingship that embraces all of humanity would have arisen automatically in paradise apart from sin, but was disrupted and cut off when paradise was lost; it now returns in Christ through humanity's salvation and renewal of life in regeneration.

For this reason, Christ's kingship is emphasized from the very time of his appearance, even before the rich treasure of the work of salvation is unfolded. John the Baptist appears as Jesus' forerunner and herald, and the first thing he cries out is: "Repent, for the kingdom, the kingdom of heaven, is at hand" [see Matt 3:2]. Shortly thereafter, when Jesus begins his preaching, he likewise first proclaims his *kingship*; and like John the Baptist he testifies: "Repent, for the kingdom of heaven is at hand" [Matt 4:17]. When his time on earth was drawing to a close, he openly and solemnly said to Rome's governor: "You say that I am a king. For this purpose I have come into the world." And more strongly yet: "For this purpose I was born" [see John 18:37]. Jesus therefore sums up the entire [purpose of] his coming in this one, all-governing idea of kingship.

The world was without its real, true King. Nations had their kings, and there was even an emperor in Rome, but the real, true idea of exalted kingship was not actualized in any of them. Jesus brought the fulfillment of that high idea. This was not incidental to his coming but was the main purpose. It was the exalted goal of his mission. For this purpose he was born, and for this purpose he had come into the world. This was the true, actual kingdom—not a kingdom as the sinful world had fabricated it, but the kingdom as it was ordained by God and would represent God's exalted authority. This is why it is referred to as the kingdom of Christ, or the kingdom of God, or the kingdom of heaven. This was the kingdom that Jesus established. This kingdom would be set in motion through his coming. This kingdom would be brought to its fulfillment through him. Of this kingdom John testified that it was at hand in Jesus. And Jesus himself testified that it was in order to be King in this kingdom that he had been sent by the Father, had been born in Israel, and had entered the world.

All of these things were weakened and deprived of their actual meaning, however, when people began to spiritualize the kingdom. Jesus' kingship was reduced to its prophetic glory. It is true that Jesus also bore witness, that he also unfolded for us the nature of spiritual life. People clung to this and supposed that the kingdom he had come to establish consisted exclusively in the power of the truth to drive back the power of the lie, as well as in the power of greater holiness to drive back the power of sin.

In other words, the words *kingdom*, *kingship*, and *king* were no longer understood as realities, but only in a figurative sense. Just as we say that the truth governs the lie and virtue governs vice, so Jesus was understood to have dominion because his position in the spiritual arena was higher than that of other religious founders. In reality, there was no kingdom; people merely spoke of it figuratively as a kingdom. In reality, Jesus was no King, but he was figuratively given this honorific title. Nevertheless, this conflicts entirely with what Scripture depicts for us prophetically in the Old Testament and historically in the New. This spiritualization crept imperceptibly into our circles as well and was the cause for the widespread waning of the glory of Jesus' kingship. This is something to which we will return later on.

This spiritual, figurative understanding seemed to have support especially in what Scripture itself testifies about this kingdom and about Jesus' kingship, to counter the national and material understanding [of the kingdom] as it had established itself among the Jews in those days. Especially in Jesus' time, the Jews claimed entirely for themselves as the Jewish nation the great prophecy of the King on whose shoulder shall be the government, and whose "name shall be called Wonderful Counselor, Mighty God, Everlasting Father" [see Isa 9:6]. The Messiah would come, but to be the king of the Jews—Israel's national king who would bring Israel victory over the Gentiles. For that reason they could not picture the Messiah's kingship in any other way than with a throne of ivory like Solomon had in his palace in Jerusalem, with the entire nation of Israel reaching for the sword to establish dominion under this king's banner over all the nations roundabout.

This exclusive, national, and pervasively false understanding of the Messianic kingship was so deeply rooted in Israel during Jesus' time on earth that even his own disciples continued to ask, "Lord, will you at this time restore the kingdom to Israel?" [Acts 1:6] until the very end, until his resurrection, and even until the Mount of Olives right before he ascended. In her tenderness, the mother of two apostles asked about the positions of honor her children would hold in the newly established kingdom of Israel [see Matt 20:21]. Given these circumstances, Jesus could not do anything except point time and again to the spiritual character of his kingship over against the earthly and worldly understanding of his kingdom. But these repeated and insistent explanations of Jesus led people in the end to spiritualize his kingship completely and thereby to destroy it completely, since they understood the name of king to be no more than figurative.

§ 3   There was no warrant for this at all, however. Jesus' words, "All authority in heaven and on earth has been given to me" [Matt 28:18], in themselves already entirely overturn this understanding. What Jesus opposed, and was forced to oppose in the given circumstances, was twofold: (1) every understanding that made Israel, rather than the world, the aim of God's work of grace; and (2) the supposition that his kingship would, like the imperium that existed among the nations, depend on external violence. As a people, Israel was chosen from the other nations to bear God's revelation, to foreshadow and prepare what would come, and to bring forth the Messiah. This was not an election to dominion, but an election to service. God was the God of the entire world and of the entire human race.

God did not so love Israel, but the world, that he sent his only Son so that everyone—Jew, Greek, or barbarian—who believed in him would have eternal life [see John 3:16]. It would have been unthinkable and impossible for the almighty God—to whom the entire earth, the entire world, and the entire human race belong—to have aimed his work of grace at the small, insignificant Jewish nation alone. His work of grace could not have aimed at anything less than the entire world and comprehended anything less than the whole human race. Israel's honor was not that it took the world's place before God, but that it was called to serve the world by foreshadowing and preparing redemption. If, at the end of all things, Israel were on this account still to occupy a place of honor among the other nations, that would apply to the true Israel that was converted to Jesus alone and could be manifested only after the other nations had been called to salvation.

The Jews' mistake was that they refused to serve to bring salvation into the world; they wanted to have dominion over all other nations and to show grace only to those within the human race who were willing to be incorporated into Israel by the sign of circumcision. Instead of seeking to be the instrument for the honor of the Messiah, they wanted the honor of the Messiah to raise their national glory to a higher level.

This turned out to be Israel's downfall. It was the Jews' national sin that they wanted dominion instead of service; and when in the end they cruelly cried out, "Crucify, crucify him!" before Gabbatha [Luke 23:21], they merely applied to Jesus the logical consequence of this, their deepest national sin. Jesus himself had emphasized these things as clearly as could be: "I, your King, have come not to be served but to serve" [see Matt 20:28]. This statement reached to the very core of Israel's national sin. If Israel was called to dominion rather than service of Israel's King, it would apply even more strongly that he was called to dominion rather than service. But conversely, since the King of Israel testified that he had come not to have dominion but to serve, this was even more true of the King's people, who, like him, had a service to complete under the ordination of God and who were to have no thoughts of exercising dominion over the other nations.

What filled a Jew's heart in Jesus' time constituted pillaging the sacred. It was an attempt to claim for itself as a nation the sacred things of God that had been entrusted to Israel for the sake of blessing the world and making it serve the honor of God, to elevate itself over the world, to pursue its own exaltation, and to position itself in order to gain dominion over all nations on earth. Supposedly the Jews were to become great, and the Jewish nation was to become great. Everything ordained by God was not to serve their carrying out the counsel of God for the entire world, but to elevate the Jewish nation to the highest honor.

Jesus' struggle with the Jews' national spirit, which in his days had mastered the heart of the entire nation of Israel, was thus a struggle for the sacred things of God, for the Lord's exalted ordination, for the glory of his work of grace, for the salvation of the whole world, and for the establishment of that spiritual kingdom. [This kingdom] would not be enclosed within the narrow boundaries of Palestine, but would instead embrace in holy unity the entire human race insofar as those who were still on earth—and those who had already entered glory, or those who were yet to be born—held onto God. His kingdom was not like that of the nations [see 1 Sam 8:19-20]. In his kingdom, every division among the nations in fact fell away. The separation that the Tower of Babel had produced became undone in his kingship. He would not be King over one nation or some nations, nor over the people of Israel. His kingship aimed at an undivided humanity, at our entire human race.

§ 4   This brings us to a second contrast. The contrast aimed at the Jews was one that proclaimed Jesus to be not the King of the Jews but the King of a people drawn from all the nations, so that his kingdom extended across the entire world. But a second contrast was directed not against the Jews, but against the other nations, against the earthly kingdoms, against the kings "like all the other nations" [see 1 Sam 8:19-20]. Jesus expressed this contrast in two statements. The first was when he said: "The kingdom of God is not coming in ways that can be observed ... for behold, the kingdom of God is in the midst of you" [Luke 17:20-21]; and the second was when he testified to Pilate: "My kingdom is not of this world. If my kingdom were of this world, my servants would have been fighting" [John 18:36].

As it had developed among the nations, the power of a sovereign was marked by the ostentatious splendor of his throne and crown, outward show far and wide, and symbolic banners and shields everywhere. This ostentatious public face was meant to impress upon others that he was elevated far above normal human beings. Things neither could nor can be any other way for an earthly kingdom. We are not defending the exaggerated wealth or boundless splendor in which the kingdom of Louis XIV, or the Roman Empire, and later the Napoleonic Empire, sought their power.

Nevertheless, in our earthly situation, those who wear a crown simply may not live as normal citizens do, but must reflect in the wealth of their palace the exaltedness and honor of their kingdom or empire. The crown and the throne must impress, and in our earthly state this is also true in terms of what can be seen and what catches our eyes. The sovereign's position is elevated far above that of even his highest subject, and for that reason his court must surpass the highest standard of life. This necessity is based on the nature and character of our earthly household, society, and state.

Since, however, Jesus' kingdom does not derive its character from earthly society but from a higher life existence, his disciples should have been deeply aware of the truth that Jesus' kingship left no room for such pageantry; and they should have been able to recognize the greatness of Jesus' kingship even without any ostentation. Its measure of honor was not according to the eye but the soul, and it was for this greatness and glory that his disciples should have reached.

Things are no different for the other defining characteristic of kingship on earth, namely, the display of power and the violence of weapons. In the current earthly situation, one cannot imagine a kingdom—if it is a more or less considerable nation-state, at least—that has no disposal over such an external power. In our situation, every power that has dominion constantly meets malevolent resistance or dangers from an external threat, so that an armed power is indispensable for breaking this resistance and maintaining order and safety.

If Jesus had accepted a kingship over the one nation of the Jews, over the Israelite people, he too would have had to arm his people so as to battle the Roman emperor's power. He says it himself: "If my kingdom were of this world, my servants would have been fighting [with the sword]" [John 18:36]. However, precisely because Jesus' kingship was not of the sinful order of this earth but of a spiritual-holy order, Jesus' regime simply could not be one of coercion or violence. If it had involved a power struggle, that struggle would at any rate not have arrayed a new earthly power against an already existing earthly power, but twelve legions of angels would have come to battle the legions fighting under the Roman eagle. As we will see later on, such a battle is in no way to be excluded from the end times. When it was first established, however, Jesus' kingdom did not appear as such. Jesus' kingship was not mechanical, but it worked from one spirit upon another. Jesus did not enter into battle for a defective earthly kingdom that would incorporate all people into it through violence. He placed the ideal and true kingship over against this earth's defective and fabricated kingship. This was why he said to Pilate that he was born to be King, so as to testify to what is true.

However, because we wish to elevate and display clearly the universal and ideal character of Jesus' kingship, we ought to protest all the more against every attempt on the part of quasi-faith or unbelief to undo the reality of Jesus' kingship because of its spiritual character by watering it down to some kind of influence that proceeded from him into the religious and ethical arena.

III.5

UNIVERSALLY HUMAN

And he put all things under his feet and gave him as head over all things to the church, which is his body, the fullness of him who fills all in all.

EPHESIANS 1:22–23

Jesus came from Israel, but he was not the King of the Jews. Salvation was from the Jews, but at the same time it was to be carried out into the world and to be a blessing to all nations and peoples. The inscription above the cross was therefore false. It reflected neither Jesus' own testimony about his kingship nor the prophetic and historical testimony about this kingship. "I have other sheep that are not of this fold. I must bring them also, and they will listen to my voice. So there will be one flock, one shepherd" [John 10:16]. This is the key to explaining the mystery in this relationship. When Jesus appeared, he joined himself closely to Israel and instructed his disciples to do the same. He had been sent to the lost sheep of Israel, and was not allowed to give the children's bread to the dogs [see Matt 15:21–28]. That Jesus began in Israel followed from Israel's election and calling. Israel was God's chosen people, but chosen in order to prepare itself for the salvation coming in Christ—and chosen to receive it once it had come, not for Israel's own sake, but for the sake of God's honor, thereby to cause it to flow to all peoples and nations.

§ 1

God's ordination was clear and transparent. He first formed and presented a special nation within the human race that could make straight in the wilderness a highway for our God and prepare the way of the Lord in the desert, which represented the life of the nations [see Isa 40:3]. All Israel should therefore have honored Christ at his coming and acknowledged that, when the Messiah appeared, its special calling had been completed and brought to an end, and that its task was now to retreat from its separation and take its place among the nations once again; and thus, notwithstanding its spiritually privileged position, it might be incorporated together with believers from all nations into the one body of Christ. The Jewish nation was to come to an end, and the entire body of the Lord gathered out of the entire human race was to bear the historical stamp that reads "the Israel of God."

Israel, however, did not do so. The Jewish nation refused to decrease so that its King alone would increase [see John 3:30]. Instead, it exalted itself so as to make its King disappear and to retain the place of honor for itself. This led to a break between the Jewish nation and its King. Jesus himself emphatically highlighted this break in the parable of the tenants [see Matt 21:33–41]. When the son, the heir, appeared at the vineyard, "they took him and threw him out of the vineyard and killed him" [Matt 21:39]. As a result, the vineyard itself was taken away from the tenants and given to others. This was fulfilled at Pentecost. In Peter's vision in Joppa, and when Christ appeared to Paul on the road to Damascus, Israel's blessing was solemnly transferred to the pagan world. Israel refused to become universal and directed toward all of humanity.

But salvation was to be universal and for all who believed in God throughout the entire world. So the Jewish nation underwent spiritual suicide because it hung onto its national exclusiveness. Then the vines and branches from which new life would shoot forth were cut off from the root and stump of Israel, and they were newly grafted in among the nations. For that reason, those who are of Israel can partake of salvation; and in the final scene, Israel's excellence and giftedness will even be able to flourish once again, but the kingdom of heaven has shed its Jewish cover and has entered the scene in its universally human character. Every knee shall bow, and every tongue shall confess, and this song of honor will go out for the Lamb of God: "You were slain, and by your blood you ransomed people for God from every tribe and language and people and nation" [Rev 5:9]. This is the glorious fulfillment of the promise given to

Abraham at Ur of the Chaldeans that all the families on the earth would be blessed in him [see Gen 12:3].

This universally human character of Christ's kingship must be maintained strictly and unrelentingly, and we always have to be on guard lest such Jewish particularism return once more in a new form, as has in fact already happened repeatedly in various spiritualist sects. Pious believers joined together in groups that separated themselves completely from human life, had absolutely no desire for universally human life, separated Jesus' kingship from universally human life, and caused the old Jewish leaven to return once again. In such sects, Jesus became the King of a single circle or group, just like the Jews had tried to bring him down to the level of a king over one nation instead of the King who ruled over the kingdom of the world.

The sin of particularism returned time and again, even though the Lord our God, the Creator of all nations, could not claim anything less for his kingdom than the entire world and all nations in their diversity. That false particularism led people to place themselves outside of the stream of life. The world's life stream then dug a channel for itself that Christians did not enter, and so they shrunk and began to grow moldy. Fresh winds no longer passed through the forest to purify the air. All Christian activity was deprived of its strength. Nothing was perceived anymore of the royal power that Christ exercised over the world. And those who set the tone in the life of the world mocked those weaklings who hid and crawled away; and instead of bowing their knees before Jesus' kingship, they smiled down in derision on the throne to which he laid claim.

Things could be no other way, because this revival of the ancient Jewish particularism that occurred in the circle of Christian living stands diametrically opposed to the revelation of the old and new covenants. It is not true that the promise of new life came first to Abraham as the patriarch of the Jewish nation; it had already been made to Adam and Eve in paradise. The seed of the woman, understood universally rather than as the seed of one particular nation, will crush the head of the serpent. The promise of salvation that Abraham later receives is not a special privilege for his seed, but for all the families on the earth [see Gen 12:3].

§ 2

In the book of Psalms, the name of the Lord is glorified over the entire earth. Psalm 100 sings: "Make a joyful noise to the LORD, all the earth! Serve the LORD with gladness! Come into his presence with singing!" [Psa 100:1–2]. Psalm 98 says: "Make a joyful noise to the LORD, all the earth;

break forth into joyous song and sing praises" [Psa 98:4]. From Israel a call always rises up to God, but from Israel it spreads among all nations.

The Savior in Daniel's visions is not a Jew, but a Son of Man [see Dan 7:13]. The prophet similarly says that *Lo-ammi*—that is, what was not the people of the Lord—would become the people of the Lord [see Hos 1–2]. Everything will culminate in the new earth under the new heavens.

Simeon prophesies in the temple that Mary's little child will be salvation for Israel, but also a light for the nations [see Luke 2:30–32]. And when Christ appears, as John the Baptist announced beforehand, salvation will not come to Abraham's physical descendants because God could raise up children of Abraham even from the stones of the desert [see Matt 3:9]. The apostle John is also unambiguous when he says, not that God so loved the Jewish nation, but that he loved the world so as to give his only Son to that world [see John 3:16]. Paul testifies throughout that the true Israel is not from the Jewish nation alone, but from the whole world. And this is confirmed by the outcome that when the light of Christ shines, Palestine is pushed back into darkness while the pagan world is illuminated. Jesus himself had testified, after all, that all power was given to him not specifically over Israel, but over heaven and over the earth [see Matt 28:18]; and even John the Baptist already pointed to him as the Lamb of God who takes away not the sin of Israel, but of the world [see John 1:29]. The apostle John later adopted this broad view when he testified that Christ is the propitiation not only for our sins (that is, those of the Jews), but for the sins of the whole world [see 1 John 2:2].

One would therefore degrade, belittle, and shortchange the kingship of Jesus if one were anxiously to limit it to one particular group, to confine it within tight boundaries, and to refuse to acknowledge that his is a kingship that extends over the whole world. His kingship indeed does find its core in the circle of the regenerated, in those who were transferred from the world to a higher life. But this regenerated group may never be understood as if it stands outside of the world or has been taken out of it. Rather, the group that constitutes the center of Jesus' royal dominion is a human group, not the circle of a special nation. Those who have been incorporated into that group not only remain people in the full sense of the term, but they even display at a higher level what it is to be human. They are not spiritual phantoms who do not belong here, but they must dwell on earth as human beings in a more noble sense. Similarly, the future of the world, the future of humanity, the future of the human race does not depend on what happens outside of that group; this future lies within that holy group.

That group therefore remains bound to the universally human life with all its threads and fibers. It must affect all relationships of that universally human life. In a long, fearsome struggle, the members of Christ's body must spiritually conquer that world for him. All the treasures, all the talents that God created in our human race and caused to flourish from it must be consecrated to the name of Christ. Humanity was the greatest product in God's creation. It was only with humanity, whom God created in his own image, that the creation of the world was completed. From that world and that humanity the highest honor of God had to arise with which his work of creation would be completed and crowned. This is why the kingship of God's only Son could be a kingship only over the entire kingdom of humanity in a rich and full sense, and it had to encompass and comprehend this entire earth, this entire world, this entire higher creaturely life. Abraham was for the Jews and the Gentiles, and Moses was the man of God in Israel. Jesus is the *Ecce Homo*! [see John 19:5], the Son of God and the Son of Man, the King over all human life that is already being unveiled on this earth and in this world, and that will be fully unveiled only at the end of days.

However, this does not mean that what is true of humanity applies necessarily to every human person individually. The world, humanity, is the three measures of flour into which leaven is placed, but the leaven does not immediately work on every bit of flour [see Matt 13:33]. In just the same way, the gospel began to affect only a small part of humanity. This fact, however, does not change the goal of Christ's kingship in any way. §3

A drowning victim may be pulled onto shore with rigid limbs and closed eyes, and hardly any sign of breathing. Nevertheless, if even a small tremor is felt in the heart and people try to restore the victim's breath in the lungs and the spirit's life in the brain, that may well begin in a very small part of the body—yet that does not separate the small heart from the body in any way. Instead, the heart is stimulated to greater activity so as to preserve the entire body.

That is the way things are in this case as well. Jesus found humanity's body when it was, as it were, half dead. It hardly gave any sign of life in the higher sense. And when he awakens the spirit of life in a small part of humanity's body once more, this is not to separate from the rest of the body the part that has been awakened, but rather to bless the whole body through it. This constitutes the very reason, however, why Jesus' kingship had to be organic in nature. As our King, Jesus had to enter into an organic bond with us and exercise his power over us within an organic relationship. God rules over both the small family of the household as well as the large family of the human race. Nevertheless, he rules the family of the household through the father as the head of the family, and he similarly rules humanity through Christ as the Head, the natural and organic Head of the large family of human life. In both cases God's rule is instrumental—coming through others. His rule over the small family, as well as the large family, passes through a Head. Yet in both cases that Head must stand in an organic bond with both the small and large family—a father's organic bond with his small family derives from the fact that he procreated his offspring, while Christ's bond with his large family derives from the fact that, as the Eternal Word, he created everything and wants to incorporate everything into himself as Savior.

This is also why, as our King, Christ is emphatically presented under the name of Head. In current usage, the title Head has largely been deprived of its organic significance. Earlier we pointed to the title *headmaster*, which lacks any kind of organic connection because a master is as such not the father of the students and has no relationship to them by blood or birth. The students do not constitute a body with organic connections, and so the master cannot be a head, since a head without a body is inconceivable apart from decapitation. *Master* was a natural title, but *head* is a senseless name taken from linguistic usage that arose in our unnatural relationships. In 1 Chronicles 29:11, God himself is called the Head over all things: "Yours is the kingdom, O LORD, and you are exalted as head above all." This is because everything owes its origin to God. But the unnatural use of the word *head* does appear, for example, when Numbers 14:4 records that the rebellious people in the wilderness cried out: "Let us choose a head and go back to Egypt." This misuse owes its origin to the sad fact that organic bonds were increasingly weakened everywhere, organic relationships disappeared, and a mechanical relationship took their place with a view to restoring the communal bond and unity. They had lost the natural head, they appointed heads for themselves, and so the head they received was *made*.

What we are told about Christ's headship may never be understood in that way. In fact, every possibility of doing so is cut off because Christ is referred to throughout as the "Head of the body." The apostle writes to the church at Ephesus that God seated Christ as King "at his right hand in the heavenly places, far above all rule and authority and power and dominion, and above every name that is named, not only in this age but also in the one to come. And he put all things under his feet" [Eph 1:20–22]. This is a description of Jesus' kingship. Of this King it is further said: "[God] gave him as head over all things to the church, which is his body, the fullness of him who fills all in all" [Eph 1:22–23]. The apostle develops this further when he writes later in this letter that the members of the church have to "grow up into him who is the head" [see Eph 4:15], and when he testifies of this Head that "from him the whole body, joined and held together by every joint with which it is equipped, when each part is working properly, makes the body grow so that it builds itself up in love" [Eph 4:16]. Christ is "the head of the church, even as the husband is the head of the wife" with whom he becomes one flesh [see Eph 5:23]. In Colossians 1:18, it is repeated once more that Jesus is the Head of the body; and in Colossians 2:19, we are warned not to lose the organic bond with the Head because our life will necessarily die out when we do not hold fast "to the head, from whom the whole body, nourished and knit together through its joints and ligaments, grows with a growth that is from God."

The organic character of the bond that binds us to our King and that §4 binds our King to us could not have been expressed in a stronger way, but in the end this is no more than the development of what Jesus himself indicated when he spoke of the vine and the branches [see John 15]. This latter image is not taken from the human body, but from plants. However, what is common to them both is that branches and shoots also sprout organically from the stump and grow organically from the root. Jesus expresses this same bond in yet another way when, in John 20:17, he calls those who are his own his "brothers." This looks back to his own Sonship and to the fact that those who are his own are born from the same Father whose only begotten Son he is. Paul similarly calls Jesus "the firstborn among many brothers" [Rom 8:29]; and the honorific name of brothers, which is subsequently applied to all believers, points to that same organic connection. The apostle Paul in particular applied this connection to our relationship to Christ, so that he speaks of "being planted together with Christ" [see Rom 6:5 KJV], so that what befell him befalls us and what was true for him applies to us as well, both in his death and in his glorification. The apostle goes so far as to testify that our life is hidden with God in

Christ, and on one occasion he even calls the body "Christ" [see Col 2:17] (that is, that mystical body now envisioned as including the Head).

There is thus no doubt at all that Scripture teaches us that the organic bond dominates everything here, and we should not even for a second imagine Jesus' kingship in terms of a mechanical kingship—as is and must be the case among the kings of the earth. The organic bond between us and our King is also not limited to the spiritual relationship, but includes our human nature together with our body. The Word became flesh [see John 1:14], and he who denies that Christ has come in the flesh is the antichrist, as John says [see 1 John 4:2-3]. He took on the flesh and blood of children [see Heb 2:14]. His was a resurrection not only of the spirit, but also of the body. Now that he sits enthroned at God's right hand, Christ is not like the angels in a spiritual sense alone, but he is enthroned as the Son of Man in our nature and in that glorious body to which he will transform our lowly body, "by the power that enables him even to subject all things to himself" [Phil 3:21].

The organic fellowship and connectedness extend further in all kinds of ways. He was not simply set up as and appointed to be King over us, but he is our King because he has naturally and clearly become our Head, the Head of the body that consists of regenerated humanity. This organic unity between us and our King extends even to the point that his glory will one day communicate itself to us through the development of life, and we will be kings together with him. Especially the [book of] Revelation emphasizes this when those who have been saved sing and confess: "You have made us kings and priests to our God, and we will reign as kings on the earth" [see Rev 5:10]. Already in the salutation in Revelation, it says: He "who loves us and has freed us from our sins by his blood and made us a kingdom, priests to his God and Father" [Rev 1:5-6]. Peter also testified: "You are a chosen race, a royal priesthood, a holy nation, a people for his own possession, that you may proclaim the excellencies of him who called you out of darkness into his marvelous light" [1 Pet 2:9]. This is also the reason why we call this body the *mystical body* of Christ, because the life of the Head and the life of the members are united more intimately than with a normal body. What glows with radiance in the Head is itself communicated to the entire body. There is no appearance or shadow of any artificial composition or subjection. All the glory of Jesus' kingship arises from life itself, and he is the one who infuses and maintains that new life through the Spirit. Whatever he feels, he causes his entire mystical body to feel. Without the Head, the body would not be a body but a corpse, and we could not think of Christ as Head without thinking of that wondrous body whose Head he is.

III.6

THE SECOND ADAM

Thus it is written, "The first man Adam became a living being; the last Adam became a life-giving spirit."

1 CORINTHIANS 15:45

§ 1   Since Christ's kingship has both a universally human (and thus not national-Jewish) and organic character, a difficulty arises that requires further discussion. The organic bond between the Head and the members of the mystical body exists as such only between Christ and those who have been given to him by the Father. Even if this group is broadened to include all believers, the sum total of those who confess Christ still constitutes not even one quarter of the world's population. Thus, even if this group is taken most broadly and generously, it is still with no more than a comparatively small part of the human race that Christ has this organic bond consisting of a mystical body. We therefore cannot suppress the question concerning how this limited organic bond can be reconciled with the universally human character of his kingship.

The apostle Paul clarified this question when he spoke of the first and second Adam. He uses the name Adam in the sense of the head of a race, one who continues living as part of that entire race and corresponds to its type. Listen to what the apostle testifies to us in this matter. He identifies two heads, described as the first and last Adam, who differ in that the first became a living soul while the latter became a life-giving spirit. He adds that he is speaking about the first man Adam, and in this connection about the second Adam, in order to demonstrate that he is discussing a sacred matter that pertains to the entire human race. The source of the difference between the first and second Adam as head of a race is that the first man taken from the earth was earthly, while the second man is the Lord from heaven. A human race, so the apostle continues, comes from each of these Adams. "As was the man of dust, so also are those who are of dust, and as is the man of heaven, so also are those who are of heaven" [1 Cor 15:48].

Can we apply this to different people, such that we might say: "There are some who belong to Adam I, and others to Adam II"? No, this is not the case. Paul considers everyone who belongs to the second Adam, and has passed from death to life, to belong by nature to the first Adam. Paul himself admits that he and all Christians with him first bore the image of the first Adam, but that all who belong to Jesus will now equally bear the image of the second Adam. They already bear this image in their soul, and one day they will have it also in the body. After all, this entire discourse on the second Adam is found in 1 Corinthians 15, a rich chapter whose overarching topic is the resurrection of the dead. In its continuity and context, therefore, the entire pericope or sentence reads as follows: "Thus it is written, 'The first man Adam became a living being'; the last Adam became a life-giving spirit. But it is not the spiritual that is first but the natural, and then the spiritual. The first man was from the earth, a man of dust; the second man is from heaven. As was the man of dust, so also are those who are of the dust, and as is the man of heaven, so also are those who are of heaven. Just as we have borne the image of the man of dust, we shall also bear the image of the man of heaven. I tell you this, brothers: flesh and blood cannot inherit the kingdom of God, nor does the perishable inherit the imperishable" [1 Cor 15:45–50].

The change in the nature of our human race [which the apostle describes] can best be compared to the grafting of a noble shoot onto a wild understock. This is not meant to suggest that the two are entirely the same, but as a metaphor it helps to clarify the distinction for us. One can carefully graft a slip from a nobler scion onto a tree that is wild by nature and prune its wild branches. From then on, the noble shoot draws its life sap from the wild trunk and turns it into noble sap. As a result, the scion begins to grow and expand; new branches and twigs, new leaves, new buds, and new fruit are formed. The character of this new growth is that of the nobler shoot, and if the sap of that shoot's new growth could speak, it would say: "I was wild and came from that wild rootstock, but the

§ 2

life-giving and ennobling spirit of the noble shoot caused me to share in the quality of the nobler shoot."

In the same way, the salvation of the human race is not a matter of individual branches or leaves but concerns the preservation and salvation of the trunk. Every year again the leaves of a tree die off in autumn and its branches are pruned, but the trunk or tree remains one and the same—the very same organism. If we compare humanity and the human race with such a family tree, our question does not concern every twig, leaf, and blossom, but concerns the outcome for the very family tree that is the human race. And just as it is not the wild branches that still sprout below the graft but only what grows on the nobler shoot that is determinative for the character, type, and preservation of the tree when it is grafted, so too what is decisive for the preservation and eternal future of the human race is not the buds that still grow on the wild stump below the graft, but only the buds that appear on the nobler shoot above.

For that reason, we could say that, as the second Adam, Christ has been grafted into the trunk of the human race that once was good but then became wild. The fruit and consequence of this grafting is that whatever buds and grows above the place of the graft now bears the character that separates the nobler shoot from the wild trunk. Christ is the life-giving spirit who introduces his Spirit into the new buds. As soon as the graft has been made, the heavenly Gardener no longer considers that tree wild but noble; he no longer concerns himself with what grows from the root, but with the fine buds sprouting out from the grafted shoot. As far as God is concerned, it is no longer the wild rootstock of the first Adam but the noble bud from the second Adam that counts as the human race. A transition, a transformation, a change in form has taken place. At one time the old understock was the human race, but from now on our human race is what grows on the grafted part of the tree. What is remarkable is that new life is not planted next to the old and wild tree as a new cutting, but new life grows from that old life and draws the life sap from the old trunk and makes it new and ennobles it.

§ 3   None of the forces from the original creation of our human race are abandoned or undone. Only the wild character that permeated our entire life as a result of sin is undone, but that life as such remains with all its saps and powers. The natural life from the first Adam, because it had become wild, could no longer govern the character of our life. Anything in our human race that still bears this wild character, persists in it, and refuses through the graft of the noble shoot to transform itself into nobler branches, leaves, and fruits, is dismissed, ceases to count, decomposes, and is devoted to death.

From the time the graft is made, it is no longer the first Adam who governs, determines, and specifies the nature of the life of our race—it is the second Adam. The first Adam with his wild branches had been dismissed, and his place as the head of the human race is now taken by the second Adam. Whereas the first Adam stood at the outset, at the beginning, when our human race had just been created and was starting to grow, Christ, the second Adam, did not come as the second Head of the race until the growth of the human race was well underway. He takes on our nature. He is grafted onto the old Adamic trunk. But as soon as the graft has been made, the new bud no longer grows in the line of the first Adam but in conformity with the second Adam. At first it is tiny and small and can hardly be noticed. Those who have no eye for it or know nothing about grafting will even fail to notice a graft on a grown trunk, because it is so small and hard to see. But gradually the noble scion and what sprouts from it become stronger, and once the gardener has pruned the wild branches from the old understock, the new graft will grow more and more and become the actual tree.

All analogies fail when they are carried too far; the present analogy fails because, with respect to the human race, the pruning of the growth on the old, wild trunk will occur not in history but on the day of judgment. But when that day comes and the wild branches have been chopped off for good, the tree—the trunk that is the human race—is preserved in the nobler part that grows from the graft. Not the tree, but the wild branches are lost. What is eternally lost is nothing more than loose branches and twigs, never the tree itself. What is lost will fall from the human race, and the human race as God's most noble creation will remain forever as the result of that graft.

Therefore, although as the Head of the mystical body Christ has an organic bond only with those who have passed from death to life, nevertheless his organic bond with our entire human race consists in that organic connection with the part of humanity that has come to life for the simple reason that only those who have life live. Whatever does not find life but remains in death enters into a state of decomposition, and from God's perspective it no longer counts as a part of the living human race. The noble shoot, however, continues to draw to itself the life sap from the wild trunk, and in the same way Christ does not abandon the rootstock of the human race but draws to himself all the powers and talents that God placed in it at creation. His life-giving Spirit extends not only to those who have been called, but to their powers and talents as well. If you distinguish the persons from their powers and talents, the result is that, as the second Adam, Christ is the one who through his life-giving Spirit is the new Head who saves, renews, and causes our human race to blossom into higher life—both in those who have been called, as well as in their powers, gifts, and talents.

One must discard the erroneous supposition that Christ preserves some branches from the human race in order to save them to eternal life as individuals and isolated people, thereafter to abandon the human race with all the gifts and talents created in it by God and to devote it to destruction. It is not a matter of some people but a body, an organically united whole, that is saved. Under Christ as the new Head, that organic body constitutes the real human race from which individuals may fall away even though it continues to be preserved as a race, as a unity, as an organic body. This all-governing fact will be manifested to the eyes of all only at the final day, and at the present time it appears still to conflict with what we see before our eyes. But this fact can and may be understood in this way only if you seek to follow the apostle Paul in honoring Christ as the second Adam, that is, as the new Head of the human race.

§ 4   Even so, there is more that needs to be said, however. Jesus' work on the human race could as such be compared to the influence exercised on the course of life by any great and powerful reformer. For that reason, Scripture points us to two further elements in order to secure the organic bond between Christ and us. The first is his resurrection from the dead, the second is his eternal Sonship.

Christ is "the firstborn among many brothers" [Rom 8:29], and also in this respect he is called the second Adam. The first Adam brought death to all his descendants and thus to the entire human race, while the second Adam brought to light the life in which the human race shall once again flourish to the honor of God. Here, too, there is organic kinship. The first Adam gave us the life that we have by nature, but over that natural life now hovers the shadow of death. In precisely the same way, the second Adam gives life—a life that has been elevated above death and therefore bears an imperishable and incorruptible character. Through his resurrection and by the power of the Spirit, Jesus unveiled the life that triumphs over death; and it is this same newly obtained resurrection life that he now shares with his own through the Spirit.

Those who belong to him do not receive this new life from elsewhere, but from him alone. Just as the first Adam was the head of our human race because he gave it life from his loins, even so Christ, the second Adam, is now the Head of a renewed humanity because he too gives us life from himself—but he is a Head in a much higher way because that life has an incorruptible character. Adam fell from his position as the head of the human race because through his fall he caused death to enter the life that flows from him to his offspring, while Christ remains the Head of the human race because he undid the seed of death in our natural life and raised and renewed life itself so that it can no longer perish.

Only if you see this will you understand the profound meaning of the following words from Paul: "Christ has been raised from the dead, the firstfruits of those who have fallen asleep. For as by a man"—that is, by human fault—"came death, by a man [(nota bene: it does not say by one man)] has come also the resurrection of the dead. For as in Adam all die, so also in Christ shall all be made alive" [1 Cor 15:20-22]. All, that is, who will be revealed as belonging to that humanity that has been saved and restored. Yet a rule has been instituted for this, such that everyone will be made alive in his order: Christ the firstborn, then those who belong to Christ in the future that he brings. Adam is the firstborn in natural life, but also the firstborn in sin and in death; Christ, the second Adam, is the firstborn in spiritual life and the firstborn in the coming glory.

The apostle summarizes all of this in his letter to Colossae: "He is the head of the body, the church. He is the beginning, the firstborn from the dead, that in everything he might be preeminent" [Col 1:18]. The apostle therefore indicates the precise moment when the change in the form of our human race takes place. This was not at Bethlehem nor on Golgotha, but when Christ arose from the grave and triumphed over death. In his resurrection, new life broke through. First, sin had to be undone on Golgotha, and only then could death be overcome at the opened grave. The other members of the body do not receive this new life on their own as Christ received it, but they receive it from him. It is his new life that he communicates to those who are his, and in this way he forms his mystical body.

All the same, Scripture sees the roots and fibers of the organic bond § 5
between Christ and the new humanity sprouting forth from even deeper ground. He is the second Adam because he generated humanity's new life,

just like Adam generated the natural life of our entire human race after he had been driven from paradise. Christ, however, is more. While he can be compared to Adam as the one who generated life and was the head of the race, there is something by virtue of which Christ far surpasses the first Adam. The apostle expresses this as follows: "He is before all things, and in him all things hold together" [Col 1:17]. This means that Christ is also before Adam, and that Adam existed through him and became the first head of our human race in him, "for"—as it says in Colossians 1:16—"by him all things were created, in heaven and on earth, visible and invisible, whether thrones or dominions or rulers or authorities—all things [(including the human race and the first Adam)] were created through him and for him." After all, "For in him all the fullness of God was pleased to dwell"— the fullness, that is, of all power and might [Col 1:19].

Christ's organic bond with regenerated humanity thereby gains a much deeper basis. He has all power and authority over every creature because the one who creates powerfully and freely is lord and master over his creation, to do and deal with it as it pleases him. According to the ordinance of God, the very fact of creation is the root from which the organic bond between the Triune God and his creation arises. Whatever owes its origin and preservation, its being and nature, to its Creator is in its very existence organically connected to its God. To create is not to imitate or fabricate in the way we human beings can produce all kinds of things materially and spiritually. To create is to cause something to arise directly from one's wisdom, will, and ability, that is, from the deeds of the Lord. These deeds of the Lord are all spiritual in their nature. In God's spiritual deeds lie both the root and cause of all creaturely existence, both material and spiritual; and the bond is therefore never imposed mechanically but comes from existence itself and is therefore organic.

Scripture applies these very same norms to the bond that, once it has been made, eternally connects us to Christ as the one who generated the new life that is in the human race. As a type, Christ is not only a lawgiver like Moses, not only a prophet like Elijah or Isaiah; nor is he a patriarch like Abraham, the father of all believers. He is more. He stands much higher. "Before Abraham was, I am," Christ himself testified [John 8:58]. He is before all creatures, including Adam. And if we go back to the deepest root from which all things, including our human race, arose, we cannot stop at Adam but must go back behind Adam to Christ. Once we make this step, Christ is no longer grafted onto humanity's trunk in the middle of history, but our human race has already been organically connected to the eternal Word from the very time of creation. New life was thus not grafted onto a trunk alien to Christ, but onto a trunk *that he himself had planted*.

This is why the apostle John introduces his Gospel, the good news of salvation, with the following solemn confession: "In the beginning was the Word, and the Word was with God, and the Word was God. All things were made through him, and without him was not any thing made that was made" [John 1:1, 3]. Then he specifically writes: "In the Word was life, and the life was the light of men" [John 1:4]. That Word became flesh and lived among us. The Word-become-flesh is Christ, who would later testify: "I am the vine; you are the branches" [John 15:5].

Therefore, the organic bond between Christ's kingship and regenerated humanity and our human race, as it will one day shine in glory, has three levels. First, it is most visible in the bond that binds the Head to the members in the mystical body. Second, the mystical body finds its origin, in a deeper sense, in the new life that Jesus unveiled through his resurrection and now grafted onto the trunk of our human race. But, third, in respect to both the mystical body as well as the resurrection life, that organic bond finds its deepest ground and explanation in the realities that our King is the eternal Word; and along with all other things, our human race with everything entrusted to it as a spiritual treasure has been created through him.

BOTH HEAD
AND KING

And no one can say "Jesus is Lord" except in the Holy Spirit.

1 CORINTHIANS 12:3B

§ 1   Until now, the words *Head* and *King* have been used synonymously, but our understanding will be served by paying attention to the distinction between them. You will sense immediately that the Lord can say to those who are his own, "You will sit with me on my throne, as I also sit down with my Father on his throne" [see Rev 3:21] and, "You will reign with me as kings" [see Rev 5:10]. But it would make no sense for him to say, "You will be head, as I also am the Head." The considerable difference between these words is that head refers to the natural and spontaneous authority over the body and everything that belongs to it, while king expresses the possession of power as dignity and dominion. For this reason, a head remains a head even if in exceptional circumstances it cannot function with the body, while a king stops being a king as soon as his rule is undone. A father remains the head of his family even after he has been taken away from his family in exile; a king ceases being a king as soon as another power drives him out of the country.

This is what makes Christ the Head, not of *all* people but only of those who have been incorporated into his congregation through him, have received new life from him, and share in the atonement in him. For that reason, Scripture also calls him the Head of the congregation. The congregation forms the core of his government. What will become a reality for the entire human race and for the world only at his return and after the day of judgment is already now operative in that congregation. Because the congregation forms a body, it cannot be imagined without a head, and no one can be the Head of the congregation except Christ. The Head automatically belongs to the congregation as the mystical body. It is inseparable from it. And everything that our own head is for our natural body, Christ is also that for the body of his congregation. Its sense of who and what it is comes from him alone. He governs and directs the course of this body's movements. He sees the dangers to which this body is exposed and averts them. He feeds the body with spiritual food and gives it spiritual drink to drink. He cares for that body and maintains it. Without him that body cannot exist for even a moment. Between Christ and his congregation, therefore, the organic bond possesses a very intimate character. He is for the body of his congregation what he as yet cannot be for whatever still lies outside his congregation.

All the same, one may never conclude from this that Christ can be the Head of his congregation without also being its King. His congregation is not outside of, but included within, the kingdom of heaven. Those who belong to Christ and are members of his mystical body have entered the kingdom of heaven. Jesus' kingship also extends to them. It can even be said that the congregation of the faithful forms Christ's bodyguard in his kingdom. They are not simply his members but his soldiers. They each have to fight the Lord's battle in their own way. The congregation is not a private institution attached to Jesus' kingdom. It forms the living center of the kingdom through which Christ makes the Spirit's power go forth among people across the entire world and throughout all history. The congregation forms the indispensable component in his kingdom; and it is only in the congregation that his royal honor and majesty are not only at work, but also acknowledged and honored.

For the moment we will leave aside the congregation of those who have attained glory in order to restrict ourselves to the congregation as it exists on this earth.

Even if Christ's royal majesty extends much further than the congregation, it is only within that congregation as such that people know about and acknowledge that kingship, understand what it is, and honor and celebrate Christ as King. In that congregation, his regiment functions purely and powerfully. He rules it through his Word and Spirit. And while numerous spirits and people exalt themselves against Christ outside of the congregation in order to resist his royal dominion, within the congregation his royal dominion is confessed from one century into the next. It honors him not only as its highest Prophet and only High Priest, but also as its eternal King. He is its Head automatically. This is not something that first needs to be acknowledged and confessed. It is a fact that was given when the congregation came into being. But that he, as the Head of the congregation, is also its King and is to be honored as its King is not a natural fact. This honor comes to him only after people acknowledge and confess it.

He is and remains its Head because those who have been given to him by the Father cannot be torn from his hand. But when it wanders into error, the congregation can push Christ's kingship into the background as it does so often at the present time. From God's perspective, he never stops reigning over it and being its King; and yet kingship presupposes two things: (1) that a King reigns, and (2) that his dominion is acknowledged and honored. In the case of our heavenly King there cannot be any shortcoming in regard to the former, but for the latter there can be. Even when the head over a family encounters disobedience and a refusal of subjection, he remains the father and head of his family, but his authority thereby suffers. Similarly, Christ remains the Head of his congregation even when it strays from him; yet when the congregation gets sidetracked, it loses the sense of his royal dominion and lives on as if it had no King.

§ 2   As a rule, Scripture refers to Christ's kingship over and in his congregation by calling him its Lord. In all of the apostolic writings, Lord is the fixed and regular expression for referring not to the Triune God, but to Christ. He is also called its King whenever the congregation is mentioned in connection with Christ's dominion over the world; but whenever the congregation and believers are considered in their own right, Scripture always speaks of our Lord Jesus Christ. The title Lord in fact expresses the essence of the mutual relationship so clearly that the apostle testifies that "no one can say 'Jesus is Lord' except in the Holy Spirit" [1 Cor 12:3]. By this he means that only those who have been incorporated into the body of Christ through the work of the Holy Spirit can acknowledge him as their Lord, not with words but in deeds and in truth. Others can speak about "the Lord Jesus" as well, but they cannot comprehend and fathom what it means to call Christ Lord; only those who have been united with Christ can do this.

Therefore, whenever the term the Lord occurs in the apostolic writings, it should be understood not as a reference to the Triune God or the Father, but very specifically and almost always as a reference to Christ. There are exceptions when this highest name is still applied to Yahweh in quotations from the Old Testament, but they are very rare and occur most often in citations from the Old Testament. The rule remains that the name Lord as such and without any further designation is to be understood of Christ and him alone. When it says, "Where the Spirit of the Lord is, there is freedom" [2 Cor 3:17], this refers to the Spirit of Christ. When it says, "Everyone who calls on the name of the Lord will be saved" [Joel 2:32], this is transferred to Christ [Rom 10:13]. And when Scripture explains that "there are varieties of service, but the same Lord" [1 Cor 12:5], the context makes it clear that this refers specifically to Christ. Similarly, when it says, "Be strong in the Lord and in the strength of his might" [Eph 6:10], this applies to Christ as well. Indeed, the repeated expression "in the Lord" points not to hidden communion with the Triune Being, but quite specifically to the intimate relationship in which those who have been saved stand toward Christ.

In Malachi 1:6, Yahweh asks: "If then I am a father, where is my honor? And if I am a Lord, where is my fear?" In the Old Testament, the word *Lord* expressed the dominion that God has over all creation, and here too we see the same distinction as that between Christ's headship and lordship. God is Father insofar as he gave existence to all creatures. But alongside this there is a second relationship that is not one of a Father but of a Lord. Everything is his. Everything exists through him and for him alone. He alone exercises the exalted divine regiment over all creatures. As a son must honor his father, so all creatures must honor their God.

But there is more. God is also the Lord, the Commander, the Governor over all creation, and in that capacity all creatures must fear him. With Christ things are the same way. Once again, the mystical body owes its existence to him, and this comes to expression when we profess that he is the Head of the body just as God is the Father of all creatures. But as Yahweh is also Possessor, Owner, the absolute Designer over all creatures, so too Christ is the Lord of those who are his and he has all authority over them so that they must honor him not only as their Head but also as their Lord.

Insofar as he is their Head, they are his members; insofar as he is the Lord of all, they are his servants. They exist for his honor, his glory, and are called to devote themselves and all that is theirs to him, place this in his service, and offer this to him as a sacrifice. While the expression *Head of the congregation* points more to what proceeds and flows from Christ to the congregation, the expression *Lord* points to what he as Lord can expect and claim from those who are his. A king receives tribute from his subjects, he claims homage and honor from his people, and he demands that those who can fight join his army in order to cast down all opposition against the glory of his name. The word *subject* does not occur in Scripture. In dogmatics, it has become customary to say that Christ cannot be a King without any subjects, but this word is not found in Scripture. It is suited more to the kings of the nations than to the much nobler kingship of God or of Christ. Scripture does say that the congregation must submit to Christ, but this means only that it has to obey his high command. However, the word *subject* is never used to express the essence of a believer. Instead, the words *(man)servant* and *(maid)servant* and *soldier* are used for this purpose, and then always in connection with Christ's lordship.

§ 3   The expression *servant of Christ* should not be misunderstood. Misunderstandings could have been avoided if the translators had chosen to translate the word not as *servant* but as *slave* or *serf*, as it should have been. They chose the word *servant* because *slave* has a negative ring in our ears and would be inappropriate for describing our relationship to Christ. But whenever we read the word *servant* in the apostolic writings, we have to remember always that in those days being a servant was completely different than today. Nowadays servants are free people who hire themselves out by a service contract; and this was also the rule in Israel, as is evident from the parable of the tenants. But all of Paul's letters were written to churches in pagan cities like Rome, Corinth, Ephesus, Colossae, and so on; and in that pagan world slavery did exist and was widely practiced at the time. Someone could be born as a slave or sold as a slave. This implied that the slave's lord had a complete right of disposal over him or her. Before their lord, slaves were not people but property, possessions, and they belonged body and soul to their master. Slaves had no rights in civil society. Their lord could discipline them as he pleased, sell and trade them, and to a certain extent he even had the right of disposal over his slaves' lives.

In Greek, such a slave was called a *doulos*, whereas a hireling was called a *diakonos*. The relationship to Christ is sometimes described with the word *diakonos*, but then in reference to an appointed office-bearer in the church. Those in the church of Christ who care for the poor we call *deacons*, because this word derives from the word *diakonos*. However, when the apostle was not referring to an office but to the relationship that every member of the congregation has with Christ as his Lord, he used the word *doulos*, which refers not to a free servant but to a slave, so that it could be translated with what we used to refer to in our country during the Middle Ages as a serf. While our translators have avoided the word *slave* because of its ignoble associations and substituted the word *(man)servant* and *(maid)servant* in its place, we should never forget that the expression *servant of Christ* has a much deeper significance than the word *servant* at first seems to convey to us.

Our Catechism was sensitive to this and therefore incorporated the word *belong*, and our belonging to Christ is called our only comfort in life and death.[1] According to the Heidelberger, that only comfort is that I belong, body and soul, both in life and in death, to my faithful Savior Jesus Christ. The word *belong* points to property, to a possession. Christ owns us. We are his possession, and in that sense the word *serf* would have been most accurate. At first we did not belong to Christ but were under the power of another lord who had dominion over us. Jesus, however, bought us from the power of our former lord and master. As it says in 1 Corinthians 6:20: "You were bought with a price," and again in 1 Corinthians 7:23: "You were bought with a price; do not become slaves of men." Jesus paid the ransom to set us free. He paid, as the apostle Peter testifies, not with gold or silver but with his precious blood [see 1 Pet 1:18]. Through that payment and ransom we are now saved from our former state of dependence, and we have become Christ's property and changed into his possession. Satan was the ruler of this world. His power reigned over us, but now we have been freed from his power. There is no longer any bond that ties us to him. We are freedmen in respect to him.

We were not freed to be our own lord and master, however, but to exchange one lord and master for another. Instead of Satan, it is now Christ who is the Lord and Master over our hearts. We now belong to him in

---

1. Here Kuyper uses the word *lijfeigene*, a serf, referring to someone whose body belonged to a master, who lacked physical freedom. We are serfs of Christ, the property and possession owned by Christ, which is our only comfort in life and in death. The Dutch text of the catechism actually uses the word *eigendom*, referring to ownership or possession, and in the translation of this sentence the word is rendered as "belong" and "belonging." See also Heidelberg Catechism, Lord's Day 1, Q&A 1, in *RC* 2:771, "What is your only comfort in life and in death? That I, with body and soul, both in life and in death am not my own, but belong to my faithful Savior Jesus Christ."

body and soul, with our entire person and all our powers and gifts. We do not exist for ourselves, but we must exist, live, endure, bear, and suffer for him.

This is the profound meaning and significance of calling Christ our Lord. We ourselves cannot exercise any right, because he has every right over us. We may no longer seek or aim at anything of our own besides what we are from Christ, because we belong entirely to him with all that is in us and with us. His will determines what we must will. Over against his will there is no room for any independent will of our own. We are completely in him. In him we lose ourselves. It is precisely when we lose ourselves in him that we gain the full freedom of the children of God. A fish stranded on the beach is not free, but a fish in water is free even though it is then fully enclosed in water on all sides. In precisely the same way, only when we have first been incorporated into Christ and taken up in Christ do we regain our true life and do we continue to enjoy it, as often and as long as we ourselves are no longer anything and Christ has become everything for us.

§ 4 Here our relationship to Christ as our Lord is grounded in the work of salvation itself, not as something incidental but as something flowing directly from Christ's appearance as the Messiah. Christ's lordship goes back to the work of creation. By virtue of our creation we are God's possession. We belong entirely to God and exist entirely for his honor; we respect no will but his will, and we accept our lot from his most sacred disposition. That was paradise. That was our original state. Through sin, however, people broke free from this relationship. They insisted on pushing through their own will against the will of God. They tried to live not for God, but for themselves. They attempted to become their own lord and their own master. For that reason, sinners merely think that they have reached their goal and become free. This is an illusion, however, and not the reality. By separating themselves from God, people became slaves of sin and were transferred into the service of the tempter. They do not know this, they do not admit it, they deny it. But the fact remains that they did the will of the Tempter and therefore came under his dominion.

By sacrificing himself, Christ broke this dominion over our sinful heart, and that bond with which Satan tied us to himself has slipped from our necks. Nevertheless, people cannot continue in that position. They cannot live on their own. People are destined and made to be the vehicle and instrument of a willpower that stands above them. This is why Christ exercises dominion over those who have been saved. He takes them up as his own into his life circle. Through his Spirit he spurs them on to exist and live for him alone.

This is what is being expressed when it says that Christ has become their Lord and that they are his possession and his man- and maidservants. To express this, it is the word *Lord* rather than *King* that is used because, according to our earthly standards, a lord is more than a king. In our earthly arrangement, a king can command his subjects, although not in a full sense; the lord of a slave meets no resistance and has, without any condition or restriction, complete control over him. The expression *the Lord* therefore includes Christ's kingship over those who are his, but it is much stronger and includes a right of control that is much more complete. The ultimate goal of Christ's lordship is to lead us back into the lordship of the Triune God so that God may be all in all. But before this final goal has been reached, the rule is given to Christ and he is the "King of kings and Lord of lords" [1 Tim 6:15; Rev 19:16]. For those who have a deep understanding of the distinction between the meaning of a lord and a king, the title *our Lord* becomes much more penetrating, encompassing, and comprehensive. His lordship is, so to speak, a kingship of a higher degree.

The very same thing is expressed when those who are saved are called Christ's *soldiers*. Christ is then depicted for us as our General. And especially in the days when Paul wrote his letters, this implied that a soldier denied his own will under the threat of the strictest discipline and knew no greater glory than to fulfill his general's will precisely and in full submission. Today that relationship has changed in many ways, but those who read Scripture must understand this expression as it applied at that time. The concept of a soldier of Jesus Christ included two thoughts. First, a soldier relinquished his will entirely, so that his only directive was found in his general's order and command. In addition to this, the soldier was bound to devote all his courage, all his forces, all his zeal, and even his life, to his general. If necessary, he had to face death undauntedly for his general and commander and die for his general. Included in this, of course, was every lesser form of suffering and devotion.

The only difference between the terms *serf* and *soldier* is that the word *doulos*—or serf—aimed more at what Christ did for us, while the word *soldier* emphasized instead what we have to do for Christ. These two words agree, however, in that they both definitely express Jesus' dominion and

Jesus' kingship over those whom he has saved. Those who do accept Jesus as their Savior and boast in their calling to eternal life, but fail to deduce immediately from it that Christ is their Lord, their King, their complete Commander, and the absolute Controller over their life and lot—over their powers and abilities—run the serious risk of making their names illegible in the book of life.

THE CURSE ON CAPERNAUM

And Jesus came and said to them, "All authority in heaven and on earth has been given to me."

MATTHEW 28:18

Christ is therefore the King of his own people and the Head of the con- §1 gregation, which is his body. He expressed this figuratively when he said: "I am the vine; you are the branches" [John 15:5], and depicted it with the metaphor of the shepherd with the sheep of his flock. In this bond between King and people, Head and body, Vine and branches, Shepherd and sheep, lies the very core of Jesus' high calling. However, because this bond is at first entirely spiritual, some people understood these things in no more than a figurative sense, as if nothing more was being expressed than that Christ, through his Spirit, exercises a certain influence on the hearts of those who acknowledge him as their Savior. A significant number even trivialize the significance of this bond so much that they explain Jesus' influence on the hearts of those who are his as being the near equivalent of the influence that one person exercises on another, albeit to a somewhat higher degree. They claim that the influence that Jesus' Spirit exercises on the spirit of those who are his is intended to confirm their faith, to clarify their hope, and to keep ablaze the fire of their love. This spiritual and moral influence, so they say, is then called "Jesus' kingship over our hearts," while the resulting richer atmosphere is depicted in terms of "the kingdom of heaven."

On the basis of this standpoint, as so many have taken it, it follows that the figurative titles of King and Head can be abandoned. After all, from this perspective they are only meaningless names, and the congregation derives no benefit from them. What reason would there be not to abolish these obsolete names, and instead to speak clearly, briefly, and simply of Jesus' *influence*—that is, of Jesus' spiritual influence on the hearts of those who confess him? In that case, all mysticism would fall away. Then one would speak of the influence of Jesus' example, the influence of his Word, and the influence of that institution he called into being that is now known as the church, whose influence has gone forth upon the world and especially upon those who confess him. You will sense, however, that this is nothing but a premeditated destruction of Jesus' kingship, the very thing against which we are here protesting. [To do so] would be to oppose Scripture, to oppose Jesus himself; it would be to dissolve the most sacred in the melting pot of the common moral notions held by this rationalizing world.

Not the modern moral teachers, however, but Jesus himself and his apostles must teach us how we are to conceive of his kingship in a way that corresponds to reality. When we listen to their teaching, it soon becomes evident and clear as day that Jesus' kingship includes something entirely different than moral-spiritual influence His kingship has to do with power, authority, and majesty—indeed, a nearly boundless measure of power. This came to light first when Jesus made his announcement of doom over Capernaum. The announcement went as follows: "And you, Capernaum, who are [were] exalted to heaven, will be brought down to Hades" [Matt 11:23 NKJV].

These words include two elements: (1) that Jesus refers to his three-year stay in Capernaum as its having been "exalted to heaven"; and (2) that Jesus was authorized to pronounce an irrevocable judgment over this city. This judgment on Capernaum has been fulfilled; the city has disappeared entirely from the face of the earth and no longer exists. This kind of appalling declaration far surpasses the boundaries of what a spiritual leader, moral teacher, and religious founder could say. Any spiritual leader, moral teacher, or religious founder who places himself so far in the foreground as to call his residence in a given city an honor that "exalts it to heaven" would show by that one statement alone that morally he ought to humble himself in his pride. And anyone would be considered mad if they pronounced the judgment of hell on a city that refused to acknowledge his importance.

That is why one should never pass too quickly over such strong statements of Jesus. These are words that no one would ever have placed on his lips. These are words that have the mark of authenticity, in complete departure from the usual. These are words that highlight Jesus' self-consciousness as the one who has been clothed with an authority and dignity that far surpass all the exaltation and majesty of the earth's sovereigns.

What we have said is not exhaustive, however, because Jesus dares also to say to the inhabitants of Capernaum: "I tell you that it will be more tolerable on the day of judgment for the land of Sodom than for you" [Matt 11:24]. Throughout the Scriptures, the sin of Sodom is branded as the greatest abomination, and we can be thankful to add that moral public opinion still points to Sodom as the city in which human self-abasement had reached its deepest depths. But, pray tell, why would you then want to persuade us that the import of Jesus' kingship is merely spiritual and moral? What do you think would happen to a moral preacher today who dares to exalt himself so highly as to say that falling into the sin of Sodom is less serious than daring to reject him? Jesus, your holy Jesus, however, said this and nothing less.

Jesus himself appears to have been impressed for some time with the effect that the harsh words he spoke over Capernaum—an effect that reversed every relationship—must have had on his audience. The sharp contrast between the common, moral view of Israel's leading men and the position betrayed in Jesus' words regarding Capernaum penetrated him so deeply that, as the story goes on to relate, he sought to unburden himself from the oppressiveness of these words by lifting up his soul to his Father and saying: "I thank you, Father, Lord of heaven and earth, that you have hidden these things from the wise and understanding and revealed them to little children," to the simple ones who follow me [Matt 11:25]. The connection between this prayer and the judgment pronounced on Capernaum finds a ready psychological explanation. What Jesus had said about Capernaum was completely contrary to the accepted moral standards. It came from a higher order, an order that does not take life on earth on its own but that puts earth and heaven together and considers them according to a higher and more sacred ordinance. The teachings and moral admonitions of the wise and prudent of this world stood diametrically

§ 2

opposed to this ordinance, however, and only the children—that is, the simple people among his followers—could follow these higher ordinances without being offended. For this reason Jesus addressed his Father as "Lord of heaven and earth," an expression that points to a higher ordination and sharply contrasts the moral and spiritual leaders in normal life (that is, "the wise and understanding") with the people—exposed and therefore open before him—who had joined him and are here called children. To make it even clearer that this was a matter of higher ordinances, Jesus even adds: "Yes, Father, for such was your gracious will" [Matt 11:26].

When Jesus lifted up his soul to his Father, he apparently did not whisper these words in quiet and seclusion, but in spiritual ecstasy he pronounced them in his disciples' hearing. For how else would they have been reported to us in the Gospel? Jesus does not end there, but he turns to his disciples and speaks these all-decisive words: "All things have been handed over to me by my Father" [Matt 11:27]. The doom he pronounced over Capernaum because its inhabitants had rejected him was not simply expressing an expectation of how things would transpire. It was not only a prophecy that this was the way things would occur. Instead, it was a judicial sentence being pronounced by the One who had the authority to make such a judgment, since the Father had given him authority and had given him all things.

As if to explain more clearly to his disciples the remarkable element in this, Jesus points to his entirely unique position: "No one knows the Son except the Father, and no one knows the Father except the Son and anyone to whom the Son chooses to reveal him" [Matt 11:27]. This entailed the declaration not of the divine mystery, but of his authority through which he was authorized to pronounce such a judgment. Neither the inhabitants of Capernaum nor even his disciples could understand this. His amazing power is of such a nature that only the Father knows it, since among people no one understands who the Son is. Not one creature knows the Son, but only the Father does. And connected to this, no one knows the Father except the Son, and only those who are willing to learn from the Son who the Father is and what his ordinances are can be introduced to the mystery of heaven and earth. At the end [of the pericope], Jesus returns to this mystery of the ordinances of a higher order comprehending both heaven and earth. There is a twofold spiritual yoke. On the one hand, we find the yoke of the wise and prudent world that pushes people down and causes them to be bent over as they walk; and on the other hand, we discover the yoke of higher ordinances that brings rest and causes the soul to be revived. This constitutes the reason why, shortly after pronouncing judgment upon Capernaum, which had rejected him, Jesus immediately added the following appeal: "Come to me, all who labor and are heavy laden, and I will give you rest. For my yoke is easy, and my burden is light" [Matt 11:28, 30].

Understood in its context, this declaration about Capernaum constitutes one of the most important statements that the Gospel offers us regarding his kingship. The name or title of *king* is not found here. The words "all things have been handed over to me" should therefore not be taken on their own, something that easily happens when texts are memorized in isolation. Instead, the all-decisive declaration that all things have been handed over to him must be taken in the context of what was said just before about Capernaum, and what was said immediately after concerning the two yokes. These words contain a revelation of a royal authority and royal power that binds Jesus' authority, as well as his power, directly to his person in such a way as to prevent any comparison between him and other moral teachers, spiritual revivalists, and religious founders. It is revelatory of another world, of a different higher order. It depicts a special kingdom, entirely distinct from the kingdom of the world. The door is opened to give you insight from afar into the kingdom of heaven as it stands over against the kingdom of the earth and nevertheless still comes to have dominion over that earth as well. That kingdom is the kingdom of heaven in which, as Jesus himself testifies here, one cannot imagine any other king than him.

Moreover, this particular testimony that all things have been given to him by the Father is not an isolated case. It comes up repeatedly in different forms and other contexts. John the Baptist had already declared: "The Father loves the Son and has given all things into his hand" (John 3:35); and Jesus himself repeated three more times what he had said on the occasion of the pronouncement of doom over Capernaum. The first time was at Bethesda, when he testified: "The Father has given me authority to execute judgment," not because he was the Son of God but, as it explicitly says, "because he is the Son of Man" [see John 5:27]. This entire appointment of Jesus as Judge, one day to execute judgment upon all those in the grave, coincides with what he declared at Capernaum about all things having been handed over to him. From the superiority extended to him over all things flows his power to judge, and in this passage it is this power to judge that

§ 3

303

comes out most forcefully. However, this immediately expands the power of Jesus' kingship from the circle of those who are his to all people.

Now we are used to a judicial authority that has a certain independent place next to that of the king. Unthinking constitutional law experts have even proclaimed that sovereignty is not singular but is divided into three parts, one of which is judicial authority. This erroneous teaching has also been adopted by many Christians, such that they no longer sense, even in Jesus, the direct relationship that exists between his judicial authority and his kingship. But in Jesus' day, and especially in Israel, this was unthinkable. Kings at that time held judicial authority in their hands, as we can recall from Solomon's first judgment. The one who exercised the highest judicial authority was the king in so doing, by virtue of that authority—just as today some constitutional law experts quite rightly teach that judicial authorization flows from the Crown, explaining why judgments today continue to be pronounced in the name of the king. We are thus inconsistent when we acknowledge Jesus' judicial authority but see in it something other than an attribute of his kingship. On the contrary, wherever Jesus is spoken of as the Judge who will render a verdict that cannot be appealed, that judicial authority is a most certain and clear indication of his royal sovereignty.

Jesus himself is the incontestable witness for this point. Nowhere does Scripture speak more decidedly of Jesus' majesty as Judge than in Matthew 25:31. What do we read there? Once again, the text speaks not of the Son of God but of the Son of Man. "When the Son of Man comes in his glory, and all the angels with him, then he will sit on his glorious throne. Before him will be gathered all the nations" [Matt 25:31-32]. This verse does not say that *all who confess him* will be gathered before him, but that the *entire human race* will be gathered. And when the judgment, the verdict, is rendered, it explicitly says: "Then the King will say to those on his right" [Matt 25:34], and again in verse 40: "And the King will answer them." Here also the two realities are placed together: (1) his power of judgment that extends not only over those who confess his name, but also over the entire earth, over all nations; and (2) his kingship as it flows from this judicial authority. The King and Judge are one and the same person. The King himself is Judge. The Judge from whom there is no higher appeal or right of pardon can be none other than the King. Jesus' excellence as Judge, or King-Judge, is preached throughout the apostolic writings. "We must all appear before the judgment seat of Christ" [2 Cor 5:10] is the basic thrust of everything the apostles reveal to us about the end of days, and in the Revelation that came to John on Patmos the same theme returns time and again. "Then I saw heaven opened, and behold, a white horse! The one sitting on it is called Faithful and True, and in righteousness he judges" [Rev 19:11].

Shortly before Gethsemane, in his high priestly prayer, testifying not to men, but to the Father, Jesus solemnly confirms that he has been authority over all things: "Father, the hour has come; glorify your Son that the Son may glorify you, since you have given him authority over all flesh" [John 17:1–2]. This seals that part of our confession with an even holier seal. A superficial reading can lead one to think that what Jesus said in the past about "his authority over all things" and about his judicial authority should not be understood all too literally; suggesting that one should sooner understand it in the sense that in the end spirit will triumph over matter, and that in this way Jesus' spirit, as the most richly and purely sophisticated spirit, of itself executes a judgment over all spiritual life. It hardly needs to be said that a careful study of the context in which Jesus made these statements, and of the manner in which he made them, eliminates each and every possibility for such an interpretation. For Jesus, all boasting, even the semblance of the same, is excluded. That is why it is so significant, especially for eliminating these kinds of interpretations, that shortly before he went to Gethsemane and Golgotha—at the sacred moment when he lifted his apostles and his church up to his Father in his high priestly prayer—Jesus not only maintained the powerful awareness that power over all flesh had been given to him, but he even emphasized it at the very beginning of his prayer as the ground on which that prayer rested.

For Jesus, even this did not suffice. In the last words he spoke before he ascended from the Mount of Olives, Jesus repeated it one more time: "All authority in heaven and on earth has been given to me" [Matt 28:18]. This pronouncement is so direct, so significant, and so clear, that unbelieving [biblical] criticism could only conclude that it is inauthentic. This is, of course, the method that the [higher critics] always apply. When Jesus speaks about the spiritual and moral life of everyday, they are willing accept what it says. In those cases, they consider what they read in the Gospels to be genuine. After all, this pleases those who deny Jesus' kingship and suits their view of Jesus' brilliance as a spiritual leader, a moral teacher, and a religious founder. Anything in Jesus' words that betrays a

§ 4

much higher, more elevated, and more majestic sense of self, however, conflicts with the image of him they give us. For that reason, they first weakened these elements through a false interpretation, then emptied them of their real meaning by interpreting them figuratively, and finally made them suspect and declared them to be false. And many church members who are not acquainted with this background accept these things.

However, the very effort made by the critics to eliminate and undo such statements on the part of Jesus elevates their importance for us. Jesus' last word before his ascension into heaven obviously had to have great weight and a far-reaching significance. It was his last will and testament to his disciples. The disciples were still obsessed with the idea that Jesus would be King, but King only of Israel; and so we read that even at that last moment they still asked him: "Lord, will you at this time restore the kingdom to Israel?" [Acts 1:6]. Countering this restriction, Jesus straightaway gives the command to preach his name to the end of the earth. In just the same way, on the mount in Galilee he had said: "All authority in heaven and on earth has been given to me," only to conclude forthwith: "Go therefore and make disciples of all nations" [Matt 28:18-19]. It goes without saying that these things were all intended to expand his kingdom spiritually, because his kingship can be recognized only where his kingdom is spiritually expanded. This was also why Jesus had said in his high priestly prayer: "You have given him authority over all flesh, to give eternal life to all whom you have given him" [John 17:2]. And here, too, he says: "All authority in heaven and on earth has been given to me. Go therefore and make disciples of all nations, teaching them to observe all that I have commanded you, and seal them with my baptism" [see Matt 28:18-20].

Although the intention remains to save people, the world, humanity, our human race—and thus to cause the spiritual kingdom to triumph— the expressions pointing to Jesus' royal authority have such far-reaching significance that they include the right of control and determination over everything that impels the lot of nations and of the human race. Not a single one of these expressions has any kind of restriction. Nowhere is his authority limited to the spiritual terrain. From beginning to end, the words are comprehensive and include all things. It is clear that the entire course of affairs, the entire course of history, the destiny of nations in every area, all [serve to] influence people's readiness, or lack thereof, to open their hearts to Jesus. It is also clear that the church's lot on this earth is determined by all kinds of external events. There are, for example, vast regions in Asia Minor and northern Africa where the church, which used to flourish there, has altogether disappeared with the passing of time. In like manner, it is hence also clear that the future of the church, and so also the future of the heavenly kingdom, could only be secured by a King who possessed an authority that extended not only to spiritual matters but also a power over all of these events that determine the lot of nations.

To section off the course of spiritual things from the course of earthly events is a false spiritualism that the entire course of history refutes. And when one keeps this undeniable connection between spiritual and earthly things in mind while reading and rereading Jesus' firm claims that: "All things have been handed over to me by my Father" [Matt 11:27], "You have given me authority over all flesh" [John 17:2], and, "All authority in heaven and on earth has been given to me" [Matt 28:18], then one cannot help but reject every interpretation that tries to exclude anything whatsoever. You will take it for certain that Jesus presents himself as the Shepherd of the sheep, as the Head of the congregation, but then also as the King in his majesty. The sovereignty he has been granted is not nominal, but is clothed with all the authority and power that is necessary to maintain and complete his kingdom.

III.9

THE SPIRITS SUBJECTED TO HIM

And he put all things under his feet.

Ephesians 1:22a

§ 1   Jesus' judgment seat contains proof that his kingship is in no way restricted to believers but extends to all human beings. That Christ will be seated as Judge at the final judgment is a consequence of his kingly authority, and regarding the sentence he will pronounce in the final judgment it is emphatically testified that it will be declared upon all who are in the grave. Similarly, Jesus declared elsewhere that not only "the sheep" but also "the goats" would appear before his judgment seat [see Matt 25:31–46]. If Jesus' judicial authority extended only to believers who will be saved unto eternal life, there would be virtually no judgment at all but only acquittal and pardon. The profound seriousness of the final judgment is owing to the day when those who did not accept him and opposed his cause first appear before Christ. For that reason, there is no advantage for the unbelieving world to keep their distance from Christ in this life and pretend that he is not their concern. It is not up to the unbelieving world to decide whether they will have anything to do with Christ. This is something that Christ himself determines according to the authority he received from the Father. And one day the hour will arrive when the thousands upon thousands of those who refused to recognize Jesus' kingship here on earth must nonetheless appear before him and be subjected eternally to the exercising of his judicial authority. The denied, rejected, or forgotten Savior will be their Judge, and he will then also manifest himself as their King.

This is something we need to emphasize, because the view that makes Christ simply the Head of the congregation and King over only those who are his own has gained more and more acceptance over the course of the past years. The claim was that we can speak only of a spiritual dominion on the part of Christ over the spirits. This spiritual authority in turn manifested itself only to those who came to faith in Christ. For that reason, Jesus' kingly dominion could extend over them alone, and this very circumstance was taken as proof that this kingship could consist only in exercising influences leading to holier living. Because his kingship was limited to believers alone, it was in fact destroyed and lowered to a nominal title of honor.

That this whole idea is untenable is immediately demonstrated when we point out in response that Christ now already holds—and will continue to hold—the highest judicial authority over all unbelievers as well, and thus over the entire human race. It surely cannot suffice to allude simply to spiritual influences, after all; their not engaging Christ or their rejection of him shows that these influences failed to work or to penetrate far enough. Still, the control over the destiny—over the ups and downs—of all of them has been put in Christ's hands. It follows from this that he also knows all unbelievers, knows them in their inner existence, and knows them in all that they have done, whether good or evil, in order to be able one day to pronounce a sentence upon them. Thus Christ has an authority that extends over all people, presupposes knowledge of the lives of all, and will one day be exercised over them in divine majesty without the possibility of appeal.

On the whole, too little attention is devoted to the great significance of Jesus' judicial authority. The entire Christian church has confessed throughout the centuries, and continues to do so even now, that Christ is "seated at the right hand of God; from there he will come to judge the living and the dead." Scripture repeatedly points out that not only the eternal destiny of those who have been saved, but also the eternal destiny of those who are lost will be decided in this final judgment. It is clear to everyone, therefore, that the final judgment will also extend to the Lord's enemies— and this final judgment would be inconceivable in Christ's kingdom unless everyone's life and existence were uncovered before him. Not only his kingship as such, but most decidedly also his kingship over unbelievers follows from the fact that the Father has given to the Son the right to pronounce the judgment.

From this it is apparent that Christ's kingship does not concern individual people, but the entire human race. According to Psalm 2, Christ has received the nations as his heritage and the ends of the earth as his possession [see Psa 2:8], and all sovereigns on earth are called to kiss the Son with the kiss of loyalty and to pay him homage lest they "perish in the way, for his wrath is quickly kindled" [Psa 2:12]. Even if the congregation of believers remains his mystical body and in that capacity forms the center of his most focused influence, Christ's honor is not limited to the fact that he is the Head of the congregation. It is true that, after the final judgment has been rendered, all who are saved will be incorporated into that mystical body; and the new humanity, once those who are lost have fallen away, will be one with that body. But until that hour arrives, a distinction must be drawn. The kingship of Christ, insofar as it pertains to this earth, falls into two spheres: the sphere of believers, in which he spiritually already has dominion at the present time; and the sphere of the as yet unregenerate world, which, together with all things, has been put "in subjection under his feet" [Heb 2:8]. Here, too, we find proof that Christ's dominion is in no way limited to salvation unto eternal life; he exercises his royal authority over our human life in its entirety, in every sphere where humanity is active and develops its power. It is not the case that the only question occupying Christ was, "Will this or that soul be saved or lost?" as if that question could be fully separated from the rest of our life. Such a divorce and separation in our human life is entirely unimaginable. Our human life is a single system in which all its gears and sprockets mesh together. The question about the life of our soul cannot be isolated from all the other questions governing our life. And this is why Jesus' kingship cannot and may not be understood as dominion over one part of life. Since everything in our personal life is connected, Jesus' dominion must also extend over everything in that life. His dominion must involve an authority that governs the entire development of our personal life, as well as human life in general.

§ 2   This is even more evident when, in considering Christ's kingship, we look not only to his sitting as Judge in the final judgment but also to his dominion over the spirit world. Just like his judicial supremacy, Christ's highest exaltation above the spiritual powers in the human world is emphatically taught in the apostolic writings. Jesus himself already revealed his authority over the angelic world when he testified that when the Son of Man appears for judgment, he will come as a King "and all the angels with him" [Matt 25:31]. Therefore, the angels are without exception presented as his bodyguards, as following him, and as subjected to his ordinance.

A prelude to this bliss could be seen already at Bethlehem, when the angels descended to greet the newborn King with jubilant singing. If the angels are subjected to Christ, this must per se be true also of demons, since they were originally angels as well but fell from their state. In line with this, we see throughout the Gospels that Jesus has power over the demons—such an authority, in fact, that he casts them out and that they cannot withstand the effect of his authoritative Word. In the desert, Jesus took on the head of the demons, and conquered him as well. At Golgotha, Satan's power was broken for good, so that with this victory Christ's anticipated supremacy over the entire demon kingdom became effective. Before the temptation and before Golgotha, Satan could still try to maintain a certain independence within his own sphere of unholy activity, but at Golgotha this came to an end. He does still exist, and he is still busy working; his power will not be undone once and for all until the last day. At the present time, however, he has no more than a subordinate power that he can exercise only under the supremacy of Christ. And when it says that all things have been subjected to the feet of God's anointed King, this includes the demonic kingdom.

This most remarkable aspect of Jesus' kingly power is emphatically placed in the foreground by the apostle. In Ephesians 1:20-23, Paul testifies that the Father has "raised him from the dead and seated him at his right hand in the heavenly places, far above all rule and authority and power and dominion, and above every name that is named, not only in this age but also in the one to come. And he put all things under his feet." In Colossians 1:16, the apostle deduces Christ's kingly authority from the fact that "by him all things were created, in heaven and on earth, visible and invisible, whether thrones or dominions or rulers or authorities—all things were created through him and for him." And in 1 Corinthians 15:25, the apostle declares that Christ "must reign until he has put all his enemies under his feet"—that is, until all things are put in subjection under his feet by destroying every rule and every authority and every power.

In these passages, two things are being declared: First, not all spirits in the spirit world are equal, but some have been clothed with higher authority. The higher authority that some spirits in the spirit world possess is in turn indicated with titles and functions derived from life on earth. Some have a throne, others rule as governments do, others are clothed with dominion, and yet others have a special authority and power at their disposal. But as high as their position may be, the authority and dominion of all of them are entirely overshadowed by the majesty with which the Mediator has been clothed. He alone is enthroned at God's right hand, high above all others. This is the first thing being declared.

The second is that Christ's kingly dominion not only far surpasses the function and glory of all those exalted spirits, but also that all these spirits—even the most exalted among them—are not placed alongside Jesus but are subjected to his kingly authority, indeed, placed at his feet. This means, of course, that sacred spirits, the pure angels, and among them even the sacred angels, bow down before him willingly and of their own accord. But it also means that the evil spirits, the demons in the demonic sphere, and among them even those spirits who have been clothed with great power—in particular, Satan, their head—resist Christ's supremacy, set themselves against him as his enemies, meet him in battle and are restrained by him; and [it means] that in the end all their authority and power and dominion will be destroyed. The final one is death, because "The last enemy to be destroyed is death" [1 Cor 15:26].

§ 3   That Ephesians 1:20-23 is not talking about earthly kings and governments is evident from what the apostle Peter writes: "Jesus Christ, who has gone into heaven and is at the right hand of God, with angels, authorities, and powers having been subjected to him" [1 Pet 3:21-22]. This does not refer to human rulers, but to angels; it is inappropriate to understand what is written thereafter about "authorities and powers" as anything but the spirit world. The addition regarding powers and authorities likewise confirms this. With regard to people, it is still possible to speak of "thrones, rulers, and dominions" [see Col 1:16]; but although it has lately become customary to speak rather impersonally of *educators*[1] instead of

---

1. Kuyper uses the word *leerkrachten* (sing., *leerkracht*), referring here to someone who is qualified to instruct, particularly in a school. Because the Dutch term employs the word *kracht*, a wooden rendering of it would be "teaching powers." That second component of "power" is what Kuyper now proceeds to compare in the world of angels.

teachers, a *power* is not a human office, a human dignity, a human title of honor. Only in the spirit world can an order exist with room not only for rulers and dominions, but also specifically for powers.

In light of this, it can only mean that the apostle Paul is speaking of "powers and authorities not only in this age but also in the one to come" [see Eph 1:21]. From this addition people have indeed tried to conclude that the apostle, in the first place, meant kings and government on earth, and then mentioned also the spirits vested with power as a simple addition.

The context, however, does not allow this interpretation, and there is an entirely different reason why he added these words. The addition speaks about a Mediator—it speaks about the authority that this Mediator, seated at God's right hand, exercises from the world that is above over the earth below and that has been concentrated in his congregation. A steady activity also proceeds from that spirit world upon this world, something that is true of both the fallen spirits as well as the spirits that remained holy. This passage therefore speaks of the spirit world not as it exists and functions in the invisible world as separated from the visible world, but first of all insofar as that spirit world also influences this earth and the world of man. Only as such can it be compared to the authority of Christ, because this passage is speaking of his authority as well only insofar as it influences human life. This passage then tells us first of all that the comparable authority and power of these spirits are of less worth than Christ's power, but also that all these influencing activities, which proceed from the spirit world to this earth, no longer work independently but are subjected to the kingly dominion of Christ.

The fact that many do not immediately perceive this when they first read what the apostle writes must be attributed to their erroneous understanding of the relationship between heaven and earth. Many imagine human life on earth to stand entirely on its own, and think of the world of angels before the throne of God as completely separate and infinitely distant from life on earth, and from which possibly in the distant past a single person descended to earth in order to communicate what God had commanded him to announce to us. They think of our world and the spirit world as if they are two entirely distinct spheres that come in contact with each other only on extremely rare occasions.

This view cannot stand before Scripture, however; especially in respect to the world of the fallen spirits, everyone who knows Scripture is quick to admit this. The demon world cannot be disconnected from our human life, and it cannot have been only on rare occasions that an influence went out from this wicked spirit world upon our human world over the course of the centuries.

In the Lord's Prayer, Jesus himself teaches us the petition to "Lead us not into temptation, but deliver us from the Evil One" as a daily plea to be made by every Christian; and this petition makes no sense unless an evil operation and influence came to us day in and day out from the demonic world and attempted to penetrate into our midst. The apostle says that the Devil still prowls around like a roaring lion, seeking someone to devour [see 1 Pet 5:8]. During his sojourn on earth, Jesus constantly came into contact with devils and battled with them, and after him his apostles did the same. From our own experience we know the evil temptations that come to us from the demonic world; and the deeper that we as children of God enter into the holy life, the more aware we become that the demonic world almost never leaves us alone but is always at work with its evil and unholy forces in our own hearts, in our families, in our entire surroundings.

§ 4   Strangely, however, although Christianity in general acknowledges, confesses, and experiences this in regard to the evil angels, on the whole there is a silence regarding the work and influence of the good angels. It was especially with the Reformation that the good angels came to be forgotten. This can be explained from the fact that reverence for angels had turned to invocation of angels in order to influence Christ through their influence. The Reformers reacted to this by positing that Christ is our only Advocate and that we need the intercession of neither saints nor angels to intervene between us and Christ. They did not intend to argue that angels do not pray for us or that saints do not remember us in their pleading. They stated only that we ourselves, as redeemed children of God, have admission and access to the throne of grace, and that we therefore have no need for an intermediary to assure us of Christ's love and intercession. For he "always lives to make intercession for us" [see Heb 7:25]. But as is more often the case, we have a tendency to exaggerate, regardless of which direction people turn, and to fall into one of two extremes. First, the mediation and significance of the angels was overemphasized, and people saw in them a kind of intermediary between us and Christ. This was countered in the time of the Reformation, but then the pendulum swung too far to the other side so that the hosts of angels were banished from our religion entirely.

There are some among us who no longer reckon with angels anymore. They may believe that they exist, but they see them to be little more than a glorious ornament to God's magnificence. This clearly conflicts with what Scripture teaches us about the angel world. "The angel of the LORD encamps around those who fear him, and delivers them" [Psa 34:7]. And Jesus himself testified: "See that you do not despise one of these little ones. For I tell you that in heaven their angels always see the face of my Father who is in heaven" [Matt 18:10].

It is also absurd to confess a steady operation and influence on the part of the wicked, fallen angels, while denying every similar influence and work on the part of the good angels. Wicked angels could not exercise influence were it not the case that the exercise of such an influence lies as such in their very nature and calling as angels. For that reason, it makes no sense to maintain that Satan and his demons do have such an influence, but to discount all influence in the case of the pure, holy angels. This is a point that we set forth more extensively in the articles that were later published separately as *The Angels of God*, so that we need not dwell on it here but can simply refer to that work.[2]

No life on earth, whether in nature or in the human world, is an independent life that exists entirely on its own. In nature, we know how the sun (and to a certain degree the moon and many stars as well) does not simply exercise influence upon the situation on this earth, but in fact governs it. This is no different for the spirit world. Also in the spiritual realm, the higher spirit world is active on our spiritual life. The real spiritual battle and struggle is not carried out here on earth but in the invisible world, and what we perceive on earth is only the consequence and aftereffect of what occurs in the latter. For that reason, it would be entirely inconceivable for Christ to have dominion as King over the spiritual domain of this world unless he, as King, had dominion also over both the good spirits as well as the evil spirits of the invisible world. Jesus' dominion in the world of the demons and angels was not added to his kingship over this world, as if it were an incidental honor given to him by the Father to increase his splendor. Rather, since the spirit world above works upon the spirit world on earth, for Christ to rule down here it was entirely necessary for him to

---

2. Kuyper identifies this work here as *Tractaat van de engelen Gods*, almost certainly in reference to the most recent title from Kuyper on the subject of angels, *De engelen Gods* (Amsterdam: Höveker & Wormser, 1902). For more information, see *AKB*, 1902.07, 336–37; and 1923.06, 521.

receive dominion over the invisible spirit world as well. If he did not have complete power in the spirit world, he would not be able to exercise his spiritual power on earth.

Thus it was precisely in this logical context that the apostle Paul first says that Christ has received authority over angels and demons, and that in that capacity he has been given to the congregation as its Head. Gas or electrical lighting illuminates the entire city throughout the night, but whoever keeps these lights burning must be lord and master where that gas or electricity is produced. In precisely the same way, Christ must be lord and master over all the powers and authorities that make it possible for the light to break through in this earth's spiritual life. For that reason, in order that he might be Head of the spirits and the King of humanity, he was given the highest authority, supremacy, and right of control over all the spiritual factors in the invisible world that work and exercise influence upon this world.

Christ thus received authority and dominion (1) over regenerated humanity, (2) over the as yet unregenerated humanity that resists him, and also (3) over the world of the demons and holy spirits—and it is only by his dominion over these three spheres that his eternal and awesome kingship can exist.

III.10

KING AS MEDIATOR

To the King of the ages, immortal, invisible, the only God, be honor and glory forever and ever. Amen.

1 TIMOTHY 1:17

Christus is thus, first of all, the Head of his mystical body. In the second place, he is the Judge of the entire human race. Third, he is the Lord of the angels. At the present time his dominion still encounters resistance in the world of humanity as well as that of the angels. We still live in the period of struggle. The struggle has not yet been completed. But once it has been completed, the outcome will be that Christ will reign as victor in the entire spiritual sphere, which includes both people and angels. All resistance will be broken. In the human world, every person who is not in Christ will no longer count. Our human race will then consist only in regenerated humanity. Similarly in the angel world, after the demons have been expelled, only the host of good angels will continue to exercise their influence. Regenerated humanity, together with the host of good angels, will constitute the spiritual world unto eternity; and in that world, consisting of human beings and angels, the *man* Christ Jesus shall be King. At its creation, humanity was made a little lower than the angels [see Psa 8:5], but when humanity fulfills its calling, it will end up far above them. For this reason, the Letter to the Hebrews says with respect to Christ that he has "become as much superior to angels as the name he has inherited is more excellent than theirs" [Heb 1:4]. The writer describes

§ 1

the angels as ministering spirits [Heb 1:14]; while he describes Christ as "the radiance of the glory of God and the exact imprint of his nature," who "upholds the universe by the word of his power" [Heb 1:3]. As he is seated at God's right hand, Christ must thus always be considered in his three-fold significance: as Head of the congregation, as Judge of the whole earth, and as Lord of the angels—clothed with such majesty that he can subject the entire spiritual order of creation to himself, break every resistance in that spiritual order, and assure himself of the final complete triumph in the whole of the spiritual creation.

The question now arises automatically how we are to understand the relationship between Christ's dominion, as it comprehends the entire world of human beings and spirit, and the original dominion that belongs to the Triune God. One should never imagine the almighty God to have divested himself of his authority and dominion or to have withdrawn from his providential design for creation, simply to watch how Christ would administer the government of the universe in his name. That would be to put Christ in the place of the Almighty, to dethrone the Triune God, so that Christ alone would rule on the throne. In this way we would end up worshiping a God who, in human terms, has abdicated and become an inactive God—a God, that is, who looked from a distance at how things were going, but distanced himself from influencing the course of events. [Christ's government] would then be an intermediate regime, set up temporarily since in the end he will return the kingdom to the Father, although for now it begins with Jesus' ascension into heaven and does not end until Jesus returns to judge [see 1 Cor 15:28].

There have been mystical sects who indeed saw things this way, and even now some still understand the lordship of Jesus as the King anointed by God. In reaction to the one extreme that understands the almighty God's kingly dominion to be temporarily dormant for the sake of Christ's kingship, another extreme gradually arose among more and more people, where they refused to understand Christ's kingship in anything more than a metaphorical sense in order that God's dominion might stand undisturbed.

A dilemma was thus created. There can be only one King. If Christ is that King, God stops being our King. Or conversely, if God remains King, then Christ's kingship can be a kingship in name only. It seemed impossible to imagine the kingship of the Triune God and the kingship of Christ as existing simultaneously. This is why there always were and there continue to be groups whose members expect everything from Christ alone, so that damage is done to the worship of the Triune God. By way of reaction, there arose much broader groups whose members expected everything from God's providential ordination, so that Christ's kingly dominion was all but abandoned.

Scripture will have nothing to do with such a contrast. While it says in Revelation 15:3, "Great and amazing are your deeds, O Lord God the Almighty! Just and true are your ways, O King of the nations!" Paul similarly cries out in 1 Timothy 1:17, "To the King of the ages, immortal, invisible, the only God, be honor and glory forever and ever!" Depicted just as decidedly and sharply outlined alongside it is the kingship of Christ, who is "the faithful witness, the firstborn of the dead, and the ruler of kings on earth" [Rev 1:5]. Indeed, Christ is seated "far above all rule and authority and power and dominion, and above every name that is named, not only in this age but also in the one to come" [Eph 1:21]. We must therefore understand Christ's kingship in such a way that God's kingdom remains. Scripture expresses how they are combined when it says that Christ is seated in heaven at the right hand of the Father, at God's right hand.

"Seated at God's right hand" [see Eph 1:20] is a figurative expression, § 2 and like all metaphors it is derived from this earth—specifically from the situation in the East in the time of Jesus. Eastern countries in particular used to have a grand vizier, and in some countries in the East this is still the case today. The grand vizier is the person who rules in the king's realm and administers all things in his name. The grand vizier held and still holds the highest office under the sovereign. While there may be ministers and a cabinet, the grand vizier's place is much higher than that of these lower officials. Even today, the grand vizier in Turkey, and he alone, carries the title *His Highness*. The grand vizier has the full confidence of his sovereign, and his sovereign puts all his authority at his disposal. And even though the dominion remains the sovereign's so that he can depose his grand vizier at any given moment, as long as someone is grand vizier he remains the one through whom the sovereign exercises his dominion. The grand vizier's entirely unique position earns him the highest seat of honor at solemn occasions, on the throne to the right of the sovereign. This is why the standard expression for the grand vizier's high position of honor is to say that he sits at the king's right hand.

Israel's prophets, and later the apostles as well, applied this expression to Christ. It was not as if they imagined it to express his majesty in its fullness, for nothing on earth can be compared with Jesus' dominion; but they still used it because a metaphor was necessary and because our earthly society did not produce another image that expressed subordinate dominion better than the position of a grand vizier in the East.

Still, it was no more than a metaphor. No Eastern sovereign had at his disposal a majesty like the majesty of God. The grand vizier of an Eastern sovereign was not his son, but a stranger. Grand viziers were frequently deposed and replaced, and then they returned to the position of a common subject. All of these additional circumstances are already sufficient to show that there is a difference in principle between the dominion of a grand vizier and the kingship of Christ. Jesus is King, but a grand vizier is no more than a paid official. As a metaphor, Jesus' session at God's right hand may for that reason never be extended any further except to indicate that no creatures are clothed with the same majesty as Christ, and that the Triune God exercises his dominion through him.

The basic principle, therefore, remains that Christ's kingly dominion is a matter of transferred, imposed, and instrumental dominion. God's dominion is self-existent and original; Christ's dominion is the result of an act of God by which Christ was anointed to be King and clothed with authority. However, this should never be understood as if, by anointing Christ as King over his kingdom, God distanced himself from his majesty. God Almighty is and remains the King of kings. His dominion is and remains the highest dominion. And where Christ serves as the instrument through whom God exercises his dominion, it always remains God, and God alone, from whom that dominion proceeds.

When a mother entrusts the care of her children to her nanny, the nanny does rule in the nursery—but never in such a way that the mother no longer has a say over her children. Rather, it is by virtue of her authority as a mother that she appoints the nanny over her children—the nanny has to follow her orders and rule in her spirit. And whenever the mother shows up in the nursery, no one would think her authority to be broken or even diminished in any way by the nanny.

In a school with multiple classrooms, a master cannot be present in all of them at once, and so he appoints teachers over the lower classes who have authority in their classroom over the children entrusted to them. The responsibility, however, remains the master's; students as well as teachers know that the head of the school has authority in all classrooms. Things are the same way for a king who places a general at the head of his army as it moves out. Every soldier and every officer in that army must obey the general and carry out his orders, but none will ever imagine the king to have distanced himself from his authority.

In times of war, a ship's command is held by a senior officer. But when the entire fleet sets sail under the high command of an admiral, the entire crew knows that the admiral has the entire fleet in his power and that each ship's commander owes his authority to him alone. Similarly, neither the admiral nor the commanders ever imagine that the authority with which they have been vested ever precludes or destroys the supreme authority of the country's sovereign.

These examples taken from our earthly life thus illustrate how a supreme authority can be exercised only through other authorities—without a sovereign, father, general, or admiral ever laying aside his dominion over land, family, army, or fleet. The authority of those who use others to exercise that authority instead remains unharmed and intact, and no damage at all is done to that original authority. In precisely the same way, the supreme majesty of the Triune God remains entirely what it was and is, even though Christ acts as Mediator in order to exercise his divine authority over the world of human beings and the world of angels in his Father's name.

A father's authority does not replace God's authority over the child, and both father and son understand all too well that God reigns over them. The authority of the king who reigns by the grace of God does not replace God's authority over land and people, and both sovereign and nation understand all too well—insofar as they serve God—that God remains their Lord and Master. Similarly, Christ's dominion does not replace the supreme dominion of the Almighty; and Christ's honor continues to be seeking nothing but his Father's honor, finding satisfaction in nothing other than the will of the Father, and bringing those who are his to the Father rather than keeping them from him. As such, all derived authority—whether that of a father in his family, of a sovereign over his land, or of Jesus as King of the kingdom of God—rests in the authority of God Almighty and finds its starting point in it, remains subjected to it, and does not annul but serves it and seeks to bring glory to it.

§ 3

Despite the remarkable similarity between the derived authority of a father or a king and the authority of Christ as King over the kingdom of God, two far-reaching differences still remain. The first difference is that the authority of a father and a king is limited, while Christ's kingship encompasses everything. The second difference is that the authority of a father and an earthly king is often flawed and even exercised against God's will, while Christ's authority in the kingdom of God is always pure and holy and never exercised except according to God's will. In what follows, we will expand briefly on these two differences.

A father must care for his children, guarantee them their life essentials, guide and nurture them, and thereby equip them to function independently in the world. A father is limited, however, in terms of the means at his disposal. He must receive the bread from God in order to be able to distribute it to his children. He has only a partial power over their health and welfare. He is not always with them. He does not have power over all the influences that affect his children from all sides. He needs all kinds of help to protect his children, to lead them, and to instruct them. Above all, no matter how close he is to his children, and even if they are flesh of his flesh and blood of his blood, his access to their heart is only very indirect. Neither their inner life nor their destiny in life is in his hand. To the extent that a father exercises God's authority over his children, he does so only in part. Never could the father be said to be the instrument through which God exercises all his divine authority over that child. This is what we wish to say about the first difference.

The second difference is even stronger. Because a father is himself a sinful and flawed man, he cannot be anything but a sinful and flawed instrument for the exercise of divine authority. It even happens frequently that a father not only exercises the authority bestowed on him in a most flawed manner, but he also abuses this authority, causing his children to go against God's will. There are, unfortunately, fathers who break down God's authority in their children instead of building it up. There have even been fathers who urged their children to go against God. They did this not only by being a bad example and providing deficient nurture, but even by intentionally cultivating unholy principles and sowing ungodly seed in their children's hearts. What we have said about fathers also applies to sovereigns throughout the earth. Their authority, too, is limited and is exercised apart from the inner life of their subjects. And furthermore, it often turns against the honor of God instead of cultivating and confirming reverence for divine authority in their subjects.

These two impediments, however, are entirely absent from the kingship of Christ. His influence on our heart knows no limits. Nothing in our existence or inner life is hidden from his authority and influence. In order to make this clear, Jesus himself said that to him and him alone—not to fathers or kings—all things were handed over [see Matt 11:27]. Indeed, he said that all authority in heaven and on earth stood at his disposal [see Matt 28:18]. In the case of fathers and sovereigns there can and must be a supplement, but such a supplement can never exist with Christ. His dominion fully encompasses the whole existence of those who are his. The Lamb was slain, so the angels of God sang, "to receive power and wealth and wisdom and might and honor and glory and blessing" [Rev 5:12]. Furthermore, it is inconceivable for Jesus to exercise divine authority in a flawed manner. His authority can never fall short when it is exercised, wrong can never be done, and it is especially the case that the exercise of divine authority through Christ can never go against the honor of God or against his holy will. The exercise of all other entrusted authority is limited, flawed, and sinful; but when Christ exercises the Father's authority, it is all-encompassing, perfect, and most holy. This means that no supplement is needed or even possible with Christ's dominion, and in his leadership it is precisely that divine authority that comes to constant and complete expression.

This can be the case only because Christ is God's only Son, who himself shares in the divine nature. Admittedly, Jesus and his apostles do clearly state that he was clothed with this kingly authority as the *Son of Man*. As the *Son of God*, as the second person of the Holy Trinity, no authority could have been given to him since he has that authority in and of himself. Nevertheless, also as the Son of Man he continues to carry his divine nature in him. He humbled himself with respect to the state of divine glory and was found in the form of a humbled humanity, but he could not put off his divine nature. It may have been veiled, it may have been muffled, but it never departed from him for even a moment. This is the very reason why divine authority reigns at the same time also in his kingly dominion as the Son of Man. In him the two are inseparable from each other. We cannot penetrate deeper into this, for who can even haltingly describe the relationship in the divine Triune Being between Father, Son, and Holy Spirit?

§ 4

For that reason, it is enough for us that when the apostles portray that divine dominion for us, they always go back to the divine power through which Christ as the Son of God created all things, while being and remaining the reflection of God's glory and the express image of God's being. Because of that, we not only owe our origin to him, but even now continue to exist through him. Thus there can be no separation or contrast between the authority of God and the authority of Christ.

But his being Mediator is part of his being King. Our spirit's direct communion with the Spirit of God was broken through sin. Sin became a hindrance. God's authority, understood here in its most holy sense, could not come into its own in us while we were sinners. It could be exercised over us, but not in us in a holy sense. In that breach, the Mediator now makes provision. When the Lamb is slain, he breaks through the toxic cloud of sin that hindered God's justice from coming to clarity. And as one of us, as the Son of Man, he now enters into a life of communion with our sinful human race. Through this, Christ granted us a rapprochement to the divine life that we did not have directly with God himself. He could thereby cause divine authority to penetrate to and in us in a much more intimate way than is now possible in our communion with the Father in our flawed state.

Things cannot remain this way, of course. The final goal must be for us to be subjected directly not only to him *through* whom all things are, but also to him *from* whom all things are. Divine authority must in the end penetrate into us without intermediary from the Triune God directly and govern us completely. The apostle also testifies that that is what is going to happen. Until the end of history, the mediatorship will remain indispensable. But once the end has come, the mediatorship will fall away and Christ will hand his dominion over to the Father insofar as it flows out of his mediatorship; thus in the end every division will be destroyed and God will be all in all [see 1 Cor 15:28]. Then God's authority will govern directly the hearts of all without any intermediary, and in glorious harmony the world of men and of angels will together form that spiritual creation in which the Triune God will have spiritual dominion. This does not mean that Christ's kingly dominion will fall away. After all, he remains the Son of God and the Head of the mystical body. But the veil of his mediatorship will fall away; it will have borne its fruit; and [we] will no longer be united with the Father through the Mediator, but in sweet communion we will be united with the Triune God in Christ.

THE MESSIAH

I saw in the night visions, and behold, with the clouds of heaven there came one like a son of man, and he came to the Ancient of Days and was presented before him. And to him was given dominion and glory and a kingdom, that all peoples, nations, and languages should serve him; his dominion is an everlasting dominion, which shall not pass away, and his kingdom one that shall not be destroyed.

DANIEL 7:13–14

The kingship of Christ does not replace the Father's dominion, but serves §1
as its instrument. It is through the kingly majesty of Christ that justice is
done to the kingship of the Triune God. This is confirmed by the prophecy
regarding Israel and by the connection Jesus had to Israel. He is not only
our Mediator, but also our Messiah. In itself it would be quite conceivable
for the Son of God to have assumed our nature through a new creation as
in paradise. Why could the Word not become flesh without being connected to the human race that already existed? Elsewhere we discussed the
similar question about why God the Lord did not destroy this human race
after it had fallen into sin and set up in its place another race, a new one.[1]
However, this is not the way things happened. There were theophanies,

---

1. Kuyper discusses God's "long-suffering" in deciding not to abandon Adam and
   Eve to eternal damnation and to "have created a second human pair in their place"
   in *CG* 1.33.1. God's commitment to his creation is a significant background to this
   point, which Kuyper revisits in a number of places in *CG*.

as when the Lord appeared in human form to Abraham, Hagar, or Jacob. Yet they passed and did not continue. That was not the incarnation.

Instead, the incarnation is a direct connection to the existing human race as it had sunk down into sin. Within that human race the connection was specifically made to Israel as a nation, within Israel more specifically to the house and line of David, and within the house of David to Mary, blessed among women [see Luke 1:42]. Alongside this line in the generations of Israel, there is also prophecy in Israel. These two lines run parallel to each other. From the human race a single branch is set apart in Abraham, the father of all believers; from that branch the house of David will bud; and on the stem of David's house Mary will finally grow as its flower. This is what we can call the line according to the flesh. But alongside it there is an entirely different line since, beginning in paradise, there is the prophecy of a Messiah who is first likewise connected to Israel through Abraham; and this line is not of the flesh but of the spirit.

In Israel's history, the two lines of flesh and spirit are interwoven at one time, run parallel at another time, and sometimes even oppose each other. In David they are one, with Rehoboam they are separated, and in Manasseh they collide. However, in the end these two lines found their fulfillment when the Messiah appeared on the banks of the Jordan, at Capernaum, and in the temple of Jerusalem. Here God did not simply establish a connection with our human nature, but also with the existing human race.

God's work in paradise was not nullified in order for a second work of creation to be set up in its place. Satan does not take away the first humanity of paradise as his spoil, leaving God the Lord, after the failure of the first, to make another attempt with a second human race. No, in spite of its leprous condition, the first human race of paradise was torn away from Satan, then purified from its leprosy, and finally taken up in the kingdom of glory once it had been purified. In the incarnation, therefore, a connection was made to a sinful race. But this sinful condition was the very reason why God the Lord could not be all in all within that race.

Consequently, the spiritual dominion of the Triune God over this race could not yet be direct. And this was what made it necessary for an intermediary to appear—a Messiah—who would himself be both God as well as a member of the existing human race, who would be the Head of that race insofar as it would be regenerated. This was the very thing achieved and revealed in Christ's kingly dominion.

Two periods can be distinguished within it. The first period begins with Bethlehem and will end when the last judgment has been rendered and the kingdom of glory appears. This is followed by a second period, when the kingdom of glory has come and nothing exists on a new earth, under new heavens, except for a regenerated humanity. In the first period, sin and grace function side by side; and although grace has the upper hand, sin and all its demonic powers are not yet rooted out and burned. The last enemy has not yet been overcome. The struggle that seeks to subject all the enemies of God to the feet of the Messiah still continues today. But one day it will end. Then the power of Satan and sin will be not only overcome, but also destroyed. Then the human race, pruned and shaken, will have emerged sinless and pure from the new shoot. Then the struggle will end so that the kingdom of eternal peace may enter. In the first period there is the circle of God's kingdom as foreshadowed in David—who fought God's war—and then follows the second period of Christ's kingly dominion as foreshadowed in Solomon's kingdom of peace.

At the present time it is the first period that still continues. The present generation lives in that period. Thus the reconnection of the spiritual life of our generation to the Triune God is present in Christ, and through him in its members, but that connection has not yet been reestablished with the human race as such. That is why the mediatorial dominion of Christ is an instrumental dominion, in which the Redeemer covers what is sinful in us and is himself one with the Father. But once the battle and the struggle has passed and sin has been abolished for good, the Father himself will connect to the regenerated human race and the Triune God will be all and in all—that is, not only in some from our race, but in the entire human race as such. Even then Christ may remain the Head of regenerated humanity and the King of the race that is his people, but the intermediary will no longer be needed. At that time the connection will be complete. God and humanity will be one in Christ. "They will all be one, just as you, Father, are in me, and I in you" [see John 17:21]. At that time the high priestly prayer will have been heard and applied, not as it is at the present time—to individuals alone—but to what God had set before his eyes as the goal of his holy kingdom when he first created our human race.

For that reason, the Messiah does not appear suddenly after paradise in our human race, but his coming is preceded by a long preparation. This preparation occurs according to the flesh in Abraham and his seed, in the people of Israel, in the tribe of Judah, in the house of David, in

§ 2

the family from which Mary was born, and finally, in Mary as the virgin mother. From paradise on, the prophetic line runs parallel to the spiritual line. The prophetic line passes from Abraham to the nation of Israel, and it perpetuates itself in this nation until the time when David's house is thrown down, the greater part of Israel wanders about in exile, and even the temple is destroyed. The remarkable thing about this prophecy is that it continually prophesies two things: both the restoration of God's own dominion over his people, and the coming of a Messiah, of an intermediary, a Mediator, who stands between God and his people and will initially exercise that kingly rule himself.

Once again, there are two elements. On the one hand, God himself must be King; and on the other hand, a Messiah will appear who solely for God and to his glory exercises this kingly dominion in his name—yet without there ever being for even a moment any kind of conflict between the two. Also in the Messiah's dominion, it is God's dominion that is asserted. Psalm 96 does not announce the coming of a messiah, but of Yahweh himself: "Yahweh reigns! Yes, the world is established; it shall never be moved; he will judge the peoples with equity. Let the heavens be glad, and let the earth rejoice; let the sea roar, and all that fills it before Yahweh, for he comes, for he comes to judge the earth" [see Psa 96:10–11, 13]. Similarly, in Psalm 98 we read: "Make a joyful noise to the LORD, all the earth; break forth into joyous song and sing praises before the LORD, for he comes to judge the earth. He will judge the world with righteousness, and the peoples with equity" [Psa 98:4, 9]. Isaiah too says: "Your God will come with vengeance, with the recompense of God. He will come and save you" [Isa 35:4]. This is expressed more powerfully yet in Isaiah 40: "O Zion, herald of good news; lift up your voice with strength, O Jerusalem, herald of good news; lift it up, fear not; say to the cities of Judah, 'Behold your God!' Behold, the Lord GOD comes with might, and his recompense before him" [see Isa 40:9–10]. Or also in Isaiah 52: "The LORD will go before you, and the God of Israel will be your rear guard" [Isa 52:12]. The Lord testifies to the same in Ezekiel: "For thus says the Lord GOD: Behold, I, I myself will search for my sheep and will seek them out as a shepherd seeks out his flock" [Ezek 34:11–12]. We thus find the clear and plain declaration that Yahweh himself will draw near to his people and assert his kingly dominion.

A single line runs through all revelation: In sin, humanity separates itself from communion with God, but God will heal that broken communion again. Humanity withdrew from God, but God seeks out that humanity again; as humanity strays, God follows it, seeks it out, and does not rest until that original communion has been fully restored. The entire work of revelation can be summed up as the Father of the spirits drawing near to the spirit of men. Although Satan attempted to take God down from his throne in the fall of humanity, God himself counters him and does not rest until humanity once again bows down in worship before his footstool. For this reason, Christ's intervening kingly dominion can never replace or limit the kingly dominion of the Triune God. Revelation knows of one goal alone: the restoration of God's complete dominion over man, whom he created in his image.

When Scripture goes on to explain how and in what way God's dominion over humanity will be restored, starting already in paradise the prospect is that this can be done only by the Son of Man, who is presented in the promise of paradise as the Seed of the woman. With that, Scripture inserts the prophecy of Jesus' instrumental kingship as intermediary into the prophecy that God would come to his people. This inserted prophecy expands until it assumes in Israel the character of the messianic prophecy—that is, the prediction of a King-Priest born from Israel who will extend his dominion over all nations and peoples; one who, after a hard and frightful struggle in which he himself initially succumbs, will in the end sit in judgment and then establish the kingdom of eternal peace. That prophecy unites the two ideas that Yahweh himself will reign over his people, and that Yahweh will do this through a Mediator. From the one side, it is said: "I, Yahweh, will search for my sheep as a shepherd" [see Ezek 34:11–12]; but from the other side, it is also said simultaneously: "I will set up over them one shepherd, my servant David, and he will be their shepherd" [see Ezek 34:23]. In Ezekiel 34:24, the two even go together: "I, the LORD, will be their God, and my servant David shall be prince among them." The two notions of a direct dominion and of an instrumental dominion therefore go together without the one excluding the other. Also in the dominion held by the great King who will appear as the Messiah, it is God's dominion that affirms itself.

This distinction between, and integration of, Yahweh's own dominion and the Messiah's conferred dominion can be seen historically in life itself in the course of history. It was revealed already to Abraham that kings would come from his loins. Jacob, when blessing his sons, mentions

§ 3

the scepter of Judah, and he speaks of a Shiloh that will come,[2] to whom the nations will subject themselves [see Gen 49:10]. When Israel is on the way to Canaan, Balaam too sings of a "shout of a king" among them [Num 23:21]. Even Moses already points out what it will mean for the people to have a king.

Despite these elements, in the first part of Israel's history there is no sign of the King himself. The Messiah does not yet come, but neither does his example or type. There is only one dominating thought throughout this initial period of history: Yahweh's dominion. Abraham could have taken the title of king when he settled in Canaan. He who with his allies entered into battle with Chedorlaomer and defeated him was at least as powerful as Melchizedek, the King of Salem. At that time many other kings in the area were no doubt less powerful than Abraham. Abraham, however, never adopts the title of king. We see the same thing with Isaac, and later with Jacob. This point comes out more powerfully still at the exodus from Egypt. By that time, Abraham's line had grown into a great and numerous nation, which could place troops on the battlefield by the thousands and ten thousands. This nation's head was Moses. Not Aaron the priest, but Moses remained the leader and commander of the entire nation until his death. He did not gain this position patriarchally, since he did not receive this exercise of authority along family lines but by appointment from God. Nothing would have been more obvious for Moses than to adopt or receive the title of a sovereign. Yet even here, there continues to be no kingship. This is all the more significant because Moses not only led and delivered the nation, but he also organized it and placed it under fixed laws.

Despite all these things, in Israel a pure and direct theocracy continued. Yahweh himself is Israel's King, and there is no king under him. After Moses dies, Joshua arises as an energetic general. He defeats most of the kings in Canaan at that time and takes over their cities and fortified places, but he too does not have the title of king. In Israel, it is Yahweh alone who is honored as King. Under the rule of the judges this does not change. One judge after another arises and is honored as leader among a broader

---

2. The meaning of the Hebrew here, rendered in the SV as "totdat Silo komt" and in the NKJV as "Until Shiloh comes," is debated. See for example the note in the (NKJV) *New Geneva Study Bible* (Nelson: 1995): "Some understand 'Shiloh' as a place-name ('until Judah's leadership comes to Shiloh,' cf. Josh. 18:1) or as a reference to tribute ('until tribute is brought to Judah'). More plausibly (and consistent with the ancient translations), others see this as a reference to a coming Judahite ruler."

or narrower group; the notion of kingship arises only in connection with Abimelech in Shechem, though it has no endorsement among the pious people [see Judges 9].

It is only under Samuel that things begin to change. When the seer grew old, the people began to have other needs and called out for a king like the other nations [see 1 Sam 8:20], and it is from this point in time onwards that kingly authority in Israel appears distinct from Yahweh's kingly dominion. However, it is precisely at this point that the contrast emerges between what here on earth is called a king and the King whom God intended in the messianic prophecy and foreshadowed in an earthly example.

The kingship of the other nations stands in irreconcilable conflict with Yahweh's kingship. Samuel is told very bluntly: "They have not rejected you, but they have rejected me from being king over them" [1 Sam 8:7]. Israel's first king was a complete fraud. Saul's kingship stands diametrically opposed not only to Yahweh's kingship, but also to the messianic kingship. For that reason he is defeated, and his kingship is abolished.

Only then does God himself first establish Israel's foreshadowing kingship. David, son of Jesse, is called to leave his flock. He is anointed and strengthened to conduct Israel's battles, and in spite of resistance his kingship is ultimately acknowledged throughout all Israel. This king is crowned with the covenant promise that God will build a house for him, and that in this Davidic house the kingship will one day have a lasting and eternal character. But when God himself institutes this kingship, theocracy does not fall away. Yahweh remains the King of Israel; and David, as "a man after God's own heart" [1 Sam 13:14], exercises God's supreme dominion.

After David, the second phase of the foreshadowing messianic kingship appears in his son, Solomon. The first phase was marked by battle and struggle. After it, in the second phase, the glory of peace would break through under the Messiah-King, and this greater glory is foreshadowed in Solomon's reign.

Not long after, however, every illusion is taken away from Israel that the messianic kingdom had already arrived in David's natural house. Already with Rehoboam the ideal of the kingship of the Messiah is separated from the actual monarchy as it exists in Jerusalem. The greatest part of the nation falls away. There is a dramatic increase in idolatry. Some of the kings from David's house follow along and even fan the flames of the people's wicked departure from Yahweh. Better kings did appear among them who restored the theocracy so that God's covenant with David might remain forever. But as exalted as a number of these kings may have been, the pious nation slowly comes to realize that the true King did not appear in this line of kings. As a result, the prophecy of Jesus' kingship automatically begins to separate itself more and more from the real kingship as it exists in Jerusalem, as it takes on an ideal-spiritual character, and fosters the expectation of a Messiah who would come as if through a miracle and in whom God himself will draw near to his people.

§ 4   In the meantime, however, the separation between the ideal and what the people see before their eyes goes even further, since the kingship of David's house finally perishes in its entirety, the nation itself is driven out in exile, and the temple on Zion is destroyed. Everything in the holy land is now gone. There is no longer a king, there is no longer a free nation, there is no longer a theocracy, there is no temple anymore, and there is no atoning sacrifice. There would not have been a more powerful way to drive Israel from the reality to the ideal. It is especially because of the exile that the messianic prophecy of Jesus' kingship—as something coming from above, as possessing a spiritual character, and as destined to entail dominion over all nations—comes through more clearly and plainly in the prophecies. In the Psalms, and in the Former Prophets as well, there are clear indications that leave no doubt about this. But initially the messianic prophecy of Jesus' kingship is still shrouded in a mystical veil. The ideal and the personal character of the Messiah-kingship only acquires solid contours during and after the exile. Not that it is separated from the house of David. Instead, the conviction grows in certainty that the Messiah will be a shoot from David's house. But the earthly splendor is dimmed, and the greatness of the messianic King descends to the Man of Sorrows [Isa 53:3], to the "Shepherd who will be pierced" [see Zech 12–13]. All that remained is a severed trunk, and from that stump a little shoot will come forth.

The idea of reconciliation, the idea of a priest, comes to be mingled with the idea of a King; and the majesty of the King who is to come is no longer derived from Solomon's ivory throne nor from David's war trophies, but comes from his higher origin. The divine nature of this ideal King begins to shine. "Therefore God, your God, has anointed you with the oil of gladness" [Psa 45:7]. Although this King will be as great as God, he will be despised according to the world's standards and cast away by the world. On earth, the Messiah will become the suffering Messiah. Sorrow and death are part and parcel of the picture prophecy paints for us. With that, his image is no longer tied to Israel alone. His dominion will become one that encompasses all nations, but only after his resurrection. Only then will the battle against all evil powers be initiated, and only after that final battle has run its course can the glory of the kingdom of peace break forth, whose praises are sung by one prophet after another.

However, four centuries passed before this richly developed promise of the Messiah was fulfilled. In those four centuries the voice of prophecy was silenced, Israel took an entirely different form as a nation state and fell one more time, and these events led to a complete change in Israel's messianic expectation. What in prophecy had gained a more spiritual, universal, and ideal character, was over the course of those four centuries reduced again to something national and understood pragmatically. The Messiah was now thought to be the one who would come to deliver the Jews from their oppressors, from Herod the Idumean and the Roman legions that governed the whole land. They again lost sight of any higher notion; every ideal portrayal disappeared; and the spiritual became bleak. So when the spiritual Messiah himself finally appeared, two mutually exclusive views collided head on: (1) from Jesus' side, a messianic kingship that, with its point of departure in the divine nature, aimed to restore God's supreme dominion in a spiritual sense over all nations and peoples and therefore had to attain glory through suffering; and (2) from the side of the people, the expectation of the liberation and reestablishment of the Jewish nation state, in order eventually to move out with many soldiers and subject the nations all around as in the days of David. The Jewish nation state went down in the struggle between these two diametrically opposed views. When Christ appeared, that nation state had fulfilled and served its calling. What remained was not Judaism but the glory of its Messiah who did indeed suffer death, but who precisely through overcoming death established in his own person Yahweh's spiritual dominion over all nations and people.

III.12

KING OF ISRAEL

You worship what you do not know; we worship what we know, for salvation is from the Jews.

JOHN 4:22

§ 1 Initially in Israel there was an absolute government by God, a direct theocracy. God was King, and he alone. Then the idea of a Davidic kingship emerged, which—in spite of its appearance in an earthly form—from the outset exhibited an ideal line as well. Because of Israel's unfaithfulness, tribulation, and exile, and as the fruit of prophecy that broke through most powerfully especially during those years, the earthly kingship soon falls away. And in the end, there is no longer a king from the house of David. From that time on, however, the messianic expectation assumes a more spiritual character, and the national understanding of the Davidic kingship transforms into an ideal view of the Messiah as the King of God's kingdom.

As time passes, however, the Jewish nation state is revived in Canaan. The Maccabees amaze with their heroic deeds; once more the national understanding of the Messiah displaces the ideal of the King over the kingdom of God. Especially when, shortly thereafter, the Jews found themselves once more under foreign domination, the entire nation clung once again to the national view of the Messiah. The national Messiah became the Jews' ideal, and this led to their exalted self-understanding that fed the Jewish national pride as supposed heirs to world dominion.

All nations could take shelter within Israel's tents, provided that the tents remained Jewish.

This resulted in the powerful propaganda for winning proselytes, to which Jesus also referred when he said: "You travel across sea and land to make a single proselyte, and when he becomes a proselyte, you make him twice as much a child of hell as yourselves" [Matt 23:15]. Your illusion of a Messiah who will satisfy your national pride rises like a wall between you and the true Messiah, and it hinders you from entering his kingdom. And while the ears and hearts of the Gentiles whom you circumcise would otherwise have been open to the true Messiah, you cut off them as well from me and therefore from eternal salvation.

As a result, when John the Baptist finally appears, the entire nation of Israel is encrusted within its national exclusivity so completely that, even shortly before his ascension, Jesus still has to hear one of his disciples ask: "Lord, will you at this time restore the kingdom to Israel?" [Acts 1:6]. [For the same reason] Paul was still forced to oppose Peter publicly at Antioch; this Jewish idea, which lived on in the Jews recently converted to Christianity, animated Peter as well.

Especially the activities of Herod the Idumean, of Edomite descent, drew the spirit of the Jews away from the shameful present to a glorious future in which the second David would sit enthroned in Jerusalem and from his base in Zion subject the nations, not in a figurative sense but in a real sense. The Jews were the holy nation, while the *Goyim*—that is, the nations—were unclean. Gentiles could come into Israel only through proselyte baptism. Their baptism represented a break with their own people, and even their own family, in order to come into Israel and to be incorporated entirely into Israel. Salvation would soon arrive in that nation of Israel. Salvation would then extend from Israel over the entire earth, so that all nations would be converted to Judaism or else be subjected to the Jews. Those who resisted would perish. And, finally, it would be this kingdom of glory over which the King from David's house, not the Roman Emperor, would wave his scepter and from which the worship of Yahweh in Zion's temple would drive out all idolatry.

In this way, the stream of spiritual life ebbed away under prophetic expectation. Only the icy crust, left behind from the stream as it ran off, still recalled those figurative expressions in which prophecy had sung the praises of its high and holy ideal. The spirit of prophecy lost its power over the nation's soul, and in its place Pharisaism made itself the master of the nation's proud soul. This Pharisaism was so deeply hypocritical not because it intentionally lied, but because it presented itself as the bearer of the messianic expectation while in fact it allowed every high and holy ideal of revelation to be petrified into a legalistic, formal service and into the illusion of the nation's self-conceit.

John the Baptist was the first to make an irreparable break in that national pride through his baptism. After all, John's baptism represented nothing less than a testimony to Israel that Israel itself was unclean, signifying that it was not at all the case that the unclean Gentiles had to enter Israel, but rather that both Jews and Gentiles were unclean—both had to enter the true kingdom that would soon come in Jesus through the baptism of the washing away of sins.

That baptism in itself contained the program of the things to come. While that baptism in the Jordan seemed so simple, it was the most radical condemnation imaginable of Israel's national expectation and pride. While the Jews called out to the Gentiles: "I am holier than you, come over to me," John first called the Jews themselves and testified to them: "You yourselves are unclean, be baptized therefore in order to enter the holy kingdom of him who is coming, the strap of whose sandal I am not worthy to untie." These two baptisms thus seemed to stand over against each other as if they were on one level—the baptism of John to call the Jews into the kingdom of the Messiah, over against proselyte baptism to bring Gentiles into Judaism.

However, this was merely the appearance. Proselyte baptism was a purely outward baptism. Pharisees clung to the outward washing with water and the ceremonies accompanying it in a truly formalistic fashion. But the baptism of John was completely different. It was a sign, and nothing more than a sign, of repentance and the washing away of sins, with an allusion to the One who would baptize with the Holy Spirit and with fire. John's baptism thus simultaneously broke through the formalism of the Pharisees and led people from petrified religious forms to the spiritual core of true religion. John summed this up when he solemnly announced that the kingdom of heaven, not the restoration of the kingdom of the Jews, was at hand.

§ 2   That Jesus came to be baptized by John had great significance, therefore, in that he himself, born as a Jew and thus a member of the Jewish state, by his baptism at the Jordan solemnly broke the false national expectation that the Jews harbored at that time. He imposed a ban on that entire false national expectation and assumed his position as the pretender, so to speak, to the throne of the true messianic kingdom. His baptism in the Jordan represented in principle a full condemnation of, and direct break with, Pharisaism, as well as the revelation of the spiritual kingdom in which he would appear as the King anointed by God.

In all that he did, however, Jesus did not in any way sever the bonds connecting him to Israel's past. "Salvation is from the Jews" [John 4:22], as he told the Samaritan woman. He sent his disciples out into all of Israel's towns and cities. He himself never brought his testimony anywhere except in Israel. To the pagan woman from the region of Sidon he uttered the harsh words: "It is not right to take the children's bread and throw it to the dogs" [Matt 15:26]. Time and again he referred back to the revelation given to Israel in the patriarchs, Moses, the psalmists, and the prophets. Instead of escaping from Palestine, he himself sought the place of his departure in Jerusalem. The sign "The King of the Jews" that Pilate had nailed on the cross may have been reflective of the Jews' false national perspective, and yet it hid a deep and real meaning. For the kingdom of heaven did arise from Israel.

From everything we know about Jesus' short life on earth, it is apparent in many ways that he could appear only in Israel. [This was related] both to his origin in Israel, as well as the circumstance that only in Israel did he find the disciples with whose spirit his testimony could make a connection—the context, so to speak, in which he could work. Jesus' origin and his context are of equal importance here. Nothing in itself would have prevented the incarnation of the eternal Word from occurring in Rome, with a Roman woman as the virgin mother. As such, God's omnipotence was not bound in any way. From a human perspective, it would even have been more impressive had Jesus appeared in the very midst of the world power of that time, than when he appeared as he did in remote Galilee and in the forgotten towns of Palestine.

This was not the way God had ordained it, however. In his ordination everything is prepared, everything is organically connected to the past, and everything is historically determined. The highest revelation does not suddenly intrude upon the world of that time, but connects to the course of revelation from the very beginning of time. It is a single work of God that began in the entire course of revelation and then attained its climax in the coming of the One promised to the fathers. The messianic line goes forth from Abraham. It passes over to the tribe of Judah. It attaches itself to the house of David. And after a history of centuries, it culminates in Mary, blessed among women. Mary was the product of this sacred history of many centuries. Mary's position, compared to the women of other nations and even the other women from Israel, was exalted not because of what she herself had accomplished, but because God had chosen her for this. In her, the nobility of women shone at its brightest.

But even the bond by which Jesus was connected through Mary to David, Judah, and Abraham was not enough for him. In order to be the Son of Man, his historical connection had to reach back all the way to Adam, the dethroned head of the fallen human race. While the genealogy in Matthew 1 goes back to Abraham, the genealogy of Luke 3 extends back to Adam. In this latter genealogy, the separation begins already with Seth. His line continues through Noah, to Shem, and then to Abraham. Jesus cannot simply enter human history somewhere in the middle as a foreign element. His genealogical root must go back to the first Adam, from whom came the entire human race—all of humanity. Only in this way was he really one with us. And only in this way could he become the Head not only of some in Israel who had repented, but the Head of regenerated humanity; and only in this way could the effect of his sacrifice on the cross go back to the very beginning of original sin. According to one legend, the physical remains of Adam rested under Mount Golgotha, so that some drops of the Man of Sorrows drained through a crack in the hill onto Adam's physical remains. Without subscribing to this legend, we can nevertheless ponder the profound thought that because he came from Adam, the atoning power of Christ's blood goes back all the way to Adam. He died not as the atonement for our sins alone—that is, the sins of the Jews—but in order to bring atonement for the sins of the whole world, for our entire race, for those from all of humanity who have been born again.

§ 3   Even if our King is historically connected in Adam to humanity, in Abraham to Israel, in Judah and in David to the kingly type, and in Mary to the blessed women from among Israel's ennobled humanity, one can never conclude from this that salvation was the result of human holiness. The fact alone that Tamar and Bathsheba are included in the genealogy suffices to reject any such interpretation. Instead, it is the case that his historical origin took all honor away from man and assigned all glory to God alone, since Israel was not distinguished from the nations by its holy existence but only by what God had worked for and in Israel. God's work—not man's work—in preparing the coming of our King was hardly limited to his origin, but it came out in an even more powerful way in what we have chosen to call the *context* that was indispensable so that Jesus' coming might achieve its goal.

Everyone lives in a milieu, an environment, a life circle whose life he shares and in which alone his life can come to its fullest expression. This includes our religious world, our moral world, the world of our thoughts and ideas, and the world of people in whose midst we function and live our lives. If there is no affinity, no agreement, no connection between our life and the world around us, our destiny will be like that of a plant that you pot in foreign soil. We will neither flourish nor grow, and we will influence nothing. No one experiences this more bitterly than those who are sent to preach Christ among pagans or Muslims. They first imagine that things will proceed automatically, since a certain need for salvation resides in every heart. But they soon meet with disappointment, especially because they largely fail to establish any contact with the religious and spiritual life of these pagans and Muslims. They are different; they live differently, they feel differently, they think differently.

The same thing would have happened to our King if no human context had been prepared in Israel with which he could establish a connection. Our King would not have found it in Athens or Rome. Nowhere on earth could [this context] have arisen out of normal human development. It could not have been there, had God not prepared it himself. And this is what God did indeed accomplish when he set Abraham apart and established the nation of Israel. Jesus came to bring the kingdom of heaven. Something out of heaven therefore had to enter this earthly life and make the preparations necessary for Jesus' coming. This occurred through the entire revelation that God had given to Abraham and Israel and through that special course of life that God arranged for Israel by the influence of his miraculous power.

The very first thing that was needed was a group, a nation, a milieu in which the one true God would be known and acknowledged, and in which all idolatry would be renounced. This context had to be governed by monotheism, a result that was indeed achieved in Israel at the time when our King appeared. Before the exile, this was not the case. Until the exile, the worship of Baal had the upper hand in ten of the twelve tribes; and even in the kingdom of Judah the most banal forms of idolatry arose time and again, often even encouraged and propagated by

Judah's kings. In the end, however, this evil was overcome. Under Ezra and Nehemiah, as well as in the time of the Maccabees, the rejuvenated Jewish nation broke completely with idolatry, and as a matter of principle it followed monotheism in its entire existence and lifeview. Even today the confession of this monotheism by the Jews—insofar as they have remained religious, at least—is their highest and most sought after title of honor, the pride of their strength. The apostles who went out among the Gentiles once more called out: "Keep yourselves from idols" [1 John 5:21], but Jesus never waged war on idolatry. In Israel, idolatry had been overcome, and Jesus appeared among a people who as a group confessed the one true God.

The situation in the moral world that Jesus found in Israel was similar. In former times, the deep moral corruption that accompanied Asiatic idolatry in the worship of Ashtoreth and Baal had also penetrated deeply among the Jews. In the pagan world there was no sense of a divine ordinance of purity regarding morality to which every human creature was automatically subject. This explains the terrible immorality that reigned throughout the entire pagan world and made prevalent the service of the senses in terms of luxury and wantonness, and even the most unnatural of sins. Just read in Romans 1 about how the apostle, who lived within this very pagan world, encountered it at Corinth, Athens, and Rome. It was in Israel alone that things were different. With this we do not mean to claim that all kinds of sin could not be found in Israel, or to deny that at his court in Tiberias Herod rivaled the Roman emperor in wantonness. But Israel did recognize a law of God, a higher ordinance for life, and this law and this ordinance had fostered a moral zeal that could not be found elsewhere. Moral zeal could be found in the pagan world among individuals, but not in the nation's public opinion. And although the formalism of Pharisaism caused this zeal for God's law to petrify in Israel and removed its heartbeat, in all of Israel's ranks and levels there remained the rooted conviction that we cannot form a law unto ourselves according to our own wants and likes, but that we are subjected to the law that God has imposed on us. This alone could produce the awareness of sin—a sense of guilt—and for that reason it was in such a context alone that Jesus could appear as the Lamb of God who takes away the sin of the world.

§ 4   Precisely the same holds true for the world of thought. Holy Scripture had been entrusted to Israel. Israel had been given a complete worldview in that Scripture—a proper view on the present, and a proper perspective on the ideal for which we must strive. The Psalms in particular show the state of mind in which the pious people in Israel lived by virtue of that revelation; and in contrast to the flaws of the present, the prophets gave most wonderful portrayals of the future ideal as it would be realized one day through God. This can be summed up in the messianic ideal as the psalmists and prophets depicted it for us with ever sharper lines and with ever deeper colors. And even though this high ideal in the Israel that Jesus found had been distorted through a one-sided patriotism and the Jews' national exclusiveness, Israel was the only place where the expectation of the second David continued unabated. From the Law, the Psalms, and the Prophets, Israel learned the thoughts, terms, words, and expressions that would be necessary in order to understand the kingdom of heaven. These made discussion and the exchange of ideas possible, such that Jesus could present himself not as a stranger, but as the one promised to the fathers, as the Messiah on whom the entirety of Israel's history was focused. At the very beginning of his ministry he therefore begins by reading the promises from Isaiah's prophecies, and then he declares: "Today this Scripture has been fulfilled in your hearing" [Luke 4:21]. This is Jesus' connection to the world of Israel's thought.

Finally, there is also the personal milieu. Had Jesus died, had he suffered, had he been raised and ascended into heaven without leaving anybody behind to serve as his witnesses, everything would have returned to its former state after he had left. Only by growing branches could this Vine bloom and bear fruit. To this end, *people* were needed who would form a fixed association around him and be able to bring his testimony out into the world after his departure. Jesus found these men in Israel, and all of the apostles including Paul were of Jewish origin. Nevertheless, Jesus did not find these people in Jerusalem or even in Judea, but specifically in Galilee. This was the northernmost region, where the Pharisees had exercised significantly less influence through their petrified legalism. The inhabitants of that region were those who did not know the law [see John 7:49]—that is, a group in which Israel's spirit did live on, but without the change in direction that the Pharisees had managed to push through in Judea. Although for that reason the true confession had been watered down in many of them, there continued to be some people for whom that spirit of Israel still retained some of its prophetic brilliance. These were the men and women who joined Jesus immediately and with complete devotion, thereby offering him the associates he needed.

With this, we do not mean to deny that much of that national leaven still lay hidden within that limited group as well. The apostles' restless questions about establishing the kingdom of Israel and [James' and John's] mother's question as to which high position her sons would hold in the new kingdom remained a barrier between Jesus and his followers to the very end. That is why this had to be resisted, and all kinds of erroneous views uprooted from that small group before the full and clear sense of the kingdom of heaven could break through within it. However, the elements necessary for making that connection were there. As slowly as things may have progressed, in the end those associates eventually reached a proper understanding of Jesus' coming; and after Jesus ascended, that group not only promoted his cause but also carried it out into the entire world. Thus our King comes as the Son of Man by virtue of his descent from Adam, Abraham, and David; and when he appears in Israel, he finds prepared for him: monotheism, also the acknowledgement of God's law, the thought-world to which he can connect, and the group of people who assimilate his Spirit and understand his Word, and can carry it forth.

III.13

JOHN THE BAPTIST

Repent, for the kingdom of heaven is at hand.

MATTHEW 3:2

Before the Messiah came to earth, John the Baptist had a special call-   § 1
ing closely connected to the preparation made for our King throughout
Israel's entire history. In order for Immanuel's coming to achieve its goal, it
was indispensable that a religious and moral atmosphere, a thought- and
idea-world, and a personal group, be prepared to which he could connect.
This indispensable preparation was established with Abraham's being set
apart and in Israel's history; and it is remarkable how the Diaspora—that
is, the dispersion of the Jews throughout the countries to the east and west
of Palestine, especially along the Euphrates, in Egypt, in Greece, and in
Italy—presented an immediate point of connection for the apostles and
evangelists when they brought the gospel to the Gentiles. Not only did the
preaching of the gospel as a rule go forth from the synagogues, but the
synagogues were also responsible for supplying the serious Gentiles with
knowledge of Israel's revelation. And although not many of them were
circumcised, a considerable number of men and women, especially from
the higher classes, nevertheless feared God and attended the synagogue.
In Capernaum, the Jewish synagogue was even built by a Gentile. It is thus
entirely justified to speak of two forms of preparation that went forth
from Israel: one in Palestine, for the King's own coming; the other in the
Diaspora, intended for his apostles.

As important as this general preparation for Immanuel's coming in Israel may have been, a final preparation was needed shortly before he arrived, for which reason John the Baptist appeared. In prophecy it had already been pointed out that such a forerunner would come. There was the voice of one crying in the wilderness: "Prepare the way of the LORD; make straight in the desert a highway for our God" [Isa 40:3]. Even Malachi spoke the following words: "Behold, I send my messenger, and he will prepare the way before me" [Mal 3:1]. And more pointedly: "Behold, I will send you Elijah the prophet before the great and awesome day of the LORD comes" [Mal 4:5]. John the Baptist thus came before Jesus in order to announce his imminent coming, to begin to sift the spirits, to gather together everything built up in the history and prophecy of Israel with respect to the ideal view of the Messiah, and to place it decisively and forcefully over against the false, nationalist perspective. In John, everything that has been prepared in Israel's history and in prophecy is finally drawn together into a single focal point. John declares to Israel that God is able to raise up children for Abraham from the stones of the rock desert [see Matt 3:9], which is like a slap in the face to the false, physical patriotism that derived its honor from its ancestry. John applied the proselyte baptism to the Jews themselves, which is the break with their national pride. The false baptism by which Gentiles were incorporated into the Jews did not save but corrupted them; and as Jesus said with sharp words, it made them children of hell rather than children of God [see Matt 23:15]. By contrast, true baptism was the baptism that brought over first the Jew and then the Gentile from their unholy state into the kingdom of God. But this was also the very reason why John could administer this baptism only for a limited time, in expectation of the One who would baptize with the fire of the Holy Spirit. Finally, John the Baptist dashed all expectations of a return of Solomon's earthly glory in the form of a Davidic kingdom established in Jerusalem when he announced the arrival of a King whose kingdom was not earthly but heavenly in nature. "Repent, for the kingdom of heaven is at hand" [Matt 3:2].

For that reason, the significance of John in the spiritual ordination of providence can hardly be overestimated. His preaching did not simply summarize prophecy and abridge it; his preaching was an act. He addressed the reigning disposition of the [people's] spirits with a forceful hand. He agitated people's minds throughout the land. That agitation began to sort out the spirits. In Jerusalem people looked at him with troubled eyes. Herod trembled. The Sanhedrin was disquieted. However, John's appearance made such an impression on the nation that [the authorities] dared not oppose him and left him be at the Jordan, and a group was formed throughout almost the entire country that chose for John and against conventional spirituality. Before he came, the spirit of the entire nation was shackled by the bonds of that official spirituality. By his coming and by what he did, John freed the spirits in a segment of the nation, called them back from the form and symbol to the core of the matter, reintroduced the higher and more ideal view of the Messiah, and joined himself to the great prophets who had arisen before, during, and shortly after the exile. When Jesus came, he could connect to that spiritually liberated segment of Israel that had been called back to the ideal. Through his baptism and his preaching, John introduced Israel the bride to the coming Bridegroom.

In John, all of these elements are summed up in the gospel of the kingdom, in his announcement that the kingdom of heaven was at hand. This was why Jesus himself, when he appeared, summarized the content of the gospel with similar expressions and likewise began by announcing that the kingdom of heaven was at hand. §2

A kingdom belongs to a King. For that reason, the preaching does not begin by announcing the Savior, the Reconciler, the Redeemer, but places the King in the foreground. This King would bring salvation and an all-surpassing bliss to the nations. He would indeed also save us from sin and reconcile us with God, and be our surety unto eternal life—yet these things do not precede his kingship, but follow from it. Jesus will also be our Prophet and High Priest, but not in order to become King and establish his kingdom through that. Rather, the converse applies. Christ is our King, he establishes his kingdom, and as King he is also Prophet and Priest so that the establishment of his kingdom may succeed.

This element has not received the attention it deserves. People, when hearing the word kingdom, have not duly considered that no kingdom exists without a king, and that their speaking of the kingdom of heaven presupposes the heavenly King. John also proclaimed Jesus to be the Lamb of God who takes away the sin of the world, but he did this only in the presence of Jesus' future disciples. To them he gave deeper instruction. But his initial general announcement, made to all the people, was and remained the proclamation of our King, whose kingdom is at hand, and the strap of whose sandal he is not worthy to untie, because of Jesus' kingly dignity.

The kingdom took center stage, and with it the King. All other elements followed from it. Christ was Priest after the order of Melchizedek; but Melchizedek, too, was first a king and then a priest as king. Jesus' prophetic calling comes and passes. His high priestly act was completed on Golgotha. But he is and remains King. In that kingship lies his essential exaltation. "For this purpose," that is, to be King, as Jesus himself said to Pilate, "I was born, and for this purpose I have come into the world" [John 18:37]. From the very beginning his unsurpassable majesty is concentrated in his kingship. Before he goes to Golgotha, he enters Jerusalem on the foal of a donkey while the people shout: "Hosanna to the Son of David!" [Matt 21:9]—that is, while they honor him as King. It is a misunderstanding of Scripture if, with John's preaching, one were to think of the kingdom alone and lose sight of the King. The preaching of the kingdom included the preaching of the King, and in that preaching the announcement of the King took center stage. Without the King there is no kingdom. The kingdom is not established before the King arrives, so that he can then enter it. He himself brings the kingdom in his own person. He establishes it. It is established only when he appears.

This must receive particular emphasis because, regrettably, even among those who confess Christ, the view has found acceptance that instead turns the kingdom of heaven into some kind of a spiritual order without any relationship to Jesus' kingship. This view has come to us from the broad circle of those who appeal for justice and equity and who gush with spiritual ideals, but who refuse to bow their knees before Jesus and, because they feel nothing for his kingship, refuse to honor him as King. They carry on in a general and figurative sense about the kingdom of the spirit, about a kingdom of the ideal, about a kingdom of justice, and imagine that the expression *kingdom of heaven* is to be understood in a similarly figurative sense. As long as justice triumphs and high moral ideals gain entrance, they think that the spirit's kingdom is already coming into its dominion. They understand the kingdom entirely outside of Jesus' personal dominion. As they imagine it, the kingdom, the spiritual kingdom, would gradually have come even if Jesus had never appeared. It is a kingdom on its own that must of itself gradually achieve victory and triumph. And although they acknowledge that Jesus also numbers among those who advanced the spirit's kingdom, they understand this as referring only to his moral, spiritual, and religious influence; and they refuse to connect that influence in a direct and unbreakable bond with Jesus' kingship. This is why even those who honor Jesus as nothing more than a rabbi from Nazareth, and even doubt his complete sinlessness, can gush about the kingdom of heaven. As they understand it, the kingdom was not established by Jesus. Its establishment is something to which all noble figures from among the nations contributed. Christ also contributed his part, but only in that sense.

This view is entirely contrary to what has been revealed to us in Scripture. The kingdom of heaven was at hand only when Jesus was about to come. The kingdom enters when the King comes. It is a kingdom announced in prophecy, with its roots in the history of Israel and the house of David. It is a kingdom that cannot be imagined without a King, is concentrated in the King, enters the world only when he appears, and attains to the manifestation of its glory through him and him alone.

The view that understands a kingdom of the spirit figuratively was entirely foreign to Israel. It came from the Greco-Roman world rather than the world of the Israelites. It is an abstraction that is entirely misplaced in the exposition of Scripture. For John the Baptist and for Jesus, a kingdom without a King in the most proper sense is an inner contradiction.

We Westerners speak figuratively of a mineral kingdom, a plant kingdom, an animal kingdom, as well as a kingdom of the arts and sciences, the kingdom of truth, and the kingdom of justice. The French even speak of *la règne de la mode*, the kingdom of fashion. Following old Latin usage and the former form of our state, scholars frequently refer to a *respublica litterarum*, that is, a republic of letters. Anything that formed a self-enclosed whole with regulated laws was presented as a kingdom. People have gone so far as to call the lion the king of the animal kingdom, the cedar the king of the plant kingdom, and gold the king of the mineral kingdom. However, this remained a figurative, symbolic way of speaking, where no personal king is involved. When they transferred this to the kingdom of truth, the kingdom of the good, and the kingdom of the beautiful as well, people ended up with just as figurative a view of the kingdom of heaven that was entirely in line with the dominion of the good, true, and beautiful. The façade of the opera house at Frankfurt am Main bears the large inscription 'Dedicated to the good, the true, and the beautiful." In fact, all too many people have equated the "kingdom of heaven" with this notion. They maintained that just like Plato, Aristotle, Solon, and Lycurgus, Jesus also—in an even more elevated sense—contributed to the establishment of this kingdom, but everything was understood figuratively.

§ 3

This figurative, symbolic view is unprecedented in the East, however, and never appears in Scripture. Trees are said figuratively to have been seeking a king [see Judg 9:8–15], but the word *kingdom* never occurs in Scripture in the figurative sense that we often ascribe to it. Especially when we come to man in what we call the *organic kingdom*, we cannot conceive of a kingdom, as a summary of the whole, that does not include conscious legislation, conscious government, a conscious judiciary, and a conscious struggle against those enemies seeking to overturn the kingdom. And since this conscious regiment of a kingdom can be imagined to exist only in a personal king, the kingdom of heaven may and can be understood only as a kingdom with its King, established through its King, maintained through its King, ruled by its King, and protected from its enemies by its King. In the same way, Jesus appears in Scripture as the King of the kingdom of God, as the King who establishes, maintains, rules, and defends the kingdom of heaven, and who as the King of that kingdom will one day be seated as Judge to judge the living and the dead—who with this judgment will also strike the final blow to his enemies so that they all will have to subject themselves to him. For this reason we must strictly and uncompromisingly maintain that John's announcement that "the kingdom of heaven is at hand," which was later taken over by Jesus himself, included the announcement of the Messiah—that is, the announcement of the King who would bring the kingdom to us.

It is worth noting that the expression *kingdom of heaven* is found only in the Gospel of Matthew, and that the phrase *kingdom of God* is found in the parallel passages of the other Gospels. These expressions refer to the same thing, albeit with a somewhat different wording. The expression *kingdom of God* explicitly mentions the King. There is a kingdom in which God himself is King. And if Matthew, too, had chosen this form, the figurative understanding [of the kingdom] would presumably never even have arisen, for the expression that specifies *of heaven* rather than *of God* has led to that understanding more than anything else has. It cannot be maintained, of course, that the phrase *kingdom of God* is used to the exclusion rather than inclusion of Jesus' kingship. The kingdom of God functions and maintains itself precisely in that kingship of Christ. Instead, the expression *kingdom of God* has a wider scope; it expresses that God himself would come to us in Christ and that Christ would not be a normal descendant of David. [He would be] a descendant and sprout from David in whom the eternal Word who was God and was with God would himself assume flesh, our nature, and as such come from the line of David.

This goes back to something we explained earlier. Originally there was no earthly king in Israel, because God himself was King of Israel in a fully theocratic sense. For that reason, it represented a departure from God as its King when Israel called out for an earthly king in the days of Samuel. Saul fell, and it was in David that God himself first raised up a kingly house that would flow into the kingship of God once again at the end and would thereby restore the original situation. Prophecy had already clearly foretold that this would happen through one who himself would be "Counselor, Mighty God" [Isa 9:6], and who as Immanuel would cause God himself to rule in his dominion. John's announcement that a full theocracy would return shortly after him through the coming of the kingdom of God thus implied both the fulfillment of prophecy as well as a contrast to what Israel erroneously desired. Israel had rejected the kingdom of God. Then an earthly kingdom came. But God's ordination had guided things such that, in connecting to David's earthly kingship, the theocratic kingship of God would in the end return in the mystery that was gradually unveiled—namely, that God would one day reveal himself in a shoot from David's house.

§ 4

John's announcement of the kingdom of God, or the kingdom of heaven, was diametrically opposed to the expectation the Jews harbored at the time. Their national exclusivity was rejected because God is King not only over Israel, but over our entire human race; and God would reveal himself as King not by once more crowning a Jew from the house of David, but by sending his only Son and revealing himself in him to Israel and to the entire world. It was God's chosen people who would receive revelation and who as a symbol would bear salvation. But once this calling had been fulfilled and this task completed, what arose from Israel had to flow into the entire world so that humanity would take the place of Israel.

Understood in this way, Israel would retain a place of honor among the nations, but of its own accord it would have to distance itself from its entirely singular and exceptional position. It was not to become a Jewish kingship, subjecting all nations and peoples to the Jewish nation state, but the Jewish nation state had to be incorporated into God's kingdom over the entire human race. That did indeed happen, but against Israel's will and choice. It even resisted this transition with violence. It nailed Christ to the cross and thereby brought upon itself the judgment that came as few as thirty years later in the destruction of Jerusalem. All the same, the Jews have still continued as a nation ever since. While the surrounding nations have all disappeared without a trace, the Jewish nation still exists and it has even grown to some twelve million in number. Furthermore, it always still has extraordinary intellectual gifts—which it obviously receives from God alone. But in spite of these things, it has ended up outside of the boundary of the kingdom of heaven. Many Jews did enter within the boundary, but as a nation Israel excluded itself. This was the necessary result contained in John's announcement that the kingdom of God was about to be established not only over Israel but over the entire world, and that this kingdom would not be of the earth but of heaven.

The King thus stands in the foreground. That King is God himself. God himself reveals himself in the Son of his love. Christ thus appears as King in his name, and it is through him that God once again reigns as King. The present era of Christ's reign will last until kingly authority has once again been restored factually and actually in all the spheres of the human spirit; then the Son will hand over the kingdom to the Father so that the Triune God may be all in all. Jesus himself expresses these things when he says: "My kingdom is not of this world" [John 18:36]. The kingdom of God and the kingdom of Christ are one.

For that reason, all figurative interpretations must be discarded. In Christ, the King appears personally. From him proceeds a law for the kingdom as he revealed it especially in his kingdom parables. One day he will, as the King of that kingdom, sit in judgment as Judge. It is he who personally fights the battle for that kingdom in order to subject and render powerless all enemies who resist it. Therefore, it may never be said that this kingdom has a purely spiritual character. Initially it does not come "with signs to be observed" [Luke 17:20]. For our King, there is no throne upon earth. He has no magnificent retinue. He has no armed forces that march out ahead of him. On earth there will be no crown of diamonds pressed upon his head. But this purely spiritual character of the kingdom over which he is King will not last forever. Once the spiritual struggle approaches its culmination, his kingdom will also dawn physically. Nature will be filled with turmoil, the existing situation will undergo violent change, and very terrifying things will happen such that the whole earth will melt, only to be arrayed thereafter in its splendor as the new earth under the new heaven. While we cannot yet develop this fully, we do need to point it out already in the present context. This is because every figurative understanding of the kingdom of heaven necessarily and automatically has led and must lead also to rejecting the last judgment as a figment of the imagination; it will discard everything in prophecy, in Jesus' words, in the apostolic letters, and in the Revelation of John that points to the physical events awaiting at the end of days.

III.14

TRIUMPH OF THE HIGHER ORDER

So that what is mortal may be swallowed up by life.

2 Corinthians 5:4

§ 1   Clear insight into Christ's kingly dominion is best gained by paying careful attention to the dominion exercised by the life-principle in those orders or kingdoms of nature that have their own life.

Nature is not dull and monotonous but infinitely diverse. But in spite of that diversity a certain order does remain through which the phenomena we observe can be divided into particular groups that are then given the name of *orders* or *kingdoms*. In terms of rank, the lowest kingdom is the so-called mineral kingdom, which is then followed by the plant kingdom and the animal kingdom. *Mineral kingdom* is definitely not a very appropriate name, and to identify it as the *inorganic* kingdom is at any rate more correct. To this lowest of nature's kingdoms belongs whatever does not display a functioning life-seed of its own. Whether this also applies to crystals cannot be considered here, since we have no time to enter into the details.

We will limit ourselves to nature's three kingdoms in general. There are boundaries between each of these kingdoms, but it is not always possible for us to draw them tightly. For the present purpose, however, it is enough if we include whatever lives from a principle of its own as a part of the plant and animal kingdoms, while we include that which lacks such a life-principle as part of the inorganic kingdom, which used to be called the mineral kingdom. The possession of life comes to clear expression first in the plant kingdom; and in a higher measure, this life-principle is displayed in the animal kingdom—more clearly, in fact, the higher one ascends among the different animal species. The life-principle comes out most strongly in the human race, which in its lower disposition is always included as a part of the animal kingdom. However, humanity's place is not exhausted with the animal kingdom, because with humanity that life-principle assumes the higher form of a spirit. Through their spirits, human beings are in turn related to the higher spirit world, and in the order or kingdom of the spiritual it is Christ who occupies the highest place. He is the Lord of the angels and the Son of Man, and as such he reigns over the entire order of spiritual life, both here and above. And because he is the eternal Word, the entire spiritual world may exist *from* the Father, but then only *through* Christ.

Beginning at the bottom, therefore, we find the following ladder in creation. First is the kingdom of matter, then the plant world, then the animal kingdom; in the animal kingdom appears the world of humanity; humanity is related to the world of the spirits; Christ is the Head of that spirit world; and in Christ, the divine has been united through a holy mediatorship with what is created. There is thus a concatenation that is made up of all the orders of lower nature together with the spirit world, and it reaches its highest point in Christ. A universe proceeded from God's mighty creative Word, rises from the lower to the higher in every sphere until it ends in Christ, and is reunited to the Triune God in and through Christ. It begins with the unconscious and inorganic, ascends through all levels and stages to divine-human life-consciousness in Christ, and seals in him creation's bond with God.

Each higher order governs the next order below it—that is, plants over the material order; animals over the material and plant orders; man over the material, plant, and animal orders; the human spirit over all of the above, as well as over the animal element in humanity; and Christ over all of these things, as well as the spiritual element in man, until Christ too hands over the kingdom to the Father that God may be all and in all [see 1 Cor 15:28]. Since that rule applies, it is clear that Christ's authoritative power reigns royally throughout all creation along its entire scale, and that all things in heaven and on earth have been handed over to him [see Matt 11:27]. In the miracles he performed, Christ intervened from without and displayed in many ways his authority over the material world, over the plant world, over the animal world, over the world of humanity, and over the evil spirits he cast out.

From the very beginning that bond was there, although it was concealed and internal, for all things—that is, all kingdoms and orders of nature—were created through him and hold together through him [see Col 1:16–17]. Through his mediatorship he elevates this bond, which encompasses and enlists everything, to the highest spiritual consciousness. And once his mediatorship has been completed, at the last judgment the transition of this broken world into the kingdom of glory will occur through great events proceeding from him into all of nature's kingdoms. His kingly dominion, rooted in the fact that all things were created through the eternal Word, therefore penetrates all spheres of creation; and in the end it will become clear that nothing in heaven or on earth is excluded from that kingly dominion.

§ 2 In nature's kingdoms we see life arising in a manner entirely inexplicable to us; and as soon as life manifests itself in its first, lowest, and weakest form, it exercises dominion over whatever is lower in creation. The tiny seed of a plant may be small, but soon it reigns over the material elements around it. A plant sprouts and builds itself up from the germ of the seed and in so doing avails itself of the material elements found in the soil and in the air. The plant processes those materials, transforms them to fit its own nature, governs them, and in propagation perpetuates its life so as to govern the material elements again and again and to subject the material elements to itself. Only when a plant's life weakens and it is no longer capable of exercising its total dominion over the material elements in the soil and in the air does its life begin to be threatened. The material element begins to resist its dominion, takes back its own power again, and if this process is allowed to continue it finally extinguishes the life in that plant that then withers, hardens, and dies. Death enters.

This is also how things go with animals. Animals too have life in them, and their life is of a higher kind and a higher order than that of plants. Through the life residing in its essence, the animal world uses what is found both in the material world as well as in the plant world in order to build and maintain itself. There are indeed parasites in the plant world that live on other plants, and in the animal world one animal may devour another. However, these are exceptions to the rule that plants live on the material found in the soil and in the air, while animals live on both the material and plant worlds. This, too, implies dominion. Plants serve animals. Animals propagate themselves in order to continue their dominion over the plant world. But once again, we see the same thing happening here as in the plant world. Animals can weaken, and the material and plant world can attack the animal world when it finds itself in that weakened state. Plant tissues can wreak havoc in an animal's body. And even where that does not happen, the animal's life can still surrender its power of dominion. Then life dies in the animal as well, and decomposition and rotting set in. Once again, the end is death.

When you go on to consider humanity, you will observe the same in their world as with animals, insofar as humanity forms a part of the animal kingdom. People, too, grow from a life-seed that uses and governs the elements from the material and plant worlds. But in the case of human beings, something more exalted manifests itself, and this is what gives the human race dominion over the animal world as well. Here too you see a struggle. Poisonous plants and wild animals threaten human life, and the plant and animal kingdoms even attack human life in the form of bacilli and microbes, maggots and tapeworms. But where these elements of a lower order succeed in attaching themselves to the human body and manage to develop independently within it so that the body's life-power can no longer control and resist their festering, there you will see destruction enter and human life waste away; death will follow. Also, if a person's life-power declines so that he or she dies, the chemical materials, the plant residues, and the animals that have nestled themselves in the body will all of a sudden reclaim their dominion over the body so that the process of decomposition sets in.

In the case of human beings, however, there is more. Just as in animals, there is a soul as life-element in human beings, but the soul or life element in human beings also has a spiritual character. This spiritual element in people has dominion over the lower elements that they share with the animals. The dominion that a person's spirit has over the lower animal element in one's soul reveals one's full worth and strength as a human being. The more that one's spirit exercises its dominion—over not only the material, plant, and animal elements in one's body, but also over the lower elements of the soul—the higher one stands as a human being. And conversely, the less that the spirit's dominion succeeds in subjecting the animal element in one's soul, the more one diminishes in value as a human being and reverts back to an animal existence. What Scripture reveals to us about the beast arising from the sea [see Rev 13:1 and 15:2] and about the animals of the godless kingdoms means simply that even people—taken collectively as the human race—can sink from the higher spiritual order down to the lower animal order. It is thus common to say of someone who has lost all control over the animal life within himself that he is a beast of a man. This expression is not symbolic or figurative, but literal. When a person's higher order recedes into the background, nothing remains except the lower order that one has in common with the life of the soul as it is found in animals, such that one's affinity to the animal approaches conformity. This, too, wreaks havoc and decay, and culminates in death. For this reason, Scripture presents the results of sin as the death of the spirit in man. Death cannot act as a power here or enter any domain unless the higher part of the soul that exercises dominion over the lower part is broken and deprived of its dominion. Christ's resurrection can even be said to have been nothing other than the complete dominion of his holy, spiritual life over the lower orders of nature that had entered into battle with him and attempted to destroy his body. They failed to succeed because the inner life-power emanating from his spirit remained unbroken.

§ 3   Poisons, parasites, and debauchery—powers rooted in the plant and animal kingdoms—may well destroy one's body, and the animal in us may bring us down spiritually. But this law—that the higher perishes as soon as what belongs to a lower order triumphs over it—which also holds for humanity, does not sufficiently explain the breaking of the power of the spirit. Breaking of the power of the human spirit did not occur apart from the plant and animal kingdoms, since in the account of the fall we read about the fruit of a tree and about a snake. All the same, that destruction was in principle brought about through influence from an entirely different kingdom, namely, the kingdom of the spirit.

Although we usually only take note of three kingdoms—of the material, of plants, and of animals—the kingdom of the spirit may not be forgotten. The human race through its spirit is in contact with the spirit world as well, such that the spirit world can also exercise an effect on humanity. Even the world of angels is of a lower order than humanity when compared to the latter's state in the glorious consummation. Humanity was created a little lower than the angels [see Psa 8:5], but at the consummation it is human beings rather than angels who will be crowned with glory. Scripture explicitly says that we will judge the angels [see 1 Cor 6:3], rather than that the angels will judge us.

The explanation for this is that the angels were created as complete, not needing development, but that we are intended for a gradual development that will be completed only steadily. We begin lower, but end up higher. In paradise, humans were actually lower than the spirits in the exalted spirit world; but in potential—that is, according to their capacity—they were more. The activity proceeding from that exalted spirit world can serve our higher development unto glory insofar as the angels are sent out for the sake of those who will inherit salvation. Christ himself says of little children that their angels always see the face of the Father who is in heaven [see Matt 18:10]. An invincible army of exalted spirits assembles around those who seek to do God's will; and eternity will reveal for the first time what we owe to the higher spirit world for our being numbered among the saved and for our sanctification. But a destructive element can also reach us from that exalted spirit world. In that exalted spirit world, a demonic kingdom stands opposed to a holy kingdom, and this demonic world is organized under a spirit that is better equipped than any other spirit—namely, under Satan. Just like the plant and animal worlds, this Satan or Devil forces himself upon us in order to become a parasite in us, a parasite on our spirit.

Being purely spirit, that demonic parasite has no control on the plant world. However, it can come into contact with the animal world, such as when Jesus sent a number of demons into a herd of swine so that they rushed down the steep bank and drowned in the sea [see Matt 8:28–34]. However, it is on humanity alone that this spiritual parasite has its proper grip, since the life of the human race has a spiritual element as well. Just like a parasite nestles in the body, so the demonic parasite nestles in our spirit. This was especially true in Jesus' day, as is evident from the many demon-possessed men and women whom Jesus met during his travels; a possessed person is someone in whose soul a demonic spirit has managed to nestle as a parasite in order to speak through that person's mouth and to live off that person's spirit.

All of these things, however, are no more than the aftereffect of Satan's first intrusion into our human race. Everything was decided at this first intrusion. At that time, he unraveled the natural bond between the human spirit and God, and he cast a net of dependence over the human spirit. That influence has continued ever since, and it will continue until it is undone through Christ at the end of time. Here, too, dominion was reversed. Because humanity's potential was of a higher order, humanity had dominion over the spirit world and should have kept it. But even though it was of a lower order, the demonic world rose up in rebellion. It gained dominion over the human race. And if another ordinance of God had not intervened, the demonic world would gradually have undone everything higher in humanity, would have pushed it back into its animal life, and would have made it vegetate like a plant. This, too, would have been the result of the fixed law that, when the higher weakens, the lower immediately returns to trying to break down its dominion and to gain dominion over the higher.

That is why our human dominion could be restored only by the entrance of the eternal Word into our nature. Once it had been weakened by the fall, the human spirit was no longer able to shake off the demonic yoke or to regain its dominion in the spirit world. And only because the human spirit reappears in unweakened, unbroken, and unassailable form in a child could the Son of Man undo the tyranny of this demonic parasite. Death entered, although this did not mean that all life was extinguished all at once. On the contrary, animal life survived, and spiritual life continued as the flickering flame of a dying nightlight.

The result was that the animal life within the human being gained the upper hand, and the destructive power of the material, plant, and animal worlds hurled itself upon the human race in order to weaken it bodily with all kinds of illnesses and dangers, until it would be forced in the end to give up the fight and physical death would come as well. In human society a similar weakening, poisoning, and destruction also manifested itself and threw that society into total disarray. Most frightening of all was that even the spiritual within the human being was poisoned, and Satan forced human beings to serve his glory instead of the honor of God.

§ 4 The parasites of the lower orders and kingdoms thus penetrated further and further into the higher creaturely order so that the whole world came to be faced with the question whether the higher order would indeed regain its dominion, or whether it was doomed to succumb to the dominion exercised by the lower order. Would the plant and animal worlds continue to bring man down physically? Would the animal in us continue to keep the spiritual in us in subjection to it? And would the demonic world poison our spirit from then on? Or, would humanity's spirit be equipped to break with Satan, and so to recapture its dominion over all the lower orders of creation? The question was not whether God Almighty could break the resistance offered by the lower orders. If need be, his omnipotence, which created it all, could cause everything to return to nothing and then turn and create a new world.

No, the question concerned the human spirit. The question was whether the human spirit could restore its original strength and thus recapture the original, bestowed dominion that it once had over all of creation's lower orders. This is the reason why it is constantly the Son of Man who appears in the foreground in this new struggle. That Son of Man was God, but he had humbled himself, lowered himself, and assumed the form of man—of a servant, in fact. And the wondrous thing about this salvation is that, in the Son of Man, the spiritual has remained entirely unweakened and unbroken, and that his Spirit extends and maintains dominion over all of creation's lower orders. In the miracles he performs, he does this provisionally over the plant kingdom, over the animal kingdom, and over the kingdom of the demons. But this display of recaptured human dominion served only to begin the battle and to show his supremacy.

This triumph on the periphery, however, did not mean the salvation of our human race. At the very heart and center of human life, the battle had to be fought spiritually. This took place in the temptation, in the spiritual duel between the Son of Man and the ruler of this world. This explains why he fasted in order to suppress the animal part, why wild animals lingered about, and finally, why Satan's first temptation was about bread. When it became clear that the Son of Man could not be wounded or hurt spiritually, Satan had no other option than to cause Jesus to disappear and, if possible, to destroy him through death. This was indeed how Satan planned things, and Jesus entered death. But it was precisely in his death that the spirit of the Son of Man proved to be invulnerable. He devoured death through the power of his spiritual life. He arose, and in Christ's resurrection the power of the higher order over all of creation's lower orders was restored. The life of the spirit undid death. The life of the spirit broke through in the glorified body, and at that hour it began the great process of taking up in Jesus what was salvageable in the world and making it like him. That power is what carries the souls and regenerates them unto eternal life, that is, to a life that is no longer governed by a lower kingdom but governs that kingdom. An entirely different order penetrates human society. And the prophets foretell the moment at which, on this earth, once it has been renewed, a new humanity will shine. And, glorified according to the body, [humanity] will shake off every dominion exercised by the lower kingdoms over this body; and once it has been glorified like Jesus himself and even crowned as king, will stand before God.

Here, too, there is organization. It is not a matter of every person on their own, but of the entire human race in one body—and in that body Christ as its Head who engenders the spirit, guides and governs everything belonging to this body. That is his kingship. It is thus a kingship that begins in the human spirit, but which subjects all lower kingdoms of nature to itself through this human spirit in order to extend over all of these kingdoms—that is, over all of creation. It is a recreation encompassing human beings in their life and in the life of society, but extending also to the lower orders of animal, plant, and material life. It is a kingship that can still be hindered for a time, but one that incessantly penetrates further and will manifest itself at the close of the age as a complete dominion governing all created things. And once this has been completed, everything falls away that stood between the Triune God and the human race as it was created in his image, everything that had obstructed their full, rich, and intimate communion. Then Christ's mediatorship will be accomplished as well. In Christ the Triune God will exercise dominion over our entire race and through our race over all of creation; and then he will be all in all.

And what other than life itself will have triumphed?—the wondrous principle of life that first arises in plants, is more richly unfolded in animals, and finds consummation in the human race. The life that was constantly impaired by the continued proliferation of the lower kingdoms and deprived once more of its power, that life was the Son of Man himself—life in its highest and richest manifestation. And that life, which presents itself invincibly in the Son of Man, has devoured the material and thereby triumphed over death. "The last enemy to be destroyed is death" [1 Cor 15:26], and he who overcomes death is in principle life itself, in the highest manifestation of its power. When God will once more be all in all, then life will again flow forth pure and unpolluted from the Fount of life and fill his entire creation.

We trust that what we said earlier in our first section, about the manifestation of Christ's kingly dominion also in the increasing power that humanity's spirit has gained over nature, will now be understood in its deeper significance.

CONNECTION WITH LIFE

For as the Father has life in himself, so he has granted the Son also to have life in himself.

JOHN 5:26

The apostle testifies to us that in the eternal Word—that is, in the Son— is life, and that this life is the light of men [see John 1:4]. We could substitute *higher consciousness* for light, but the meaning remains the same. In Christ is life, and from that life comes all higher flourishing, and thus our salvation as well. Christ gives us a further explanation of this when he says that the Son has life in himself [see John 5:26], and that we by contrast receive life from him alone. He goes before us as the one who "gives life to the world" [John 6:33]. He calls himself the "way, the truth, and the life" [John 14:6]. This explains the principle, "Whoever has the Son has life; whoever does not have the Son of God does not have life" [1 John 5:12]. To be incorporated into Christ is to pass from death to life. And Christ is at once the Bread of Life, that is, the Bread through which anyone who at one time received life continues to live. Paul goes so far as to say that our life has been hidden with Christ in God, and that Christ is our life [see Col 3:3–4].

    Since, in contrast with that life, Scripture depicts all unholiness, all injustice, all inner weakening of our higher existence with the image of

§ 1

death, it automatically follows that our King's dominion must be one of life over death; and we must seek to explain the essence of that dominion on the basis of life. While death reigned from Adam to Moses [see Rom 5:14], life will now reign in those who are in Christ. When Jesus came, it was not so much about the words he spoke but about his very person, not so much about what goes forth from him but about Jesus Christ himself. At the end, the entire struggle against him was concentrated on that one goal of destroying his life; his kingship arose from the fact that the life he had in himself could not be destroyed, but instead broke through death and was glorified in his resurrection. The last enemy to be overcome is for that reason neither sin, nor even Satan, but death—that is, the antithesis of life. Grace begins with life as its first milestone, and the last milestone will not be reached until life has done away with death.

The dominion exercised by the kings on this earth is different. It is external. A command goes forth. The king's subjects hear this command. They conform their will to that command and carry it out. Or, if they do not carry it out, the king coerces those subjects by a show of force.

Jesus' dominion, however, is one that arises internally from life itself and reposes in life. What Christ our King communicates to us is his life. Those who receive his life are born again and as such are members of his body—a metaphor that is once again derived from life. When they have life, they will also listen to his word and carry it out with their will that has been set free. This is a result, however—a consequence. It is the second phase. But the starting point, the beginning, is found in life; and for that reason, in Christ's kingship it is, above all, life—that is, his life—that has dominion in us and makes him our King.

Christ's life may well be life in its highest and richest manifestation, the only life that remains unshaken; but in its basic character, it remains one with the life that creatures possess. It is life of the highest order within created life; and it is from this life that the kingdom—the one elevated high above all of nature's kingdoms—arises; but this life nonetheless follows the law governing all of life and is connected with all lower orders of life. He, the Christ, assumed our human nature not only according to the soul, but also the body. And our human body is in turn directly connected with both the animal and plant kingdoms. There is a progression between the orders of creation. Lowest in rank is the life of plants, followed in the second place by the life that animals have. For it is not in plants, but in animals that life manifests itself in a soul.[1] After all, Scripture teaches us throughout that animals have a soul. But in humanity, the life of the soul ascends once again to reach a higher order, a spiritual order.

In the spirit world, that spiritual order was initially elevated above us [human beings] because it already was in a state of completion, but the human spirit will in the end surpass the spirit world. That higher order represented by man's spiritual life then finds its highest manifestation in Christ, and in Christ we have a direct connection to the life of God.

There is thus a so-called scale, a life-ladder, where life ascends higher and higher with every rung, but in such a way that even on the lowest rung life remains the great mystery. After all, Psalm 104 says even of plants and animals that their spark was lit "by the Spirit of God" [see Psa 104:30]. From God, through God, and unto God, the aforementioned law applies to the whole scale of life. The second law is that within this range of the lowest, the higher, and the highest life, the higher always rests upon the lower and must govern the lowest. And as long as the higher remains intact and undamaged, it indeed really does govern the lowest. Conversely, however, when life of a higher order decays and collapses, life of the lower order begins to take control over the higher life and thereby kills it. When a plant takes control over an animal, the animal will die. When a plant or animal takes control over a person, that person will die physically. And when the animal soul in a person takes control over his spirit, that person will die spiritually.

This is why human life could become incorruptible and develop into eternal life only if a spiritual life of a higher order were to take root in humanity—a life, that is, that spiritually could not succumb, and that physically could break through death. This took place in him who, as our King, possesses such dominion over life's lower orders that no life of a lower order could triumph any longer over what was higher. Our King, who has life in himself and is our life, has dominion over all of creation's orders. He has dominion over the spirit world, over the world of humanity, over life in the animal and plant kingdoms. He has dominion over the life of plants, bodies, souls, and spirits. And all things have been subjected to him so that "in him all things hold together" [Col 1:17].

It is only when we come back to life that Christ's kingly dominion is displayed to us in its full splendor and glory. His birth, his miracles, his

§ 2

---

1. See *PR* 1.II.2.2.

death, his resurrection, his headship over angels and people, his power over all things (that is, over the entire creation)—they begin to form a coherent whole only when you trace your way back to the very core of his power, that is, to that life of the highest, all-encompassing order which was in him. One can analyze everything. We have been able to discover the cause and origin for everything, except for life. Whether it be the life of plants or animals, of people or angels, life remains equally mysterious—the greatest mystery eluding every attempt at an answer. Life suddenly appears at creation, and the question, "Who lit the spark of life?" still cannot be answered in any other way except: It is God who did it. All life within creation is an immediate testimony to God's influence, whether it be the life of the nations or the life of the archangel Michael.

Across all of creation's orders, kingdoms, and ranks, life in its essence remains one and the same. There is development from the lower to the higher. First, life creeps and crawls. Then it moves and progresses with a higher sense. Slowly it develops into an ever clearer consciousness, becomes spiritual in nature, and begins to reveal that it is related to God's life. And, finally, in Christ it appears in that higher, kingly form through which it is at once human and divine. Again, all of these transitions from lower to a higher only come about through an act of God. Animals did not come from plants, people did not come from animals, angels did not come from people, and Christ did not come from the created spiritual world. Every time again we are confronted with a mystery. There is a separate mystery in the creation of plants, a particular mystery in the creation of animals, a special order in the creation of angels and people. So too, there is a distinct mystery in the incarnation of the Word. But across this entire series of mysteries, God himself connects what is higher to what is lower. Animals cannot have life without there being plant life. In humanity there is a connection to animal life. People and angels are similarly connected, and Christ came only when he took on our human nature.

The dominion exercised by Christ, as the one who has in himself the highest and unshakable life, is thus not a bestowed dominion but one that organically and automatically extends over the entire creation. His kingdom cannot be shaken for the very reason that it was not formed and imposed externally, but is rooted in his life; and because of this highest life, it automatically exercises dominion over all life of a lower order. Christ is not given a scepter so that he may subject all other things to himself through the power of that scepter with a show of an external supremacy.

The metaphor used to describe him and his dominion remains that of the Head of the body. The dominion exercised by our head over our members is not one where the head gives external commands to the members to which they incline their wills in obedience. Rather, our mind's dominion over our senses and members happens automatically and internally. When the head wants to walk, the feet move automatically. When we want to grab something, our hands move automatically toward the object we want to grab. When we want to see something, our eyes turn automatically to the object we are looking for. In us, too, a dominion is at work that passes automatically from the brain in our head to our body's other members and nerves.

This is the metaphor that Scripture emphasizes in order to give us an understanding of the essence and manner of the operation of Christ's kingly dominion, which differs so widely from the dominion exercised by earthly kings. The kingdom of heaven is within you. By means of this very life that your King pours out into you and circulates throughout your entire being like the blood pumping through your arteries, he establishes, exercises, and maintains his dominion in you. However, with this you neither can nor may isolate and separate yourself from the rest of creation. You are a part of that creation; you share in the life of even creation's lower orders, and for that reason Christ's kingly dominion is not restricted and limited to your spiritual life. It penetrates all orders and levels of creation.

Here, too—and in fact, especially here—all that is lower is subjected to the higher. Christ had dominion over the plant and animal kingdoms. We never read that Christ was sick; the dominion that his life exercised over his body was too superior for that to happen. In his resurrection he showed how that power of his life over his body even broke through death. And it is only when you understand Christ's kingly dominion in its most complete sense, which you do automatically when you take your starting point in his life, that you can begin to understand the otherwise so mysterious words that power has been given to him "over all things in heaven and on earth" [see Eph 1:10].

It is worth noting in this context that in everything Christ did and said, §3 he seldom retreated to the abstract and spiritual; he seldom uttered tenets; and he uttered dogmas only by way of exception. In all that he did, said, and preached, Jesus was almost always active within the creaturely life he found round about him. We see our King occupied with creaturely life in the spirit world, with the normal activities of human life, but just as much with the life in the lower orders of creation, in the plant and animal worlds and even the material kingdom. Already from of old, a connection was made in Israel to the higher life of the tabernacle and temple in that produce from the field and animal sacrifices were dedicated to God in the holy place. Jesus in no way undid that connection. Instead, we see that even in the Sermon on the Mount, Jesus directs the crowds to the lilies of the field that neither toil nor spin but that God himself clothes with a glory far surpassing the glory of Solomon and his palace. Similarly, he points to the birds of the air that neither sow nor reap, and yet they are fed only by our Father who is in heaven [see Matt 6:26–29]. In reference to his break with Israel, Jesus similarly takes an image from the animal world: Just as a hen gathers her chicks under wings, so I, your King, wanted to gather you together, O Jerusalem, but you were unwilling [see Matt 23:37]. Jesus further permits John the Baptist to present him by using the image of the Lamb of God: Behold, the Lamb of God, who takes away the sin of the world [see John 1:29]. And in the vision of heaven in the Revelation given on Patmos, this unique image is taken over in terms of the heavenly spheres: John sees "a Lamb standing, as though it had been slain" [Rev 5:6].

The images for what is worthy of worship in the higher order are always taken from creation's lower order. Jesus presents himself as the Bread of Life. And when he is about to be taken from his disciples, when he is about to embark upon the road to Golgotha, and when fixed signs for the new covenant are to be instituted, Jesus once again reaches back to the plant world for both the bread and the wine and impresses the sacramental seal upon them.

We noted earlier that the same is true for his miracles. He performs miracles in the plant world when the bread is multiplied and the fig tree withers, and miracles in the animal world when the disciples are amazed by a miraculous catch of fish or when the small fish are multiplied for a crowd of 5,000. Jesus rarely ever acts in the abstract; he almost always occupies himself with what is concretely visible. The two lower orders of creation, namely, the plant and animal kingdoms, are not at all forgotten but are placed in the foreground and constantly present new material for the existence of higher powers and for the unveiling of holy mysteries.

That Jesus connected with the ordinary life around him is even more powerfully emphasized in his parables, which are almost always presented to us as *kingdom* parables. In these parables, too, we are directed to what yeast does in flour, to the amazing mustard seed, to the sowing of seed in the field, and to what comes from that seed as a result of the ground on which it falls. We are defined by the wheat and the weeds, and the gathering of the harvest [see Matt 13:24-30]. Catching fish is used as a metaphor [see Matt 4:19], and the same is true of what happens to the fish after the catch has been made when they are sorted [Matt 13:47-50]. In his parables, Jesus connects with ordinary human life—with what happens when a field is bought, with laborers hired to work in a vineyard, with a woman who loses a coin in her house, with a king who holds a wedding feast, with the maidens who await the royal procession with oil lamps.

The image that is emphasized more powerfully than all others, however, is that of the shepherd and his sheep. We are the sheep of his pasture, as was already sung in the Psalms [see Psa 100:3]. There are other sheep, which Jesus must add to his flock. There shall be one flock and one Shepherd [see John 10:16]. The prowling wolf will be kept at bay. And when Jesus foretells the last judgment he will render, he says that the Son of Man will be seated as King and will separate the sheep from the goats [see Matt 25:31–46].

Jesus himself said that he spoke in parables in order to cast a veil over the holy and spiritual [see Matt 13:13–16]. Taken on its own, however, his constant use of new images derived from the lower order of created life to describe the kingdom is indicative of the connection he makes with that lower life. Because of the similarities, all of these references to created things must contain a purpose and idea if they are to serve as images. What this purpose might be is something that we do not need to guess at. In Matthew 13:35, it is explicitly explained to us that Jesus spoke in parables to utter what had been hidden since the foundation of the world. What could this mean, except that all of nature's lower orders contained a prophecy of the highest order that was still to be revealed? What else could this mean except that one of God's thoughts has governed the entire work of creation; and that in creation's kingdoms, this single, holy, and highest thought of God was first expressed coarsely, then increasingly refined in creation's progression to a higher order, and in the end fully expressed in the highest order of creation? It should also always be remembered that those who know a higher order discover its foundations in the lower orders that preceded them, and that those who finally enter the highest order clearly see the connection that exists with all the lower orders of creation.

Understood in this way, the kingdom of heaven is the highest order to which created life can ascend. This is why it is said repeatedly that the

§ 4

kingdom is not far away and that we will enter into that kingdom; and this can only mean that we will come under the dominion that Christ our King exercises over that highest order. Just as humanity was called to be king on earth and to have dominion over nature's three lower kingdoms of matter, plants, and animals—indeed, just as humanity as such in a sense still exercises kingship over these three kingdoms of nature—so too, the order, or if you will, the kingdom of the angels, and the kingdom of the sanctified human race are now placed under Christ as King. And in that kingdom of the highest order, God's principle for all of creation came to realization. Christ is the Head of humans and angels; humanity is the head of the visible, created things on earth; animals reign over the plant kingdom; and plants reign over the mineral kingdom. All of them are subsumed under Jesus' kingship, and together they form a continuous line of dominion. Understood in this way, all the kingdoms of a lower order already were able to—and had to—contain within themselves the basic features of the higher and highest [orders] because God had placed them there.

So Jesus found in nature and in his surroundings all the images he needed to illustrate for us the nature and essence of his kingship. Jesus did not have to come up with these images; they were already there from the very foundation of the world. Jesus used them because he saw them there, and he pointed them out to us so that we too might see them.

Therefore, regardless of where we turn, we may never build a wall of separation between the kingdom of heaven and the lower orders of creation, as if all of that would no longer affect us once we enter the kingdom. Doing that would introduce a false spiritualism that finds no support anywhere in Scripture. It is not the case that only souls will be saved, or that at the very most humanity will be saved as a race. Our King's dominion must include all of creation, and for that reason all orders and kingdoms in creation must be saved from the oppression under which they now groan. "The whole creation has been groaning together in the pains of childbirth until now, waiting for the freedom of the glory of the children of God," knowing that "the whole creation will be set free from its bondage to corruption" [see Rom 8:21-22]. Jesus himself testifies that he will drink the wine anew with us in the kingdom of his Father [see Matt 26:29], and all the prophecies about the kingdom of glory point consistently to an influence of Christ's kingly power that will extend over all of creation. Israel's prophets already prophesied about a future where the desert would bloom like a rose, where predators would cease to be ferocious, and where a child would play over the hole of the cobra [for example, Isa 11:6–8; 35:1–2]. Things are no different when you turn from the prophetic to the apostolic Scriptures. They constantly point to a future in which the whole earth will be renewed and the glory of the Lord will radiate from a new heaven over a new earth.

It is never about the soul without it also being about the body. Christ's resurrection from the dead is so seminal to the entire gospel that we are told repeatedly that our mortal body will put on immortality and that our humbled body will also be made like Jesus' glorified body. This will not happen of itself, but by an act of our King—an act that is a consequence of that amazing power through which he can subject all things, even the material, to himself. The addition of the words kingdom *of heaven* may not mislead us for even a single moment to conclude from these words that death will separate us forever from the visible. The apostle Paul in particular draws a straight line from Christ's resurrection not only to our *spiritual* resurrection, but also to our *bodily* resurrection on the last day and to the glory that will follow. That same line he finally traces through to the entire creation that now groans in futility. When Revelation presents us with visions in which the final showdown in the mystery of salvation is depicted for us, it is as if we see before our very own eyes how Christ's kingly power extends to all the kingdoms of nature; it governs the seas and the earth and the heavens, and it sets them free from their counterfeit order so as to arrange them after the order of God's will.

Because Jesus' kingship is rooted in the very principle of life, and because all of life—stretching from the lower all the way to the higher [order]—is united in its starting point in the mystery of God's omnipotence, nothing that lives can or may be excluded from his kingly dominion. Furthermore, the all-encompassing character and the all-pervasive power of Jesus' kingship, both of them with respect to the entire creation, must be upheld tooth and nail against the one-sided spiritualism that is interested only in the fenced-off arena of the spiritual. Those who are unspiritual see only the trunk and the branches, the leaf and the blossom, but Jesus sees the root of the trunk hidden under the earth's surface; and it is to this root of all higher life that he constantly directs our attention with all of creation's kingdoms of a lower order. A tree that blossoms from its unsevered and undamaged root system—not a tree in the sense of a severed trunk—will one day, under his kingly dominion, be the image of the glorified creation.

A TEMPORARY SITUATION

For what will it profit a man if he gains the whole world and forfeits his soul? Or what shall a man give in return for his soul?

MATTHEW 16:26

§ 1   The kingdom of heaven is a kingdom because it is founded by a King and by his spiritual ordinance is monarchical in its design. It could not be any other way, because the kingdom is not only moral but above everything else is religious in nature, finding bliss and glory in the direct subjection of every creature to the ordinance of God. For that reason, God's dominion must be complete in that kingdom; God must govern it completely. Consequently, the Lord God must be King in it; and his all-encompassing, supreme rule over heaven and earth is expressed in this royal name insofar as that supreme rule extends to spiritual beings that are endowed with a consciousness and a will—that is, to angels and people.

This does not exclude but sooner presupposes his dominion over inanimate creation. In the dominion he exercises over matter and over the elemental forces of nature, however, the kingly character of God's supreme governance does not come to light. Kingship entails that there are conscious subjects over whom the king rules by force or because they are willing and do not want things to be any other way. In the kingdom of heaven, the latter alone applies. "Your people will be wholly glad and willing when you to your great battle summon them."[1] The father-child relationship is used to express the personal relationship between this King and the people over whom he reigns. And the King's rule reaches to the furthest ends of the conscious existence of his subjects. Once the kingdom of heaven has been fully realized in its holy ideal, the conscious life of those who have entered it is fully unfolded in its richest expressions. And it is God, as our King, who governs this complete unfolding along all its lines and in all its forms. Just as the sun is dominant in our solar system, so God is dominant throughout his entire spiritual kingdom. There is no void, no lack or shortcoming, nor even a shadow of anything unholy or unhappy. The kingdom exists in complete purity. And all of inanimate creation will then only have this one goal: namely, to bring to light the glory of that kingdom in everything that is external and visible.

That is not how things are at present. That will have to wait for the end of time, when night is no more—that is, when time will be swallowed up in eternity. Until then, the kingdom exists holy and as the ideal that shall come for now only in the heavens; for which reason it is referred to on earth as the *kingdom of heaven*. But in the meantime it began to be realized, albeit imperfectly, on earth as well. The current situation is one in which born-again sinners live as new people, even though the sin of their inner life has not yet been cut off for good; living as children of God, even though the bondage of corruption has not yet been entirely undone. Sin still clings to these new people, and they still live in the state of misery. Although God has become their King, he is not yet everything in them.

A temporary situation prevails, such that Christ's kingship functions vicariously in the place of God's direct kingship. Because he is not only the Son of God and God himself, but also the Son of Man, Christ can have direct communion with his elect even though sin still clings to them; he can reign over us even though we are still in the state of misery instead of glory. He took our sin upon himself and entered our misery. This is why Jesus repeatedly speaks of "my kingdom" [see Luke 22:30; John 18:36], because he is the one who entered the kingdom of heaven—the kingdom of God— as the vicarious King. He is Mediator and King. And it is only when all sin has been destroyed and the last enemy overcome, when all misery has

---

1. Psalm 110, stanza 3, from *Het Boek der Psalmen, nevens de gezangen, bij de Hervormde Kerk van Nederland in gebruik* (Amsterdam: J. Brandt en Zoon, en P. Proost, 1851), 304; see also *Book of Praise: Anglo-Genevan Psalter* (Winnipeg: Premier, 2014), 275.

been turned to glory, that his regency will end, that God himself will be all and in all, and that the kingdom will be handed over to God the Father. Christ will remain the Head of the body; that is something he will remain forever. But the supreme kingship of the Triune God will then be direct.

The basic difference between these two is that Christ's vicarious kingship aims to prepare and bring about the situation necessary for God's direct kingship to come. At the present time, there is still impurity within and enemies without. Sin and misery have not yet been destroyed. The removal of these things does not occur all at once, but a long process must first run its course. Accordingly, in the vision on Patmos, the angel cried out: "The harvest of the earth must first fully ripen" (Rev 14:15). Those who will fall away must first be ripe for destruction, while those who will enter must first be ripe for glory. In that situation, the kingship can be exercised only by him who, being God, is at the same time the Son of Man, and in this way have direct contact with our human existence. That is why Jesus himself says in Matthew 25:31–40 that when the spiritual process of ripening has been completed, the Son of Man—not the Son of God!—will sit as King on his glorious throne and will pronounce the judgment and complete the process of sorting (Matt 25:34).

§ 2   Related to this is that our King is at the same time our greatest Prophet and our only High Priest. In a kingdom that is not purely spiritual, authority and dominion are increasingly being separated from the spiritual factors of the nation's life. In the order of Melchizedek, kingship and priesthood were still united because that order had arisen from the father's rule over his family. In families, fathers have not only the authority to rule, but also the spiritual responsibility to lead their families spiritually. In fatherhood, authority and spiritual leadership are united. For that reason, when kingship first arose, the priest also had to function as the king; and Scripture depicts this original position for us in the order of Melchizedek. Psalm 110 therefore prophesies about the Messiah: "The Lord has sworn and will not change his mind, 'You are a priest forever after the order of Melchizedek'" [Psa 110:4]. These words come only after the preceding verses have declared the Messiah's kingship: "Sit at my right hand, until I make your enemies your footstool" [Psa 110:1].

Caesaropapism, which continues to exist most powerfully in Russia, but partially in a number of Lutheran countries as well, still attempts to unite kingship and priesthood since the king is declared at the same time to be the supreme bishop, the *summus episcopus*.[2] Such caesaropapism, however, is nothing but the assumption of authority against Christ's church. In this system, kingly power and episcopal majesty are joined in a bond that is entirely external, and there is no internal unity at all. Even if the king himself is a thoroughgoing unbeliever, he remains the supreme bishop. If matters are conducted as they should be, however, royal authority and spiritual majesty are kept further apart. The one comes gradually to be separated from the other.

So too in Israel, priests functioned independently of the kingship, while prophets functioned between kings and priests. The task of the prophets was to cause the lofty ideal to shine in all its brilliance under the guidance of the Spirit, while the priests were to make atonement for the sins of the people by offering sacrifices. The one, full office is therefore split into two. On the one side there is the kingship intended to exercise authority and to rule the people, and on the other side there are the two spiritual offices of prophet and priest intended to assume spiritual leadership over the people. The king was there for outward life, while the prophet and priest were for inner life.

In the kingdom of heaven, of course, this separation was not allowed to continue. The separation had come from the division in our life—from the separation between the higher and lower life of the people, from the personal lack of holiness on the part of so many of the kings throughout the earth. As a result, the strength through which kingship could exist was that of external violence. The unwilling were not convinced and converted spiritually, but were compelled by the strong arm [of force] to acknowledge the authority of the king and submit to it. But in the kingdom of Christ, all of this fell away. His rule is spiritual. He does not coerce externally, but regenerates and convinces internally. He lays claim to the inner life. "My kingdom is not coming in ways that can be observed. It is within you" [see Luke 17:20–21]. Christ exercises dominion over God's children with spiritual factors. He lays a claim on their soul, addresses them in their spiritual life, and transforms them in such a way that they turn to him in their entire inner existence and are incorporated into his mystical body.

As a result, there was no room for an independent prophet or priest alongside the King. This King could not be King unless he was

---

2. For Kuyper's critique of caesaropapism, see *OP* §32, pp. 35–36.

automatically a Prophet for our conscious life, and a Priest for our ethical life. It is only because he is our Prophet and Priest that he can be our King. In him these three offices fuse together into one, all-encompassing office. In him the three lines of Israel's threefold office come together in a higher unity. He gives in full measure what the prophets in Israel gave only in a preparatory way: namely, the full revelation of truth about heaven and the situation here on earth, and about the divine ideal toward which everything is moving and for which everything is being ripened. Similarly, in a real and full way he gives what Israel's priests could only depict figuratively: namely, the sinner's reconciliation with a holy God. He does not offer a lamb, but he is himself the Lamb that takes away the sin of the world. And once he as Priest has made atonement for us and as Prophet has given us clear insight into what is and was and shall be, only then will the spiritual and royal power, through which he is able to exercise dominion over the spirits with complete authority, be effective and achieve its goal. Here we see a purely spiritual power that will rule unconstrained. Yet in order to be able to rule, it does not resort to driving back the spiritual agitation and overwhelming the spirits by means of the sword; but it conquers the subjects internally, seizes their very essence and never lets go of them again, and completes their spiritual edification in such a way that they become living stones for the temple in which God will dwell.

This is why, in Christ, King and Prophet had to be one. In the vision on Patmos we see the very opposite with the power of the Antichrist. First comes the beast from the sea, in which the kingly power of the Antichrist presents itself. But it is followed by another beast from the earth, and the bestial human figure that appears therein is not a king but a prophet. It is only a prophet, and it prepares itself to lead the people spiritually so that they may worship the image of the kingly power of the Antichrist, receive his mark, and exclude all those without that mark from its trade and activity, that is, from its social community.

§ 3   Although the kingdom brought by Christ is called a kingdom because it is monarchical-spiritual in nature and because it is ruled by a King, it nevertheless assumes a most particular form. It was of one sort as it came into existence by God's design, but in the course of its historical development it assumes a most particular form. It is a kingdom with boundaries that determine what does and does not belong to it. Like other kingdoms, it too has its own territory, and beyond that territory is an area that falls under an entirely different dispensation. In order to enter this kingdom, one must cross the boundary delineating what belongs to it from what belongs to the area beyond it. People can draw near to it, and even be not far from it, while failing to take the last step to cross the boundary and remaining on the outside.

This is entirely in line with the words spoken to the scribe: "You are not far from the kingdom of God" [Mark 12:34]; although this man did not take the final step, so that he failed to enter and instead remained in the area close to, but still beyond, the border.

With this, any conception that sees the kingdom as something vague is of course excluded. There is no nebulous spiritual area that passes imperceptibly into another area, and to which one can just attribute whatever has a shadow of the true, the good, and the beautiful. It is a kingdom that itself makes clear where it is and is not, and this means that it always demands a transition. It demands a transference from the kingdom of Satan into the kingdom of the Son of Love. It requires being drawn from the power of darkness to the kingdom in which the wonderful light shines—a transition from death to life.

Especially that final expression of Scripture draws a very clear line and understands the contrast between what is inside and outside the kingdom in a most concrete sense. This constitutes the reason why John the Baptist, as well as Jesus himself at the beginning of his ministry, placed such a heavy emphasis on that transition, on being transferred and transported from the unholy into the kingdom of Christ. The kingdom of Christ initially did not yet exist, not even in Israel. But then it came and was at hand. All who feared God were then called to pass over and enter that kingdom through repentance. [They were called] to seal this transference and repentance symbolically by submitting to [John's] baptism in the Jordan, and later by following Christ's baptism with fire. Talk of a gradual transition was out of the question. What had been did not flow imperceptibly into what would come. There was a break, there was a departure from the place where they once stood in order to pass over into the new place awaiting them, in order to enter the kingdom of heaven.

If you think of this kingdom of heaven according to God's design—in its ideal conception and as it will one day be at the end of the age—you will see before you a kingdom of total beatitude, holiness, and glory.

Two things will have been accomplished. The first accomplishment will be the exclusion and banishment of everything that arose from the demonic world, from human sin, and from the misery following sin—

in both the spirit world and the human world—which had nestled in a place within creation over against God and set itself up in hostility against him. And in the second place, there will be no return to the pre-fall situation in paradise; human development had only just begun in paradise and had not yet reached its full consummation. When sin and misery are banished, it will not be the life of paradise that returns, but instead the created world will appear as it has developed perfectly and completely. In paradise, the human race could still fall; but in the situation of the kingdom of God in its consummation, this possibility will be excluded. The holy angels and the people who are saved will be elevated above the danger of falling into sin; and everything that would have developed richly from humanity if it had not fallen will, after the last day, not exist in the kingdom of heaven as potentiality but will attain complete and total realization. The power and influence of Satan over our human race will be undone, and humanity will no longer be abandoned to its own free choice. Instead, everything that has spiritual life will then live in its spiritual existence under the dominion of Christ the King.

A relapse is unimaginable. No one can tear from Christ's hand what has been given to him by the Father. The high ideal will then be realized. All fruit will be ripened. God's perfection will be reflected in a perfected creation. "God saw that it was good," originally pronounced at creation, will then apply also to what has come from creation. There is no longer anything that stands in the way. The "holy, holy, holy!" sung in the song of praise will then arise out of the pure holiness of the spirits. And God will be all and in all.

But at the present time this is not how things are. In fact, even in the heavens the manifestation of perfect glory still awaits. The battle still continues in the spirit world as well. Michael and his angels are still battling the dragon and his followers. Similarly, on earth the kingdom begins also by being enclosed within very restricted borders. There is a small flock, a circle of a few faithful people. In fact, that battle continues even within that circle, despite how small it is. But for this King, a nation is slowly being formed, a peculiar people, a people given to him; but that people stands like a small multitude over against the mighty nations of the earth. And although this small multitude grew after Jesus ascended, and although Jesus at present has subjects among all peoples and nations—even now, that group among the children of men, who made the decisive transition and who entered the kingdom of heaven, cannot compare in either number or power to the great multitude outside the kingdom. Moreover, over the course of its history, the glory of the kingdom was manifested and unveiled only in part. On the surface the world hates God's child because it could not satisfy his high demand, but the outward manifestation of glory is still being restrained. Misery continues, and the misery of those who entered the kingdom has in fact increased for the very reason that they entered it. And not only does the glory still linger, but the effect of the kingdom's holy character can for now also reach only a small beginning of its lofty radiance. As our Catechism says, even the best and most pious reach only a small beginning of full obedience on earth, and only in their death do they finally die to sin.[3]

The battle—which always precedes the complete revelation of the kingdom of heaven in the spirit world—as a struggle between the evil and the holy spirits, therefore finds its antitype on earth in a twofold struggle. The first struggle is between those who fear God and those who oppose him. But the second struggle occurs among King Jesus' own subjects. Sin has an effect. The demonic world still attempts to seduce our King's subjects to unfaithfulness. And a relapse of his subjects is forestalled only because of the overwhelming power of the spiritual dominion proceeding from Christ. It is not they themselves who persevere; it is their King who extends his protective hand over them. All the same, the kingdom manifests itself in them in a rather flawed form. Because those who have been incorporated into Jesus are born of God, they can no longer commit Adam's sin and fall away; but the radiance of glory is still dampened because of sin.

But even though this means that our King's reign still remains restricted, it is not limited in its extent to the new life of those who have been born again. By working spiritually on those who are his, Christ works spiritually upon the entire conscious life of the human race through them. His people are not taken out of the world, but are preserved in the world. They therefore remain in contact and communion with the world, and they exercise influence on the development of humanity's conscious life. The dominion of our King is not limited by the borders of his kingdom, but is at work beyond those borders as well. When pagan countries like Japan and China unite to end their former cruelties and barbarities

---

3. The sentence is a paraphrastic conflation of Heidelberg Catechism, Lord's Day 44, A 114, and Lord's Day 16, A 42.

in war on land and sea, in order to make room for higher human ideals even in battle, this is the fruit of Christ's dominion. He was the one who caused this deeper understanding to enter his people; through his people it passed into the general human consciousness; and through the power of human society this perspective triumphed well beyond the actual borders of the kingdom.

This holds true for every terrain. Had Christ not brought his kingdom to this earth, human development would never have become what it is now. From him, the stimulus for higher development went forth upon his people, and from his people upon human society in general, so that it is not humanity itself but Christ who through the power of his Spirit brought us to this more elevated position. In realms like that of ancient Egypt or China, whose process of development passed through a struggle lasting many centuries, we see what happens to that development when it is left up to human beings. Conversely, in the way human life has developed until now in Christian Europe and America, we see how much that development owes to Christ's work for having attained this high level. Even if that development is accompanied by many lamentable things, and even if it may not be denied that a frightening level of development was attained also in unholy things, one cannot dispute the reality that more lofty sentiments also gained ground. [It cannot be denied] that the power of the human spirit (now understood positively) has expanded in an encouraging way under the banner of the cross, although that cross was in fact denied.

These developments did not happen apart from Christ. It is through the power and influence that proceeded from him and his people that this result was achieved. Just as the Netherlands has colonies outside of the kingdom, so Christ's kingdom has the entire world as its colony, while he works on that world in a way that brings blessing, soothes, and energizes. Already among the nations of the earth, the influence of a powerful and energetic nation is not restricted to its borders but extends well beyond them. Think only of the influence upon all nations exercised by the French spirit, or that of England and Germany. In the same way, the dominion of the spirit of our King is not limited to his kingdom in a narrower sense, but presses over those borders and extends over our entire human life.

THE EXISTING ORDER MAINTAINED

Let every person be subject to the governing authorities. For there is no authority except from God, and those that exist have been instituted by God.

ROMANS 13:1

Must Christ's kingly dominion be understood so comprehensively that we consider all authority on earth to derive from him after the time of his ascension? And more specifically, do governments owe their authority to Christ after Jesus' ascension? Is it through Christ that not only the Christian emperor of Germany rules, but also the pagan emperor of Japan? This question was of quintessential importance particularly in bygone centuries because the "Vicar of Christ" claimed to have authority over thrones and crowns. But even though the theory of the papacy's supreme authority has passed into near oblivion, this question remains important; and we have to determine whether authority on earth has a sphere of its own, or whether all worldly authority among people is now to be considered as proceeding from our Mediator.

§ 1

Our discussion at this point is not about the authority of the church. No one denies that all church authority comes to us from Christ. Our question concerns worldly authority alone, that is, the authority exercised by one person over another, not only among Christians but also among pagans and Muslims. Authority is exercised by fathers and mothers over their children, by husbands over their wives, by ruling sovereigns over their public servants and appointees, by judges in their courts, by generals over their armies, by admirals over their fleets, by teachers over their students, by employers over their employees, by masters or mistresses over their servants, by those with genius and talent in the spheres in which they excel. Wherever a number of people live in groups, there is one who leads while the others follow. Without such dominion exercised by an appointed or inherent authority, no ordered society is possible nor will there be development and advance.

Superior power exists in the plant and animal kingdoms as well, but there it is grounded in violence alone. For that reason, it is only among people that a higher society developed where authority took the place of violence, and where authority may well use a show of force if necessary while its foundation nevertheless remains moral. That king is lost who knows no other way to maintain his position except through the power of the sword. The nerve of a king's superior power resides not in his soldiers or police force, but in the conscience of his subjects. As long as only a number of his subjects rise up in rebellion against him, he can counter them with violence—but even then, he has to presume that the greatest majority remain faithful to him and will continue to honor his authority. Even the troops who must suppress a rebellion represent no support for his authority unless he can count on them to remain faithful to him. The use of violence is incidental; and a sovereign can find the basis for his dominion only in his subjects' fidelity, which in turn arises in their conscience from the conviction that they are to honor and obey their king because they must honor and obey God's will.

The power that rests on this foundation has the character of authority, and this authority is like the cement of our entire human society. Should one say (keeping the church outside of the discussion) that this authority among people is laid upon those who are invested with it by the Triune God, or does it come from Christ as the King over the kingdom of God? And if this authority in former times proceeded from the Triune God, must we confess that after Jesus' ascension it no longer proceeds from the Triune God but from the exalted Messiah, seated at the right hand of the Father?

The answer is that both before and after Jesus' ascension, all worldly authority among people proceeds from the Triune God rather than from Christ. Kings rule by the grace of God, not by the grace of Christ. The dominion exercised by the kings of the earth is, just like Christ's spiritual dominion, allotted to them by the Triune God. Jesus is the King in his kingdom, and they are king in the kingdom to which they have been appointed. In both cases this is by virtue of the ordinance, appointment, and regulation of the Triune God. Christ's dominion far surpasses the dominion of the kings. Their kingdom cannot in any way be compared with Christ's kingship in terms of scope, time, or inner strength; all the same, their kingdom stands alongside rather than below it. Christ is not the King of kings and Lord of lords because he is the one who appoints kings and lords, but because among all kings and lords he is the highest, most excellent, and most eminent in every respect, and because he will one day sit in spiritual judgment on them and be their Judge. But the source, the origin of their authority is not to be found in Christ. That origin, that source lies in the Triune God, in the Father, the Son, and the Holy Spirit—in the Son, therefore, insofar as he is one in essence with the Father and the Holy Spirit, but not in the Son of Man, not in the Mediator, not in the King of God's kingdom as such.

We feel this most poignantly when we begin by considering parental authority, which stands on a continuum with the authority exercised by governments. In terms of its origin, parental authority lies entirely outside the work of salvation. It arises through procreation as far as the parents are concerned, and through birth as far as the children are concerned. Both procreation and birth were part of the original creation ordinance. As such, it would have been entirely possible for God to have created all people directly, just as he did with Adam. And why not? After all, this is how things are in the angel world. Angels do not marry. Jesus himself said that in heaven no one, not even those saved, would be given in marriage [see Matt 22:30]. The reproduction of one creature from another is something found on this earth alone. We see it in the plant kingdom, characterized by sowing seeds. We likewise see it in the animal world, where one animal is born of another or emerges from an egg.

§ 2

And this is the way God ordained things to be for the human race at creation. After Adam had been created, Eve did indeed come from a distinct creative act. But after Adam and Eve, every person has a father and a mother. A father and mother's authority over the child born to them is derived from the fact of this child's birth.

In the case of animals, the birth relationship does not lead to authority. As soon as a young animal ceases to be dependent, it goes its own way, looks for its own food, and soon it no longer even recognizes its own mother. And for an animal to recognize its father even for a short time is highly exceptional.

For human beings, things start in the same way, but they soon take on an entirely different form. At first a child is not even aware of his or her dependence. Newborn animals are initially at a much higher state of development than newborn children are. Babies know and perceive nothing. They cannot walk and cannot find their mother. They are carried, they pass through the first stage of life without any consciousness of what is happening, and they are totally helpless. Furthermore, young children are not only much less developed than young animals are, but when they do begin to develop and grow, this happens at a much slower pace. By the time they have reached the age of one, young animals often already find their own way around, while children of that age are still dependent on a mother's care for everything. It takes at least seven years, and often as many as ten, before children begin to achieve a certain level of independence; and the greatest majority by far cannot be independent and supply their own needs until they have been under care for a period of some fifteen or sixteen years. What is more, young animals need only to develop physically and for the rest are driven by instinct; whereas young children need, in addition to physical development, spiritual development as well. This not only produces a second need and dependence, but also creates an entirely different bond between children and their parents. Some animals no longer recognize their mother within a matter of months. By contrast, in the case of children a much tighter bond comes to be woven between their heart and that of their parents during the course of the years. Parental authority, as well as the children's recognition of that same authority, is founded on the child's persistent state of dependence and the spiritual bond that unites the hearts of parents and their children.

With what we have just written, we do not mean to claim that these things happen in our children outside of sin and grace and that they entirely bypass the work of salvation. On the contrary, by the very nature of the case, sin in both parents and children constantly undermines this authority. The sins of fathers and mothers very often weaken their care for and authority over the child, while conversely, the sin in children's hearts diminishes their obedience and incites them to disobedience or even rebellion. Conversely, it is also true that grace counters the corrupting effects of sin in both parents and children, and it places parental authority on a much firmer foundation. Baptism also functions as a support for that authority. But even if we must acknowledge that sin and grace also have an effect on this authority, grace is not its foundation. This is powerfully evident in the paternal authority that is at a much higher level in China, for example, than in Christian Europe. Even when he is forty or fifty years of age, no son in China will ever sit down in his father's presence unless his father has invited him to do so. In China, respect for one's father, and to a certain degree for one's mother as well, is the very nerve of all moral development. And even if there may be other reasons to wrangle about the state of this relationship in China today, in any case it proves that paternal authority can flourish and endure in a nation whose national life is estranged from every influence of special grace.

Since these two ordinances are grounded in creation and not in the work of grace—that is, the ordinance that no human being is created separately but all are born of parents, and the ordinance of the utter helplessness of newborn child, followed by their rather slow development— it necessarily follows that the parental authority arising from both of these ordinances derives from him who created the earth and everything in it, and not from the Mediator. When that authority is threatened to be disrupted, it may be restored by the Mediator and sanctified in practice; but as such this authority forms an independent sphere that, rooted in the natural order, exists independently of saving faith, has continued to exist even in non-Christianized countries and regions, and at times has even survived more strongly in pagan countries than in Christian countries. To our knowledge, no one has ever claimed that parental authority derives from Christ and flows from his kingly administration. If one thinks back to the centuries preceding Christ's coming and considers life in that world where Christian baptism had not yet been received, it is parental authority in particular that forms the starting point for all of human society. Down through the centuries and in every place, human society has developed out of family life; this family life consistently found its principal connective bond in the authority that both parents, or the father, or the mother, exercise over their children. Since parental authority is not derived from Christ but from the creation ordinance, it follows immediately from this fact that the further structuring of social and political life in the nations cannot flow from Christ. It must be explained on the basis of the ordination and arrangement of God's providence.

§ 3

Patriarchal authority arose automatically from the family and from the authority exercised by parents, and that patriarchal bond imperceptibly changed into a tribal bond. In these patriarchal circles and tribes, a need was felt not only for a certain amount of order and regulation, but also for some kind of unity that would supply a stronger defense against third parties. Among the many forms of authority that manifested themselves, there was also the authority of a single head—yet that authority had nothing to do with Christ's coming down to the earth. It existed already before he came, and after his coming it remained what it had been before his coming. What is more, it persisted even among the tribes that remained outside the sphere of baptism. Since the bond uniting peoples and nations gradually arose from this tribal bond long before Christ was born in Bethlehem, and since the formation of these nations of old occurred without any connection to Christ, it is difficult to see why what applies to a father's authority over his children would not be just as true for the authority that a government exercises over an entire nation. We do admit that the authority of governments was instituted because of sin. Had there been no sin, the authority arising directly from the family would have sufficed, no violence would have been committed, no violence would have had to be combated, and the greater part of what we call politics would not have arisen. Nations would not have been divided, as when speech was confused at Babel. Civil authority is therefore a corrective intended to counter the disruptive effects of sin. However, civil authority still did not arise by virtue of the special work of salvation; it flowed from common grace.

Grace has a twofold character.[1] It is saving with a view to eternal life, but it also restores temporarily with a view to life here on earth. Insofar as grace is saving, it saves only the elect; but its temporal restoration extends to include the entire human race. For that reason, the government's activity must not be explained in terms of saving grace but in terms of common grace—insofar as even civic life and the related authority of governments arose among all nations, both before and after Christ appeared on earth, and even remained where Christ's name was never mentioned at all. The corrective [to sin supplied] by civil authority was directed to human society as it existed by virtue of the creation ordinance. The form that this civil authority had to assume was indicated by flaw that sin introduced into the life that arose owing to that ordinance. The ordinance defined it. Sin influenced it. The creational ordinance for human society

---

1.   See here especially *CG* 1.30, "Forms of Grace."

and the disruption inflicted by sin, taken together, designated the basic lines along which the state ought to be organized, so that by the very nature of the case the organization of the state occurred entirely outside of the work of salvation.

If you imagine for a moment that salvation had never come in Christ, the state would still have appeared, a government would still have arisen, and this government would still have exercised its authority. Anything that would nonetheless exist even if Christ had never come cannot be explained from Christ, but must find the origin and source of its existence in a divine ordinance that was instituted by the Creator of our human race for the entire human race.

We do not mean to deny in the least that Christ has an influence on the state as it now exists, or that those who confess Christ are inspired through Christ also in their activities related to political administration. (This is something to which we will give extensive attention in the chapters forming the third part of the present work.) However, this is like a graft on a new trunk, while the trunk on which that graft is made has its own origin and can never be explained from that scion.

It is also remarkable that the apostles, whose constant concern was to elevate Christ's kingly authority as high as possible, never point to Christ when they discuss authority in the order of this world but always draw a connection to God. Especially significant is what the apostle Paul writes to the church at Rome in regard to this matter. He writes: "Let every person be subject to the governing authorities. For there is no authority except from God, and those that exist have been instituted by God. Therefore whoever resists the authorities resists what God has appointed, and those who resist will incur judgment" [Rom 13:1–2]. In this passage, the name *God* is thus emphasized as many as three times; and later on, the government is called the servant of God another three times, without Christ's name ever appearing in this context at all. In his testimony before Pilate, Jesus himself declared that the governor would not have had power over him unless it had been given to him from above [see John 19:11]. Note carefully that Jesus does not say, "unless power had been given to you from me," but "unless it had been given you from above." Jesus continually subjected himself to the authority that God had instituted.

Israel's greatest sin, which Jesus' disciples harbored for some time as well, was to think of the Messiah as a worldly power who would raise Israel to exercise dominion over the nations, and to think of Israel's King as some kind of emperor who would rule over all sovereigns. Jesus never claimed that the worldly power of the Davidic kingship had been transferred to him. He never reached for control over Israel, but instead he himself constantly recognized the de facto ruling sovereignty and demanded of his disciples that they recognize that sovereignty as well. His descent from the flesh of David was thus in no way intended as a means to inherit the worldly authority that David once exercised. David's kingship is worldly and its meaning is no more than national-symbolic. Israel was the image and prototype of the kingdom of God; and more specifically, David only foreshadowed what Christ would be in the spiritual kingdom.

This is why Jesus and his apostles allowed the existing order to continue unimpaired and undisturbed. They lived and acted within that existing order. They made no attempt to introduce another state of affairs in its place; and concerning the powers that be, the apostle says that they are from God. That was how things were, and that is how things still are at the present time.

The arrangement for our human life was given in creation itself, for both our body and our spirit, for the individual person as well as for human society. Even at the present time, human life perpetuates itself in following the ordinance of this arrangement. And all the basic lines of this original arrangement were fixed before the work of salvation, and therefore apart from it. For this reason, they may not be explained from and derived from Christ, but out of and from the wisdom and omnipotence of the Triune God, the Creator of all creatures.

The fundamental design of creation did not adjust to the work of salvation, but the work of salvation molded itself according to that design. God the Lord ordained them both: first, the work of creation according to the ordinance instituted by him, and after that the work of salvation—the latter in part through common grace, and in part through special grace. In this second work, the Lord God directed himself according to the principles of the first work. Thus Christ was appointed Head of the church and King of God's kingdom through a decree of God, and it is through just as holy a decree of God that one person's authority over another has been established in the worldly regiment—ranging from the authority exercised by parents over their children to that which a government has over its nation. Both Christ, as the King of the kingdom of God, as well as the sovereigns of the kingdoms of the earth, reign by the grace of God.

THE SALVATION OF THE WORLD

But if anyone has the world's goods and sees his brother in need, yet closes his heart against him, how does God's love abide in him?

1 JOHN 3:17

Christ's kingship was placed in the foreground immediately in the announcement that the angel Gabriel made to Mary. In his song of praise, Zechariah said about John the Baptist: "And you, child, will be called the prophet of the Most High" [Luke 1:76], but about Jesus the angel testified even before he had been born: "He will be great and will be called the Son of the Most High. And the Lord God will give to him the throne of his father David, and he will reign over the house of Jacob forever, and of his kingdom there will be no end" [Luke 1:32]. Jesus would also be Prophet, but John went ahead of Jesus as the prophet while Jesus came as King. Jesus would also be Priest, but that priesthood initially remains in the background while his kingly majesty and calling—because they govern his entire life and encompass all other things—are announced to Mary by the angel to the exclusion of every other office. Similarly, the wise men from the East went to Jerusalem with the message that a great King had been born in Israel, and that they had seen his star in the eastern skies. Then John the Baptist came to introduce the coming of the kingdom of heaven, and to prepare the multitudes for the coming of the King who

§ 1

would hold the scepter in that kingdom. Jesus was condemned by the Sanhedrin and sentenced by Pilate on account of his kingship. It was the title of King that was nailed above the cross as a mocking gesture. It was as King that he ascended into heaven and is now seated at the right hand of the Father. And when the end of all things is depicted in a series of visions in the Revelation on Patmos, it is time and time again Jesus who, as King of kings and Lord of lords, comes riding on the white horse of victory, drives his enemies back, and brings triumph to God's cause.

He is thus first of all King—King from beginning to end. His kingship is emphasized time and again, and it is from this kingship first of all that his honor as the Savior flows. It is not the case that he is first nothing more than a savior and a physician who then ascends to kingly power later on; but it is by virtue of his kingship that he can be the Savior who brings us salvation. It is not the Savior who becomes King, but the King becomes Savior and can be our Savior only by virtue of the fact that he is King. Christ is the Savior. He is the Savior of the body, but also the Savior of the world. He "did not come to judge the world but to save the world" [John 12:47]. The judgment will not fail to come, but it has to wait until the end has come. If Jesus had appeared immediately as Judge, there would have been no room for his work of salvation.

The distinction between his first and second coming is not only one of time; it concerns more their respective nature and character. His first coming was not to judge, but to save. His second coming will not be to save, but to judge. The distinct and opposite goal determined the specific form in which Jesus first appeared in Bethlehem, and it will likewise determine the specific form in which he will come to judge. He first came as Savior; later he will come as Judge; but in both cases he is the King who fulfills his calling and completes his task, and who brings about, whether as Savior or as Judge, the salvation of the world. Salvation is brought about the first time by healing and restoring what is sick, the other time by winnowing out what proved to be incurable and destroying it.

Jesus does not accomplish this work of salvation mechanically; he is not like a physician who prescribes a medicine and then goes away, and [he is] even less like a goldsmith who restores a precious stone that has suffered damage and then returns it to its owner. Rather, this work of salvation is brought about organically. This means that Jesus himself enters the world that he will save. He does not descend to the world and touch its surface with the soles of his feet alone, only to ascend to heaven once more.

Jesus enters the very life of that world—he moves among that world and among the children of men; not as some alien figure from heaven, nor as an angel or messenger from above, but as a human being he lives and acts among human beings. He does not come as a newly created person who presents himself to our historic Adamic race as a distinct human being who will be the founder and forefather of a new human race. No, he partook of the flesh and blood of children [see Heb 2:14], and the blood of the fallen Adamic race coursed through his veins. In order to save the world, he allowed himself to be included in the world in such a way that he himself now belonged to the world, shared in its life, and could exercise his power on it from within. This very thing was indicative of his kingship.

Our queen is the queen of the Netherlands, but not the queen of Java or Sumatra.[1] Java and Sumatra are colonies subjected to her crown. We, however, are her nation. The history of our ancestors is closely interwoven with the history of her ancestors. We share a communal life with our queen. She is our queen and we are her people.

With Christ, things are this way as well. The world was not transferred to Jesus as a colony and subjected to his authority as a foreigner. He came to us, entered our life, and became one of us. He is thus our King and we are his people, and it is as our King in that more narrow and organic sense that he will save the world. The life that he has in common with us, we have in common with him. And from this one life that we have in common proceeds the power that expels poison, that heals the sick, and that will separate us from what cannot be healed, so that one day—when no blemish or wrinkle will disfigure the world and nothing unclean or unholy will be found in it—we will celebrate our redemption and that of the world, world without end. That is when the work of salvation will be completed and the redemption of the world accomplished.

It is not the case that this world must pass away so that another may be set up in its place. This world must remain. It must not be destroyed, but saved. It must be renewed and recreated, but in its essence and order it remains the very same world to which we now belong and in which we live—the world of all the preceding generations, the world that God once saw and declared to be good. God does not forsake the work of his hands [see Psa 138:8]. God does not allow his work to be frustrated. It may seem

---

1. At the time Kuyper wrote these words, the reigning monarch of the Netherlands was Queen Wilhelmina, who reigned from 23 November 1890–4 September 1948.

like everything has been lost, but this false impression will be revealed for what it is. Everything that Satan and sin have wrought upon the world in order to bring it to corruption will pass away one day, but the world will continue as world. What will pass away is the "present form of this world" [1 Cor 7:31], but not the world in its essence. That essence will remain as the "new earth under the new heavens" [see Rev 21:1], and God will forever be the glory of his creational work.

§ 2   In order to bring about that salvation of the world, Jesus took hold of that world by taking hold of humanity, which is the crown of creation here on earth. In this world, people are the creatures that govern and have dominion over all things. There is inanimate nature. In the midst of this nature that lacks a soul, life manifests itself in the created plants and in animals that do have a soul. But creation is still not complete. Creation's edifice still had no façade or cornice, and it was not completed until man appeared in paradise to accept from God's hand the scepter over the entire creation. In this way all the parts of the creation of this world are integrated. Inanimate nature serves the things created with a soul; the plant world feeds the animal kingdom; the animal kingdom, together with the plant kingdom, is subjected to humanity—only when these four orders are taken together can we speak of the life of the world; and it is this life of the world that must be saved.[2]

In light of the above, we see why, when he appeared on this earth, Jesus took hold of it in terms of humanity. He entered our human race, becoming one of us, and within our human race took Adam's place. While Adam was, by the very nature of the case, appointed king of humanity in paradise, Jesus becomes the Head of humanity, the King of our race, in his place.

People are not all alike. One person differs from another. Some among us are greater, others less so. Those who are greater have dominion over those who are lesser, and this dominion that arises as a matter of course binds us together as one. The effect that one person can have upon another is not restricted to our time on earth. Powerful spirits continue to have an effect even after they have departed from us. This influence emanating from those more powerful spirits unites the generations and forms peoples and nations. And if, among these powerful persons, there is one

---

2. For Kuyper's elaboration of the fourfold order of creation (inorganic, vegetative, animal, human), see *PR* 1.III.14.1.

who surpasses each and every other one in terms of power and spirit so as to exercise dominion over them all through their spirit, both now and in the following generations, then that all-surpassing spirit is the King of all, the King of the spirits, the King of our race, the King of humanity in this world—not only in name and title, but also in truth and in fact, because he has kingly power over all and subjects everyone's spirit to his majesty.

Adam originally occupied this place, and he could have maintained it had he not fallen away. When he fell, everything lay in shattered ruins, precisely because at that point we had become a kingdom without a king. This lasted until Jesus came to this world and entered our human race. For from that hour, our humanity, our world once more had a King, its own King—the Spirit that surpassed all other spirits in power and therefore naturally had dominion. The world did not perceive this, and in kingly residences this went unnoticed. Israel itself failed to understand this, and the disciples also hardly understood its significance. Nevertheless, this was how things really were.

From the moment that Jesus was conceived in the womb of the virgin Mary and began his being as a child to be born of a woman, he belonged to the human race and was part of our family. That said, his spirit surpassed the human race in strength—not simply in part but the whole. And this was what made him our King. He did not become our King upon his ascension, but he was already our King from the very beginning because the strength and power of his spirit and truth instantly surpassed all others in its potential. It was only after his ascension that this kingship could be outwardly manifested in its radiance. Initially it would remain hidden, just like the ability to speak lies hidden within a newborn child. But that kingly superiority was not something that first had to be won. It was already there from the very moment of his conception. This is the mystery of the eternal Sonship. The Word became flesh; God was revealed in the flesh.

Nothing created in our human race, therefore, can exist or arise that would surpass Jesus. He was above all things, he is above all things, and he will always be above all things. This is why he had dominion and authority over every human spirit by the very nature of the case, without this dominion having been transferred to him. For a time there may be opposition, there may be resistance, and there may be struggle; but the final outcome must and will seal his dominion and break down every opposition;

and one day the hour will come when every knee shall bow to him and every tongue confess him as the Master, Lord, and King of all.

§ 3   Between Bethlehem and that blissful final outcome, however, a long historical process intervenes that has been continuing for twenty centuries already and can continue for many more. It is a matter not only of the salvation of humanity, but of the salvation of the world. After entering the human race, Jesus had to subject the world as well to his kingly authority. That world does not stand on its own, but is connected to the world of the spirits, which includes both God's holy angels as well as the fallen angels of Satan's armies. As our King, Jesus must also supply to that spirit world what is necessary to save our world. This is something he can do by virtue of the fact that he is at once the Lord of the angels.

We must therefore distinguish: (1) what Jesus does as King for and in individual people; (2) what he does as King for and in human society; (3) what he does as King in order to subject to humanity the life of the world that exists beyond the human race; and finally (4) how, as King, he fights in order to bring down the power of sin and Satan. The first (that is, the adding and saving of individuals) reaches the deepest spiritual level, because here God's power directly turns around the spirit in a person's soul. With elect individuals it comes down finally to personal regeneration. To speak of repentance is not strong enough. Repentance is the personal-conscious effect of regeneration, but the reversal in life that objectively occurs in being born again is a mystical act of God, one that defies any and every explanation. Through regeneration, the person who has undergone that reversal becomes a subject of King Jesus without realizing it, while personal faith produces a conscious relationship between regeneration and that atonement accomplished once for all. In this way the subject becomes one who has also been bought by the blood of the Lamb, and as such this person becomes a subject and possession of Jesus in both soul and body.

The body, too, has a place in this discussion. The army of spirits surrounding God's throne would indeed be increased in number if nothing more happened than that the separated souls of the elect, after dying, entered heaven. But that would not do justice to the very thing God created in human beings that made them entirely different from the angels. The significance of the difference between the world of human beings and the world of angels is that the visible and the invisible has been united in the human race. Inanimate creation is visible. The angelic world is invisible. But these two have been interwoven in humankind. This is why, in order to become our King, Jesus also had to assume the flesh and blood of children [see Heb 2:14]. This is why not only the soul, but also the body had to suffer. And this is why his love had to be sealed in the shedding of his blood.

That the Word became flesh is the starting point for the salvation of our human race. The resurrection became necessary and possible only through the incarnation; and even the ascension is nothing other than the necessary consequence of the victory he won over death, not only spiritually but also physically. It is a complete mystery with a view to Scripture how so many dear, pious people could imagine Jesus' kingship as a triumph in his glorified body, even at the present time, while conceiving of those who have died as continuing to exist only in terms of the soul. The incarnation demands resurrection, ascension, and Jesus' reign at God's right hand in his glorified body.

From this it necessarily follows that the redeemed will, in their turn, partake of the resurrection through the blood of the Lamb; and their humiliated bodies, too, will one day be made like Christ's glorified body through him. This now proves that Christ's kingship is not limited to the invisible, but extends to the visible as well, and that all one-sided spiritualism must therefore be condemned. After all, our body is not the fruit of an isolated creation. The whole work of creation is like a single chain whose individual links have been joined together. With regard to their body, human beings were created from the dust of the earth. Their creation is the last in a series of individual creative acts. What had been created in plants and animals had to precede it, in order to point to what would be both much richer and much nobler in the human body. And even if today we scientifically analyze the human body, or the nutrition, maintenance, care, and healing of the body, it constantly appears that virtually everything existing in the visible sphere outside of human beings entertains a certain relationship with what we observe in and around the human body. Therefore, if Jesus' kingship is to extend to the entire person and guarantee the full glorification of the whole person in both soul and body, you neither can nor may isolate Christ in any way from all other visible things that have been created. Instead, it is required that in your confession you subject also the entire visible world to Jesus' kingship and make room for it there.

All of this in its entirety holds true for human society as well. With the phrase "human society," we are not here referring to the social aspect, but rather to the rich, organic life that results when a multitude of people live together in a mutual relationship. During the eighth century, tens of thousands of lonely hermits wandered about in the Libyan desert, searching for greater holiness by separating themselves from everyday life. But even if we refrain from judging the motivation driving them, one need only compare these wandering hermits with the rich human life along the Nile to perceive instantly that human society is something entirely different, much richer, and much more exalted than the life of many individuals out there on their own.

Whatever arises in such a human society, in family and society, in agriculture, industry, and commerce, in science and art, in moral development and especially in religious elevation, has been planted as a seed in the human world by God himself. He created not only individual people but a world of people, and his wisdom shines in that world of people. Sin may well have affected this society as well and poisoned and spoiled its life, but God does not for this reason abandon the treasure that he created in the human world. Rather, through his plan of salvation that human world must be purified from whatever is unclean, unholy, and satanic, and after that be raised up to a higher and richer development so as to cause the full riches of human society to shine one day in boundless splendor on the new earth and under the new heaven at the end of time.

If this is so, the human world cannot lie outside of Jesus' kingship in its organic development. If this is true, Jesus' kingship must extend not only to our soul and body, but also to our society as the world of humankind. Only when we understand things in this way can we do full justice to what Scripture says, namely, that God gave his Son in order to save the world. Every attempt to understand *world* as referring to the souls of the elect alone fails to appreciate the deeper significance of God's work of salvation. Concerning this work of salvation, Scripture repeatedly emphasizes that it includes our entire human existence in terms of soul, body, and society.

Even with this, however, we have not yet reached the outermost border of Jesus' kingdom. Our human world is not limited to this earth as we know it. It also includes the multitudes of martyrs and saints who are already singing praises before the throne; furthermore, our human world, here on earth as well as above, is in contact with the spirit world. Just as our human world has a relationship with the entire visible creation because of our bodily existence, so we as spiritual beings are in contact with the invisible world of spirits, both holy and unholy spirits. In that regard, of what benefit would it be if our King freed our souls, bringing us and our society into the glory of the new earth, but could not exercise his authority in the spirit world? His power must be able to resist, break, and destroy whatever in that spirit world is bent upon our destruction, and conversely, to be able to place in his service whatever in the spirit world is sympathetic to us, and to make it cooperate for the salvation of the world of humanity.

In saying so we have approached the full extent of Christ's kingship. It is a kingship for the soul, a kingship for our body, and in connection with this, a kingship for the entire visible creation. In the third place, his is a kingship that permeates human society in its entirety, in every domain and in every mode of existence. And in the fourth place, it is a kingship that reigns in the spirit world, in order thereby to save our world in a fuller and richer sense. The exposition of this will occupy us later, together with pointing out the obligations that flow from this for ourselves. But before doing that, we must first discuss the two distinct periods in which this kingship of Christ manifests its authority: the period of the gradual process in which we are currently living, and then the final period that, completely differently and with superior strength, will bring this great process to its consummation.

PREPARATION, ESTABLISHMENT, DEVELOPMENT, AND CONSUMMATION

The coming of the lawless one is by the activity of Satan with all power and false signs and wonders.

2 Thessalonians 2:9

§ 1   Christ's kingship takes its starting point in humanity—and this not only for the soul, but also for the body. In its work on the latter, it also extends to the world of the visible. Furthermore, since a person is not merely an individual, but also a member of the human race, [Christ's] kingly dominion establishes itself not only in the hearts of individuals, but also in society. The human race undergoes both good and evil influences from the spirit world; and therefore, as our King, Christ must have dominion over the world of the spirits as well. Only when it is understood in this full scope can Christ's kingship save the world so as to ensure that Christ's appearance on earth achieves its goal.

     As we pointed out at the end of the last chapter, however, even if we have managed to ascertain the extent of the terrain of his kingship, it is just as necessary to consider the distinction that can be made in the work of that kingship as it passes through several different periods. These distinct periods are four in number. The period of preparation for this kingdom begins in paradise and runs through to John the Baptist. In the second place, there is the period of its establishment, beginning at Bethlehem and ending with the ascension from the Mount of Olives. Third is the period of development over the course of the world's history. And, finally, a fourth period of an entirely different character will come, the period of consummation, which will begin with what Jesus' return will introduce and which will end when the kingdom is handed over to the Father.

It catches our attention that each of these four periods indeed has an entirely distinct character, and in each case Christ forms the sharp dividing line. In the first period, Christ is not yet on earth. In the second period, he comes to earth. In the third, he departs from the earth again. And in the fourth, he returns once more to earth. The kingdom is really just one kingdom in all four periods, but its operation differs according to the relationship between King and his kingdom.

In the first period—under the Old Testament dispensation, if you will— the King announces his arrival to us, gives us premonitions of it, and completes all preparations for it. In the second period, he appears and reveals the extent of his power for a moment, only to let it be submerged in his death; then he causes it to triumph just as decisively in his resurrection. Since this brings a temporary end to the establishment of his kingdom, he returns to where he came from and now reigns over his kingdom from on high. This situation will last until the struggle between Christ and the adversary has been fought to its end and the yeast has worked its way through the three measures of flour. Once this point has been reached and the harvest of the earth is ripe, the King will return in order to bring all resistance to nothing "with the breath of his mouth" [see 2 Thess 2:8]. [He will then] cause the kingship—which will be handed over to the Father in its completed state—to break through in all of its splendor. The first two periods are already behind us. We are now living in the third period. The fourth and final period still awaits us, and it remains the expectation of everyone who holds on to Christian hope in faith and love.

The period of preparation presents the need for Christ's kingship, depicts it symbolically, and both gives it shape historically in Israel and also provides it with a point of connection in the person and house of David. It even creates a group of people who are equipped to receive the King.

The first provision for the work of preparation comes already in paradise, continues in the days of Noah, and becomes active when Abram is called. Then with new divisions and choices, the contrast that had already manifested itself with Cain and Abel is continued in Jacob and Esau, finally to establish itself in the tribe of Judah and in the house of Israel.

This continuous process of dividing and choosing is intended to show that while humanity may withdraw from God's authority, the Lord in his sovereign design places his hand on one part of the human race time and again, incorporates it into his covenant, subjects one generation after another to his majesty within that covenant, and thereby brings nearer and nearer the rise of the kingdom of heaven over against the kingdom of the world.

In Israel's existence as a nation, this work of preparation is at the same time symbolic. The symbolism is found not only in the temple worship, but also in the nation's very existence, because Israel's existence as a nation does not constitute the kingdom of Christ but only portrays and displays it in symbolic form. Prophetically, it leads people to understand that what is yet to come will be a kingdom. To make it clear that the Davidic kingship and Israel's existence as a nation are not real but symbolic, David dies, his hereditary kingship is brought down, and his people must leave their land in exile. Everything concrete and real is taken away. What remains is the idea alone, the prophecy, the spiritual form. This idea, this prophecy, this spiritual form in the end demands fulfillment and realization, something that indeed happens when the holy Child is born in Bethlehem. This Child could come to a land, among a people, and in spiritual surroundings as they were found only in Israel at that time as the product of history. Those who had no eyes to see spiritually looked back to the line of David, Solomon, and Rehoboam; and those who had no ears to hear spiritually tried to bring Israel's former existence back and to choose Israel's triumph over the nations as their ideal. Yet those who did have ears to hear what the Spirit spoke let go of the shell to grasp the pearl, and thereby passed from Israel's symbolic existence as a nation to the full spiritual reality of the kingdom of heaven. That preparation did not happen outside of Christ. The King anointed by God over Zion was himself active in all these things. As it says in Isaiah 63: "In all their affliction he was afflicted, and the angel of his presence saved them; in his love and in his pity he redeemed them; he lifted them up and carried them all the days of old. And so he became their Savior" [see Isa 63:8–9].

When the preparations had been completed, the second period arrived: namely, the establishment of the kingdom of Christ, when the One promised by the Father was born of Mary in Bethlehem. In John the Baptist the prophecy of preparation once more came to a narrow focus; then Jesus himself came and declared that the prophetic period had come to an end and that the kingdom of heaven itself was now at hand. And in the years during which the King of God's kingdom sojourned on earth, he revealed the majesty of this kingdom in every sphere of human life. The full scope of this kingdom had already been foreshadowed in the period of preparation. Personally, the elect were raised to life. After all, who can enjoy the Psalms without feeling that it is a redeemed soul who wrestles there to grab hold of salvation? But even beyond the terrain of the spiritual and invisible, the Lord's power intervened in the visible order. Beginning with the Red Sea, miracles were Israel's means of deliverance. Such miracles intervened time and again in the visible world, and they constantly accompanied Israel in its pilgrimage throughout the course of history. The King's power over the material world as well as nature had to be displayed already during the period of preparation, and this not only as a revelation of power but also as a means to salvation. The old covenant miracles are almost without exception and by nature designed to save. But this was not all. The King whom God had anointed had to impress his stamp on human society already during the period of preparation, and he expressed in practical ways his influence and effect on human society—first in the society of the patriarchs and then in Israel's existence as a nation.

§ 2

Finally, as far as the fourth terrain of the King's battles with unholy powers is concerned, this struggle was depicted in Israel's struggle with the nations around them. These nations were governed by the spirit of the demonic, as is evident in the idolatry, fortune-telling, and sorcery that they practiced. And although, because of its size, Israel was nothing compared to the powerful nations of Egypt, Assyria, Babylon, and Persia, Israel's independence was honorably maintained as long as it held onto God. During Solomon's reign it even seemed as if Israel already had dominion over the demonic power of the nations.

The same things are even more apparent when, in that second period of establishment, the King himself is finally born and the kingdom of heaven enters. During this period, too, there is activity in the four terrains: (1) in the soul, (2) in the body and in all that is visible, (3) in human society, and (4) in the battle with the demonic powers. During the three years of his sojourn on earth, the King of God's kingdom caused his kingly majesty to shine brightly in each of those four terrains. He calls his disciples, and they surrender to him. He teaches the crowds and attracts them with his words, and later the apostle can testify: "We have seen his glory, glory as of the only Son from the Father" [John 1:14]. The circle of those who join him is not large, but those who do join him are called to life and will soon bear witness to him throughout the world—first of all in the words they speak, but also, continuing to this day, through the words they wrote down and left us as our spiritual inheritance.

Jesus does not restrict himself to the spiritual operation upon the soul, however; he also addresses the body. Those who are sick, he heals. To the blind he restores sight. The lame man takes up his mat and walks at [Jesus'] command. At times the healing of bodily afflictions seems to take on greater proportions in his work than does the saving of souls. And, finally, he revealed his greatest power over the body when he called the dead back to life, and when he himself rose from the dead and appeared to his people in his glorified body.

Christ's kingly power extends from the body further out to all things visible in nature. He shows his dominion over the plant kingdom at the wedding at Cana, in the multiplication of bread, and in the curse on the fig tree. Similarly, he shows his power over the animal kingdom when the wild animals surround him in the wilderness, and with the miraculous catch of fish. Indeed, he even manages to subject the elemental forces of nature to his power; and when a storm breaks out on the Sea of Gennesaret, he calms it through his powerful word.

When he comes to this earth, the King does not overturn human society as such. He does not do what the Anabaptists throughout history have tried to do, namely, to introduce a new state of affairs for social life. He does not touch the family relationships, the employer-employee relationships, the relationships between a nation and its government; rather, he honors them and lets them be. Jesus does attempt to introduce a more holy spirit that can work in all of these relationships. He fights against enslavement to the sensible and visible. He sanctifies marriage so that it receives a nobler form. He raises the position of women, who in the East had always lived under oppression. He gives children a place of prominence. He shows compassion to the poor, feeding the five thousand. He places all of life under religion's exaltation, and in all things he points to the high and holy ideal in the law of his God and summarizes that ideal in the power of love. He thus allows what had arisen from the ordinance of life to continue, but pours another spirit into it so that he can exercise his kingly dominion also in society through that holier spirit. When Christian groups begin to form, you soon observe that their social image begins to change and is no longer what it was before that time.

Fourthly, Jesus likewise acts as King when it comes to the relationship to the spirit world. God's holy angels herald Jesus' coming, and they make repeated appearances during his short life on earth. Jesus himself refers to those angels in the Lord's Prayer. He explains that the angel world rejoices when a sinner passes into the kingdom of heaven. He says that the angels, who have been sent to serve us, dwell in the Father's presence. Conversely, from the very outset he goes to battle with the unholy spirits. In the wilderness, he answers the ruler of this world at the first temptation. He casts demons out from those who are possessed. And from the very beginning of his ministry, just as John the Baptist had done before him, he speaks out openly against the brood of vipers in order to break the power by which Satan—without actual demon possession—nevertheless held captive the spirits of many people and groups. Jesus even involved his apostles in that struggle with the demonic forces. They too were called to break down the demonic kingdom; and even the first time they were sent out into Israel, their fixed assignment included casting out demons. That this struggle would not be ended with the departure of his apostles is most clear in the daily prayer to "deliver us from the Evil One," which Jesus placed forever on the lips of his disciples and of those whom he has redeemed.

Consequently, in both the preparation for Christ's kingship in Israel as well as in the establishment of that kingdom in the period between Bethlehem and the ascension, activity occurred in four areas: spiritually in the soul; physically in the material world; socially in society; and anti-demonically in the spirit world. More significantly, the activity in each of the four terrains was consistently brought about by way of a direct intervention on the part of a supernatural power. The entire process is permeated with miracles.

If we may leave aside for the moment the third period of development in which we currently live and move directly to the fourth and final period of consummation, we see that Jesus' kingly activity is once again of the same character. We will treat the latter more extensively when we examine the Revelation to John. Already now, however, it can be noted that in the period of consummation as well, the character of Christ's activity will be partly spiritual, partly material, partly social, and partly anti-demonic, and that even then the activity will be mostly supernatural in kind.

Thus, the deeper we delve into this topic, it becomes more and more untenable to maintain that Jesus' activity in his kingdom is and will remain purely spiritual in nature. Instead, we must conclude that the King's activity in the kingdom of God has a predominantly supernatural character; that miracles are indispensable; and that both body and soul, as well as the forces of the spirit world and of nature, are under the dominion of that supernatural activity. What we call *miracles* were not incidental, but took place on center stage. This applies to the activity on all four terrains—at least in regard to the first two periods, as well as the fourth or last period. Miracles have a leading role in the preparation, establishment, and consummation of the kingdom; and it is on the whole only through miracles that everything comes to be in the course of history. Unique to the third period of *development*, therefore, is the fact that miracles in this period increasingly disappear, and natural development in large part replaces supernatural interventions.

This is not to suggest that supernatural works fell away entirely. In fact, in the spiritual arena they continue all the time. Regeneration is something that always comes to the soul supernaturally, and without regeneration no one can enter life. Those who are not born of water and the Spirit cannot even see God's kingdom [see John 3:5]. And if you were to ask Jesus how, from where, and in what way our souls are regenerated, he would answer that it is as with the gusts of wind that blow upon the sails. You hear the wind's sound, but you do not know where it comes from or where it is going [see John 3:8]. Similarly, we would not dare to deny that miracles at times still occur in the physical arena as well. Many things that have been called miracles in that sense can be explained by an operation that comes subjectively to a person's nervous system from faith, but even then, faith must be strengthened supernaturally through special grace in order for this effect to be achieved. However, there also are healings that do not admit of this explanation.

The question that is decisive for the character of the kingship of Jesus during this third period is therefore not whether a miraculous healing or rescue was recorded in history here and there, from time to time. The question is entirely different: One must ask whether the supernatural display of Christ's power is still the rule of thumb that it was in the first and second period. Do miracles constitute, also during this third period, the regular acts of power by which Jesus announces, promotes, and maintains his kingly majesty? Can we say accordingly of these last eighteen centuries that, as was the case in the Old and New Testament, the history of Christianity has been one continuous story of miracles? Has it up until now substantially remained one powerful, impressive display of miraculous and supernatural work? When one poses the question this way—which also happens to be the only correct way—there can be no doubt about what the answer is. When it comes to the material and demonic arena, supernatural interventions recede almost entirely into the background during this period of development as the history of God's kingdom increasingly assumes the character of the yeast that works its way through the three measures of flour.

If we were to give a brief explanation of the character of the activity brought about in the third period, throughout the four different sectors over which it continues to extend, it would be as follows: In the arena of the soul's life, that activity remains like it was before—that is, of a supernatural nature, first in regeneration, and additionally in the leading of grace. It is true that, by virtue of the covenant of grace, spiritual life is now borne along—more than before—by the generations, and therefore also by the ministry of the church and by spiritual community. Nonetheless, spiritual life remains in its inception and development the fruit of the work of the Holy Spirit, and the Spirit's work in the life of grace is of course supernatural. The immediate rule of our King continues to exist, and our King exercises this rule over the spirits through the Holy Spirit.

In the second place, as far as the operation on the body and on all of the nature residing behind it is concerned: by managing to enter the cultural life of art and science, Christian activity has discovered and detected the means to heal numerous diseases and to place all kinds of natural forces in its service. The scale of this activity is such that in magnitude it far surpasses the benefit derived from the supernatural activity that used to occur. The truth of this statement is immediately evident when you compare the means for healing and for exercising dominion over nature that Christian Europe now has at its disposal with the situation before Christianity entered the world, or else with the situation still found in the pagan regions of Asia and Africa.

Next, with respect to the third terrain formed by human society, the rule still holds true that Christianity does not overturn the existing order of things, but through its spiritual power elevates and ennobles that order to a much higher level.

Finally, with respect to the anti-demonic work of Jesus' kingship, in Christian countries Satan's influence continues to operate, although as a governing power it has already been broken once and for all. In the moral sphere, Satan's power is still at work and even on the increase, since it constantly opposes the moral power of Christianity. But as a spiritual power, the demonic is no longer in any Christian country what it once was even in Europe, and still often continues to be in pagan countries.

III.20

THE RETURN
OF THE KING

Then I saw in the right hand of him who was seated on the throne a scroll written within and on the back, sealed with seven seals.

REVELATION 5:1

Christ our King prepared his kingship in Israel, a kingship whose roots   § 1
reached all the way back to paradise. He established it two thousand years
ago when he was incarnated in Israel. Over the course of the centuries, he
has gradually caused his kingship to develop and extend over all of human
life. But one day, the third period of gradual development will come to
an end as well, and the last period of consummation will arrive with his
great return.

What Holy Scripture reveals and announces clearly in this respect may
not be obscured, veiled, or spiritualized. We must be certain and express
clearly that the period of gradual development in which we now live will
one day come to an end and pass over into the last period, which is that of
a supernatural manifestation of power encompassing not only the whole
world but the entire universe as well. The final victory cannot be brought
about gradually, because [the path of gradual development] will end in
failure. When it is clear and evident in the course of history that natural,
gradual development does not and cannot lead to the final goal, then—and
only then—will our King intervene in a completely supernatural manner

so as to neutralize all resistance and to cause the full glory of his kingship to break through.

Before this happens, however, it must be determined and demonstrated that [this process of] gradual development was unable to lead to its triumph. One should not be able to say afterward: "If only it had pleased God to leave humanity to its own natural development, everything still would have worked out on its own." No, the facts of history must show that humanity was incapable of this on its own. Humanity must therefore be given time. Time to absorb the blessing that Christianity brings. Time to test every method and manner of saving itself with the gospel's help. Once it is clear after this generous passage of time that humanity failed—because its very life root has been poisoned and because the demonic power finds novel ways and means in every new development to enter humanity's veins and spoil it from within—then and only then will Christ suddenly arrest this period of gradual development, fermentation, and influence, and intervene with his full kingly power. And [he will do] this no longer to save but to judge, and to bring about the consummation of his kingdom with supernatural power.

Why this is so can be explained as follows: Humanity was created as a single unit, and was therefore represented by a natural head—that is, in Adam. Sin broke that organic unity. After the fall, humanity no longer had a head or king, and for that reason it fell into continuous fragmentation and disintegration so that one of two things had to happen. Either humanity had to continue on the path of disintegration until its unity ceased to be significant, or humanity had to receive a new Head and God had to provide it with a new King.

It was the latter that occurred. In Christ, humanity once more received a King, but in the second Adam it received a King who was much more glorious than the first Adam. What comes as a result of the fall is not the same thing that would have come if there had been no fall, but it is something much more glorious. This is what moved Augustine to speak of the *felix culpa*, the happy fall.[1]

---

1. See Augustine, *The Augustine Catechism: The Enchiridion on Faith, Hope, and Charity*, trans. Bruce Harbert, ed. Boniface Ramsey (Hyde Park, NY: New City Press, 1999), 8.27, p. 60: "[God] judged it better to bring good out of evil than to allow nothing evil to exist." The phrase *felix culpa* appears in the text of the Exultet, a hymn traditionally sung during the Easter Vigil: "O happy fault that earned for us so great, so glorious a Redeemer!" (*O felix culpa, quæ talem ac tantum méruit habére Redemptórem!*).

The gift to the human race of so glorious a King began with the exalted life of humanity being drawn together in the existence of a single, chosen people as a nation. This occurred in Israel. In this chosen nation, the idea of a holy kingship slowly began to arise. That kingship was not real, since everything in Israel was only a shadow and image of the things to come. However, the idea did begin to take root. The nation's ideal became a Son of Man, not taken from the human race itself but introduced into it as its spiritual Head. Already with Daniel we see that the expression *Son of Man* becomes fixed. Then that King finally appears in Israel, but with him the symbolic and foreshadowing nature of what had existed becomes evident.

As we noted back in the last chapter, the shell split open and the pearl became visible. When this happened, Israel as a nation fell. In the place of the physical Israel descending from Abraham came the spiritual Israel comprising those who had been regenerated. Christ is the real King of that [people of] Israel. He forms his people, and he unites them into one body with himself as their Head. This spiritual Israel is made up of people from every family, nation, tongue, and language.

This created a division in the life of the human race. On the one side stand those people who really do live from Christ as their King, who are ruled and protected by him; while on the other side stand those who refuse to subject themselves to him as their King. And although the followers of Christ and subjects of the King increase in number and expand from thousands to millions, that contrast does not fall away. One part of the human race hardens itself in its rejection of the King. This is how things are now, and this is how things will continue until the end. The demonic power attaches itself to that rebellious part of the human race. The tempter wants to be the ruler of this world once again, to place and maintain his kingdom over against Christ, and even to bring the kingdom of Christ down. Our King will bring an end to this when he returns. He will arrest humanity's history with his return and bring it to an end. He will undo and crush for good the power of the demonic. And as Judge, he will judge the living and the dead, gathering into his kingdom the entire human race wherever his kingship has permeated it, and cutting off from the stem of our human race all those individual branches, leaves, and withered blossoms that persisted in their rejection of his kingship. Therefore, at the end nothing will remain except the kingdom of Christ. Whatever still constitutes the human race will be subject to him. Then the kingdom of glory will arrive. It will be a kingdom of glory because all of nature and the entire spirit world will then be taken up in complete harmony with our sanctified human race in the unity of life and dominion established by our King.

§ 2   In the visions that came to John on Patmos, Scripture makes known the final events that will accompany Jesus' return, that will be decided in the last judgment, and that will bring the consummation of Jesus' kingdom and the kingdom of glory. Therefore, we will not have a clear understanding of Christ's kingship unless we consider these visions. There is no doubt a void in the believers' world of thought because they draw so little comfort and courage from the revelations that came to John as they are presented to them in Scripture. Yet even though the last period of consummation is depicted for us particularly in the Revelation of John, the final event is announced just as definitively to us in the Prophets, in the Gospels, and in the apostolic Letters.

Nowhere does Scripture suggest that the consummation will occur through a gradual spiritual development. Scripture teaches repeatedly that the course of history will one day be arrested for good, and at that time the high and holy ideal will be realized through a supernatural intervention encompassing both the entire invisible world as well as the entire visible world.

Joel, the first of the prophets, already announced a day when "the harvest is ripe," when the sickle will be put in that harvest, and the day of the LORD will come (Joel 3:13). That the LORD's coming will not only be a spiritual act but also have an effect on nature and its elemental forces is clear from the fact that Joel writes not only that the Spirit will be poured out, but also that there will be "wonders in the heavens and on the earth, blood and fire and columns of smoke. The sun shall be turned to darkness, and the moon to blood, before the great and awesome day of the LORD comes" [Joel 2:30–31]. In 3:15, Joel repeats that when the day of the LORD is near, "The sun and the moon [will be] darkened, and the stars [will] withdraw their shining."

Jesus himself, no less emphatically than Israel's prophets, announced that final day to his disciples shortly before his death. Just read Matthew 24:27–31: "For as the lightning comes from the east and shines as far as the west, so will be the coming of the Son of Man. Immediately after the tribulation of those days the sun will be darkened, and the moon will not give its light, and the stars will fall from heaven, and the powers of the heavens will be shaken. Then will appear in heaven the sign of the

Son of Man, and then all the tribes of the earth will mourn, and they will see the Son of Man coming on the clouds of heaven with power and great glory. And he will send out his angels with a loud trumpet call, and they will gather his elect from the four winds, from one end of heaven to the other" [Matt 24:27, 29–31]. This is followed in Matthew 25:31–46 by just as decisive an announcement of the judgment that will follow immediately upon Christ's return: "When the Son of Man comes in his glory, and all the angels with him, then he will sit on his glorious throne. Before him will be gathered all the nations, and he will separate people one from another as a shepherd separates the sheep from the goats. And these will go away into eternal punishment, but the righteous into eternal life" [Matt 25:31–32, 46]. At Jesus' ascension the disciples hear this announcement once more, this time not from Jesus but from the angels: "Two men stood by them in white robes, and said, 'Men of Galilee, why do you stand looking into heaven? This Jesus, who was taken up from you into heaven, will come in the same way as you saw him go into heaven'" [Acts 1:10–11].

In the Letters of the apostles, Jesus' return likewise forms a fixed component of the gospel that they carried out into the world. "In a moment," as it says in 1 Corinthians 15:52, "in the twinkling of an eye, at the last trumpet ... the trumpet will sound, and the dead will be raised imperishable. When the perishable puts on the imperishable, and the mortal puts on immortality, then shall come to pass the saying that is written: 'Death is swallowed up in victory'" [1 Cor 15:52, 54]. And similarly in 1 Thessalonians 4:16: "The Lord himself will descend from heaven with a cry of command, with the voice of an archangel, and with the sound of the trumpet of God. And the dead in Christ will rise first." The apostle in fact confesses ever more clearly that there will first be a time of development and fermentation, and only after this time has passed will the Lord return. Thus he says in 2 Thessalonians 2:7–8: "For the mystery of lawlessness is already at work. Only he who now restrains it will do so until he is out of the way. And then the lawless one will be revealed, whom the Lord Jesus will kill with the breath of his mouth and bring to nothing by the appearance of his coming." That the Lord's return will be accompanied by a supernatural intervention in the existing order, even in nature, is emphatically expressed by Peter in these words: "The day of the Lord will come like a thief, and then the heavens will pass away with a roar, and the heavenly bodies will be burned up and dissolved, and the earth and the works that are done on it will be exposed. The heavens will be set on fire and dissolved, and the heavenly bodies will melt as they burn" [2 Pet 3:10, 12]. Then the kingdom of glory will come in, since "according to his promise we are waiting for new heavens and a new earth in which righteousness dwells" [2 Pet 3:13]. This will be the fulfillment of the ancient prophecy found in Isaiah 65:17: "For behold, I create new heavens and a new earth, and the former things shall not be remembered or come into mind."

§ 3   Even if the Revelation of John had not been included in the New Testament as its capstone, the prophecy of the old covenant, Jesus' own testimony, and the clear statements in the apostolic Letters would still have cemented the Lord's return firmly within the structure of our Christian confession. One cannot imagine a fully developed confession without an article on Jesus' return on the clouds of heaven. For that reason, the twelve articles of the Christian faith include the confession that "He ascended into heaven, from which he will come to judge the living and the dead," and all Christian churches without distinction have accepted these twelve articles. During the last nine centuries, however, the churches have done little more than nominally to confess Jesus' return. Virtually every century there were indeed small groups and circles that cast themselves all too one-sidedly upon this one element of the confession, and they soon lapsed into all kinds of fantasies. However, aside from what happens in these groups or sects, the Lord's return has hardly animated the preaching and it did not receive its full due in the faith of a single church.

The confession of Jesus' return did revive in times of pressure and persecution. That is also how it was during the Reformation in those countries where the Reformation either managed to maintain itself with the greatest of difficulties or where, even worse, it dissipated shortly after it had arisen. In such frightening and upsetting times people again reached for the promise of Jesus' return. But soon after the position of the different churches over against and alongside each other had become settled in the seventeenth century, people once again began to feel at home in the world, turned the end of all things into a very distant prospect, and turned the confession of the future Jesus would bring into an all but dead part of our confession. This is how things went in the Greek churches, in the Roman churches, in the Lutheran churches, and in the Reformed churches. And even the Baptists—who are the heirs to the Anabaptist party of old that had been filled with zeal for the doctrine of the last things—were soon all too content with the calm progression of history.

Mystically inclined or fanatical people recurrently arose in reaction to this cool indifference toward "the last things," or else talented song-writers were attracted by the gripping visions of Jesus' return. In our own country we have the example of Da Costa.[2] New groups were also formed, such as the Latter-day Saints and others, who expected within their own lifetime the future that the Lord would bring within a few years.[3] But in the broad stream of the church's life, the waters hardly even rippled under the gusts of these eschatological winds.

Indeed, in broad Christian circles people gradually fell away into entirely anti-Scriptural views and imagined that the separated souls of those who had fallen asleep were destined to lead to no more than a spiritual existence in the Father's house throughout all eternity. They no longer thought that the dead would be raised, that a final judgment would actually happen, or that the body would be glorified from the humiliated state it had obtained in death and the grave. When the confession of Jesus' return was lost sight of, everything tied to it gradually faded into the background as well. And even though there was always a remnant of Christians who had a deeper understanding of things, who were immersed in the doctrine of the last things, who strengthened their faith by it and delighted in it, for the vast majority of Christians beliefs concerning the last things became less and less an essential component of their faith convictions. As they saw it, the material remains of the dead had already been dealt with in the grave. As far as they were concerned, the dead now exist simply as immortal souls in the house of the Father, which awaits them as well. [They believed] that things would continue in this way century after century until the world's life stopped and heaven's life alone remained. Being reunited back in heaven with those they had lost here was at least as important for them as living in the service of the glorified King.

People hardly gave any thought to his being a King anymore. At most, they spoke of a Friend so faithful, who has saved and rescued us, and whom we ought to thank for that salvation. But with the exception of a sermon or song here and there, or apart from the deathbed or at the

---

2. Isaac da Costa (1798–1860) was a renowned Jewish poet who studied with Willem Bilderdijk and, after his mentor's death, became a leader among the Reformed in the Netherlands.

3. The Church of Jesus Christ of Latter-day Saints, also known informally as the Mormon Church, traces its origins to Joseph Smith (1805–44) in the United States of America in the late 1820s.

open grave, mention was hardly made anymore of the kingdom of glory, of a new earth under a new heaven, of our return in a glorified body, of Christ's victory over his adversaries, of his judgment over the living and the dead, and of our entry into the full glory of Christ's kingly regiment. The first thing the church abandoned was the doctrine of the last things, trading it in for a superficial, one-sidedly spiritual view that found its origin among unbelieving groups.

As a result, the Revelation of John no longer connected with the church. The church no longer felt anything for it. It no longer understood it. It found no food in it for its faith. And when persecution ceased, the church no longer felt any need for the comfort that this last book in Holy Scripture had to offer. Believers did continue to find much that was beautiful in the seven letters to the seven churches of Asia Minor, and the description of the new Jerusalem and the heavenly paradise still had great appeal for them because of its poetic beauty. But what comes between the seven letters and the depiction of the new Jerusalem no longer fascinated them. They no longer read it. They no longer knew it. And, just like the article of Jesus' return in the twelve articles of the faith, it became a dead letter.

Since there is no New Testament book in which Christ's kingship shines as radiantly as in the visions that came to John on Patmos, allowing the doctrine of the last things to slip away damaged more than anything else the honoring of Jesus' kingship. The tendency throughout was to honor Jesus only as Savior and Mediator, and especially to understand his kingdom in an exclusively spiritual sense as the dominion of his highly religious and moral ideas. The majority of people increasingly lost sight of the fact that Jesus' kingly majesty would unfold in a display of power over all creatures—not only over human beings as conscious, spiritual creatures, but also over inanimate creatures throughout the entire kingdom of nature. This included the elements and even the rich spirit world that stands outside of the circle of human life. Belief waned with regard to the miracles with which Jesus displayed this power during his time on earth, and people no longer understood that this same miraculous power would burst through much more gloriously at the end of time, to reveal Christ's kingly majesty. People were content to honor Jesus spiritually in every way, with one person still praising him as Redeemer while another recognized him only as a religious genius. But supernaturalists and modernists were united in agreeing that they did not expect a new, much higher, and much more awesome manifestation of our King's power in the future. Even the last judgment was to be understood only in terms of Jesus' work in our consciences.

At the very least, abandoning the teaching of Jesus's second coming contributed to the undermining of many Christians' sound beliefs regarding the life-giving power of Jesus' kingship as a kingship that has to do with all things in heaven and on earth.

THE REVELATION ON PATMOS

And he said to me, "These words are trustworthy and true. And the Lord, the God of the spirits of the prophets, has sent his angel to show his servants what must soon take place."

REVELATION 22:6

§ 1   Without going deeply into the doctrine of the last things, we still cannot conclude this second part without a further exposition of what the Revelation of John tells us about Christ's kingship. It should be emphasized that the visions John received on Patmos were first of all intended for the Christians living at that time. Their lot was hard. As a small group, as a small flock in the fullest sense of the word, they stood in the middle of a world that turned against them with the power of the government, with its erudition and with its social pursuits. If those first Christians had been content with a modest place alongside that life of the world, they would have been tolerated. Surely there would be room for the Christian religion alongside the many other religions of those days! After all, the Jews with their Old Testament religion were not only tolerated even in Rome, but they had even received a place of honor there. The Christians, however, refused to be satisfied with this. They were not content to place their Christian religion on par with the pagan and Jewish religions. Their aim was much higher, and they strove for much more.

They were the nation of the King, and Christ their King had to have dominion over all peoples and nations. All other religion had to be destroyed. The Christian religion was the religion for the world. It was the only true worship, the only pure worship, the only form of worship to be tolerated. For that reason, every temple had to be razed, every priesthood abolished, every idolatry exposed for what it was, and every human soul claimed for the honor of Christ. Equal standing was out of the question. Even subordinating the other religions would not suffice. Every other religion had to disappear because it was sinful and an insult to God. Nothing was to survive except Christianity, and the dominion of the King of Christianity was to be recognized and honored throughout the entire earth.

So originally it was not the pagans who attacked the Christians, but the Christians who, with their confession, launched an attack on all existing religions. For that reason, peace was unimaginable. A struggle had to arise, and in that struggle either Christianity or paganism would succumb. It would be a struggle between the Christian King and the emperor. It would be a struggle between the Christian faith and pagan philosophy; a struggle between Christian social morals and the moral teaching of pagan society.

Especially during the first century, that struggle really did seem a desperate cause for the Christians. What did their small flock represent in the face of the power of the Roman emperor? Did not all kinds of pagan philosophy enter the Christian confession as early as the first century through the teachings of the Nicolaitans, the Docetists, and the Gnostics?[1] And above all, was not their holy lifeview at risk of being weakened and poisoned in the younger generation by the lower moral teachings of pagan society?

With all of this in the background, Christ appeared to John on Patmos in order to depict, with fascinating images given in a series of visions, the course that history would take, the suffering that the Christians would endure, but also the victory that would be theirs in the end. If you provide certainty that the frightening struggle will end in triumph, remove all doubt concerning the outcome of that struggle, and supply clear signs to show that the course of that history necessarily has to lead to the desired

---

1. These are heretical groups who taught, respectively, that immoral behavior was acceptable for Christians living in the end times, that Jesus Christ only seemed to be incarnate in human form, and that the material world was fundamentally evil.

outcome, then the weakest will feel the courage of a hero aroused within them; those who must die as martyrs in that struggle will do so with a cry of jubilation on their lips; and they will find comfort in their overwhelmed soul before they climb the pyre or are thrown to the animals.

The entire Revelation given on Patmos must be considered from this perspective. It is first of all directed to that generation of Christians living at that time; it seeks to reveal the certainty of the final victory to the believers suffering at that time; and it wants to give courage through that certain future to the sinking soul and give comfort to those who are perishing in the struggle.

Therefore, everything is directed to supplying such certainty. No room was to be left for doubt or hesitation, and this explains why Christ himself appeared, why the assurance that things will indeed happen in this way was repeated, and why this solemn assurance was given one more time at the end: "These words are trustworthy and true. And the Lord, the God of the spirits of the prophets, has sent his angel to show his servants what must soon take place" [Rev 22:6]. The assurance in this verse is reinforced by the announcement that "If anyone adds to the words of the prophecy of this book, God will add to him the plagues described in this book, and if anyone takes away from the words of the book of this prophecy, God will take away his share in the book of life and in the holy city" [see Rev 22:18-19]. In the midst of a struggle that from a human perspective could end only in the complete defeat and extinction of the Christians, they needed a firm conviction and a certain knowledge that the outcome would be the very opposite, and an unshakable hope that the final victory would belong to Christ their King. And that certainty, that sure knowledge, that foundation of hope was what the King gave to John on Patmos, and through John to a suffering, persecuted, and hard-pressed Christianity. Those visions were one of the means for the triumph of Christianity.

§ 2   The visions had to satisfy two requirements. First of all, they had to display throughout history what the end would be, and in that end, whose would be the final victory. Secondly, the visions had to emphasize the initial triumph that already then awaited them and would soon take place. That is why these visions gave a panoramic overview of the entire course of history, and in this they depict the final victory so clearly from afar that it becomes the horizon for the searching eye of faith. The imminent fall of Jerusalem had to be depicted; and from that fixed point the line of history is drawn straight through to the end point when Christ will return, when all opposition against him will be broken, when the last judgment will come, and when the glory is revealed.

It is not important whether years or centuries intervene between [the fall of Jerusalem and the return of Christ]. Is not a thousand days for the Lord like one day [see 2 Pet 3:8]? The point was to show that that power of the King was already at work in that period. It would not begin at a later time, but already then—soon, in the fall of Jerusalem, and later on in the fall of pagan Rome—so that the believers, while peering over the panoramic course of history beginning with [the fall of Jerusalem and Rome], would have the final victory of Christ our King depicted for them in clear lines.

With respect to the former, [that is, the fall of Jerusalem and Rome], it is repeatedly declared that the things portrayed "must soon take place." The power display depicted in these visions is not something that will happen hundreds of years later. No, that display of power will begin soon. The visions do not refer to what will begin to unfold at a much later time, but they point plainly and clearly to a beginning in this manifestation of power that is most imminent. The two great powers facing the first Christians were Judaism and the pagan imperial power. Both powers, which are represented in Jerusalem and imperial Rome, respectively, would already come under attack; and their fall is depicted with clear images. The addition, "where their Lord was crucified," (Rev 11:8) points to the city outside of whose walls Golgotha lay; while the words, "the seven heads are seven mountains on which the woman is seated," in [Rev] 17:9 are just as decidedly an allusion to ancient Rome, which was known throughout the world as the city with the seven mountains.

Even this announcement regarding the fall of Jerusalem and Rome should not be understood to mean that Christ's kingly power had not already begun to work earlier; nor does it mean that his power would be displayed only in such great events. It goes without saying that Christ's kingly power also works in normal life without interruption and without ceasing, both in the experiences of the churches and in the personal condition of believers' souls. Just read how in the letters to the churches in Asia Minor Jesus himself constantly testifies about what he will do as the Head of all, and how he also influences particular individuals with the specific purpose of protecting those churches. This is clear in the letter to Thyatira, where it says about the woman Jezebel: "I gave her time to repent, but she refuses to repent of her sexual immorality. Behold, I will throw her onto a sickbed, and those who commit adultery with her I will throw into great tribulation, unless they repent of her works, and I will strike her children dead. And all the churches will know that I am he who searches mind and heart" [Rev 2:21-23].

Although these verses leave no doubt that the Revelation of John in no way intends to overlook or disparage Christ's quiet influence on regular life, the visions speak throughout of an intention to cause our King's power to radiate in the great and powerful events of this world; these are placed as milestones on the path of history and will bring a visible change and perceptible turn in the course of events. This is how everybody considers his or her life, since in our memory we attach the most value to the things that introduced a remarkable change in the course of our life and destiny. All nations similarly describe their history in this way as well, since for the benefit of the next generation they commit to print precisely those events that determined their situation and set them on new paths.

Similarly, the intention of those visions given on Patmos is to encourage and comfort the churches as they live under terrifying pressure by focusing all attention especially on the coming manifestations of Jesus' power, which—in startling interventions brought about throughout the course of history—displayed to the eyes of all that Jesus' continuously progressing victory could not be resisted.

There is no doubt that when Christianity entered history, it was confronted with the two major powers of Judaism and paganism—symbolized in Jerusalem and imperial Rome—over which it had to triumph or else to which it would succumb; thus there was no way to display Christ's kingly power more visibly than in the fall of Jerusalem in the first century and in the fatal blow that Rome's imperial power would soon suffer.

The visions could not stop there, however. In every struggle the chance [of victory or defeat] can rise or fall. Although it became clear that Christianity would soon see Jerusalem and Rome fall, this as such contained no guarantee that fortune would not take another turn. And of what use would the fall of Jerusalem and Rome be to Christ's kingly power if other powers were to arise soon thereafter and bring complete defeat to the Christian religion with a new wave of attacks? The visions given on Patmos could therefore strengthen the church of the living God decisively only if they revealed clearly that there would be victory not only in the beginning, but that there would also be total victory in the end. As long and dark as the tunnel of vision was through which they looked from the fall of Jerusalem and Rome on through to the end, at that end there had to be, at the most distant point of the diorama, a very bright and clear light.

Furthermore, whatever the historical distance may have been, it had to be made clear that, at that end, all unholy powers would unite one more time against our King, with every instrument turning on him so as to bring his kingdom down; but also that our King would with irresistible majesty strike every one of those unholy powers one after the other, casting them down until one day all enemies would be subjected under his feet. And then, behind the arena on which this last battle would occur, the full splendor of the kingdom of glory would rise before the soul's eye. Thus salvation, which had been the aim of God's eternal design for heaven and earth, could shine in the wedding of the Lamb—or if you will, in the new Jerusalem and in the paradise of God.

This is the very guarantee that the believers of those days received in the visions on Patmos. It was the announcement of the imminent victory over Jerusalem, of the imminent fall of the Roman Empire. Thereafter it announced the long, dark history leading to the end. But that end was described in clear, impassioned images. The beauty [of these images] entices, the enormous struggle—in which their King would triumph—delights, and the full assurance with which that final victory will be sealed gives peace.

Even this was not all that was being revealed. It was insufficient [simply] to demonstrate what would soon take place and what that final triumph would one day look like. The things that would happen in the intervening time, too, had to be indicated already then. This explains why repeated attempts have been made to discern in the visions given on Patmos the special events from the entire course of the world's history that have occurred throughout the ages up until the present time. Such attempts can even be seen in the annotations to the authorized Dutch Bible. One is justified in assuming that everything that has happened since Patmos and awaits us until Jesus returns is comprehended in these visions depicting the course of history for us. Where people go wrong, however, is that they attempt to connect every verse to a specific event in history, while the visions actually do no more than give an overview of the characteristics that would emerge continuously, and in an ascending process, from this struggle that will last many centuries. Jesus clearly states that the specific hour when all these things will occur is not known to anyone, not even the angels or the Son of God, for the fact that "the Father has

§ 3

fixed the time or seasons by his own authority" permits no other interpretation of these visions [see Acts 1:7]. The visions form a single unit since they arise from the scroll with the seven seals [Rev 5:1]; and the successive appearance of the seven angels, the seven trumpets, and the seven bowls no doubt announces a historical process. However, the assumption that in this revelation the events to come are foretold century by century and year by year is something entirely different from the assumption that they depict the character that will manifest itself in the course of the events as they continue and progress through the centuries. The faith is not about dates, names, and isolated facts, but about a spiritual struggle that will be on display in the course of history with increasing clarity; and the latter is the very thing presented in the visions from Patmos.

There are five main elements to the character of that struggle.

(1) First, there is a process that grows in intensity. Similar events return again and again, but every time they return, the same struggle manifests itself with increasing ferocity. The outpouring of God's wrath begins with normal phenomena like the rise of wars, dreadful pestilence, and terrible famine. But with every wave of history the destruction becomes more and more drastic. Initially destruction strikes only a part of the world, often a third. But then it continues, until finally nothing endures, nothing is spared, and everything perishes; the destructive powers, at the same time, are more and more frightening in their nature as well.

(2) Alongside this characteristic of an increasingly intense process, another equally constant and clear characteristic is that the struggle is not only waged spiritually, but it also comes with violence; and not only the world of man, but also that of nature—that is, in the firmament and on earth—are taken up in this struggle. The power of the King of the kingdom of God is not restricted to the arena of the spirits, but also attacks nature and the visible world. The sun and the moon, the sea and the rivers, and the bodies of people and animals are all involved. It becomes ever clearer that the struggle is one that encompasses all creatures, the whole earth, and in the end, the entire universe.

(3) In addition to this continually intensifying process and the increasingly universal nature of the struggle, the third characteristic to emerge is that the apostate are continually given the opportunity to repent and worship God. Among fallen believers there is partial success, but the world hardens itself. When our King continues to call the apostate world to repentance through his judgments, they harden themselves in their

evil, blaspheme the God who brings these plagues upon them, and chew on their tongues in pain while they continue to curse the Almighty.

(4) It is just as certain from these visions that the anti-Christian power is constantly given the opportunity to show what it can do. It organizes itself more and more powerfully. It establishes its anti-Christian kingdom over against the kingdom of Christ. Within its kingdom, it also imitates Christ's kingdom. It works through kings and false prophets, and finally impresses its sign upon all its followers, excluding even from normal life and from trade and commerce those who do not have the mark of the beast. In the end, the man of lawlessness will set himself up as God in the temple of God and claim the whole world for himself. Christ will indeed triumph, but first his enemy must be given the opportunity to deploy the fullness of his power against Christ. Only when the anti-Christian power has exerted its greatest force and unfolded all of its unholy potential will the final battle be worthy of Christ; then he will celebrate a suitable victory after destroying that power in its full deployment.

(5) In addition to the above, the fifth characteristic governing all the visions is that whatever is done through either the Antichrist or our King, even though it is played out on earth, still receives its driving force from the spirit world and not from the earth. On the part of Christ, this is because he sits at God's right hand. He does not fight alone, but with the armies of God's angels [at his side]. And whatever our King does has its starting point in what happened in the palace of our God, in the heavens. The entire holy drama is enacted according to what has been written in the scroll with the seven seals, and every new impulse for the execution of the drama comes from the throne of God's majesty. Life does not begin on earth and extend upward to heaven, but the vision begins time and again by placing us in the heavens before the throne of God. It is from the throne of God that every new movement in the enormous drama has its starting point.

On the part of the anti-Christian power, however, things occur in precisely the same way. Here, too, the activity undertaken against Christ does not find its starting point in humanity's sin. The battle that breaks out on earth against the kingdom of Christ is only the outcome and result of the enmity in which Satan hardens himself against the living God. This is indicated vividly by the red dragon (that is, Satan) being cast down from the world of the spirits upon the earth. Even before the red dragon was cast down, much influence proceeded from Satan to the human world, but it is only from that point in time that Satan himself becomes active. He imitates the incarnation of the Word by himself becoming incarnate in a man, and by setting up the blasphemous worship of him—Satan—and of his image, in the place of the worship of God Almighty and of the exact imprint of God's nature [see Heb 1:3]. In this way, the false incarnation stands over against the real incarnation, the false prophet over against the true Prophet, the king anointed by Satan over against the King anointed by God. It is only then that the great argument between Christ and Satan can be decided. It is only in this way that demons and angels, Satan and Christ, death and life, sin and holiness, hell and paradise come to stand over against each other fundamentally and with both of their respective powers fully deployed. Things cannot go any further. This is where history ends. There can be no more history to follow. Time is finished; eternity takes over. And the final outcome is that God will be all and in all, and every unholy power will sink away into the pit of destruction.

THE TWO KINGDOMS

And the devil who had deceived them was thrown into the lake of fire and sulfur where the beast and the false prophet were, and they will be tormented day and night forever and ever.

REVELATION 20:10

Nothing has done more damage to the church's confession of Jesus' kingship than the marked increase in the indifference toward the spirit world, whether toward angels or of demons. It is not as if the believing congregation would go along in denying that such a spirit world exists. This would be impossible, as long as they still persevere in their belief in Holy Scripture. Scripture teaches the existence of a spirit world and its influence on our world's life so clearly and extensively that the acknowledgement of a spirit world's existence had to remain. Even if the recognition came to expression only in the petition of the Lord's Prayer that God's will be done on earth as it is in heaven, together with the petition: "Lead us not into temptation, but deliver us from the Evil One," those who still pray the Lord's Prayer as the most sacred prayer by that very fact automatically confess their belief in the existence of good angels as well as demons.

§ 1

But this purely outward confession is powerless unless it is paired with the acknowledgement that these spirits exercise an influence on our own destiny and soul. It is especially here, however, that many fall short.

423

Faithful believers, much more than many of them imagine, are also under the sway of public opinion and generally accepted notions. People often think that they take their instruction from Scripture alone, but public opinion also has an incredibly marked, albeit imperceptible, influence on believers' interpretation of that Scripture. In the days of Luther and Calvin there still was a shared sense that Satan exists, and everyone read and understood Scripture in such a way that left room for Satan's influence on the destiny of the world and on the human heart.

After belief in [the existence of] spirits had disappeared entirely from public opinion, especially in the eighteenth century, however, it began to weaken in believing circles as well. At present, people still accept the existence and influence of the spirit world when they read Scripture, but once they close the Bible they no longer take any account of it in their lives. Even in the preaching of decidedly believing pastors, the spirit world is only seldom given conscious attention. The spirit world ceased to be a fixed element in education. One still hears of it in connection with the [story of the] angel choirs [see Luke 2:13-14], as well as with the last petition in the Lord's Prayer. But, for the rest, neither the angel world nor the demon world is ever referred to except as a token. Even in regard to spiritual events, virtually no attention is devoted any longer to the demonic powers. It is as if human beings do it all, accomplish everything, and as if no created powers are at work in history aside from them. It is remarkable that, during this same time period, the clear understanding of Jesus' kingship as well as the clear understanding of the power of the spirit world, while not completely worn away in the minds of the congregation, did at least become half illegible. What has also happened during this time is that the last book of Holy Scripture, in which both Christ's kingship and the demonic world are most clearly presented, is left unread by all too large a segment of the congregation. Even where believers do still read through it chapter by chapter, it has ceased as a book to occupy an indispensable place in their thought.

There are many reasons, therefore, to give conscious attention to the relationship between Christ's kingship and the influence of the spirit world. What was visible of Jesus' kingship while he lived on earth remains under a veil. The rule of our King during these centuries of quiet process can only be seen through the eyes of faith. And the full majesty of Christ's kingship will radiate throughout heaven and earth only when the last battle has been fought; when the eternal victory is guaranteed; and when, once the final victory has come, our King will have subjected the last enemy to his feet on the new earth and under a new heaven.

Scripture expresses this by juxtaposing one kingdom with another kingdom. Jesus spoke emphatically of Satan's kingdom when he asked: "If Satan casts out Satan, how will his kingdom stand?" [see Matt 12:26]. Satan is not alone and does not stand on his own. Satan has a power beneath him at his disposal. As long as that power remains united and in subjection to him, it constitutes a kingdom; if one part of it turns against another, that kingdom cannot remain standing. §2

That is why this kingdom is called a power. The grace of God consists in this, that "he has delivered us from the power of darkness and transferred us to the kingdom of his beloved Son" [see Col 1:13]. These words are often understood to mean that we have been delivered from the hand of Satan, from his greater power. That cannot be what this verse means, however. "Transferred" means being taken from one domain and placed in another. The "power of darkness" is thus the terrain of Satan's kingdom, and it is from this domain that those who are saved are taken away, transferred, relocated, and translated to the domain of the kingdom of Christ (or kingdom of heaven).

In this verse, the essence of Satan's kingdom is located in darkness, as the opposite of the light, which is the life principle of Christ's kingdom. In this kingdom of darkness, the prince Beelzebul has a powerful host at his disposal that fights for him as his army in order to defend his kingdom, a host that consists entirely of fallen angels, demons, and evil spirits. Because the prince of this kingdom of darkness has extended his power over the entire earth, he has manifested himself as the "ruler of this world," a title that Jesus himself applies to him. The prince of darkness said to Jesus that all the earth's kingdoms were in his power, and that he could give them to whomever he pleased [see Matt 4:8–9]. *Ruler of this world* is not a title he has by virtue of being a prince of his own kingdom, but a title that he won for himself when he, as the prince of the kingdom of darkness, took the earth for himself as a colony. The earth initially did not belong to his kingdom but to the kingdom of God, and it is from God that he wrested it. He tore it away from the kingdom of God and annexed it to his kingdom. Scripture even depicts the mighty battle between God and Satan as involving nothing else than the possession of the earth. Through the seduction and temptation in paradise, Satan caused humanity to succumb, broke its power, and tore the power over this earth away from the human race, [who were] the governors God had appointed. This situation will continue until God sends his Son to beat back Satan's dominion on this earth, and to establish God's dominion once more—this time forever!—thereby to regain it for the sake of the kingdom of God.

The word *kingdom* may not be understood figuratively or symbolically for either Christ or Satan. In respect to both of them, the word is meant in its proper sense. Both kingdoms are organized powers. They both are controlled, managed, and guided according to a set plan. Satan sets himself slyly and cunningly against the counsel of God. It goes without saying that Satan remains a creature in terms of his strength and power, although among all creatures the highest power imaginable has been granted to him. We know of no spirit who was more richly endowed before his fall and more magnificently equipped than this created spirit, and it is this superiority of the gifts with which he was endowed that caused him to think so foolishly that he could compare himself with God. By the very nature of the case, that folly implied that he would have to try to obtain and conquer for himself whatever he could from all that has been created. He had no terrain, life sphere, or region of power of his own. He was the highest creature, but he always remained a created being; and as such, he was created for no other purpose than to serve God and to bring glory to his majesty.

Because he was unfaithful in this service, he deprived and robbed himself of God; he similarly stole and robbed of the glory of God whatever he took with him from the spirit world as well. What he took with him was already organized, just like everything else that exists in God's creation is created in organic coherence. The lower spirits whom he seduced immediately came under his power, in a mutual relationship with him. His superiority soon gave him the power to exercise total dominion over all lower evil spirits and to make them subservient to him. The demons do not each fight on their own in some kind of guerilla warfare, but they are incorporated in his army and fight their battle together. They direct all their power and potency to the increase of Satan's honor over against the honor of the God against whom they are fighting. Satan managed to capture our human race for this unholy service as well. And although common grace, as well as salvation—which began as early as paradise—have continually prevented Satan from becoming the complete master over this earth, he still gathered the life of this world under his banner, subjected the pagan nations to the dominion of his spirit, managed to penetrate the rule of earthly kings, and thus became the ruler of this world.

Satan's kingdom therefore consists of two parts: his kingdom proper consisted in the fallen spirit world, while the earth formed a colony that he had taken. In the kingdom of the earth, he had caused his power to penetrate further and further. People often imagine the earth as something neutral and think that the battle between Satan and God will be played out exclusively in people's hearts. If this were true, the earth would remain the same before the fall, after the fall, and after the work of redemption. The stage on which the drama was to take place, so to speak, would have remained one and the same; and the only difference would have been that humanity was alienated first from paradise, then alienated itself spiritually from God, and now, due to Christ's coming, is being partially won back for God.

However, this is not the teaching of Scripture. In fact, many suspect that before man was created, the break Satan caused in the spirit world when he abandoned God already had shaken the entire creation and thus also the earth; and they suggest that this is the explanation for the words in Genesis 1:2 that the earth was "without form and void." According to this view, paradise would simply have been an oasis in a vast wilderness, and humanity would have been called into existence in that paradise. Whether this interpretation is accurate or not, it is in any case certain that the fall was soon followed by the curse, a curse that caused paradise to disappear and impaired the entire kingdom of the earth in its mode of existence so that it began to bring forth thorns and thistles [see Gen 3:18]. And death, appalling death, made its entry into the world.[1] Not only is man's spirit tempted to commit apostasy, but his body, which is organically related to his spirit, also loses the higher radiance of its life. Sickness and disease arise, as do all kinds of suffering and misery—and these are in no way limited to our soul alone, but without a doubt extend to our physical existence and to society as it develops outside of us. And even beyond humanity, the elemental forces of nature are unleashed and desolation is wreaked over the earth's entire surface.

Of course, we can disregard all that has invaded the countries in Europe from the Germanic religions, most famously in the so-called witch trials. These things have nothing to do with Scripture. Similarly, all that

§ 3

---

1. See CG 1.35.1.

crept in from Persian dualism must be left entirely out of the discussion here. In Scripture, Satan and his henchmen are perpetually seen as beings created by God himself, who exist through [God's] power alone and will in the end be subjected to his power once more.

Nevertheless, it remains within the essence of the spirit's nature to exercise power and influence also over visible things, on visible nature, on what lies before one's eyes. The spirit of a person cannot be separated from the person's physical existence, and a person's physical existence can likewise not be separated from the rest of nature. Everything is related. An organic connection exists between all things. That is why Satan's power, once it has broken out in this world, gradually impairs all of creation. Today natural science and psychology teach us more and more clearly that the human spirit is related to the human body, and further that an organic relationship exists between all of nature's kingdoms—even between the organic kingdoms of nature and the material world, to the deepest depths of the earth and the tiniest elements of nature. This was expressed of old in the fact that humanity's fall in the spirit was followed by the curse that came upon this entire earth in all of nature's kingdoms. Therefore, the kingdom of Satan extends everywhere and attempts more and more to encompass everything.

The model for the kingdom of Satan is and remains the kingdom of God. Just as God exercises dominion over spirits and people, exercises dominion over spirit and matter, and encompasses all of creation, so Satan wants to establish his kingdom against God. Satan wants to destroy God's power; and once God's power has been completely broken, Satan's ultimate goal is to set himself up in God's place, to become and to be and to remain what God himself is—that is, the Commander over all things, the King over all creation, the Lord over all creatures. What gives this battle such majestic proportions is that God Almighty did not crush Satan with his superior power once Satan had risen up in flagrant rebellion against him; but he gave Satan room and even allowed him to develop his power enormously, in order to enter the principal battle with him only later, and in that principal battle finally to defeat him and destroy him. Satan is and remains a spirit, and he must for that reason be conquered spiritually. He must be crushed with violence and superior power not immediately, but only when he can emerge with full armor, be spiritually attacked in the human heart, and in this way be destroyed spiritually. Only in this way can the spiritual supremacy of the light over the darkness be made evident—by the victory of the truth over the lie and the triumph of life over death. It is not just that Satan must be conquered, but in that victory over Satan, the exalted glory of God's righteousness must radiate at one and the same time.

In this terrifying struggle of the ages, Satan constantly tries to remain behind the scenes. When thieves break in, they want to go unnoticed. Assassins hide themselves until the very last moment. Robbers look out over the road from a place where they can remain unseen. So too, Satan's objective is to hide himself, to cloak himself, to veil himself, and to perform his work while in hiding. He is and remains the prince of darkness, whose strength resides in that darkness. Satan never laughs more than when he sees how the wise men of this world insist that Satan and a demon kingdom do not exist, and when even among believers those who do take account of his devilish schemes represent no more than an exception. He loves it when people forget him, when no one speaks about him, when people keep quiet about his work so that no one is on the lookout for his ruses and traps. There is no better time for Satan than when people in general claim that everything that was at one time confessed about devils and demons, even in Scripture, rests on pure fantasy. It is then that he can work without interruption, eventually to show himself only when his goal has already been attained.

§ 4

But this is the very reason why the Prince of Light must rise up in action against this prince of darkness. A King must appear to attack the ruler of this world and then to destroy his kingdom. Humanity on its own is not equipped for this battle. Whatever enters the battle with the prince of darkness with his organized demonic power must itself be an organized power as well.

In order to be freed, humanity must itself also be able to function under a King; and since the spirit of Satan is much more powerful than the human spirit, this King must not only be man, but as the Son of Man he must at the same time bear the divine perfection of power. Only that kind of a King is powerful enough and able not only to beat Satan back for himself personally, but also to cause the very foundations of his kingdom to shake and to pry them loose. Whoever is going to rise up in action against Satan must be able to descend as low as him and to aim as high as him. In order to wrest the colony (that is, this earth) from the grasp of Satan, Satan's power must be struck a blow at the very foundations of its own spiritual kingdom. Not only must his power among people on earth be broken, but he must also be taken down from the throne he has erected in his world of spirits. God's Hero must both drive the ruler of this world away and must become King over all the kings of the earth himself; he must be the Lord and Head over the angels so as to fight the last battle in the world of the spirits as well.

And it is in this context that Christ's kingship first appears in its full reality. He does not appear as a King who will hover high above humanity and subject them to himself through coercion. On the contrary, he becomes one of us—a human being just as we are. He organically incorporates all the elect into his mystical body, and he rules over them by ruling in them and making them spiritually free. The humanity that has been transferred by him forms one power—a whole, an organic unity together with him—and he is a King unlike our earthly kings, but the kind of King who exercises complete authority in all. Whatever he as King incorporates is forever wrested away from Satan's power. A sacred oasis of heavenly life thus begins to form in the midst of that unholy life. From this holy focal point, Christ as our King expands his power and influence further and further throughout the earth, while wrestling in the spirit world along with his holy angels, in order to stifle Satan's influence and work on earth.

But just as Christ was led by the Spirit into the wilderness at the beginning of his ministry in order to attack Satan personally, so the end cannot come until he has once more personally engaged the struggle with the prince of demons. Satan is indeed released, agitated, and challenged to exalt himself in his full power and with his full armor against the kingdom of Christ one final time, and then the last duel will come. On the one side stands Satan, who thinks that he has once more made himself the master of the world in the Antichrist and in his false prophet; and over against him stands the King on a white horse, with the armies of heaven surrounding him, who judges and makes war in righteousness, clothed in a robe dipped in blood, and the name by which he is called is the Word of God [see Rev 19:11-14]. And this King will slay Satan and his demons with the breath of his mouth, and the hallelujahs will be lifted up in all the heavens: "Hallelujah! For the Lord our God the Almighty reigns" [Rev 19:6]. The King has power over people, power over spirits, power over soul and body, power over all of nature's forces and elements. The poison of apostasy and sin, of lies and darkness, of misery and death, is undone even to the remotest hidden corners. It is not as if Satan never existed. Instead, a glory will now break out that is much greater than the glory that once radiated in paradise. There will be a new earth under a new heaven, and the surprising outcome will be that Satan as the prince of darkness will actually not have accomplished anything except a greater manifestation of God's glory, which would never have reached these heights had Satan not rebelled. This is something that can be brought about only by the appearance of our King. Kingdom against kingdom, Prince against prince, Ruler against ruler, King against king! And this is why the radiance of Jesus' kingship can only wane in your faith whenever belief in the rebellion and resistance of the prince of darkness loses for you the clarity that God sealed unto you in his Word.

History places the seal upon this. Those heroes of faith who most deeply experienced in their souls that their battle was not against flesh and blood, not against human beings, but "against the spiritual forces of evil in the heavenly places" [Eph 6:12]—were they not the very same people who felt the greatest need for the kingship of Christ, and who magnified Christ's kingship with highest praise? There is a cloud of witnesses, from the man of Tarsus to the man of Worms, who cried out: "Here I stand, I can do no other. May God help me!"[2]

---

2. This is traditionally identified as the concluding confession of Martin Luther in his testimony before Charles V at the Imperial Diet of Worms in 1521.

III.23

MYSTICAL AND INSTRUMENTAL

Who will transform our lowly body to be like his glorious body, by the authority that enables him even to subject all things to himself.

PHILIPPIANS 3:21

§ 1   We may not pass over in complete silence the way in which we should think about how Jesus exercises his kingly authority. The apostle testifies to us that he has "the power that enables him even to subject all things to himself" [Phil 3:21]. In Revelation, Christ himself speaks about the sword of his mouth [see (Rev 2:16)]. Of Christ it is said that he will kill the man of lawlessness "with the breath of his mouth" [2 Thess 2:8]. He is likewise depicted for us with a sharp sickle in his hand to swing across the harvest of the earth [see Rev 14:14, 16]. On Patmos a song of praise is sung that "the Lamb is worthy to receive power" [see (Rev 5:12)], and that "the power of Christ has come" [see (Rev 12:10]. The Letter to the Hebrews tells us that Christ "upholds the universe by the word of his power" [Heb 1:3]. The apostle's fervent prayer is that the power of Christ may dwell in him [2 Cor 12:9]; and when he delivers a man to destruction, he does so "with the power of our Lord Jesus" (1 Cor 5:4). Already during his sojourn on earth, we repeatedly read that power went out from him (Luke 8:46), and that he cast out unclean spirits with power and authority (Luke 9:1). When he departed from the earth, he left us with the following words of comfort: "All authority in heaven and on earth has been given to me" [Matt 28:18].

This series of quotations indeed confirms the conviction that Christ's authority is extensive enough for him to carry out his office as King; but a general testimony such as this one does not satisfy us, so that it is worth our while to investigate in somewhat greater detail the way in which Christ exercises his authority. With this we do not mean to claim that we could ever completely dissect the exercise of his authority and understand it fully. Even when it comes to physical power, ultimately something inexplicable always remains that we just have to accept. And especially in all spiritual power there is always at bottom a kind of mystery that defies all further explanation. The power of love, the power of faith, and the power of a hero's courage fascinate us, even though we cannot fathom these; so how could we ever be able to investigate the very roots of the miraculous power that was and is at work in Christ? But even if we already know at the very outset that the mystery confronting us cannot be fully solved, this limitation to our knowledge need not hinder us from trying to gain a general understanding of the way in which Christ exercises his power as our King.

It goes without saying that one must draw a distinction between the work that Jesus himself does directly, and the work that he brings about through the servants and subjects he has ordained. Furthermore, when it comes to those servants, we should think not only of people but also of angels. Earthly kings use an entire army of officials to administer their rule, and they have armed forces at their disposal. Through those officials they have their orders delivered to the parties concerned, and they enforce obedience to these orders through a show of force. In the case of Christ's kingship, up to a certain point things are similar in that he too, by virtue of his kingly majesty, gave some to be apostles, others to be evangelists, to be overseers, to be shepherds and teachers, in order to tend his flock. The duty given to these servants was not only to preach the gospel and to convey the command to believers, but they also were clothed with a certain authority. With this authority they exercise discipline, and by means of that discipline a certain spiritual dominion is maintained here on earth. These servants of the Word, all these overseers and deacons from all churches scattered throughout the whole world, form an innumerable army of thousands and even tens of thousands of office-bearers who stand in service to Christ in his kingly regiment, and who indeed exercise a part of that rule in the name of Jesus insofar as they are faithful to him.

Nevertheless, this multitude of human servants is still small compared to the immense host of angels who always stand at his service in the spirit world. The angels are servants who are always faithful to him and stand ready to carry out the commands of his mouth, are not bound by any earthly obstacles, and are sent again and again "to serve for the sake of those who are to inherit salvation" [Heb 1:14]. You would therefore make a mistake if you imagine our King to be completely isolated at God's right hand. On the contrary, no earthly emperor or king, with the full array of his officials and with his armed forces fully deployed, can even come close to the innumerable servants, soldiers, and subjects who stand under our King.

Therefore, even if we were to perceive nothing else of the miraculous power Jesus himself exercised, it would still be hard for us to overestimate his dominion. Through the course of the centuries, his disciples increased from twelve, to thousands, and even tens of thousands; and the twelve legions of angels about which he spoke shortly before his death have by now expanded to become the host of heaven. His position is in no way one of isolation, but even in the higher spheres he is surrounded by his mighty angels [see 2 Thess 1:7].

§ 2 The exercise of this authority by Jesus' servants on earth and by his mighty angels is nevertheless deserving of further explanation. After all, the regular channels that earthly kings have available to them in their civil servants are absent. The highest advisers of an earthly king appear to him in person in order to listen to his wishes, to give counsel, and to deliberate with him. Written orders are then prepared, and a vast system of clerks and messengers is in place to make the king's will and orders known to his subjects via couriers, mail, telegraph, and the printed press. It further needs to be noted that earthly kings nominate their public servants and appoint their army chiefs with written orders, and that a hierarchical relationship exists among them whereby authority moves from one person to another.

None of these elements can be found with King Jesus, however. He is not on earth, but sits enthroned in heaven. And none of his servants has seen the King, has ever heard his voice, or has ever received a personal, daily order from him. The church on earth does, of course, have a certain organization through which his servants are appointed and through which oversight and discipline are exercised in it, but in these things there is no personal, visible contact with the King. He remains in heaven; and the church's entire organization on earth, among people, runs on its own. This is why abuse has so often crept in, and why that organization so often has been totally corrupted. As a result, his servants on earth frequently have not only faded away into inactivity, but in the end formed themselves into a group that opposed the King, persecuted his faithful servants, and oppressed them.

The organization of this King's servants on earth, compared with the organization of a government available to an earthly king, seems highly flawed. There is no personal contact, no direct ad hoc orders are given, no direct and personal appointments are made, and the possibility even exists that this organization on earth will in fact turn against what was its very goal. Our King did leave his Word with his church and demanded that it live according to that Word and draw its power from that Word. However, that Word is no Qur'an. The Word is a historical product. It arose in Israel over the course of the centuries, and therefore it has a historical and Eastern character. It does not contain a fixed set of laws and decisions; it recounts history, recounts God's powerful acts, and contains the prophets' pronouncements and testimonies—yet without them being in such a ready form that they could be considered to form a law book in which one only has to turn to the appropriate article to meet every situation. As great as the authority of the Word may be, in character it differs completely from the law book of an earthly sovereign; it exercises its influence in an entirely different manner. It works upon the [human] spirit to conform them to Jesus' will—but then in a way that differs entirely from the way this is achieved with earthly laws or decisions.

One consequence of this different character is that opinions can differ widely regarding the meaning and interpretation of this Word; that both academic as well as spiritual study is required to understand the Word and to apply it to life; and that with the Word, a lofty, spiritual guidance is demanded that cannot come from people, but only from the King himself.

Even if we limit ourselves to the usual organization of the church on earth and to the rule she exercises in Jesus' name, we cannot but acknowledge an invisible involvement on the part of the King himself that has a fully mystical character and cannot be explained on the basis of earthly institutions. A mystical intervention on the part of our King is just as indispensable for the angels. The King must know his angel forces and must know which angel is suited to which task. He has to communicate his orders to all his angels so that they know their task, and the King himself must so protect and lead his angels that they carry out his high command according to his will. Just this part of the King's domain, as it is administered by the office-bearers or servants chosen from among angels and people, consequently requires the King to have what it takes to know down to the finest details what happens on earth and to be able to ordain, guide, and regulate all things in such a way that his will is done, that his command is carried out, and that his kingly authority is maintained.

§ 3   In addition to the authority that King Jesus exercises by means of his subjects, officials, and angels, the mystical glow of our King's *direct* operation on the entire course of our human life is even greater. Our King is not a passive King who, seated at the right hand of the Father, merely watches and waits to see what will become of the service of his followers; but he really does exercise dominion, he does have an effect on what happens in this world, and he exercises his kingly dominion personally.

Many fail to see this. They think that Jesus ascended into heaven and now dwells in the Father's house where he is in communion with the angels and saints, but has no direct influence on the things that happen here below. As they see it, Jesus instituted his church, left us his Word, gave us the sacraments as a gift, and further applies the fruit of his sacrifice before the Father; but otherwise he waits to see what will happen on earth, looks on while these events occur, passively tolerates what happens, and so awaits the end of all things when he will one more time intervene in the course of events.

Others do assume a strong communion between Jesus and the souls whom he has redeemed and who themselves enjoy that communion with their Savior, but this occurs entirely apart from his kingly authority and even apart from his kingly office. What they have in mind is rather the High Priest of their confession, who now lives to pray for them and prepares a place for them in the Father's house. But for this second group, too, Jesus as King is no more than a *roi fainéant*—one who is King in name only, that is, who awaits what will occur without actually having a dominion to exercise on earth.

There are still others who do not even admit this mystical communion, and who imagine that Jesus left behind nothing more than the memory of his appearance on earth; that the impression made by his life, suffering, and death continues; that his example still wins and draws people to him;

and that the Word he left us does make itself the master over our hearts as a picture of a holy ideal. But for the rest, they do not believe that Jesus, with premeditation and full consciousness, exercises any direct influence on earth. As far as they are concerned, kingship may possibly await Jesus at his return, but that he is King during the centuries between his ascension and his return on the clouds of heaven is for them out of the question. Jesus, so they say, does possess the title of "King" as an honorific title, and is even King over the angels and saints in heaven, but not over human life on earth. We may already have some communion with Jesus' Spirit through his Word, in the example he left for us, and through the memory of his sojourn on earth; and one day an entirely new form of communion with Jesus will be unfolded for us in the Father's house when we shall see him as he is. But, so it is argued, while we live here on earth, we have nothing but the history and the ideal, and all personal contact with Jesus is a matter of the imagination and fiction. This position in the end destroys Jesus' kingship in a practical sense, or at the very least renders it inactive; and it makes Jesus' position equal to that of all those saints now departed who have been taken up into glory.

This entire perspective runs counter to what Scripture reveals to us. You have only to open your Bible to Jesus' letters to the congregations in Asia Minor in the second and third chapters of Revelation to sense the contrast. In these letters, Jesus himself addresses these churches in a way that makes it clear that he knows even the smallest details about them; judges what they do and do not do down to the small and sundry affairs; holds their destiny in his hands; and so, knowing their future, already judges them with kingly authority, pronounces punishments and blessings over them, threatens them or enriches them with promises, and holds their future in his hand. There is simply no way that Jesus sits back passively at any point in time. Jesus is present in the congregation, Jesus knows her, Jesus judges her past and present situation, and even knows the different heresies that have arisen in her. And he tells the church that if she does not repent, he will intervene, exercise his authority against her, and finally remove her lampstand from her.

This is in every respect the very same picture that the apostles paint in their letters. Jesus is the King; Jesus is the Lord who strengthens whomever needs to be strengthened in order to do his will. As King, Jesus has dominion over every person, over every servant, in every corner of life. When he acts, it is always the Lord, the King, who stands in the foreground and causes both individual people and his church to experience his work and operation. Indeed, does not Jesus himself forestall every notion that construes his kingship as something existing only in name and title, when he introduced his command to baptize the nations with the solemn declaration that all authority in heaven and on earth had been given to him? Note carefully that he says not only *in heaven*, but also *on earth*. His majesty would not only radiate among the saints in heaven, but would also be manifested on earth. As his apostles said after they performed their first miraculous healing, not they themselves but Jesus had brought healing [see Acts 3:16].

Jesus therefore has the power to draw near to the soul, to influence human spirits, to guide them, to direct them, and to steer them according to his will. All distance is absent here. As our Catechism says: "According to His human nature He is now not on earth, but according to His Godhead, majesty, grace, and Spirit, He is at no time absent from us."[1] There is no such thing as distance in the spiritual. On a spiritual level, earth and heaven together form a single spiritual unity. There is nothing that separates us from our King, or our King from us. He not only knows that a church exists on earth, but within that church he also knows each and every person who belongs to him. With divine compassion, he shares in their sufferings and struggles. Their life is hidden in him. And every morning and every evening his guiding power comes upon their souls from on high.

Moreover, Jesus' kingly rule does not act only upon individuals, but it likewise encompasses the course, the lot, and the path of an entire congregation and even of the entire church as it exists on earth. And since the lot of his church on earth continually depends on and is governed by the destiny of the nations and peoples, his influence and activity likewise extends to the history and destiny of the nations. The latter is not limited to—and does not even primarily apply to—the wars that nations fight and the changes that [their borders] undergo; but it extends also to their inner degeneration, development, and transformation. A nation's lot is governed by the spirits that have dominion in that nation, in its religious, moral, scientific, artistic, and social fields. The struggle of these spirits leads to the nation's disposition, its aspirations, and its spiritual decline or rise; these are inextricably tied to the disposition of those spirits that have dominion in the church of that particular land.

---

1. Heidelberg Catechism, Lord's Day 17, A 47, *RC* 2:780.

The church's lot is therefore tied closely to the development that the spirits undergo in each nation. If Jesus is to rule his church as King, he also has to exercise dominion over the whole spiritual development that every nation undergoes. The one cannot be separated from the other, and those who deny Jesus' kingly authority over the peoples and nations by that very fact deny his kingly authority over the church. For that reason, we must hold unconditionally to what we confess in our Catechism: "Christ ascended into heaven for this end, that He might there appear as the Head of His Church, by whom the Father governs all things."[2]

Our King therefore exercises a ruling, steering, and guiding authority not only on individual believers, but on the entire life of the world, on people and circumstances, on the course of history and events, on the development of nature, and on the spirits that acquire authority among the nations. You cannot reach this point if you limit yourself to the lasting effects of Jesus' sojourn on earth, or with the memory of his life and death. Furthermore, the mystical communion between believers and their Savior is the delight of their soul, but it still is not his kingly rule. In order for us to grasp this kingly dominion as a necessary truth governing the world's entire destiny, Jesus as he is seated at the Father's right hand must have at his disposal an authority, a power, an influence, an impact that cannot be obstructed by anything. [It must be one] that has no boundaries and that is at work in everything—in order to subject all things to him, to make them accessible to him, to unlock them for him, and to place them under his kingly authority. Those who honor in our King nothing other than the capacities implanted in human nature when the first man was created, will not be able to find that power, authority, ability in him, even if they understand those capacities of our human nature in their most developed state. That is why the apostles, whenever they illustrate this kingly regiment to us, always go back to the divinity of the Mediator, of whom we confess that "he is before all things, and in him all things hold together" [Col 1:17].

---

2. Heidelberg Catechism, Lord's Day 19, A 50, RC 2:780.

THE ÜBERMENSCH

Therefore God has highly exalted him and bestowed on him the name that is above every name.

PHILIPPIANS 2:9

§ 1   Christ's kingly authority goes forth from a specific place. As our Mediator, the Son of God cannot be imagined separately from his human nature. It was in the body that he arose from the dead, and it was in the body that he ascended into heaven. He did not put off that body at his ascension or even thereafter. He lives in that body. He came to earth in that body. He will return to judge in that body. A body must be somewhere; it is bound to a certain place. And as it was manifested to us, so too the body of Jesus, and therefore our Mediator in that body, appears to cause his actions to proceed from a specific point in the universe.

With this we do not mean to deny that even created spirits, including human souls, occupy some kind of place somewhere. But whenever we speak of spirits, there are countless other things that can easily confuse us. This is why we specifically emphasized Jesus' existence in his body, because it alone suffices to confirm to everyone that Jesus indeed exists in a place. Where that holy residence might be is something that we will find difficult to describe in greater detail. That our King is "seated on the throne, at the right hand of the Father" [see Rev 8:1] is no further indication as to where he now dwells. After all, the expression *right hand* is metaphorical. God is spirit—he has no body, and he therefore has no right hand. This metaphorical expression depicts the majesty and ability of the Lord of lords, but it does not specifically indicate a place to which we can direct our eye or on which we can rest our searching gaze. The same holds true for the expression "my Father's house." Similarly, the indication that our King is enthroned in heaven does not give us a clear and fixed perspective, either. Our thoughts are directed upward to what is above, and we continue to use this same expression even though we know that someone on the other side of the globe also points upward—although, from our perspective, the heavens to which that person points in fact lie below us. This should not make us feel uncertain as long as we remember that we have no language available for describing the spiritual except for what we apply in a figurative sense by way of images derived from the material world.

We know virtually nothing about the distance separating the heavens of God's glory from the earth, and there is no basis for the assumption that the heavens of God's glory (also called the third heaven) lie far above the last fixed star. In fact, to think in that way is rather counterintuitive. Those outermost stars are so immeasurably far from us that even their light rays need thousands of years to reach us. Thus when the psalmist sings: "To you, O LORD, I lift up my soul" [Psa 25:1], this cannot mean that our soul in its outpouring bridges that immeasurable distance in order to find God. God's omnipresence is not sufficient for us at this point. This is why we must think of a single focal point for God's majesty, worship him as our Father in heaven, and in the *sursum corda* (that is, lift up your hearts above) imagine God to be in his majestic palace.

But it is impossible for us to go further than this. Where, in which sphere, in which direction the heavens of God's glory may exist, how far away they are from the earth, and any other attempt at a more specific local definition escapes us entirely. Nor can we say anything definite about the way in which the transition from this world to the glorious heavens occurs. We do not know how Christ ascended; nor do we know how the soul of someone who has died in Christ reaches the Father's house; nor do we know the path taken by our prayers when they leave our lips and rise up to the Exalted One. All these things escape us because they involve an entirely different order of affairs concerning which we have no knowledge or conception. These are mysteries that the future alone will unveil to us. It is therefore entirely impossible for us to determine anything more about where King Jesus resides, about the place in which he is now found, about the sphere surrounding him, or about his current physical existence. We do know that he is surrounded by his holy angels and that the saints enjoy his close presence, but both the angels and the saints have a purely spiritual existence, and therefore tell us nothing whatsoever about the visible and material existence of our Savior and King.

The only thing Scripture allows us to conclude is that our King's material existence is no longer the same as his former material existence on earth. After all, the apostle testifies that "flesh and blood cannot inherit the imperishable" [see 1 Cor 15:50]. The body is and remains the same, but it exists in a totally different form. His existence is a physical existence in a glorified form. Jesus' appearance to Paul on the road to Damascus and to John on the island of Patmos already show us that, although the body's basic character remains the same, the appearance of the earthly body is very different from the manifestation of the heavenly body.

§ 2   There are two things that must be noted in this regard. First is the distinction between the physical in its seed and in its consummation, and second is the distinction between what the human body derives from its earthly and from its heavenly sphere of life. We can already see this first distinction between the physical in its initial state and its full development in people when we compare a primitive African cannibal to noble Solomon as he is seated on his throne.[1] Both are human, but in their appearance they are most different and diverse. If this is already true of their outward appearance, it applies all the more to the knowledge, work, and power of a person in his initial and lowest development compared to someone who is high on the developmental scale.

For the purposes of this chapter, we will leave Adam's paradise situation out of the discussion. Humanity now lives in a condition of humiliation; and accordingly, what Christ took on from Mary was not the humanity of paradise but the flesh and blood of children, that is, of our humiliated body. If you compare the knowledge, work, and power of that state of humiliation in a primitive tribe that is still at the lowest level of development with the knowledge, work, and power at our disposal in a Christianized Europe and America, you will immediately sense that a deep gulf separates someone whose capacities have not been developed and remain hidden, from someone in whom the capacities that were once

---

1. For more on Kuyper's problematic judgments based on racial and ethnic stereotypes, see the volume editors' introduction to *CG*, as well as *CG* 1.12.10n4 and 1.41.1n3.

hidden have now been revealed. If you compare humanity's situation four thousand years ago with the current situation, you will see an immeasurable advance in human power.

This advance in no way means, however, that this development has already run its course. In fact, the past century documents how remarkably human power and capabilities have increased over the course of time. We can therefore only imagine how much more powerful the development will be when another two or three centuries have passed, and how remarkable that development will be by the time it has reached its endpoint. When you think of the human existence of our King Jesus as he is in heaven, it speaks for itself that you have to imagine human development to have run its full course in him, and that even the higher development of the power that has been reached on earth gives us no more than a faint idea of the development of the human power with which Christ is enthroned in the kingdom of glory. Therefore we may not think of our King as one of our own, or measure his knowledge, work, and power according to what is at our disposal; but we must imagine his human existence in its perfection, in the complete flourishing of all the gifts and powers that reside as nascent spores in our human nature.

The truth of this becomes even more evident when you remove the humiliation from the picture. Had humanity's paradise situation been able to unfold and flourish without interruption, our being human would have displayed very different miracles than it has thus far. Yet these are the very miracles that you have to imagine in the glorified Christ. Not only does Christ live in the highest degree of development that humanity will reach on earth at the end of the age, but his existence is also more glorious. Everything that God had planted as a seed in Adam at creation, and which would have flourished in us if sin had not intervened, came to its full and glorious flourishing in Christ. Nothing more lies hidden within him. In his glory, flourishing is consummated. For that reason, we cannot even begin to imagine what knowledge, work, and power are at the disposal of Christ as our King according to his human nature. In Adam we see a power over nature that we have lost. Even in our current humiliated condition, our knowledge has gradually expanded incredibly, our authority over nature has increased miraculously, and the distance that once divided people has almost been undone entirely with telegraphs, telephones, and wireless communications; thus we cannot imagine the glorified human existence of our King to be anything other than a triumph over nearly everything that still hampers and limits us in our daily life. We read time and again that already when Jesus appeared on earth, a power went forth from him to triumph over nature; while his miracles testify to how his position before nature is entirely different from our own. If only we imagine what this would look like in its perfected state, we should understand that we may not think Christ's human existence to be anything less than something that far surpasses us in terms of knowledge, work, and power.

§ 3   The second distinction is the radical difference between what we have by virtue of our earthly sphere, and what is at the disposal of our King in the much higher sphere he has entered. More than people seem to be aware, our life is governed by our surroundings, by nature around us, by the atmosphere in which we live, by the influence exercised upon us by the earth that we inhabit. However, you need only compare the dismal existence of an Eskimo in the polar regions, or the life of an African under the scorching heat of the tropics, with the life of a European in a moderate climate in order to understand the enormous influence that the region where we live exerts upon us both physically and spiritually. If the gap between different regions on the earth alone is already that wide, how much greater should the difference be if you were to compare a person living on this earth with a human existence in entirely different spheres of the universe?

The situation in the heavens is of an entirely different nature than it is here on earth. The two can hardly be compared with each other. Although there is a material nature even in the heavenly spheres, it must have an entirely different and much more ethereal character. If there is air, the air must be totally different, much more refined. A totally different kind of light must shine there. The body is no longer maintained through food there, for as the apostle says, the stomach will be destroyed [see 1 Cor 6:13]. There will be no giving or taking in marriage. Distance will be no more. It is not the paradise of earth, but a heavenly paradise. It shines in all its splendor and glory, and even the most beautiful thing produced on earth will fade into insignificance compared with the majesty and radiance of life in the heavenly spheres. Nevertheless, humanity as it was created is also directed to that glory. Jesus did not exchange his body for another, but his one and the same physical existence has passed from what it had become on earth to what it could become in the higher spheres. And this not in part, but the whole.

A caterpillar's metamorphosis into a butterfly can give us some idea as to what that transition looks like; although this picture of our transformation from an earthly to a heavenly existence will not yet be complete, because both caterpillar and butterfly still belong to our earthly dispensation.

In the kingdom of glory, everything earthly falls away, together with every resulting limitation, hindrance, and obstacle. People will no longer die, but they will also no longer need rest or sleep. Life will awaken in full luminosity, and it will continue without interruption throughout the ages. It is an eternal existence that will experience no decline or weakening. There will be no pain or suffering. There will be no tears, but angelic smiles all around. How then can you have any idea, any conception at all, of the all-pervasive knowledge, the all-encompassing work, and the all-governing authority that your King already has at his disposal according to his human nature as he is seated at God's right hand?

This point needed to be emphasized, because nothing forms a greater obstacle to the recognition of Jesus' kingly authority than when people imagine him to exist in our current, earthly form. We are limited, we are of this earth, we are restricted in all kinds of ways. And even if we think of someone who far outshines all other people, he or she remains always a person with earthly limitations. If you think of your King in the same way, as if he were one of us, as if he were subject like we are to all kinds of earthly limitations and imperfections, the only outcome possible is for your perspective on Jesus' majesty to be so modest that you have difficulty explaining his dominion over all things. You then find yourself faced with a choice between two errors: either you will depict his kingship as being purely spiritual and thus deprive it of the real dominion of its authority, or you will derive his kingship exclusively from his divine nature and thereby separate his kingship entirely from the Mediator, from the man Jesus. This situation can be avoided if you do not think of your King's human existence in terms of a model taken from this earth, but understand it according to that exalted, complete existence of human nature. There all of our nature's latent capacities have reached their full development and received from the heavenly sphere—which differs vastly from the sphere of this earth—an authority and majesty that far surpass the highest form that human existence can assume on this earth in the sphere we now inhabit.

Our King's human existence no doubt remains creaturely in character, and therefore finite in nature. After all, the authority he has at his

§ 4

disposal as Mediator, and thus also as our King, is not original but has been given to him by the Father. Of course, the background formed by his divine nature may never be forgotten when our King exercises this authority. However, Christ's human nature is always in the foreground; and, as we saw, Scripture repeatedly emphasizes that he is our King as the Son of Man. Once we lose sight of this, there will be no exaltation. The "therefore God has highly exalted him" of Philippians 2:9 then disappears. This is why it is so important not to form an earthly conception of our King's human existence in the state of glory and exaltation, but to imagine all earthly limitations and restrictions to be absent—and thus conceive of that human existence in its consummation and [perceive] the powers inherent to it flourishing fully.

We must do this not only when we think of Jesus but also when we think of ourselves, since one day [Christ] "will transform our lowly body to be like his glorious body, by the power that enables him even to subject all things to himself" [Phil 3:21]. How much more should we remember this for Christ! Although a complete and glorified existence will also be ours one day, so that we will reign as kings together with Jesus upon his throne, still the Son of Man surpasses us by far.

Even among ourselves we see how one person surpasses another in terms of their gifts and talents. There is no equality among people. What is a quiet housekeeper compared to a philosopher like Augustine when it comes to knowledge? What is a farmer behind his plow compared to men such as Plato or Kant when it comes to knowledge? Similar distinctions could be drawn for artistic intuition and talent, willpower and resilience, courage and resolution. No two people are identical: There are some who are of a lower standing; then there are normal people; then there are those of a higher order; and, finally, there are geniuses and heroes who surpass everyone. This difference cannot be annulled in the state of glory, since it is connected to what God implanted as a seed in every person at creation. And although these different capacities will emerge entirely differently in the state of glory than they do here on earth, even in the state of glory some will surpass others in terms of knowledge, work, and power.

This applies in a much greater measure, of course, to the Head of humanity, to the Son of Man, to him who was destined to become the King of all in the kingdom of God. What Jesus received according to his human existence far surpasses anything even the most noble and best among us will ever receive. He became one of us, but none of us can be compared with the Son of Man in terms of what is in us as a seed and in terms of our capacity. Only in him has human existence reached its complete and highest perfection. He has not only been appointed as our King, but by his very nature he is greater than all of us. In him is found the highest level that our human existence can reach according to God's ordinance. He is the King of all because of his inherent superiority. He is the genius of all geniuses, the hero of all heroes, the wisdom of all the wise, the strongest of all the strong, the one who incarnates whatever may ever have radiated among people as noble and ideal.

As a result, you have to think of his human existence in the state of glory not only as being complete compared to the incompleteness of our development and as having been glorified by passing from the earthly into the heavenly paradise, but also as having been perfected and fully developed in the entirely unique sense in which the Son of Man—who alone surpasses all humanity in his capacity—must display the highest glory. Only those who one day will see the King as he really is will fully understand the depths of the humiliation he entered for our sake. And when one day he appears at his return on the clouds of heaven, we will see a glorified man whose human majesty will far overshadow all other human existence and will blind every eye. So much has been said these last few years about the *Übermensch*.[2] Well then, our King is the only *Übermensch*.

---

2. With this German term, Kuyper is likely referring to the philosophy of Friedrich Nietzsche (1844-1900). A central concept in his philosophy was that of the *Übermensch*, the superhuman or overman. Because it entailed an aggressive this-worldliness, this concept was set in contrast to the other-worldliness attributed to Christianity. This entire chapter sets forth the consummative glory of the exalted King Jesus Christ as an explicit alternative to Nietzsche's *Übermensch*.

III.25

KNOWLEDGE AND AUTHORITY

Beloved, we are God's children now, and what we will be has not yet appeared; but we know that when he appears we shall be like him, because we shall see him as he is.

1 JOHN 3:2

§ 1   We can therefore never overestimate what our King knows, is capable of, and does, by virtue of being the Son of Man—that is, according to his human nature. And in any case, our human existence on earth may never serve as the measure for this. In our exalted King we find what has reached completion rather than what is still gradually developing. In him the form does not correspond to this earthly sphere, but to the sphere of the heavens. In him it is not the ordinary that shines, but the highest apex of the potential that belongs to our nature by virtue of its creation. And in him all of this radiates with the special exaltation and eminence, the entirely unique majesty and excellence that result from our Messiah having been highly exalted [see Phil 2:9]. One reason he is King is that he far surpasses everything; and for that reason, whenever we explain his kingly rule, we must always place this singular exaltation of his human existence in the foreground. When Jesus himself said that he would come soon in order to judge as the Son of Man, we may not understand this to mean anything other than that he exercises his kingly regiment in the first place as man—while we still have to remember how much greater human knowledge and power become when a person enters the state of glory.

Especially with regard to knowledge, we find instruction at this point particularly in 1 Corinthians 13. The apostle says that when we die, we do not take the knowledge gained on earth with us in order to supplement it in heaven; no, in the state of glory our knowledge will assume an entirely different character. "For we know in part and we prophesy in part, but when the perfect comes, the partial will pass away" [1 Cor 13:9–10]. Prophecies, languages, knowledge, as he further testifies in verse eight, will all pass away. The distinction between the knowledge we gain on earth (some of us more than others) and the knowledge of heaven can be compared to an adult who discards the conceptions he had as a child and now views and understands things in a completely different way. Our current knowledge and our knowledge in the state of glory will differ not only in degree, but also in essence. On earth we must be content with knowledge deriving from appearances. Now we see only the image of things in a mirror, and therefore dimly (without clarity). But in the state of glory, things will be entirely different. Then we will see the essence of things, face to face [see 1 Cor 13:11–12]. Then we will know them just as God knows us—that is, immediately, by direct perception. He knows us immediately, and then we too will know things just as immediately. We will know them just as we ourselves are known. The only thing we will take with us into the state of glory is our faith, hope, and love. All other things were in part, and they will for that reason pass away; and although we will still have knowledge in the state of glory, that knowledge will be totally different in kind and will be obtained in an entirely different way.

Instinct and what Scripture calls wisdom (*hokhmah*) give us some understanding of that other kind of knowledge; and even among animals we can observe a form of immediate knowledge. A spider that spins its first web does so straightaway with the perfect proportions. It never went to school for this, never saw another spider do it, and used no pattern or calculations; but it completed that work of art, which no person can duplicate, just like that and all by itself. Furthermore, we see much more of this instinct among the primitive indigenous people groups than in our society.

Similarly, the author of Proverbs constantly points to wisdom not as something learned from books or taken over from the educated, but as something that is of itself propagated among ordinary people in communal life. Most often the ones who lack this wisdom and are lost when it comes to practical matters are university graduates, PhDs, and professors. There is, of course, a tendency to exaggerate this anecdotally, but there still is a kernel of truth here. The wisdom that Solomon refers to is in fact found much more in villages than in our highly intellectualized life in our cities. We encounter a similar phenomenon in artistic vision—the way an artist can intuitively cut through to the soul or essence of a thing. And when we read that Adam gave every animal its own name when he saw the different species, no one will suppose that he undertook some kind of zoological study in paradise but will understand instead that he still had the instinctive capacity to see into the very nature of these animals. Every animal knows its enemies. A little mouse that has never even seen a cat kill a mouse will quickly flee into its hole when it sees one, and it is no different when a sparrow sees a hawk. Even in clairvoyance, ancient oracles, mind reading, and in the premonitions primitive people groups have of imminent bad weather we find a whole series of phenomena analogous to this wisdom.

All of these examples pertain to an immediate knowledge that is gained with the first observation and perception of the object. Such knowledge is on the decline among us, however. On earth, we humans can gain only an initial grasp of things through such instinctive knowledge. And when we want to probe more deeply into our knowledge of them, the instinctive recedes into the background so that we are forced to follow the difficult and often painful path of scholarly study through gradual analysis, comparison, and summary. What a swallow, ant, or beaver does instinctively, an architect must first learn in steps—namely, how to build a house.

§ 2   For that reason, we may never compare the knowledge of our King as he is seated at God's right hand with our erudition and scholarship, and certainly not with the way we acquire knowledge. In the state of glory, Christ's human knowledge—that is, even apart from his divine omnipotence—is suddenly transformed into a complete, immediate, and direct knowledge of persons, things, and affairs. And whereas, according to 1 Corinthians 13:9–12, the saints already have a similar immediate knowledge, in our King that knowledge has been raised to the highest level of perfection so that in this too he has been highly exalted [see Phil 2:9].

We do not know the extent of this knowledge or the degree to which it is limited by distance. We also do not know the extent of this knowledge as it is found in angels and saints. In us, at any rate, in this earthly dispensation, the limitations imposed by distance are quite painful. We often do notice what happens next door or to our neighbors. Every wall that divides one room from another blocks our perceptions. Only in clairvoyance, and recently also with x-rays, do we have the ability to look through walls and from afar. Moreover, we may observe that the limitation posed by distance is much less of a hindrance to us than it was to the previous generations. We have already come so far that we can know every evening what happened around the world earlier that day. Further, we may be certain that this limitation on our knowledge imposed by distance will largely be absent in the state of glory. We read that during his time on earth, Jesus said to Nathanael: "Before Philip called you, when you were under the fig tree, I saw you" [John 1:48]. Among the saints, who one day will form a crowd numbering millions upon millions, we also cannot imagine any communion if their interaction with each other were to be bound by this limitation.

That is why we must suppose that for our King, as he is in the state of glory, these boundaries for the most part disappear. And if even angels have knowledge of people and places on earth, as can be seen from the fact that they were sent out to particular people and to specific places they managed to find, we need to consider the possibility that by virtue of his human nature our King already has a much greater knowledge of our human situation than we commonly assume.

We will attempt to go no further than what has been revealed to us. The extent of knowledge that our human nature can attain in the state of glory remains a mystery to us while we still live on earth. Our position is too low to gain a clear conception of it. The most we can do is to consider similar phenomena that we observe in nature and relate them to what Scripture reveals to us about this knowledge in passages like 1 Corinthians 13. All the same, we should not forget that another apostle says that believers have the anointing of the Holy One, and through that they know all things (1 John 2:20).

On the basis of these data, we neither may nor can come to any other conclusion than that the knowledge of the saints, and even more so the knowledge of the Son of Man in the state of glory, is of a different kind than our earthly knowledge, is acquired in another way, and far surpasses all our knowledge. Whereas an earthly king in his palace does not see his nation, but is informed of the situation in the many reports prepared by his officials, it is certain that our King, seated at God's right hand, has no need for such means; he himself oversees the entire situation of his kingdom immediately and directly. Similarly, he needs no means to have contact with the angel world. This world, as well, he knows and comprehends with immediate vision. The same is true, of course, for the world of demons. Our King does not wait on reports to tell him about things that are going on, happening, and being prepared in the satanic world. He grasps, comprehends, and knows also the demonic world by immediate perception. Here too all mystery will fall away in the state of glory.

§ 3   What holds true for the knowledge of the Son of Man in his state of kingly majesty holds true for his power and authority as well. In this respect, too, we can see that already while he lived on earth, his power far surpassed the normal power and capacity of people in their humiliated state. A power went forth from him to heal, so we read. And Jesus knew when such a power went out from him, for when the woman who had suffered from a discharge of blood was healed without anybody in the crowd noticing it, Jesus himself testified that a power had gone forth from him [see Mark 5:24–34].

The power that is in each one of us varies widely. Even among animal tamers, an ability manifests itself that is entirely foreign to most other people. There are great differences between the personal power each person can exercise. Some people can gain control over others with a single look and overpower them entirely. Others can captivate in the most literal sense of the word. Similarly, one sees entire people groups during the heroic period of their history manifest a driving force and power to perform valorous acts that later weaken and ultimately dissipate. Think only of what our own Dutch nation accomplished in the time of its greatest flourishing in the sixteenth and seventeenth centuries, and compare that to the discouragement and powerlessness manifested during the eighteenth and first half of the nineteenth centuries. We can further point out how the power and authority of an adult male in the prime of his life far surpasses the power of a child or old man. In fact, even in perilous circumstances a person at times can suddenly have such a power at his disposal that we say he outdid himself. A latent power is suddenly awakened in that person at a specific point in time that surprises everyone, including himself.

But if we see in these examples alone that it is difficult to establish a fixed measure for the power and authority that can proceed from our human nature, we must conclude that, by the very nature of the case, our power in the state of glory should in this respect also far surpass what humanity possesses in the state of humiliation, since in the state of glory nearly everything that still binds and limits us on earth will disappear. Just like a child is inferior to an adult, an adult on earth will be totally inferior to the glorified person when they will one day shine in the glorified body with a sanctified spirit.

But there is more. Just as we acquire knowledge with the use of various means, our earthly situation similarly requires us to exercise our power and authority over nature and fellow humanity by using various means. On earth, a king does not rule in his land and over his people by his own hand, but through the many intermediaries he appoints—that is, through his officials, police corps, soldiers, and bureaucrats. Things are no different when it comes to our power and authority. The increase in our strength and power over nature is extraordinary and astonishing; and in its struggle with nature, humanity hardly shrinks back before anything anymore. Humanity's dominion over nature has taken on gigantic proportions compared to earlier times. Since nothing suggests that this process has ground to a halt, and instead the expectation is that our power over nature will only increase and even reach previously unknown heights in the coming centuries, it would seem that humanity's dominion over nature—given in creation as no more than a seed—knows virtually no boundaries, even if some such boundaries do indeed exist.

All the same, notwithstanding the enormous strides made in humanity's power over nature, the exercise of that power is and remains bound to these means. We need to apply a host of either coarse or more refined tools in order to ensure that we have control over nature. It is through these rougher or more refined tools that we put nature's very power in our service, in order to subject nature to our will through them. Without tools, without means, when standing before nature with nothing but the strength of their body, people are and remain without power.

When a shipwrecked vessel drifts on the open sea without a rudder, without oars, and without a compass, even the most skilled captain is immobilized, powerless, and delivered over to the capriciousness of the waves. Without a locomotive or rails, even the smartest engineer cannot move his train. Every exercise of power depends on those tools or means, and without those aids every attempt to exercise power is in vain. Even the farmer cannot get anything done in his field without a plough or spade, and without a bit and bridle even the best rider will eventually fall from his horse. An immediate power may still manifest itself in animal tamers or hypnotists; but for the rest, when we have no means, no tools, and no aids of any other kind, we are limited in every way to the little we can move with our feet and can lift or twist with our hands—the most clumsy way of exercising our power.

If, in the state of glory, means are no longer used in regard to our power, so that a glorified person's strength is applied directly and immediately to the chosen object, then it is worth noting that this is something that also increases humanity's power. When what we now dimly see at work in the remarkable courage of the heroes of antiquity, in animal tamers, and in hypnotists, becomes the rule and is raised to a level of complete perfection, only then will the image of God in humanity begin to radiate in all its brightness. While remaining in its finite and thus limited circle, humankind will be able to exercise dominion over nature through their willpower alone. Likewise, nature will no longer wrestle with humanity in the state of glory, but will submit to its scepter.

If you transfer this thought to our King, you will understand how he can have dominion and rule and carry out his will. Then you will no longer think of your glorified King as if he were deep in thought at God's right hand and bound by his earthly limitations, but you will conceive of him as a Potentate of Potentates, a King of kings—who, with the immediate knowledge he has of his kingdom, not only gives his commands to his subjects so that they may carry them out, but also acts with power and brings to pass whatever pleases him. He is not merely a Savior from the curse who presented his offering to the Father for the redeemed and waits to watch how the struggle between the good and evil spirits develops over time. No, he is a King who has and exercises power, who sees everything, comprehends everything, guides, leads, and governs everything, applies his power whenever necessary, and causes his power to be effective irresistibly and immediately.

It cannot be denied that all these things come to pass because of the background formed by Christ's divine nature. This, too, is something we will treat explicitly later on. But, for the moment we had to counter the suggestion that his entire kingly rule must be explained almost exclusively from his divine attributes—as well as the notion that the Son's human nature would continue to be bound to our earthly limitations even in the state of glory—so that we would think of our King, seated on the throne in his human nature, as if he were like us as we now live here on earth. If this were indeed true, nothing would have been conferred or given to Christ, and he would not have been highly exalted because he would already have possessed all of his divine attributes of himself by virtue of being the Son of God. The Mediator, the Son of Man, would then be something merely incidental in him, something that exuded no power; and it would be to the Son of God, to the Second Person of the Trinity set apart from his humanity, that we would have to direct ourselves in prayer. The two natures in the glorified King would then stand alongside each other, and his human nature would be deprived of almost all of its significance for his kingly rule.

We can avoid this misconception only if we form a clear impression for ourselves of the great difference between human existence here on earth and human existence as it will be bestowed on us one day in the kingdom of glory when we are raised up in our glorified body. What our existence will be like is still a mystery to us at the present time. "Beloved," writes the apostle, "what we will be has not yet appeared; but we know that when he appears we shall be like him, because we shall see him as he is" [1 John 3:2]. Our King is now already enthroned in his glorified body. He already possesses the full glory that awaits us at the end of the age. And not only that but, to the extent that there will be differences also in ability and aptitude among the saved in that state of glory, our King is clothed with the highest glory and his knowledge and ability are the full manifestation of the image and likeness of God according to which humanity was created. Only when we understand this will Christ no longer be just the Prophet who gave his Word, or only the High Priest who lives to pray for us, but also our King in glory and majesty who, not only through his angels and his servants and subjects on earth, but also immediately and directly himself, manifests his authority and power and exercises his kingly rule without any created power being able to resist him in his dominion.

III.26

DIVINE CAPACITY

And he is before all things, and in him all things hold together. And he is the head of the body, the church. He is the beginning, the firstborn from the dead, that in everything he might be preeminent. For in him all the fullness of God was pleased to dwell.

COLOSSIANS 1:17–19

§ 1   We intentionally attempted to explain the exercise of the kingly rule of the Son of Man, in the first place, from information regarding his human nature. This was not to suggest that our King is a human person who has been joined to the divine persons. The Son of God took on our human nature, not human personhood. At bottom, the Mediator's *I* always remains the Son of God. However, this does not mean that the Son of God, as Son of Man, was bound in the exercise of his authority to the boundaries of the finite that are always associated with our human nature.

This was why it seemed advisable to us to gain clear insight into the way Christ exercises his kingly rule, to ascend from the smaller to the greater, and so to consider and contemplate first of all what human nature itself could already bestow on him in terms of knowledge, work, and the exercise of his power. We may not imagine even for a moment that the Mediator's human nature lost its significance through and on account of his ascension into heaven, as if the divine nature were at work only from that moment on.

This was why we demonstrated at length that the human nature that Jesus assumed may not be measured according to this nature as it is found in ordinary people, especially not in their current humiliated state.

If the human nature of some is much more richly endowed than that of others; if it is capable of much more now, twenty centuries after the birth of Christ, than it was twenty centuries before Bethlehem; if it would have been capable of more yet, had we remained without sin; and finally, if it (presumably) will manifest itself as even more richly gifted in the state of glory—then we may conclude that we would be hard pressed to over-estimate how the human nature in our King now functions in its sinless, complete, and elevated state in glory.

The knowledge, inner workings, and power available in the Mediator's human nature far surpass what is possible for the human nature of people on earth, even among the greatest heroes and geniuses. Also Jesus' human nature remains finite in its functions, but these functions extend themselves over a much larger and richer domain than ours can. This holds also when it comes to distance, which has already been reduced so much for us compared to our fathers, but of course present much less an impediment to him who is "highly exalted" [Phil 2:9].

All the same, we neither can nor may probe more deeply than this. After all, we do not have all the details regarding Christ's kingly rule to distinguish sharply which parts are owing to the functions of his human nature and which must be traced back directly to our Mediator's divine nature. Already during Jesus' appearance upon earth, people so easily ended up on the wrong path when making that distinction. If we imagine Jesus' human nature, when he performed a miracle, to have been just as limited as it is in us, we will soon be tempted to derive anything that is extraordinary in Christ from his divine nature alone. Yet it is clear that his human nature, too, was operative and functioning here; that believers, too, are given the ability to do extraordinary things; and that it has been foretold even of the Antichrist that he will succeed in extending his influence by way of extraordinary signs [see Matt 24:24].

Whenever we speak of human nature, we must also distinguish between what it possesses by virtue of its created potential and what it can already bring about. Since there clearly is much more in our potential that remains hidden than has actually already become visible, we must always remember concerning the Mediator in his glorified state that his human nature can perform everything that has potentially been implanted in that nature according to the ordinance of creation. The technical term *potential* stands in contrast to the term *actual*; the latter refers to what has already become actualized at one time or in a specific person. Using this terminology, we therefore have to confess that every potential in our human nature has been fully actualized in our glorified King; while in us—as we dwell in our humiliated state here on earth—the actual is at a much lower level than the potential. In its potentiality, the image and likeness of God is complete; while, in its actuality, it is no more than highly flawed in respect to holy intent as well as with respect to its knowledge and its exercise of power. We can also express this by saying that the image and likeness of God in a human person's being, knowledge, and ability reaches its consummation first in the glorified King, according to the rule he himself spoke: "You therefore must be perfect, as your heavenly Father is perfect" [Matt 5:48]. Only the Son of Man is himself "the image of the invisible God" [Col 1:15].

§ 2   But as lofty a conception as we may have of the functioning of our King's perfected human nature when he exercises his authority and kingship, there is no doubt that it is hardly adequate for explaining the full extent of the display of his authority. The kingly rule of Christ is in no way limited to some isolated acts accomplished with respect to people, spirits, and inanimate nature; it is just as much a matter of appropriating and engaging these individual acts within the general administration of providence as it extends throughout the entire earth and universe. If you separate the two so that the general administration of providence over peoples and nations, over individual people, and over all of nature, runs its own course entirely removed from Christ; and if you place Christ's individual acts aimed at carrying out his kingly regiment alongside [the general administration of providence]; then the unity and mutual bond between them will be lost, and the entire history of the world following his ascension will become altogether inexplicable.

For this reason, the church has always confessed that a distinction ought to be maintained in Christ's kingly regiment between the general kingdom extending to all things and the particular kingdom involving the church and believers. Our Catechism thus confesses in answer 50: "Christ ascended into heaven for this end, that He might there appear as the Head of His Church, by whom the Father governs all things."[1] Only then can

---

1.   Heidelberg Catechism, Lord's Day 19, A 50, *RC* 2:780.

you do full justice to Jesus' claims that all things have been handed over to him by the Father [see Matt 11:27] and that all authority in heaven and on earth has been given to him [see Matt 28:18]. When we read this, we sense immediately that this does not apply to the functions of his human nature, and that in this context we ought rather to return to the background formed by Christ's divine nature.

The extensive exposition of the way his human nature functions was therefore not at all intended to deny the knowledge, work, and exercise of power of the Son of God in our King. As we have already stated, anyone who understands that the Son of God is not a human person—the man Jesus—but only took on our human nature, cannot doubt for a moment that in the Son of Man it is the Son of God who is and remains what may be referred to as the subject, the agent, the *I*. This is not the place to discuss either the mystery of the Holy Trinity or the mystery of the union of the two natures in Christ; but it is certain that our King, also as the Son of Man, is and remains the Son of God, the Second Person in the Holy Trinity. And even if the glory that he now has may have been hidden in the state of humiliation he assumed on earth for our sake, Scripture still specifically emphasizes that this hiddenness, humbling, ultimate humiliation ended with his ascension. He was exalted, highly exalted in fact [see Phil 2:9], so that the full radiance of his divine Sonship could shine once more in its entire splendor.

In the mystery of the Holy Trinity, with regard to the exercise of his power, great emphasis is placed on the fact that all things are from the Father and through the Son. This is how things went at creation, and this is how they still proceed in the administration of providence. Therefore, whenever the apostles want to give us the proper perspective on Christ's kingly rule, they always go back to the creation of all things in order to make it clear that it is through the Son alone that all things received their being, form, mode of existence, and operation. In fact, the apostle John began his entire Gospel with the statement that the Word was with God in the beginning, that the Word was God, and that all things were created through the Word, that is, through the Son of God [see John 1:1–3]. The apostle Paul, too, testifies to us indefatigably that all the fullness dwells in the Son of God, that he alone is the pure image of our God, that all things in heaven and on earth, visible or invisible, were created through him and for him, and that all things hold together in him [see Col 1:15–19]. Indeed, it is from the Father that all wisdom, every decree, all power and authority, all government and direction go forth. This is because he is the fount of life, the source of authority, the origin of everything that will become; yet it is always confessed that nothing proceeding from the Father comes into being except *through the Son*. In the Father, all things are one; and it is only through the Son that all things flourish in their individuality and multiformity. Therefore, nothing is excluded from the work of the Son of God. He has set his mark on all created things. Similarly, all that happens in this world or in the entire universe happens through him. It was not just that all things were created through him, but all things also exist in their current form and shape through the Son of God alone.

§ 3   We may indeed be placed before an unsolvable mystery with regard to the period of Christ's humiliation, since we cannot understand how, at the very moment when he nearly collapsed in his deadly sorrow in Gethsemane, he still bore all things through his Word of power. When it comes to his state of glory, however, we are no longer faced with an impenetrable mystery. In this state of glorification, our King is the Son of Man and our Mediator; but at the very same time he shines forth in his majesty as the God who is both omniscient and omnipotent! Of course, the elect alone belong to our King's spiritual subjects, but in a wider sense every person and every spirit is subjected to him. There is no person or angel over whom Christ's scepter does not extend as his subjects.

Of course, only the angels and believers recognize that they are his subjects, but in reality every creature is subject to his authority. What is true for an animate and conscious creature is true also for inanimate creation: both on earth and beyond it, inanimate creation is subjected to Christ, and he has it under his complete power and authority. In respect to the functioning of his human nature, we already pointed out that his knowledge is much greater than ours; all the same, the knowledge he has as Son of Man is and remains limited. In the Son of God, by contrast, every limitation and boundary disappears. Nothing is hidden from him. He sees through everything, and even in your personal life nothing remains hidden from him.

That reality is the only thing that allows you to explain his regiment over the church and over believers. God's omniscience means that every person here on earth is known to him by name. He knows their past and present, their inner being, and their outward destiny in life. This alone provides the conditions for the close relationship between our King and each of his spiritual subjects. He lives to pray for us, not only in the general sense that he prays for the church as a whole or for believers as a group, but such that he knows all the tribulations of the hearts of all his people and lifts them up in prayer. He appoints his servants in his church—by the participation of people, admittedly, but still in such a way that every one of them has been raised up, set apart, and appointed to their office. This, too, is something that one cannot imagine, had not everyone been known to him by name. There is no shred of evidence in the gospel that, before Paul became a follower of Jesus, he ever had personal contact with Jesus while he lived on earth. All the same, the events on the road to Damascus reveal that Jesus knew this Saul of Tarsus, understood him, knew what was in him, knew that he was kicking against the goads, and also knew that he was on his way to Damascus at that very moment. We are to understand the appointment of all his servants in just as specific and literal a sense.

The knowledge Jesus has regarding his own and regarding those whom he will call is not enough. All kinds of outside influences are working on the church and on believers. There are influences of a national nature, influences of a historical character, influences of a social character, influences from public opinion, influences of scholarship and art, and influences of the spirit of the age. Believers do not float like drops of oil on top of the water; they live in the world, and they are inserted into and connected with the life of the world via the numerous bonds of birth, family, office, commerce, and so on. If you deny that your King has knowledge or awareness of all these things, how would he be able to see to the specific needs of the church and believers in the face of those influences?

For that reason, we must simply acknowledge that our King sees all these things; recognizes the danger in them; knows how they will turn out; and understands with a divine certainty how the dangers are to be intercepted and how everything is to be thwarted, guided, and engaged for the benefit of those who belong to him. If our lot as believers often depends on the history of our nation and on what is being stirred up in the nations of this world pertaining to our own nation's life, how then can you imagine our King's rule without the "roar of nations like the roaring of mighty waters" [see Isa 17:12] being completely known to him? A spiritual dominion cannot be exercised if his omniscience does not unveil for our King everything that is hidden; and those who claim that our King's dominion is spiritual and insist that it occurs entirely apart from the dominion of the world are contradicting themselves. In our personal lives, the one cannot be separated from the other, and neither can they be separated from the lofty administration of Christ's church on earth.

§ 4   This all-encompassing knowledge of things would not suffice if our King were not able, at the same time, to influence and to guide all these things. If the administration of providence was entirely beyond his reach, he could repeatedly attempt to thwart the danger threatening us, but he would ultimately be powerless before it and just have to let things happen. This is the reason why our Catechism so strongly emphasizes that Christ is the one "by whom the Father governs all things."[2] Even the administration of providence is not something belonging to only the First Person of the holy Triune Being; rather, even though it proceeds from the Father, it works through the Son and in the Holy Spirit. Our King thus has the administration of providence in his hand, and it does not operate except through him.

When, in our struggle with Spain, the lot of his church in our lands went back and forth repeatedly depended on the outcome of this battle or that on land and sea, he did not wait passively to see how things would turn out; but he himself was at work in it, even exercised leadership, and ensured the victory.[3]

This is also how it is with one's personal life destiny. Your spiritual growth is constantly governed by what you encounter in life. If the course of your life unfolded entirely apart from your King—so that, although he knew about it, he still would not be able to guide or change anything in it—your spiritual development would elude him and he would be powerless with respect to it. For that reason alone he is, in the fullest sense of the word, your spiritual Shepherd and Leader and your Mediator who guides you to salvation, because as the Son of God he is active also in the administration of providence on behalf of your personal life. He is not at all passive.

Here too, omniscience is not enough. Here too, his omniscience must be united with his omnipotence so that he can realize the goal of his spiritual leadership. The same holds for the world of the spirits. The spirit world as well is constantly at work, influencing in numerous ways the spirit of the age, one's nation, one's life circle, and even one's heart. If your

---

2.   Heidelberg Catechism, Lord's Day 19, A 50, *RC* 2:780.
3.   Kuyper refers here to the Dutch Revolt (1568–1648) against the Roman Catholic King Philip II of Spain.

King had nothing more than knowledge of all these things and lacked the authority and power to exercise any influence on them and to respond to them, whatever he accomplished for our spiritual nurture could have been spoiled and destroyed by that spirit world. This is why Scripture stresses so emphatically to us that everything, including all influencing factors, in the current but also in the coming world, are subject to him.

If this seems to conflict with the presence of so much that is lamentable in the world, in the church, and in the spirit world; with the fact that any opposition is not broken all at once; with the great amount of unfaithfulness, even among his servants; and with the fact that our King constantly seems to be unable to avert all this misery and danger—we need to point out that our salvation is indeed the goal of Christ's kingly rule, but that its primary goal is the glorification of the Triune God. And as we have already demonstrated extensively, it is to God's honor not to destroy every opposition with brute force and superior power immediately, but to [take on and] overturn every opponent and enemy in a principled struggle. Thus we also see why our King constantly ordains things in such a way that this opposition arises and is even allowed to arise, so that the principial enmity may be overcome more gloriously than it otherwise would have.

Our King does the same in your personal life. He allows you to be attacked by all kinds of spirits and to spend all your strength, and leads you through very tough times—so that, as a better and more holy fruit, you may be ripened for the harvest of his kingdom.

Thus, everything in his kingdom is connected with everything else. The lot of the world is connected to your personal lot. The lot of your nation is connected with your own spiritual existence. The church's lot on earth experiences its ups and downs. At one time there is growth and glory, but it is followed by a time of faithlessness, apostasy, and decline. And the reins are not in the hands of people, but in the firm hand of our King who governs all things with his hand. This pervasive and all-encompassing regiment he now exercises as our Mediator, so that, once the last enemy has been subjected under his feet, in order to remain the Head of saved humanity, he will deliver the kingly dominion back to God [see 1 Cor 15:24].

III.27

THE HOLY SPIRIT

If anyone loves me, he will keep my word, and my Father will love him, and we
will come to him and make our home with him.

JOHN 14:23

§ 1   Christ's kingly rule over his spiritual, that is, actual subjects—the members of his mystical body who were redeemed by his blood and for whom
the Lord paid the ransom—has a special, unique, and entirely mystical
character. This special relationship was brought about through the outpouring of the Holy Spirit. It was clear from what Jesus himself said about
it in his final conversations with his disciples that the Holy Spirit would
be poured out, that the outpouring would take place shortly after Jesus
departed from the earth, and that it would occur through our King.

He prayed to the Father that his disciples might have another Counselor
who would never abandon them but remain with them forever (John 14:16).
That Counselor was the Holy Spirit, whom they knew, who would dwell in
them and they in him (14:17). They would then no longer be orphans because, as he said, "You are in me, and I in you" (14:20). The Father would
love them, and Christ would come with the Father and make their home
with him (14:23).

The preceding testifies to a very special relationship that our King
would enter with his people, one that would be much closer, much more
intimate, and much more significant than the relationship in which the
King would come to stand with those who are indifferent or even hostile

toward him. This distinction derives from the fact that his regiment is brought to bear only within the innermost being of his spiritual subjects. This penetration to the inner depth of their soul's life is expressed in various ways, but with increasingly potent locutions. We hear about the Vine with its branches; we hear about the members and the Head of the one body; we see that Christ himself makes his home with them, and in fact dwells in them just as they dwell in him. The apostolic Letters express this with the image of the temple. The heart, the soul of those who are saved by Christ has become the temple of the Lord. The separation between people and their God is undone. God himself lives in those who believe. God's house, God's temple, God's dwelling place is no longer on Mount Zion, but in the heart of those who belong to Jesus because they have been bought with his blood.

The historical turning point in this respect is the outpouring of the Holy Spirit on the tenth day after Jesus' ascension. In paradise, there initially was nothing that separated God from humanity. There was communion, there was interaction, there was contact, and everything was prepared for the most intimate community to be established. In the human soul, the flower's bud had only to open and the Spirit's breath would fill it, bringing God's being in us and our being in God to fruition.

This did not happen, however. The sepals of the bud did not open up, and the twig from which it sprouted turned away. Not only was that close communion thwarted, but outward contact was broken off as well. God and humanity went their separate ways, instead of humanity drawing near to God. Sin is separation from God, disconnection from God, the closure of the heart to God. We read in Isaiah 18:4 that the Lord says: "I will quietly look from my dwelling"; these words may have been directed to Cush, but they perfectly express the relationship between God and humanity after the fall. People go their own way and God watches them go, but then he follows them with his eyes and beckons them to come back. But the cord that bound the human heart to the heart of their God has weakened and has been severed almost completely. The intimate communion is gone. Things begin to fall apart, and in the end humanity closes itself up within itself. Two inner lives are formed in complete separation from each other: the most blissful inner life in the Holy Trinity, and the life of the human soul as it is now subjected to death and the curse and sin. Humanity wants to keep it that way and defies God, refusing to return. It is as if humanity wants China's Great Wall to separate its life from the life of God. People will still want to have gods; but they will imagine, portray, and make them themselves. In paradise the world belonged to God, with plenty of room for humankind; but now the world would belong to humankind, with some room left for the gods as well—that is, until humanity decided that it also had had enough of these gods, smashed its own idols, pushed it all to the side, and embracing total atheism, became convinced that they could go it alone. The crude and blunt opposition between God and humanity was therefore pointed and immediate.

The original situation in paradise was one where God sat on the throne with humankind kneeling as subjects before his footstool; but now humanity has placed itself on a throne of its own, while the almighty God is quarantined high above us in his own dwelling, condemned to silence. The separation, the isolation, between God and humanity was driven to its utmost limits. In the pagan world of antiquity this happened while bowing to sensual pleasure and false philosophy; and now, in many respects, this has happened once again as people pledge allegiance to an extreme materialism. This is something that the idealists of our day do manage to escape. With them, however, they once again have a god fashioned in the image of humankind rather than a humanity created in the image of God.

§ 2   The work of the Christ in this regard cannot be complete until the very root of sin, the curse, and death has been undone. That victory did not come with the cross or the resurrection. The cross removes the curse and supplies the ransom for the guilt of our sin, and life triumphed over death in the resurrection. But in spite of these accomplishments, the estrangement and separation had not been undone, and the close communion of God living in us and we living in God had not yet been reinstated. That close communion was indeed brought about in Christ, but not in us. It was something that needed to happen. It was the very purpose [of creation] and the original situation [in paradise]. That original situation had to be restored; and after having been restored, it was to be elevated to its highest point of development and reach its fullest consummation. Not only did the break have to be undone, but the unity also had to be so fully restored that nothing would remind one that the break ever existed—such that in its place would come a close communion, much more exalted than the communion begun in paradise and without the possibility of a new break in the future.

That could happen only when God the Holy Spirit, through Christ exalted at the right hand of God, descended to enter the circle of those who are his, and in such a way that he could never be separated from them again. By this he would create an entirely new situation characterized by the wonderful circumstance that Christ with the Father would dwell in the hearts of his people, so that the heart of God's children would be a temple or a dwelling place of the Holy Spirit. This is the closest communion one can imagine. When our heart has become a dwelling place of God and God himself dwells in the heart of his people, all separation and alienation will be undone and replaced with the greatest intimacy imaginable between God's life and human life. *Immanuel* dawns, not only in the person of the Mediator, but through him in his entire mystical body. It is no longer a God far away, but a God close by—indeed, a God who dwells within our own heart.

This is something that could be brought about only through the Holy Spirit's descent into Christ's body. In the wonderful mystery of the Holy Trinity, the Holy Spirit is always that person of the divine essence who enters a created being. Everything is from the Father, through the Son, but life itself first came as a result of the Holy Spirit's work.

This is true not only for humanity, but for all creatures. It is just as true for plants as it is for animals, for all talents and gifts, for any creature that moves on the earth, and for the angelic world. In all these cases, however, it is never more than an operation of the Holy Spirit. They are powers that proceed from him, influences that go forth from the Holy Spirit to the created beings and sustain their life force.

This is not [the same as] the Holy Spirit's entrance into people in order to implant God's life in them and to cause their life in God to flourish. Wherever people live or have lived on this earth, the Holy Spirit has always been at work on behalf of their natural life, their talents, and their gifts. Even at the present time, the Holy Spirit's work is not limited to the circle of believers but expands beyond it and extends to all people, including atheists and hardened sinners. No one can fall or stray so far that every spark of light that ever shone in him, even in his sin, does not come from the Holy Spirit. In fact, we cannot even imagine human life without and apart from the Holy Spirit.

All the same, this is no more than an outward operation of the Holy Spirit that has nothing to do with humanity's inner being, occurs entirely apart from our being aware and conscious of it, and does not undo our separation from God in any way. The Holy Spirit's entering into a person, the Holy Spirit's living with a person, and his establishing a holy communion between a person's heart and God's heart was called into being bears an entirely different and distinct character. In order for these things to happen, a temple to God first had to be prepared and opened in the human heart. In Christ, this situation was present according to his human nature. There was no moment during his life on earth when he was separated from the Holy Spirit. The Holy Spirit was given to him without measure. The temple was in him. The Holy Spirit lived in that temple. It was thus also in the person of Jesus, again by virtue of his human nature, that the separation was undone, and that the full and close communion with God, once more by virtue of his human nature, was made perfect. This did not happen gradually but very suddenly, from the very moment when the virgin's womb conceived him.

§ 3   Though estranged and separated from God, God did not wait for the manger in Bethlehem to come to humankind. The entire history of the Old Testament in fact forms a continuous attempt on the part of the Holy One to draw near to the human race he had created—to draw near in the Word he had revealed, in the visions he gave to his messengers, in the miraculous deeds he brought to pass, in the call of the patriarchs, in sending Moses and the other prophets, in establishing his people Israel, in the choice of Jerusalem, in the holy worship on Mount Zion.

These things could only be preparatory, however. For one thing, all of these operations involved individual people and left the masses unaffected. On the other hand, they never got beyond the outward and the symbolic. That God's dwelling was in Zion was a particularly clear indication that he had not yet made his home once more in human hearts. Worship like it happened on Mount Zion would have been unthinkable in paradise, and we similarly read that there is no temple in the new Jerusalem. These things speak for themselves. A stone temple built high upon Mount Zion with the holy of holies hidden behind the curtain clearly indicated that there was no inner and intimate communion between God and humanity. This was why the union between God and people could be portrayed only symbolically in a temple built of stone.

This was why Jesus expressly stated that his body would replace the temple on Zion. It could be no other way. At the very moment when the union between God and humanity was brought about in Jesus' human heart, even though it was only one human heart, the temple had fulfilled its purpose. And there was no longer any reason for the temple to exist when God made his home in the hearts of believers through the outpouring of the Holy Spirit on the disciples in an antechamber of that temple on the day of Pentecost. Tents are abandoned when a fixed dwelling has been prepared and is ready to use.

Related to this is that the Holy Spirit did perform special operations in the days of the patriarchs and Israel, but this was always limited to light that shone and power that was manifested. And even though these often involved hidden exchanges, they did not involve the Spirit's indwelling in the heart. God does not just let Israel be, but he constantly entered more and more deeply into Israel's life.

All the same, God did not prepare his temple in the heart of Israel. We see instead how Israel as a nation constantly strayed to follow the idols of the pagan nations. The prophet Isaiah was even forced to isolate himself completely from the nation and to withdraw to a small circle of believers and "to bind up the testimony" among them, as Scripture expresses it [Isa 8:16].

The first improvement in the situation came with the terrifying exile. Because when the hour of deliverance had finally come, the part of the nation of Israel that had strayed from God stayed behind in Babylon, and only those who feared the name of the Lord returned. But also in the new Jewish state that was founded by Ezra and Nehemiah and later elevated to great splendor by the Maccabean princes, the separation from God continued. Even prophecy gradually came to an end. The special operations of the Holy Spirit were less frequent. And when prophecy revived once more in John the Baptist, it was clear that the old contrast still existed: there was a great mass of people who were spiritually deaf and dead, and only small, scattered groups of people who hungered for righteousness.

The outpouring of the Holy Spirit is therefore entirely distinct. All of the Holy Spirit's works performed before that time in the days of our fathers were of an entirely different character. And also after the great feast of Pentecost—when mention is made of being baptized with the Holy Spirit, but the miracle of Pentecost is never repeated—we see that no more than a few people are brought to salvation, or that those who already have been now come to a deeper understanding of their spiritual life. Earlier there were indeed activities and powers that went forth from the Holy Spirit: revelations, visions, dreams, the bestowal of gifts and talents, the raising up of heroes and courageous witnesses, and the guidance of specific people on the path of righteousness—but on the day of Pentecost things were totally different. Now the Third Person of the Holy

Trinity descended, God the Holy Spirit entered the circle of the redeemed to dwell in them from that time on, to make his home in them, to form their hearts into a dwelling place, and to make the union of God and humanity a reality. As a result, "God in us, and we in God" became the motto of all higher life.

§ 4   Consider now the high priestly prayer that Jesus lifted up to the Father in the terrifying hours before he went to Gethsemane: "Father, I pray for them, that they may all be one, just as you, Father, are in me, and I in you, that they may also be one in us. I in them, and you in me" [see John 17:21, 23]. Add to this the promise he made to his disciples at that same hour: "We will come to him and make our home with him" [John 14:23]. Connect the preceding with Jesus' pledge that it was to their advantage that he was leaving them, since it was only by departing from them that he could send the Holy Spirit, the Counselor, and take what was his and make it known to them [see John 16:7, 14].

All of the foregoing makes it clear to you that Christ himself was fully aware that he would first have to be seated as King on the throne of glory before he could destroy the separation between God and humanity and restore intimate communion between them. That full communion between God and humanity could not be restored unless all sin, everything unholy, was first driven from the human heart. Our holy God could not dwell where sin dwelled. That was why the first communion between God and humanity could occur only in Christ himself, the one who had taken on our human nature but was without sin. As such, this communion would not have begun until after our death, when death would have made us dead to all sin. Therefore, intimate communion with God, the indwelling of God in the heart of our temple, would have been inconceivable until the Lord's return. The disciples were intimately connected with Jesus through faith and officially adorned with the gifts of the Spirit. But, despite this, their hearts could not have become God's dwelling place if the great and mighty miracle of the outpouring of the Holy Spirit had not occurred shortly after Jesus ascended into heaven.

How was that outpouring possible and even imaginable in the circle of believers who, however much they honored Christ, still carried sin in their hearts? The apostle John gives this answer to that question: "No one born of God makes a practice of sinning, for God's seed abides in him, and he cannot keep on sinning because he has been born of God" [1 John 3:9]; such a person has been "anointed by the Holy One" [1 John 2:20]. The apostle

Paul similarly explains to us from the experience of his own soul: "Now if I do what I do not want, it is no longer I who do it, but sin that dwells within me" [Rom 7:20].

These words remain shrouded in mystery unless you know and understand the mystical union of believers with Christ. Everything, therefore, comes down to that mystical union: the mystical union that Christ established as our King and still maintains among us as our King. It is only by virtue of being our King that he is the Head of the body. As the Head of the body he causes his life to flow forth into all the members of that body. There is only one life in that entire body, the life of Christ, and the apostle testifies about this life that it is hidden in Christ with God [see Col 3:3]. Since the Holy Spirit is the Mediator's Spirit, he makes his dwelling not only in the Head, but in the entire body as well and in everyone who is incorporated as a living member in that mystical body. Insofar as Christ as the Head of the body reigns in that believing congregation, there is no sin in that congregation, it is a holy congregation; they are the *saints* (as they are called time and again), and the temple has been prepared that God can choose for his dwelling place. Everything was ready for the mystical body even before Jesus' ascension, but it was only when he had ascended and received the Holy Spirit from the Father to give to his own that the temple was ready.

Only then for the first time could he as Head pour out the Holy Spirit in the temple—that is, in his body—so that, on the day of Pentecost God once and for all time came near to us in the most complete sense, after all division and alienation had been undone. He came not only to those who lived at that time, but to all who would one day be members of that body. Did not Christ in his high priestly prayer plead not only for his disciples, "but also for those who will believe in me through their word" [John 17:20]? Election defines the mystical body, while the covenant of grace causes it to grow throughout the centuries into the saved human race.

Through Christ's kingly dominion, therefore—now understood in a spiritual sense—the mystical body was established and the living members of the body who are hidden in Christ have a holy life separated from all sin; they have prepared in their hearts the dwelling place, the temple of the Holy One, and now in that temple they also receive God's presence and indwelling in their innermost being. In the conflicts that will necessarily arise within believers between their holy existence and the sin that remains in them, with the struggles that cause them to progress in grace, and with all the battles they have with the world—their King is near as he leads and supports them, comforts and sanctifies them. Similarly, on account of his kingly rule, no one who stumbles can ever fall from grace. This, too, is why the body of Christ grows continually; why his church remains standing despite great oppression, grief, and persecution; and why a seal can be placed on [Scripture's] words that no one will ever be able to pluck either those who belong to him, or his church taken as a whole, from the Father's hand.

SUMMARY

For he must reign until he has put all his enemies under his feet.

1 CORINTHIANS 15:25

When, at the end of this third series, we now look back on the road we have already traveled, Christ's kingship displays itself to us in all its majesty. The starting point is and must remain the kingship that the Triune God bestowed on humanity in paradise. Humanity lost that kingship with its apostasy from God. This same kingship returns in Christ and is restored in him, and it is even elevated above the glory it had in its original state.

§ 1

The kingship that was bestowed on humanity in paradise no doubt included humanity's dominion over all of nature—that is, over everything that dwells here on earth other than humanity. That majestic dominion was symbolically expressed in the majesty with which Adam had all the animals appear before him and expressed their character and essence in a name. This dominion extended beyond this, however. Although at creation humanity was indeed placed below the angels, at the end we will judge the angels and be elevated above them. This circumstance is to be explained from the fact that the angels are complete all at once, while humanity must travel a long road of development before its potential is fully manifested at the end of that road. Initially humanity was less than the angels, but humanity will end up standing above them. Angels are not objects of our veneration but ministering spirits who try to look into our salvation and yet cannot themselves penetrate it. The authority of humanity over the angelic world was thus added to the dominion that humanity had over the entire world at its creation.

Even though creation consists of different parts, these parts mutually cohere. According to the original arrangement, the unity of that coherence comes to expression in humanity as the creature that gathers everything else—all other creatures—under its dominion, so as to moreover consecrate, in a priestly fashion, the entire creation to God, and dedicate it to him, in a kingly fashion, forever. That humanity in paradise could be destined to so high a dominion is to be explained from its creation in the image and likeness of God. Through its creation in God's image, humanity could one day—because it came from God—become perfect just like its Father in heaven is perfect. Both as individuals and as the entire human race, humanity was meant to be a temple to God, a dwelling place of the Holy One, so that God would be in humanity and humanity in God: God all and in all, with humanity as the vicegerent under the Triune God.

Humanity thus has a very lofty place in the plan of creation, as well as in the ideal that was to be realized, toward which this plan aimed. According to Scripture, nothing in creation can be greater than what has been apportioned to the human race. Had humanity from the moment of creation progressed without interruption directly to the complete fulfillment of its ideal destination, its immediate dominion over the visible would automatically have placed it in a world of miracles. In that world of miracles, humanity would have developed in terms of its unique essence in a holy manner; humanity would even have subjected the spirit world. And in the end, earth and heaven, the material and the spiritual world, all things visible and invisible, would together have lifted up hallelujahs to the Triune God, because the humanity that God created in his own image would have willfully subjected itself to God in such a manner that the ideal of "God who is all and in all" would have been realized.

This program for creation—regarding the kingship that was to be exercised by a sinless humanity—included the holy plan regarding Christ's kingship. God remains true to himself. He does not change. Even if his creation is disrupted, his counsel is not undone. And when that disruption came and creation's entire original plan appeared to have gone up in smoke, God's work continued in peace; and we see that, in the end, the original plan of creation will still be executed as God had ordained it. Christ's kingship simply takes the place of the kingship that humanity had lost; it is not of a different kind, but entirely the same. That is why the Word became flesh; and why our King assumed our human nature; and why he was like us in every respect except, of course, for the sin that brought about this disruption. The kingship of Christ, in his position as Mediator, constitutes a dominion over nature and over the spirit world; that dominion makes creation into a unity, so that as Priest he presents it to God and as King he subjects it to the Triune God. The outcome is once more that God's dwelling place or holy temple will be manifested in humanity; and when all things have been completed and reached their end, this kingdom too will be delivered to God so that he may be all and in all.

What gives us assurance is that Christ's kingship did not enter as a foreign element into the life of creation; but it grew within creation, was demanded by it, and arose naturally as it were according to God's exalted ordination. The disruption that entered did not begin with humanity, but came from the spirit world. The spirit world knew that it would itself be subjected to humanity, and this stimulated the spirit world to turn humanity against God so that his plan would be reversed—that is, so that humanity would be subjected to the powerful prince who has dominion over the spirit world. Behind humanity's fall, therefore, stands the fall and apostasy of Satan. It was Satan who first rose up in rebellion. Accordingly, we may assume that, in connection with this event, a disruption occurred upon the earth and in nature already before humanity appeared in paradise; and this explains why it says that "the earth was without form and void, and darkness was over the face of the deep" [Gen 1:2]. Another consequence of Satan's change was the fall of humanity. Humanity also fell, but it did not fall in the same way that Satan did. Because the spirit world was not intended to undergo a process of development, Satan's fall immediately represented a complete fall, such that there was no possibility for the demon world to be saved and recovered. Humanity, by contrast, did have to undergo a process of development. For that reason, humanity's fall was not immediately a complete fall. The fall of humanity did allow for the possibility of recovery. That is why Satan launched an enormous spiritual battle against the saints immediately after the fall. Satan attempted persistently to draw humanity further away from God; while God conversely displayed an all-surpassing compassion in order to draw the human race back to himself, to free it from Satan's embrace, and to carry out and complete his plan for humanity.

At first, Satan's scheme is effective. Sin gains the upper hand. The curse perpetuates the disruption of nature, paradise is lost, and people are

§ 2

introduced to a world that produces for them thorns and thistles—although, by the sweat of their face, people can still draw out of that world what they need in order to sustain their life. But at the same time, sin also proceeds from the human heart to permeate society; and all of human society—in family, tribe, people, and nation—increasingly comes under the dominion of Satan's influence. Things are so serious that ultimately a situation occurs where it appears that this world's life has been torn completely out of God's hands, so that Satan may be called the ruler of this world, placing himself directly over and against the original kingship that once belonged to humanity. Humanity's kingship is gone. Rather than being the king of creation, humanity is now a slave to sin and a servant to the ruler of this world.

In spite of this, already in paradise itself God continues with his original creation plan. According to God's will, counsel, and ordination, not Satan but humanity was supposed to be the ruler of this world below as well as the ruler of the spirit world above. Already in paradise, God's grace begins to operate in order to reveal how Satan and his authority will fall in the end, and how humanity will still triumph notwithstanding the fall, in spite of the curse, and despite its humiliated state.

This could not be brought about, however, by the fallen human race itself. The fall had broken humanity's power and devoured humanity's glory. The human race was no longer united, and in its division humanity became weak and powerless so that it could not resist Satan's power. That is why God destined his only Son to enter the life of this world; to take on our human nature; to gather, as the Head of humanity, the split, divided, and scattered world into a unity once again; and to unite it in one body. This Son was to destroy the world's sin through his blood so that it no longer stands guilty before the Holy One, and thereafter to raise up in his own person the kingship that humanity had lost. This meant that the Son would have to fight Satan and his demons and drive them back. He would plant new life in those who have been redeemed. He would make their heart a dwelling place for God. And finally, through these things he would realize the original plan of creation in order that the human race, created in God's image, would exercise dominion over the visible and invisible world, so that through humanity as his instrument God would be all and in all in the entire creation gathered in a holy unity.

Everything will thus be directed toward undoing the disruption caused by Satan. God will triumph—and humanity through God—and his counsel will stand. At the end of all things, it will be clear not only that the disruption caused by Satan was entirely unable to undo God's ordination, but in fact the effect of Satan's work was that God's virtues shone in even greater glory and the final triumph surpassed what paradise had promised.

This restored kingship—which transfers to the Son of Man from the human race as a whole in Christ—is inaugurated with the declaration that the Seed of the woman will crush the head of Satan; and this becomes the all-determining factor in the history of our human race. When Memphis and Thebes, Nineveh and Babylon, Athens and Rome, have each played their successive roles, then a spiritual sphere proceeds from Jerusalem that calls into existence—first in Europe and then in America—an entirely new and much more elevated human society.

§ 3

The preparation for that turn in world history came in the creation of Israel as God's holy nation. It was established by being set apart and separated as a part of the whole. The process of separation began with Noah, or in part already with Seth; while the call of the first patriarch from the heart of Asia to the coast of the Mediterranean Sea laid the foundation for the Israel that was to come. After Israel finally began as a nation under Moses, under David and his house [the original] theocracy developed into a symbolic kingship—but a kingship that would fall so as to make it clear that it was symbolic rather than the proper kingship itself. The idea of a king nevertheless did take root in Israel, to which the Messianic prophecy then bound itself; while the mighty declaration, "I have set my King on Zion, my holy hill" [Psa 2:6], caused the expectation of a King to arise in the hearts of all who feared God. Everything awaited, anticipated, and longed for the King who was to come—the King who, according to the ordination of God, was already there in the heavens but waited for a time before assuming our human nature. Before he could come, the history of the nations had to have reached the required point; while the terrain had to be prepared in Israel that would enable Christ to display his power and to connect with our human race.

The Son of Man then came according to his name: Immanuel. He was not a man from among humanity, but the Son of God who assumed our human nature. Here lay the mystery—yet one that would gradually be unveiled. It was clear by now that the ideal of "God who is all and in all" could not be realized by humanity drawing near to God, but only by God himself drawing so near to humanity that, in the Son, God united himself with the human race by assuming our human nature. It was not we with

477

God, but God with us. Things could begin only with Immanuel, God with us. Humanity was unable to assume the divine nature, but God could take on human nature. The radiance of God's image could not become one with this image; but he who was the radiance of the invisible God could unite himself in one person with the radiance of that image. And when the end of the age has come and God is all and in all, the glory will not be due to man, but to God. We did not seek God, but instead alienated ourselves from him. He was the one who approached us, came close to us, entered our nature, and turned our heart into his temple and dwelling place. This is why Bethlehem surpassed paradise by far, and why Bethlehem alone could realize what had been foreshadowed in paradise but had not yet been realized.

When Christ came to earth, humanity's authority over nature and the spirit world—that is, the kingship ordained in the life of paradise—was immediately manifest in him. The evangelist Mark is always symbolized with a lion, the king of the forest; his Gospel in particular displays Jesus' kingly activity in his kingly authority over nature, humanity, and the spirit world. Kingly authority is evident in his word; kingly majesty is evident in his activity; kingly authority is evident in his miracles and his dominion over the demons; and kingly majesty is no less evident in the way he resists and denounces the tempter, faces off against his enemies, and willingly takes his cross upon himself. Above all, there is kingly power evident in his breaking the bonds of death when he arose from the dead and then ascended in glory to heaven. Already during his sojourn on earth, then, humanity's original dominion could be found in this Son of Man; humanity's kingly authority over all creatures was restored; and humanity's complete union with the Triune God was realized.

§ 4   These things were still local in nature, however. They were tied to a particular land and place, and they shone within a very limited group in just one nation among many others. But all of this changed completely with Jesus' ascension. When he ascended, he placed himself upon the throne, high above all peoples and nations, above every sphere in the spirit world—in a word, above everything that has been created. From this point forward, his twofold rule would function: on the one hand, his kingly dominion over those who are regenerated and believe; and on the other hand, his kingly dominion over all that God created, over the visible and invisible in heaven and on earth. From this hour, he became the

Head of the mystical body, while the Triune God rules all things through the Mediator.

In order to establish the first dominion, he incorporates into himself those who have been redeemed; takes them up as living members of his mystical body; causes life to flow from him into that body; and as the Head of a sanctified humanity, he governs, defends, and exalts that body. He establishes his church on earth; and even though this church is just the earthly part of his mystical body to the extent that it still tarries on earth, the regenerated members of that church constitute its key ingredient, so that the church and the mystical body often appear to be one; and they will indeed be one in the church triumphant. He pours out his Holy Spirit in the mystical body, and that in itself produces a situation where humanity on earth already experiences union with God through God's work in the human heart as his temple. But neither the church nor the mystical body are extricated or isolated from the world. Both stand and live in the life of the world, and they form its center and core with a view to the eternal ideal. The dominion of our King over his mystical body, and the dominion of the Son of Man over all authorities, are fully intertwined with each other. Because he bears all things through the word of his power, he can order and direct all things in such a way that his church continues to stand without being crushed to death. And because he is the Head of the mystical body, he can cause all kinds of powers and influences to proceed from that body and enter the development of the human race in the world, to raise up our whole life to a higher level. These two very distinct elements of his kingly dominion both affect each other. He has authority over those who belong to him soul and body, in terms of the destiny of their lives and their inner development. In the very same way, he has authority over whatever moves and lives in the world and over whatever is being devised in the spirit world.

On the one hand, our King directly exercises his dominion himself; and on the other hand, he exercises it by his high command and direction through the angels, office-bearers on earth, and spiritual subjects. Our King exercises this latter dominion in such a way, however, that he enlists his subjects into his service, appoints office-bearers, commands and commissions his angels, and grants his servants the powers they need to complete their task. That period in which our King exercises this activity is the period of development in a process lasting many centuries, during the course of which he guides his kingdom toward consummation;

calls into existence every capacity; and further tolerates, allows, and even incites his enemies to display their greatest power so that, when it comes, his victory will be complete.

Once this point has been reached, then comes the consummation. That consummation is not part of the regular course of events, but will conclude that history. It is at this moment that our King will return to the earth; the last enemy will be subjected under his feet and judged; and after the judgment has been rendered, the kingdom of glory will appear. He will thus display his kingly authority over all spirits—whether the spirits of people, of angels, or of demons. Then he will reveal his power over our body by resurrecting it in a glorified form. Then he will reveal his kingly power over the whole earth by renewing it under a new heaven. And when all these things have been completed and the ordination and counsel of God will have triumphed in every way, creation—regained and now glorified—will be handed over to the Triune God so that God will be all and in all. Rather than a purely spiritual exercise of power among believers, Christ's kingship is a dominion over the world and over everything that has been created; and the history of this world and of the entire creation will revolve around the kingship of Christ as the center governing all things.

This is what the world does not see, understand, or know. The world will undergo the influences and the power of his kingship unawares, until, to its horror and surprise, it will see in the end as with its own eyes how it had been blind to what propelled and governed its own course. But, for that reason, those whose eyes have been opened to that kingly majesty, and who served him here in his kingdom—once the hour of their separation from this earth arrives—will be met above by their King.

BIBLIOGRAPHY

Augustine. *The Augustine Catechism: The Enchiridion on Faith, Hope, and Charity*. Translated by Bruce Harbert. Edited by Boniface Ramsey. Hyde Park, NY: New City Press, 1999.

Bank, Jan, and Maarten van Buuren. *Dutch Culture in a European Perspective*. Vol. 3, *1900: The Age of Bourgeois Culture*. Translated by Lynne Richards and John Rudge. Assen: Van Gorcum, 2004.

Book of Praise: Anglo-Genevan Psalter. Winnipeg: Premier, 2014.

Brewer, E. Cobham. *Character Sketches of Romance, Fiction and the Drama*. Vol. 1. Edited by Marion Harland. New York: Selmar Hess, 1902.

Centraal Bureau Voor de Statistiek. Uitkomsten der negende tienjaarlijksche volkstelling in het Koninkrijk der Nederlanden gehouden op den een en dertigsten December 1909. The Hague, 1910–1911.

Dennison, James T., Jr., ed. *Reformed Confessions of the 16th and 17th Centuries in English Translation*. 4 vols. Grand Rapids: Reformation Heritage Books, 2008–2014.

Esposito, John L., ed. *The Oxford Encyclopedia of the Islamic World*. 6 vols. Oxford: Oxford University Press, 2009.

Flammarion, Camille. *Les Forces naturelles inconnues*. Paris: Ernest Flammarion, 1921.

Herrick, Jim. *Against the Faith: Essays on Deists, Skeptics, and Atheists*. Buffalo, NY: Prometheus, 1985.

Het Boek der Psalmen, nevens de gezangen, bij de Hervormde Kerk van Nederland in gebruik. Amsterdam: J. Brandt en Zoon, en P. Proost, 1851.

Honderich, Ted. *The Oxford Companion to Philosophy*. 2nd ed. New York: Oxford University Press, 2005.

Hughes, Thomas Patrick. *Dictionary of Islam*. London: W. H. Allen, 1885.

Hurgronje, Christiaan Snouck. *The Holy War "Made in Germany."* New York: G. P. Putnam's Sons, 1915.

Jones, R. J. Barry, ed. *Routledge Encyclopedia of International Economy*. Vol. 2. New York: Routledge, 2001.

Kuipers, Tjitze. *Abraham Kuyper: An Annotated Bibliography 1857–2010*. Translated by Clifford Anderson and Dagmare Houniet. Brill's Series in Church History 55. Leiden: Brill, 2011.

Kuyper, Abraham. *Abraham Kuyper: A Centennial Reader*. Edited by James D. Bratt. Grand Rapids: Eerdmans, 1998.

———. *Common Grace: God's Gifts for a Fallen World.* Translated by Nelson D. Kloosterman and Ed M. van der Maas. Edited by Jordan J. Ballor and Stephen J. Grabill. 3 vols. Bellingham, WA: Lexham Press, 2015–2017.

———. *De engelen Gods*. Amsterdam: Höveker & Wormser, 1902.

———. *Encyclopedia of Sacred Theology*. Translated by J. Hendrick DeVries. New York: Scribner's, 1898.

———. *Om de Oude Wereldzee*. 2 vols. Amsterdam: Van Holkema & Warendorf, 1907–1908.

Luther, Martin. *Lectures on Genesis: Chapters 31–37*. Translated by Paul D. Pahl. Edited by Jaroslav Pelikan and Helmut T. Lehmann. Luther's Works 6. Saint Louis: Concordia, 1969.

Macauley Jackson, Samuel, ed. *The New Schaff-Herzog Encyclopedia of Religious Knowledge*. 13 vols. Grand Rapids: Baker, 1949–50. Originally published in 12 vols., 1908–12.

Myers, William Henry. *Human Personality and Its Survival of Bodily Death*. Edited and abridged by Leopold Hamilton Myers. London: Longmans, Green & Co., 1906.

Parrinder, Geoffrey. *The Routledge Dictionary of Religious and Spiritual Quotations*. New York: Routledge, 2001.

The Qur'an: A New Translation. Translated by M. A. Abdel Haleem. Oxford World's Classics. Oxford: Oxford University Press, 2004.

Schleiermacher, Friedrich. *The Christian Faith*. Edited by H. R. Mackintosh and J. S. Stewart. 2nd ed. Berlin, 1830. New York: T&T Clark, 1999.

Schroeder, Carl J. *In Quest of Pentecost: Jodocus van Lodenstein and the Dutch Second Reformation*. Lanham, MD: University Press of America, 2001.

Schwartz, A. "The Literature of Holland during the Nineteenth Century." *Macmillan's Magazine* 33 (November 1875–April 1876): 155–164, 267–274.

Wright, George Frederick. *The Ice Age in North America and its Bearings Upon the Antiquity of Man*. 5th ed. New York: D. Appleton, 1911.

———. *Greenland Icefields and Life in the North Atlantic*. New York: D. Appleton, 1896.

———. *Asiatic Russia*. New York: McClure, Phillips & Co., 1902.

———. *Scientific Confirmations of Old Testament History*. Oberlin, OH: Bibliotheca Sacra, 1906.

ABOUT ABRAHAM KUYPER (1837–1920)

Abraham Kuyper's life began in the small Dutch village of Maassluis on October 29, 1837. During his first pastorate, he developed a deep devotion to Jesus Christ and a strong commitment to Reformed theology that profoundly influenced his later careers. He labored tirelessly, publishing two newspapers, leading a reform movement out of the state church, founding the Free University of Amsterdam, and serving as prime minister of the Netherlands. He died on November 8, 1920, after relentlessly endeavoring to integrate his faith and life. Kuyper's emphasis on worldview formation has had a transforming influence upon evangelicalism, both through the diaspora of the Dutch Reformed churches, and those they have inspired.

In the mid-nineteenth-century Dutch political arena, the increasing sympathy for the "No God, no master!" dictum of the French Revolution greatly concerned Kuyper. To desire freedom from an oppressive government or heretical religion was one thing, but to eradicate religion from politics as spheres of mutual influence was, for Kuyper, unthinkable. Because man is sinful, he reasoned, a state that derives its power from men cannot avoid the vices of fallen human impulses. True limited government flourishes best when people recognize their sinful condition and acknowledge God's divine authority. In Kuyper's words, "The sovereignty of the state as the power that protects the individual and that defines the mutual relationships among the visible spheres, rises high above them by its right to command and compel. But within these spheres ... another authority rules, an authority that descends directly from God apart from the state. This authority the state does not confer but acknowledges."

ABOUT THE CONTRIBUTORS

Clifford Anderson (Ph.D., Princeton Theological Seminary) is director, scholarly communications at the Vanderbilt University Libraries. He holds an M.Div. from Harvard Divinity School and a Th.M. as well as a Ph.D. from Princeton Theological Seminary. Currently, he serves as the chair of the Abraham Kuyper Center Advisory Board at Princeton Theological Seminary in Princeton, NJ.

Albert Gootjes (Ph.D., Calvin Theological Seminary) is a post-doctoral researcher in the Spinoza's Web project with the Department of Philosophy and Religious Studies at Utrecht University. He is currently working on an intellectual biography of the physician, philosopher, and theologian Lambertus van Velthuysen (1622–1685) and his Utrecht Cartesian network (the "Collegie der sçavanten"). He is the author of *Claude Pajon (1626–1685) and the Academy of Saumur: The First Controversy over Grace* (Brill) and has translated numerous works in Reformation history and theology.

Nelson D. Kloosterman (Th.D., Theological University of the Reformed Churches [Liberated], Kampen, the Netherlands) is ethics consultant and executive director of Worldview Resources International, a service organization whose mission is to produce and provide resources designed to assist in understanding and applying a Christian worldview to responsible living in a global culture. He has served as minister and professor for more than thirty years and has translated dozens of works on Reformed theology and ethics.

John H. Kok (Ph.D., Vrije Universiteit Amsterdam) is professor of philosophy emeritus at Dordt College in Sioux Center, IA, and managing director of Dordt College Press. He also served as dean for research and scholarship and director of the Andreas Center for Reformed Scholarship and Service until his retirement in 2014. He is author, editor, and translator of numerous works, including studies of and works by D. H. Th. Vollenhoven, one of the originators of Reformational philosophy, as well as his mentor, Calvin Seerveld.

SUBJECT/AUTHOR INDEX

SCRIPTURE INDEX

Old Testament

New Testament